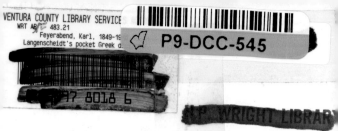

LANGENSCHEIDT'S
POCKET
DICTIONARIES

LANGENSCHEIDT'S POCKET GREEK DICTIONARY

CLASSICAL GREEK-ENGLISH

By
DR. KARL FEYERABEND

PREFACE

This Pocket Dictionary is not intended to compete with any of the larger Lexicons, but as it contains all the words which occur in the selections commonly read in schools, and also those of the Greek New Testament, it will perhaps prove useful to beginners, and may also lend occasional service to more advanced students.

Those who use the book should observe that, as a rule, the quantity of doubtful vowels (α, ι, υ) is only indicated when these are long (ᾱ, ῑ, ῡ); when they are short, the mark of quantity is omitted, except in some special cases. Where no mark is found, it is to be assumed that they are short.

As the Substantives ending in -εύς regularly form Genitive in -έως, this termination has been omitted. This applies also to the words ending in -ις with the Genitive in -εως. Unless some other form, such as -ιδος, -ιος, is given, the form in -εως is to be taken for granted.

Some Remarks
on the History of Greek Sounds

As the Greek language, though its tradition is unbroken from Homer and Hesiod down to its present form of Romaic or Modern Greek, has gone through marked changes in grammar and vocabulary, its pronunciation as a living tongue has, in the course of so many centuries, suffered no less considerable alterations.

When in the 15th century, after a long eclipse, the knowledge and study of Greek was once more brought within the intellectual horizon of the western nations of Europe by Byzantine scholars driven from their country, the bearers of the new learning brought with them the mode of pronunciation to which they were accustomed. But soon the observation forced itself on western students that the Byzantine pronunciation was at a wide distance from the written tradition of the language, and did not correspond to the sounds which people were accustomed to give to Greek words in their Latin form, such as *ecclesia* or *alphabetum*. And when it was found out that many passages in ancient authors pointed to another pronunciation, there arose strong doubts as to the authority of Byzantine tradition. Already in 1512, Aldus Manutius the Elder published a small treatise on the faulty pronunciation of some vowels and diphthongs; but the chief champion for a more correct rendering of Greek sounds was the famous Desiderius Erasmus. Though in his own practice he still adhered to the traditional method, yet his (Latin) Dialogue on the right pronunciation of the Latin and Greek languages, 1528, furnished for the first time scientific arguments for the fact that the phonetic system of the period of Plato must have been widely different from that of the Byzantines.

In England, the views of Erasmus, who was a reformer only in word, not in deed, were carried into practical effect by John Cheke and Thos. Smith. Sir J. Cheke, professor of Greek at Cambridge and one of the tutors of the prince, afterwards Edward VI, is chiefly distinguished for his exertions in introducing the study of Greek language and literature into his country. But having dictated to his pupils a certain mode of pronouncing, he was violently assailed on that account by Stephen Gardiner, bishop of Winchester, then Chancellor of the University. Yet, notwithstanding the veto of this arbitrary prelate, the system of Cheke prevailed, and still prevails. Gardiner had strictly forbidden the distinction between αι and ε; ει, οι and ι in pronouncing under penalty of expulsion from the University (1542).

On the Continent, at the close of the 16th century, the Erasmians had made good their case at all the chief seats of classical learning, led by such men as Theodore Beza and Henry Estienne (Stephanus). In all the schools and universities of Europe the so-called Erasmian pronunciation is in use, only modified by the peculiar phonetic systems of the different languages; and at present the modern Greeks are the only nation that apply the sounds of their vernacular speech to the language of their forefathers.

Specimen of modern Greek pronunciation

(the opening lines of Homer's Iliad):

Μῆνιν ἄειδε, θεά, Πηληιάδεω Ἀχιλῆος
mi'nin ai'dhɐ̆ thɐ̆a' pili'iadhǐ̆ɐ̆' aɕili'ɐ̆s

οὐλομένην, ἣ μυρί' Ἀχαιοῖς ἄλγε' ἔθηκεν,
ū'lomɐ̆ni'n i mi'ri aɕi'is a'lyɐ̆ ɐ̆thi'kɐ̆n

πολλὰς δ' ἰφθίμους ψυχὰς Ἄϊδι προΐαψεν
po'las dh i'fthimū's psiɕa's aidhi' proia'psɐ̆n

ἡρώων, αὐτοὺς δὲ ἑλώρια τεῦχε κύνεσσιν
i'roɐ̆'n aftu's dhɐ̆ ɐ̆lo'ria tɐ̆'fɕɐ̆ kinɐ̆'sin

οἰωνοῖσί τε πᾶσι. Διὸς δ' ἐτελείετο βουλή
i'ɐ̆ni'si tɐ̆ pa'si dhiɐ̆'s dh ɐ̆tɐ̆li'ɐ̆tɐ̆ vū'li

ἐξ οὗ δὴ τὰ πρῶτα διαστήτην ἐρίσαντε
ɐ̆'ks ū dhi' ta pro'ta dhia'stiti'n ɐ̆risa'ntɐ̆

Ἀτρεΐδης τε ἄναξ ἀνδρῶν καὶ δῖος Ἀχιλλεύς.
a'trɐ̆idhi's tɐ̆ ana'ks andhro'n kɐ̆ dhi'ɐ̆s aɕi'lɐ̆fs.

VIII

Specimen of the usual pronunciation of Greek in England.

Μῆνιν ἄειδε, θεά, Πηληιάδεω Ἀχιλῆος
mī'nin āā'dĕ thĕā' pīlī'ādyŏ' ăkilĕ̄os

οὐλομένην, ἣ μυρί' Ἀχαιοῖς ἄλγε' ἔθηκεν,
āūlŏmĕnī'n hī mjū'ri ăkaiŏis ä'lgĕ ŏthī'kĕn

πολλὰς δ' ἰφθίμους ψυχὰς Ἄϊδι προΐαψεν
pŏ'llăs d ĭfthāimāūs psjūkă's ĕidăi prŏiä'psĕn

ἡρώων, αὐτοὺς δὲ ἑλώρια τεῦχε κύνεσσιν
hī'rŏ̄o'n āūtū's dĕ hĕlŏ̄'riă tjū'kĕ̆ kjūnĕ̆'sin

οἰωνοῖσί τε πᾶσι. Διὸς δ' ἐτελείετο βουλή
ŏi'ŏnŏi'si tĕ̆ pē̄'si daiŏ's d ĕtĕ̆lai'ĕtŏ bāū'lī

ἐξ οὗ δὴ τὰ πρῶτα διαστήτην ἐρίσαντε
ĕ'ks hāū dī' tă prŏ̄'tă diāstītī'n ĝrisă'ntĕ̆

Ἀτρείδης τε ἄναξ ἀνδρῶν καὶ δῖος Ἀχιλλεύς.
ă'traidī's tĕ̆ ănă'ks ăndrŏ̄'n kāi dai'ŏs ăki'ljūs.

(*Hom. Il. I, 1—7.*)

Key to the Transcription.

a̱ deep a, half-long, French *bas.*	ǫ open o, half-long, as in French *homme.*
ā̱ = aw in *law.*	ŏ open o, short, French *poste.*
ă = a in *can.*	ū close u, long, as in *true, fool.*
a = a in *far.*	jū = u in *music.*
ē = a in *fate.*	aī = i in *mine.*
ę open e, half-long ⎫ as in *bet, chess.*	āū = ow in *how.*
ĕ „ „ short ⎭	ŏi = oi in *coin.*
I = ee in *keen.*	dh = th in *this.*
i = i in *mint.*	g as in *get.*
i̧ close i, half-long, as in French *dit.*	th = th in *think.*
	v = v in *very.*
Ĭ close i, short, as in French *histoire.*	y = y in *year.*
ō = o in *note.*	ɥ = ch in Germ. *ach.*
ŏ = o in *not.*	ꭓ = ch in Germ. *ich.*

A

A, α (ἄλφα) first letter of the alphabet; as a numeral α' = 1, ͺα = 1000.

ᾱ Dor. = ῃ; ᾱ Dor. = ῇ.

ᾱ, ἀᾱ int. ah, alas, woe.

ἀ-ᾱατος 2 invulnerable, inviolated; infallible.

ἀ-ᾱγής 2 unbroken; infrangible.

ἄ-απτος 2 untouched; unapproachable.

ἀ-άσχετος 2 = ἄσχετος.

ἀάω, ἀάζω to hurt, infatuate, befool.

ἀ-βάκέω to be unknowing or insuspicious.

ἀ-βᾰρής 2 not burdensome.

ἀ-βᾰσάνιστος 2 unexamined, untested. [ent.]

ἀ-βᾰσίλευτος 2 independ-]

ἄ-βᾰτος 2 impassible; inaccessible; consecrated.

ἀ-βέβαιος 2 unsure, unsteady, precarious.

ἀ-βελτερίᾱ, ἡ silliness; awkwardness. [stupid.]

ἀ-βέλτερος 3 and 2 silly,]

ἀ-βίωτος 2 not worth living, intolerable.

ἀ-βλᾰβής 2 innoxious, harmless; unhurt. [unused.]

ἀ-βλής, ῆτος not yet shot,]

ἄ-βλητος 2 unwounded.

ἀ-βληχρός 3 weak, delicate; slow.

ἀ-βουλέω to be unwilling.

ἀ-βούλητος 2 involuntary; undesired.

ἀ-βουλίᾱ, ἡ thoughtlessness; helplessness.

ἄ-βουλος 2 unadvised; careless. [voluptuary.]

ἀβρο-δίαιτος 2 weakling,]

ἄ-βρομος 2 roaring, noisy.

ἀβρός 3 luxurious; delicate, weak; elegant.

ἀβροσύνη, ἀβρότης, ἡ luxuriousness; elegance.

ἀ-βροτάζω to miss, fail.

ἄ-βροτος 3 and 2 immortal; divine; holy.

ἀβρύνω to spoil; to adorn; M. to boast.

ἄ-βυσσος 2 unfathomable; abyss, nether world.

ἀγάζομαι see ἄγαμαι.

ἀγᾰθο-εργίᾱ, ἡ deserving deed.

ἀγᾰθο-εργός, ὁ benefactor.

ἀγᾰθός 2 good, proper; apt; useful; brave, strong; noble, well-born; wise; honest, righteous; patriotic. — τὸ ἀγαθόν the good, good fortune; welfare; benefit, interest. [bounty.]

ἀγᾰθωσύνη, ἡ goodness,]

ἀγαίομαι = ἄγαμαι.

ἀγᾰ-κλεής 2, ἀγᾰ-κλειτός 3, ἀγᾰ-κλῠτός 3 highly renowned, glorious, illustrious.

ἀγαλλιάω and *M.* to rejoice. shout.

ἀγάλλω to adorn, glorify; *P.* to glory, exult.

ἄγαλμα, τό ornament; splendid work; statue.

ἀγαλματο-ποιός, ὁ sculptor.

ἄγαμαι *P.* to wonder, stare; to admire, praise; to annoy; to be jealous; to be indignant or angry. [ingly.]

ἀγαμένως *adv.* approvingly.

ἄ-γάμος 2 unmarried; ill-fated. [too much.]

ἄγᾱν *adv.* much; entirely;

ἀγανακτέω to be uneasy, vexed, or discontented.

ἀγανακτητός 3 irritating.

ἀγάν-νιφος 2 covered with snow. [cheering.]

ἀγᾱνός 3 friendly, gentle;

ἀγᾱνο-φροσῦνη, ἡ gentleness, meekness.

ἀ.ᾱνό-φρων 2 tenderhearted, meek.

ἀγάομαι = ἄγαμαι.

ἀγάπάζω (and *M.*). ἀγάπάω to welcome; to treat kindly; to love, esteem; to be contented, to acquiesce.

ἀγάπη, ἡ love, charity; agape.

ἀγαπ-ήνωρ, ορος manly.

ἀγαπητός 3 beloved; amiable; welcome; sufficient; manly.

ἀγαπητῶς sufficiently; scarcely.

ἀγάρ-ροος (-ρους) 2 gushing vigorously.

ἀγά-στονος 2 rushing vehemently.

ἀγαστός 3 admirable.

ἀ-γαυός 3 illustrious; high. noble. [proud.]

ἀ-γαυρός 3 admirable;

ἀγγᾰρεύω to send as courier. [mail-service.]

ἀγγαρήιον, τό Persian

ἄγγᾰρος, ἀγγᾰρήιος, ὁ courier, riding postman.

ἀγγεῖον, τό vessel, receptacle. urn. [order.]

ἀγγελίᾱ, ἡ message, news;

ἀγγελίης, ὁ messenger.

ἀγγελιη-φόρος, ὁ messagebearer; chamberlain.

ἀγγέλλω to announce, report; to tell, order.

ἄγγελμα, τό = ἀγγελία.

ἄγγελος, ὁ, ἡ messenger; envoy; angel.

ἀγγήιον, τό and ἄγγος, τό = ἀγγεῖον. [come!]

ἄγε, ἄγετε well then! up!

ἀγείρω to gather, collect; to ask alms.

ἀγελαῖος 3 gregarious, forming a flock.

ἀγε-λείη, ἡ driver or dispenser of booty. [band.]

ἀγέλη, ἡ herd. flock; troop;

ἀγεληδόν *adv.* in herds.

ἀ-γενεᾱ-λόγητος 2 without pedigree.

ἀ-γένειος 2 beardless.

ἀ-γενής, ἀ-γεννής 2 unborn; not noble, plebeian, mean. unmanly.

ἀ-γένητος, ἀ-γέννητος 2 unborn, uncreated; ignoble, mean.

ἀ-γέραστος 2 without a gift of honour, disregarded.

ἄγερσις, ἡ collection, gathering.

ἀγέρωχος 2 valiant, gallant; impetuous.

ἄ-γευστος 2 untasted; inexperienced.

ἄγη, ἡ astonishment; envy.

ἀγ-ηλατέω to banish.

ἀγ-ηνορίη, ἡ manliness; haughtiness.

ἀγ-ήνωρ, ορος manly, magnanimous; haughty.

ἀ-γήραος 2, ἀγήρᾱτος 2. ἀγήρως, ων not ageing. imperishable.

ἀγητός 3 = ἀγαστός.

ἀγιάζω, ἁγίζω to consecrate.

ἁγιασμός, ὁ sanctification.

ἁγῑνέω to lead; to carry, convey.   [rable.

ἅγιος 3 holy, sacred. venerable.

ἁγιότης, ἡ, ἁγιωσύνη, ἡ holiness, sanctity.

ἀγκάζομαι M. to lift up (in the arms), to embrace.

ἀγ-καλέω = ἀνακαλέω.

ἀγκάλη, ἡ, ἀγκαλίς, ίδος, ἡ, ἀγκοίνη, ἡ elbow, bent arm.

ἀγκάς adv. in the arms.

ἄγκιστρον, τό fishing-hook.

ἀγ-κλίνω = ἀνακλίνω.

ἄγκος, τό ravine, glen.

ἀγ-κρεμάννῡμι = ἀνακρεμάννῡμι.   [thong.

ἀγκῠλη, ἡ bend, loop, noose;

ἀγκυλο-μήτης, ου cunning, deceitful, artful.

ἀγκῠλος 3 crooked, curved.

ἀγκυλό-τοξος 2 with curved bow.   [crooked beak.

ἀγκυλο-χείλης, ου with

ἄγκῡρα, ἡ anchor; support.

ἀγκών, ῶνος, ὁ curve, bend; elbow; projection; glen.

ἀγλᾱΐᾱ, ἡ splendour, pomp, magnificence; delight; pride.   [make a show.

ἀγλαΐζομαι to shine, to

ἀγλάϊσμα, τό ornament.

ἀγλαό-καρπος 2 bearing splendid fruit.

ἀγλαός 3 splendid, shining; magnificent.

ἀγλα-ώψ, ῶπος bright, beaming.

ἄ-γλωσσος 2 barbarous, foreign.   [not fulled.

ἄ-γναφος 2 not carded,

ἁγνείᾱ, ἡ purity, chastity.

ἁγνεύω to be pure or chaste; to abhor.

ἁγνίζω to purify, expiate.

ἁγνισμός, ὁ purification, expiation.

ἀ-γνοέω to ignore, not to know; to mistake; to overlook, to wink at; to doubt; to err unconsciously.

ἀ-γνόημα, τό, ἄ-γνοια, ἡ ignorance; indiscernibleness; mistake.

ἁγνός 3 pure, chaste; holy, sacred; purifying.

ἁγνότης, ἡ purity.

ἄγνῡμι to break (in pieces).

ἀ-γνωμονέω to act thoughtlessly.

ἀ-γνωμοσύνη, ἡ want of judgment, imprudence; misunderstanding; obstinacy; regardlessness.

ἀ-γνώμων 2 imprudent; regardless, unfair; obstinate; not knowing, mistaking.

ἀ-γνώς, ῶτος unknown,

strange; not knowing, ignorant. [obscurity.]

ἀ-γνωσία, ἡ ignorance;

ἄ-γνωστος, ἄγνωτος 2 unknown; unrecognisable, unintelligible.

ἄ-γονος 2 unborn; childless; barren.

ἀγορά, ἡ meeting, congregation, assembly; council; speech; eloquence; market-place, market; victuals; commerce, trade.

ἀγοράζω to frequent a market-place; to buy or sell (in the market).

ἀγοραῖος 2 belonging to a public assembly or a market; street-lounger.

ἀγορά-νόμος, ὁ surveyor of the market.

ἀγοράομαι to speak in an assembly or publicly; to tell, order. [purveyor.]

ἀγοραστής, οῦ, ὁ buyer,

ἀγορεύω = ἀγοράομαι.

ἀγορῆθεν adv. from an assembly. [sembly.]

ἀγορήνδε adv. into an as-

ἀγορητής, οῦ, ὁ public speaker, orator.

ἀγορητύς, ύος, ἡ gift of speaking.

ἀγός, ὁ leader, captain.

ἄγος[1], τό abomination, blood-guiltiness, capital crime; expiation.

ἄγος[2], τό reverence, awe.

ἀγοστός, ὁ palm of the hand. [capture, game.]

ἄγρα, ἡ chase, hunting;

ἀ-γράμμᾰτος 2 unlettered.

ἄ-γραπτος 2 unwritten.

ἀγρ-αυλέω to dwell in the open air.

ἀγρ-αυλος 2 dwelling in the fields, rural. [neutral.]

ἄ-γράφος 2 unwritten;

ἀγρευτής, οῦ, ὁ hunter.

ἀγρεύω, ἀγρέω to hunt, catch; ἄγρει, ἀγρεῖτε up! come on!

ἀγριαίνω to grow angry.

ἀγρι-έλαιος, ἡ wild olive, oleaster.

ἄγριος 3 rural; wild; brutal, cruel; malignant; furious, passionate.

ἀγριότης, ητος, ἡ wildness, rudeness.

ἀγριό-φωνος 2 with a harsh voice.

ἀγριόω to infuriate; P. to grow angry, enraged, or cruel. [in the fields.]

ἀγρο-βότης, ου, ὁ feeding

ἀγρόθεν adv. from the field or country.

ἀγρ-οικίᾱ, ἡ rusticity, boorishness.

ἀγρ-οικος or ἀγρ-οῖκος 2 rustic, boorish, churlish: untilled.

ἀγροιώτης = ἀγρότης.

ἀγρόνδε adv. to the country.

ἀγρο-νόμος 2 living in the country; agriculturist.

ἀγρό-νομος 2 used for pasture. [estate, farm.]

ἀγρός, ὁ field, arable land;

ἀγρότερος 3 wild; country-loving.

ἀγρότης, ου, ὁ countryman, rustic. [or awake.]

ἀγρ-υπνέω to be sleepless

ἀγρ-υπνία, ἡ sleeplessness.

ἄγρ-υπνος 2 sleepless, wakeful.

ἀγρώσσω to hunt, catch.

ἄγρωστις, ἡ field-grass, green provender. [street.]

ἀγυιά, ἡ way, road, path,

ἀγυιεύς, ὁ protector of the roads (Apollo).

ἀ-γύμναστος 2 untrained, unskilled; unplagued.

ἄγυρις, ἡ congregation, meeting; troop.

ἀγυρτάζω to beg, collect.

ἀγύρτης, ου, ὁ beggar, tramp; buffoon.

ἀγχέ-μαχος 2 fighting hand to hand.

ἄγχι adv. and prp. near, at hand, close by; comp. ἆσσον, ἀσσοτέρω, sup. ἄγχιστος. [sea-girt.]

ἀγχί-ἁλος 2 near the sea;

ἀγχι-βαθής 2 deep near the shore. [to the gods.]

ἀγχί-θεος 2 godlike, akin

ἀγχι-μαχητής, οὗ = ἀγ-χέμαχος. [close to.]

ἀγχί-μολον adv. near,

ἀγχί-νοια, ἡ presence of mind, sagacity.

ἀγχί-νοος 2 ready of mind, ingenious. [bouring.]

ἀγχί-πτολις, ὁ, ἡ neigh-

ἀγχιστεία (-στεία), ἡ near relationship; succession.

ἀγχιστεύς, ὁ next of kin; heir apparent.

ἀγχιστήρ, ῆρος, ὁ accomplice. [gether.]

ἀγχιστῖνος 3 close to-

ἀγχί-στροφος 2 quick-changing.

ἀγχόθεν adv. from near.

ἀγχόθι adv. = ἄγχι.

ἀγχόνη, ἡ throttling, strangulation; rope.

ἀγχοῦ adv. near; comp. ἀγχότερος; sup., adv. ἀγχότατα, ἀγχοτάτω nearest.

ἄγχω to throttle, strangle.

ἀγχ-ώμαλος 2 nearly equal, undecided.

ἄγω trans. to lead away, off, on, towards, to conduct, drive, bring, convey, fetch, to take along: to estimate; to direct, command, rule, instruct, guide; to keep (a festival), to spend. — intr. to march, move, pass. — M. to lead or take (on, along) with one or for oneself.

ἀγωγεύς, ὁ conveyer, forwarder.

ἀγωγή, ἡ abduction, transport, the leading away; departure, march; a leading, direction; education, discipline; manner of life.

ἀγώγιμος 2 transportable (τὰ ἀ-α cargo); outlawed.

ἀγωγός, ὁ, ἡ leader, guide.

ἀγών, ῶνος, ὁ assembly; meeting-place, place of combat, arena, lists; prize-combat, contest; lawsuit; exertion, labour, struggle, danger. [θέτης.]

ἀγων-άρχης, ου = ἀγωνο-

ἀγωνία, ἡ struggle, contention, labour; fear, agony.

ἀγωνιάω to vie, compete, cope; to be irritated or harassed.

ἀγωνίζομαι to fight, contend; to carry on a lawsuit; to speak publicly; to strive, to exert oneself.

ἀγώνιος 2 belonging to a (prize-)combat.

ἀγώνισις, ἡ combat.

ἀγώνισμα, τό contest; lawsuit; prize, splendid or showy thing; exploit, bravery.   [competition.]

ἀγωνισμός, ὁ contention,]

ἀγωνιστής, οῦ, ὁ prizefighter, rival, champion; advocate, defender.

ἀγωνο-θετέω to arrange a prize-combat; to (act as) umpire.

ἀγωνο-θέτης, ὁ arranger of combat, umpire.

ἀδαγμός, ὁ an itching, biting.

ἀ-δαημονίη, ἡ ignorance, inexperience.   [norant.]

ἀ-δαήμων, ἀδαής 2 ig-]

ἀ-δάκρῦτος 2 tearless; unwept; adv. ἀδακρυτί.

ἀδαμάντινος 2 and 3 of steel, steely.

ἀ-δάμας, αντος, ὁ steel.

ἀ-δάμαστος, ἀ-δάμᾱτος 2 untamed; invincible, inexorable; unwedded.

ἀ-δάπανος 2 gratuitous.

ἄ-δαστος 2 not yet distributed.

ἀδδεής = ἀδεής.

ἀδδέω = ἀδέω.

ἄδδην = ἄδην.

ἀ-δεής 2 fearless, undaunted; impudent; safe, dangerless; unpunished.

ἄδεια, ἡ fearlessness, security; impunity, safe-conduct; permission, liberty; latitude.

ἀ-δεής = ἀδεής.

ἀ-δείμαντος 2 intrepid.

ἄ-δειπνος 2 dinnerless, unfed.   [cide.]

ἀδελφεο-κτόνος, ὁ fratri-]

ἀδελφή, ἡ sister.

ἀδελφιδέος, ἀδελφιδοῦς, ὁ nephew.

ἀδελφιδή, ἡ niece.

ἀδελφός 3 brotherly, fellow-like; coupled; ὁ brother.

ἀδελφότης, ητος, ἡ brotherhood.

ἄ-δερκτος 2 not seeing.

ἄ-δεσμος 2 unfettered.

ἀ-δευκής 2 bitter, unkind; ignominious.

ἀ-δέψητος 2 untanned.

ἀδέω to be satiated; to surfeit.   [or at a loss.]

ἀ-δηλέω to be uncertain]

ἄ-δηλος 2 unseen, invisible, secret, obscure, dark; unknown; uncertain.

ἀ-δηλότης, ητος, ἡ uncertainty.

ἀδημονέω to be uneasy, distressed, or haunted.

ἄδην, ἄδην (ἄδδην) adv enough, sufficiently, abundantly, to the fill.

ἀ-δῇος 2 uninfested.

ἀ-δήρῑτος 2 unfought, undisputed.

Ἅιδης, ου, ὁ Hades; the nether world.

ἀδη-φάγος 2 voracious, devouring.

ἀ-δῄωτος 2 unwasted.

ἀ-διάβατος 2 impassable.

ἀ-διάκρῐτος 2 indiscernible.

ἀ-διάλειπτος 2 incessant, continuous. [cilable.]

ἀ-διάλλακτος 2 irreconcilable.

ἀ-διάλῠτος 2 indissoluble.

ἀ-διάφθαρτος 2, ἀδιάφθορος 2 incorruptible; unbribable; imperishable.

ἀ-διήγητος 2 indescribable.

ἀδῐκέω to act unjustly or lawlessly; to sin; to be wrong; to injure, wrong, maltreat; to offend. — P. to be wronged.

ἀδίκημα, τό, ἀδικίᾱ, ἡ, ἀδίκιον, τό wrong, injury; offenc ; undue gain.

ἄ-δῐκος 2 unjust, unlawful; dishonest; wrong, foul; unserviceable.

ἀδῑνός, ἀδινός 3 agitated, vehement, loud, sonorous, restless, palpitating; copious, crowded. [lated.]

ἀ-διόρθωτος 2 not regulated.

ἀ-δμής, ῆτος and ἄ-δμητος uncurbed; unmarried.

ἀ-δόκητος 2 unexpected.

ἀ-δοκίμαστος 2 untried; under age.

ἀ-δόκιμος 2 untried, unfit; insignificant. [tattle.]

ἀδολεσχέω to prat(tl)e.

ἀδολέσχης, ου, ὁ prattler.

ἀδολεσχίᾱ, ἡ prating, gossip. [nuine, pure.]

ἄ-δολος 2 guileless; genuine, pure.

ἀ-δόξαστος 2 certain, unquestionable.

ἀ-δοξέω to be ill-famed.

ἀ-δοξίᾱ, ἡ ill repute, disrepute.

ἄ-δοξος 2 inglorious.

ἄδος, ἅδος, τό satiety.

ἄ-δρηστος 2 not running away. [growth, stout.]

ἀδρός 3 grown up, in full growth, stout.

ἀδροτής, ῆτος, ἡ full vigour, ripeness; rich gift.

ἀδρύνω to make ripe.

ἀ-δῠναμίᾱ, ἡ and ἀ-δῠνασίᾱ, ἡ impotence, weakness.

ἀ-δῠνᾰτέω to be unable.

ἀ-δῠνᾰτος 2 unable; inefficient; feeble, weak; frail; invalid, cripple; poor, needy; impossible.

ἄ-δῠτον, τό holy place, sanctuary.

ᾄδω = ἀείδω.

ἄ-δωρος 2 without gifts; not giving, unyielding; unbribed.

ἀεθλεύω etc. = ἀθλ.

ἀεί, αἰεί adv. always, ever, for ever; every time.

ἀει-γενέτης 2, ἀει-γενής 2 ever-existing, immortal.

ἀ-ειδής 2 shapeless; invisible. [praise, announce.]

ἀείδω to sing, sound; to praise, announce.

ἀ-εικία, ἡ ill-treatment.

ἀ-εικέλιος 3 and 2, ἀ-εικής 2 improper; impertinent, unmannerly, shameful; ugly; wretched.

ἀεικίζω to maltreat, dishonour; to deface.

ἀεί-μνηστος 2 not to be forgotten, memorable.

ἀεί-ναος = ἀέναος.

ἀεί-ρῠτος 2 ever-flowing.

ἀείρω = αἴρω.

ἄεισμα = ᾆσμα.

ἀεί-φρουρος 2 keeping in perpetual imprisonment.
ἀεκαζόμενος 3 unwilling.
ἀεκήλιος = ἀεικέλιος.
ἀ-έκητι *adv.* against the will.
ἀ-έκων = ἄκων.
ἀέλιος = ἥλιος.
ἄελλα, ἡ storm, whirlwind, eddy.
ἀελλαῖος 3, ἀελλάς, άδος, ἡ swift as a storm, stormy.
ἀελλής 2 crowded (eddying).
ἀελλό-πος, ἀελλό-πους, ποδος = ἀελλαῖος.
ἀ-ελπής = ἄελπτος.
ἀ-ελπτέω not to hope.
ἄ-ελπτος 2 unhoped for.
ἀε-νάος 2 and ἀε-ναων 3 ever-flowing.
ἀέξω = αὐξω.
ἀ-εργία, ἀ-εργός see ἀργ.
ἄ-ερκτος 2 unfenced.
ἀερο-βατέω to walk in the air. [trotting, fleet.]
ἀερσί-πους, ποδος swift-
ἄεσα, ἄσα (*aor.*) to sleep, to rest at night.
ἀεσι-φροσύνη, ἡ silliness.
ἀεσί-φρων 2 silly, foolish.
ἀετός, ὁ eagle. [leather.]
ἀζαλέος 3 dry; of dry
ἄζη, ἡ mould, dirt.
ἄ-ζηλος 2 unenvied; miserable, wretched.
ἀ-ζήλωτος 2 unenviable.
ἀ-ζήμιος 2 unpunished; blameless; not punishing.
ἀ-ζηχής 2 unceasing.
ἄ-ζῡμος 2 unleavened.
ἄζω to dry up. — *P.* to be parched.

ἄζω and *P.* ἄζομαι to stand in awe (of), to dread, revere, worship. [less.]
ἀ-ηδής 2 unpleasant, cheer-
ἀ-ηδία, ἡ displeasure; disgust, odiousness. [gale.]
ἀηδών, όνος, ἡ nightin-
ἀ-ήθεια, ἡ unwontedness.
ἀ-ηθέσσω to be unaccustomed. [common.]
ἀ-ήθης 2 unwonted; un-
ἄημα, τό a blast, wind.
ἄημι to blow, to breathe. — *P.* to be agitated.
ἀήρ, έρος, ὁ, ἡ air; mist, cloud.
ἀήσυλος = αἴσυλος.
ἀήτης, ου, ὁ a blast, wind.
ἄητος 2 stormy, raging; panting. [invincible.]
ἀ-ήττητος 2 unconquered,
ἀ-θανασία, ἡ immortality.
ἀ-θανατίζω to make immortal; to believe in immortality. [everlasting.]
ἀ-θάνατος 2 immortal,
ἄ-θαπτος 2 unburied.
ἀ-θέατος 2 not seeing; unseen.
ἀ-θεεί *adv.* without God.
ἀ-θέμιστος 2, ἀ-θεμίστιος 2, ἀ-θέμιτος 2 lawless, illegal; criminal, wicked; illicit.
ἄ-θεος 2 godless, infidel, atheist; god-forgotten.
ἀ-θεράπευτος 2 untended, neglected.
ἀθερίζω to despise, disdain. [warmth.]
ἄ-θερμος 2 without
ἄ-θεσμος 2 = ἀθέμιστος.
ἀ-θέσφατος 2 unspeakably huge, enormous.

ἀ-ϑετέω to do away with, reject. [moval.]

ἀ-ϑέτησις, ἡ abolition, re-, ἀϑηρη-λοιγός, ὁ winnowing-fan. [or game.]

ἄ-ϑηρος 2 without beasts]

ἄ-ϑικτος 2 untouched.

ἀϑλεύω and ἀϑλέω to contend, fight (for a prize); to toil, struggle; to suffer.

ἄϑλησις, εως, ἡ combat.

ἀϑλητήρ, ῆρος, ὁ and ἀϑλητής, οῦ, ὁ prize-fighter, pugilist, athlete; champion. [ched, distressed.]

ἄϑλιος 3 miserable, wret-, ἀϑλιότης, ητος, ἡ wretchedness, drudgery.

ἀϑλο-ϑέτης, ου, ὁ arranger of a contest, umpire.

ἄϑλον, τό prize; = ἄϑλος.

ἄϑλος, ὁ contest, combat; labour, toil; distress.

ἀϑλο-φόρος 2 prize-bearer.

ἀϑρέω to look at, observe, view; to consider.

ἀϑροίζω, ἀϑροίζω to gather, collect, assemble.

ἄϑροισις, εως, ἡ and ἄϑροισμα, τό collection, a compiling, amassing.

ἀ-ϑρόος, ἀ-ϑρόος 3 gathered, crowded; in one body, all at once.

ἀ-ϑῡμέω to despond, to be discouraged; to be fretful.

ἀ-ϑῡμίᾱ, ἡ dejection, despondency; fretfulness.

ἄ-ϑῡμος 2 desponding, faint-hearted; fretful, without spirit.

ἄϑυρμα, τό toy, plaything.

ἀϑύρμάτιον, τό little toy.

ἀϑυρο-στομέω to speak freely. [lous.]

ἀ-ϑυρό-στομος 2 garru-]

ἀϑύρω to play, to amuse oneself.

ἄ-ϑῠτος 2 unsacrificed; not having sacrificed.

ἀ-ϑῷος 2 unpunished; unhurt, spared; innocent, guiltless.

ἀ-ϑωράκιστος 2 unmailed.

αἰ, αἴ conj. if, oh that.

αἴ, αἰαῖ int. woe! alas!

αἶα, ἡ earth, land.

αἰάζω to lament, wail.

αἰᾱνής 2 everlasting; painful, afflicting; dismal, gloomy.

αἰγάνέη, ἡ javelin.

αἴγειος, αἴγεος 3 of goats.

αἴγειρος, ἡ black poplar.

αἰγί-ἀλός ὁ beach, shore.

αἰγί-βοτος 2 browsed or grazed by goats.

αἰγι-κορεύς, ὁ goat-herd.

αἰγί-λιψ, ιπος, ὁ, ἡ steep, precipitous; storm-beaten.

αἰγί-οχος 2 ægis-bearing.

αἰγί-πους, πουν, gen. ποδος goat-footed.

αἰγίς, ίδος, ἡ shield of Jupiter or Minerva; breastplate of leather; storm.

αἴγλη, ἡ brightness, lustre; daylight; torch.

αἰγλήεις 3 bright, brilliant. [faced.]

αἰγο-πρόσωπος 2 goat-]

αἰγῠπιός, ὁ vulture.

αἰδέομαι P. M. to be ashamed (of); to shun, fear; to revere, respect; to pardon; to reconcile.

ἀ-ίδηλος 2 absconding, undoing, destroying; invisible, dark; ugly.

αἰδήμων = αἰδοῖος.

ἀΐδιος 2 everlasting.

αἰδοῖον, τό pudenda.

αἰδοῖος 3 shame-faced, bashful; modest; chaste; venerable, respectable.

αἴδομαι = αἰδέομαι.

αἰδό-φρων 2 merciful.

ἀ-ιδρείη, ἡ ignorance, silliness.

ἄ-ιδρις 2 ignorant, silly.

αἰδώς, οῦς, ἡ shame; modesty; decency; respect, awe; reverence, veneration; ignominy, disgrace; pudenda.

αἰεί = ἀεί.   [νής.]

αἰει-γενέτης, ου = ἀειγε-

αἰέλ-ουρος, ὁ. ἡ cat.

αἰέν = ἀεί.

αἰε-νάων = ἀέναος.

αἰέν-υπνος 2 lulling in eternal sleep.

αἰετός = ἀετός.

αἰζήιος, αἰζηός 2 vigorous, robust, young; young man.   [distinct.]

αἴζηλος 2 conspicuous,

ἄητος = ἄητος.

αἰθαλόεις 3 sooty; smoky, blackened.

αἴθε int. oh that!

αἰθέριος 2 and 3 ethereal, aerial.

αἰθήρ, έρος, ἡ or ὁ the upper air, clear sky.

αἴθουσα, ἡ vestibule, colonnade, hall.

αἴθ-οψ, οπος sparkling, shining; fiery, ardent.

αἴθρη, ἡ, αἰθρίᾱ, ἡ brightness of the sky; bright, blue sky.

αἰθρη-γενέτης, ου, αἰθρη-γενής 2 ether-born; clearing up; chilling.

αἴθρος, ὁ chill, hoar-frost.

αἴθυια, ἡ diver, water-hen.

αἴθω trans. to kindle, fire, burn; intr. and P. to flame, burn, shine.

αἴθων 2 burning; sparkling, shining, ruddy; tawny; fiery, hot.

αἴκ', αἴκε = εἰ ἄν (ἐάν).

αἰκάλλω to flatter.

αἰκή, ἡ rush, impact, press.

αἰκής 2 = ἀεικής.

αἰκίᾱ, ἡ ill-treatment.

αἰκίζω = ἀεικίζω. [=αἰκία.]

αἴκισμα, τό and αἰκισμός, ὁ

αἰκῶς = ἀεικῶς shamefully.

αἴλινος, ὁ plaintive cry, wailing.

αἷμα, τό blood; bloodshed; murder; murderous weapon; life, vigour, strength; kindred, blood-relationship.

αἱμάς, άδος, ἡ effusion of blood.   [fence.]

αἱμᾰσιά, ἡ thornbush;

αἱμάσσω to make bloody, to sprinkle or stain with blood.   [shed.]

αἱμᾰτ-εκχῠσίᾱ, ἡ blood-

αἱμᾰτηρός 3, αἱμᾰτόεις 3 bloody, bleeding; blood-red.

αἱμᾰτόω = αἱμάσσω.

αἱμᾰτώδης 2 bloodlike; blood-red.   [blood.]

αἱμο-βαφής 2 steeped in

αἱμο-ρροέω to be affected with a flux of blood.

αἱμο-φόρυκτος 2 bloody, raw.

αἱμὅλιος 2, αἱμὅλος 3 flattering, charming; artful, wily. [pert.]

αἵμων, ονος knowing, ex-

αἰν-αρέτης, ου, ὁ mischievously brave.

αἴνεσις, εως, ἡ = αἴνη.

αἰνέω to praise, laud; to approve, assent, agree (to); promise; persuade.

αἴνη, ἡ praise, renown.

αἴνιγμα, τό riddle.

αἰνίζομαι M. = αἰνέω.

αἰνίσσομαι M. to speak in riddles, to hint.

αἰνόθεν αἰνῶς adv. more than horrid, most horribly.

αἰνό-μορος 2 ill-fated.

αἰνο-παθής 2 hard-suffering.

αἶνος, ὁ ingenious speech; saying, by-word; praise, encomium.

αἰνός 3 horrible, dreadful; destructive, pernicious; miserable.

αἴνὕμαι M. to take; to lay hold of, seize.

αἴξ or αἶξ, αἰγός, ὁ, ἡ goat. [to and fro.]

αἰόλλω to move quickly

αἰολο-θώρηξ, ηκος with a shining breast-plate.

αἰόλος 3 swift, movable; wriggling; flitting; shining, glittering, bright; party-coloured; stained.

αἰολό-στομος 2 ambiguous in speech. [αἰπύς.]

αἰπήεις 3, αἰπήεις 3 =

αἰπόλιον, τό herd of goats.

αἰπόλος 2 feeding goats; goatherd, shepherd.

αἰπός 3, αἰπύς 3 high, steep, precipitous; sudden, past help; troublesome.

αἴρεσις, εως, ἡ a taking, capture; option, choice, election; inclination; cast of mind; sect, party; heresy.

αἱρετίζω to choose.

αἱρετικός 3 heretical.

αἱρετός 3 takable, conquerable, superable; intelligible, comprehensible; chosen; eligible, acceptable; desirable.

αἱρέω Act. to take, seize; to overtake, catch, join; to take away; to capture, conquer, subdue; to kill; to convict; to understand. — M. to take or seize for oneself; to get, win, receive, enjoy; to choose, prefer; to wish.

αἴρω trans. to raise, lift, elevate, erect; to render prominent, to extol, enhance, heighten, praise; to take away, remove, carry away; to take, seize, fetch, get; to show, to manifest. — intr. to set out, put to sea, set sail. — P. to rise, mount, soar; to set out; to grow, increase; to grow excited. — M. to lift up, carry away, seize; to get, win, gain, obtain; to take in hand, undertake, undergo.

αἶσα, ἡ due portion, share; the due; fate, destiny,

lot; duration of life, lifetime.

αἰσθάνομαι *M.* to feel, perceive; to notice, observe, to become sensible; to know, understand.

αἴσθησις, εως, ἡ sensation, perception, feeling; sense; knowledge, consciousness.

αἰσθητήριον, τό organ of sense.

αἰσθητός 3 perceptible.

αἴσθομαι = αἰσθάνομαι.

ἀΐσθω to breathe, expire.

αἴσιμος 2 and 3 fatal; due, fit, just, convenient.

αἴσιος 2 and 3 auspicious, lucky.

ἀΐσσω *intr.* to move quickly; to run, rush, dash; to fly away, to hurry up; to rise, soar up; to pounce. — *trans.* to wave.

ἄ-ϊστος 2 unseen, invisible.   [hilate.]

ἀ-ϊστόω to destroy, anni-)

αἴσυλος 2 mischievous.

αἰσυ-μνητήρ, ῆρος and αἰσυ-μνήτης, ου, ὁ judge, umpire; ruler.

αἶσχος, τό disgrace, shame, ignominy; ugliness.

αἰσχρο-κέρδεια and -ίᾱ, ἡ love of gain, greediness.

αἰσχρο-κερδής 2 greedy of gain, covetous.

αἰσχρο-λογίᾱ, ἡ foul talk.

αἰσχρός 3 disgracing; ugly; shameful, base, ignominious, lewd; reviling; unfit.

αἰσχρότης, ητος, ἡ ugliness; infamy.

αἰσχύνη, ἡ shame, dis-

grace; violation; sense of shame or honour, reverence.

αἰσχυντηρός 3 bashful.

αἰσχύνω to disfigure, deform; to ravish, disgrace, defame; to confound, to put to the blush. — *P.* to be ashamed, to get ashamed.

αἰτέω to ask, demand, desire; to beg. — *M.* to ask, demand for oneself.

αἴτημα, τό and αἴτησις, εως, ἡ demand, request, entreaty.

αἰτητός 3 asked for, wanted.

αἰτίᾱ, ἡ cause, reason, motive, occasion, inducement; guilt, imputation, charge, reproach; αἰτίαν ἔχειν to have a cause or reason; to be in fault; to be charged with.   [charge.]

αἰτίᾱμα, τό imputation,)

αἰτιάομαι *M.* to accuse, impeach; to blame; to pretend, allege, feign.

αἰτίζω to ask, beg.

αἴτιος 3 causing, chargeable, guilty; ὁ αἴτιος doer, author; culprit; τὸ αἴτιον = αἰτία.

αἰτίωμα, τό = αἰτίαμα.

αἰφνίδιος 2 sudden.

αἰχμάζω to throw a lance.

αἰχμ-αλωσίᾱ, ἡ captivity.

αἰχμ-αλωτεύω, -ίζω to make prisoner of war.

αἰχμ-αλωτίς, ίδος, ἡ female captive, slave.

αἰχμ-άλωτος 2 prisoner of war, captive, captured; slave.   [war, battle.]

αἰχμή, ἡ point, edge; lance;)

αἰχμητής, οῦ, ὁ spearman, warrior.

αἰχμο-φόρος, ὁ lance-bearer. [denly.]

αἶφα adv. quickly, sud-

αἰφηρός 3 quick, swift.

ἀΐω to perceive, observe, see, hear, feel; to know.

αἰών, ῶνος, ὁ, ἡ space of time, duration, period; age, lifetime; eternity; spirit of the age.

αἰώνιος 2 and 3 eternal.

αἰώρα, ἡ suspension, swing.

αἰωρέω to lift up, swing. — P. to be suspended, to hover, hang, soar (aloft), float; to be anxious or in suspense; to rise.

ἀ-καθαρσία, ἡ impurity

ἀ-κάθαρτος 2 uncleaned; unatoned; unclean.

ἀ-καιρέομαι to find no opportunity.

ἀ-καιρία, ἡ wrong or unseasonable time; importunity.

ἄ-καιρος 2 unseasonable, inopportune, importunate.

ἀ-κάκητα, ὁ helper, redeemer.

ἄ-κακος 2 guileless; harmless, innocent. [flowing.]

ἀκάλα-ρρείτης, ου soft-

ἀ-κάλυπτος 2 uncovered.

ἀ-κάμας, αντος and ἀ-κάμᾰτος 2 and 3 untired, indefatigable.

ἄκανθα, ἡ thorn(-bush), thistle; acacia; spine, backbone.

ἀκανθώδης 2 thorny.

ἀ-καρπία, ἡ unfruitfulness.

ἄ-καρπος 2 fruitless, barren. [unrequited.]

ἀ-κάρπωτος 2 fruitless,

ἀ-κατάγνωστος 2 blameless. [veiled.]

ἀ-κατακάλυπτος 2 un-

ἀ-κατάκρῐτος 2 undoomed.

ἀ-κατάλῠτος 2 imperishable.

ἀ-κατάπαστος 2 insatiable.

ἀ-κατάπαυστος 2 restless, incessant.

ἀ-καταστασία, ἡ unrest, confusion. [unsteady.]

ἀ-κατάστᾰτος 2 unstable,

ἀ-κατάσχετος 2 indomitable, unruly. [tious.]

ἀ-κατάψευστος 2 not ficti-

ἄκᾰτος, ἡ and ἄκάτιον, τό light boat or ship, pirate's vessel; sail.

ἄ-καυστος 2 unburnt.

ἀκαχίζω to trouble, afflict, grieve. [pointed.]

ἀκαχμένος 3 sharpened,

ἀκείομαι = ἀκέομαι.

ἀ-κέλευστος 2 unbidden.

ἀκέομαι M. to heal, cure; to amend; to reconcile.

ἀ-κέραιος 2 unmixed, pure; uninjured, entire, untouched, fresh.

ἀ-κερδής 2 gainless, unprofitable; bad.

ἀ-κερσε-κόμης, ου with unshorn hair. [ing.]

ἄκεσις, εως, ἡ cure, heal-

ἄκεσμα, τό remedy, medicine. [appeaser.]

ἀκεστήρ, ῆρος, ὁ healer,

ἀκεστός 3 curable; placable. [head.]

ἀ-κέφᾰλος 2 without a

ἀκέων, ουσα, ον silent, still.

ἀ-κήδεστος 2, ἀ-κηδής 2 uncared for, neglected; unburied; careless, secure; unfeeling.

ἀ-κηδέω to neglect.

ἀ-κήλητος 2 inflexible; incurable.

ἀκήν adv. silently.

ἀ-κηράσιος 2, ἀ-κήρᾶτος 2, ἀ-κήριος[1] = ἀκέραιος.

ἀ-κήριος[2] 2 lifeless; heartless, cowardly.

ἀ-κήρυκτος 2 unannounced, unknown; without a herald's conduct; without mediation, irreconcilable.

ἀ-κίβδηλος 2 unadulterated, sincere.

ἀκιδνός 3 tiny, weak.

ἄ-κῑκυς, υος 2 powerless, feeble.

ἀκῑνάκης, ου dagger.

ἀ-κίνδῡνος 2 without danger, safe; unfailing.

ἀ-κίνητος 2 unmoved; immovable, firm, steady; inflexible; not to be touched, not to be divulged.

ἀ-κίχητος 2 unattainable.

ἀκκίζομαι to behave affectedly.

ἄ-κλαυ(σ)τος 2 unwept, tearless, unpunished.

ἀ-κλεής, ἀ-κλειής 2 inglorious, obscure.

ἄ-κλειστος 2, ἄ-κλῃστος 2 not shut, unlocked.

ἄ-κληρος 2 shareless; needy. [drawing lots.]

ἀ-κληρωτί adv. without

ἄ-κλητος 2 uncalled.

ἀ-κλῑνής 2 unswerving.

ἀκμάζω to bloom, flourish, to be in vigour or in the prime of life; to abound (in).

ἀκμαῖος 3 full-grown, ripe; vigorous, at the prime; in time.

ἄ-κματος 2 = ἀκάματος.

ἀκμή, ἡ point, edge; highest point, prime, bloom, climax, pitch, vigour, maturity.

ἀκμήν adv. even now.

ἀκμηνός 3 full-grown.

ἀ-κμής, ῆτος untiring.

ἀκμό-θετον, τό anvilblock.

ἄκμων, ονος, ὁ anvil.

ἄκνηστις, ιος, ἡ spine, back-bone.

ἀκοή, ἡ sense of hearing; listening; ear; hearsay, report, rumour; sermon, preaching.

ἀ-κοινώνητος 2 unsocial.

ἀ-κοίτης, ου, ὁ consort, husband.   [wife.]

ἄ-κοιτις, ιος, ἡ consort,

ἀ-κολάκευτος 2 not flattered.   [ness, debauch.]

ἀ-κολασίᾱ, ἡ licentious-

ἀ-κολασταίνω to be licentious.

ἀ-κόλαστος 2 unrestrained, licentious, dissolute.

ἄκολος, ἡ bit, morsel.

ἀ-κολουθέω to follow, attend; to join; to obey.

ἀ-κόλουθος 2 following, attending; follower, attendant; convenient. agreeing.

ἀ-κομιστίη, ἡ want of tending or nursing.

ἀκονάω to sharpen.

ἀκόνη, ἡ whetstone.

ἀ-κονῑτί *adv.* without dust; without pains.

ἀκοντίζω to throw a (spear), to dart; to hit, wound.

ἀκόντιον, τό javelin, spear.

ἀκόντισις, ἡ, ἀκόντισμα, τό throwing spears.

ἀκοντιστής, οῦ, ὁ darter, spearman.

ἄ-κοπος 2 without pains; unwearied, not wearying.

ἀ-κόρεστος 2, ἀ-κόρητος 2 insatiable, unsated; greedy; insolent.

ἄκος, τό remedy; healing.

ἀ-κοσμέω to be disorderly, to offend.

ἀ-κόσμητος 2 without order, disorderly, confused; unprovided.

ἀ-κοσμία, ἡ disorder, confusion; unruliness.

ἄ-κοσμος 2 disorderly; refractory.

ἀκουάζομαι to be invited.

ἀκουή = ἀκοή. [or heir.]

ἄ-κουρος 2 without a son]

ἀκούσιος 2 = ἄκων.

ἀκουσμα, τό anything heard; report; treat *or* feast for the ears; instruction.

ἀκουστός 3 audible.

ἀκούω to hear, know; to listen to; to obey; to be called *or* reputed.

ἄκρα, ἡ end, point, top, height; castle; headland.

ἀκρ-αής 2 blowing strongly.

ἀκραιφνής 2 pure, fresh, vigorous. [unfinished: vain.]

ἄ-κραντος 2 unfulfilled,

ἀ-κρασία and ἀ-κράτεια, ἡ incontinence, intemperance. [moderate.]

ἀ-κρατής 2 impotent; im-]

ἀκρᾱτο-ποσία, ἡ drinking of unmixed wine.

ἀκρᾱτο-πότης, ου, ὁ drinker of unmixed wine.

ἄ-κρᾱτος 2 unmixed, pure; purified; strong, vigorous; perfect. [τής.]

ἀ-κράτωρ, ορος = ἀκρα-]

ἀκρητο- see ἀκρατο-.

ἀκρίβεια, ἡ accuracy, exactness, precision; strictness, severity, discipline; parsimony; perfection.

ἀκρῑβής 2 exact, accurate, careful; severe; adequate, proper; tight(ly fitting); parsimonious, frugal, scanty; perfect.

ἀκρῑβο-λογέομαι *M.* to be precise in language.

ἀκρῑβόω to know *or* examine thoroughly.

ἄκρις, ιος, ἡ = ἄκρα.

ἀκρίς, ίδος, ἡ locust.

ἀ-κρισία, ἡ disorder.

ἀκρῑτό-μῡθος 2 talking immoderately.

ἄ-κρῑτος 2 without judgment, arbitrary; unsevered, confused; untried, unjudged; undecided; immoderate, countless. [dense foliage.]

ἀκρόᾱμα, τό anything heard; treat *or* feast for the ears.

ἀκροάομαι *M.* to hear; listen; obey. [obedience.]

ἀκρόασις, εως, ἡ a hearing;

ἀκροατήριον, τό audience; lecture-room.

ἀκροατής, οῦ, ὁ hearer, listener. [mish.

ἀκρο-βολίζομαι M. to skir-

ἀκρο-βόλισις, εως, ἡ and ἀκρο-βολισμός, ὁ a skir-mish(ing). [misher.

ἀκρο-βολιστής, οῦ. ὁ skir-

ἀκρο-βυστία, ἡ foreskin; the gentiles. [ner-stone.

ἀκρο-γωνιαῖος(λίθος) cor-

ἀκρό-δρυον, τό fruit-tree.

ἀκρο-θίνιον, τό firstling, first-fruit; votive gift; booty.

ἀκρο-κελαινιάω to be (-come) black on the surface.

ἀκρό-κομος 2 shock-headed, high-tufted.

ἀκρο-μάνής 2 stark raging, madcap.

ἀκρό-πολις, εως, ἡ upper city, castle, citadel.

ἀκρο-πόλος 2 high, lofty.

ἀκρο-πόρος 2 piercing through.

ἄκρος 3 pointed; extreme, upper, topmost; egregious, excellent. — τὸ ἄκρον height, top, summit, ex-tremity, border, skirt, sur-face; castle. [inclined.

ἀκρο-σφαλής 2 tottering;

ἀκρο-τελεύτιον, τό ex-treme end (of a verse).

ἀκρο-φύσιον, τό spout of a pair of bellows. [ice.

ἀ-κρύσταλλος 2 clear of

ἀκρ-ωνυχία, ἡ tip of the nail; top. [mountain.

ἀκρ-ώρεια, ἡ top of a

ἀκρωτηριάζω and M. to

take off the fore part or extremities; to mutilate.

ἀκρωτήριον, τό point, height, top, peak; projec-tion; promontory; beak; gable; extremity.

ἀ-κτένιστος 2 uncombed.

ἀ-κτέριστος 2 unburied; unconsecrated.

ἀκτή, ἡ coast, shore, beach; neck of land; elevation.

ἀκτή, ἡ groats, meal.

ἀ-κτήμων 2 without pro-perty, poor.

ἀκτίς, ῖνος, ἡ ray, beam; light, splendour; heat.

ἄκυλος, ἡ esculent acorn.

ἄ-κῦρος 2 without autho-rity, annulled; invalid, powerless.

ἀ-κῦρόω to abolish, cancel.

ἀκωκή, ἡ point, edge.

ἀ-κώλῦτος 2 unhindered.

ἄκων, οντος, ὁ javelin.

ἄκων, ουσα, ον against one's will, involuntary, un-willing; undesigning; un-welcome.

ἄλα, τό = ἅλς.

ἀλάβαστρος, ὁ and ἀλά-βαστρον, τό onyx, ala-baster; salve-box.

ἅλαδε adv. to the sea, sea-ward(s).

ἀλαζονεία, ἡ boasting, swaggering, brag.

ἀλαζονικός 3 and ἀλαζών, όνος, ὁ, ἡ braggart, swag-gerer, impostor; vagabond.

ἀλαλά, ἡ, ἀλαλαγμός, ὁ and ἀλαλητός, ὁ war-cry; shout. [the war-cry.

ἀλαλάζω and M. to raise

ἀ-λάλητος 2 unspeakable.

ἄ-λάλος 2 speechless, dumb.

ἀλαλύκτημαι (from ἀλυκτέω) to be in fear or anguish.

ἀ-λάμπετος 2 and ἀ-λαμπής 2 lustreless.

ἀλάομαι to wander, stray, err, rove, ramble about; to doubt.

ἀλαός 2 blind; blinding.

ἀλαο-σκοπίη, ἡ vain watch.

ἀλαόω to make blind.

ἀ-λάπαδνός 3 weak, feeble.

ἀ-λάπάζω to empty, exhaust; to overwhelm, destroy, kill.

ἅλας, ατος, τό = ἅλς.

ἀλαστέω to be angry, to hate, resent.

ἀ-λάστορος 2 and ἀ-λάστωρ, ορος, ὁ avenger, tormenter; fiend, villain, rascal.

ἄ-λαστος 2 unbearable; unceasing, lasting; memorable; wicked, hateful.

ἀλάτᾱς = ἀλήτης.

ἀλαωτύς, ύος, ἡ act of blinding.

ἀλγεινός 3 painful, afflicting, grievous; evil; unpleasant; vehement; difficult; suffering.

ἀλγέω to feel pain, to suffer; to be afflicted, grieved, or sad.

ἀλγηδών, όνος, ἡ, ἄλγημα, τό. ἄλγησις, εως, ἡ, ἄλγος, τό pain, grief, sorrow.

ἀλγύνω to grieve, cause pain; P. = ἀλγέω.

ἀλδαίνω to strengthen, invigorate.

ἀλδήσκω to grow, thrive.

ἀλέᾱ¹, ἡ heat (of the sun).

ἀλέᾱ², ἡ avoidance, escape.

ἀλεγεινός = ἀλγεινός.

ἀ-λέγω, ἀλεγίζω, ἀλεγύνω, to care for, mind, attend (to); to heed. [ing.]

ἀλεεινός 3 warm, warm-]

ἀλείνω = ἀλέομαι.

ἀλεής 2 in the noontide heat. [= ἄλευρον.]

ἀλείατα from ἄλειαρ, τό]

ἄλειμμα, τό salve.

ἄλεισον, τό cup, bowl.

ἀλείτης, ου, ὁ offender, sinner.

ἄλειφαρ, ατος, τό salve oil.

ἀ-λείφω to anoint; besmear.

ἄλειψις, εως, ἡ unction, anointing.

ἀλεκτορο-φωνίᾱ, ἡ cockcrow.

ἄ-λεκτρος 2 unwedded; illicit, illegitimate.

ἀλεκτρυών, όνος and ἀ-λέκτωρ, ορος, ὁ cock.

ἀλέκω = ἀλέξω.

ἀλεξ-άνεμος 2 keeping off the wind.

ἀλέξησις, εως, ἡ a keeping off, defence.

ἀλεξητήρ, ῆρος and ἀλεξήτωρ, ορος, ὁ protector, guardian, helper.

ἀλεξί-κακος 2 keeping off evil. [from death.]

ἀλεξί-μορος 2 defending]

ἀλέξω to keep off; to guard, protect, defend, help. — M. to defend oneself; to assist; to requite.

ἀλέομαι *M.* to turn aside; to avoid, shun, escape.

ἀλέτης, ου, ὁ, ἀλετρίς, ίδος, ἡ grinding.

ἀλετρεύω = ἀλέω.

ἀλεύομαι = ἀλέομαι.

ἄλευρον, τό meal, flour.

ἀλέω to grind, pound.

ἀλεωρή, ἡ escape; protection. [madness.]

ἄλη, ἡ a wandering about;

ἀλήθεια, ἡ truth; veracity; uprightness; reality; propriety.

ἀληθεύω to speak the truth.

ἀ-ληθής 2 true; sincere, frank; real, genuine, proper; actual. — *adv.* ἀληθῶς, ἀληθές truly, really, indeed. [θεύω.]

ἀληθίζομαι *M.* = ἀλη-]

ἀληθινός 3 = ἀληθής.

ἀλήθω = ἀλέω.

ἀ-λήϊος 2 not wealthy.

ἄλημα, τό and ἀλήμων 2 arrant knave; vagabond, fugitive. [inconceivable.]

ἄ-ληπτος 2 unattainable;

ἀλής 2 crowded, in a mass; altogether.

ἀλητεύω = ἀλάομαι.

ἀλήτης, ου, ὁ = ἄλημα.

ἄλθομαι *P.* to get cured or healed.

ἁλίᾱ, ἡ assembly.

ἁλιάδης, ου, ὁ = ἁλιεύς.

ἁλι-αής 2 blowing seaward. [incessant.]

ἀ-λίαστος 2 unyielding;

ἀ-λίγκιος 2 like, equal.

ἁλιεύς, ὁ fisherman; mariner, sailor. [fishermen.]

ἁλιευτικός 3 belonging to]

ἁλιεύω to fish.

ἁλίζω to assemble.

ἁλίζω to salt.

ἄ-λιθος 2 without stones.

ἁλί-κλυστος 2 sea-girt.

ἁλί-κτυπος 2 sea-beaten.

ἀ-λίμενος 2 harbourless.

ἀ-λιμενότης, ητος, ἡ harbourlessness. [the sea.]

ἁλι-μῡρήεις 3 flowing into]

ἅλινος 3 (made) of salt.

ἅλιος = ἥλιος.

ἅλιος[1] 3 vain, fruitless.

ἅλιος[2] 3 belonging to the sea, sea-. [tured.]

ἁλιο-τρεφής 2 sea-nur-]

ἁλιόω to frustrate, make fruitless. [adorned.]

ἀ-λιπαρής 2 plain, un-]

ἁλι-πλαγκτος 2 wandering over the sea.

ἁλί-πλακτος 2 sea-beaten.

ἁλί-πλοος 2 floating in the sea. [purple.]

ἁλι-πόρφυρος 2 of sea-]

ἁλί-ρροθος 2 in the roaring sea. [fully; amply, enough.]

ἅλις *adv.* in crowds, plenti-]

ἁλίσγημα, τό pollution.

ἁλίσκομαι to be taken, caught, captured, conquered, or subdued; to be found (out), apprehended, or convicted. [offend.]

ἀλιταίνω and *M.* to sin,]

ἀλιτήμων 2, ἀλιτήριος 2, ἀλιτηρός 2, ἀλιτρός 2 trespassing, offending, sinning, wicked; offender; rascal.

ἀλιτρίᾱ, ἡ wickedness.

ἄλκαρ, τό defence, protection.

ἀλκή, ἡ defensive power, force, prowess; guard, defence, delivery.

ἀλκῑμος 2 fit for battle, warlike, martial; valiant.

ἀλκτήρ, ῆρος, ὁ defender, protector.

ἀλκυών, όνος, ὁ kingfisher.

ἀλλά conj. but. yet, however; notwithstanding; at least; but, except; why, well, certainly, well then.

ἀλλαγή, ἡ change, alteration.

ἀλλάσσω to change, alter, transmute; requite. — M. to take in exchange.

ἀλλαχῇ, ἀλλαχόθι, ἀλλαχοῦ adv. elsewhere; to another place.

ἀλλαχόθεν adv. from another place.   [place.]

ἀλλαχόσε adv. to another]

ἀλ-λέγω = ἀναλέγω.

ἄλλη adv. = ἀλλαχῇ; otherwise.

ἀλλ-ηγορέω to speak metaphorically, to allegorize.

ἀλληλο-φαγία, ἡ the eating one another.

ἀλληλο-φθορία, ἡ mutual destruction.   [other.]

ἀλλήλων one another, each]

ἄλλην adv. to another place.   [reign.]

ἀλλο-γενής 2 alien, fo-]

ἀλλό-γλωσσος 2 of a foreign language, foreign.

ἀλλο-γνοέω to mistake, not to know. [unknown.]

ἀλλό-γνωτος 2 strange.]

ἀλλο-δᾰπός 3 strange, foreign, outlandish.

ἀλλο-ειδής 2 looking differently.   [ther place.]

ἀλλό-θεν adv. from ano-]

ἄλλοθι adv. elsewhere; far from; else.

ἀλλό-θροος 2 speaking another language; foreign.

ἀλλοῖος 3 different, heterogeneous; changed.

ἀλλοιόω to change, alter.

ἀλλοίωσις, εως, ἡ permutation, change.

ἀλλό-κοτος 2 different; uncommon, strange; unnatural.

ἄλλομαι M. to spring, jump, leap; to fly, run.

ἀλλο-πρόσ-αλλος, ὁ changeable, fickle.

ἄλλος, η, ο another, the other; different, strange, foreign; inconvenient, false. — adv. ἄλλως otherwise (better or worse); in vain, at random; merely, simply; else, besides, already; ἄλλως τε καί especially, above all.   [place.]

ἄλλοσε adv. to another]

ἄλλοτε adv. at another time.

ἀλλοτριο-ἐπίσκοπος, ὁ meddler, busy-body.

ἀλλότριος 3 belonging to others; foreign, alien, not related; hostile, adverse; changed, strange; inconvenient.   [trangement.]

ἀλλοτριότης, ητος, ἡ es-]

ἀλλοτριόω to estrange, alienate; to transfer; to rob.

ἀλλοτρίωσις, εως, ἡ rejection.

ἄλ-λοφος 2 crestless.

2*

ἀλλο-φρονέω to think otherwise or wrongly; to be absent in mind.

ἀλλό-φῦλος 2 of another tribe, foreign.

ἄλλῠδις adv. elsewhither.

ἀλλύεσκε see ἀναλύω.

ἄλλως see ἄλλος.

ἅλμα, τό jump, leap, bound.

ἅλμη, ἡ sea-water; brine; saltness.

ἁλμῠρός 3 salt, bitter, sea-.

ἀλοάω to thrash. [liver.]

ἄ-λοβος 2 without lobe of the

ἀ-λογέω to take no heed or notice of, to neglect.

ἀ-λογίᾱ, ἡ disregard; want of reason.

ἀ-λόγιστος 2 unreasonable, absurd; unfathomable.

ἄ-λογος 2 without reason, silly; unexpected; speechless.

ἀλόη, ἡ aloe.

ἁλόθεν adv. from the sea.

ἀλοιάω = ἀλοάω.

ἀλοιφή, ἡ fat, grease; salve.

ἄλοξ, οκος, ἡ furrow; cornland.

ἁλοσ-ύδνη, ἡ sea-born.

ἀλουργής 2 dyed with purple. [dirt.]

ἀ-λουσίᾱ, ἡ unwashedness,

ἄ-λουτος 2 unwashed, dirty.

ἄ-λοχος, ἡ wife, spouse.

ἅλς, ἁλός, ὁ salt; ἡ saltwater, sea. [forest.]

ἄλσος, τό (sacred) grove,

ἁλῠκός 2 salt, briny.

ἁλυκτάζω = ἀλύω.

ἄ-λῡπος and ἀ-λύπητος 2 without pain or grief, easy; not grieving.

ἄ-λῠρος 2 without a lyre, songless.

ἅλῠσις, εως, ἡ chain.

ἀ-λῠσιτελής 2 useless; injurious.

ἀλύσκω, ἀλυσκάζω, ἀ-λυσκάνω to turn aside, escape.

ἀλύσσω = ἀλύω.

ἄ-λῠτος 2 inseparable; infinite.

ἀλύω to be unsteady, beside oneself, troubled, excited.

ἄλφα, τό first letter of the alphabet. [quire.]

ἀλφάνω to earn, gain, ac-

ἀλφεσί-βοιος 3 bringing in cattle; much-wooed.

ἀλφηστής, οῦ, ὁ laborious, industrious; eating bread.

ἄλφῐτον, τό barley-meal; bread. [of barley-meal.]

ἀλφῐτο-ποιΐᾱ, ἡ making

ἀλωή, ἡ thrashing-floor; orchard, cornfield.

ἄλων, ωνος, ἡ = ἅλως.

ἀλωπεκῆ and ἀλωπεκίς, ίδος, ἡ foxskin.

ἀλώπηξ, εκος, ἡ fox.

ἅλως, ω and ωος, ἡ thrashing-floor; corn.

ἁλώσιμος 2, ἁλωτός 3 easily won or conquered or understood.

ἅλωσις, εως, ἡ a taking, capture; conquest.

ἀμ = ἀνά.

ἅμα adv. and prp. together, at the same time, at once, jointly, with.

ἀ-μαθής 2 ignorant, unlearned, unlettered; inexperienced; incalculable.

ἀ-μᾰθίᾱ, ἡ ignorance; in-experience.

ἄμᾰθος, ἡ sand.

ἀμᾰθύνω to reduce to dust.

ἀ-μαιμάκετος 3 huge; raging.

ἀ-μαλδύνω to destroy.

ἀμαλλο-δετήρ, ῆρος, ὁ binder of sheaves.

ἄ-μᾰλός 3 soft, feeble, delicate. [carriage.]

ἅμαξα, ἄμαξα, ἡ waggon.

ἁμαξεύω to drive (a cart). — P. to be frequented by waggons. [gon.]

ἁμαξιαῖος 3 filling a waggon.

ἁμαξίς, ίδος, ἡ a little waggon. [waggons; road.]

ἁμαξ-ιτός practicable for)

ἆμαρ = ἦμαρ.

ἀ-μάραντος 2, ἀ-μαράντινος 2 unfading.

ἀ-μάρη, ἡ trench, ditch.

ἁμαρτάνω to miss the mark, err, fail, mistake, lose; to offend, trespass. sin.

ἁμαρτάς, άδος, ἡ, ἁμάρτημα, τό, ἁμαρτίᾱ, ἡ transgression, sin, offence, error.

ἁμαρτέω = ὁμαρτέω.

ἁμ-αρτῇ adv at the same time, at once.

ἁμαρτο-επής 2 speaking falsehood or at random.

ἀ-μάρτυρος 2 unattested.

ἁμαρτωλός 2 sinful; sinner. [with.]

ἁμα-τροχάω to run along)

ἁμα-τροχίη, ἡ collision of waggons.

ἀ-μαυρός 3 dark, dim; blind; feeble, gloomy; indifferent.

ἀμαυρόω to darken, weaken.

ἀ-μάχητος 2, ἄ-μαχος 2 (adv. ἀμαχεί, ἀμαχητί) without fighting; peaceful; unconquerable. [gather.]

ἀμάω to mow, reap; to)

ἄμ-βᾰσις = ἀνάβασις.

ἀμ-βᾰτός 2 = ἀναβατός.

ἀμ-βλήδην adv. bubbling up.

ἀμβλύνω to blunt, dull; to lessen, discourage.

ἀμβλύς 3 blunt, dull; slack, feeble, weak. [sighted.]

ἀμβλυώττω to be dim-)

ἀμ-βολάδην = ἀμβλήδην.

ἀμβροσίᾱ, ἡ food of the gods. [immortal, divine.]

ἀμβρόσιος 3, ἄμβροτος 2)

ἀμ-μώσας see ἀναβοάω.

ἀ-μέγαρτος 2 unenvied; unhappy, miserable.

ἀ-μέθυστος, ἡ amethyst.

ἀμείβω and M. to change, alter; to exchange; to pass, cross; to reply, answer; to requite. [(of a roof).]

ἀμείβων, οντος, ὁ rafter)

ἀ-μείλικτος 2, ἀ-μείλιχος 2 harsh, severe; relentless.

ἀμείνων 2 (comp. of ἀγαθός) better, abler, nobler; stronger, more valiant.

ἀ-μειξίᾱ, ἡ = ἀμιξία.

ἀμέλγω to milk, drain.

ἀμέλει adv. never mind; of course. [negligence.]

ἀ-μέλεια, ἡ carelessness,)

ἀ-μελέτητος 2 unpractised, unskilled.

ἀ-μελέω to be careless, heedless; to neglect, overlook, omit.

ἀ-μελής 2 careless, negligent; neglected.

ἄ-μεμπτος 2 blameless; contented.

ἄμεναι for ἀέμεναι, see ἄω.

ἀ-μενηνός 2 feeble, weak, powerless, swooning; unsteady.

ἀμενηνόω to make weak.

ἀμέρᾱ, ἡ = ἡμέρα.

ἀ-μέρδω to rob, deprive; to blind. — P. to get or become deprived (of).

ἀ-μερής 2 indivisible.

ἀ-μέριμνος 2 free from care; neglected.

ἀμέριος = ἡμέριος.

ἀ-μετάθετος 2 unalterable.

ἀ-μετακίνητος 2 immovable.

ἀ-μεταμέλητος 2, ἀ-μετανόητος 2 impenitent.

ἀμέτερος = ἡμέτερος.

ἀ-μέτρητος, ἄ-μετρος 2 unmeasured, immense; boundless.

ἀ-μετρία, ἡ want of measure or moderation.

ἀμετρο-επής 2 immoderate talker.   [anyhow.)

ἀμῇ, ἀμῇ adv. somehow,)

ἀ-μήνῑτος 2 not angry.

ἀμητήρ, ῆρος, ὁ reaper.

ἄμητος, ὁ reaping, harvest, crop.   [unmotherly.)

ἀ-μήτωρ, ορος motherless;)

ἀ-μηχάνέω to be at a loss, helpless, or embarrassed.

ἀ-μηχάνίᾱ, ὁ embarrassment, helplessness.

ἀ-μήχανος 2 helpless, embarrassed, puzzled; impossible, unattainable; incre-

dible; indescribable; unco querable; inflexible; irreversible, inevitable.

ἀ-μίαντος 2 undefiled.

ἀ-μίγής, ἄ-μῑκτος 2 unmixed; unsociable; incompatible.

ἅμιλλα, ἡ rivalry, contest; combat; striving, desire.

ἀμιλλάομαι M. and P. to contend, rival, strive.

ἀμίλλημα, τό = ἅμιλλα.

ἀμιλλητήρ, ῆρος, ὁ competitor, rival.

ἀ-μῑξίᾱ, ἡ want of traffic; unsociableness.

ἄμ-ιππος 2 fleet as a horse; companion of a horse-soldier.

ἄ-μισθος 2 unpaid.

ἀ-μιτρο-χίτων, ωνος in a girdless coat.   [smoking.)

ἀμιχθάλόεις 3 reeking,)

ἅμμα, τό knot, noose.

ἄμμε = ἡμᾶς; ἄμμες = ἡμεῖς.

ἄμ-μιγα = ἀναμίξ.

ἀμ-μίγνῡμι = ἀναμίγνυμι.

ἀμ-μορίη, ἡ a having no share; misfortune.

ἄμ-μορος 2 without lot, unfortunate.   [ground.)

ἄμμος, ἡ sand; riding-)

ἀ-μνάστέω = ἀμνηστέω.

ἀ-μνημονέω to be forgetful; to pardon.

ἀ-μνηστέω = ἀμνημονέω. P. to fall into oblivion.

ἀμνίον, τό offering-bowl.

ἀμνός, ὁ, ἡ lamb.

ἀ-μογητί adv. without toil or trouble.

ἀμοθεί adv. unanimously

ἀμόθεν (ἀμ.) *adv.* from anywhere.

ἀμοιβαῖος 3 and 2, ἀμοιβάς, άδος alternate.

ἀμοιβή, ἡ change, exchange; reply, answer; recompense, return.

ἀμοιβηδίς *adv.* alternately.

ἀμοιβός 2 substitute, equivalent.

ἄ-μοιρος 2 shareless, free from; unfortunate. [light.]

ἀμολγός, ὁ darkness; twi-]

ἄμορος = ἄμμορος.

ἄ-μορφος 2 deformed, ugly.

ἀμός, ἁμός 3 our, ours; my, mine.

ἄ-μοτον, *adv.* incessantly.

ἀμοῦ *adv.* anywhere.

ἄ-μουσος 2 destitute of the Muses, illiterate, rude.

ἄ-μοχθος 2 without pains or trouble; lazy.

ἀμπαυ- see ἀναπαυ-.

ἀμπείρω see ἀναπείρω.

ἀμπέλινος 3 of the vine.

ἀμπελόεις 3 rich in vines.

ἄμπελος, ἡ vine.

ἀμπελ-ουργός, ὁ vine-dresser.

ἀμπελών, ῶνος, ὁ vineyard.

ἀμπεπαλών see ἀναπάλλω.

ἀμ-περές = διαμπερές.

ἀμπ-εχόνη, ἡ clothing, upper garment.

ἀμπ-έχω to enclose, surround; to clothe. — *P.* to be clothed.

ἀμ-πηδάω = ἀναπηδάω.

ἀμπ-ίσχω = ἀμφέχω.

ἀμπλάκημα, τό offence.

ἀμπλακίσκω to offend; to fail, miss.

ἀμ-πνέω = ἀναπνέω.

ἀμ-πνοή, ἡ breath.

ἀμπν- see ἀναπν-.

ἀμπυκτήριον, τό bridle.

ἄμπυξ, ὕκος, ὁ wheel; circlet; diadem. [tide.]

ἄμπωτις, εως, ἡ ebb, low]

ἀμυγδάλινος 3 of almonds.

ἄμυγμα, τό a tearing, rending. [once.]

ἄμυδις *adv.* together, at]

ἀμυδρός 3 dim, indistinct.

ἀ-μύητος 2 uninitiated; gaping.

ἀ-μύθητος 2 unspeakable.

ἀ-μύμων 2 blameless.

ἀμύνάθω = ἀμύνω.

ἀμύντωρ, ορος, ὁ defender; avenger.

ἀμύνω to keep off, ward off, defend; to aid; to requite and *M* to defend oneself; to resist; to requite. [rate.]

ἀμύσσω to scratch, lace-]

ἀμφ-ἀγαπάζω to cherish, foster, befriend.

ἀμφ-αγείρομαι *M.* to assemble around one.

ἀμ-φάδιος 3 manifest, public, known; *adv.* ἀμφαδά, ἀμφαδόν, ἀμφαδίην.

ἀμφ-αΐσσομαι *M.* to rush on or charge from all sides.

ἀμφ-άκης = ἀμφήκης.

ἀμφ-αλείφω to anoint all over. [rattle about.]

ἀμφ-αραβέω to clink or]

ἀμ-φασίη, ἡ speechlessness. [round.]

ἀμφ-αϋτέω to sound all]

ἀμφ-αφάω and *M.* to touch all round; to handle.

ἀμφ-έπω = ἀμφιέπω.

ἀμφ-έρχομαι to surround.

ἀμφ-ηγερέθομαι = ἀμφαγείρομαι.

ἀμφ-ήκης 2 double-edged.

ἀμφ-ῆμαι to sit all round.

ἀμφ-ηρεφής 2 covered all round, shut. [oars.]

ἀμφ-ηρικός 2 with double

ἀμφ-ήριστος 2 disputed, controverted; undecided.

ἀμφί adv. on both or all sides, around; about. — prp. with gen. near, round, about; concerning, for; with dat. at, about; round; because of; by means of; with acc. round, about, along, at, near; concerning; during.

ἀμφί-αλος 2 sea-girt; between two seas. [sides.]

ἀμφ-ϊάχω to sound on all

ἀμφι-βαίνω to walk around, to encompass; to bestride; to protect.

ἀμφι-βάλλω to throw or put round; to embrace; to ensnare. — M. to put on.

ἀμφί-βασις, εως, ἡ protection. [net.]

ἀμφί-βληστρον, τό fishing-

ἀμφι-βολίᾱ, ἡ doubt.

ἀμφί-βολος 2 shot upon on all sides; ambiguous, doubtful; undecided, helpless. [whole man.]

ἀμφί-βροτος 3 covering the

ἀμφι-γνοέω to be uncertain or doubtful. [both sides.]

ἀμφι-γυήεις 3 strong on

ἀμφί-γυος 2 double-pointed; = ἀμφιγυήεις.

ἀμφι-δαίω intr. to burn around.

ἀμφί-δασυς 3 tasselled all round.

ἀμφι-δέαι, αἱ ligatures, clasps, bracelets.

ἀμφι-δέξιος 2 skilled with both hands, very dexterous; ambiguous.

ἀμφι-δήρῑτος 2 disputed, doubtful. [round.]

ἀμφι-δῑνέω to roll all

ἀμφί-δρομος 2 running round.

ἀμφι-δρυφής 2 and ἀμφί-δρυφος 2 scratched on all sides.

ἀμφί-δυμος 2 double.

ἀμφι-δύομαι M. to put on oneself.

ἀμφι-έζω, ἀμφι-έννῡμι and M. to put on, to dress oneself. [rounded.]

ἀμφι-έλισσα, ἡ double-

ἀμφι-έπω to be busy about; take care of; to tend, protect. [ment.]

ἀμφι-εσμα, τό dress, rai-

ἀμφι-εύω to singe all round.

ἀμφ-ιζάνω to sit around, to stick to.

ἀμφι-θαλής 2 with both parents living. [dled.]

ἀμφί-θετος 2 double-han-

ἀμφι-θέω to run round.

ἀμφί-θηκτος 2 double-edged.

ἀμφί-θρεπτος 2 congealed around. [doors.]

ἀμφί-θυρος 2 with double

ἀμφι-καλύπτω to cover, wrap; to veil up, hide; to enclose, envelop, shelter.

ἀμφι-κεάζω to cleave off around.

ἀμφί-κειμαι to lie around, to embrace, to lean on.

ἀμφί-κίων 2 with pillars all round.

ἀμφί-κλυστος 2 washed around by waves.

ἀμφί-κομος 2 with dense foliage.

ἀμφί-κτίονες, οἱ confiners, neighbours. [handled.]

ἀμφί-κύπελλος 2 double-

ἀμφι-λαφής 2 wide, large, huge: copious.

ἀμφι-λαχαίνω to dig or hoe round. [tercate.]

ἀμφι-λέγω to dispute, al-

ἀμφί-λογος 2 disputed, doubtful; altercating.

ἀμφί-λοφος 2 enclosing the nape. [light.]

ἀμφι-λύκη, ἡ dawn, twi-

ἀμφι-μαίομαι to wipe all round. [round.]

ἀμφι-βάσιη, ἡ to fight]

ἀμφι-μάχομαι to fight]

ἀμφι-μέλᾱς, αινα, αν wrapped in darkness.

ἀμφι-μῡκάομαι to roar, low around.

ἀμφι-νεικής, ἀμφι-νείκητος 2 courted by warriors.

ἀμφι-νέμομαι to dwell around.

ἀμφι-νοέω = ἀμφιγνοέω.

ἀμφι-ξέω to smooth all round. [hover around.]

ἀμφι-πέλομαι to surround,

ἀμφι-πένομαι = ἀμφιέπω.

ἀμφι-περι-στέφω to surround on all sides.

ἀμφι-περι-στρωφάω to manage (a horse) round about.

ἀμφι-πίπτω to fall upon.

ἀμφί-πλεκτος 2 entwined, entangled. [around.]

ἀμφι-πλήκτος surging]

ἀμφι-πλήξ, ῆγος double-hitting.

ἀμφι-πολεύω = ἀμφιέπω.

ἀμφι-πολέω to move about with.

ἀμφί-πολος 2 attending, serving; servant. [ἕπω.]

ἀμφι-πονέομαι M. = ἀμφι-]

ἀμφι-ποτάομαι M. to flit around. [by a blaze.]

ἀμφί-πῠρος 2 surrounded]

ἀμφί-ῤῤῠτος flowed around.

ἀμφίς adv. on both sides, round about, on all sides; asunder, apart; far, remote; in two, twofold, differently. — prp. with gen. around; far from, side-ways; with acc. and dat. round about.

ἀμφισ-βάσίη, ἡ = ἀμφισ-βήτησις.

ἀμφισ-βητέω (-βᾰτέω) to altercate; to contradict, dispute, doubt; to assert, claim.

ἀμφισ-βητήσιμος 2, ἀμφισ-βήτητος 2 controverted, disputed, doubtful.

ἀμφισ-βήτησις, εως, ἡ controversy, dispute, doubt.

ἀμφί-ίσταμαι M. to stand around, enclose.

ἀμφί-στομος 2 double-mouthed; double.

ἀμφι-στρατάομαι M. to besiege, beleaguer.

ἀμφι-στρεφής 2 turning or twisting to all sides.

ἀμφι-τάμνω to cut off all round. [or on.]

ἀμφι-τίθημι to put round]

ἀμφι-τρέμω to tremble all over. [openings or outlets.]

ἀμφι-τρής, ῆτος with two]

ἀμφι-τρομέω to tremble for. [crest.]

ἀμφι-φάλος 2 with double]

ἀμφι-φοβέομαι P. to flee on all parts or sides.

ἀμφι-φορεύς, ὁ two-handled pitcher; urn; pail; measure (for fluids).

ἀμφι-φράζομαι M. to consider carefully.

ἀμφι-χάσκω to yawn round.

ἀμφι-χέω to pour or spread around. — P. to flow out, to surround, embrace.

ἀμφί-χῠτος 2 heaped up on both sides.

ἀμφόδιον, τό, ἄμφ-οδον, τό street; quarter of a town.

ἀμφορεύς, ὁ = ἀμφιφορεύς.

ἀμφότερος 3 both, either.

ἀμφοτέρωθεν adv. from or on both sides.

ἀμφοτέρωθι adv. on both sides. [way.]

ἀμφοτέρως adv. in either]

ἀμφοτέρωσε adv. to both sides. [the ground.]

ἀμφ-ουδίς adv. up from]

ἄμφω, ἀμφοῖν both.

ἄμφ-ωτος 2 two-eared, two-handled. [blameless.]

ἀ-μώμητος 2, ἄ-μωμος 2]

ἄμωμον, τό amomum.

ἀμῶς adv. anyhow.

ἄν particle denoting possibility.

ἄν = ἐάν.

ἀνά adv. upwards, above, on high, on the top, thereon. — prp. with dat. on, upon; with acc. up, upwards; through, throughout, along; about; during; up to, according to, with. [up!]

ἄνα for ἀνάστηθι up! get]

ἀνα-βχθμός, ὁ step, stairs.

ἀνα-βαίνω intr. to go up, mount, ascend; to go up the country; to embark, set off; to land; to mount a horse; to enter, appear; to increase to; to pass, end. — trans. to ascend, mount; to step through, bestride; to bring up; to cause to ascend.

ἀνα-βάλλω to throw up; to put back, defer, delay. — M. to put on; to take upon oneself, to undergo, incur; to begin, lift up one's voice.

ἀνά-βασις, εως, ἡ a going up, ascent; inland expedition; ascending steps, stairs; cavalry.

ἀνα-βάτης, ου, ὁ horseman. [swiftly.]

ἀνα-βᾰτικός 3 mounting]

ἀνα-βῐβάζω to cause to go up or ascend, to lead up; to produce. — M. to cause to appear in court; to take up.

ἀνα-βιόω and ἀνα-βιώσκομαι M. to return to life; to call back to life.

ἀνα-βλαστάνω to shoot or blossom up again.

ἀνα-βλέπω to look up or back (upon); to regain sight.

ἀνά-βλεψις, εως, ἡ recovery of sight.

ἀνά-βλησις, εως, ἡ delay.

ἀνα-βοάω to cry out, shout, scream. call. [delay.]

ἀνα-βολή, ἡ mound; cloak;

ἀνα-βραχεῖν to clink; to fly open with a clink.

ἀνα-βρόχω to swallow back. — P. to flow back.

ἀνα-βρῡχάομαι M. to raise a roaring. [ment.]

ἀνά-γαιον, τό upper apart-

ἀν-αγγέλλω to report, give information (about).

ἀνα-γεννάομαι to be born anew.

ἀνα-γιγνώσκω to know again, recognize; to understand thoroughly; to read. recite; to persuade.

ἀναγκάζω to compel, force, urge, ask; to persuade; to prove, demonstrate.

ἀναγκαίη, ἡ = ἀνάγκη.

ἀναγκαῖος 3 and 2 necessary, requisite, wanted, indispensable; inevitable, urgent, violent, compulsory; scanty; related, friendly, allied; forced; bondsman. [forced.]

ἀναγκαστός 3 compelled,

ἀνάγκη, ἡ necessity, constraint, compulsion; fate, law of nature; means of coercion, violence, torture, confinement; need, distress.

ἀνα-γνάμπτω to bend back or round. [guilt.]

ἀν-αγνος 2 stained with

ἀνα-γνωρίζω to recognize, acknowledge.

ἀνα-γνωρισμός, ὁ recognition; recital.

ἀν-αγόρευσις, εως, ἡ publication, proclamation.

ἀν-αγορεύω to proclaim publicly. [down.]

ἀνά-γραπτος 2 written

ἀνα-γραφεύς, ὁ secretary.

ἀνα-γραφή, ἡ record, document.

ἀνα-γράφω to write down, record, enter; inscribe.

ἀν-άγω to lead or bring up (the country, to the high sea); to lift up, raise, exalt; to lead or bring back; intr. to set sail; to retire. — M. and P. to put to sea, to depart; to set about a thing.

ἀν-αγωγή, ἡ departure, putting to sea.

ἀν-άγωγος 2 uneducated, untrained. [contention.]

ἀν-αγώνιστος 2 refusing

ἀνα-δαίω to divide anew.

ἀνα-δασμός, ὁ distribution.

ἀνα-δείκνῡμι, or -ύω to show forth; to reveal, make public; to appoint.

ἀνά-δειξις, εως, ἡ publication; appointment.

ἀνα-δέχομαι = ἀναδέχομαι. [ther or sister.]

ἀν-άδελφος 2 without bro-

ἀνα-δέρχομαι to look up.

ἀνα-δέσμη, ἡ headband.

ἀνα-δέχομαι M. to take up, snatch up; to undergo, bear, endure; to promise: to warrant: to accept, receive.

ἀνα-δέω to tie to, to fasten; to tie round, wreath. — M. also to take (a ship) in tow.

ἀνα-διδάσκω to teach better or thoroughly.

ἀνα-δίδωμι to give forth, to yield; to deliver, distribute; *intr.* to burst forth, bubble up.

ἀνα-διπλόω to make double.

ἀνά-δοτος 2 given back.

ἀνα-δύομαι to rise, emerge; to retire, recede, retreat; to hesitate; to shun, to avoid doing. [wooer's gifts.]

ἀν-άεδνος 2 without a]

ἀν-αείρω to lift up, draw up; to carry off, obtain.

ἀνα-ζάω to revive, return to life. [again; to start.]

ἀνα-ζεύγνῡμι to harness]

ἀνα-ζέω to boil up.

ἀνα-ζητέω to search; to inquire after.

ἀνα-ζώννῡμι to gird up.

ἀνα-ζωπῠρέω to refresh, revive.

ἀνα-θάλλω to cause to sprout, to renew.

ἀνα-θαρρέω to regain one's courage. [anew.]

ἀνα-θαρρύνω to encourage]

ἀνά-θεμα, τό execration; an execrated one.

ἀναθεματίζω to execrate.

ἀνά-θεσις, εως, ἡ dedication. [ly.]

ἀνα-θεωρέω to view closely.

ἀνα-θηλέω to become green again.

ἀνά-θημα, τό consecrated gift, monument; addition.

ἀνα-θορῠβέω to make a noise, to applaud.

ἀν-αθρέω to observe exactly, to examine.

ἀνα-θρώσκω to spring or jump up. [ness.]

ἀν-αίδεια, ἡ shameless-]

ἀν-αιδής 2 shameless, regardless, impudent.

ἀν-αίμων 2 bloodless.

ἀν-αιμωτί *adv.* without bloodshed.

ἀν-αίνομαι *M.* to refuse, decline; to deny.

ἀν-αίρεσις, εως, ἡ a lifting up, gathering; burial; destruction, murder.

ἀν-αιρέω to take or lift up; to bury; to give an oracle, to prophesy; to take away, abrogate, abolish, remove; to destroy, kill. — *M.* to lift up for oneself; to bury; to accept, receive, obtain, take away; to undergo, undertake.

ἀν-αισθησία, ἡ insensibility, dulness.

ἀν-αισθητέω to be dull.

ἀν-αίσθητος 2 unfeeling, dull; painless. [use.]

ἀν-αισῑμόω to consume,]

ἀν-αισίμωμα, τό expense for maintenance.

ἀν-αΐσσω to start up.

ἀν-αισχυντέω to be shameless or impudent.

ἀν-αισχυντία, ἡ impudence. [shameless.]

ἀν-αίσχυντος 2 impudent,]

ἀν-αίτιος 2 guiltless, innocent. [upright.]

ἀνα-καθίζω and *M.* to sit]

ἀνα-καινίζω, ἀνα-καινόω to renew. [newal.]

ἀνα-καίνωσις, εως, ἡ re-]

ἀνα-καίω to kindle.

ἀνα-κᾰλέω to call up, to summon; to call back; to cry. — M. to call to assistance; to summon; to sound the retreat. [unveil.]

ἀνα-κᾰλύπτω to uncover,

ἀνα-κάμπτω intr. to bend back; to return.

ἀν-ἄκανθος 2 boneless.

ἀνα-κάπτω to snap up, wallow.

ἀνά-κειμαι M. to be laid up, offered, or dedicated; to be erected; to belong to, to depend on.

ἀνακεῖον, τό upper story, upper apartment.

ἀνάκειον, τό prison.

ἀνα-κεράννῡμι to mix up.

ἀνα-κεφᾰλαιόω to comprehend.

ἀνα-κηκίω to spout up.

ἀνα-κηρύσσω to proclaim.

ἀνα-κινδῡνεύω to risk again.

ἀνα-κῑνέω to move or swing upwards; to stir.

ἀνα-κίνησις, εως, ἡ commotion.

ἀνα-κλαίω to weep aloud, burst into tears.

ἀνα-κλάω to bend or break back. [cation.]

ἀνά-κλησις, εως, ἡ invo-

ἀνα-κλίνω trans. to lean against; to open; to cause to recline. — P. to lie or lean back.

ἀνα-κογχῠλιάζω to gargle.

ἀνα-κοινόω to communicate, impart; to consult, take counsel (with).

ἀνα-κομῐδή, ἡ restitution.

ἀνα-κομίζω to carry up or back; to bring back. — M. to carry up for oneself; to recover. [(a spear).]

ἀν-ακοντίζω to throw up

ἀνα-κόπτω to thrust or push back, to check.

ἀνα-κουφίζω to lift up; to relieve. [alleviation.]

ἀνα-κούφισις, εως, ἡ relief,

ἀνα-κράζω to cry out, shout. [up.]

ἀνα-κρεμάννῡμι to hang

ἀνα-κρίνω to question, examine; to judge. — M. to litigate.

ἀνά-κρισις, εως, ἡ questioning, examination; remonstrance.

ἀνά-κρουσις, εως, ἡ the pushing back.

ἀνα-κρούω to thrust back. — M. to row back slowly.

ἀνα-κτάομαι M. to acquire or obtain again, to regain.

ἀνακτόριος 3 lordly.

ἀνάκτορον, τό sanctuary.

ἀνα-κυκλέω to revolve.

ἀνα-κυμβᾰλιάζω to tumble rattling. [to emerge.]

ἀνα-κύπτω to rise out of,

ἀνα-κωκύω to wail aloud.

ἀνακῶς adv. carefully.

ἀνακωχεύω to hold back, stop, check; to anchor on the high sea; to preserve, retain; to keep quiet.

ἀνακωχή, ἡ cessation; armistice. [war-cry.]

ἀν-ἀλᾰλάζω to raise the

ἀνα-λαμβάνω to take or lift up; to seize; to take along with or upon one or

into one's service; to undergo, take in hand; to
take again, regain; to
restore, encourage; to re-
trieve, retract. — *M.* to
undergo, incur; to recover.

ἀνα-λάμπω to flame up.

ἀν-αλγησίᾱ, ἡ unfeeling-
ness, dulness.

ἀν-άλγητος 2 unfeeling;
painless.

ἀνα-λέγω to pick up, ga-
ther, collect; to recount.
— *M.* to pick up for oneself; to read.

ἀνα-λείχω to lick up.

ἀνά-ληψις, εως, ἡ a taking
up, regaining, repairing;
ascension.

ἀν-αλίσκω to spend, con-
sume, use up, waste; to
kill.

ἀν-αλκείη, ἡ cowardice.

ἀν-αλκις, ιδος weak, cow-
ardly.   [conformity.]

ἀνα-λογίᾱ, ἡ proportion.]

ἀνα-λογίζομαι to count
up, calculate; to consider.

ἀνα-λογισμός, ὁ delibera-
tion, reasoning; — ἀνα-
λογίᾱ.   [proportionate.]

ἀνά-λογος 2 answering,]

ἄν-αλος 2 unsalted.

ἀν-ᾱλόω = ἀναλίσκω.

ἄν-αλτος 2 insatiable.

ἀνά-λῠσις, εως, ἡ disso-
lution, end; start.

ἀνα-λύω to dissolve, de-
tach, unloose; to deliver;
to set out; to return; to
die. — *M.* to compensate.

ἀν-άλωμα, τό, ἀν-άλωσις,
εως. ἡ expense, cost.

ἀν-άλωτος 2 unconquer-
able.

ἀνα-μαιμάω   to rage
through.   [out.]

ἀνα-μανθάνω to search]

ἀν-ἁμάξευτος impassable
for waggons.

ἀν-ἁμάρτητος 2 faultless,
unfailing; unswerving.

ἀνα-μάσσω to wipe off on.

ἀνα-μάχομαι to renew
battle; to begin anew.

ἀνα-μένω to await; to wait,
stay; to delay; to endure.

ἀνά-μεσος 2 midland.

ἀνα-μετρέω to measure
back; to measure out.

ἀνά-μῑγδα *adv.* = ἀναμίξ.

ἀνα-μίγνῡμι to mix up to-
gether, to intermix.

ἀνα-μιμνῄσκω to remind,
mention. — *P.* to remem-
ber.

ἀνα-μίμνω = ἀναμένω.

ἀνα-μίξ *adv.* mixed up,
promiscuously.

ἀνα-μίσγω = ἀναμίγνῡμι.

ἀνά-μνησις, εως, ἡ remem-
brance.

ἀνα-μορμύρω to rush or
foam up.   [able.]

ἀν-αμπλάκητος 2 inevit-]

ἀν-αμφί-λογος 2, ἀν-
αμφισ-βήτητος 2 undis-
puted.

ἀν-ανδρίᾱ, ἡ unmanliness.

ἄν-ανδρος 2 unmanly, cow-
ardly; without men.

ἀνα-νέμομαι to count up,
enumerate.   [anew.]

ἀνα-νέομαι *M.* to rise]

ἀνα-νεόω and *M.* to renew.

ἀνα-νεύω to deny, refuse.

ἀνα-νήφω to become sober again.

ἀν-αντα *adv.* up-hill.

ἀν-ανταγώνιστος without a rival. [difficult.]

ἀν-άντης 2 up-hill, steep;

ἀν-αντίρρητος 2 indisputable.

ἄναξ, ἄνακτος, ὁ lord, nobleman, king, prince, ruler, master.

ἀνα-ξηραίνω to dry up.

ἀν-άξιος 2 and 3 unworthy, not deserving; vile, contemptible.

ἀνα-ξῠνόω = ἀνακοινόω.

ἀναξῠρίδες, αἱ Persian trousers.

ἀνα-οίγω = ἀνοίγω.

ἀνά-πᾰλιν *adv.* invertedly; back again.

ἀνα-πάλλω to swing up. — *P.* to spring up.

ἀνά-παυλα and ἀνά-παυσις, εως, ἡ rest, recreation, pause.

ἀνα-παυ(σ)τήριος 2 fit for resting.

ἀνα-παύω to cause to cease or leave off, to stop, finish; to bring to rest. — *M.* to leave off, cease, repose; to come to rest. [seduce.]

ἀνα-πείθω to persuade,

ἀνα-πειράομαι *M.* to try, to exercise, train (soldiers).

ἀνα-πείρω to spit, broach.

ἀνα-πεμπάζομαι *M.* to think over. [back.]

ἀνα-πέμπω to send up or

ἀνα-πετάννῡμι to spread out, to open. [away.]

ἀνα-πέτομαι to fly up or

ἀνα-πηδάω to jump up or forth. [pled.]

ἀνά-πηρος 2 maimed, crip-

ἀνα-πίμπλημι to fill up, fulfil, perform; to suffer; to infect.

ἀνα-πίπτω to fall back, to recede, retire; to lie down to table; to lack courage. [κητος.]

ἀν-απλάκητος=ἀναμπλά-

ἀνα-πλάσσω to shape, reshape, restore. [back.]

ἀνα-πλέω to sail up or

ἀνά-πλεως, ων filled up, full; infected.

ἀνα-πληρόω to fill up, complete.

ἀνά-πλοος, ὁ a sailing upwards. ascent up stream; landing-place.

ἀνα-πλώω = ἀναπλέω.

ἀνά-πνευσις, εως, ἡ a breathing again; recovery.

ἀνα-πνέω to breathe again; to recover.

ἀνα-πνοή, ἡ breathing: recovery. rest. [back.]

ἀνα-ποδίζω to call or bring

ἀν-άποινος 2 without ransom, gratis.

ἀνα-πολέω to repeat.

ἀν-απολόγητος 2 inexcusable.

ἀνα-πράσσω to exact, levy.

ἀνα-πρήθω to let burst forth.

ἀνα-πτερόω to lend wings; to incite, instigate.

ἀνα-πτύσσω to unfold, develop; to disclose, unveil.

ἀνα-πτύω to spit or spout up.

ἀν-άπτω to hang up, fasten, attach; to kindle.

ἀνα-πυνθάνομαι *M.* to inquire, search, learn.

ἀνά-πυστος 2 known, notorious.

ἄν-αρθρος 2 enfeebled.

ἀν-αρίθμητος and ἀν-άριθμος 2 numberless, countless; immense.

ἀν-άριστος 2 without breakfast.

ἄν-αρκτος 2 not governed, independent. [harmony.]

ἀν-αρμοστέω to be in disharmostíā, ἡ disharmony. [unfit.]

ἀν-αρμοστία, ἡ disharmony. [unfit.]

ἀν-άρμοστος 2 discordant.

ἀν-αρπάζω to tear or snatch up, to draw up or out; to sweep away, take by force; to rob, destroy. [torn away.]

ἀν-άρπαστος 2 snatched or

ἀνα-ρρήγνῡμι to rend, break, tear open; to tear in pieces; to break forth.

ἀνά-ρρησις, εως, ἡ publication.

ἀνα-ρριπτέω, ἀναρρίπτω to throw up, to whirl up; to dice; to risk. [back.]

ἀνα-ρροιβδέω to swallow

ἀνα-ρρώννῡμι to strengthen or encourage again.

ἀν-άρσιος 2 and 3 reluctant, hostile; repulsive.

ἀν-αρτάω to hang up; to suspend; to make dependent upon; to delay. — *M.* to be prepared to do.

ἀν-άρτιος 2 uneven, odd.

ἀν-αρχία, ἡ anarchy, licentiousness, disobedience.

ἄν-αρχος 2 without a leader. [stir to rebellion.]

ἀνα-σείω to shake up; to

ἀνα-σεύομαι *M.* to spout up. [πέω.]

ἀνα-σκέπτομαι = ἀνασκο-

ἀνα-σκευάζω to pack up; to transport, convey, to clear away. — *M.* to remove, escape. [σταυρόω.]

ἀνα-σκολοπίζω = ἀνα-

ἀνα-σκοπέω to consider exactly.

ἀνά-σπαστος and ἀνα-σπαστός 2 drawn back or opened (door); dragged along, exile.

ἀνα-σπάω to draw up or back, to tear up, to open; λόγους to boast; to drag away. [queen.]

ἄνασσα, ἡ mistress, lady,

ἀνάσσω and *M.* to rule, reign, sway, to be lord or master.

ἀν-άσσω = ἀναΐσσω.

ἀνα-στάδόν *adv.* upright, standing.

ἀνά-στᾰσις, εως, ἡ a setting up; resurrection; expulsion, evacuation, ruin; the getting up; departure.

ἀνά-στᾰτος 2 expelled, exiled; destroyed, wasted; submissive; rebelling.

ἀνα-στᾰτόω to raise up, to seduce. [crucify.]

ἀνα-σταυρόω to impale,

ἀνα-στέλλω to drive or keep back.

ἀνα-στενάζω, ἀνα-στενᾱχίζω, ἀνα-στενᾱχω, ἀνα-στένω to groan, heave sighs, bewail.

ἀνα-στρέφω to turn over, up, back, or about; to upset, throw down; to lead back; intr. to return, to face. — M. and P. = Act. intr.: to wander, rove; to dwell, sojourn; to behave.

ἀνα-στροφή, ἡ a turning back, return; a dwelling in; mode of life. [and fro.

ἀνα-στρωφάω to turn to

ἀνα-σύρομαι to pull up one's clothes, to bare oneself.

ἀνα-σχετός 2 tolerable.

ἀνα-σχίζω to rip up, slit.

ἀνα-σῴζω and M. to save; to recover, restore; to recall to memory.

ἀνα-ταράσσω to stir up, disturb. [again.

ἀνα-τάσσομαι to arrange

ἀν-ἀτεί adv. see ἄνατος.

ἀνα-τείνω to stretch or hold up, to raise; to extend, spread; intr. and M. to stretch out or up, to expand. [wall).

ἀνα-τειχίζω to rebuild (a

ἀνα-τειχισμός, ὁ a rebuilding.

ἀνα-τέλλω to raise, bring forth, produce; intr. to rise, grow, issue.

ἀνα-τέμνω to cut up, dissect.

ἀν-ᾱτί adv. see ἄνατος.

ἀνα-τίθημι to set up, erect, consecrate, dedicate; to put or lay on, load with; to ascribe, impute, charge; to put back, remove. — M. to shift, transpose, al-

ter; to retract; to expose, narrate. [price).

ἀνα-τιμάω to enhance (the

ἀνα-τλῆναι to bear, suffer.

ἀνα-τολή, ἡ sunrise, east.

ἄν-ατος 2 unhurt, uninjured.

ἀνα-τρέπω to upset, overthrow, destroy, ruin; to stir up. — M. and P. to fall down backwards; to perish.

ἀνα-τρέφω to bring up, nourish; to feed again.

ἀνα-τρέχω to run up or back, to ascend, rise; to sprout, shoot up.

ἀνα-τρίβω to rub well.

ἀνα-τροπή, ἡ subversion, downfall.

ἄν-αυδος, ἀν-αύδητος 2 speechless; unutterable, unheard of.

ἀνα-φαίνω to cause to shine or flash up; to show, to make appear, reveal. — P. to appear, to become conspicuous.

ἀνα-φανδά and ἀνα-φανδόν adv. openly, conspicuously.

ἀνα-φέρω to carry, convey, bring up; to offer; to lift up, raise, heave; to carry or bring back; to refer, ascribe. propose; to bear, suffer; intr. to rise, recover; to refer to; to give an account. — M. and P. to draw a long breath.

ἀνα-φεύγω to flee up or back; to be absolved.

ἀνα-φλύω to bubble up.

ἀνα-φορέω = ἀναφέρω.

ἀνα-φράζομαι *M.* to recognize. [one's senses.]

ἀνα-φρονέω to recover.

ἀνα-φύρω to mix up; to soil. [to puff up.]

ἀνα-φῡσάω to blow out;

ἀνα-φύω to let grow, bring forth; *intr.* and *M.* to grow; to sprout (again).

ἀνα-φωνέω to proclaim, recite. [tire, recede.]

ἀνα-χάζω and *M.* to re-

ἀνα-χαιτίζω to throw off; to overthrow.

ἀνα-χέω to pour upon. — *P.* to flow out, to empty oneself. [wantonness.]

ἀνά-χῠσις, εως, ἡ excess,

ἀνα-χωρέω to retire, retreat, withdraw; to return; to pass over, to be transferred.

ἀνα-χώρησις, εως, ἡ a going back, retreat, departure; recess, refuge.

ἀνα-χωρίζω to lead back.

ἀνα-ψηφίζω to cause to vote again. [recreation.]

ἀνά-ψυξις, ἡ a refreshing,

ἀνα-ψύχω to cool, refresh. — *P.* to recover. [tisfy.]

ἀνδάνω to please; to sa-

ἄν-δῐχα *adv.* asunder.

ἀνδρ-ᾰγᾰθίᾱ, ἡ manliness, valour, honesty.

ἀνδρ-ᾰγᾰθίζομαι to act the gentleman.

ἀνδρ-άγρια, τά spoil. booty.

ἀνδρᾰκάς *adv.* man by man, one by one.

ἀνδρᾰποδίζω to kidnap, enslave.

ἀνδρᾰποδισμός, ὁ kidnapping, enslavement.

ἀνδραποδιστής, οῦ, ὁ kidnapper, enslaver.

ἀνδράποδον, τό slave; slavish man. [servile, mean.]

ἀνδραποδώδης 2 slavish;

ἀνδρ-αχθής 2 burdening a man. [lour, courage.]

ἀνδρείᾱ, ἡ manliness, va-

ἀνδρεῖος 3 of a man; manly, valiant, brave.

ἀνδρειότης, ητος, ἡ = ἀνδρεία. [slaying.]

ἀνδρεϊ-φόντης, ου, ὁ man-

ἀνδρεών = ἀνδρών.

ἀνδρηΐη, ἀνδρήϊος = ἀνδρεία. ἀνδρεῖος. [nish.]

ἀνδρηλᾰτέω to exile, ba-

ἀνδρίᾱ, ἡ = ἀνδρεία.

ἀνδριαντο-ποιέω to make statues. [tor.]

ἀνδριαντο-ποιός, ὁ sculp-

ἀνδριάς, άντος, ὁ statue.

ἀνδρίζομαι to prove a man.

ἀνδρικός 3 = ἀνδρεῖος.

ἀνδρό-γῠνος, ὁ man-woman, hermaphrodite, eunuch. [man, artefact.]

ἀνδρό-κμητος 2 made by

ἀνδρο-κτασίᾱ, ἡ manslaughter.

ἀνδρο-κτόνος 2 man-slaying, husband-slaying.

ἀνδρόμεος 3 human.

ἀνδρο-μήκης 2 of a man's height. [man.]

ἀνδρόομαι *P.* to become a

ἀνδρό-σφιγξ, ιγγος. ὁ a man-sphinx. [δρεία.]

ἀνδροτής, ητος. ἡ = ἀν-

ἀνδρο-φάγος 2 eating men, cannibal.

ἀνδρο-φθόρος 2 man-destroying.

ἀνδρό-φθορος 2 slain.

ἀνδρο-φόνος 2 man-killing.

ἀνδρώδης 2 = ἀνδρεῖος.

ἀνδρών, ῶνος, ὁ apartment for males.

ἀν-δύομαι = ἀναδύομαι.

ἀν-εγείρω to awake, rouse. — P. to be roused; to wake up.   [reproach.]

ἀν-έγκλητος 2 free from

ἀν-έδην adv. let loose; freely; simply, without ceremony: sluggishly.

ἀν-έεδνος = ἀνάεδνος.

ἀν-εθέλητος 2 unwished for.

ἀν-ειλέω and ἀν-είλλω to keep, press or urge back.

ἀν-ειμένος 3 let loose, licentious; without restraint.

ἄν-ειμι to go up, to rise; to return.   [ing.]

ἀν-είμων 2 without cloth-]

ἀν-ειπεῖν to proclaim, announce.

ἀν-είργω to keep back.

ἀν-είρομαι to inquire of or about, ask.

ἀν-ειρύω = ἀνερύω.

ἀν-είρω to fasten or tie to.

ἀν-ειρωτάω = ἀνερωτάω.

ἀν-έκαθεν adv. from on high; of old.   [let.]

ἀν-έκβατος 2 without out-]

ἀν-εκδιήγητος 2 indescribable.

ἀν-έκδοτος 2 unmarried.

ἀν-εκλάλητος unspeakable.   [ible.]

ἀν-έκλειπτος inexhaust-]

ἀν-εκπίμπλημι to fill anew.

ἀν-έκπληκτος 2 undaunted, intrepid.

ἀν-εκτός 2, ἀνεκτέος 3 bearable.

ἀν-έλεγκτος 2 not examined; irrefutable.

ἀν-ελεήμων 2 and ἀν-έλεος 2 unmerciful.

ἀν-ελευθερία, ἡ slavish mind, meanness, shabbiness.

ἀν-ελεύθερος 2 ignoble, mean.

ἀν-ελίσσω to unroll, open.

ἀν-έλκω, -ύω to draw up, back, or out.

ἀν-έλπιστος 2 unhoped for; hopeless, despairing.

ἀ-νεμέσητος 2 blameless, free from reproach.

ἀνεμίζω to agitate with the wind.   [as the wind.]

ἀνεμόεις 3 windy; swift]

ἄνεμος, ὁ wind, storm.

ἀνεμο-σκεπής 2 screening from the wind.

ἀνεμο-τρεφής fed by the wind.   [tile, vain.]

ἀνεμώλιος 2 windy; fu-]

ἀν-ένδεκτος 2 inadmissible.

ἀν-εξέλεγκτος 2 = ἀν-έλεγκτος.   [able.]

ἀν-εξερεύνητος 2 inscrut-]

ἀν-εξέταστος not examined; not scrutinized; without inquiry.

ἀν-εξεύρετος 2 not to be found out.

ἀνεξί-κακος 2 forbearing.

ἀν-εξιχνίαστος 2 untraceable.   [no cause for shame.]

ἀν-επαίσχυντος 2 having]

ἀν-επαχθής 2 not molesting, without constraint; indulgent.

ἀν-επιβούλευτον, τό unwariness, harmlessness.

ἀν-επιδεής 2 not needy.

ἀν-επιεικής 2 unyielding, unfair. [κλητος.]

ἀν-επίκλητος 2 = ἀνέγ-]

ἀν-επίληπτος 2 unattacked; blameless.

ἀν-επίσκεπτος 2 unnoticed; inconsiderate.

ἀν-επιστημοσύνη, ἡ ignorance. [unskilled]

ἀν-επιστήμων 2 ignorant,]

ἀν-επίτακτος 2 unconstrained.

ἀν-επιτήδειος 2 unfit, inconvenient; adverse.

ἀν-επιτίμητος 2 not censured. [reproach.]

ἀν-επίφθονος 2 free from]

ἀν-έραμαι P. to fall in love again.

ἀν-ερεθίζω to excite, provoke. — P. to strive anew.

ἀν-ερείπομαι M. to snatch off.

ἀν-ερευνάω to trace out.

ἀν-έρομαι = ἀνείρομαι.

ἀν-ερύω to draw up.

ἀν-έρχομαι to go up, rise; to come; to come back, return, to come home.

ἀν-ερωτάω to question.

ἄν-εσις, εως, ἡ cessation; relaxation.

ἀν-έστιος 2 homeless.

ἀν-ετάζω to search, inquire thoroughly (into).

ἄνευ prp. with gen. without; away from, far from; besides.

ἄνευθεν adv. apart, asunder; = ἄνευ.

ἀν-εύθετος 2 inconvenient.

ἀν-εύθυνος 2 irresponsible.

ἀν-ευρίσκω to find out.

ἀν-ευφημέω to cry aloud.

ἀ-νέφελος 2 cloudless; uncovered. [ed.]

ἀν-εχέγγυος 2 unwarrant-]

ἀν-έχω to hold or lift up; to support, to exalt, honour; to restrain, stop; intr. to project, reach; to emerge, come up; to stop, stay, persist. — M. to hold up; to rise; to stand upright: to keep one's ground; to hold out; to bear, admit; to keep one's temper.

ἀνεψιά, ἡ female cousin.

ἀνεψιός, ὁ male cousin.

ἄνεω, ἄνεῳ (from ἄνεως) silent, mute. [again.]

ἀν-ηβάω to grow young]

ἀν-ηγέομαι M. to count up, relate.

ἄνηθον, τό anise; dill.

ἀν-ήκεστος 2 incurable, irreparable; inexorable; immoderate. [not knowing.]

ἀν-ήκοος 2 not hearing;]

ἀν-ηκουστέω not to listen (to). [horrible.]

ἀν-ήκουστος 2 unheard of,]

ἀν-ήκω to be come; to reach to; to rest or depend on; to become, to beseem.

ἀν-ήλιος 2 sunless.

ἀν-ήμελκτος 2 unmilked.

ἀν-ήμερος 2 untamed, wild.

ἀν-ήνεμος 2 calm.

ἀν-ήνοθα perf. to gush forth, mount up.

ἀν-ήνῠ(σ)τος 2 unfeasible; unsuccessful, endless.

ἀν-ήνωρ 2 unmanly.

ἀνήρ, ὁ man, male; husband; warrior, hero: man (as opp. to gods and beasts).

ἀν-ήριθμος 2 = ἀνάριθμος. [untilled.]

ἀν-ήροτος 2 unploughed,]

ἄνησον = ἄνηθον.

ἀνθ-αιρέομαι M. to choose instead of. [tend, rival.]

ἀνθ-αμιλλάομαι P. to con-]

ἀνθ-άπτομαι to lay hold of, to seize in turns; to manage, carry on; to blame.

ἀνθ-έλκω to draw to the other side.

ἀνθέμιον, τό flower.

ἀνθεμόεις 3 flowery.

ἀνθερεών, ῶνος, ὁ chin.

ἀνθέριξ, ικος, ὁ awn; ear of corn; stalk.

ἀνθέω to bloom, blossom, flourish; to shine.

ἀνθ-ήλιος 2 = ἀντήλιος.

ἀνθηρός 3 blooming, fresh; gay; violent. [turn.]

ἀνθ-ησσάομαι to yield in]

ἀνθίζω to deck as with flowers. [able.]

ἀνθινός 3 flowery; veget-]

ἀνθ-ίστημι to set against, oppose; intr. and P. to oppose oneself, resist.

ἀνθ-ομολογέομαι M. to concede or grant in turn; to confess; to praise.

ἀνθ-οπλίζομαι to arm oneself against.

ἀνθ-ορμέω to ride at anchor opposite.

ἄνθος, τό flower. blossom.

ἀνθ-οσμίας, ου sweet-scented, fragrant. [coal.]

ἀνθρᾱκιά, ἡ burning char-]

ἄνθραξ, ᾱκος, ὁ (living) coal. [serving.]

ἀνθρωπ-άρεσκος 2 time-]

ἀνθρώπειος 3 and ἀνθρώπινος 3 human; sublunar. [man; wretch.]

ἀνθρώπιον, τό child of]

ἀνθρωπο-ειδής 2 in the shape of man. [slaying.]

ἀνθρωπο-κτόνος 2 man-]

ἄνθρωπος, ὁ man (as opp. to gods and beasts), human being, anyone; husband; inhabitant; slave; ἡ ἄ. woman, concubine.

ἀνθρωπο-φᾱγέω to be a man-eater. [man species.]

ἀνθρωπο-φῠής 2 of hu-]

ἀνθ-υπάγω to accuse in turn. [consul.]

ἀνθ-ῠπᾰτεύω to be pro-]

ἀνθ-ῠπᾰτος, ὁ proconsul.

ἀνθ-υποπτεύομαι P. to be suspected in turn.

ἀνῑ́ᾱ, ἡ vexation, annoyance; pain, grief.

ἀνῑάζω to vex, annoy, tease; to be ill-humoured or grieved.

ἀν-ῑάομαι M. to heal again.

ἀνῑᾱρός 3 distressing, molesting, grieving; adverse; melancholy.

ἀν-ῑᾱτος 2 incurable.

ἀνῑάω to distress, vex; to grieve, molest, annoy.

ἀν-ίδρῠτος 2 restless, unsteady; unsociable.

ἀν-ιδρωτί adv. without sweat.

ἀν-ίερος 2 unholy, wicked.

ἀν-ίημι to send up; to raise, produce; to let loose, relax, dismiss, detach, neglect, omit; to incite; to admit, permit, remit; *intr.* to slacken, cease. — *P.* to be loose, free, *or* licentious; to be exposed, sacrificed, *or* abandoned.

ἀνιηρός 3 = ἀνιαρός.

ἀ-νίκητος 2 unconquered; invincible.

ἀν-ίλεως 2 unmerciful.

ἀν-ιμάω to pull up.

ἄν-ιππος 2 unmounted; not fit for horses.

ἀ-νιπτό-πους, ποδος with unwashed feet.

ἄ-νιπτος 2 unwashed.

ἄν-ισος 2 unequal.

ἀν-ισότης, ητος, ἡ inequality.

ἀν-ισόω to equalize.

ἀν-ίστημι to set up, erect, build; to raise, rouse, stir up; to drive away, dislodge; to raise from the dead; to excite; *intr.* and *P.* to be driven away; to rise, get up; to come forth, appear; to start; to recover oneself. [to), investigate.]

ἀν-ιστορέω to inquire (in-}

ἀν-ίσχω = ἀνέχω.

ἀν-ίσωσις, ἡ equilibration.

ἀν-ιχνεύω to trace back, descry.

ἀν-νέομαι = ἀνανέομαι.

ἄν-οδος[1], ἡ way up; march up.

ἄν-οδος[2] 2 impassable.

ἀ-νοήμων 2 unwise.

ἀ-νόητος 2 foolish, silly; inconceivable.

ἄ-νοια, ἡ folly, imprudence.

ἀν-οίγνῦμι, ἀν-οίγω to open, uncover, disclose.

ἀν-οιδέω to swell up.

ἀν-οικίζομαι to settle in the up-country; to lie inland.

ἀν-οικοδομέω to rebuild, build.

ἄν-οικος 2 houseless, homeless. [pitied.]

ἄν-οικτος 2 pitiless; un-}

ἀν-οιμωκτί *adv.* without wailing, with impunity.

ἄν-οιξις, ἡ an opening.

ἀν-οιστέος 3 to be reported.

ἀν-οιστός 3 reported; pending. [see ἀναχ.]

ἀν-οκωχεύω, ἀν-οκωχή}

ἀν-όλβιος and ἄν-ολβος 2 unfortunate, miserable.

ἀν-όλεθρος 2 unhurt.

ἀν-ολκή, ἡ a drawing up.

ἀν-ολολύζω to cry out, scream, shout. [bewail.]

ἀν-ολοφύρομαι *M.* to wail,}

ἄν-ομβρος 2 without rain.

ἀ-νομέω to act contrary to law.

ἀ-νομία, ἡ lawlessness.

ἀν-όμματος 2 eyeless.

ἀν-όμοιος 2 unequal, unlike. [equality.]

ἀν-ομοιότης, ητος, ἡ in-}

ἀν-ομολογέω and *M.* to agree (again).

ἀν-ομολογούμενος 3 inconsistent, contradictory.

ἄ-νομος 2 lawless, wicked; pagan. [enjoying.]

ἀν-όνητος 2 useless; un-}

ἄ-νοος 2 foolish.

ἀν-οπαῖα *adv.* through the smoke-hole (or up in the air, or unnoticed).

ἄν-οπλος 2 unarmed.

ἀν-ορθόω to set up, to set right; to rebuild, restore.

ἄν-ορμος 2 harbourless.

ἀν-όρνῦμαι *M.* to rise.

ἀν-ορούω to start or leap up.

ἀν-όσιος 2 unholy, wicked.

ἀν-οσιότης, ητος, ἡ wickedness.

ἄ-νοσος 2 free from disease.

ἄ-νόστιμος and ἄ-νοστος 2 not returning.

ἀν-ούτατος 2 unwounded, *adv.* ἀνουτητί. [mistice.]

ἀν-οχή, ἡ patience; ar-

ἀν-σχετός = ἀνασχετός.

ἄντα *adv.* opposite, over against, to the face; straight on; against, before.

ἀντ-ἀγοράζω to buy in return.

ἀντ-ἀγωνίζομαι *M.* to fight or struggle against; to contend.

ἀντ-ἀγωνιστής, οῦ, ὁ adversary, rival. [return.]

ἀντ-ἀδικέω to wrong in

ἀνταῖος 3 opposed, in front.

ἀντ-αίρω (-αείρω) and *M.* to lift in defence; to withstand. [turn.]

ἀντ-αιτέω to ask in re-

ἀνταχαῖος, ὁ sturgeon.

ἀντ-ἀκούω to hear in turn.

ἀντ-ἀλλάσσω to exchange, to give or take in exchange.

ἀντ-ἀμείβομαι *M.* to answer, reply; = ἀντ-αλλάσσω.

ἀντ-ἀμύνομαι *M.* to defend or revenge oneself, to resist, to requite.

ἀντ-ἀναβιβάζω to bring up or cause to go up against.

ἀντ-ἀνάγω to lead up against, to lead to the high sea; *intr. M.* and *P.* to sail to meet.

ἀντ-ἀναιρέω to neutralize.

ἀντ-ἀναμένω to wait in turn.

ἀντ-ἀναπίμπλημι, ἀντ-ἀναπληρόω to fill or complete in turn.

ἀντ-ἄνειμι to go up against.

ἀντ-ἀνίσταμαι *M.* to rise up against.

ἀντ-ἄξιος 3 equivalent.

ἀντ-ἀξιόω to claim in return. [in return.]

ἀντ-ἀπαιτέω to demand

ἀντ-ἀποδίδωμι to give back, requite; to correspond.

ἀντ-ἀπόδοσις, ἡ and ἀντ-ἀπόδομα, τό a giving back in turn, requital.

ἀντ-ἀποκρίνομαι *M.* to answer against; to litigate.

ἀντ-ἀποκτείνω to kill in return. [in return.]

ἀντ-ἀπόλλῦμι to destroy

ἀντ-ἀποφαίνω to adduce as a counter-evidence.

ἀντ-ἀρκέω to be a match for. [come in return.]

ἀντ-ἀσπάζομαι *M.* to wel-

ἀντ-ἀτιμάζω to defame in return. [accost.]

ἀντ-αυδάω to answer; to

ἀντάω = ἀντιάω.

ἀντ-ειπεῖν see ἀντιλέγω.

ἀντ-είρομαι = ἀντέρομαι.

ἀντ-εισάγω to import in return. [in return.]

ἀντ-εκπέμπω to send out]

ἀντ-εκπλέω to sail out against. [against.]

ἀντ-εκτρέχω to sally out]

ἀντ-ελπίζω to hope in return. [roads against.]

ἀντ-εμβάλλω to make in-]

ἀντ-εμβιβάζω to change the crew. [requital.]

ἀντ-εμπίπλημι to fill in]

ἀντ-εμπίπρημι to set on fire in revenge.

ἀντ-έξειμι, ἀντ-εξέρχομαι to march out against.

ἀντ-εξόρμησις, ἡ a starting against.

ἀντ-επάγω to lead to attack in turn; to march against. [out against.]

ἀντ-επανάγομαι to sail]

ἀντ-έπειμι, ἀντ-επέξειμι, ἀντ-επεξελαύνω, ἀντ-επεξέρχομαι = ἀντέξειμι.

ἀντ-επεξάγω to extend the line of battle likewise.

ἀντ-επιβουλεύω to form counter-designs.

ἀντ-επιθῡμέω to desire in turn. [return.]

ἀντ-επικουρέω to help in]

ἀντ-επιμελέομαι P. to make counter-preparations.

ἀντ-επιτάσσω to enjoin in turn. [fortify against.]

ἀντ-επιτειχίζομαι M. to]

ἀντ-επιτίθημι to order in return. [in love.]

ἀντ-εραστής, οῦ, ὁ rival]

ἀντ-ερείδω to stand firm against.

ἀντ-ερεῖν see ἀντιλέγω.

ἀντ-έρομαι to ask in return. [return.]

ἀντ-έρως, ωτος, ὁ love in]

ἀντ-ευεργετέω, ἀντ-ευποιέω to benefit in return.

ἀντ-έχω to hold against, to object; to keep off; to bear, sustain; to suffice; to keep one's ground. — M. to object in defence; to cling to; to aim at; to be attached to; to take care of.

ἀντή, ἡ supplication.

ἀντ-ήλιος 2 eastern.

ἄντην adv. opposite, over against, face to face; in front, openly.

ἀντήρης 2 opposite, adverse. [beam.]

ἀντηρίς, ίδος, ἡ supporting]

ἀντήστις, εως, ἡ a meeting.

ἀντί prp. with gen. opposite, over against, before; in return of, for the sake of, instead of, for.

ἀντιάζω = ἀντιάω.

ἀντι-άνειρα, ἡ manlike.

ἀντιάω to go or advance to meet; to approach, meet; to attack; to accept, partake; to experience; to solicit, entreat. — M. to partake. [foot against.]

ἀντι-βαίνω to set one's]

ἀντι-βάλλω to throw in turn; to exchange.

ἀντί-βιος 3 hostile, using force; adv. ἀντιβίην with force, in battle.

ἀντι-βλέπω to look straight at.

ἀντι-βοηθέω to assist in turn; to assist the adversary.

ἀντι-βολέω to go to meet, approach, meet; to partake, join in; to solicit, entreat.

ἀντι-βόλησις, ἡ and ἀντι-βολίᾱ, ἡ entreaty.

ἀντι-γενεηλογέω to devise another pedigree.

ἀντι-γραφή, ἡ counter-writ, accusatory libel, protest, counter-plea.

ἀντί-γραφον, τό copy.

ἀντι-γράφω to write in answer; to remonstrate, protest.   [turn.]

ἀντι-δάκνω to bite in return.

ἀντι-δέομαι P. to beg in turn.

ἀντι-διατίθεμαι to resist.

ἀντι-δίδωμι to give in return, to give back, repay, requite; to atone for; to offer exchange of property.

ἀντι-δῑκέω to be at law, to litigate.

ἀντί-δῐκος, ὁ opponent, adversary.   [property.]

ἀντί-δοσις, ἡ exchange of

ἀντι-δράω to requite.

ἀντι-δωρέομαι M. to present with in return.

ἀντί-θεος 3 godlike.

ἀντι-θεράπεύω to honour in return.

ἀντί-θεσις, ἡ opposition, the contrary.

ἀντι-θέω to run to meet; to rival in running.

ἀντί-θῠρον, τό vestibule, floor.   [against.]

ἀντι-κάθημαι to sit over

ἀντι-καθίζομαι to be seated over against.

ἀντι-καθίστημι to oppose, to place in lieu of; to encourage; intr. and P. to resist; to be placed in lieu of.

ἀντι-κακουργέω to injure in turn.   [turn.]

ἀντι-κάλέω to invite in

ἀντι-καταλλάσσομαι M. to exchange for.

ἀντί-κειμαι to be opposed.

ἀντι-κελεύω to request in turn.

ἀντι-κλαίω to weep in turn.

ἀντι-κόπτω, ἀντι-κρούω to resist, struggle against.

ἀντι-κρῠ́, ἀντι-κρυς over against, against, to the face; straight on; outright, thoroughly, really.

ἀντι-κῠρω to meet, to fall in with.   [weak part.]

ἀντι-λαβή, ἡ handle, hold;

ἀντι-λαμβάνω to take or receive in turn; to take part with; to hold fast. — M. to take hold of, to lay claim to, to seize, to take care of.

ἀντι-λέγω to gainsay, deny, dispute; to resist; to reply.

ἀντί-λεκτος 2 disputed, controverted.

ἀντί-ληψις, ἡ a receiving in return; seizure, claim; objection; a falling sick, infection; an aiding.

ἀντι-λογέω = ἀντιλέγω.

ἀντι-λογίᾱ, ἡ gainsaying, rejoinder, contradiction; law-suit; contention, enmity.

ἀντι-λογίζομαι M. to consider against.

ἀντι-λογικός 3 controversial, sophistical. [turn.

ἀντι-λοιδορέω to revile.in]

ἀντί-λυρος lyre-like.

ἀντί-λυτρον, τό ransom.

ἀντι-μάχομαι M. to be opposed in battle. [turn.

ἀντι-μέλλω to await in]

ἀντι-μέμφομαι M. to blame in turn. [out again.

ἀντι-μετρέω to measure]

ἀντι-μέτωπος 2 with opposed fronts.

ἀντι-μηχᾰνάομαι M. to devise counter-practises.

ἀντι-μίμησις, ἡ imitation on the other side.

ἀντι-μισθία, ἡ requital.

ἀντι-ναυπηγέω to build ships against; to take preventive measures in shipbuilding.

ἀντί-ξοος 2 hostile, opposed.

ἀντιόομαι P. to resist.

ἀντίος 3 opposite, confronting; opposed, contrary.

ἀντιο-στᾰτέω to resist.

ἀντιόω = ἀντιάω.

ἀντί-πᾰλος 2 wrestling against; rival, contrary, adversary; counterpoising, equivalent, counter-balanced. [pare.

ἀντι-παραβάλλω to com-]

ἀντι-παραγγέλλω to command in turn. [against.

ἀντι-παρχθέω to run past]

ἀντι-παρακᾰλέω to encourage in turn.

ἀντι-παρακελεύομαι M. to exhort in turn.

ἀντι-παραλῠπέω to injure in turn.

ἀντι-παραπλέω to sail along on the other side.

ἀντι-παρασκευάζομαι M. to make counter-preparations. [ter-preparation.

ἀντι-παρασκευή, ἡ coun-]

ἀντι-παρατάσσω to draw out in array against.

ἀντι-παρατίθημι to oppose, to compare.

ἀντί-πάρειμι to march parallel to.

ἀντι-παρεξάγω to lead to battle against. [πάρειμι.

ἀντι-παρέρχομαι = ἀντι-]

ἀντι-παρέχω to offer in turn. [turn.

ἀντι-πάσχω to suffer in]

ἀντι-πᾰτᾰγέω to outsound.

ἀντι-πέμπω to send against, in return, back, or in supply.

ἀντι-πέραια, τά the opposite coast.

ἀντι-πέρᾱν, ἀντι-πέρᾱς adv. over against, opposite.

ἀντί-πετρος 2 hard as stone.

ἀντι-πίπτω to fall out differently.

ἀντι-πλέω to sail against.

ἀντι-πλήξ, ῆγος wavebeaten. [turn.

ἀντι-πληρόω to man in]

ἀντι-ποθέω to long for in turn.

ἀντι-ποιέω to do in turn. — M. to claim; to rival; to contend. [atoning.

ἀντί-ποινος 2 requiting,]

ἀντι-πολεμέω to make war against.

ἀντι-πόλεμος, ὁ enemy.

ἀντι-πολιορκέω to besiege in turn. [march against.]

ἀντι-πορεύομαι P. to} ἀντί-πορος 2 opposite.

ἀντι-πράσσω (-πρήσσω) to counter-act.

ἀντι-πρεσβεύομαι M. to send ambassadors in turn.

ἀντι-πρόειμι, ἀντι-πρόσ-ειμι to advance against.

ἀντι-προσερρήθην (from ἀντιπροσαγορεύω) to requite salutation. [face.]

ἀντι-πρόσωπος 2 face to face

ἀντι-προτείνω to stretch forth in turn.

ἀντί-πρωρος prow to prow.

ἀντί-πυλος 2 with opposite doors.

ἀντί-ρροπος 2 counterpoising, outweighing.

ἀντι-σήκωσις, ἡ equilibrium. [an equal footing.]

ἀντ-ισόομαι P. to be on}

ἀντί-σπαστος 2 spasmodic.

ἀντί-σταθμος 2 equal in weight. [adverse party.]

ἀντι-στασιάζω to form an}

ἀντι-στασιώτης, ου, ὁ political adversary.

ἀντι-στατέω to resist.

ἀντι-στοιχέω to stand opposite in array.

ἀντι-στρατεύομαι M. to take the field against.

ἀντι-στράτηγος, ὁ general of the enemies.

ἀντι-στρατοπεδεύομαι M. to encamp over against.

ἀντί-στροφος 2 corresponding. [firm in turn]

ἀντ-ισχυρίζομαι M. to af-}

ἀντ-ίσχω = ἀντέχω.

ἀντί-ταξις, ἡ opposite line of battle.

ἀντι-τάσσω to range in battle agai st. [pose.]

ἀντι-τείνω to resist, op-}

ἀντι-τείχισμα, τό counter-fortification.

ἀντι-τεχνάομαι M. to form a counter-scheme.

ἀντι-τέχνησις, ἡ counter-practise.

ἀντί-τεχνος, ὁ rival in art.

ἀντι-τίθημι to set against, oppose, compare; to compensate, give for.

ἀντι-τιμάω to honour in return. — M. to make a counter-proposal of a fine.

ἀντι-τιμωρέομαι M. to revenge oneself in turn.

ἀντι-τίνω to atone for, suffer punishment.

ἀντι-τολμάω to act boldly in turn. [rows in return.]

ἀντι-τοξεύω to shoot ar-}

ἀντι-τορέω to bore through.

ἄν-τιτος 2 requited.

ἀντι-τυγχάνω to get in return.

ἀντί-τυπος 2 repulsive; echoing; ἀντί-τυπον, τό exact representation, prototype.

ἀντι-τύπτω to beat in turn.

ἀντι-φερίζω to think oneself equal.

ἀντι-φέρω to set against, oppose. — M. to resist, cope with.

ἀντί-φημι to gainsay.

ἀντι-φιλέω to love in return.

ἀντί-φονος 2 murdering in return. [caution.]

ἀντι-φῦλᾰκή, ἡ mutual/ ἀντι-φῠλάττομαι M. to be on one's guard against.

ἀντι-φωνέω to reply, gainsay. [turn.]

ἀντι-χαίρω to be glad in/ ἀντι-χᾰρίζομαι M. to oblige or favour in turn.

ἀντι-χειροτονέω to vote against.

ἀντι-χράω to suffice.

ἀντί-χριστος, ὁ antichrist.

ἀντλέω to draw water; to empty.

ἄντλημα, τό bucket.

ἀντλίᾱ, ἡ and ἄντλος, ὁ bilge-water; bottom of a ship. [turn.]

ἀντ-οικτίζω to pity in/ ἀν-τολή = ἀνατολή.

ἀντ-όμνῦμι to swear in turn. [anew.]

ἀντ-ονομάζω to name/ ἀντ-ορύσσω to dig a countermine. [in turn.]

ἀντ-οφείλω to be indebted/ ἀντ-οφθαλμέω to withstand to the face.

ἀν-τρέπω = ἀνατρέπω.

ἄντρον, τό cave, grotto, cavern.

ἀντρώδης 2 cavernous.

ἄντυξ, υγος, ἡ circle, rim, edge; rail of a chariot.

ἀντ-υποκρίνομαι M. to answer in return.

ἀντ-υπουργέω to return kindness.

ἀντ-ωμοσίᾱ, ἡ plaintiff's oath; bill of indictment.

ἀντ-ωνέομαι M. to outbid.

ἀντ-ωφελέω to help in return. [drought.]

ἀν-υδρίᾱ, ἡ want of water,/ ἄν-υδρος 2 without water, dry; ἡ ἄ. desert.

ἀν-ὑμέναιος 2 without nuptial song, unwedded.

ἀνῠμι = ἀνύω.

ἀ-νύμφευτος and ἄ-νυμφος 2 unmarried; ill-married.

ἀν-υπέρβλητος 2 insurpassable, insuperable.

ἀν-υπόδητος 2 unshod, barefoot.

ἀν-υπόκρῐτος 2 guileless.

ἀν-ύποπτος 2 unsuspected; unsuspecting. [ible.]

ἀν-υπόστᾰτος 2 irresist-/ ἀν-υπότακτος 2 not subjected; disobedient.

ἄνῠσις, εως, ἡ achievement, success.

ἀνυστός 3 to be accomplished, feasible.

ἀνῠτω and ἀνύτω = ἀνύω.

ἀν-ῠφαίνω to weave anew.

ἀνύω and ἀνύω to accomplish, complete, achieve, perform, effect; to travel over, advance; to consume, finish.

ἄνω = ἀνύω

ἄνω adv. up, upwards, on high, above, aloft; up country, northwards; beyond; ἀνωτέρω higher up; ἀνωτάτω upmost, highest up.

ἄνωγα and ἀνώγω to command, order, advise.

ἀνώ-γαιον, τό and ἀνώγεων, ω, τό upper story or apartment; granary.

ἀν-ώδῠνος 2 free from pain, painless; soothing pain.

ἄνωθεν *adv.* from on high, from above; above; downward; ever since; anew.

ἀν-ωθέω to push up or back. — *M.* to ward off.

ἀν-ώϊστος 2 unexpected; *adv.* ἀνωϊστί. [able.]

ἀν-ώλεθρος 2 imperish-]
ἀν-ωμαλίᾱ, ἡ unevenness, inequality. [equal.]
ἀν-ώμᾰλος 2 uneven, un-]

ἀν-ωμοτί *adv.* unsworn.

ἀν-ώνῠμος 2 without name.

ἀν-ωρίᾱ, ἡ wrong or unseasonable time.

ἀν-ωρος 2 untimely.

ἀνωτερικός 3 situated higher up.

ἀν-ωφελής and ἀν-ωφέ-]
λητος 2 useless, hurtful.
ἄ-ξενος 2 inhospitable.

ἄ-ξεστος 2 unpolished.

ἀξίᾱ, ἡ worth, value, price; dignity, honour; merit, desert; the due.

ἀξι-ἀφήγητος 2 worth relating. [thy.]

ἀξι-έπαινος 2 praisewor-]
ἀξίνη, ἡ axe, hatchet.

ἀξιο-βίωτος 2 worth living for. [able.]

ἀξιο-θαύμαστος 2 admir-]
ἀξιο-θέᾱτος 2 worth seeing.

ἀξιό-λογος 2 worth naming; important; just, proper. [battle.]

ἀξιό-μᾰχος a match for in]
ἀξιο-μνημόνευτος 2 memorable. [tory.]

ἀξιό-νῑκος 2 deserving vic-]

ἀξιό-πιστος 2 trustworthy.

ἄξιος 3 worth, equivalent, compensating; worthy, precious; due, convenient, deserving; right and proper; cheap. [notice.]

ἀξιό-σκεπτος 2 worthy of]
ἀξιο-στράτηγος 2 worthy of being general.

ἀξιο-τέκμαρτος 2 demonstrative.

ἀξιό-χρεως, ων 2 considerable; sufficient; authentic; proper, convenient, worthy.

ἀξιόω to rate, estimate; to think worthy, esteem; to request, claim; to suppose, take for true.

ἀξίωμα, τό, ἀξίωσις, ἡ valuation, estimation; dignity, rank, credit; consideration; importance; request, will; opinion.

ἄ-ξῠλος 2 not cleared of wood; scantily wooded.

ἄξων, ονος, ὁ axle.

ἀοιδή, ἡ song, myth, legend.

ἀοιδιάω to sing.

ἀοίδῐμος 2 celebrated in song; notorious.

ἀοιδός, ὁ, ἡ singer, poet; conjurer.

ἀ-οίκητος 2 uninhabited.

ἄ-οικος 2 houseless, homeless, poor; uninhabitable.

ἄ-οινος 2 without wine; disdaining wine.

ἄ-οκνος 2 unhesitating; eager, willing. [crowds.]

ἀ-ολλής 2 all together, in]
ἀ-ολλίζω to assemble.

ἄορ, ἄορος, τό sword.

ἀ-όρᾱτος 2 unseeing; invisible.

ἀ-όριστος 2 undefined.

ἀορτήρ, ῆρος, ὁ baldrick, shoulder-belt. [protector.]

ἀοσσητήρ, ῆρος, ὁ helper,]

ἄ-ουτος 2 unwounded.

ἀ-οχλησίᾱ, ἡ ease.

ἀπ-αγγελίᾱ, ἡ report.

ἀπ-αγγέλλω to report, announce, relate, declare; to praise.

ἀ-παγής 2 not solid.

ἀπ-αγῑνέω to carry off; to pay.

ἀπ-αγορεύω to forbid, deny, dissuade; to fail, fall short, to be worn out.

ἀπ-αγριόομαι P. to become wild or savage.

ἀπ-άγχω to strangle. — M. to hang oneself.

ἀπ-άγω to lead or carry on or away; to remove; to march off, go away; to lead up, back, or home. — M. to take with one.

ἀπ-αγωγή, ἡ a leading off, taking home; payment; motion of arrest.

ἀπ-ἀδεῖν see ἀφανδάνω.

ἀπ-ᾄδω to sing out of tune.

ἀπ-αείρω = ἀπαίρω.

ἀπ-ἀθᾱνᾱτίζω to make immortal.

ἀ-παθής 2 without pain, not suffering; uninjured; unfeeling, dull; impatient; unaccustomed.

ἀ-παιδευσίᾱ, ἡ want of education, coarseness.

ἀ-παίδευτος 2 uneducated, rude.

ἀ-παιδίᾱ, ἡ childlessness.

ἀπ-αίνυμαι to take from, withdraw.

ἀπ-αίρω to lift away, to take or snatch away; to cause to start; intr. to start, march or sail away. — M. to go away.

ἄ-παις, αιδος childless.

ἀπ-αΐσσω = ἀπᾴσσω.

ἀπ-αισχύνομαι to renounce for shame.

ἀπ-αιτέω, ἀπ-αιτίζω to demand back, reclaim.

ἀπ-αίτησις, ἡ reclamation.

ἀπ-ακρῑβόω to work exactly.

ἀ-πάλαμνος 2 awkward, wavering. inactive. [dull.]

ἀπ-αλγέω to forget; to be]

ἀπ-αλείφω to blot out.

ἀπ-αλέξω to ward off; to defend from. — M. to defend oneself. [thoroughly.]

ἀπ-άλθομαι to be cured]

ἀπ-αλλαγή, ἡ separation; retreat; deliverance.

ἀπ-αλλαξείω to wish for deliverance. [λαγή.]

ἀπ-άλλαξις, ἡ = ἀπαλ-]

ἀπ-αλλάσσω to set free, release, deliver, dismiss, remove, separate; intr. to get off, to get clear. — P. to go away, depart; to be delivered or released.

ἀπ-αλλοτριόω to estrange.

ἀπ-αλοιάω to crush.

ἀπαλός 3 soft, tender, delicate.

ἀπαλότης, ητος, ἡ softness, tenderness; effeminacy.

ἀπαλο-τρεφής 2 well-fed.

ἀπ-αμάω to cut off, mow.

ἀπ-αμβλύνω to blunt, weaken. [τάνω.]

ἀπ-αμβροτεῖν see ἀφαμαρτ-

ἀπ-αμείβομαι to answer.

ἀπ-αμελέω to neglect utterly or altogether.

ἀπ-αμύνω to ward off. — M. to repel; to defend oneself. [to refuse.]

ἀπ-αναίνομαι M. to deny;

ἀπ-αναισχυντέω to do with the utmost impudence.

ἀπ-αναλίσκω to consume, waste; to kill.

ἀπ-άνωθεν adv from afar, far off; aside, apart; without (with gen.).

ἀπ-ανίστημι to cause to rise or depart; intr. and M. to rise, depart, emigrate.

ἀπ-αντάω to come or go to meet, to meet; to advance against; to come to pass, to happen.

ἀπάντη adv. everywhere.

ἀπ-άντησις, ἡ meeting.

ἀπ-αντικρύ, ἀπ-αντίον adv. right over against.

ἀπ-ανύω to finish.

ἅπαξ adv. once; at once, once for all; for the first time.

ἀπ-αξιόω to think unworthy; to detest, reject.

ἀ-παράβατος 2 imperishable. [ρέω.]

ἀπ-αραιρῆσθαι see ἀφαι-

ἀ-παραίτητος 2 inexorable; inevitable. [for.]

ἀ-παράκλητος 2 uncalled

ἀ-παρασκεύαστος 2 and ἀ-παράσκευος 2 unprepared, unarmed.

ἀπ-αράσσω to dash down, to strike or cut off.

ἀπ-αρέσκω to displease. — M. to reconcile fully.

ἀπ-αριθμέω to count over.

ἀπ-αρίθμησις, ἡ a numbering.

ἀπ-αρκέω to suffice.

ἀπ-αρνέομαι P. and M. to deny; to disown, refuse.

ἄπ-αρνος 2 denying.

ἀπ-αρτάω to hang (up), attach; to put away, remove. [cisely.]

ἀπ-αρτί adv. exactly, precisely, pre-

ἀπ-άρτι adv. just now, at once. [amount.]

ἀπαρτι-λογία, ἡ full

ἀπ-αρτισμός, ὁ consummation, completion.

ἀπ-αρύω to skim off.

ἀπ-αρχή, ἡ firstlings, first-fruit. [sacred act.]

ἀπ-άρχομαι to begin a

ἅπας, ἅπασα, ἅπαν all, all together; whole, entire; each, every.

ἀπ-ᾴσσω to leap down; to rush away; to digress.

ἄ-παστος 2 not having tasted. [beguile.]

ἀπατάω to cheat, deceive,

ἀπ-άτερθεν adv. asunder, apart; far from (with gen.).

ἀπατεών, ῶνος, ὁ cheat.

ἀπάτη, ἡ cheating, deceit, fraud.

ἀπατήλιος 2 and ἀπατηλός 3 and 2 deceitful. [roughly.]

ἀπ-ατιμάω to despise tho-

ἀ-πάτωρ, ορος fatherless.

ἀπ-αύγασμα, τό reflection, image.

ἀπ-αυδάω to forbid.

ἀπ-αυθαδίζομαι, ἀπ-αυθαδιάζομαι *M.* to be overweening. [away, to rob.]

ἀπ-αυράω to take or snatch]

ἄ-παυστος 2 incessant.

ἀπ-αυτομολέω to desert, go over.

ἀπαφίσκω to beguile.

ἄ-πεδος 2 even, flat.

ἀ-πείθεια, ἡ disobedience.

ἀ-πειθέω to disobey; to be an unbeliever.

ἀ-πειθής 2 disobedient; unbelieving.

ἀπ-εικάζω to copy, portray; to describe; to compare.

ἀπ-εικότως *adv.* unjustly.

ἀπ-ειλέω[1] to press hard.

ἀπειλέω[2] to threaten, menace; to boast; to promise.

ἀπειλή, ἡ and ἀπείλημα, τό menace, threat; boast.

ἀπειλητήρ, ῆρος, ὁ braggart.

ἀπειλητήριος 2 and ἀπειλητικός 3 threatening.

ἄπ-ειμι[1] to be away or absent; to be wanting.

ἄπ-ειμι[2] to go away, to leave; to go over; to return.

ἀπ-εῖπον to tell plainly, pronounce; to forbid, deny, refuse; to renounce, resign; *intr.* to fail, fall short. — *M.* to fail; to refuse; to renounce.

ἀ-πείραστος, ἀ-πείρατος, ἀ-πείρητος 2 untried, unattempted; not having tried; inexperienced.

ἀπ-είργω (ἀπ-ειργαθεῖν) to keep away, separate, define; to remove; to encompass, confine.

ἀ-πειρέσιος = ἄπειρος.

ἀπ-πειρία, ἡ inexperience, ignorance.

ἀπειρό-κακος 2 wanting bad experience. [nered.]

ἀπειρό-καλος 2 ill-man-]

ἄ-πειρος 2, ἀ-πείρων 2 unlimited, boundless, innumerable; unexperienced, ignorant.

ἀπ-εκδέχομαι to await.

ἀπ-εκδύομαι to put off one's clothes; to overcome.

ἀπ-εκλανθάνομαι *M.* to forget entirely.

ἀπ-ελαύνω, -ελάω to drive or turn away; to exclude; *intr.* to march or ride off.

ἀπ-ελεγμός, ὁ ill repute.

ἀ-πέλεθρος 2 immense.

ἀπ-ελεύθερος 2 freedman.

ἀπ-ελπίζω to despair; to hope from.

ἀπ-εμέω to spit out.

ἀπ-εμπολάω to sell.

ἀπ-έναντι, ἀπ-εναντίον *adv.* over against. [arms.]

ἀπ-εναρίζω to deprive of]

ἀπ-ενιαυτίζω to be absent for a year.

ἀπ-εννέπω to forbid.

ἀπ-έοικα to be unlike; ἀπεικώς unlikely, unnatural; unfair.

ἄπερ just as.

ἀ-πέραντος 2 infinite, endless; impassable.

ἀπ-εργάζομαι *M.* to work off; to contrive, construct, finish.

ἀπ-εργασίᾱ, ἡ a finish(ing), completing, causing.

ἀπ-έργω = ἀπείργω.

ἀπ-έρδω to complete.

ἀπερ-εί just as, like.

ἀπ-ερείδομαι M. to support oneself upon, to lean on; to turn to; to insist upon.

ἀπερείσιος 2 = ἀπειρέσιος.

ἀ-περίοπτος 2 reckless.

ἀ-περίσκεπτος 2 inconsiderate.

ἀ-περίσπαστος 2 undistracted, unmoved. [cised.]

ἀ-περίτμητος 2 uncircum-]

ἀ-περίτροπος 2 unconcerned.

ἀπ-ερύκω to keep off or away. — M. to abstain.

ἀπ-έρχομαι to go away, depart; to go over; to return.

ἀπ-ερωεύς, ὁ destroyer, thwarter. [recoil.]

ἀπ-ερωέω to withdraw,]

ἀπ-εσσούᾱ = ἀπεσσύη (from ἀποσεύω) he is gone (dead).

ἀπ-εστώ, οῦς, ἡ absence.

ἀ-πευθής 2 inscrutable; ignorant.

ἀπ-ευθύνω to straighten; direct; judge; to bind back.

ἀπ-ευνάζω to lull to sleep.

ἀπ-εύχομαι M. to execrate; to avert by praying.

ἀπ-εφθός 2 refined.

ἀπ-εχθαίρω to hate; to make hateful.

ἀπ-εχθάνομαι M. to become hated or odious; to turn enemy. [tred.]

ἀπ-έχθεια, ἡ enmity, ha-]

ἀπ-εχθής 2 odious, hateful; hostile.

ἀπ-έχω to hold off; prohibit; to have one's share (ἀπέχει: it is enough); to be distant or far. — M. to abstain, desist.

ἀπ-ηλεγέως adv. bluntly.

ἀπ-ηλιξ, ικος elderly.

ἀπ-ηλιώτης, ου, ὁ east wind.

ἀ-πήμαντος 2 unhurt; without pain; harmless; wholesome.

ἀπήνη, ἡ waggon.

ἀπ-ηνής 2 unfriendly, harsh.

ἀ-πηρος 2 unmaimed.

ἀπ-ήωρος 2 hovering far.

ἀπ-ιάλλω to send away.

ἀ-πίθανος 2 incredible, unlikely.

ἀ-πιθέω = ἀπειθέω.

ἀ-πῑνύσσω to be unconscious or senseless.

ἄπιος 3 far away, distant.

ἀπ-ῑπόω to squeeze out.

ἀπ-ῑσόω to make equal.

ἀ-πιστέω not to believe; to doubt; to mistrust; to disobey.

ἀ-πιστίᾱ, ἡ disbelief; doubt; mistrust; perfidy.

ἄ-πιστος 2 unreliable, perfidious; incredible; doubtful; unbelieving, distrustful; disobedient.

ἀπ-ισχυρίζομαι M. to reject strongly.

ἀπ-ίσχω = ἀπέχω.

ἀ-πλατος 2 unapproachable; horrible.

ἄ-πλετος 2 immense.

ἀ-πληστίᾱ, ἡ insatiability.

ἄ-πληστος 2 insatiate; infinite.

ἄ-πλοια, ἡ no sailing, calm.

ἀπλοΐζομαι M. to act honestly.

ἀπλοΐς, ίδος, ἡ onefold.

ἀπλόος, ἀπλοῦς 3 onefold, single; simple, plain; sincere, honest; sound; ἀπλῶς plainly, simply; decidedly, without ceremony, in a word.

ἄ-πλοος, ἄπλους 2 unnavigable; unfit for sea, unseaworthy.

ἀπλότης, ητος, ἡ simplicity; honesty.

ἄ-πνευστος 2 breathless.

ἀπό adv. off, away; back. — prep. (with gen.) from, away from; from above; far from; asunder from; since, immediately after; on the part of, by means of, because of, with; after.

ἀπο-βάθρᾱ, ἡ gangway; ladder.

ἀπο-βαίνω to step off, alight, dismount, descend, land; to turn out, end, come to pass, happen, succeed; to prove, become; trans. to disembark.

ἀπο-βάλλω to throw off, to drop; to get clear of the shore; to drive away; to lose.

ἀπο-βάπτω to dip in.

ἀπό-βασις, ἡ a landing, disembarking. [embark.]

ἀπο-βιβάζω trans. to dis-)

ἀπο-βλάπτω to injure. — P. to be robbed of.

ἀπο-βλαστάνω to sprout forth.

ἀπο-βλάστημα, τό descendant. [gard.]

ἀπο-βλέπω to look at, re-)

ἀπό-βλητος 2 rejectable.

ἀπο-βλύζω to spirt out.

ἀπο-βολή, ἡ a casting away; loss.

ἀπο-βρίζω to sleep.

ἀπο-γεισόω to provide with a sheltering roof.

ἀπο-γεύομαι M. to taste; to try. [by dikes.]

ἀπο-γεφυρόω to dam up)

ἀπο-γίγνομαι M. to be absent or away; to get lost; to depart this life.

ἀπο-γιγνώσκω to absolve; to give up, resign; to despair; to reject, acquit.

ἀπό-γνοια, ἡ despair.

ἀπό-γονος 2 descendant.

ἀπο-γραφή, ἡ list, catalogue, register; census; indictment of fraud in taxpaying.

ἀπο-γράφω to write down, register, enlist; to depose, give evidence; to bring an action against. — M. to get enlisted or registered; to sign; to note down; to cause to be recorded; to bring in a law-suit. [feeble.]

ἀπο-γυιόω to lame, en-)

ἀπο-γυμνόω to make bare, to strip of (clothes).

ἀπο-δαίομαι M. to assign; to portion off, single out.

ἀπο-δάσμιος 2 parted off.

ἀπο-δειδίσσομαι to frighten from.

ἀπο-δείκνῡμι, -ὕω to show forth, exhibit, set forth; to manifest; to prove, demonstrate; to appoint, designate. [age.]

ἀπο-δειλιάω to lose courage.

ἀπό-δειξις, ἡ a showing forth, statement, proof.

ἀπο-δειροτομέω to behead; butcher.

ἀπο-δείρω = ἀποδέρω.

ἀπο-δεκατόω to tithe.

ἀπό-δεκτος 2 welcome.

ἀπό-δερμα, τό stripped-off skin.

ἀπο-δέρω to flay, skin (off).

ἀπο-δέχομαι M. to accept, receive; to perceive, understand; to approve of, acknowledge, believe; to be attached to.

ἀπο-δέω[1] to tie to.

ἀπο-δέω[2] to want, lack; to be behind.

ἀπο-δημέω to be absent or abroad; to depart, emigrate.

ἀπο-δημητής, οῦ, ὁ inclined to or fond of travelling.

ἀπο-δημίᾱ, ἡ absence from home, travel abroad.

ἀπό-δημος 2 abroad, travelling.

ἀπο-διδράσκω to run away; to shun, avoid; to be lost (out of sight).

ἀπο-δίδωμι to give away or back, to return, requite, pay off; to perform, accomplish; to surrender, deliver; to concede; to abandon. — M. to sell, let out.

ἀπο-δίεμαι to frighten away.

ἀπο-δικέω to defend oneself in court.

ἀπο-δῑνέω to thrash out.

ἀπο-διο-πομπέομαι M. to expiate. [guish.]

ἀπο-διορίζω to distinguish.

ἀπο-διώκω to chase, expel.

ἀπο-δοκέω to displease.

ἀπο-δοκιμάζω to disapprove, reject; abrogate; turn out; to ostracize.

ἀπό-δοσις, ἡ return, payment.

ἀπο-δοχή, ἡ a receiving back; approbation.

ἀπο-δοχμόω to bend sideways. [flight.]

ἀπό-δρᾱσις, ἡ escape.

ἀπο-δρύφω to rub off, gall.

ἀπο-δύνω = ἀποδύω M.

ἀπ-οδύρομαι to lament, bewail. [ing-room.]

ἀπο-δυτήριον, τό undressing-room.

ἀπο-δύω to undress, strip off. — M. and ἀπο-δύνω to undress oneself. [from.]

ἀπο-είκω to withdraw.

ἀπο-εργάθω, ἀπο-έργω = ἀπείργω.

ἀπο-ζάω to eke out existence, to earn a scanty livelihood.

ἀπ-όζω to give odour.

ἀπο-θαρρέω to gain courage. [at, marvel.]

ἀπο-θαυμάζω to wonder.

ἀπόθεν = ἀπωθεν.

ἀπό-θεσις, ἡ a laying aside, keeping.

ἀπό-θεστος 2 despised.

ἀπό-θετος 2 hidden; precious.

ἀπο-θέω to run away.

4*

ἀπο-θήκη, ἡ granary, receptacle, magazine. [up.]

ἀπο-θησαυρίζω to store]

ἀπο-θλίβω to press hard.

ἀπο-θνήσκω to die; to be killed. [or down.]

ἀπο-θρῴσκω to leap up]

ἀπο-θύμιος 2 disagreeable.

ἀπο-θύω to sacrifice.

ἀπ-οικέω to dwell afar (off); emigrate. [ment.]

ἀπ-οικία, ἡ colony, settle-]

ἀπ-οικίζω to transplant; send away; colonize.

ἀπ-οικίς, ίδος, ἡ = ἀποικία.

ἀπ-οικοδομέω to wall up, block up.

ἄπ-οικος 2 emigrant, colonist, settler; ἡ ἄ. colony.

ἀπ-οικτίζομαι M. to lament.

ἀπ-οιμώζω to bewail.

ἄ-ποινα, τό ransom, fine for homicide; compensation.

ἀπ-οίχομαι M. to be gone; to be far from; to go away.

ἀπο-καθαίρω to wipe off, to clean(se).

ἀπο-κάθαρσις, ἡ lustration; secretion.

ἀπο-κάθημαι to sit apart.

ἀπο-καθίστημι (-καθιστάνω) to restore, reestablish; intr. and P. to be restored.

ἀπο-καίνυμαι to surpass.

ἀπο-καίριος 2 = ἄκαιρος.

ἀπο-καίω to burn off or out; to cause to freeze.

ἀπο-καλέω to call away, aside or back; to name, give names. [uncover.]

ἀπο-καλύπτω to unveil,]

ἀπο-κάλυψις, ἡ revelation.

ἀπο-κάμνω to grow tired; to abandon from weariness.

ἀπο-κάπω to breathe out.

ἀπο-καρᾱ-δοκίᾱ, ἡ a yearning, expectation.

ἀπο-καταλλάσσω to reconcile anew. [ration.]

ἀπο-κατάστασις, ἡ resto-]

ἀπο-καυλίζω to break off.

ἀπο-κάω = ἀποκαίω.

ἀπό-κειμαι to lie apart or in store, to be ready.

ἀπο-κείρω to shear off; to cut in pieces.

ἀπο-κεφαλίζω to behead.

ἀπο-κηδεύω to mourn the due time. [being careful.]

ἀπο-κηδέω to relent in]

ἀπο-κινδύνευσις, ἡ risk, dangerous attempt.

ἀπο-κινδῡνεύω to venture, attempt, try. [drive away.]

ἀπο-κῑνέω to remove; to]

ἀπο-κλαίω to burst into tears, to weep oneself out.

ἀπό-κλεισις, ἡ a shutting off, exclusion.

ἀπο-κλείω to shut or lock up, in, or out; to exclude, refrain; to cut off, intercept [lot(s).]

ἀπο-κληρόω to draw by]

ἀπό-κλησις = ἀπόκλεισις.

ἀπο-κλίνω to turn as de, divert; intr. and P. to deviate; to stoop, fall; to incline to.

ἀπο-κλύζω to wash away.

ἀπο-κναίω to rub off, to torment.

ἀπ-οκνέω to hesitate; to give up from fear.

ἀπ-όκνησις, ἡ a shrinking from, aversion. [enough.]

ἀπο-κοιμάομαι P. to sleep

ἀπο-κοιτέω to be absent at night. [by swimming.]

ἀπο-κολυμβάω to escape

ἀπο-κομιδή, ἡ retreat.

ἀπο-κομίζω to carry away or back. — M. to fetch back. — P. to depart.

ἀπο-κοπή, ἡ abolition.

ἀπο-κόπτω to cut off.

ἀπο-κορΰφόω to answer concisely or briefly.

ἀπο-κοσμέω to clear away.

ἀπο-κοτταβίζω to fling the last drops of wine from a cup.

ἀπο-κρατέω to surpass.

ἀπο-κρεμάννῡμι to let hang down. [precipitous.]

ἀπό-κρημνος 2 sloping,

ἀπό-κριμα, τό answer; sentence.

ἀπο-κρΐνω to separate; to select; to vary, distinguish. — P. and M. to part, separate (oneself). — M. to answer, return sentence; to take up the word.

ἀπό-κρισις, ἡ answer.

ἀπό-κροτος 2 hard.

ἀπο-κρούω to strike off or back, to ward off.

ἀπο-κρύπτω to hide from; conceal; to lose from sight. — M. to hide oneself; to conceal. [cret.]

ἀπό-κρῡφος 2 hidden, se-

ἀπο-κτείνω, -κτιννΰω, -κτίννῡμι to kill, slay.

ἀπο-κυέω, -κύω to bring forth, give birth.

ἀπο-κυλίω to roll off.

ἀπο-κωλύω to hinder, prevent. [lot.]

ἀπο-λαγχάνω to get by]

ἀπο-λαμβάνω to take away or apart; to separate; to cut off; to retain, hinder; to accept, receive; to regain.

ἀπο-λαμπρΰνομαι P. to become famous.

ἀπο-λάμπω to shine far, reflect (light).

ἀπό-λαυσις, ἡ enjoyment, advantage. [profit.]

ἀπο-λαΰω to enjoy, to

ἀπο-λέγω to pick out, select. [down.]

ἀπο-λείβομαι P. to drip

ἀπο-λείπω to leave, lose, relinquish; to leave behind; to leave a distance; to omit; to go away, to leave off; to fail, fall short, to be wanting. — P. to remain, to be left, to remain behind; to miss; to stay away; to be severed.

ἀπο-λείχω to lick off.

ἀπό-λειψις, ἡ a leaving, retreat, depart. [choice.]

ἀπό-λεκτος 2 chosen out,

ἀ-πόλεμος 2 unwarlike.

ἀπο-λέπω to peel or cut off.

ἀπο-λήγω to leave off, cease, end.

ἀπό-ληψις, ἡ an intercepting, a cutting off.

ἄ-πολις 2 townless; homeless. [to slip.]

ἀπ-ολισθάνω to glide off,

ἀπο-λιχμάω to lick off.

ἀπ-όλλῡμι (-ύω) to ruin, destroy, undo; to kill; to

lose. — *M.* (and *perf.* ἀπό-λωλα) to be ruined, undone, destroyed or lost, to perish, die.

ἀπο-λογέομαι *M.* to defend or justify oneself; to defend.

ἀπο-λογία, ἡ defence.

ἀπο-λογίζομαι *M.* to give an account (of); to discuss; to calculate, enumerate.

ἀπό-λογος, ὁ tale; fable.

ἀπο-λούω to wash off.

ἀπ-ολοφύρομαι *M.* to bewail enough.

ἀπο-λῡμαίνομαι *M.* to clean(se) oneself.

ἀπο-λῡμαντήρ, ῆρος, ὁ one who clears tables, consumer, destroyer.

ἀπό-λῠσις, ἡ release, absolution. [release.]

ἀπο-λῠτικός 3 disposed to]

ἀπο-λύτρωσις, ἡ a ransoming, redemption.

ἀπο-λύω to loosen, set free, deliver; to dismiss, acquit; to absolve. — *M.* to free or justify oneself; to redeem, ransom. — *M.* and *P.* to depart.

ἀπο-λωβάω to insult.

ἀπο-μανθάνω to unlearn.

ἀπο-μαραίνομαι *P.* to wither, dry up.

ἀπο-μάσσω to scrape or wipe off.

ἀπο-μαστῑγόω to scourge.

ἀπο-μᾰτᾰΐζω to behave indecently.

ἀπο-μάχομαι *M.* to fight from; to ward off; to repudiate.

ἀπό-μᾰχος 2 unfit for battle.

ἀπο-μετρέω to measure out.

ἀπο-μηκύνω to lengthen or draw out. [wrath.]

ἀπο-μηνΐω to prolong]

ἀπο-μῑμέομαι *M.* to copy, counterfeit.

ἀπο-μιμνήσκομαι *P.* to remember, bear in mind.

ἀπό-μισθος 2 without pay; paid off. [for hire.]

ἀπο-μισθόω to put out]

ἀπο-μνημονεύματα, τά memoirs, memorable things.

ἀπο-μνημονεύω to keep in memory; to recount.

ἀπο-μνησῐκᾰκέω to resent an evil.

ἀπ-όμνῡμι to swear; to disclaim upon oath.

ἀπο-μονόω to leave alone; to exclude. [or clean.]

ἀπ-ομόργνῡμι to wipe off]

ἀπο-μῡθέομαι *M.* to dissuade (from).

ἀπο-ναίω to transplant; to send home. — *M.* to emigrate.

ἀπο-νέμω to allot, assign.

ἀπο-νέομαι to go away; to return.

ἀ-πόνητος 2 without pains, easy; unpunished. — *adv.* ἀπονητί. [bathe.]

ἀπο-νίζω to wash off; to]

ἀπ-ονίνᾰμαι *M.* to enjoy.

ἀπο-νίπτω = ἀπονίζω.

ἀπο-νοσέομαι *P.* to be desperate. [foolhardiness.]

ἀπό-νοια, ἡ folly; despair;]

ἄ-πονος 2 inactive, lazy; easy.

ἀπο-νοστέω to return home.

ἀπο-νόσφιν asunder, apart; far from.

ἀπο-νοσφίζω to put asunder; to deprive; to shun.

ἀπό-ξενος 2 inhospitable.

ἀπο-ξενόω to estrange. — P. to live abroad.

ἀπο-ξέω to smooth, polish; to cut off.

ἀπο-ξηραίνω to dry up.

ἀπ-οξύνω to sharpen, point.

ἀπο-ξῠρέω to shear off.

ἀπο-ξύω to shave off.

ἀπο-παπταίνω to look about timidly.

ἀπο-παύω to cause to leave off, to stop. — M. to leave off, cease.

ἀπό-πειρα, ἡ proof, trial, experiment.   [prove.]

ἀπο-πειράω and P. to try,

ἀπο-πέμπω to send away or back, to dismiss. — M. to get rid of.

ἀπό-πεμψις, ἡ dismissal.

ἀπο-πέτομαι M. to fly away or back.

ἀπο-πήγνῡμι to cause to freeze. — P. to congeal, curdle.

ἀπο-πηδάω to leap off or away; to desert.

ἀπο-πίμπλημι to fill up, complete; to supply; to satisfy.

ἀπο-πίνω to drink of.

ἀπο-πίπτω to fall down.

ἀπο-πλάζω, ἀπο-πλανάω to lead astray. — P. to go astray, to be cast away.

ἀπο-πλέω to sail off or home.

ἀπό-πληκτος 2 struck by apoplexy; benumbed.

ἀπο-πληρόω = ἀποπίμπλη-μι.   [benumbed.]

ἀπο-πλήσσομαι P. to be)

ἀπό-πλοος, -πλους, ὁ a sailing away.

ἀπο-πλύνω to rinse off.

ἀπο-πλώω = ἀποπλέω.

ἀπο-πνέω (-πνείω) to breathe forth, exhale; to blow from.   [strangle.]

ἀπο-πνίγω to choke,)

ἀπό-πολις 2 banished.

ἀπο-πορεύομαι P. to depart, go away.

ἀπο-πρίω to saw off.

ἀπο-πρό adv. far away; far from.

ἀπο-προαιρέω to take away from before.

ἀπό-προθεν adv. from afar.

ἀπό-προθι adv. far off.

ἀπο-προΐημι to send far (away); to shoot forth; to let drop.

ἀπό-πτολις = ἀπόπολις.

ἀπ-οπτος 2 seen from afar; invisible.

ἀπό-πτυστος 2 detested.

ἀπο-πτύω to spit out.

ἀπο-πυνθάνομαι to question, inquire after.

ἀπορέω to be embarrassed, perplexed, at a loss or helpless; to be distressed or needy.   [or indestructible.]

ἀ-πόρθητος 2 not sacked)

ἀπ-ορθόω to make straight; to direct.

ἀπορία, ἡ embarrassment, perplexity; doubt; need; difficulty, impassableness.

ἀπ-όρνῠμαι *M.* to start, depart.

ἄ-πορος 2 impassable; difficult; irresistible; impossible; extravagant; helpless; needy, poor; unable.

ἀπ-ορούω to leap off, rebound.

ἀπο-ρραθῡμέω to leave off from timidity.

ἀπο-ρραίνω to spirt about.

ἀπο-ρραίω to tear from.

ἀπο-ρράπτω to sew up.

ἀπο-ρρέω to flow off or down; to vanish.

ἀπο-ρρήγνῡμι to break off, to sever.

ἀπό-ρρητος 2 forbidden; unspeakable; secret; abominable. [from, recoil.]

ἀπο-ρρῑγέω to shrink]

ἀπο-ρρίπτω, -τέω to throw away, reject; to despise.

ἀπο-ρροή and ἀπό-ρροια, ἡ a flowing off or out.

ἀπο-ρροιβδέω to shriek out.

ἀπο-ρρώξ, ῶγος, ὁ, ἡ steep, abrupt; a flowing out; wine of the first press.

ἀπ-ορφανίζομαι *P.* to become an orphan.

ἀπ-ορχέομαι *M.* to lose in dancing.

ἀπο-σᾰλεύω to anchor in the open sea. [lustrate.]

ἀπο-σᾰφέω to explain, il-]

ἀπο-σβέννῡμι to extinguish; *intr.* and *P.* to be extinguished; to expire.

ἀπο-σείω to shake off.

ἀπο-σεύομαι *M.* and *P.* to run away.

ἀπο-σημαίνω to announce by signs, to signal. — *M.* to perceive; to seal; to confiscate. [to freeze off.]

ἀπο-σήπομαι *P.* to rot off;]

ἀπο-σῑμόω to turn aside.

ἀπο-σιωπάω to grow speechless. [by trenches]

ἀπο-σκάπτω to bar (off)]

ἀπο-σκεδάννῡμι to scatter, chase; to remove, dismiss.

ἀπο-σκευάζω to clear away. — *M.* to pack up.

ἀπο-σκηνόω to be encamped apart.

ἀπο-σκήπτω to fling on; *intr.* to burst forth; to end.

ἀπο-σκίασμα, τό adumbration; trace. [δάννῡμι.]

ἀπο-σκίδνημι = ἀποσκε-]

ἀπο-σκοπέω to look at away from; to regard.

ἀπο-σκυδμαίνω to be wroth or angry.

ἀπο-σκώπτω to scoff.

ἀπό-σπασμα, τό morsel.

ἀπο-σπάω to tear or pull off, to sever; *intr.* and *P.* to go away, part.

ἀπο-σπένδω to pour out (a libation).

ἀπο-σπεύδω to dissuade; to prevent; to frustrate.

ἀπο-στᾰδά, -δόν *adv.* from afar.

ἀπο-στάζω to let drip.

ἀπο-στᾰσίᾱ, ἡ, ἀπόστᾰσις, ἡ a standing away; rebellion, apostasy.

ἀπο-στάσιον, τό (bill of) divorce.

ἀπο-στᾰτέω to stand away; to differ; to apostatize

ἀπο-σταυρόω to palisade.

ἀπο-στεγάζω to unroof.

ἀπο-στείχω to step away, back.

ἀπο-στέλλω to send away or out; to forward; to send back; to chase.

ἀπο-στερέω to deprive; to withhold; to rob, snatch away.

ἀπο-στέρησις, ἡ deprivation. [ρέω.]

ἀπο-στερίσκω = ἀποστε-

ἀπο-στίλβω to shine.

ἀπο-στολεύς, ὁ commissary of the fleet.

ἀπο-στολή, ἡ a sending; apostle's office.

ἀπό-στολος, ὁ messenger; traveller; apostle; naval expedition. [to question.]

ἀπο-στοματίζω to recite;

ἀπο-στρατοπεδεύομαι M. to encamp at a distance.

ἀπο-στρέφω to turn away or back; to tie to the back; to bring back; to cause to return; to drive away or back; to turn to. — intr. and P. to turn away or round; to return; to abhor; to apostatize.

ἀπο-στροφή, ἡ turning away, averting; flight, escape; help; refuge.

ἀπό-στροφος 2 averted.

ἀπο-στυγέω to abhor, detest. [back.]

ἀπο-στυφελίζω to push

ἀπο-συλάω to rob, spoil.

ἀπο-συνάγωγος 2 ejected from the synagogue.

ἀπο-σύρω to tear off.

ἀπο-σφακελίζω to die of mortification.

ἀπο-σφάλλω to mislead; to frustrate. — P. to miss, fail.

ἀπο-σφάττω to slay, slaughter. [sever.]

ἀπο-σχίζω to split off; to]

ἀπο-σῴζω to save, shelter.

ἀπο-τακτός 2 appropriated

ἀπο-τάμνω = ἀποτέμνω.

ἀπο-τάσσω to range apart; to assign specially. — M. to depart from. [a ditch.]

ἀπο-τάφρευω to fortify by]

ἀπο-τείνω to stretch out, lengthen; to reach to; to aim at. — P. to be extended.

ἀπο-τειχίζω to separate or surround by a wall; to wall round or in; to fortify.

ἀπο-τείχισις, ἡ, ἀπο-τείχισμα, τό a blockading; circumvallation. [(intr.).]

ἀπο-τελευτάω to end]

ἀπο-τελέω to finish, achieve, satisfy, effect, pay, fulfil.

ἀπο-τέμνω to cut off; to tear off; to separate; to make one's own.

ἀπο-τήκομαι to melt away; to vanish.

ἀπο-τηλοῦ adv. far.

ἀ-ποτίβατος = ἀπρόσβατος.

ἀπο-τίθημι to put away, aside, or down. — M. to put away, remove; to omit; to defer.

ἀπο-τίλλω to pluck out.

ἀπο-τῑμάω to value, tax. — *M.* to get payment.

ἀπο-τινάσσω to shake off.

ἀπο-τίνω (-τίνῡμι) to pay off, atone, requite. — *M.* to exact, punish; to avenge.

ἀπο-τμήγω = ἀποτέμνω.

ἄ-ποτμος 2 unhappy.

ἀπο-τολμάω to venture, dare; to tell freely.

ἀπο-τομή, ἡ a cutting off.

ἀπο-τομία, ἡ steepness.

ἀπό-τομος 2 steep, precipitous; severe.

ἄ-ποτος 2 not drinking; undrinkable.

ἀπο-τρέπω to turn away or back; to restrain, dissuade; to prevent. — *P.* and *M. intr.* to turn away or back; to return, fly; to desist, shun.

ἀπο-τρέχω to run away.

ἀπο-τρίβω to rub or scour off. — *M.* to efface. [evil.]

ἀπο-τρόπαιος 2 averting,]

ἀπο-τροπή, ἡ an averting, deterring, prevention; aversion.

ἀπό-τροπος 2 averted, banished; averting, horrible.

ἀπό-τροφος 2 brought up abroad.

ἀπο-τρύω to undo, vex.

ἀπο-τρωπάω = ἀποτρέπω.

ἀπο-τυγχάνω to miss, lose, fail. [death.]

ἀπο-τυμπανίζω to beat to]

ἀπο-τύπτομαι *M.* to cease mourning.

ἀπ-ούρας see ἀπαυράω.

ἀπ-ουρίζω to alter boundary-stones; to lessen.

ἀπ-ουρος 2 distant.

ἄ-πους, ἄπουν, -ποδος footless; lame.

ἀπ-ουσία, ἡ absence.

ἀπο-φαίνω to show forth, point out, to bring to light; to prove, explain; to describe; to appoint. — *P.* to appear.

ἀπο-φάσκω = ἀπόφημι.

ἀπο-φέρω to carry off or away; to carry, lead, take, bring back or up; to transmit; to indicate.

ἀπο-φεύγω to flee from, escape; to avoid; to be acquitted.

ἀπό-φημι to speak out, declare; to deny; to refuse.

ἀπο-φθέγγομαι *M.* to speak plainly. [sentence.]

ἀπό-φθεγμα, τό a saying,]

ἀπο-φθείρω to destroy, undo, ruin.

ἀπο-φθίνῠθω to perish; to lose.

ἀπο-φθίνω, -φθίω to destroy; to perish. [slight.]

ἀπο-φλαυρίζω to despise,]

ἀπο-φοιτάω to go away.

ἀπο-φορά, ἡ tribute, tax.

ἀπο-φορτίζομαι *M.* to unburden oneself.

ἀπο-φράγνῡμι to bar, block up, stop, intrench. [up.]

ἀπό-φραξις, ἡ a blocking]

ἀπο-φῠγή, ἡ escape, flight; refuge.

ἀπο-φώλιος 2 void, vain, useless. [draw.]

ἀπο-χάζομαι *M.* to with-]

ἀπο-χειρο-βίωτος 2 living by manual labour.

ἀπο-χέω to pour out; to throw down.

ἀπο-χόω to dam up.

ἀπο-χράω to suffice. — P. to be contented. — M. to use out; to misuse; to kill.

ἀπό-χρησις, ἡ misuse; consumption.

ἀπο-χρώντως adv. sufficiently.   [lame.]

ἀπο-χωλόω to make quite}

ἀπο-χώννῡμι = ἀποχόω.

ἀπο-χωρέω to go away; to retreat.   [retreat.]

ἀπο-χώρησις, ἡ return,}

ἀπο-χωρίζω to part, separate. — P. to part.

ἀπο-φάω to wipe off.

ἀπο-ψηφίζομαι M. to countervote, reject; to acquit. — P. to be rejected.

ἀπο-ψῑλόω to make bald; to deprive.

ἄπ-οψις, ἡ view, prospect.

ἀπο-ψύχω to breathe out, swoon; to cool, refresh; to dry up.

ἀ-πρᾱγμοσύνη, ἡ inactivity; non-intervention.

ἀ-πρᾱγμων 2 inactive; peace-loving; without pains, easy.

ἄ-πρᾱκτος, ἄπρηκτος 2 effecting nothing, useless; inactive; not done, untried; impossible; unconquerable, incurable.

ἀ-πρᾱξίᾱ, ἡ inaction.

ἀ-πρεπής 2 unbecoming.

ἀ-πρίατος 2 and 3, adv. ἀπριάτην, unbought, gratuitous.   [incessantly.]

ἀπρίξ adv. holding fast;}

ἀ-πρόθῡμος 2 disinclined.

ἄ-προικος 2 dowerless.

ἀ-προμήθεια, ἡ imprudence.

ἀ-προνόητος 2 heedless.

ἀ-προσδόκητος 2 unexpected; not expecting.

ἀ-προσήγορος 2 not to be accosted; unkind.

ἀ-πρόσῑτος 2 inaccessible.

ἀ-πρόσκοπος 2 innocent; blameless.

ἀ-πρόσμαχος 2 invincible.

ἀ-πρόσμῑκτος 2 without intercourse.

ἀ-προσόμῑλος 2 unsociable.

ἀ-προσωπο-λήπτως adv. without respect of persons.

ἀ-προτί-μαστος 2 untouched.

ἀ-προφάσιστος 2 unevasive; unreserved.   [able.]

ἀ-προφύλακτος 2 inevit-}

ἄ-πταιστος 2 without stumbling.

ἄ-πτερος 2, ἄ-πτην, ῆνος unwinged; not flying away.

ἄ-πτο-επής 2 prattling boldly.

ἀ-πτόλεμος 2 = ἀπόλεμος.

ἅπτω to fasten, attach, fix; to kindle. — M. to touch, grasp, seize, lay hold of; to try; to perceive; to mention; to undertake. — P. to be kindled, to take fire.

ἀ-πύλωτος 2 not closed by a gate.

ἀ-πύργωτος 2 not fortified (by towers).

ἄ-πυρος 2, ἄ-πύρωτος 2 not touched by fire, uncooked, new.

ἄ-πυστος 2 not remembered or known, inaudible; not knowing.

ἀπύω = ἠπύω. [far away.]

ἄπωθεν adv. from afar;

ἀπ-ωθέω to thrust away. — M. to drive away or back; to ward off, repel; to despise. [ruin, loss.]

ἀπ-ώλεια, ἡ destruction,

ἀπ-ώμοτος 2 abjured, abjurable; who abjures.

ἄπ-ωσις, ἡ a driving away.

ἀπ-ωστός 3 expelled, driven away.

ἀπωτάτω adv. farthest off.

ἀπωτέρω adv. farther off.

ἄρα part. of affirmation: then; farther; moreover.

ἆρα part. of interrogation = lat. num or -ne; ἆρ' οὐ = nonne.

ἀρά, ἡ prayer; curse; destruction, revenge.

ἀράβέω to rattle, clatter.

ἄράβος, ὁ and ἀραγμός, ὁ a rattling, clashing, din.

ἀραιός 3 thin, narrow, slender; weak.

ἀραῖος 3 and 2 cursing, dire; accursed.

ἀραίρηκα see αἱρέω.

ἄράομαι M. to pray, implore; to wish; to curse.

ἀραρίσκω to join, put together, fit with; to fix; to build, fit out; intr. to be joined, fastened, or fitted, to suit; to be equipped; to please.

ἀράσσω to strike, knock, hammer, dash. [cursed.]

ἀρᾱτός 3 prayed for; ac-

ἀράχνη, ἡ spider. [cobweb.]

ἀράχνιον, τό spider's web,

ἀργᾰλέος 3 heavy, troublesome, grievous.

ἀργεϊ-φόντης, ου, ὁ epithet of Hermes; swift messenger or killer of Argus.

ἀργεννός 3 = ἀργής.

ἀργεστής, οῦ white; clearing up.

ἀργέω to be idle or inactive.

ἀργής, ῆτος or έτος white, shining, bright.

ἀργίᾱ, ἡ laziness, leisure.

ἀργι-κέραυνος 2 with bright flashes of lightning.

ἀργῐλώδης 2 clayish.

ἀργινόεις 3 = ἀργής.

ἀργι-όδους, ὀδοντος with white teeth.

ἀργί-πους, ποδος with white feet, fleet.

ἄργμα, τό firstlings of an offering. [Argives.]

ἀργολίζω to side with the]

ἀργός[1] 3 bright, white; swift.

ἀργός[2] 2 lazy, idle; useless; not done; untilled. [silver.]

ἀργύρειος, ἀργύρεος 3 of

ἀργύριον, τό silver; silver coin; money; silver-mine.

ἀργυρο-δίνης, ου eddying like silver. [nails.]

ἀργυρό-ηλος 2 with silver]

ἀργυρο-κόπος, ὁ silversmith. [money.]

ἀργυρο-λογέω to exact]

ἀργυρο-λογίᾱ, ἡ the levying of money. [money.]

ἀργυρο-λόγος 2 exacting]

ἀργυρό-πεζα, ἡ, ἀργυρό-πους, ποδος silver-footed.

ἀργύρος, ὁ silver; money.

ἀργῠρό-τοξος 2 with silver bow. [with money.]

ἀργῠρ-ώνητος 2 bought

ἀργῠφεος 3, ἄργῠφος 2 silver-white.

ἄρδην adv. on high, upwards; from on high; utterly, entirely.

ἄρδις, ἡ arrow-head.

ἀρδμός, ὁ watering-place.

ἄρδω to water, irrigate.

ἀρετή, ἡ = ἀρά.

ἀρείων 2 better; braver.

ἄ-ρεκτος 2 unfinished.

ἀρέομαι = ἀράομαι.

ἀρεσκεία, ἡ pleasing disposition.

ἀρέσκω and M. to please, amend, compensate, satisfy. — P. to be agreeable or pleasant; to be pleased or satisfied.

ἀρεστός 3 agreeable, acceptable. [thrive.]

ἀρετάω to be good, to

ἀρετή, ἡ goodness, excellence, perfection, merit, fitness; bravery, valour; virtue.

ἀρήγω to help, aid.

ἀρηγών, όνος, ὁ, ἡ helper.

ἀρηΐ-θοος 2 swift in war.

ἀρηΐ-κτάμενος 3, ἀρηΐφατος 2 killed in battle.

ἀρηΐ-φιλος 2 loved by Ares. [whelmed.]

ἀρημένος 3 damaged, over-

ἀρήν, ἀρνός, ὁ, ἡ lamb, sheep.

ἄρηξις, ἡ help, defence.

ἀρητήρ, ῆρος, ὁ one praying, priest.

ἄ-ρητος 2 unspeakable.

ἀρητός = ἀρατός.

ἀρθμέω to be joined together.

ἄρθμιος 3 united, joined; friend; concordant.

ἄρθρον, τό joint; limb.

ἀρθρόω to articulate.

ἀρί-γνωτος 2 and 3 easy to be known; well-known.

ἀρί-δείκετος 2 excellent.

ἀρί-δηλος 2, ἀρίζηλος 2 and 3 most distinct, conspicuous, clear, excellent.

ἀριθμέω to number, count up; to class. [cal.]

ἀριθμητικός 3 arithmeti-

ἀριθμός, ὁ number; amount, quantity; a counting, muster. [splendid.]

ἀρι-πρεπής 2 eminent,

ἀριστάω to breakfast.

ἀριστεία, ἡ heroic deed; heroism. [ward, prize.]

ἀριστεῖον, τό victor's re-

ἀριστερός 3 left, to the left; ἡ ά. the left hand; sinister, ominous; clumsy.

ἀριστεύς, ὁ the best or noblest one; prince, hero.

ἀριστεύω to be the best (one), to excel.

ἀριστίνδην adv. according to noble birth.

ἀριστο-κρατέομαι P. to live in an aristocracy.

ἀριστο-κρατίᾱ, ἡ aristocracy. [cratical.]

ἀριστο-κρατικός 3 aristo-

ἀριστό-μαντις, ὁ the best of the seers.

ἄριστον, τό breakfast.

ἀριστο-ποιέομαι M. to (get one's) breakfast.

ἄριστος 3 the best, bravest or noblest; aristocrat.

ἀριστό-χειρ, ειρος with the bravest hand. [pery.]

ἀρι-σφαλής 2 very slippery.

ἀρι-φράδής 2 very manifest, easily known.

ἄρκεσις, ἡ help, service.

ἀρκετός 3 sufficient.

ἀρκέω to keep or ward off; to help, assist; to be enough, to suffice; to be able. — P. to be contented or satisfied.

ἄρκιος 3 sufficient, sure.

ἄρκος, τό defence; solace.

ἀρκούντως adv. sufficiently, enough.

ἀρκτέον from ἄρχομαι to begin; to be ruled.

ἄρκτος, ὁ, ἡ bear.

ἀρκτ-οὖρος, ὁ bearherd.

ἄρκυς, υος, ἡ net, snare.

ἀρκύ-στατος 3 and 2 ensnared.

ἅρμα, τό waggon, team.

ἁρμ-άμαξα, ἡ coach, travelling carriage.

ἁρμάτειος 3 belonging to a waggon. [waggon.]

ἁρματ-ηλάτέω to drive a]

ἁρματ-ηλάτης, ὁ charioteer. [wright.]

ἁρματο-πηγός, ὁ cart-]

ἁρμόδιος 3 fitting.

ἁρμόζω = ἁρμόττω.

ἁρμονίᾱ, ἡ joint, union; cramp, clasp; treaty, decree; harmony, proportion. [peg.]

ἁρμός, ὁ joint; groove; slit;]

ἁρμοστήρ, ῆρος, ὁ and ἁρμοστής, οῦ, ὁ governor, prefect, magistrate.

ἁρμόττω to fit together, join, adjust; to betroth, marry; intr. to fit, suit, become, to be convenient. — M. to be betrothed, married. [sheep.]

ἄρνειος 3 of a lamb or]

ἀρνειός, ὁ ram.

ἀρνέομαι to deny, disown, refuse; to despise.

ἀρνευτήρ, ῆρος, ὁ diver.

ἀρνήσιμος 2 to be denied.

ἄρνησις, ἡ denial.

ἀρνίον, τό young lamb.

ἄρνυμαι to gain, earn, obtain, carry off.

ἄροσις, ἡ arable land.

ἀροτήρ, ῆρος, ὁ ploughman.

ἄροτος, ὁ ploughing, husbandry; engendering; produce of the fields.

ἀροτριάω = ἀρόω.

ἄροτρον, τό plough.

ἄρουρα, ἡ plough-land, field, soil; acre.

ἀρουραῖος 3 rustic.

ἀρόω to plough, till; beget, sow.

ἁρπαγή, ἡ and ἁρπαγμός, ὁ a robbing, plundering; spoil, plunder.

ἁρπάζω to snatch, seize, rob, plunder; to do in haste.

ἁρπακτήρ, ῆρος, ὁ robber.

ἁρπαλέος 3 greedy; pleasant. [robbing.]

ἅρπαξ, αγος rapacious,]

ἁρπεδόνη, ἡ lace, rope, string.

ἅρπη, ἡ falcon; sickle.

ἅρπυια, ἡ whirlwind; harpy.

ἀρραβών, ῶνος, ὁ pledge, deposit.

ἄ-ρράφος 2 unsewed, without a seam.

ἄ-ρρηκτος 2 unbreakable, not to be broken or tired.

ἄρρην = ἄρσην.

ἄ-ρρητος 2 unsaid; unknown; unspeakable, secret, holy; abominable.

ἄ-ρρυθμος 2 without rhythm or proportion.

ἀρρωδέω = ὀρρωδέω.

ἄ-ρρώξ, ῶγος untorn.

ἀ-ρρωστέω to be weak, invalid, or sick.

ἀ-ρρώστημα, τό and ἀ-ρρωστίᾱ, ἡ weakness, sickness, depression.

ἄ-ρρωστος 2 weak, sickly, languid.   [derast.]

ἀρσενο-κοίτης, ου, ὁ pe-

ἄρσην, εν, ενος male; manly, vigorous, strong.

ἀρτάβη, ἡ bushel (a Persian measure).

ἀρτάνη, ἡ rope, sling.

ἀρτάω, -έω to fasten, fix; to hang up. — P. to depend on. — M. to prepare.

ἀρτεμής 2 sound, fresh.

ἀρτέμων, ονος or ωνος, ὁ top-sail.   [ear.]

ἄρτημα, τό pendant of the

ἀρτηρίᾱ, ἡ artery, vein; air-pipe. [the other day.]

ἄρτι adv. just now; lately,

ἀρτι-γέννητος 2 new-born.

ἀρτι-επής 2 ready of speech.

ἀρτί-κολλος 2 close-glued.

ἄρτιος 3 fit; ready; proper, perfect; even (of numbers);

ἀρτίως = ἄρτι.

ἀρτί-πους (-πος), ποδος sound or swift of foot.

ἄρτῐσις, ἡ adjustment.

ἀρτί-φρων 2 sensible, intelligent.   [spread.]

ἀρτί-χριστος 2 newly

ἀρτο-κόπος, ὁ bread-baker.

ἀρτο-ποιίᾱ, ἡ bread-baking.

ἄρτος, ὁ bread.

ἀρτύνᾱς, ου, ὁ arranger.

ἀρτύνω, ἀρτύω to join; to arrange, prepare; to devise.   [for liquids.]

ἀρυστήρ, ῆρος, ὁ measure

ἀρύω, ἀρύτω, ἀρύσσω to draw (water).

ἀρχ-άγγελος, ὁ archangel.

ἀρχαιό-γονος 2 ancient, primeval.   [stories.]

ἀρχαιο-λογέω to tell old

ἀρχαιό-πλουτος 2 rich of old.

ἀρχαῖος 3 ancient, primeval, old, time-honoured, antiquated; former, bygone.   [fashioned.]

ἀρχαιό-τροπος 2 old-

ἀρχ-αιρεσίᾱ, ἡ election of magistrates.

ἀρχεῖον, τό government-house, town-hall. [making.]

ἀρχέ-κακος 2 mischief-

ἀρχέ-λᾱος 2 leading the people.   [of wealth.]

ἀρχέ-πλουτος 2 founder

ἀρχεύω to lead, rule.

ἀρχή, ἡ beginning, commencement, origin; firstling; cause, motive, principle, element; leadership, power, rule, magistrate, office, government; territory, empire.

ἀρχ-ηγετέω, -εύω to begin with; to rule.

ἀρχ-ηγέτης, ου and ἀρχηγός, ὁ ruler, leader, head; author, founder.

ἀρχῆθεν adv. of old, originally.

ἀρχίδιον, τό minor office.

ἀρχ-ιερατικός 3 pontifical.

ἀρχ-ιερεύς, ὁ and ἀρχιέρεως, ω, ὁ high priest, pontiff. [authoritative.]

ἀρχικός 3 commanding,)

ἀρχι-ποιμήν, ένος, ὁ chief shepherd.

ἀρχι-συνάγωγος, ὁ head of the synagogue.

ἀρχι-τέκτων, ονος, ὁ builder, architect, engineer.

ἀρχι-τελώνης, ου, ὁ chief publican. [steward.]

ἀρχι-τρίκλῑνος, ὁ chief)

ἀρχός, ὁ leader, prince.

ἄρχω to be the first, to lead on, to guide; to begin; to cause; to be at the head (of), to lead, rule, govern, domineer; to be archon. — P. to be ruled, governed, subject, to obey. — M. to begin, try.

ἄρχων, οντος, ὁ leader, ruler, chief; archon, magistrate.

ἀρωγή, ἡ protection, help.

ἀρωγός 2 helping, aiding; helper.

ἄρωμα, τό spice.

ἀρώσιμος 2 to be sown.

ἀ-σάλευτος 2 unshaken.

ἀ-σάμινθος, ἡ bathing-tub.

ἀ-σάομαι P. to be disgusted.

ἀ-σάφεια, ἡ indistinctness.

ἀ-σαφής 2 indistinct, uncertain, dubious.

ἄ-σβεστος 2 unquenchable; endless.

ἀ-σέβεια, ἡ, ἀσέβημα, τό impiety, wickedness.

ἀ-σεβέω to be godless or wicked.

ἀ-σεβής 2 ungodly, wicked.

ἀσελγαίνω to be licentious.

ἀσέλγεια, ἡ licentiousness, lewdness.

ἀσελγής 2 licentious, lewd.

ἀ-σέληνος 2 moonless.

ἀσέπτέω = ἀσεβέω.

ἄση, ἡ, surfeit, woe. [der.]

ἀ-σήμαντος 2 without lea-)

ἄ-σημος 2 and ἀ-σήμων 2 without mark or sign; uncoined: indistinct, unintelligible; obscure.

ἀ-σθένεια, ἡ and ἀ-σθένημα, τό weakness; illness; neediness.

ἀ-σθενής 2 weak, feeble; sick; poor, insignificant.

ἄσθμα, τό shortness of breath, panting.

ἀσθμαίνω to gasp, pant.

ἀ-σινής 2 unhurt; innoxious, harmless.

ἄσις, ἡ mud, mire.

ἀ-σῑτέω to fast, hunger.

ἀ-σῑτίᾱ, ἡ a fasting, hunger. [hungry.]

ἄ-σῑτος 2 without food,)

ἀ-σκελής 2 weak; incessant.

ἄ-σκεπαρνος 2 unhewn.

ἄ-σκεπτος 2 not considered, not examined; inconsiderate.

ἀ-σκευής 2, ἄ-σκευος 2 unprepared; unprotected.

ἀσκέω to work out artificially; to adorn; to practise, exercise, train, drill; to endeavour, strive. [maged.

ἀ-σκηθής 2 unhurt, unda-

ἄσκησις, ἡ practise, training; athletic trade.

ἀσκητής, οῦ, ὁ athlete.

ἀσκητός 3 curiously or artificially wrought; wanting practise; trained.

ἄ-σκοπος 2 inconsiderate; unseen, invisible; unmeasurable; unexpected.

ἀσκός, ὁ hide; leather bag.

ᾆσμα, τό song.

ἄσμενος 3 willing, ready, glad; saved.

ἄ-σοφος 2 unwise, foolish.

ἀσπάζομαι M. to welcome, greet, salute, hail; to visit; to take leave; to hug, caress, love. [kick.

ἀ-σπαίρω to jerk, struggle,

ἄ-σπαρτος 2 unsown.

ἀσπάσιος, ἀσπαστός 3 welcome, longed for; delighted, glad, willing.

ἀσπασμός, ὁ greeting, embrace.

ἄ-σπερμος 2 without issue.

ἀ-σπερχές adv. eagerly, zealously; incessantly.

ἄ-σπετος 2 unspeakable, incessant, immense.

ἀσπιδιώτης, ου, ὁ shield-bearing.

ἄ-σπιλος 2 unstained.

ἀσπίς, ίδος, ἡ shield; hoplite; adder.

ἀσπιστήρ, ῆρος and ἀσπιστής, οῦ, ὁ shield-bearer, warrior.

ἄ-σπλαγχνος 2 heartless; cowardly.

ἄ-σπονδος 2 without treaty or truce; implacable.

ἄ-σπορος 2 unsown.

ἀ-σπουδί adv. without zeal or struggle.

ἄσσα = ἅτινα (ὅστις).

ἄσσα = τινά (τὶς).

ἀσσάριον, τό small coin.

ἄσσω = ἀΐσσω.

ἀ-στάθμητος 2 unsteady; unmeasurable.

ἀ-στακτός 2(adv. ἀστακτί) gushing freely.

ἀ-στασίαστος 2 without party-contests.

ἀ-στατέω to be unstable.

ἀσταφίς, ίδος, ἡ raisin.

ἀ-στάχυς, υος, ὁ ear of corn. [shelter.

ἀ-στέγαστος 2 without

ἀστεῖος 3 of a town, townlike, polite, accomplished.

ἀ-στείπτος 2 untrodden.

ἀ-στεμφής 2 firm, steady.

ἀ-στένακτος 2 without a sigh. [out love.

ἀ-στεργής 2 unkind, with-

ἀστερόεις 3 starry, starred; sparkling.

ἀστεροπή, ἡ lightning.

ἀστεροπητής, ὁ lightener.

ἀ-στεφάνωτος 2 not wreathed. [male citizen.

ἀστή, ἡ townswoman, fe-

ἀστήρ, έρος, ὁ star.

ἀ-στήρικτος 2 unsupported, weak.

ἀ-στιβής 2 untrodden; inaccessible. [man.

ἀστικός 3 of a town; towns-

ἄ-στικτος 2 untatooed.

ἄ-στομος 2 hard-mouthed.

ἄ-στοργος 2 unkind.

ἀστός, ὁ townsman, citizen

ἀ-στοχέω to miss, fail.

ἀστόω = ἀϊστόω.

ἀστραβή, ἡ pack-saddle; saddled mule.

ἀστράγαλίζω to dice.

ἀστράγαλος, ὁ joint of the spine; ankle-bone; die, dice.

ἀστραπή = ἀστεροπή.

ἀστράπτω to flash, lighten, shine.   [from service.]

ἀ-στράτευτος 2 exempt)

ἀστρο-λογία, ἡ astronomy.

ἀστρο-λόγος 2 astronomer, astrologer.   [tion.]

ἄστρον, τό star, constella-)

ἀστρο-νομία, ἡ astronomy.

ἄ-στροφος 2 not turning or looking back.

ἄ-στρωτος 2 without covering, uncovered.

ἄστυ, εως or εος, τό city, capital.

ἀστὺ-βοώτης, ου crying through the city.

ἀστυ-γείτων 2 neighbouring. [tecting, town-ruling.]

ἀστυ-νόμος 2 town-pro-)

ἀ-συγ-κρότητος 2 untrained.   [able.]

ἀ-σύμβατος 2 irreconcil-)

ἀ-σύμβλητος 2 incomprehensible.

ἀ-συμμετρία, ἡ disproportion, deformity. [tionate.]

ἀ-σύμμετρος 2 dispropor-)

ἀ-σύμφορος 2 unexpedient; useless; unfit.

ἀ-σύμφωνος 2 discordant.

ἀ-συνεσία, ἡ stupidity.

ἀ-σύνετος 2 stupid.

ἀ-σύνθετος 2 faithless, breaking treaties.

ἀ-σύντακτος 2 not arranged.

ἀ-σύφηλος 2 foolish, disgraceful, mortifying.

ἀσυχαῖος see ἡσυχαῖος.

ἀ-σφάδαστος 2 without convulsion, untrembling.

ἀσφάλεια, ἡ steadiness, safety, security, certainty, truth; safe-conduct; care.

ἀ-σφαλής 2 steadfast, incessant; safe, certain, true; careful.

ἀσφαλίζω to secure.

ἄσφαλτος, ἡ mineral pitch, asphaltum.

ἀ-σφάραγος, ὁ wind-pipe.

ἀσφόδελος, ὁ daffodil.

ἀ-σχαλάω and ἀ-σχάλλω to be grieved, vexed, or indignant.

ἄ-σχετος 2 not to be checked, incontrollable.   [seemly.]

ἀ-σχημονέω to behave un-)

ἀ-σχημοσύνη, ἡ indecency; deformity.   [miserable.]

ἀ-σχήμων 2 indecent; ugly;)

ἀ-σχολία ἡ want of leisure, occupation, business; hindrance.   [busy.]

ἄ-σχολος 2 without leisure,)

ἀ-σώματος 2 incorporeal.

ἀσωτία, ἡ debauch, gluttony.   [fligate.]

ἄ-σωτος 2 debauched, pro-)

ἀ-τακτέω to be disorderly or undisciplined.

ἄ-τακτος 2 disorderly, undisciplined, dissolute.

ἀ-ταλαίπωρος 2 without pains; indifferent.

ἀ-τάλαντος 2 equivalent.

αταλάφρων   — 67 —   ἄτλατος

ἀταλά-φρων 2 harmless, childlike.

ἀ-ταξία, ἡ want of discipline, disorder; licentiousness.

ἀτάομαι P. to be vexed.

ἀτάρ conj. but. yet, however.

ἀ-τάρακτος 2 intrepid.

ἀ-ταρβής 2, ἀ-τάρβητος 2 fearless, dauntless.

ἀ-ταρπιτός and ἀ-ταρπός, ἡ = ἀτραπιτός. [uncivil.]

ἀταρτηρός 3 mischievous.

ἀτασθαλίᾱ, ἡ recklessness.

ἀτασθάλλω to offend.

ἀτάσθαλος 2 reckless, haughty.

ἄ-ταφος 2 unburied.

ἄτε just as, as if; because, as.

ἄ-τεγκτος 2 unwetted, hard. [away.]

ἀ-τειρής 2 not to be worn

ἀ-τείχιστος 2 unfortified; not blockaded.

ἀ-τέκμαρτος 2 ambiguous, vague, uncertain.

ἄ-τεκνος 2 childless.

ἀ-τέλεια, ἡ exemption, immunity.

ἀ-τέλεστος 2 = ἀτελής; not to be fulfilled; uninitiated. [inexorable.]

ἀ-τελεύτητος 2 unfinished;

ἀ-τελής 2 unfinished; not fulfilled; endless; imperfect; unsuccessful; invalid; free from taxes.

ἀτέμβω to hurt, injure; to cheat. — P. to forfeit.

ἀ-τενής 2 strained, tight, intense; firm, persevering, inflexible, steady.

ἀτενίζω to look at intently.

ἄτερ prp. with gen. far from: without, besides; in spite of.

ἀ-τέραμνος 2 hard, inexorable.

ἄτερθεν = ἄτερ.

ἀ-τερπής 2 and ἄ-τερπος unpleasing, sad.

ἀ-τεχνίᾱ, ἡ want of skill.

ἄ-τεχνος 2 without art; ἀτέχνως plainly, without art; ἀτεχνῶς really, of course; quite, utterly.

ἀτέω to be foolhardy.

ἄτη, ἡ infatuation, delusion, stupor; guilt, wickedness; punishment; evil, woe.

ἄ-τηκτος 2 unmelted.

ἀ-τημέλητος 2 not cared for, heedless.

ἀ-τηρίᾱ, ἡ evil, ruin.

ἀτηρός 3 and ἀτήσιμος 2 ruinous; wicked.

ἀ-τίζω not to honour.

ἀ-τῑμάζω, ἀ-τῑμάω to esteem lightly, despise; to defame disgrace, insult.

ἀ-τίμητος 2 despised; not estimated.

ἀ-τῑμίᾱ ἡ dishonour, disgrace; infamy, proscription (loss of civil rights).

ἄ-τῑμος 2 unhonoured. despised; outlaw; not deigned, unworthy; dishonouring, shameful, despicable; unestimated.

ἀ-τῑμόω = ἀτιμάζω.

ἀ-τῑμώρητος 2 unpunished; helpless.

ἀτῑτάλλω to bring up.

ἄ-τῑτος 2 unavenged; unpaid.

ἄ-τλᾱτος = ἄτλητος.

5*

ἀ-τλητέω to think unbearable, to be indignant.

ἄ-τλητος 2 unbearable.

ἀτμίζω to steam, reek.

ἀτμίς, ίδος, ἡ and ἀτμός, ὁ steam, vapour, smoke.

ἄ-τοκος 2 barren.

ἀ-τολμία, ἡ despondency.

ἄ-τολμος 2 cowardly.

ἄ-τομος 2 unmowed; indivisible.   [strangeness.]

ἀ-τοπία, ἡ unusualness,}

ἄ-τοπος 2 unusual, strange; absurd; indecent, wicked.

ἄτος 2 insatiate.   [row]

ἄ-τρακτος, ὁ spindle; ar-}

ἀ-τράπιτός, ἀ-τράπός, ἡ path, road, (foot)way.

ἀ-τρέκεια, ἡ full truth.

ἀ-τρεκής 2 sure, exact, strict, true.

ἀ-τρεμάς adv. without trembling; quietly, silently; circumspectly.

ἀ-τρεμέω to keep quiet.

ἀ-τρεμής 2 unmoved, quiet.

ἀ-τρεμίζω = ἀτρεμέω.

ἄ-τρεστος 2 intrepid.

ἀ-τρῑβής, ἄ-τριπτος 2 unhurt; untrodden; unhardened.

ἄ-τρομος 2 = ἀτρεμής.

ἄ-τροφος 2 underfed.

ἄ-τρύγετος 2 unfruitful, desert; everfluctuating.

ἄ-τρῠτος 2 incessant, unabating.

ἀ-τρῠτώνη, ἡ indomitable.

ἄ-τρωτος 2 unwounded; invulnerable.

ἄττα[1], ὁ father.

ἄττα[2] = τινά.

ἄττα = ἄτινα.

ἀτταταῖ int. woe! alas!

ἀττέλεβος, ὁ unwinged locust.

ἄττης, ου, ὁ surname of Bacchus.

ἀττικίζω to side with the Athenians.

ἀττικισμός, ὁ inclination towards Athens.

ἀτύζω to alarm, harass, anguish. — P. to be frightened or benumbed; to flee.

ἀ-τῠράννευτος 2 not ruled by a tyrant.

ἀ-τῠχέω not to obtain, to miss, fail; to be unlucky or unfortunate.

ἀ-τῠχημα, τό and ἀ-τῠχία, ἡ misfortune.   [happy.]

ἀ-τῠχής 2 unfortunate, un-}

αὖ adv. back; again, once more; for another time; on the other hand; further.

αὐαίνω, αὐαίνω to dry up; to scorch. — P. to become dry, to wither.

αὐγάζω to illumine; to shine; to perceive. — M. to discern, perceive.

αὐγή, ἡ splendour, brilliancy; ray, beam; eye, glance.

αὐδάζομαι M., αὐδάω and M. to speak, utter, talk, cry, call; to order, advise.

αὐδή, ἡ voice, speech; report, rumour.

αὐδήεις 3 gifted with speech.   [back.]

αὐ-ερύω to draw or bend}

αὖθ' = αὖθι, αὖτε.

αὐθ-άδεια αὐθ-αδία, ἡ self-complacency; arrogance; obstinacy.

αὐθ-άδης 2 self-willed;

arrogant; capricious; arbitrary.

αὐθ-ᾰδίζομαι *M.* to be self-pleasing *or* arrogant.

αὐθ-αιμος 2 and αὐθ-αίμων 2 = αὐθόμαιμος.

αὐθ-αίρετος 2 self-chosen, self-made, voluntary; self-incurred.

αὐθ-έντης, ου, ὁ author, doer; murderer; executioner.

αὐθ-ήμερον *adv.* on the same day; on the spot.

αὖθι *adv.* there, on the spot.

αὐθι-γενής 2 home-born, native, indigenous.

αὖθις = αὖ.

αὐθ-όμαιμος 2 allied by blood; brother, sister.

αὔΐαχος 2 shouting together.

αὖλαξ, ᾰκος, ἡ furrow.

αὔλειος 2 belonging to the court.

αὐλέω to play on the flute. — *M.* to be entertained by fluting.

αὐλή, ἡ yard for cattle; farm-yard; court, yard-wall; dwelling, cabin; palace, residence.

αὔλημα, τό and αὔλησις, ἡ flute-playing.

αὐλητής, οῦ, ὁ flute-player.

αὐλητικός 3 concerning flute-playing.

αὐλητρίς ίδος, ἡ flute-girl.

αὐλίζομαι *M.* and *P.* to be fenced in; to camp in the open air; to pass the night.

αὔλιον, τό hurdle; farmyard; grotto. [ters; stable.]

αὖλις, ιδος, ἡ night-quar-)

αὐλός, ὁ pipe, tube; nozzle, shank; flash of blood; flute.

αὐλών, ῶνος, ὁ hollow way, ravine, defile; strait; canal, ditch.

αὐλ-ῶπις, ιδος with a tube.

αὐξάνω, αὔξω to increase, augment, enlarge, extol, to let grow. — *P.* to grow, improve, thrive.

αὔξη and αὔξησις, ἡ growth, increase, thriving.

ἄ-ϋπνος 2 sleepless.

αὔρᾱ, ἡ air, breath, breeze, draught.

αὔριον *adv.* to-morrow.

αὐσταλέος 3 dry; bristly; dirty.

αὐστηρίᾱ, αὐστηρότης, ητος, ἡ harshness, austerity.

αὐστηρός 3 harsh, sour, austere. [messenger.]

αὐτ-άγγελος 2 one's own)

αὐτ-άγρετος 2 = αὐθαίρ-ετος. [or sister.]

αὐτ-άδελφος 2 full brother)

αὐτάρ *conj.* but, yet, however; further.

αὐτ-άρκεια, ἡ self-sufficiency. independence.

αὐτ-άρκης 2 self-sufficient, independent; secure; contented.

αὖτε = αὖ.

αὐτ-επάγγελτος 2 of one's own accord.

αὐτ-ερέτης, ου, ὁ both rower and soldier.

ἀϋτέω to cry, shout; to roar, ring.

ἀϋτή, ἡ cry; war-cry; battle.

αὐτ-ήκοος 2 ear-witness.

αὐτίκα *adv.* forthwith, instantly, directly; for instance.

ἀϋτμή, ἡ and ἀϋτμήν, ένος, ὁ breath, blast, wind; odour; blaze. [war-cry.]

αὐτο-βοεί *adv.* at the first

αὐτο-γέννητος 2 self-engendered.

αὐτο-γνωμονέω to act of one's own will. [solved.]

αὐτό-γνωτος 2 self-re-

αὐτο-δαής 2 self-taught.

αὐτό-δεκα just ten.

αὐτο-δίδακτος 2 self-taught. [own jurisdiction.]

αὐτό-δῐκος 2 with one's

αὐτόδῐον *adv.* at once.

αὐτο-έντης, ου, ὁ = αὐθέντης. [same year.]

αὐτό-ετες *adv.* in the

αὐτόθεν *adv.* from the spot, thence, from here; on the spot, at once; from the beginning; therefore; without ceremony.

αὐτόθι *adv.* on the spot, there, here. [sister.]

αὐτο-κασιγνήτη, ἡ full

αὐτο-κασίγνητος, ὁ full brother. [condemned.]

αὐτο-κατάκριτος 2 self-

αὐτο-κέλευστος 2, αὐτο-κελής 2 self-bidden.

αὐτό-κλητος 2 self-called, of one's own accord.

αὐτο-κρατής 2 and αὐτο-κράτωρ 2 sovereign, absolute, independent; authorized. [suicide.]

αὐτο-κτονέω to commit

αὐτό-μᾰτος 2 and 3 self-moved; of one's own will, voluntary; accidental.

αὐτο-μολέω to go over, desert.

αὐτο-μολίᾱ, ἡ desertion.

αὐτό-μολος 2 going over, deserter. [oneself.]

αὐτο-νομέομαι to govern

αὐτο-νομίᾱ, ἡ independence.

αὐτό-νομος 2 independent.

αὐτό-νυχί *adv.* in the same night.

αὐτό-ξυλος 2 quite wooden.

αὐτό-παις, ὁ genuine child.

αὐτό-πετρος 2 of natural stone.

αὐτό-ποιος 2 self-grown.

αὐτό-πολις, ἡ free state.

αὐτο-πολίτης, ὁ citizen of a free state. [root.]

αὐτό-πρεμνος 2 with the

αὐτ-όπτης, ου, ὁ eye-witness.

αὐτός, ή, ό self, oneself, personal; by oneself, alone; together with; oneself with others; he, she, it; ὁ αὐτός the same. [same place.]

αὐτόσε *adv.* just at the

αὐτο-σταδίη, ἡ close fight.

αὐτό-στολος 2 going of oneself.

αὐτο-σφαγής 2 self-killed.

αὐτο-σχεδιάζω to improvise, act wantonly or unadvisedly; to judge superficially.

αὐτο-σχεδίη = αὐτοσταδίη.

αὐτο-σχεδόν *adv.* in close fight.

αὐτο-τελής 2 taxing oneself; arbitrary.

αὐτοῦ *adv.* in the same place; there, here; at once.

αὐτο - ουργός 2 self-working; workman.

αὐτο-φυής 2 natural.

αὐτό-φωρος 2 caught in the very act; convicted by facts.

αὐτό-χειρ, ρος with one's own hand; doer, murderer.

αὐτο-χειρία, ἡ one's own deed; murder.

αὐτο-χόωνος 2 solid, massive.

αὕτως, αὔτως adv. just so, quite so; still, only, solely; without ceremony, downright; in vain, uselessly; without reason.

αὐχενίζω to cut one's neck.

αὐχένιος 3 belonging to the nape.

αὐχέω to boast, brag.

αὔχημα, τό pride; boast; ornament.

αὐχήν, ένος, ὁ nape, neck; neck of land; strait; defile; forking.

αὔχησις, ἡ = αὔχημα.

αὐχμέω to be dry, squalid, or rugged.

αὐχμηρός 3 dry, parched; squalid, wild; dark.

αὐχμός, ὁ drought; dirt.

αὐχμώδης = αὐχμηρός.

αὔω¹, αὔω to kindle, to singe.

αὔω², αὔω to shout, call aloud, roar, sound.

ἀφ-αγνίζω to offer an atonement.   [away.\

ἀφ-αίρεσις, ἡ a taking/

ἀφ-αιρέω to take off, away, or from; to remove; to rob, deprive; to free from, to diminish. — M. to take for

oneself, to obtain, deprive, rob; to make an end of; to prevent.

ἄ-φαλος 2 without a φάλος.

ἀφ-αμαρτάνω to miss, lose.

ἀφαμαρτο-επής 2 failing in speech.

ἀφ-ανδάνω to displease.

ἀ-φάνεια, ἡ obscurity, insignificance.

ἀ-φανής 2 unseen, invisible; hidden, secret; vanished; uncertain, unknown; insignificant, obscure.

ἀ-φανίζω to make unseen, to cause to vanish, to hide, remove; to destroy, annihilate; to disfigure, deface. — P. to vanish, disappear, cease.   [ὁ a vanishing.\

ἀφάνισις, ἡ, ἀφανισμός,\

ἄ-φαντος 2 = ἀφανής.

ἀφ-άπτω to fasten, tie to, hang on. — P. to hang, to be hung on.

ἄφαρ adv. quickly, forthwith, presently.

ἄ-φαρκτος 2 = ἄφρακτος.

ἀφ-αρπάζω to snatch away; to rob.

ἀφάρτερος 3 quicker.

ἀφάσσω = ἀφάω.

ἄ-φατος 2 unutterable; horrible, huge.

ἀφαυρός 3 weak, feeble.

ἀφάω to touch, feel.

ἀ-φεγγής 2 dark, gloomy; terrible.

ἀφ-εδρών, ῶνος, ὁ a privy.

ἀ-φειδέω not to spare; to overlook, neglect.

ἀ-φειδής 2 unsparing; unmerciful, cruel; plentiful.

ἀ-φειδίᾱ, ἡ profuseness; harshness.

ἀ-φελής 2 simple, plain.

ἀφ-έλκω to draw or drag away; to seduce. [city.]

ἀφελότης, ητος, ἡ simpli-

ἄφενος, τό wealth, stores.

ἀφ-έρπω to steal away.

ἄφ-εσις, ἡ a sending away; a setting free, starting; dimission; remission.

ἄφ-ετος 2 let loose or free; sacred.

ἀφή, ἡ a kindling; a touching, touch; sense of touch; joint.

ἀφ-ηγέομαι M. to lead the way, to lead on or off; to tell, relate.

ἀφ-ήγημα, τό and ἀφ-ήγησις, ἡ tale, narration.

ἀφ-ῆμαι to sit far off.

ἀφ-ημερεύω to be absent at day.

ἀφήτωρ, ορος, ὁ archer.

ἀ-φθαρσίᾱ, ἡ immortality.

ἄ-φθαρτος 2 incorruptible, immortal. [mute.]

ἄ-φθεγκτος 2 speechless,

ἄ-φθιτος 2 = ἄφθαρτος.

ἄ-φθογγος 2 voiceless, speechless.

ἀ-φθονίᾱ, ἡ freedom from envy, readiness; abundance, plenty.

ἄ-φθονος 2 free from envy; liberal; fertile; abundant, plentiful.

ἀφ-ίημι to send off or away; to throw, shoot; to let loose, set free, acquit; to dissolve, break up; to pronounce, utter; to shed; to give up, neglect; to remit, forgive;

intr. to start; to cease. — M. to free oneself; to escape; to start.

ἀφ-ικάνω = ἀφικνέομαι.

ἀφ-ικνέομαι M. to arrive at, come to; to return; to overcome, befall.

ἀ-φιλ-άγαθος 2 averse to good men. [money.]

ἀ-φιλ-άργυρος 2 not loving

ἀ-φίλητος 2 unloved.

ἄ-φιλος 2 friendless; unfriendly, unkind; ungrateful; disagreeable.

ἄφ-ιξις, ἡ arrival; return; departure. [back.]

ἀφ-ιππεύω to ride off or

ἄφ-ιππος 2 unskilled in riding; not fit for riding.

ἀφ-ίπταμαι = ἀποπέτομαι.

ἀφ-ίστημι to put away, remove, depose; to make fall off or revolt. intr. and P. to go away; to stand aloof; to fall off, revolt; to desist, abstain, omit. — M. to get weighed out, to be paid.

ἄφλαστον, τό ornament of the curved stern of a ship.

ἀφλοισμός, ὁ foam.

ἀφνειός 2 and 3 rich, wealthy.

ἄφνω adv. suddenly.

ἀ-φόβητος, ἄ-φοβος 2 fearless; defenceless.

ἄφ-οδος ἡ departure, retreat; expedient. [to portray.]

ἀφ-ομοιόω to make like,

ἀφ-οπλίζομαι M. to put off one's armour.

ἀφ-οράω and M. to look away from; to look from afar; to behold.

ἀ-φόρητος 2 unbearable.

ἀφ-ορίζω to divide by a boundary-line; to select; to define. [away.

ἀφ-ορμάω to start, to rush

ἀφ-ορμή, ἡ starting-point; support, means, resources, capital; cause, occasion, chance.

ἄφ-ορμος 2 hastening away.

ἄ φορος 2 barren.

ἀφ-οσιόω to expiate. — M. to expiate oneself, to perform religious duties.

ἀ-φραδέω to be foolish.

ἀ-φραδής 2 foolish, silly, thoughtless; senseless.

ἀ-φραδίᾱ, ἡ thoughtlessness; ignorance.

ἀ-φραίνω = ἀφραδέω.

ἄ-φρακτος 3 unfenced; unguarded; unarmed.

ἄ-φραστος 2 unspeakable; unperceived, secret; inconceivable; unexpected.

ἀφρέω to foam.

ἀ-φρήτωρ 2 without family.

ἀφρίζω = ἀφρέω. [to love.

ἀφροδισιάζω to be given

ἀφροδίσιος 3 and 2 indulging in love; belonging to Venus.

ἀ-φρονέω to be foolish.

ἀ-φροντιστέω to be heedless or careless.

ἀ-φρόντιστος 2 thoughtless, heedless; out of one's wits.

ἀφρός, ὁ foam. [ness.

ἀ-φροσύνη, ἡ thoughtless-

ἄ-φρων 2 thoughtless, foolish, senseless; indecent.

ἀ-φυής 2 ungifted. unfit.

ἀ-φυκτος 2 inevitable.

ἀ-φύλακτέω not to be on one's guard.

ἀ-φύλακτος 2 unguarded; careless, heedless.

ἄ-φυλλος 2 leafless.

ἀφ-υπνόω to fall asleep.

ἀφυσγετός, ὁ mud, mire, rubbish.

ἀφύσσω to draw (water); to pour in; to heap up.

ἀφ-υστερέω to come too late; to withhold.

ἀ-φώνητος 2 = ἄφωνος.

ἀ-φωνίᾱ, ἡ speechlessness.

ἄ-φωνος 2 speechless, unspeakable. [arms.

ἀ-χαλκος 2 without brazen

ἄ-χαρις, ιτος 2 without grace or charm, displeasing, ungrateful; unrewarded.

ἀ-χαριστέω to be ungrateful. disobliging.

ἀ-χαριστίᾱ, ἡ ingratitude, want of charm.

ἀ-χάριστος 2, ἀ-χάριτος 2 = ἄχαρις.

ἀ-χειροποίητος 2 not made by (human) hands.

ἄ-χειρος 2 without hands; τὰ -α back.

ἀ-χείρωτος 2 unconquered.

ἄχερδος, ἡ wild pear-tree.

ἀχερωίς, ίδος, ἡ white poplar. [to mourn.

ἀχεύω, ἀχέω to be sad,

ἀχέω = ἠχέω. [angry.

ἀχθεινός 3 cumbersome;

ἀχθηδών, όνος, ἡ grief.

ἄχθομαι P. to be burdened, molested, vexed; to be sad, angry, or unwilling.

ἄχθος, τό burden, load; sorrow, grief.

ἀχθο-φόρος 2 carrying burdens. [tunic.

ἀ-χίτων, ωνος 2 without

ἀχλυόεις 3 dark, gloomy; grieving. [darkness.

ἀχλύς, ύος, ἡ mist, gloom,

ἀχλύω to grow dark.

ἄχνη, ἡ chaff; foam; dew.

ἄχνυμαι to be sorry, afflicted, or angry.

ἄ-χολος 2 what allays anger.

ἄχομαι = ἄχνυμαι.

ἀ-χόρευτος 2, ἄ-χορος 2 without a dance; joyless.

ἄχος, τό pain, sorrow, grief.

ἀ-χρεῖος 2 useless, unserviceable, weak.

ἀ-χρεόω P. to become useless.

ἀ-χρημᾰτίᾱ, ἡ want of means.

ἀ-χρήμᾰτος 2 without means, poor. [μᾰτία.

ἀ-χρημοσύνη, ἡ = ἀχρη-

ἄ-χρηστος 2 useless, unprofitable; foolish, bad, unfit; not yet employed.

ἄχρι, ἄχρις, adv. wholly, utterly; prp. with gen. and conj. until; as far as.

ἀχυρμίη, ἡ heap of chaff.

ἄχυρον, τό chaff.

ἀχώ, ἡ = ἠχώ.

ἄψ adv. back; again.

ἄ-φαυστος 2 untouched; without touching.

ἀ-φεγγής 2 unblamed.

ἀ-ψευδέω not to lie.

ἀ-ψευδής 2 truthful, trustworthy; genuine, true.

ἀψίνθιον τό and ἄψινθος, ἡ wormwood.

ἀψό-ρροος 2 flowing backwards.

ἄψορρος 2 going back.

ἄψος, τό joint, limb.

ἀ-ψόφητος and ἄ-ψοφος 2 noiseless.

ἄ-ψυκτος 2 uncooled.

ἄ-ψῡχος 2 without soul, lifeless; spiritless.

ἄω to satiate. — M. to be satisfied.

ἄ-ωρος[1] 2 untimely; unripe; ill-shaped.

ἄωρος[2] 2 invisible; pending.

ἀ-ωτέω to sleep.

ἄωτος, ὁ tuft, lock, wool, fleece.

B

B, β (βῆτα) second letter of the alphabet; as a numeral β' = 2.

βαβαί int. only look!

βάδην adv. step by step, slowly.

βαδίζω to step, pace, march.

βάδισμα, τό a marching,

βάζω to talk, say. [pace.

βαθμός, ὁ step, stair, degree. [extension.

βάθος, τό depth; height,

βάθρον, τό step, stair; threshold; ladder; bench, seat; base, pedestal; soil; foundation. [soil.

βαθύ-γαιος 2 with deep

βαθυ-δῑνήεις 3, βαθυ-δίνης 2 deep-eddying.

βαθύ-ζωνος 2 deep-girded.

βαθύ-κολπος 2 deep-bosomed. [grass.

βαθύ-λειμος 2 with high

βαθυ-λήιος 2 with deep
corn or crops.
βαθύνω to deepen.
βαθυ-ρρείτης, ου deep-
flowing.
βαθύ-ρριζος 2 deep-rooted.
βαθύς 3 deep; high; wide;
vehement.
βαθυ-σκαφής 2 deep-dug.
βαθύ-σχοινος 2 with deep
rushes.
βαίνω to take strides, to
sit astride; to go, step,
walk; to mount; to arrive,
go away; to depart, die;
(perf.) to stand fast, to be
settled. — trans. to cause
to go, to bring; to cause
to descend.
βάϊον, τό palm-branch.
βαιός 3 little, small, short;
humble.
βαίτη, ἡ coat of skin.
βακτηρία, ἡ stick, staff.
βακχεῖος and βάκχειος 3
Bacchic, in ecstasy.
βακχεύω to keep the feast
of Bacchus; to be frantic,
to be in ecstasy.
βάκχη, ἡ and βακχίς, ίδος,
ἡ Bacchante.
βάκχιος 3 and βακχιώτης,
ου = βακχεῖος. [thusiast.]
βάκχος, ὁ Bacchanal, en-
βαλαν-άγρα, ἡ key.
βαλανεῖον, τό bath; bath-
ing-house. [eating.]
βαλανη-φάγος 3 acorn-
βαλανη-φόρος 2 bearing
dates.
βάλανος, ἡ acorn; date;
chestnut; peg; door-bolt.
βαλάντιον, τό purse.

βαλαντιο-τομέω to cut
purses. [battlements.]
βαλβίς, ίδος, ἡ bar, lists;
βαλιός 3 dappled.
βάλλω to throw, cast, hurl,
shoot; to hit, wound, strike;
to dash, push; to let fall;
to put on; to meet, catch;
to put; intr. to fall; to dis-
charge; to rush. — M. to
throw around oneself; to
take to heart, bear in
mind; to deliberate.
βαμβαίνω to shake, totter.
βαναυσία, ἡ handicraft; vulgar trade. [tisan; vulgar.]
βάναυσος 2 craftsman, ar-
βάξις, ἡ speech, saying;
oracle; report, talk.
βαπτίζω to dip, wash; to
baptize.
βάπτισμα, τό and βαπτισ-
μός, ὁ baptism.
βαπτιστής, οῦ, ὁ dyer;
baptizer.
βάπτω to dip, wet; to dye;
to temper, harden.
βάραθρον, τό gulf, pit (for
criminals).
βαρβαρίζω to behave or
act like a barbarian; to
side with the Persians.
βαρβαρικός 3 and βάρβα-
ρος 2 barbarous, not Greek,
foreign, outlandish; rude,
uncivilised, cruel.
βαρβαρό-φωνος 2 with a
strange voice.
βαρβαρόω to make bar-
barous. — P. to become
barbarous.
βάρδιστος see βραδύς.
βαρέω = βαρύνω.

βάρις, ιος or ιδος, ἡ canoe, boat, raft.

βάρος, τό weight, burden, load; grief, sorrow; plenty; dignity. [sorely.]

βαρυ-άλγητος 2 grieving/

βαρυ - ᾱχής 2 groaning heavily. [thundering.]

βαρυ-βρεμέτης, ου loud/

βαρυ-βρώς, ῶτος greedily eating.

βαρύθω to be burdened.

βαρύνω to burden, load; to vex, torment. — P. to be burdened or tormented; to be vexed, annoyed, or angry. [unhappy]

βαρύ-ποτμος 2 ill-fated,/

βαρύς 3 heavy, burdensome, oppressive; weighty; deep, hollow, loud (voice); grievous, troublesome, painful; unwholesome; hard, cruel; strong, mighty.

βαρύ-στονος 2 groaning heavily, painful.

βαρυ-σύμφορος 2 oppressed by misfortune.

βαρύτης, ητος, ἡ heaviness; load, oppression; bass voice; harshness, pride.

βαρύ - τῑμος 2 precious, costly. [dejected.]

βαρύ-φῡχος 2 low-spirited,/

βασανίζω to test, try, examine; to (put to the) torture. [torture.]

βασανισμός, ὁ a torturing,/

βασανιστής, οῦ, ὁ torturer, jailer.

βάσᾰνος, ἡ touchstone; test, proof, trial; inquiry; torture.

βασίλεια, ἡ queen, princess.

βασιλείᾱ, ἡ kingdom, monarchy.

βασίλειος 2 and 3 kingly, royal, princely. — τὸ βασίλειον royal palace, court; treasury.

βασῐλεύς, ὁ king, prince, ruler; the king of Persia; lord, nobleman. [rule.]

βασῐλεύω to be king, to/

βασιληίς, ίδος, ἡ royal.

βασιλικός 3 kingly, royal, princely.

βασιλίς, ίδος and βασίλισσα, ἡ = βασίλεια.

βάσιμος 2 passable.

βάσις, ἡ step, pace; foot; basis, foundation, pedestal.

βασκαίνω to slander; to fascinate, spell.

βασκανίᾱ, ἡ slander; spell.

βάσκανος 2 slanderous, malignant; envious.

βάσκω to go.

βασσάριον, τό Libyan fox.

βαστάζω to touch; to lift up: to bear, hold up; to carry away.

βᾰτός 3 passable, accessible.

βάτος[1], ἡ thorn-bush.

βάτος[2], ὁ a measure for liquids.

βάτρᾰχος, ὁ frog.

βάτταλος, ὁ weakling.

βαττο-λογέω to prattle.

βαφεύς, ὁ dyer.

βαφή, ἡ a dipping; dyeing.

βδέλλα, ἡ leech.

βδέλυγμα, τό abomination.

βδελυγμίᾱ, ἡ a loathing, disgust.

βδελυκτός 3 abominable.

βδελῠρίᾱ, ἡ shamelessness.

βδελῠρός 3 disgusting; shameless. [detest, fear.⟨

βδελύσσομαι *P.* to abhor,⟩

βέβαιος 2 and 3 firm, steady; trusty; sure, certain.

βεβαιότης, ητος, ἡ firmness, steadiness, safety, certainty.

βεβαιόω to make firm, to confirm, assert; to fulfil. — *M.* to secure for oneself; to feel confirmed.

βεβαίωσις, ἡ confirmation.

βέβηλος 2 profane; unholy, unclean.

βεβηλόω to profane.

βεβρώθω to devour.

βείομαι = βέομαι.

βέκος, τό bread. [pon.⟨

βέλεμνον, τό missile wea-⟩

βελόνη, ἡ point of an arrow; needle.

βέλος, τό missile weapon, dart, javelin; terror.

βέλτερος 3 = βελτίων.

βέλτιστος 3 the best, noblest, or bravest.

βελτίων 2 better, braver, nobler.

βένθος, τό depth.

βέομαι I shall live.

βέρεθρον, τό = βάραθρον.

βηλός, ὁ threshold.

βῆμα, τό step, stair; raised step, stage, tribune, throne, tribunal.

βήξ, βηχός, ὁ, ἡ cough.

βήρυλλος, ἡ, ὁ beryl.

βῆσσα, ἡ glen, wooded valley.

βήσσω to cough.

βητ-άρμων, ονος, ὁ dancer.

βίᾱ, ἡ strength, force; violence.

βιάζω to force, to use violence; to overpower; to maltreat, oppress, constrain; to defy.

βίαιος 3 and 2 forcible, violent; strong, oppressive; forced. [force.⟨

βιαστής, οῦ, ὁ one using⟩

βιάω = βιάζω.

βιβάζω to cause to go; to bring; to lift up.

βιβάσθω, βιβάω, βίβημι to stride, step.

βιβλαρίδιον, βιβλιάριον, βιβλίδιον, τό little book or scroll.

βιβλίον, τό, βίβλος, ἡ bark of the papyrus; paper; book; letter. [sume.⟨

βιβρώσκω to eat up, con-⟩

βῖκος or βίκος, ὁ vessel, jug, flagon.

βιό-δωρος 2 life-giving.

βίος, ὁ life; mode of life; livelihood; means.

βιός, ὁ bow. [livelihood.⟨

βιο-στερής 2 bereft of one's⟩

βιοτεύω to live. [βίος.⟨

βιοτή, ἡ and βίοτος, ὁ =⟩

βιόω to live. — *M.* to maintain one's life; to preserve life. [endurable.⟨

βιώσιμος 2 worth living;⟩

βίωσις, ἡ mode of life.

βιωτικός 3 belonging to life, earthly.

βιωτός 3 = βιώσιμος

βλαβερός 3 noxious, hurtful.

βλάβη, ἡ and βλάβος, τό damage; hurt; loss.

βλάβω = βλάπτω.

βλᾱκείᾱ, ἡ sloth; stupidity.

βλᾱκεύω to be lazy, indolent.

βλάξ, βλᾱκός, ὁ lazy, indolent, careless; stupid.

βλάπτω to hinder; to weaken; to damage, hurt; to deceive, confound.

βλαστάνω to sprout, bud, germinate; to grow up; to be descended from; *trans.* to bring forth.

βλάστη, ἡ, βλάστημα, τό, βλάστος, ὁ sprout, bud; growth; descendant; origin.

βλασ-φημέω to blaspheme, slander. [slander.]

βλασ-φημίᾱ, ἡ blasphemy, [

βλάσ-φημος 2 blaspheming, slandering.

βλεμεαίνω to exult in.

βλέμμα, τό look, glance.

βλεπτός 3 worth seeing.

βλέπω to look at or on; to see, regard, observe; to have sight; to beware of.

βλεφαρίς, ίδος or ῖδος, ἡ eyelash.

βλέφαρον, τό eyelid; eye.

βλῆμα, τό shot; wound.

βλῆτρον, τό ring, hoop.

βληχή, ἡ a bleating.

βλίττω to cut out honeycombs.

βλοσυρός 3 grim, terrible.

βλοσυρ-ῶπις, ιδος, ἡ grim-looking.

βλωθρός 3 tall, high grown.

βλώσκω to go; to come.

βοάγριον, τό leather shield.

βοάω to cry, shout, roar, howl; to call to; to praise.

— *P.* to be known or famous.

βοεικός 3 and βόειος 3 of or for oxen, of ox-hide (shield).

βοεύς, ὁ thong of ox-leather.

βοή, ἡ cry, shout; war-cry; battle; call; sound; loud speech, voice; prayer.

βοή. ἡ ox-hide.

βοη-δρομιών, ῶνος, ὁ name of a month (September to October).

βοήθεια, ἡ help, aid, rescue, succour; protection; auxiliary force.

βοηθέω to succour, to come to the rescue, to aid, help, assist. [battle.]

βοη-θόος 2 hasting to the[

βοηθός 2 helping; assistant.

βο-ηλᾰσίᾱ, ἡ a robbing of cattle.

βο-ηλάτης, ου, ὁ driver.

βοητύς, ύος, ἡ a crying, shouting. [hole, pit.]

βόθρος, ὁ, βόθῡνος, ὁ[

βοιωτ-αρχέω to be a magistrate with the Bœotians.

βοιωτ-άρχης, ου, βοιώτ-αρχος, ὁ magistrate in Bœotia.

βοιωτιάζω to speak Bœotian; to side with the Bœotians. [ray.]

βολή, ἡ throw, shot; glance;[

βολίζω to throw the sounding-lead. [plummet.]

βολίς, ίδος, ἡ missile.[

βόλομαι = βούλομαι.

βόλος, ὁ = βολή; fishing-net.

βομβέω to sound deep, hum, huzz, ring.

βόμβος, ὁ hollow sound.

βορά, ἡ food, meat.

βόρβορος, ὁ mud, mire, dirt.

βορβορώδης 2 miry.

βορέας, ου, ὁ north wind; north.   [northern.]

βόρειος 2 and βορήιος 3)

βορρᾶς, ᾶ, ὁ = βορέας.

βόρυς, υος, ὁ gazelle.

βόσις, ἡ food.   [pasture.]

βόσκημα, τό cattle, herd;)

βόσκω to feed, nourish. — P. and M. to be fed, maintained, to graze.

βόστρυχος, ὁ lock of hair.

βοτάνη, ἡ fodder, pasture.

βοτήρ, ῆρος, ὁ shepherd.

βοτόν, τό grazing cattle.

βοτρυδόν adv. in the shape of grapes.

βότρυς, υος, ὁ grape.

βούβαλις, ιος, ἡ antelope

βού-βοτος, ἡ pasture for cattle.

βού-βρωστις, ἡ hungry evil; craving greediness.

βουβών, ῶνος, ὁ groin; abdomen.

βου-γάϊος, ὁ braggart.

βου-θερής 2 feeder of cattle.   [cattle.]

βου-θυτέω to sacrifice)

βού-θῠτος 2 belonging to a sacrifice of cattle

βού-κερως, ων horned like an ox.

βου-κολέω to feed cattle. — P. and M. to be fed, to graze.

βου-κολίη, ἡ and βου-κόλιον, τό herd of cattle.

βού-κολος, ὁ cowherd, herdsman.

βουλείᾱ, ἡ office of counsellor.

βούλευμα, τό resolution; decree, plan; wish, opinion; counsel.

βουλευτήριον, τό council-house, council-board.

βουλευτής, οῦ, ὁ counsellor, alderman.

βουλευτικός 3 belonging to counsellors.

βουλεύω to be counsellor; and M. to take counsel; to contrive, devise; to consider; to determine, resolve; to give counsel.

βουλή, ἡ will, determination; counsel, advice; project; council, senate.

βούλημα, τό, βούλησις, ἡ will, determination; purpose.

βουλη-φόρος 2 counselling.

βου-λῑμιάω to suffer from canine hunger.

βούλομαι to will, wish, want, like; to be willing or resolved; to prefer, choose; ὁ βουλόμενος anyone.

βου-λῠτός, ὁ evening, time of unyoking oxen.

βου-νόμος 2 cattle-feeding.

βουνός, ὁ hill, height.

βου-πλήξ, ῆγος, ἡ goad.

βου-πόρος 2 piercing through an ox.

βού-πρωρος 2 with the head of an ox.

βοῦς, βοός, ὁ, ἡ cow, ox, bull; cattle; ox-hide, shield of ox-hide.

βου-φονέω to kill oxen.
βου-φορβός, ὁ cowherd.
βο-ῶπις, ιδος, ἡ ox-eyed.
βραβεῖον, τό prize in a contest.
βραβεύς, ὁ, βραβευτής, οῦ, ὁ judge, umpire.
βραβεύω to be a judge, to (be) umpire; to rule.
βράγχος, ὁ hoarseness, sore-throat.   [loiter.]
βραδύνω to delay; to tarry,
βραδυ-πλοέω to sail slowly.
βραδύς 3 slow, heavy; lazy.
βραδυτής, ῆτος, ἡ slowness, tardiness.
βράσσων 2 = βραδύτερος.
βραχεῖν to rattle, ring, roar.
βράχιστος 3 = βραχύτατος.
βραχίων, ονος, ὁ arm, shoulder.
βράχος, τό shallows (spot).
βραχυ-λογίᾱ, ἡ brevity in speech.   [speech.]
βραχυ-λόγος 2 short in
βραχύς 3 short, not far off; little, shallow.
βραχύτης, ἡ shortness.
βρέμω and M. to roar, sound, clash.
βρέφος, τό unborn child; newborn child; young one, colt.   [head.]
βρεχμός, ὁ forepart of the
βρέχω to wet, sprinkle; to let rain; P. to be wetted.
βρῑαρός 3 weighty, strong.
βρίζω to sleep, slumber.
βρι-ηπύος 2 loud shouting.
βρῑθοσύνη, ἡ weight, heaviness.
βρῑθύς 3 weighty, heavy.
βρίθω and M. to be weighty

or loaded, to be bent down to teem, abound; to out weigh, prevail.
βρομέω to hum, huzz.
βρόμος, ὁ noise, huzzing, roar.
βροντάω to thunder.
βροντή, ἡ thunder; stupefaction.
βρότειος 3 and 2 = βροτός.
βροτόεις 3 bloody.   [ing.]
βροτο-λοιγός 2 man-slay-
βρότος, ὁ gore.
βροτός, ὁ, ἡ mortal, man.
βροτόω to stain with blood.
βροχή, ἡ rain.
βρόχος, ὁ rope, noose.
βρυγμός, ὁ a gnashing.
βρύκω to bite; to devour.
βρῡχάομαι M. and P. to roar, shout aloud.
βρύχω to gnash the teeth.
βρύω to sprout, bud, swell; to cause to come forth.
βρῶμα, τό and βρώμη, ἡ, βρῶσις, ἡ, βρωτύς, ύος, ἡ food, meat; an eating.
βύβλινος 3 made of byblus.
βύβλος, ἡ papyrus plant; bark of papyrus.
βύζην adv. closely, thickly.
βυθίζω to let sink; to sink.
βυθός, ὁ depth, abyss.
βύκτης, ου howling.
βυνέω = βύω.
βύρσα, ἡ skin, hide.
βυρσεύς, ὁ and βυρσο-δέψης, ου, ὁ tanner.
βύσσινος 3 of fine linen.
βυσσο-δομεύω to contrive secretly.   [depth.]
βυσσόθεν adv. from the
βυσσός, ὁ = βυθός.

βύσσος, ἡ fine linen.

βύω to cram, to stuff full.

βωθέω = βοηθέω.

βῶλος, ἡ clod of earth.

βώμιος 3 belonging to an altar.

βωμίς, ίδος, ἡ step, stair.

βωμός, ὁ raised place, step, stand, pedestal, altar.

βωστρέω to call to. [ing.]

βωτι-άνειρα, ἡ man-feed-

βώτωρ, ορος, ὁ herdsman.

Γ

Γ, γ (γάμμα) third letter of the alphabet; as a numeral γ' = 3.

γάγγραινα, ἡ gangrene, cancer.

γάζα, ἡ, γαζο-φΰλάκιον, τό treasury.

γαῖα, ἡ = γῆ.

γαιά-οχος = γαιήοχος.

γαιήιος sprung from Gaea.

γαιή-οχος 2 earth-compassing; land-protecting.

γαίω to exult.

γάλα, ακτος, τό milk.

γαλα-θηνός 2 milk-suck-ing. [drinker.]

γαλακτο-πότης, ου, ὁ milk-

γαλέη and γαλῆ, ἡ weasel; cat.

γαλήνη, ἡ calm, stillness of wind; tranquillity.

γαλόως, ω, ἡ sister-in-law.

γαμβρός, ὁ son-in-law; brother-in-law.

γαμετή, ἡ wife.

γαμέτης, ου, ὁ husband.

γαμέω to marry, take to wife. — M. to be given to wife; to give in marriage.

γαμηλιών, ῶνος, ὁ an Attic month (January to February).

γαμίζω to give in marriage. — P. to be wed.

γαμικός 3 bridal.

γαμίσκω = γαμίζω.

γάμμα the letter Gamma.

γᾱ-μόρος = γεωμόρος.

γάμος, ὁ a wedding, marriage, wedding-feast.

γαμφηλή, ἡ jaw.

γαμφ-ῶνυξ, υχος with curved talons. [bright.]

γανάω to shine, to be

γάνΰμαι M. to be delighted.

γάρ conj. for; since, as; why, what; o that!

γαργαλισμός, ὁ a tickling.

γαστήρ, στρός, ἡ belly; womb; kind of sausage.

γάστρᾱ, ἡ belly. [tony.]

γαστρι-μαργίᾱ, ἡ glut-

γαυλικός, γαυλιτικός 3 belonging to a merchant-ship. [merchant-vessel.]

γαυλός, ὁ milk-pail, bucket;

γαυριάω to pride oneself.

γδουπέω = δουπέω.

γέ conj. at least, at any rate, even, just, of course, indeed.

γέγωνα perf. to make oneself heard, to cry, shout; to proclaim.

γέεννα, ἡ hell.

γείνομαι M. to be begotten or born; to beget. [bour.]

γειτνιάω to be a neigh-

γείτων, ονος, ὁ. ἡ neighbouring; neighbour.

γελασείω to be inclined to laughing. [mocker.]
γελαστής, οῦ, ὁ laugher,
γελαστός 3 laughable.
γελάω, γελοιάω to laugh, smile, shine; to sneer at.
γελοῖος and γέλοιος 3 laughable; facetious, jesting.
γέλως, ωτος, ὁ and γέλος, ὁ laughter, laughing; joke, mocking. [laughter.]
γελωτο-ποιέω to cause
γελωτο-ποιός, ὁ jester, buffoon.
γεμίζω to fill, load.
γέμω to be full.
γενεά, ἡ birth, descent; race, family, tribe; home; generation.
γενεα-λογέω to trace a pedigree. — P. to derive one's pedigree. [pedigree.]
γενεα-λογία, ἡ genealogy;
γενέθλη, ἡ = γενεά.
γενέθλιος 2 belonging to one's birth; τὰ γενέθλια birthday or funeral festival; belonging to a family. [descent.]
γένεθλον, τό descendant;
γενειάς, άδος, ἡ beard; chin; cheek.
γενειά(σκ)ω to get a beard.
γένειον, τό chin; beard.
γενέσιος 2 = γενέθλιος.
γένεσις, ἡ origin, birth, engendering; a being, creature; race.
γενετή, ἡ birth.
γενέτης, ου, ὁ, γενέτωρ, ορος, ὁ, father; ancestor; son.
γενηΐς, ίδος, ἡ axe; shovel.

γεννάδας, ου noble.
γενναῖος 3 innate; highborn, noble, generous, highminded; genuine, sincere.
γενναιότης, ητος, ἡ nobleness, magnanimity.
γεννάω to engender, beget.
γέννημα, τό product, fruit; child; nature.
γέννησις, ἡ a begetting.
γεννητής, οῦ, ὁ begetter, parent.
γεννητός 3 begotten, born.
γεννήτωρ, ορος, ὁ = γεννητής.
γένος, τό birth, descent; race, family, kindred; descendant, child; sex, gender; one's own country; kind, species; generation.
γέντο he seized or grasped.
γένυς, υος, ἡ jaw; pl. mouth; chin; axe.
γεραιός 3 old, aged; old man; οἱ γεραίτεροι the elders, senators.
γεραίρω to honour, reward.
γέρανος, ἡ crane.
γεραός 3 = γεραιός.
γεραρός 3 reverend; stately.
γέρας, αος and ως, τό gift of honour; honour; privilege; gift, reward.
γεροντ-αγωγέω to guide an old man.
γερόντιον, τό old man.
γερουσία, ἡ council of elders, senate. [the elders.]
γερούσιος 3 belonging to
γέρρον, τό wicker-work; wicker-shield.
γερρο-φόρος, ὁ bearer of a wicker-shield.

γέρων, οντος, ὁ old; old man: *pl.* aldermen, elders, senators.

γεύω to give to taste. — *M.* to taste, to eat of; to try.

γέφῡρα, ἡ mound; bridge; battle-field.

γεφῡρόω to dam, embank; to bridge over.

γεω-γράφος, ὁ geographer.

γεώδης 2 earthy.

γεω-μέτρης, ου, ὁ surveyor, geometer.

γεω-μετρίᾱ, ἡ land-surveying, geometry. [cal.]

γεω-μετρικός 3 geometri-

γεω-μόρος, ὁ land-owner; peasant; landed proprietor.

γεω-πέδιον, γεώ-πεδον, τό piece of land.

γεω-πείνης, ου poor in land.

γεωργέω to till, cultivate.

γεωργίᾱ, ἡ agriculture; arable land.

γεωργικός 3 belonging to agriculture; farmer, skilled in farming.

γεωργός 2 tilling; husbandman; vine-dresser.

γεωρῠχέω to dig mines.

γῆ, ἡ earth, land; soil, ground, field; empire; home.

γη-γενής 2 earthborn.

γῆθεν *adv.* from the earth.

γηθέω to be glad, to rejoice.

γηθοσύνη, ἡ joy, delight.

γηθόσυνος 2 gay, glad.

γήϊνος 3 of earth.

γή-λοφος, ὁ hill.

γη-οχέω to possess land.

γηραιός 3 old, aged.

γῆρας, αος, ως, τό old age.

γηράσκω, γηράω to become old; to ripen.

γηρο-βοσκός 2 feeding one's old parents.

γηρο-τροφέω to feed in old age.

γηρο-τρόφος 2 = γηροβοσκός. [speech.]

γῆρυς, υος, ἡ voice; sound;

γήτης, ου, ὁ husbandman.

γίγνομαι to become, grow; to be born; to come in (revenue); to result, amount to; to happen, occur.

γιγνώσκω to perceive, to gain knowledge (of), to know, learn, understand; to judge, determine, decide; to think; to resolve.

γίνομαι = γίγνομαι.

γινώσκω = γιγνώσκω.

γλάγος, τό milk. [eating.]

γλακτο-φάγος 2 milk-

γλαυκιόων 3 with sparkling eyes.

γλαυκ-όμματος 2, γλαυκ-ῶπις, ιδος, ἡ bright-eyed; owl-eyed.

γλαυκός, 3 clear, bright, gleaming; bluish.

γλαῦξ, γλαύξ, κός, ἡ owl.

γλᾰφῠρός 3 hollow, convex; smoothed.

γλεῦκος, τό sweet wine.

γλήνη, ἡ eye-ball; puppet.

γλῆνος, τό ornament.

γλίσχρος 2 slippery; scanty, scarce, petty.

γλίχομαι *M.* to be fond of, to strive after.

γλοιός, ὁ resin, gum.

γλουτός, ὁ buttock.

γλυκερός 3 = γλυκύς.

γλυκύ-θῡμος 2 sweet-minded. [lovely; kind.]

γλυκύς 3 sweet, delightful,)

γλυκύτης, ητος, ἡ sweet-ness. [arrow.]

γλῠφίς, ίδος, ἡ notch of an)

γλῠφω to carve, engrave.

γλῶσσα, γλῶττα, ἡ tongue; mouth; speech; dialect.

γλωσσό-κομον, τό case for money.

γλωχίς, ῑνος, ἡ point of a nail or of an arrow.

γναθμός, ὁ and γνάθος, ἡ jaw, mouth. [flexible.]

γναμπτός 3 curved, bent;)

γνάμπτω to curve, bend.

γναφεῖον, γναφεύς see κναφεῖον. [nuine, true.]

γνήσιος 3 legitimate; ge-)

γνόφος, ὁ darkness.

γνύξ adv. with bent knees.

γνύφη, ἡ hollow, cave.

γνῶμα, τό mark, token; knowledge.

γνώμη, ἡ mind, understand-ing, reason, judgment; opinion, persuasion; dis-cretion; resolution, purpose; wish, intention; sentence, truism; advice, proposal.

γνώμων, ονος, ὁ one that knows, judge, umpire, ar-biter; overseer; sun-dial.

γνωρίζω to perceive, make out, discover; to know, to become acquainted with; to declare.

γνώριμος 2 known, fami-liar; perceptible, knowable; noble, aristocrat. [mind.]

γνωσι-μάχέω to alter one's)

γνῶσις, ἡ knowledge, wis-dom, understanding; judi-cial sentence. [knows.]

γνώστης, ου, ὁ one that)

γνωστός 3 = γνώριμος.

γνωτός 3 known; knowable; kinsman, brother, sister.

γοάω and M. to wail; to bewail.

γογγύζω to murmur, mutter.

γογγυσμός, ὁ a muttering.

γογγυστής, οῦ, ὁ mutterer.

γοή, ἡ = γόος.

γόης, ητος, ὁ enchanter, wizzard; juggler, cheater.

γοητεία, ἡ sorcery, witch-craft, delusion. [delude.]

γοητεύω to bewitch, cheat,)

γόμος, ὁ cargo, freight.

γομφίος, ὁ cheek-tooth, molar (tooth).

γόμφος, ὁ peg, nail.

γονεύς, ὁ parent, ancestor.

γονή, ἡ a begetting; birth, origin; descendant, off-spring; seed. [ductive.]

γόνιμος 2 vigorous, pro-)

γόνυ, γόνατος, τό knee.

γονυ-πετέω to fall or go down on one's knees.

γόος ὁ a wailing, lament, dirge, incantation. [fierce.]

γοργός 3 terrible, wild,)

γοργύρη, ἡ underground dungeon. [looking.]

γοργ-ῶπις, ιδος fierce-)

γοῦν (γὲ οὖν) at least, at any rate; of course; for in-stance; yet, indeed.

γουνάζομαι, γουνόομαι M. to be prostrate, to entreat, supplicate.

γουνός, ὁ angle of fruit-land; promontory; hill.

γράδιον, γραΐδιον, τό old woman. [old, knowing.]

γραῖα, ἡ old woman; adj.

γράμμα, τό letter of the alphabet; writing, writ; note-book, letter, document, catalogue; inscription; picture; pl. letters, learning.

γραμματεῖον, τό tablet, note-book; document; account-book.

γραμματεύς, ὁ scribe, writer, secretary. [tary.]

γραμματεύω to be secre-

γραμματικός 3 knowing to write and read; belonging to grammar.

γραμματιστής, οῦ, ὁ secretary; school-master.

γραμμή, ἡ stroke, line in writing.

γραπτός 3 written.

γραπτύς, ύος, ἡ a scratching, wound. [hag.]

γραῦς, γραός, ἡ old woman,

γράφεύς, ὁ writer; painter.

γραφή, ἡ picture, drawing; writing, document; bill of indictment, public prosecution.

γραφικός 3 belonging to writing or painting. [style.]

γραφίς, ίδος. ἡ writing-

γράφω to scratch, engrave; to write, draw, paint; to write down, to register; to describe; to inscribe. — M. to write for oneself, to note down; to have something painted; to indict.

γραώδης 2 like an old woman. [live.]

γρηγορέω to be awake; to

γρηῦς, γρηΰς = γραῦς.

γρύψ, γρυπός, ὁ griffin.

γύαλον, τό a hollow, curvature, bow; armour-plate; cave, grotto, den.

γύης, ου, ὁ corn-field.

γυῖον, τό joint, limb; knee, leg, arm.

γυιόω to lame.

γυμνάζω to train, exercise, accustom. [ercise.]

γυμνασία, ἡ training, ex-

γυμνασί-αρχος, ὁ training-master.

γυμνάσιον, τό exercise; place of exercise, training-school. [master.]

γυμναστής, οῦ, ὁ training-

γυμναστικός 3 belonging to training, gymnastic.

γυμνής, ῆτος and γυμνήτης, ου ὁ light-armed foot-soldier.

γυμνητεία, ἡ light infantry.

γυμνητεύω to be naked, light-armed.

γυμνητικός 3 belonging to one lightly armed.

γυμνικός 3 = γυμναστικός.

γυμνο-παιδίαι, αἱ gymnastic festival.

γυμνός 3 naked; unarmed, lightly clad or armed; bare, destitute.

γυμνότης, ητος, ἡ, γύμνωσις, ἡ nakedness, denudation.

γυμνόω to bare, denudate.

γυναικάριον, τό = γύναιον.

γυναικεῖος 3 womanly, feminine.

γυναικωνῖτις, ιδος ἡ women's apartment.

γυναι-μανής 2 devoted to women. [wench.]

γύναιον, τό little woman;

γύναιος 3 = γυναικεῖος.

γυνή, γυναικός, ἡ woman, lady; wife; mistress; widow; servant.

γυρός 3 round, curved.

γύψ, γυπός, ὁ vulture.

γύψος, ἡ chalk, gypsum.

γυψόω to besmear with gypsum.

γῶν = γοῦν.

γωνίᾱ, ἡ angle, corner; joiner's square; corner-stone.

γωνιώδης 2 angular.

γωρυτός, ὁ bow-case.

Δ

Δ, δ (δέλτα) fourth letter of the alphabet; as a numeral δ' = 4.

δᾳδοῦχος, ὁ torch-bearer.

δαήμων 2 knowing, experienced. [to know.]

δαῆναι to teach; to learn;

δαήρ, έρος. ὁ brother-in-law.

δαί; τί δαί what then? πῶς δαί how then?

δαιδάλεος 3 cunningly or curiously wrought.

δαιδάλλω to work or adorn curiously.

δαίδαλον, τό work of art.

δαΐζω to divide, tear, pierce; to kill. [battle.]

δαΐ-κτάμενος 3 killed in

δαιμονάω, δαιμονίζομαι P. to be mad or raving.

δαιμόνιος 3 divine, god-like; possessed by a demon, unfortunate; supernatural, wonderful; poor, odd, or infatuated man. — τὸ δαιμόνιον divine being, inferior deity, evil spirit, demon, devil; guardian spirit; divine operation, fate; genius (with Socrates).

δαιμονιώδης 2 devilish.

δαίμων, ονος, ὁ, ἡ divine being, (inferior) deity, guardian spirit; evil spirit, demon, devil, spectre; fate, evil, death.

δαίνῡμι to portion out; to give a feast. — M. to eat, feast.

δάϊος 3 burning, hot; pernicious, hostile; unhappy.

δαΐς, ιδος, ἡ pine-wood; torch; battle.

δαίς, δαιτός, ἡ banquet, feast; portion.

δαίτη, ἡ meal, feast.

δαιτρεύω to portion out; to carve.

δαιτρόν, τό portion.

δαιτρός, ὁ carver. [ing.]

δαιτροσύνη, ἡ art of carv-

δαιτυμών, όνος, ὁ guest, companion at table.

δαιτύς, ύος, ἡ meal.

δαΐ-φρων 2 knowing, intelligent; warlike.

δαίω¹ to kindle, set on fire. — P. to burn, blaze.

δαίω² and M. to divide, part out; to tear.

δακέ-θῡμος 2 heart-biting.

δάκνω to bite, sting; to hurt, vex.

δάκρυ, υος, δάκρῡμα, τό and δάκρυον, τό tear.

δακρύοεις 3 tearful; weeping. [in tears.

δακρυ-πλώω to be bathed)

δακρυ-ρροέω to shed tears.

δακρύω to weep; to shed tears; to weep for.

δακτύλιος, ὁ finger-ring.

δάκτυλος, ὁ finger; toe; finger's breadth; short space. [of wood.

δᾱλός, ὁ firebrand; billet)

δᾰμάζω see δαμάω.

δάμᾰλις, ἡ young cow, calf.

δάμᾱρ, δάμαρτος, ἡ wife, spouse.

δᾰμάω to tame, break; to subdue, overpower; to slay; to give in marriage.

δᾰνείζω to lend, to put out at usury. — M. to borrow.

δάνειον and δάνεισμα, τό loan. [ing, usury.

δανεισμός, ὁ money-lend-)

δανειστής, δανιστής, οῦ, ὁ money-lender, usurer.

δᾱνός 3 dry, parched.

δᾰος, τό torch.

δᾰπᾰνάω to spend; to spend on; to consume, waste.

δᾰπάνη, ἡ, δᾰπάνημα, τό a spending, expense, cost; extravagance; tribute.

δᾰπᾰνηρός 3 and δάπανος 2 expensive; extravagant.

δά-πεδον, τό soil, flat country; floor. [to devour.

δάπτω to tear in pieces;)

δαρδάπτω to pluck in pieces; to devour.

δαρεικός, ὁ Persian gold-coin.

δαρθάνω to sleep.

δᾱρός 3 = δηρός.

δᾴς, δᾳδός, ἡ = δαίς.

δά-σκιος 2 thick-shaded.

δάσμευσις, ἡ distribution.

δασμο-λογέω to exact tribute.

δασμός, ὁ division; tax, tribute. [bute.

δασμο-φόρος 2 paying tri-)

δασ-πλῆτις, ἡ hard-striking. [fleeced.

δασύ-μαλλος 2 thickly)

δασύς 3 hairy, bushy, thick grown; densely wooded; rough. [gy breast.

δασύ-στερνος 2 with shag-)

δατέομαι M. to divide, portion out; to carve; to crush.

δάφνη, ἡ laurel. [laurel.

δαφνη-φόρος 2 bearing)

δα-φοινός 2 blood-red.

δαψιλής 2 liberal, profuse; abundant.

δέ conj. but, on the other hand; further; thus; then.

δέαται he seems, δέατο he seemed. [come.

δεδίσκομαι to greet, wel-)

δεδίσσομαι M. to frighten, alarm; to get frightened.

δεδοκημένος 3 lying in wait.

δέελος 3 = δῆλος.

δέησις, ἡ prayer, entreating.

δεῖ one must, one ought; τὸ δέον, τὰ δέοντα the needful, the necessary or proper thing, the thing required. — δεῖ τινος there is need of.

δεῖγμα, τό proof, sample, specimen; show, bazaar.

δειγματίζω to expose to shame.

δειδήμων 2 timorous, cowardly.

δείδια see δείδω.

δειδίσκομαι = δεδίσκομαι.

δειδίσσομαι = δεδίσσομαι.

δείδω to be afraid, fear, apprehend. [ing meal.]

δειελιάω to take an evening

δείελος 2 belonging to the evening; evening.

δεικανάομαι to welcome.

δείκηλον, τό representation.

δείκνῦμι, -ύω to show, point out, exhibit, display; to prove, demonstrate, explain; to tell; to teach. — M. to welcome, to pledge with.

δείλη, ἡ afternoon; evening.

δειλίᾱ, ἡ cowardice.

δειλιάω to be dismayed or afraid. [evening).]

δείλομαι M. to set (towards)

δειλός 3 timid, cowardly; vile, mean; unhappy.

δεῖμα, τό fear, terror, horror.

δειμαίνω to fear, to be afraid or alarmed.

δειματόω to frighten.

δεῖνα, ὁ, ἡ, τό any one, a certain one.

δεινο-λογέομαι M. to complain vehemently.

δεινό-πους, ποδος striding fearfully.

δεινός 3 venerable; fearful, terrible, frightful, awful, dangerous; τὸ δεινόν danger, terror, distress; extraordinary; mighty, powerful; clever, skilful; unheard of, shocking, strange, wonderful, marvellous.

δεινότης, ητος, ἡ terribleness, sternness; power, ability.

δεινόω to exaggerate.

δειν-ώψ, ῶπος horrible-looking.

δεῖος, τό = δέος.

δειπνέω to take the chief meal, to dine.

δείπνηστος, ὁ meal-time.

δειπνίζω to treat at table.

δεῖπνον, τό meal, chief meal; banquet; food.

δειπνο-ποιέομαι M. to prepare a meal; to dine.

δειράς, άδος, ἡ ridge of a hill; rock.

δειρή, ἡ neck, nape.

δειρο-τομέω to cut the throat of a person; to behead.

δείρω = δέρω.

δεισι-δαιμονίᾱ, ἡ fear of the gods; religion; superstition.

δεισι-δαίμων 2 god-fearing; superstitious. [men.]

δέκα ten.

δεκαδ-αρχίᾱ, ἡ rule of ten

δεκάδ-αρχος, -άρχης, ου, ὁ commander of ten men.

δεκα-δύο twelve.

δεκα-ετής 2 ten years old.

δεκάκις adv. ten times.

δεκά-μηνος 2 ten months old.

δεκα-πέντε fifteen.

δεκά-πηχυς, υ ten cubits long or high.

δεκα-πλάσιος 3 tenfold.

δεκά-πλεθρος 2 ten plethra long. [αρχος.]

δεκ-άρχης, ου, ὁ = δεκάδ-

δεκ-αρχίᾱ, ἡ = δεκαδ-αρχία.

δεκάς, άδος, ἡ the number ten; a body of ten.

δεκαταῖος 3 on the tenth day.

δεκα-τέσσαρες, α fourteen.

δεκατευτήριον, τό custom-house.

δεκατεύω to tithe, to give or take the tenth; to consecrate.

δέκατος 3 tenth.

δεκατόω to take the tenth. — P. to give the tenth.

δεκά-φῡλος 2 divided into ten tribes.

δεκά-χῑλοι 3 ten thousand.

δεκ-έτης 2 ten years old.

δείκνῡμι = δείκνυμι.

δέχομαι = δέχομαι.

δέκτης, ου, ὁ receiver, beggar.

δεκτός 3 acceptable.

δελεάζω to entice (by a bait), to bait.

δέλεαρ, ατος, τό bait.

δέλτα, τό delta.

δελτίον, τό, δέλτος, ὁ writing-tablet.

δέλφαξ, ακος, ἡ young pig.

δελφῑνο-φόρος 2 bearing a dolphin.

δελφίς, ῑνος, ὁ dolphin.

δέμας, τό body, figure, frame, stature; adv. in the form or shape of.

δέμνιον, τό bedstead, bed.

δέμω to build.

δενδίλλω to glance at.

δένδρεον = δένδρον.

δενδρήεις 3 rich in trees.

δενδρο-κοπέω to cut trees.

δένδρον, ου and δένδρος, τό tree.   [κοπέω.]

δενδρο-τομέω = δενδρο-]

δεννάζω to revile.

δέννος, ὁ abuse, reproach.

δεξαμένη, ἡ cistern.

δεξι-βόλος, ὁ slinger.

δεξιο-λάβος, ὁ lance-bearer.

δεξιόομαι M. to give the right hand; to greet.

δεξιός 3 at the right-hand side (ἡ δεξιά the right hand; promise, agreement); prosperous, fortunate; dexterous, ready.

δεξιό-σειρος 2 near or right-hand horse.

δεξιότης, ητος, ἡ dexterity, readiness.

δεξιόφιν adv. to the right.

δεξιτερός 3 = δεξιός.

δεξίωμα, τό offering of the right hand, pledge.

δέομαι see δέω.

δέος, τό fear, awe, reverence; danger.   [to look at.]

δέρκομαι P. to look, see;]

δέρμα, τό hide, skin; leather; bag.

δερμάτινος 3 leathern.

δέρρις, ἡ hide, skin.

δέρτρον, τό caul.

δέρω to skin, flay; to cudgel.

δέσμα, τό = δεσμός.

δεσμεύω, δεσμέω to fetter; to throw into prison.

δέσμη, δεσμή, ἡ bundle.

δέσμιος 2 fettered, captive.

δεσμός, ὁ band, fillet; fetter, string, thong; cable; imprisonment.

δεσμο-φύλαξ, ακος, ὁ jailer.

δέσμωμα, τό fetter.

δεσμωτήριον, τό prison.

δεσμώτης, ου, δεσμῶτις, ιδος prisoner.

δεσπόζω to be or become master, ruler.

δέσποινα, ἡ mistress, lady.

δεσποσύνη, ἡ absolute power. [owner.]

δεσπότης, ου, ὁ lord, master,

δεσποτικός 3 imperious, despotic. [ποινα.]

δεσπότις, ιδος, ἡ = δέσ-

δετή, ἡ fagot; torch.

δεύομαι = δέομαι.

δεῦρο, δεύρω adv. hither; come hither! up!; till now, hitherto.

δεύτατος 3 the last.

δεῦτε pl. of δεῦρο.

δευτεραῖος 3 on the second or next day.

δευτερεῖα, τά second prize.

δευτερό-πρωτος 2 next to the first. [inferior.]

δεύτερος 3 second, next;

δεύω[1] to wet.

δεύω[2] = δέω.

δεχ-ήμερος 2 for ten days.

δέχομαι M. to take, accept, receive; to approve; to choose; to suffer patiently; to take for; to receive kindly; to treat; to make head against, to stand one's ground; to lie in wait.

δέφω to soften, mould, knead; to tan. [imprison.]

δέω[1] to bind, fasten, fetter,

δέω[2] to be far from; to want, lack, to be in need of.

— M. δέομαι to be behind; to be in need of; to want,

wish, strive after; to ask, to beg for.

δή adv. = ἤδη; now, already, just now; presently, at once; then; of course, indeed, manifestly; even; yet, only, therefore; as said before.

δῆγμα, τό bite, sting.

δηθά adv. long.

δῆθεν adv. manifestly, forsooth; in vain; of course, really; perhaps.

δηθύνω to tarry, loiter.

δήϊος 3 = δάϊος.

δηϊότης, ητος, ἡ enmity; battle.

δηϊόω = δηόω.

δηλαδή adv. plainly, of course. [plainly.]

δηλ-αυγῶς adv. quite

δηλέομαι M. to hurt, damage, destroy.

δήλημα, τό hurt, ruin, destruction. [stroyer.]

δηλήμων 2 pernicious; de-

δήλησις, ἡ a hurting, ruin.

δηλον-ότι adv. plainly, clearly, of course.

δῆλος 3 manifest, visible, evident, plain, clear.

δηλόω to manifest, show, signify; to explain, prove; δηλοῖ it is clear.

δήλωσις, ἡ manifestation, a pointing out, advertisement, order, proof.

δημ-αγωγέω to be a popular leader or d magogue.

δημ-αγωγός, ὁ popular leader, demagogue.

δήμ-αρχος, ὁ chief of a district.

δήμευσις, ἡ confiscation.

δημεύω to confiscate; to make known.

δημ-ηγορέω to be a public orator, to harangue the people. [speech.]

δημ-ηγορία, ἡ public

δημ-ηγορικός 3 qualified for public speaking.

δημ-ηγόρος, ὁ public orator. [ουργός.]

δημιο-εργός 2 = δημι-

δήμιος 2 belonging to the whole people, public.

δημιουργέω to carry on a trade; to work.

δημιουργία, ἡ trade; handicraft, work. [to craftsmen.]

δημιουργικός 3 belonging

δημιουργός 2 working for the common weal; craftsman, workman, artist, master; maker, creator; magistrate.

δημο-βόρος 2 consuming the people's goods.

δημο-γέρων, οντος, ὁ elder of the people. [pense.]

δημόθεν adv. at public ex-

δημο-κρᾰτέομαι P. to live in a democracy.

δημο-κρᾰτία, ἡ democracy.

δημο-κρᾰτικός 3 democratic. [the people.]

δημό-λευστος 2 stoned by

δῆμος, ὁ land, country, district; common people, community; popular assembly; democracy.

δημός, ὁ fat.

δημοσιεύω to carry on a public trade, to be in the civil service; to confiscate.

δημόσιος 3 public, of or for the state; public officer or slave. τὸ δημόσιον the commons, state, state affairs, general weal; state treasury; state prison; δημοσίᾳ publicly, in the name of the state.

δημοσιόω to confiscate.

δημο-τελής 2 public, at public expense.

δημοτεύομαι M. to belong to a demos.

δημότης, ου, ὁ man of the people, private man; fellow-citizen.

δημοτικός 3 belonging to the people, common, public, civilian.

δημοῦχος 2 inhabitant of the country; protector of the country. [mon.]

δημώδης 2 popular; com-

δήν adv. long.

δηναιός 3 long-living.

δηνάριον, τό denarius (a Roman coin).

δῆνος, τό counsel, project.

δῆος 3 = δάιος.

δηόω to treat as an enemy, to slay, fight; to rend; to destroy, waste.

δή-ποτε adv. ever, once, at some time.

δή-που, δή-πουθεν adv. indeed, certainly; perhaps.

δηριάομαι, M. and δηρίομαι M. to contend, fight.

δῆρις, ἡ strife, fight, contest.

δηρός 3 long.

δῆτα adv. certainly, indeed, of course, plainly; therefore, then.

δήω I shall find.

διά *adv.* asunder; through, throughout. — *prp.* with *gen.* through, right through, through between; during; since; by means of, arising from. with *acc.* through; during; on account of, because of, by reason of; with a view to.

δια-βᾰδίζω to go over.

δια-βαίνω to stride; to stand firm; to cross, go over, step across.

δια-βάλλω to throw over, carry across; to disunite; to slander, accuse falsely, calumniate, revile; to cheat.

διά-βᾰσις, ἡ a crossing, passage, bridge, ford, pass.

δια-βατήρια, τά offerings for a happy crossing.

δια-βᾰτός 2 passable, fordable. [sert, confirm.\

δια-βεβαιόομαι *M.* to as-\

δια-βιβάζω to lead, bring, or carry over.

δια-βιόω to live through; to pass one's life.

δια-βλέπω to look through; to look straight on or round; to consider.

δια-βοάω to cry loud or promiscuously; to cry out, proclaim.

δια-βολή, ἡ slander, calumny, false accusation, reproach; bad fame; suspicion; hatred.

διά-βολος 2 slanderous; ὁ δ. slanderer, fiend, devil.

δια-βόρος 2 eating through, consuming.

διά-βορος 2 eaten through.

δια-βουλεύομαι *M.* to consult well.

διά-βροχος 2 wet; soaked, leaky [push through.\

δια-βῡνέω to thrust or\

δι-αγγέλλω to notify, announce, send message, proclaim. — *M.* to inform one another, to pass the word of command.

δι-άγγελος, ὁ negotiator, go-between.

δια-γελάω to laugh at.

δια-γίγνομαι *M.* to continue, live on, survive, remain; to be between, elapse.

δια-γιγνώσκω to discern, distinguish; to perceive well; to resolve, determine, decide.

δι-αγκυλίζομαι, δι-αγκύλόομαι *M.* to hold the javelin in readiness.

δια-γλάφω to hollow out.

δια-γνώμη, ἡ distinction; resolution, decree, judgment, sentence. [known.\

δια-γνωρίζω to make\

διά-γνωσις, ἡ = διαγνώμη.

δια-γογγύζω to mutter promiscuously.

δι-αγορεύω to state precisely.

διά-γραμμα, τό a drawing, figure; register; decree.

δια-γράφω to draw out; paint out; to strike out, reject. [awake.\

δια-γρηγορέω to remain\

δι-άγω to lead through, over, across, or up; to pass, live, spend; to tarry, delay; to continue, keep; to accomplish.

δι-αγωγή, ἡ a leading across; course of life.

δι-αγωνίζομαι M. to contend, fight; to carry on a lawsuit; to fight to the end.

δια-δαίομαι M. to divide; to destroy.

δια-δάπτω to rend, lacerate. [bute.]

δια-δατέομαι M. to distri-

δια-δείχνῦμι to point out exactly, to explain, show.

δια-δέξιος 2 quite auspicious.

δια-δέρχομαι to see or perceive through.

δια-δέχομαι M. to receive in turn; to take up, succeed to; to relieve.

δια-δέω to fasten or bind to; to fetter. [to pieces.]

δια-δηλέομαι to tear in or

διά-δηλος 2 quite distinct, manifest.

διά-δημα, τό circlet, diadem.

δια-διδράσκω to run away, escape.

δια-δίδωμι to pass on, give over; to distribute, pay off.

δια-δικάζω to carry on a lawsuit; to pass sentence.

δια-δικαιόω to plead.

δια-δικασίᾱ, ἡ decision; action for precedence.

δια-δοχή, ἡ a taking up; succession; relief.

διά-δοχος 2 taking up, alternating; successor.

δια-δρηστεύω to run away.

δια-δύομαι to pass or slip through; to escape.

δια-είδομαι to show clearly; to appear clearly.

δια-ζάω to survive; to maintain life.

δια-ζεύγνῦμι to disjoin.

διά-ζευξις, ἡ a disjoining.

διά-ζωμα, τό girdle; apron.

δια-ζώννῦμι to cut through; to gird round.

δια-ζώω = διαζάω.

δι-άημι to blow through.

δια-θεάομαι M. to view closely.

δια-θειόω to fumigate through with brimstone.

διά-θεσις, ἡ arrangement, disposition, condition; constitution; mind.

δια-θέτης, ου, ὁ arranger.

δια-θέω to run through or about; to spread; to run in contest.

δια-θήκη, ἡ arrangement, disposition; testament; treaty, covenant.

δια-θορυβέω to trouble vehemently.

δια-θροέω to spread a report.

δια-θρῡλέω to spread abroad; to have always in one's mouth.

δια-θρύπτω to break in or to pieces; to spoil, weaken; to make vain.

διαί = διά.

διαίνω to wet, moisten.

δι-αίρεσις, ἡ division; distribution; distinction.

δι-αίρετος 2 divided.

δι-αιρέω to divide, sever, cut in two; to pull down, demolish, destroy; to distribute; to explain, interpret; to define; to decide.

δι-αϊστόω to kill, murder.

δίαιτα, ἡ life; mode of life; diet; intercourse; food; dwelling.

διαιτάω to be umpire. — P. to lead a life, to live, dwell.

διαίτημα, τό = δίαιτα.

διαιτητής, οῦ, ὁ arbiter, umpire. [thoroughly.]

δια-καθαρίζω to clean(se)]

δια-καίω to burn through.

δια-καλύπτω to cover thoroughly.

δια-καρτερέω to last out, persevere. [fute utterly.]

δια-κατελέγχομαι to con-]

δια-κεάζω to split in two.

δια-κειμαι to be in a certain condition or disposition, to be affected or disposed; to be settled.

δια-κείρω to frustrate.

δια-κελεύομαι M. to exhort, encourage, impel.

διά-κενος 2 empty between.

δια-κηρυκεύομαι M. to negotiate through a herald.

δια-κινδυνεύω to run a risk, to face danger; to make head against.

δια-κινέω to shake thoroughly; to put in disorder.

δια-κλάω to break in two.

δια-κλέπτω to steal away, to abstract, to remove by stealth; to betray.

δια-κληρόω to assign by lot; to let draw lots.

δια-κομιδή, ἡ a carrying over.

δια-κομίζω to carry over or across; to bring to an end.

διακονέω and M. to render service, to wait on, serve; to provide, attend to.

διακονία, ἡ service, attendance, business; deacon's office. [servile.]

διακονικός 3 serviceable,]

διάκονος, ὁ servant, attendant; deacon.

δι-ακοντίζομαι M. to contend in spear-throwing.

δια-κόπτω to cut or break through; to beat to pieces.

διά-κορος 2 satiated.

διακόσιοι 3 two hundred.

δια-κοσμέω to dispose, arrange.

δια-κόσμησις, ἡ, διά-κοσμος, ὁ arrangement, battle-array. [listen to.]

δι-ακούω to hear out; to]

δι-ακριβόω and M. to do accurately; to examine thoroughly; to know exactly.

δια-κριδόν adv. eminently.

δια-κρίνω to discern, separate, divide; to choose; to decide, judge. — P. and M. to be divided; to part; to dispute with one another; to be reconciled; to doubt.

διά-κρισις, ἡ separation; distinction; decision.

διά-κρουσις, ἡ delay.

δια-κρούω to hinder. — M. to push off; to deceive, elude; to delay.

διάκτορος, ὁ guide, messenger of the gods.

δια-κυκάω to mix together.

δια-κύπτω to peep through.

δια-κωλῡτής, οῦ, ὁ hinderer.

δια-κωλῡω to hinder, prevent, check; to forbid.

δια-κωμῳδέω to ridicule.

δι-ακωχή, ἡ = διοκωχή.

δια-λαγχάνω to assign by lot.

δια-λαλέω to talk over.

δια-λαμβάνω to take asunder, to separate, to take apart; to distinguish; to divide, distribute; to pause; to grasp, seize, hold fast; to deliberate. [through.]

δια-λάμπω to shine or flash]

δια-λανθάνω to be hidden, escape notice.

δια-λέγω to pick out, choose. — P. to consider; to talk with, converse, negotiate; to recite, speak (a dialect).

διά-λειμμα, τό interval, gap.

δια-λείπω to leave an interval or gap; to let pass; to leave off, desist; to lie between.

δια-λεκτικός 3 skilled in discourse; belonging to dialectics.

διά-λεκτος, ἡ conversation; speech: dialect.

δι-αλλαγή, ἡ change; reconciliation, agreement. [tor.]

δι-αλλακτής, οῦ, ὁ media-]

δι-αλλάσσω to interchange, change; to reconcile; to differ. — P. and M. to exchange between one another; to be reconciled; to be different.

δια-λογίζομαι M. to consider, reflect; to examine together.

δια-λογισμός, ὁ consideration, thought; doubt.

διά-λογος, ὁ conversation, dialogue.

δια-λοιδορέομαι P. to revile grossly. [treat.]

δια-λῡμαίνομαι M. to mal-]

διά-λῠσις, ἡ a loosing, separation, ending; a paying off, settling of accounts; reconciliation, peace.

δια-λῠτής, οῦ, ὁ destroyer.

δια-λῠτός 3 dissoluble.

δια-λύω to dissolve, divide, separate; to destroy; to end, break off; to reconcile; to pay.

δι-αμαρτάνω to miss or fail entirely; not to obtain; to go astray; to err.

δι-αμαρτίᾱ, ἡ mistake, failure, error. [witnesses.]

δια-μαρτῠρέω to refute by]

δια-μαρτῠρομαι M. to give solemn evidence (of), to conjure, to abjure.

δια-μαστῑγόω to whip well.

δια-μάχομαι M. to fight through; to fight, struggle; to endeavour.

δι-αμάω and M. to cut through; to scrape away.

δι-αμείβω to exchange; to change, alter. — M to exchange for oneself; to change one's mind.

δια-μέλλησις, ἡ a tarrying, delay.

δια-μέλλω to delay continually.

δια-μέμφομαι M. to blame severely. | tinue, persevere.)

διά-μένω to remain, con-) διά-μερίζω to divide. — P. and M. to be at variance.

διά-μερισμός, ὁ dissension.

διά-μετρέω to measure out or off; to sell. — M. to have measured out to one; to portion out among themselves. [out.)

διά-μέτρητος 2 measured)

διά-μηχανάομαι M. to contrive, devise. [tend, rival.)

δι-αμιλλάομαι P. to con-)

διά-μιμνήσκομαι to remember continually.

διά-μιστύλλω to cut in little pieces.

διά-μνημονεύω to remember well; to mention.

διά-μοιράω to portion out; to rend.

δι-αμπάξ adv. quite through.

δι-αμ-περές adv. quite through; continually; throughout; altogether.

διά-μῦθολογέω to converse. [pel.)

δι-αναγκάζω to force, com-)

δι-αναπαύω to give rest for a moment. — M. to cease for a while. [sea.)

διά-ναυμαχέω to fight at)

δι-άνδιχα adv. two ways; in either way.

διά-νέμω to distribute, portion out. — M. to divide between themselves. [to.)

διά-νεύω to nod or beckon)

διά-νέω to swim through.

δι-ανίσταμαι M. to depart from.

διά-νοέομαι P. to consider, reflect; to think, intend.

διά-νόημα, τό thought; purpose.

διά-νοια, ἡ thought, intellect, mind; opinion; intention. [plain.)

δι-ανοίγω to open; to ex-)

διά-νομή, ἡ distribution.

διά-νυκτερεύω to pass the night. [finish, accomplish.)

δι-ανύω, δι-ανύτω to)

διά-παιδεύω to educate thoroughly.

διά-παντός adv. throughout.

διά-παρα-τρῐβή, ἡ altercation. [flower.)

διά-παρθενεύω to de-)

διά-πασσαλεύω to fasten with nails.

διά-πάσσω to strew about.

διά-παύομαι P. to cease. — M. to pause.

δι-απειλέω to threaten violently. [trial.)

διά-πειρα, ἡ experiment,)

διά-πειράομαι P. to try, to make a proof (of); to know by experience. [through.)

διά-πείρω to pierce or bore)

διά-πέμπω to send over; to send to; to send about.

διά-περαίνω and M. to finish, to bring to an end.

διά-περαιόομαι P. to go over or across; to be drawn to one another.

διά-περάω to go over or across; to pass; to endure, get through. [tally.)

διά-πέρθω to destroy to-)

διά-πέτομαι M. to fly through or away.

δια-πίμπλημι to fill up (completely).

δια-πίνω to vie with one another in drinking.

δια-πίπτω to fall or go to pieces; to escape.

δια-πιστεύω to entrust.

δια-πλέκω to interweave; to weave to the end.

δια-πλέω to sail through or across. [pieces.]

δια-πλήσσω to dash to[

διά-πλους, ὁ a sailing across, passage.

δια-πνέω to blow through; to revive. [adorn.]

δια-ποικίλλω to variegate,]

δια-πολεμέω to end war; to carry on the war.

δια-πολέμησις, ἡ an ending of the war.

δια-πολιορκέω to carry a siege through. [sage.]

δια-πομπή, ἡ legacy; mes-]

δια-πονέω to toil; to work out with labour, to elaborate; to train, make hardy. — M. to endeavour; to get practised; to be vexed.

δια-πόντιος 2 transmarine.

δια-πορεύω to carry over or through. — P. to go or march through.

δι-απορέω and M. to be at a loss, to be undecided.

δια-πορθέω = διαπέρθω.

δια-πορθμεύω to carry over, across; to carry a message.

δια-πραγματεύομαι M. to examine closely; to do a thing diligently.

δια-πράσσω and M. to finish,

accomplish, effect; to procure, get; to make an appointment; to kill.

δια-πρεπής 2 conspicuous, excellent. [to adorn.]

δια-πρέπω to be eminent;]

δια-πρεσβεύομαι M. to send embassies about.

δια-πρήσσω = διαπράσσω.

δια-πρηστεύω to betray.

δια-πρίω to saw through. — P. to grow furious.

δια-πρό adv. quite through, thoroughly.

δια-πρύσιος 3 and 2 piercing; far-stretching.

δια-πτοέω, -πτοιέω to frighten or scare away.

δια-πτύσσω to disclose.

διά-πυρος 2 glowing, firy.

διά-πωλέω to sell.

δι-αράσσω to strike or knock through.

δι-αρθρόω to articulate; to form; to dissect.

δι-αριθμέω to count up. — M. to judge. [dure.]

δι-αρκέω to suffice; to en-]

δι-αρκής 2 enduring; sufficient. [ing.]

δι-αρπαγή, ἡ a plunder-]

δι-αρπάζω to tear to pieces; to rob, plunder.

δια-ρραίνω M. to drizzle down about.

δια-ρραίω to tear or dash to pieces; to destroy.

δια-ρρέω to flow through; to vanish; to melt away.

δια-ρρήγνυμι to break through; to break to or in pieces; to destroy; to rend; to pierce. — P. to burst.

διά-ρρήδην adv. expressly.

διά-ρρίπτέω, -ρρίπτω to throw through; to fling about, to distribute.

διά-ρρῖψις, ἡ a flinging about.

διά-ρροια, ἡ diarrhœa.

διά-ρροιζέω to whiz through.

διά-σαφέω, διά-σαφηνίζω to make conspicuous, to explain; to report.

διά-σείω to shake or stir violently; to extort.

διά-σεύομαι M. to rush, run, or dart through.

διά-σημαίνω to point out, mark.

διά-σημος 2 quite perceptible. [lent.

διά-σιωπάω to remain si-

διά-σκάπτω to dig through.

διά-σκαρῖφάομαι M. to scrape up.

διά-σκεδάννῦμι to scatter about; to disband; to destroy. [σκοπέω.

διά-σκέπτομαι = διά-

διά-σκευάζομαι M. to prepare for battle.

διά-σκηνέω, -όω to encamp in different quarters; to rise from the table.

διά-σκίδνημι = διασκεδάννῦμι.

διά-σκοπέω and M. to view closely, to examine, consider; to look round. [out.

διά-σκοπιάομαι M. to spy

διά-σκορπίζω to scatte about; to winnow; to waste.

διά-σμάω, -σμέω to wipe out, to rinse.

διά-σπάω to draw asunder, to tear to pieces; to sever; to scatter; to split.

διά-σπείρω to scatter about; to waste.

διά-σπορά, ἡ dispersion.

διά-σπουδάζω and M. to endeavour, do earnestly.

δι-άσσω to rush through.

διά-στᾰσις, ἡ distance; interval; dissension, discord, enmity. [lisade.

διά-σταυρόομαι M. to pa-

διά-στέλλω and M. to separate; to distinguish; to command. [distance.

διά-στημα, τό interval,

διά-στοιβάζω to stuff in between. [difference.

διά-στολή, ἡ distinction,

διά-στρέφω to turn aside, pervert; to distort; to incite (to rebellion), to stir up.

διά-στροφος 2 distorted, crippled; perverted.

διά-σύρω to mock.

διά-σφάξ, άγος, ἡ cleft, ravine.

διά-σφενδονάω to fling about from a sling. — P. to burst.

διά-σχίζω to cleave in two, to tear asunder.

διά-σώζω to save through; to preserve; to keep in memory.

διά-ταγή, ἡ and διά-ταγμα, τό arrangement, order.

διά-τάμνω = διατέμνω.

διά-ταξις, ἡ disposition, order of battle.

διά-ταράσσω to throw into confusion, to confound.

δια-τάσσω to dispose, arrange well; to draw up for battle; to arrange separately; to command.

δια-τείνω t stretch out; and *M.* to stretch oneself; to exert oneself; to affirm; to get ready for shooting.

δια-τείχισμα, τό (intermediate) fortification.

δια-τελευτάω to finish entirely.

δια-τελέω to finish, complete; to come to; to continue or keep doing.

δια-τελής 2 permanent.

δια-τέμνω to cut through; to divide.

δια-τετραίνω to perforate.

δια-τήκω to melt.

δια-τηρέω to keep, preserve; to watch; to beware (of).

δια-τίθημι to put asunder; to dispose, arrange, manage, treat; to influence. — *P.* to be disposed, to be in a mind. — *M.* to dispose of, make a testament; to sell off, to settle; to make use of.

δια-τινάσσω to shake to and fro; to shake to pieces.

δια-τμήγω to cut through; to sever; to scatter. — *P.* to be dispersed.

διά-τορος 2 pierced.

δια-τρέφω to feed through.

δια-τρέχω to run or sail through. [sides.]

δια-τρέω to flee to all

δια-τριβή, ἡ a wasting of time; a lingering, delay, stay; pastime, employment, study, conversation.

δια-τρίβω to rub away; to waste, consume; to prevent; to delay; to stay, live; to converse; to busy or occupy oneself with.

δια-τροφή, ἡ sustenance.

δια-τρόγιος 2 to be gathered in at different times.

δι-αυγάζω to shine through.

δι-αυγής 2 transparent.

δί-αυλος, ὁ double pipe.

δια-φαίνω to make shine through. — *M.* to shine through, to become visible.

δια-φάνεια, ἡ transparency.

δια-φανής 2 transparent; manifest, evident.

δια-φερόντως *adv.* differently; excellently, especially.

δια-φέρω to carry across; to bring to an end; to live: to bear; to carry different ways, to throw about; to differ, to be different, to excel; διαφέρει it makes a difference; it is of consequence τὸ διαφέρον interest, point of dispute. — *P.* to be at variance.

δια-φεύγω to flee through, escape, avoid.

διά-φευξις, ἡ escape.

δια-φημίζω to divulge.

δια-φθείρω to destroy, ruin, corrupt, spoil, waste; to bribe. — *P.* to be destroyed or lost; to perish.

δια-φθορά, ἡ destruction, ruin; corruption; seduction.

δια-φθορεύς, ὁ destroyer; seducer.

δι-αφίημι to dismiss.

7*

δια-φοιβάζω to drive mad.
δια-φοιτάω to rove about.
δια-φορά, ἡ difference; controversy.
δια-φορέω to carry over; to carry different ways; to disperse; to plunder; to tear to pieces.
διά-φορος 2 different; at variance; excellent. τὸ διάφορον difference; disagreement, dispute, object of controversy; interest, profit.
διά-φραγμα, τό partition-wall; diaphragm. [clearly.]
δια-φράζω to show or tell)
δια-φρέω to let through.
δια-φυγγάνω = διαφεύγω.
δια-φυγή, ἡ an escaping.
δια-φυή, ἡ growth between; joint, knot, partition.
δια-φυλάσσω to watch carefully, to preserve.
δια-φύομαι M. to intervene, elapse.
δια-φῡσάω to blow away.
δι-αφύσσω to draw out; to drink up; to tear out; to rend.
δια-φωνέω to sound discordantly; to disagree.
δια-φώσκω to dawn.
δια-χάζω and M. to retreat separated; to part.
δια-χειμάζω to pass the winter. [M. to slay.]
δια-χειρίζω to manage. —)
δια-χείρισις, ἡ management; direction. [by vote.]
δια-χειροτονέω to decide)
δια-χειροτονία, ἡ a voting.
δια-χέω to pour out; to

melt; to confound, frustrate; to clear up. — P. to be melted; to fall to pieces.
δια-χόω to heap up a mound.
δια-χράομαι M. to use, employ, have; to kill.
δια-χωρέω to go through (of diarrhœa).
δια-χωρίζω to separate.
δια-ψεύδω and M. to lie; to deceive. — P. to be mistaken. [cide by vote.]
δια-ψηφίζομαι M. to de-)
δια-ψήφισις, ἡ a voting.
δια-ψύχω to cool; to make dry.
δί-γλωσσος 2 speaking two languages. [teaching.]
διδακτικός 3 skilled in)
διδακτός 3 that can be taught; taught, instructed.
διδασκάλεῖον, τό school.
διδασκαλία, ἡ a teaching, instruction; a rehearsing.
διδασκαλικός 3 belonging to teaching; = διδακτικός.
διδασκάλιον, τό science.
διδάσκαλος, ὁ teacher, master.
διδάσκω to teach, instruct, train; to show, prove; to prepare a play. — P. to learn. — M. to devise, contrive; to apprentice to.
διδαχή, ἡ teaching, doctrine.
δίδημι = δέω (to bind).
διδράσκω to run.
δί-δραχμος 2 of two drachms. [brother.]
διδυμάων, ονος, ὁ twin-)
δίδυμος 3 double, twofold.
δίδωμι to give, present,

grant; to afford, pay; to consecrate, devote; to concede, permit, give over; to pardon, release; to allow.

δι-εγγυάω to give bail for; to release on bail.

δι-εγείρω to arouse.

δί-ειμι[1] (-ιέναι) to go or march through; to discuss.

δί-ειμι[2] (-εῖναι) to be continually.

δι-εῖπον to speak through; to explain, tell exactly.

δι-είργω to separate, keep asunder.

δι-είρομαι to question.

δι-ειρύω to draw across.

δι-είρω to put across.

δι-έχ, δι-έξ adv. through.

δι-εκπεράω to go or sail through, across. [through.]

δι-εκπλέω to sail out]

δι-έχπλοος, δ a sailing through; a breaking the enemy's line.

δι-εκπλώω = διεκπλέω.

δι-έχροος, δ a flowing out, outlet.

δι-ελαύνω to drive through; to pierce through; to ride or march through.

δι-ελέγχω to refute or examine thoroughly.

δι-έλκω, -ύω pull or tear asunder.

δίεμαι M. to chase, frighten away; to flee in awe.

δι-εμπολάω to sell; to betray. [intently.]

δι-ενθῦμέομαι P. to think]

δι-ενιαυτίζω to live out the year. [parate.]

δι-εξειλίσσω to sift, se-]

δι-έξειμι to go out through; to examine, peruse; to describe.

δι-εξελαύνω to drive, ride, or march through.

δι-εξερέομαι to question.

δι-εξέρχομαι to go out through, to pass through, to elapse, to come to; to go through, explain, recount. [plain, recount.]

δι-εξηγέομαι M. to ex-]

δι-εξίημι to let out through; to empty itself.

δι-έξοδος, ἡ passage, outlet, issue, event; crossroad; detailed account, recital, statement.

δι-εορτάζω to keep a feast to the end.

δι-έπω to manage, take care of, attend to; to arrange; to pass through.

δι-εργάζομαι M. to ruin, kill.

δι-έργω = διείργω.

δι-ερέσσω to row through; to row well.

δι-ερευνάω and M. to search, examine closely.

δι-ερμηνευτής, οῦ, ὁ interpreter. [translate.]

δι-ερμηνεύω to interpret,]

διερός[1] 3 fugitive, quick.

διερός[2] 3 long-lived; fresh.

δι-έρπω to step through.

δι-έρχομαι to go, walk, drive, or pass through; to arrive at; to narrate, explain; to consider.

δι-ερωτάω to question continually. [through.]

δι-εσθίω to eat or bite]

δι-ετής 2 of two years.

δι-ετήσιος 2 lasting the whole year. [years.]

δι-ετία, ἡ space of two

δι-ευλαβέομαι to take heed well. [tinually.]

δι-ευτυχέω to prosper con-

δι-έχω to keep asunder or aloof; to reach through; to be extended to; to stand apart, to be distant; τὸ διέχον interval.

δίζημαι M. to seek out, to aspire to or after; to examine.

δί-ζυξ, υγος doubly-yoked.

δίζω to doubt.

δι-ηγέομαι M. to explain, describe, narrate.

δι-ήγησις, ἡ discussion; narration.

δι-ηθέω to sift, strain through; to cleanse; to filter through.

δι-ηκονέω = διακονέω.

δι-ήκω to come through, pervade. [whole day.]

δι-ημερεύω to pass the

δι-ηνεκής 2 uninterrupted, continual; far-reaching; exact, full.

δι-ήνεμος 2 windy.

δι-θάλασσος 2 between two seas.

διθύραμβος, ὁ dithyramb.

δι-ίημι to send, thrust, or shoot through; to let pass through; to dismiss.

δι-ικνέομαι M. to go through; to reach, meet; to recount.

δι-ιπετής 2 fallen from heaven, heaven-sent.

δι-ίστημι to set apart or asunder; to divide, to set at variance; intr. and M. to stand apart or at intervals; to part; to differ; to be ajar; to remove; to quarrel.

δι-ισχυρίζομαι M. to be at ease, to abide; to affirm.

δι-φίλος 2 loved by Zeus.

δικάζω to judge, administer justice; to decide, determine. M. to plead, speak in court. [ment.]

δικαιο-κρισία, ἡ just judg-

δίκαιος 3 just; righteous, honest; legal, lawful, right, proper; useful, fit, convenient; regular; entitled to, worthy of, bound to. τὸ δίκαιον and τὰ δίκαια right, justice, privilege, lawquestion, argument, judicial proceeding.

δικαιοσύνη, ἡ, δικαιότης, ητος, ἡ justice; administration of justice.

δικαιόω to think right, to justify, judge; to condemn; to claim, desire.

δικαίωμα, τό legal axiom, right; argument, justification; legal claim; judgment; legal act.

δικαίωσις, ἡ summons at law; condemnation; legal claim; (good) pleasure, judgment; justification.

δικανικός 3 skilled in law; lawyer; lawyer-like, arrogant.

δικασ-πόλος, ὁ judge.

δικαστήριον, τό court of justice.

δικαστής, οῦ, ὁ judge.

δικαστικός 3 judicial, of a judge; skilled in law.

δίκελλα, ἡ mattock, pick-axe.

δίκη, ἡ custom, usage (δίκην after the manner of); right, law, order, justice; judgment, sentence; judicature, lawsuit, action at law, trial; fine, penalty, satisfaction; δίκην διδόναι to suffer punishment.

δι-κλίς, ίδος double-folding (door). [ful.)

δι-κρατής 2 doubly power-)

δί-κροτος 2 vessel with two decks. [in meshes.)

δικτυό-κλωστος 2 woven)

δίκτυον, τό fishing-net.

δί-λογος 2 double-tongued.

δί-λοφος 2 with two peaks.

δί-μνεως 2 worth two minæ.

δι-μοιρία, ἡ double amount.

δῑνεύω, δῑνέω to whirl or spin round (tr. and intr.).

δίνη, ἡ whirlpool, eddy.

δῑνήεις 3 eddying.

δῑνωτός 3 turned on a lathe, elaborated nicely.

διξός 3 = δισσός. [fore.)

διό (δι' ὅ) wherefore; there-)

διό-βολος 2 hurled by Zeus.

διο-γενής 2 sprung from Zeus. [to travel through.)

δι-οδεύω, δι-οδοιπορέω)

δί-οδος, ἡ passage through, thoroughfare; mountain-pass; way.

δι-οίγω to open.

δί-οιδα to know exactly.

δι-οικέω to administer, manage; to direct; to treat.

δι-οίκησις, ἡ house-keeping; management, government; province.

δι-οικίζω to let live apart; to scatter. — M. to settle apart; to change place.

δι-οίκισις, ἡ remove.

δι-οικοδομέω to bar off by a wall.

δι-οϊστέω to shoot an arrow through or across.

δι-οίχομαι to pass away, be gone. [abating.)

δι-οκωχή, ἡ a ceasing, an)

δι-όλλῡμι to destroy or ruin utterly; to forget. — P. to perish utterly.

δι-όμνῡμι and P. to swear, take an oath; to affirm solemnly.

δι-ομολογέω and M. to agree (to), grant, accord.

διόπερ = διό.

διο-πετής = διϊπετής.

δι-οπτεύω to spy about; to look about.

δι-οπτήρ, ῆρος, ὁ spy, scout.

δι-οράω to see through.

δι-όργυιος 2 two fathoms long. [right, amend.)

δι-ορθόω and M. to set)

δι-όρθωμα, τό and δι-όρ-θωσις, ἡ correction, amendment.

δι-ορίζω to divide; to distinguish; to define; to ordain; to banish. [canal.)

δι-όρυγμα, τό ditch, trench,)

δι-ορύσσω to dig through; to rake up; to undermine; to block up.

δῖος 3 shining, brilliant; excellent, noble; divine.

δι-ότι *conj.* for the reason that, since; wherefrom; that. [Zeus.]

διο-τρεφής 2 sprung from/

δι-ουρίζω = διορίζω.

δί-παλτος 2 double, twofold.

δί-πηχυς, υ of two cubits.

διπλάζω to double; to be doubled.

δίπλαξ, ακος, ἡ double-folded garment, cloak.

διπλασιάζω to double.

δι-πλάσιος 3 double, twice as much.

διπλασιόω to double.

δί-πλεθρος 2 of two plethra.

δι-πλόος, -πλοῦς 3 double, twofold: both; alternating; double-minded.

διπλόω to double.

δί-πους, ποδος two-footed.

δί-πτυξ, υχος and δί-πτυ-χος 2 folded together.

δί-πυλος 2 with two gates.

δίς *adv.* twice, double.

δισ-θανής twice dying.

δισκεύω, δισκέω to throw the disk or quoit. [quoit.]

δίσκος, ὁ disk, discus,)

δίσκ-ουρα, ων, τά quoit's cast. [number 20000.]

δισ-μυριάς, άδος, ἡ the)

δισ-μύριοι 3 twenty thousand. [ing.]

δισσ-άρχης, ου doubly rul-)

δισσός 3 double, twofold; ambiguous, doubtful.

διστάζω to doubt. [gether.]

δί-στολος 2 in pairs, to-)

δί-στομος 2 double-mouth-ed, with two entrances; two-edged.

δισ-χίλιοι 3 two thousand.

δι-τάλαντος 2 weighing two talents.

δι-ϋλίζω to strain, filter.

δι-φάσιος 3 double, twofold.

δίφάω to seek, search, dive after.

διφθέρα, ἡ skin, hide, leather; anything made of leather (coat, bag, coverlet).

διφθέρινος 3 of leather.

διρρευτής, οῦ, ὁ charioteer.

διφρ-ηλατέω to drive in a chariot. [ρευτής.]

διφρ-ηλάτης, ου, ὁ = διφ-)

δίφρος, ὁ chariot-board; chariot; chair.

διφρο-φορέομαι *P.* to be carried in a chair or litter.

δι-φυής 2 of double form.

δίχα *adv.* in two, at two, twofold; apart, asunder; at variance, different. *Prep.* with *gen.* far from; without.

διχάζω 2 to divide in two; to make disagree, disunite.

διχῇ *adv.* = δίχα.

διχθά *adv.* in two.

διχθάδιος 3 double, twofold.

διχο-γνωμονέω to differ in opinion.

διχόθεν *adv.* from two sides.

διχο-στασία, ἡ division, quarrel.

διχο-στατέω to stand asunder, to disagree.

διχο-τομέω to split in two.

διχοῦ = δίχα.

δίψα, ἡ thirst.

διψάω to thirst, to be dry.

δίψιος 3 thirsty, dry.

δί-ψῦχος 2 double-minded, doubtful. [δίεμαι.]

δίω to fear, flee. — *M.* =)

δι-ωβελίᾱ, ἡ payment of two obols.

διωγμός, ὁ = δίωξις.

δι-ώδυνος 2 very painful.

δι-ωθέω to push or tear asunder; to pierce or break through. — M. to push away from oneself, to repulse; to refuse; to break through.

διωκάθω = διώκω.

διώκτης, ου, ὁ pursuer.

διώκω to pursue, chase, drive, hunt; to expel, banish; to run after, follow, catch; to strive after; to be attached to; to prosecute, accuse; to drive a chariot; to haste. — M. to chase, drive before oneself.

δι-ώμοτος 2 bound by oath.

δίωξις, ἡ chase, pursuit; persecution; striving after.

δι-ῶρυξ, υχος, ἡ ditch, trench, canal; underground gallery.

δμῆσις, ἡ a taming.

δμήτειρα, ἡ tamer.

δμωή, ἡ female slave. servant.

δμώς, ωός, ὁ slave. [about.]

δνοπαλίζω to shake, push]

δνοφερός 3 dark, dusky.

δοάσσατο it seemed.

δόγμα, τό opinion; decree, resolution; doctrine.

δογματίζομαι P. to be subject to statutes.

δοιή, ἡ doubt.

δοιοί 3 two, both.

δοκάζω, δοκάω, δοκεύω to expect; to watch, lie in wait.

δοκέω to think, suppose, imagine; to resolve; to seem, appear; to appear to be something; δοκῶ μοι I seem to myself; methinks; δοκεῖ it seems; it seems good, it is decreed.

δόκησις, ἡ opinion; suspicion; appearance.

δοκιμάζω to prove, test, examine; to approve, to declare good.

δοκιμασίᾱ, ἡ examination, a proving; a mustering.

δοκιμαστής, οῦ, ὁ examiner.

δοκιμή, ἡ and δοκίμιον, τό examination, proof, test.

δόκιμος 2 tried, approved; esteemed; considerable.

δοκός, ἡ wooden beam.

δολερός 3 cunning, deceitful.

δολιό-μῦθος 2 artful.

δολιό-πους, ποδος of stealthy foot, dodging.

δόλιος 3 = δολερός.

δολιόω to betray, cheat.

δολίχ-αυλος 2 with a long pipe. [spear.]

δολιχ-εγχής 2 with a long]

δολιχ-ήρετμος 2 with long oars. [runner.]

δολιχο-δρόμος 2 prize-]

δολιχός 3 long, far.

δόλιχος, ὁ long course; stadium.

δολιχό-σκιος 2 casting a long shadow.

δολόεις 3 = δολερός.

δολο-μήτης, ου and δολό-μητις, ιος wily, artful.

δολο-ποιός 2 = δολερός.

δόλος, ὁ bait, inducement; cunning, deceit, treachery.

δολο-φρονέω to devise treachery.

δολο-φροσύνη, ἡ deceit, cunning, intrigue.

δολόω to cheat, entice, beguile; to disguise.

δόμα, τό gift.

δόμος, ὁ house, building; dwelling, apartment, room, hall; layer; home; family; household.

δονακεύς, ὁ thicket of canes or reeds. [canes.]

δονακό-χλοος 2 green with

δόναξ, ακος, ὁ cane, reed; arrow; shepherd's pipe.

δονέω to shake, stir, drive about. — *P.* to be agitated; to be in commotion.

δόξα, ἡ opinion, notion; expectation; false opinion, delusion, fancy; decree, project; judgment; reputation, report, estimation, honour; glory, splendour.

δοξάζω to think, believe, suppose, presume; to extol.

δοξόομαι *P.* to bear a reputation.

δορά, ἡ hide, skin.

δοράτιον, τό javelin; pole.

δορι-άλωτος 2, δορί-κτητος 2, δορί-ληπτος 2 taken in war, captive.

δορι-μαργος 2 eager for combat.

δορκάς, άδος, ἡ roe, gazelle.

δορός, ὁ leather bag.

δορπέω to take supper.

δορπηστός, ὁ supper-time, evening.

δορπίᾱ, ἡ eve of a feast.

δόρπον, τό supper.

δόρυ, ατος, τό wood, stem of a tree, beam, timber; ship; pole: shaft of a spear; spear; battle, war; spearbearer, warrior; army; booty; ἐπὶ δόρυ to the right hand. [άλωτος.]

δορυ-άλωτος 2 = δορι-

δορυ-δρέπανον, τό handle of a sickle: grappling-hook.

δορύ-ξενος, ὁ companion in arms, comrade.

δορυ-σσόης, ητος and δορυσσόος 2 brandishing a spear, warlike.

δορυ-φορέω to be a bodyguard, to attend as a guard.

δορυ-φόρος, ὁ lance-bearer; body-guard; pole-bearer.

δοσί-δικος 2 = δωσίδικος.

δόσις, ἡ act of giving; gift, present; portion.

δοτήρ, ῆρος, ὁ and δότης, ου, ὁ giver, dispenser.

δουλ-αγωγέω to lead into slavery.

δουλεία, ἡ slavery, thraldom, bondage, servility; bondmen, menials.

δούλειος 2 slavish, servile.

δούλευμα, τό slavery; slave.

δουλεύω to be a slave, to serve.

δούλη, ἡ female slave.

δουλίᾱ, ἡ = δουλεία.

δουλικός 3 and δούλιος 2 = δούλειος.

δουλιχό-δειρος 2 longnecked. [a slave.]

δουλο-πρεπής 2 befitting

δοῦλος 3 slavish, servile; enslaved, subject; ὁ, ἡ slave.

δουλοσύνη, ἡ = δουλεία.

δουλόω to enslave, subdue; to discourage.

δούλωσις, ἡ an enslaving, subjugation. [to roar.]

δουπέω to sound hollow;

δοῦπος, ὁ hollow sound, roaring, noise.

δουράτεος 3 wooden.

δουρ-ηνεκές adv. a spear's cast off. [ἀλωτός.]

δουρι-άλωτος 2 = δορι-

δουρι-κλειτός, -κλυτός 2 famous as a spearman.

δουρί-ληπτος 2 = δορί-ληπτος. [spears.]

δουρο-δόκη, ἡ case for

δοχή, ἡ banquet.

δόχμιος 3 and δοχμός 3 slanting, sideways.

δράγμα, δράγμα, τό handful; sheaf.

δραγμεύω to collect sheaves.

δραίνω to be about to do.

δράκαινα, ἡ she-dragon.

δράκων, οντος, ὁ dragon; serpent.

δρᾶμα, τό action, deed; play.

δράμημα, τό = δρόμος.

δραπετεύω to run away, escape

δραπέτης, ου, ὁ runaway, fugitive slave; falling to pieces.

δρασείω to be willing to do.

δρασμός, ὁ escape, flight.

δράσσομαι M. to grasp, seize. [enterprising.]

δραστήριος 2 active, busy,

δρατός 3 flayed.

δραχμή, ἡ drachm.

δράω to be active; to do, perform, accomplish.

δρεπάνη, ἡ = δρέπανον.

δρεπανη-φόρος 2 bearing a sickle. [shaped.]

δρεπανο-ειδής 2 sickle-

δρέπανον, τό sickle, scythe; curved sabre.

δρέπω, δρέπτω to pluck.

δρησμός, ὁ = δρασμός.

δρήστειρα, ἡ, δρηστήρ, ῆρος, ὁ worker, servant.

δρηστοσύνη, ἡ service.

δριμύς 3 piercing, biting; violent, sharp, bitter; shrewd. [wood.]

δρίος, τό thicket, brush-

δρομαῖος 3, δρομάς, άδος 2 running, fleet.

δρομεύς, ὁ runner.

δρομικός 3 running swift; τὰ δρομικά foot-race.

δρόμος, ὁ a running, course, race; δρόμῳ in rapid march, swiftly; place for running, race-course, stadium.

δροσερός 3 dewy. [water.]

δρόσος, ἡ dew, dewdrop;

δρυΐνος 3 oaken.

δρυμός, ὁ oak-wood; wood.

δρύ-οχος, ὁ rib of a ship.

δρύπτω to peel off, to scratch, tear; to snatch away.

δρῦς, ὑός, ἡ oak; tree; wood.

δρυ-τόμος 2 wood-cutter.

δρύ-φακτον, τό and δρύ-φακτος, ὁ fence, railing.

δρύφω = δρύπτω. [two.]

δυάς, άδος, ἡ the number

δυάω to drive into misery

δύη, ἡ misery, woe, pain.

δύναμαι P. to be able or capable; to be strong, mighty, or powerful; to be worth; to signify.

δύναμις, ἡ ability; might,

power, strength; military force, army; expedient, implement; talent, faculty; power of speech; miracle; influence, consequence; worth, value; meaning, signification.

δυναμόω to strengthen.

δύναςτις, ἡ = δύναμις.

δυναστεία, ἡ sovereignty, lordship, rule. [to sway.]

δυναστεύω to have power,

δυνάστης, ου. ὁ sovereign, lord, ruler, master; nobleman.

δυνατέω to be powerful.

δυνατός 3 able; strong, mighty, powerful; fit, apt; noble; possible.

δύνω = δύομαι, see δύω.

δύο two, both.

δυο-καί-δεκα = δώδεκα.

δυοκαιδεκα-μηνος 2 of twelve months.

δύρομαι = ὀδύρομαι.

δυς-αής 2 ill-blowing.

δυς-άθλιος 2 most miserable. [miserably.]

δυς-αίων, ωνος living,

δυς-άλγητος 2 unfeeling.

δυς-άλωτος 2 hard to catch.

δυς-άμμορος 2 most unhappy.

δυς-ανασχετέω to find unbearable; to be beside oneself.

δυς-άνεκτος 2 unbearable.

δυς-άνεμος 2 wind-beaten, stormy.

δυς-απάλλακτος 2 hard to ward off, stubborn.

δυς-απότρεπτος 2 hard to turn away

δυς-άρεστος 2 ill-pleased, morose.

δυς-αριστο-τόκεια, ἡ unhappy mother of a hero.

δύς-αυλος 2 uncomfortable for lodging. [bear.]

δυς-βάστακτος 2 hard to

δύς-βατος 2 impassable.

δυς-βουλία, ἡ ill counsel, folly.

δυς-γένεια, ἡ low birth.

δύς-γνωστος 2 hard to discern or know.

δυς-γοήτευτος 2 difficult to be charmed. [misery.]

δυς-δαιμονία, ἡ ill fate,

δυς-δαίμων 2 ill-fated.

δυς-διάβατος 2 hard to cross. [ugly.]

δυς-ειδής 2 misshapen,

δύς-ελπις, ιδος hopeless.

δυς-έμβατος 2 difficult of access.

δυς-έμβολος 2 impregnable, inaccessible.

δυς-εντερία, ἡ dysentery.

δυς-εξαπάτητος 2 hard to deceive. [refute.]

δυς-εξέλεγκτος hard to

δύς-ερις, ιδος quarrelsome, captious. [able.]

δυς-έριστος 2 unconquer-

δυς-ερμήνευτος 2 hard to be understood.

δύς-ερως, ωτος crossed in love; passionately loving.

δυς-έσβολος 2 = δυσέμβολος.

δυς-εύρετος 2 hard to find.

δύς-ζηλος 2 irascible.

δυς-ηλεγής 2 painful.

δυς-ηχής 2 ill-sounding, raging.

δυσ-θαλπής 2 chilly.

δυσ-θανατέω to suffer dying agonies. [dismal.]

δυσ-θέατος 2 horrible,]

δύσ-θεος 2 hated by the gods. [tend.]

δυσ-θεράπευτος 2 hard to]

δυσ-θετέομαι P. to be out of humour. [able.]

δυσ-θρήνητος 2 lament-]

δυσ-θῡμέω to be disheartened; to despond.

δυσ-θῡμίᾱ, ἡ ill humour; despondency. [desponding.]

δύσ-θῡμος 2 ill-humoured;]

δυσ-ίᾱτος 2 hard to heal, incurable. [valry.]

δύσ-ιππος 2 unfit for ca-]

δύσις, ἡ sunset; west.

δυσ-κάθαρτος 2 hard to expiate. [check.]

δυσ-κάθεκτος 2 hard to]

δυσ-κατέργαστος 2 hard to obtain by labour.

δυσ-κέλαδος 2 ill-sounding, harsh.

δυσ-κηδής 2 sad, sorry.

δυσ-κλεής 2 inglorious, infamous. [shame.]

δύσ-κλεια, ἡ bad fame,]

δυσ-κοινώνητος 2 unsociable. [or discontented.]

δυσ-κολαίνω to be peevish]

δυσ-κολίᾱ, ἡ peevishness, discontent; difficulty, perplexity.

δύσ-κολος 2 peevish, discontented, fretful; difficult, perplexing.

δυσ-κόμιστος 2 unbearable.

δύσ-κριτος 2 hard to discern or decide. [able.]

δυσ-λόγιστος 2 inconceiv-]

δυσ-μαθής 2 indocile; dull; difficult to be learnt.

δυσ-μαχέω to fight with ill luck.

δύσ-μαχος 2 hard to fight with; unconquerable.

δυσ-μεναίνω to be peevish; to be hostile. [mity.]

δυσ-μένεια, ἡ ill-will, en-]

δυσ-μενέων 3, δυσ-μενής 2 hostile, malevolent.

δυσ-μεταχείριστος 2 hard to fight with.

δυσμή, ἡ = δύσις. [mother.]

δυσ-μήτηρ, ἡ not a true]

δύσ-μοιρος 2, δύσ-μορος 2 unhappy, miserable.

δυσ-μορφίᾱ, ἡ ugliness.

δύσ-νιπτος 2 not to be washed off.

δυσ-νόητος 2 difficult to be understood.

δύσ-νοια, ἡ dislike, ill-will.

δύσ-νοος, -νους 2 hostile, malign; ill-disposed.

δύσ-νυμφος 2 ill-betrothed.

δυσ-ξύμβολος 2 unsociable. [gible, obscure.]

δυσ-ξύνετος 2 unintelli-]

δύσ-οδμος 2 ill-smelling.

δύσ-οδος 2 scarcely passable.

δύσ-οιστος 2 unbearable, hard to bear.

δύσ-ομβρος 2 with adverse showers of rain.

δύσ-οργος 2 irascible.

δυσ-οσμίᾱ, ἡ bad smell.

δυσ-ούριστος 2 driven on by bad winds. [querable.]

δυσ-πάλαιστος 2 uncon-]

δυσ-πάρευνος 2 ill-mated.

Δύσ-παρις, ὁ unlucky Paris.

δυσ-πάριτος 2 hard to pass.

δυσ-πειθής 2 disobedient, refractory. [suade.

δύσ-πειστος 2 hard to per-

δυσ-πέμφελος 2 stormy.

δυσ-πέρατος 2 hard to bring through.

δυσ-πετής 2 difficult.

δυσ-πινής 2 very dirty.

δύσ-πνοος 2 breathless; adverse (wind).

δυσ-πολέμητος 2 hard to make war upon.

δυσ-πολιόρκητος 2 hard to take by siege.

δυσ-πονής 2, δυσ-πόνητος 2, δύσ-πονος 2 toilsome, hard-earned.

δυσ-πόρευτος 2, δύσ-πορος scarcely passable. [age.

δυσ-πορία, ἡ difficult pass-

δύσ-ποτμος 2 ill-fated.

δυσ-πραξία, ἡ misfortune.

δυσ-πρόσβατος 2, δυσ-πρόσοδος 2 hardly accessible. [friendly, gloomy.

δυσ-πρόσοιστος 2 un-

δυσ-πρόσοπτος 2, δυσ-πρόσωπος 2 of ill aspect.

δύσ-ρῑγος 2 sensible to cold.

δυσ-σέβεια, ἡ impiety.

δυσ-σεβέω to be impious; to act impiously. [less.

δυσ-σεβής 2 impious, god-

δυσ-τάλᾱς, αινα, ᾱν most unhappy.

δυσ-τέκμαρτος 2 hard to conclude. [a mother.

δύσ-τεκνος 2 unhappy as

δύστηνος 2 unhappy; wretched, abominable.

δυστομέω to revile, defame.

δυσ-τράπελος 2, δύσ-τροπος 2 stubborn.

δυσ-τυχέω to be unlucky. — P. to fail. [τυχία.

δυσ-τύχημα, τό = δυσ-

δυσ-τυχής 2 unlucky, unhappy, miserable.

δυσ-τυχία, ἡ ill luck, misfortune, mishap; defeat.

δυσ-φημέω to speak words of an evil omen; to revile, slander.

δυσ-φημία, ἡ words of ill omen; a reviling; lamentation; bad fame.

δυσ-φιλής 2 hateful; ugly.

δυσ-φορέω to bear with resentment; to do unwillingly.

δύσ-φορος 2 hard to bear, heavy, oppressive; misleading.

δύσ-φρων 2 sorrowful, melancholy; hostile, ill-disposed; senseless. [stormy.

δυσ-χείμερος 2 wintry,

δυσ-χείρωμα, τό hard work.

δυσ-χείρωτος 2 hard to overcome.

δυσ-χεραίνω to be or become discontented or angry; to disapprove, reject; to make difficulties; to rouse indignation.

δυσ-χέρεια, ἡ incommodity; annoyance.

δυσ-χερής 2 hard to manage, difficult; annoying, unpleasant, vexatious; peevish, ill-affected.

δύσ-χρηστος 2 hard to use; useless.

δυσ-χωρία, ἡ disadvantageous ground.

δυσ-ώδης 2 ill-smelling.

δυσ-ώνυμος 2 bearing an ill name; ominous, ill-reputed.   [or timid.)

δυσ-ωπέομαι P. to be shy.

δυσ-ωρέω to keep a painful watch.

δύτης, ου, ὁ diver.

δύω and M. intr. to dive, sink; to enter; to perish; trans. to put on.

δύω = δύο.

δυώ-δεκα = δώδεκα.

δυωδεκά-βοιος 2 worth twelve oxen.

δυωδεκά-πολις 2 belonging to a confederation of twelve cities.   [τος.)

δυωδέκατος 3 = δωδέκα-)

δυωκαιεικοσί-μετρος 2 holding 22 measures.

δυωκαιεικοσί-πηχυς, υ 22 cubits long.

δῶ, τό = δῶμα.

δώδεκα twelve.

δωδεκά-σκῦτος 2 composed of 12 pieces of leather.

δωδέκατος 3 twelfth.

δωδεκά-φῦλον, τό the twelve tribes.

δῶμα, τό dwelling, house; palace, temple; chamber, hall; roof; family, household.   [chamber.)

δωμάτιον, τό room, bed-)

δωρεά, ἡ gift, present; gift of honour; benefit; δωρεάν adv. freely, gratis.

δωρέω and M. to give, present.

δώρημα, τό = δωρεά.

δωρητός 3 given; open to gifts.

δωριστί adv. in Dorian manner, dialect, or tune.

δωρο-δοκέω to accept presents, to get bribed.

δωρο-δόκημα, τό, δωρο-δοκία, ἡ bribe; bribery.

δωρο-δόκος 2 taking bribes.

δῶρον, τό gift, present.

δωρο-φορίᾶ, ἡ the bringing of presents.

δωσί-δικος 2 submitting to justice.

δωτήρ, ῆρος, ὁ giver.

δωτῑνάζω to collect gifts.

δωτίνη, ἡ = δῶρον.

δώτωρ, ορος, ὁ = δωτήρ.

E

E, ε (ε ψιλόν) fifth letter of the alphabet; as a numeral ε' = 5.

ἔ, mostly ἒ ἔ int. woe!

ἕ him-, her-, it-self.   [ah!)

ἑᾶ int. denoting wonder: ha!)

ἐάν conj. if, if so be that, in case that; as often as, whenever; if, whether.

ἑᾶνός 3 wrapping up; smooth, pliant.

ἑᾶνός, ὁ a woman's robe.

ἔαρ, ἔαρος, τό spring, prime.

ἐαρίζω to pass the spring.

ἐαρινός 3 belonging to spring.

ἑαυτοῦ, ῆς, οῦ of himself, herself, or itself; of oneself.

ἐάφθη = ἥφθη, see ἅπτω.

ἐάω to let, permit, allow, suffer; to let or leave alone or unnoticed; to omit, give up.

ἑβδομαῖος 3 on the seventh day.

ἑβδόματος 3 = ἕβδομος.

ἑβδομήκοντα seventy.

ἑβδομηκοντάκις seventy times.

ἕβδομος 3 seventh.

ἔβενος, ἡ ebony(-tree,-wood).

ἐγ-γείνομαι to engender in.

ἔγ - γειος 2 within the boundaries of the country; in the earth.　[mock.]

ἐγ-γελάω to laugh at,

ἐγ-γενής 2 blood-related; native; inborn.

ἐγ-γηράσκω to grow old at a place.

ἐγ-γίγνομαι M. to be born in; to happen, take place in, to arise; to be innate or infused; to intervene, pass; to be possible.

ἐγγίζω to approach, draw near.　[ἐγγύς.]

ἔγγιον and ἔγγιστα from

ἐγ-γλύσσω to have a sweetish taste.

ἐγ - γλύφω to engrave, carve, cut in.

ἐγ-γνάμπτω to bend in.

ἔγ-γονος, ὁ, ἡ relation; descendant.

ἐγ-γράφω to engrave; to write, draw, or paint in; to write down.　[to grant.]

ἐγ-γυαλίζω to hand over,

ἐγ-γυάω and M. to stand security; to betroth, engage, promise; to be betrothed.　[pledge.]

ἐγ-γύη, ἡ security, bail,

ἐγ - γυητής, οῦ, ὁ, ἔγ-γυος, ὁ warranter, surety.

ἐγγύς adv. near, in the neighbourhood, neighbouring; coming near; like, nearly; soon; at last; comp. ἐγγίω, ἐγγύτερος; superl. ἔγγιστος, ἐγγύτατος.

ἐγ - γώνιος 2 forming a (right) angle.

ἐγείρω to awaken, rouse; to stir, excite; to raise.

ἔγερσις, ἡ a rousing, raising.

ἐγερτί adv. in an exciting way.

ἐγ-καθέζομαι M. to sit down in, to encamp in.

ἐγ - κάθετος 2 suborned; watcher.

ἐγ-καθιδρύω to set up in.

ἐγ-καθίζω to set in or upon; to seat oneself in. — M. to sit on; to take one's seat.

ἐγ-καθίστημι to place, put, or set in; to establish, arrange; intr. to be established.

ἐγ - καθορμίζομαι M. to run into the harbour.

ἐγ-καίνια, τά feast of the dedication of the temple.

ἐγ-καινίζω to renew, renovate.　[to relax.]

ἐγ-κακέω to grow weary,

ἐγ-καλέω to call in; to accuse, reproach, blame, to bring a charge (against); to claim (a debt).　[ment.]

ἐγ - καλλώπισμα, τό orna-

ἐγ-καλύπτω to veil in, wrap up, hide.

ἔγ-καρπος 2 fruitful.

ἐγ-κάρσιος 3 and 2 oblique, transverse.

ἐγ-καρτερέω to persevere, persist (in); to control oneself. [trails.]

ἔγκατα, τά bowels, entrails.

ἐγ-καταδέω to bind fast in.

ἐγ-καταζεύγνῡμι to join with, to unite. [sleep in.]

ἐγ-κατακοιμάομαι P. to

ἐγ-καταλαμβάνω to catch in a place, to seize, take, apprehend, arrest; to cut off.

ἐγ-καταλέγω to gather in; to enlist.

ἐγ-καταλείπω to leave behind in a place or with one. — P. to be left behind.

ἐγ-κατάληψις, ἡ a catching, capture.

ἐγ-καταμ(ε)ίγνῡμι to mix up in; to place between.

ἐγ-καταπήγνῡμι to thrust into, to fix in.

ἐγ-κατασκήπτω to fling down into; to break out; to invade. [pieces.]

ἐγ-κατατέμνω to cut into

ἐγ-κατατίθεμαι M. to lay in or hide for oneself.

ἐγ-κατοικέω to live in or among. [in or aside.]

ἐγ-κατοικοδομέω to build

ἐγ-καυχάομαι to boast.

ἔγ-κειμαι to lie in or on, to be placed in; to press on, urge, importune, attack; to be intent upon.

ἐγ-κέλευστος 2 bidden, ordered; suborned.

ἐγ-κεντρίζω to ingraft.

ἐγ-κεράννῡμι, ἐγ-κεράω to mix in. — M. to suborn, contrive. [row.]

ἐγ-κέφαλος, ὁ brain; mar-

ἐγ-κλείω to shut in, confine; to shut fast or up.

ἔγ-κλημα, τό accusation charge, reproach, complaint controversy; fault, guilt.

ἔγ-κληρος 2 sharing, partaking; heir, heiress; destined by lot. [κλείω.]

ἐγ-κλήω, ἐγ-κληΐω = ἐγ-

ἐγ-κλίνω to bend or incline towards. — intr. and P. to be bent; to lean on; to yield; to turn to flight.

ἐγ-κοιλαίνω to hollow out.

ἔγ-κοιλος 2 hollowed out.

ἐγ-κολάπτω to cut in, engrave.

ἐγ-κομβόομαι to make one's own. [busy.]

ἐγ-κονέω to hasten; to be

ἐγ-κοπή, ἡ hindrance.

ἐγ-κόπτω to hinder, trouble; to delay.

ἐγ-κοσμέω to arrange within. [hatred.]

ἔγ-κοτος, ὁ resentment,

ἐγ-κράζω to shriek at.

ἐγ-κράτεια, ἡ self-control, temperance; induration.

ἐγ-κρατεύομαι M. to be frugal or abstemious.

ἐγ-κρατής 2 strong, stout; having mastery over; self-disciplined, sober.

ἐγ-κρίνω to choose among, to admit, adopt; to reckon among.

ἐγ-κροτέω to strike against, to beat time with the feet. — M. to strike one another.

ἐγ-κρύπτω to hide in.

ἐγ-κτάομαι M. to acquire possessions in a place.

ἔγ-κτησις, ἡ landed property in a place.

ἐγ-κυκάω to mix up in.

ἐγ-κυκλόω to move about in a circle.

ἐγ-κυλίομαι P. to wallow in, to be given to. [child.]

ἔγ-κυος 2 pregnant, with

ἐγ-κύπτω to stoop; to peep, to cast a side-glance.

ἐγ-κύρέω, ἐγ-κύρω to meet with; to fall into.

ἐγ-κωμιάζω to praise, extol, laud.

ἐγ-κώμιον, τό song of praise; glory. [battle.]

ἐγρε-μάχης 2 exciting the

ἐγρηγοράω to be awake.

ἐγρηγορτί adv. awake.

ἐγρήσσω to be awake.

ἐγ-χαλινόω to bridle.

ἐγ-χειρέω to take in hand, to undertake, to try; to attack.

ἐγ-χείρημα, τό, ἐγ-χείρησις, ἡ an undertaking, execution. [ing.]

ἐγ-χειρητικός 3 enterpris-

ἐγ-χειρίδιον, τό dagger, knife.

ἐγ-χειρίζω to hand over, deliver, entrust. — M. to take upon oneself.

ἐγχειρί-θετος 2 handed over, delivered. [eel.]

ἔγχελυς, υος and εως, ἡ

ἐγχεσί-μωρος 2 famous with the spear.

ἐγχέσ-παλος 2 lance-brandishing.

ἐγ-χέω to pour in.

ἔγχος, τό spear, lance; weapon, sword.

ἐγ-χραύω to dash or push into.

ἐγ-χρίμπτω to cause to strike against; to dash or drive against, to bring near; to approach, to come to land. — P. to touch, verge, reach to.

ἐγ-χρίω to anoint.

ἐγ-χρονίζω to tarry; to become inveterate.

ἐγ-χωρέω to give way or room; ἐγχωρεῖ it is possible.

ἐγ-χώριος 2 and 3, ἔγχωρος 2 native, indigenous; inhabitant; rustic.

ἐγώ I, myself; ἔγωγε I for my part.

ἐδανός 3 lovely, delicious.

ἐδαφίζω to level with the earth. [floor, bottom.]

ἔδαφος, τό ground, soil,

ἔδεσμα, τό food, meat, dish.

ἐδεστής, οῦ, ὁ eater.

ἐδεστός 3 eaten, consumed.

ἐδητύς, ύος, ἡ food.

ἔδνα, τά nuptial gifts; dowry.

ἕδος, τό, ἕδρα, ἡ seat, chair, bench, row; sitting-part; abode, dwelling; temple, altar, statue; foundation; base, station, stand; act of sitting, a sitting still, inaction; session.

ἑδραῖος 3 sitting still, sedentary, unmoved.

ἑδραίωμα, τό foundation, support.

ἕδρανον, τό = ἕδρα.

ἑδριάομαι M. to sit down.

ἔδω to eat, consume.

ἐδωδή, ἡ food, fodder; bait.

ἐδώδιμος 2 eatable.
ἐδώλιον, τό seat, residence; rowing-bench.
ἕε = ἕ him.
ἕεδνα, τά = ἕδνα.
ἐεδνόομαι M. to betroth.
ἐεδνωτής, οῦ, ὁ father of a bride. [twenty oxen.]
ἐεικοσά-βοιος 2 worth
ἐείκοσι = εἴκοσι.
ἐέλδομαι = ἔλδομαι.
ἐέλδωρ, τό = ἔλδωρ.
ἐέλπομαι = ἔλπομαι.
ἐεργάθω = ἐργάθω.
ἐέρση = ἔρση.
ἕζω to set, place, settle. — M. to sit down; to sit; to settle (down).
ἐθάς, άδος accustomed, wont.
ἔθειρα, ἡ hair; mane; horse-tail; plume of a helmet.
ἐθείρω to till, cultivate.
ἐθελο-θρησκεία, ἡ arbitrary worship.
ἐθελο-κακέω to be bad or cowardly on purpose.
ἐθελοντηδόν, ἐθελοντήν, ἐθελοντί adv. on purpose, willingly.
ἐθελοντήρ, ῆρος, ἐθελοντής, οῦ voluntary, willing.
ἐθελό-πονος 2 willing to work. [willing proxenus.]
ἐθελο-πρόξενος, ὁ self-
ἐθελούσιος 3 and 2 = ἐθελοντής.
ἐθέλω to be willing, to wish, want, desire, to be resolved or inclined; to be able; to have power; to be wont, to mean.
ἔθεν = ἕο, οὗ.

ἐθίζω to accustom. — P. to be accustomed.
ἐθν-άρχης, ου, ὁ governor, prefect.
ἐθνικός 3 national; gentile.
ἔθνος, τό company, band; people, nation, tribe; class of men; gentiles.
ἔθος, τό custom, manner.
ἔθω to be wont or accustomed; perf. εἴωθα, part. εἰωθώς wont, accustomed, usual.
εἰ conj. if, whether.
εἶα int. up, on, well then.
εἰαμενή, ἡ lowland, meadow(-land).
εἰανός, ὁ = ἑανός.
εἶαρ, τό = ἔαρ.
εἰαρινός 3 = ἐαρινός.
εἴβω and M. to drop. trickle.
εἰδάλιμος 3 shapely, comely.
εἶδαρ, ατος, τό food, fodder; bait.
εἶδος, τό act of seeing; appearance, shape, form; beauty; notion, idea; kind, species, description; nature.
εἴδω and M., aor. εἶδον, ἰδεῖν to see, behold, perceive, know; to have an appearance, to look, seem: to resemble; to feign. — perf. οἶδα, εἰδέναι to know, to be knowing, skilled, or cunning.
εἰδωλεῖον, τό idol's temple.
εἰδωλό-θυτος 2 offered to idols.
εἰδωλο-λατρεία, ἡ idolatry.
εἰδωλο-λάτρης, ου, ὁ idolater.
εἴδωλον, τό image, shape, phantom; vision, idol.

8*

εἶεν *adv.* well (then).

εἶθαρ *adv.* at once, forthwith, immediately.

εἴ-θε *int.* o that.

εἰκάζω to make like to; to portray; to compare: to conjecture, guess, examine. — *P.* to resemble, to be like.

εἰκάθω = εἴκω.

εἰκασία, ἡ image.

εἰκαστής, οῦ, ὁ guesser.

εἴκελος 3 like, resembling.

εἰκῇ, εἰκῆ *adv.* at random, headlessly, in vain.

εἰκός, ότος, τό probable, likely, natural, fair, reasonable. [years old.]

εἰκοσα - έτης 2 twenty

εἰκοσάκις *adv.* twenty times.

εἴκοσι twenty.

εἰκοσι-νήριτος 2 twenty times immense.

εἰκοσί-πηχυς, υ of twenty cubits. [oars.]

εἰκόσ-ορος 2 with twenty

εἰκοστός 3 the twentieth.

εἰκότως *adv.* probably, naturally, of course, fairly, reasonably.

εἴκω[1] to yield, give way, retire; to submit, resign; to grant, allow.

εἴκω[2], εἶκε it seemed good.

ἔοικα to be or look like; to seem, to have the appearance (of); to think, believe; to be fit, right, or fair.

εἰκών, όνος, ἡ likeness, image, picture, painting; simile; phantom; notion.

εἰκώς 3 = ἐοικώς.

εἰλαπινάζω to feast, dine.

εἰλαπιναστής, οῦ, ὁ companion at table.

εἰλαπίνη, ἡ feast, banquet.

εἶλαρ, τό protection, shelter.

εἰλάτινος 3 = ἐλάτινος.

εἰλέω, εἴλλω to press hard; to force together; to shut up in; to strike; to check; to drive. — *P.* to be shut up or pressed together; to be crowded, assembled, or drawn together; to go or turn about.

εἴλησις, ἡ heat of the sun.

εἰλι-κρίνεια, ἡ purity.

εἰλι-κρινής 2 sun-bright; manifest; pure, uncorrupted, genuine.

εἰλί-πους, ποδος trailing the feet.

εἴλλω see εἰλέω.

εἴλυμα, τό cover, clothing.

εἰλυφάζω, εἰλυφάω to roll along.

εἰλύω to roll, whirl; to involve, enfold. — *P.* to roll on; to crawl, creep, wind along; to cling to, couch.

εἴλω = εἰλέω.

εἵλως, ωτος and εἱλώτης, ου, ὁ Helot, Spartan serf.

εἷμα, τό garment, cover.

εἱμαρμένη, ἡ destiny.

εἵμαρται see μείρομαι.

εἰμί to be, exist, live, continue; to take place, to come to pass; to dwell, sojourn; to be in a certain state; to behave; to be real; to mean, signify; to be descended; to belong to.

εἶμι to go, come, wander,

travel, drive, sail, fly; to march, progress, advance; to go away; to retire; to arrive.

εἴν = ἐν.

εἰνα-ετής 2 (*neutr.* εἰνάετες) of nine years.

εἰνάκις = ἐνάκις nine times.

εἰνακόσιοι 3 = ἐνακόσιοι.

εἰν-άλιος 3 = ἐνάλιος.

εἰνά-νυχες *adv.* nine nights long. [law.]

εἰνατέρες, αἱ sisters-in-law.

εἴνατος 3 = ἔνατος ninth.

εἵνεκα = ἕνεκα.

εἰνί = ἐν.

εἰν-όδιος 3 = ἐνόδιος.

εἰν-οσί-γαιος, ὁ = ἐννοσίγαιος. [the leaves.]

εἰν-οσί-φυλλος 2 shaking the leaves.

εἴξασι from ἔοικα.

εἷος = ἕως.

εἶπον aor. II, inf. εἰπεῖν, belongs to ἀγορεύω.

εἰργάθω = εἴργω.

εἰργμός, ὁ prison. [jailer.]

εἰργμο-φύλαξ, ακος, ὁ

εἴργω, εἵργω, εἵργνῡμι to press, enclose, shut in, confine, include, arrest; to shut out, exclude, separate; to prohibit, hinder, prevent. — *M.* to abstain from; to spare.

εἵρερος, ὁ slavery.

εἰρεσίᾱ, ἡ a rowing.

εἴρη, ἡ place of assembly.

εἰρήν, ένος, ὁ = ἰρήν.

εἰρηναῖος 3 peaceful.

εἰρηνεύω to keep peace, to live in peace.

εἰρήνη, ἡ peace; peace-making; time of peace, rest; blessing.

εἰρηνικός 3 peaceful.

εἰρηνο-ποιέω to make peace. [maker.]

εἰρηνο-ποιός 2 and 3 peace-maker.

εἰρίνεος 2 woollen.

εἴριον, τό wool.

εἰρκτή, ἡ enclosure; prison.

εἰρο-κόμος 2 wool-dressing. [ἐρέω.]

εἴρομαι *M.* to ask, see εἴρο-πόκος 2 wool-fleeced.

εἶρος, τό wool.

εἰρύω = ἐρύω.

εἴρω[1] to say, speak, tell; to report, order; εἴρομαι = ἐρέω. [join.]

εἴρω[2] to string together, to join.

εἴρων, ωνος, ὁ dissembler.

εἰρωνείᾱ, ἡ a dissembling, disguise, mockery; evasion, pretext, irony.

εἰρωνεύομαι *M.* to dissemble, to feign ignorance.

εἰρωνικός 3 ironical.

εἰρωτάω = ἐρωτάω.

εἰς, ἐς *adv.* and *prp.* with *acc.* into, towards, in; against; until; for; for the purpose of; up to; about.

εἷς, μία, ἕν one, one alone, a single one; the same; each one, any one.

εἶσα see ἕζω. [cer, usher.]

εἰσ-αγγελεύς, ὁ announcer.

εἰσ-αγγελίᾱ, ἡ announcement; impeachment.

εἰσ-αγγέλλω to announce, report; to denounce, impeach. [place.]

εἰσ-αγείρω to gather in a.

εἰσ-άγω to lead into; to

lead up; to import; to produce; to admit, introduce; to bring before an assembly, to summon before a court. — *M.* to bring into one's house. to marry.

εἰσ-αεί *adv.* for ever.

εἰσ-αθρέω to look at, descry.

εἰσ-ακοντίζω to throw spears into or against.

εἰσ-ακούω to listen or hearken to; to obey, follow.

εἰσ-άλλομαι *M.* to leap into or upon, to assail.

εἰσάμην see ἕζω.

εἰσ-αναβαίνω to go up into.

εἰσ-ανάγω to lead up into.

εἰσ-άνειμι to go up into.

εἰσ-άντα *adv.* to the face.

εἰσ-άπαξ *adv.* at once; for once. [to drive back.)

εἰσ-αράσσω to drive into;)

εἰσ-αῦθις *adv.* for another time, hereafter.

εἰσ-αφικάνω, εἰσ-αφικνέομαι to come or go into, to arrive at.

εἰσ-βαίνω to go or come into; to lead into.

εἰσ-βάλλω to throw into; to drive into; *intr.* to throw oneself into; to fall into; to invade, make an inroad, to enter. — *M.* to put on board.

εἴσ-βασις, ἡ embarkation.

εἰσ-βατός 3 accessible.

εἰσ-βιβάζω to embark.

εἰσ-βλέπω to look at.

εἰσ-βολή, ἡ inroad, attack; entrance; pass; mouth (of a river).

εἰσ-γράφω to inscribe. — *M.* to write down for oneself; to inscribe oneself.

εἰσ-δέρχομαι to look at, behold. [admit.)

εἰσ-δέχομαι *M.* to receive,)

εἰσ-δρομή, ἡ inroad, attack.

εἰσ-δύνω, εἰσ-δύομαι to enter, to slip into; to come over, seize.

εἴσ-ειμι to come or go into, to enter; to visit; to make one's appearance; to come before the court; to come into one's mind, to seize.

εἰσ-ελαύνω, -ελάω to drive into; to enter, invade.

εἰσ-έπειτα *adv.* henceforth, in future.

εἰσ-έργνῡμι to shut up into.

εἰσ-ερύω to draw into.

εἰσ-έρχομαι = εἴσειμι.

εἰσ-έχω to stretch into, reach; to shine into.

εἴση see ἴσος.

εἰσ-ηγέομαι *M.* to lead into; to introduce, propose, advise; to instruct.

εἰσ-ήγησις, ἡ a proposing; a contriving.

εἰσ-ηγητής, οῦ, ὁ proposer; contriver.

εἰσ-ηθέω to inject, syringe.

εἰσ-θρῴσκω to leap into.

εἰσ-ιδρύω to build in.

εἰσ-ίζομαι *M.* to lie down in.

εἰσ-ίημι to send into; to put into. — *M.* to admit to oneself; to betake oneself to, to resort to.

εἴσ-ιθμη, ἡ entrance.

εἰσ-ικνέομαι *M.* to come into, arrive at.

εἰσκαλέω — 119 — εἰωθότως

εἰσ-καλέω and *M.* to call into; to summon; to invite.

εἰσ-καταβαίνω to go down into.

εἴσ-κειμαι to lie in to be put in. [proclaim.]

εἰσ-κηρύσσω to call in; to

εἰσ-κομιδή, ἡ import(ation), supply.

εἰσ-κομίζω to bring into, import, procure. — *M.* to lay in provisions. — *P.* to take shelter in a place.

ἔϊσκω = ἴσκω.

εἰσ-λεύσσω to look into, behold. [the hand.]

εἰσ-μαίομαι *M.* to put in

εἰσ-νέω to swim over to.

εἰσ-νοέω to perceive, remark. [bule; admission.]

εἴσ-οδος, ἡ entrance; vesti-

εἰσ-οικείόω to introduce as a friend.

εἰσ-οίκησις, ἡ dwelling.

εἰσ-οικίζομαι *P.* to settle oneself. [into.]

εἰσ-οικοδομέω to build

εἰσ-οιχνέω to step into.

εἰσόκε *adv.* until; as long as.

εἰσ-οπίσω *adv.* in future.

εἴσ-οπτος 2 visible.

εἰσ-οράω to look into, upon, or at; to view, behold; to descry, perceive; to consider.

εἰσ-ορμάω and *P.* to force one's way into.

ἔϊσος, ἔϊσος = ἴσος.

εἰσ-παίω to dash in. [in.]

εἰσ-πέμπω to send or bring

εἰσ-πέτομαι *M.* to fly into; to arrive at.

εἰσ-πηδάω to jump into.

εἰσ-πίπτω to fall into. rush

into; to invade, attack, fall upon; to be thrown into.

εἰσ-πλέω to sail into.

εἴσ-πλους, ὁ a sailing in; entrance of a harbour.

εἰσ-ποιέω to put in; to add; to give to be adopted.

εἰσ-πορεύομαι *P.* to go into. to enter.

εἴσ-πραξις, ἡ exaction of money. [act, collect.]

εἰσ-πράσσω and *M.* to ex-

εἰσ-ρέω to flow into.

εἰσ-τίθημι to put or place into or upon.

εἰσ-τοξεύω to shoot into.

εἰσ-τρέχω to run into.

εἰσ-φέρω to carry or bring into; to bring in; to contribute, pay (an income-tax); to bring forward, propose. — *M.* to carry with one, to import. — *P.* to get into.

εἰσ-φορά, ἡ contribution; income-tax.

εἰσ-φορέω = εἰσφέρω.

εἰσ-φρέω to let in, admit.

εἰσ-χειρίζω to hand over to.

εἰσ-χέω to pour into.

εἴσω, ἔσω *adv.* in(to a place), inward(s); within; between; within the reach of.

εἰσ-ωθέομαι *M.* to force one's way into.

εἰσ-ωπός 2 in front of.

εἶτα *adv.* then; after, further; and then, and yet; therefore.

εἴτε ... εἴτε *conj.* either ... or; whether ... or.

εἴωθα *pf.* of ἔθω.

εἰωθότως *adv.* in the wonted way.

εἵως = ἕως.

ἐκ, ἐξ *prp.* with *gen.* out of, from, from among, without, far from; since, immediately after; on the part of, because of, in consequence of; accordingly to.

ἐκά-εργος 2 working from afar. [far off.]

ἔκα-θεν *adv.* from afar.

ἑκάς *adv.* far off; *prp.* with *gen.* far from.

ἑκασταχόθεν *adv.* from every side.

ἑκασταχόθι, ἑκασταχοῦ, ἑκάστοθι *adv.* everywhere.

ἑκασταχόσε *adv.* to all sides.

ἕκαστος 3 every, every one, εἰς ἕκαστος each one.

ἑκάστοτε *adv.* every time.

ἑκατεράκις *adv.* (at) both times.

ἑκάτερθεν = ἑκατέρωθεν.

ἑκάτερος 3 each of (the) two, either; *pl.* both, both parties.

ἑκατέρωθεν *adv.* from each side. [side.]

ἑκατέρωσε *adv.* to each]

ἑκατη-βελέτης, ου, ὁ, ἑκατη-βόλος 2 far-shooting, never failing.

ἕκᾱτι = ἕκητι.

ἑκατόγ-χειρος 2 with a hundred hands.

ἑκατό-ζυγος 2 with a hundred rowing-benches.

ἑκατόμ-βη, ἡ hecatomb (a sacrifice of a hundred oxen).

ἑκατόμ-βοιος 2 worth a hundred oxen.

ἑκατόμ-πεδος 2, -ποδος 2 a hundred feet long.

ἑκατόμ-πολις 2 with a hundred towns.

ἑκατόμ-πους, ποδος with a hundred feet. [gated.]

ἑκατόμ-πυλος 2 hundred-]

ἑκατόν, οἱ, αἱ, τά a hundred.

ἑκατοντα-έτης 2 a hundred years old.

ἑκατοντα-πλασίων 2 hundredfold, centuple.

ἑκατοντ-άρχης, ου, ὁ, ἑκατόντ-αρχος, ου, ὁ centurion.

ἑκατοντάς, άδος, ἡ the number one hundred.

ἕκατος, ὁ = ἑκηβόλος.

ἑκατοστός 3 the hundredth.

ἑκατοστύς, ύος, ἡ = ἑκατοντάς.

ἐκ-βαίνω to step, go, or come out, disembark, leave; to depart from; to turn out, to happen; to digress. *trans.* to put on shore; to transgress. [tic.]

ἐκ-βακχεύω to make fran-]

ἐκ-βάλλω to throw or cast out; to expel, banish; to cast away; to fell; to strike out; to let fall, drop, to lose; to reject; to recant.

ἔκ-βασις, ἡ a disembarking, landing; egress; mountain-pass; ascent.

ἐκ-βάω = ἐκβαίνω.

ἐκ-βιάζομαι *P.* to be wrested from.

ἐκ-βιβάζω to make step out; to lead away.

ἐκ-βλαστάνω to sprout out

ἐκ-βοάω to cry out, shout.

ἐκ-βοήθεια, ἡ a marching out to aid; sally.

ἐκ-βοηθέω to march out to aid; to sally out.

ἐκ-βολή, ἡ a throwing out, expulsion, banishment; outlet, defile; digression; loss; what is cast out; a shooting forth; origin.

ἔκ-βολος 2 cast out; ὁ ἔκβολος promontory, beach.

ἐκ-βράσσω to throw up on shore, to cast ashore.

ἐκ-βρῡχάομαι M. to roar out.

ἔκ-βρωμα, τό what is eaten out. [in marriage.]

ἐκ-γαμίζω to give away)

ἐκ-γαμίσκομαι P. to be given in marriage.

ἐκ-γελάω to laugh loud.

ἐκ-γενής 2 without family.

ἐκ-γί(γ)νομαι to be born (of), to spring from, to descend from; to have gone by or elapsed; to be permitted.

ἔκ-γονος 2 descended; descendant, offspring, relation, pl. posterity.

ἐκ-δακρύω to burst into tears. [oneself up.]

ἐκ-δαπανάω P. to offer)

ἔκ-δεια, ἡ a falling short; being in arrears.

ἐκ-δείκνῡμι to show openly.

ἐκ-δέκομαι = ἐκδέχομαι.

ἔκ-δεξις, ἡ succession.

ἐκ-δέρκομαι to look out from.

ἐκ-δέρω to flay (off).

ἐκ-δέχομαι M. to take or receive from; to take upon oneself; to acquire, learn; to succeed, follow; to wait, expect.

ἐκ-δέω to fasten or bind to; to shut in. — M. to put on.

ἔκ-δηλος 2 quite plain, manifest; excellent.

ἐκ-δημέω to go or be abroad, to travel.

ἔκ-δημος 2 abroad, (away) from home. [through.]

ἐκ-διαβαίνω to step quite)

ἐκ-διαιτάομαι to depart from one's mode of life.

ἐκ-διδάσκω to teach thoroughly. [escape.]

ἐκ-διδράσκω to run away,)

ἐκ-δίδωμι to give out or up, to surrender; to give away in marriage; to lend out, to let out (on hire); intr. to run out (into).

ἐκ-διηγέομαι M. to tell to the end.

ἐκ-δικέω to avenge, punish; to defend, vindicate.

ἐκ-δίκησις, ἡ punishment, revenge. [avenging.]

ἔκ-δικος 2 lawless, unjust;)

ἐκ-διώκω to expel.

ἔκ-δοσις, ἡ a surrendering; giving in marriage.

ἔκ-δοτος 2 surrendered.

ἐκ-δοχή, ἡ expectation; succession.

ἐκ-δρομή, ἡ sally, raid; scouring party.

ἔκ-δρομος 2 skirmisher.

ἐκ-δύνω = ἐκδύομαι.

ἔκ-δυσις, ἡ a slipping out, escape; final event.

ἐκ-δύω to strip off; intr. and M. to strip oneself of, to put off; to escape.

ἐκ-δωριόομαι P. to become quite a Dorian.

ἐκεῖ adv. there; thither; then; in that case.

ἐκεῖθεν adv. thence; from that time; therefore,

ἐκεῖθι, ἐκείνη = ἐκεῖ.

ἐκεῖνος, η, ο (= Lat. ille) that.

ἐκεῖσε, adv. thither; then.

ἐκε-χειρία, ἡ armistice.

ἐκ-ζέω to boil out; to swarm with. [to avenge.]

ἐκ-ζητέω to search eagerly;

ἐκ-ζήτησις, ἡ matter of dispute. [from afar.]

ἐκη-βολία, ἡ a shooting

ἐκη-βόλος, ὁ shooter, archer.

ἔκηλος 2 quiet, at one's ease; untroubled.

ἔκητι, adv. at the pleasure of; for the sake of.

ἐκ-θαμβέομαι P to be amazed.

ἔκ-θαμβος 2 quite amazed.

ἐκ-θαυμάζω to wonder, be astonished. [the end.]

ἐκ-θεάομαι M. to see to

ἔκ-θεσις, ἡ exposure of a child.

ἔκ-θετος 2 exposed.

ἐκ-θέω to run out; to sally.

ἐκ-θηρεύω to catch.

ἐκ-θλίβω to force away.

ἐκ-θνήσκω to be dying.

ἐκ-θρῴσκω to leap out or down. [passionate.]

ἔκ-θυμος 2 courageous;

ἐκ-θύω to offer for atonement. — M. to atone for.

ἐκ-καθαίρω to cleanse, purify; to clear away.

ἐκ-καθεύδω to sleep out of doors.

ἐκ-καί-δεκα sixteen.

ἐκκαιδεκά-δωρος sixteen palms long.

ἐκκαιδεκά-πηχυς, ὁ sixteen cubits long.

ἐκ-καίω to burn out; to kindle, inflame.

ἐκ-κακέω to get tired, to grow weary.

ἐκ-καλέω to call out to oneself; to call forth, exhort, excite.

ἐκ-καλύπτω to uncover.

ἐκ-κάμνω to get tired, grow weary; to fall short.

ἐκ-καρπόομαι M. to enjoy the fruit of. [down.]

ἐκ-καταπάλλομαι to leap

ἔκ-κειμαι to be exposed, to lie there at large.

ἐκ-κενόω to empty; to unpeople, depopulate.

ἐκ-κεντέω to pierce.

ἐκ-κηρύσσω to proclaim by a herald; to banish.

ἐκ-κινέω to move out; to stir; to expel.

ἐκ-κίω to go out.

ἐκ-κλάω to break in or to pieces.

ἐκ-κλείω to shut out; to hinder, oppress.

ἐκ-κλέπτω to remove by stealth; to abduct; to deceive.

ἐκκλησία, ἡ assembly of citizens or soldiers; corporation; church; assembly-room.

ἐκ-κλησιάζω to call together an assembly; to sit in assembly.

ἐκκλησιαστής, οῦ, ὁ partaker of an assembly.

ἔκ-κλητος 2 called forth; member of an assembly.

ἐκ-κλίνω to bend aside. *intr.* to turn away; to give way; to withdraw; to degenerate.

ἐκ-κνάω to rub off.

ἐκ-κολάπτω to chisel off.

ἐκ-κολυμβάω to swim out of. [out; a saving.]

ἐκ-κομιδή, ἡ a bringing)

ἐκ-κομίζω to carry or bring away; to save.

ἐκ-κομπάζω to boast.

ἐκ-κοπή, ἡ hindrance.

ἐκ-κόπτω to knock out; to cut off or down, to fell; to demolish; to chase; to destroy.

ἐκ-κρέμαμαι *P.* to hang upon. [upon, cling to.]

ἐκ-κρεμάννυμαι to hang)

ἐκ-κρίνω to single out; to choose, select.

ἔκ-κριτος 2 chosen.

ἐκ-κρούω to beat out; to expel, drive away; to frustrate, thwart. [merset.]

ἐκ-κυβιστάω to turn a so-)

ἐκ-κυλίνδω, ἐκ-κυλίω to roll out. — *P.* to be rolled out; to tumble out of.

ἐκ-κυμαίνω to undulate; to make the front-line uneven. [lot).]

ἐκ-λαγχάνω to obtain (by)

ἐκ-λαλέω to speak or let out.

ἐκ-λαμβάνω to take out of; to choose; to receive; to perceive, understand.

ἐκ-λάμπω to shine forth.

ἐκ-λανθάνω to escape notice; to make forget. — *M.* to forget utterly.

ἐκ-λέγω to pick out, choose; to collect; to exact.

ἐκ-λείπω to leave out, omit; to forsake, abandon; to be unmindful (of), neglect; *intr.* to cease, disappear; to run short; to die; to be eclipsed.

ἔκ-λειψις, ἡ a forsaking; a disappearing; loss; eclipse.

ἐκ-λεκτός 3 selected.

ἐκ-λέπω to hatch.

ἐκ-λήγω to cease.

ἔκ-ληστις, ἡ forgetfulness.

ἐκ-λιπής 2 wanting, failing, deficient; eclipsed.

ἐκ-λογή, ἡ choice, selection.

ἐκ-λογίζομαι *M.* to calculate, consider. [ness.]

ἔκ-λυσις, ἡ release; weak-)

ἐκ-λυτήριος 2 releasing.

ἐκ-λύω to loose, set free, release, redeem; to dissolve, weaken, exhaust; to abrogate, put an end to. — *P.* to be exhausted or wearied out, to despond.

ἐκ-λωβάομαι *M.* to treat shamefully.

ἐκ-λωπίζω to uncover.

ἐκ-μαίνω to drive mad, enrage. — *P.* to rave, to be frantic.

ἐκ-μανθάνω to learn thoroughly; to learn by heart; to examine closely

ἐκ-μάσσω to wipe away.

ἐκ-μείρομαι to partake of.

ἐκ-μετρέω to measure out.

ἔκ-μηνος 2 of six months.

ἐκ-μηρύομαι *M.* to file off.

ἐκ-μῑμέομαι *M.* to imitate closely. [farm out.]

ἐκ-μισθόω to let on hire,

ἐκ-μολεῖν to go out.

ἐκ-μυζάω to suck out.

ἐκ-μυκτηρίζω to mock at.

ἐκ-νέμω and *M.* to go forth.

ἐκ-νευρίζω to unnerve.

ἐκ-νεύω to nod away; *intr.* to turn aside.

ἐκ-νέω to swim out of or away; to escape. [again.]

ἐκ-νήφω to become sober

ἐκ-νίζω to wash off; to expiate.

ἐκ-νῑκάω to become victorious; to prevail, be in use.

ἐκ-νοστέω to return again.

ἑκούσιος 2 and 3 = ἑκών.

ἐκ-παγλέομαι to be highly amazed, to wonder at.

ἔκ-παγλος 2 astonishing, frightful, terrible.

ἐκ-παιδεύω to educate thoroughly.

ἐκ-παιφάσσω to shine forth.

ἔκ-παλαι *adv.* of old, long since. [out.]

ἐκ-πάλλομαι *M.* to spirt

ἐκ-πατάσσω to knock out.

ἐκ-παύομαι *M.* to cease entirely.

ἐκ-πείθω to persuade.

ἐκ-πειράομαι *P.* and ἐκ-πειράζω to try, test.

ἐκ-πέλει = ἔξεστι it is allowed.

ἐκ-πέμπω to send out or away; to export; to convey; to chase, banish; to dismiss; to send for.

ἔκ-πεμψις, ἡ a sending away.

ἐκ-πεπταμένως *adv.* extravagantly. [end.achieve.]

ἐκ-περαίνω to bring to an

ἐκ-περάω to go or pass through or along. [terly.]

ἐκ-πέρθω to destroy ut-

ἐκ-πετάννῡμι to spread out. [forth; to rush on.]

ἐκ-πηδάω to leap out or

ἐκ-πίμπλημι to fill up; to satiate, satisfy; to spend; to atone for.

ἐκ-πίνω to drink out, to drain; to drink up.

ἐκ-πιπράσκω to sell out.

ἐκ-πίπτω to fall out of or down; to fall from, depart from; to be hissed off; to stop short; to turn out, result; to lose; to cease; to be confounded; to be banished, driven out of; to be wrecked or cast on shore; to come or sally forth; to escape; to empty itself.

ἐκ-πλέω to sail out, leave port; to swim out; to outsail.

ἔκ-πλεως, ων filled up, full; complete, abundant.

ἐκ-πλήγνῡμι = ἐκπλήσσω.

ἐκ-πληκτικός 3 terrifying.

ἔκ-πληξις, ἡ fright, terror, perplexity, consternation; awe.

ἐκ-πληρόω = ἐκπίμπλημι.

ἐκ-πλήρωσις, ἡ a filling up, completion.

ἐκ-πλήσσω to strike out, drive away; to frighten, astound. — *P.* to be out of one's senses, to be amazed, frightened or panic-struck.

ἔκ-πλοος, ὁ a sailing out; port of departure.

ἐκ-πλύνω to wash out.

ἐκ-πλώω = ἐκπλέω.

ἐκ-πνέω to breathe out, forth, or away; *intr.* to expire, to be killed; to blow along.

ἐκ-ποδών *adv.* out of the way, away.

ἐκ-ποιέω to complete, finish; to build up.

ἐκ-ποίησις, ἡ emission of seed.

ἐκ-πολεμέω to make war from; to excite to war.

ἐκ-πολιορκέω to take by assault or siege, to overpower.

ἐκ-πομπή, ἡ a sending out.

ἐκ-πονέω to work out, finish, execute; to digest; to bring to perfection; to train; to be eager.

ἐκ-πορεύομαι *P.* to march or go out. [plunder.]

ἐκ-πορθέω to devastate,]

ἐκ-πορίζω to make out; to contrive; to provide.

ἐκ-πορνεύω to be given to lewdness. [from.]

ἐκ-ποτέομαι to fly down]

ἐκ-πράττω to finish, to achieve, effect, kill; to exact punishment; to avenge. — *M.* to avenge.

ἐκ-πρεπής 2 prominent, excellent, extraordinary.

ἐκ-πρίασθαι *aor.* see ἐξωνέομαι.

ἐκ-πρίω to saw off or out.

ἐκ-προκαλέομαι *M.* to call forth to oneself.

ἐκ-προλείπω to forsake.

ἐκ-προτιμάω to honour above others. [detest.]

ἐκ-πτύω to spit out; to]

ἐκ-πυνθάνομαι *M.* to search out; to hear of.

ἐκ-πυρόω to set on fire.

ἔκ-πυστος 2 known, notorious.

ἔκ-πωμα, τό drinking-cup.

ἐκ-ραίνω to sputter out.

ἐκ-ρέω to flow out; to vanish.

ἐκ-ρήγνῡμι to break out or off, to tear in or to pieces; *intr.* and *P.* to sally forth, to burst out; to become known.

ἐκ-ριζόω to root out.

ἐκ-ρίπτω to throw out.

ἐκ-ροή, ἡ, ἔκ-ροος, ὁ outflow.

ἐκ-σαόω = ἐκ-σῴζω.

ἐκ-σείω to shake out.

ἐκ-σεύομαι *P.* to rush out, to hasten away.

ἐκ-σημαίνω to signify.

ἐκ-σμάω to wipe out or off.

ἐκ-σπάω to draw out.

ἔκ-σπονδος 2 excluded from treaty. [trance.]

ἔκ-στασις, ἡ astonishment,]

ἐκ-στέλλω to equip; to send out. [garlands.]

ἐκ-στέφω to adorn with]

ἐκ-στρατεύω and *M.* to march out to war; to end war. [encamp outside.]

ἐκ-στρατοπεδεύομαι *M.* to]

ἐκ-στρέφω to turn or pull out; to turn inside out; to change, make worse.

ἐκ-σῴζω to save.

ἐκ-τάδιος 3 and 2 far off.

ἑκταῖος 3 on the sixth day.

ἐκ-τανύω = ἐκ-τείνω.

ἐκ-ταράσσω to confound, trouble. [out in order.]

ἐκ-τάσσω to arrange, draw)

ἐκ-τείνω to stretch out, extend; to draw out; to strain; to prostrate.

ἐκ-τειχίζω to build or fortify completely.

ἐκ-τελέω to finish, bring to an end, achieve, satisfy; to spend (time).

ἐκ-τέμνω to cut out from, to cut off; to castrate.

ἐκ-τένεια, ἡ zeal.

ἐκ-τενής 2 zealous, earnest, assiduous. [trive, devise.]

ἐκ-τεχνάομαι M. to con-)

ἐκ-τίθημι to put out or outside; to explain.

ἐκ-τῑμάω to honour much.

ἔκ-τῑμος 2 not honouring.

ἐκ-τινάσσω to strike or shake out or off.

ἐκ-τίνω to pay off, requite, make amends (for). — M. to punish.

ἐκ-τιτρώσκω to miscarry.

ἔκτοθεν = ἐκτοσθεν.

ἔκτοθι adv. outside.

ἐκ-τομίας, ου, ὁ eunuch.

ἐκ-τοξεύω to shoot arrows out of; to spend in shooting.

ἐκ-τόπιος 3 and 2, ἔκτοπος 2 away from a place, distant; strange, extraordinary.

ἔκτος 3 the sixth.

ἐκτός adv. without, outside; out of, far from; without, except.

ἔκτοσε adv. outwards.

ἔκτοσθε(ν) adv. from without, outside. — prp. with gen. out of, far from.

ἐκ-τραχηλίζω to throw over the head, to throw down.

ἐκ-τρέπω to turn away or aside, divert; to drive away; to sprain; to dissuade from; to lead to. — P. and M. to turn (oneself) aside from; to deviate: to avoid.

ἐκ-τρέφω to feed, rear up.

ἐκ-τρέχω to run out; to sally forth; to degenerate.

ἐκ-τρίβω to rub out of; to destroy by rubbing.

ἐκ-τροπή, ἡ a turning off or aside; digression; sideway.

ἐκ-τρυχόω to wear out.

ἔκ-τρωμα, τό abortion.

ἐκ-τυφλόω to make blind.

ἐκ-τύφλωσις, ἡ a making blind.

ἑκυρά, ἡ mother-in-law.

ἑκυρός, ὁ father-in-law.

ἐκ-φαίνω to show forth, to bring to light, reveal, betray. — P. to appear, come to light.

ἐκ-φανής 2 manifest.

ἔκ-φασις, ἡ a saying.

ἐκ-φαυλίζω to make bad, depreciate.

ἐκ-φέρω to carry out of or away; to bury; to begin (war); to carry off (a prize); to steal; to lead out or away; to accomplish; to speak out, tell; to produce; to bring to light; to proclaim, publish; to put to sea; to run ahead. — *P.* to come forth; to come to; to be agitated. [escape.]

ἐκ-φεύγω to flee away,)

ἔκ-φημι to speak out.

ἐκ-φθίνω to consume, destroy. [*P.* to fear.]

ἐκ-φοβέω to frighten. —)

ἔκ-φοβος 2 frightened.

ἐκ-φοιτάω to go out or away.

ἐκ-φορά, ἡ burial.

ἐκ-φορέω = ἐκφέρω,

ἐκ-φόριον, τό produce, crop; rent. [known.]

ἔκ-φορος 2 to be made)

ἐκ-φορτίζω to sell away.

ἐκ-φροντίζω to devise; to deliberate.

ἔκ-φρων 2 senseless, mad.

ἐκ-φυλάσσω to watch carefully.

ἐκ-φύω to cause to grow out of; to produce, beget; *intr.* and *M.* to grow from; to be born from.

ἐκ-χέω to pour out, shed, spill; to lavish, squander, spoil. — *P.* to stream out; to indulge in.

ἐκ-χράω[1] to suffice.

ἐκ-χράω[2] to declare; to give oracle.

ἐκ-χώννῡμι to heap up earth; to fill with mud.

ἐκ-χωρέω to go away, depart; to make way. [last.]

ἐκ-ψύχω to breathe one's)

ἑκών, οὖσα, όν voluntary, willing; on purpose.

ἐλάα, ἐλαία, ἡ olive-tree; olive. [olive-wood.]

ἐλάϊνος, ἐλάϊνος 3 of)

ἔλαιον, τό olive-oil.

ἔλαιος, ὁ wild olive-tree.

ἐλαιών, ῶνος, ὁ olive-garden.

ἔλασις, ἡ a driving, chasing; a riding, march, expedition; attack.

ἐλασσόω to make less, to damage. — *P.* to become smaller, to decrease; to be a loser, to come short of.

ἐλάσσων 2 *comp.* of ἐλαχύς.

ἐλαστρέω to drive, row.

ἐλάτη, ἡ pine, fir; oar; canoe. [waggoner.]

ἐλατήρ, ῆρος, ὁ driver,)

ἐλάτινος 3 of pine-wood.

ἐλαττονέω to be or have less.

ἐλάττωμα, τό loss, want.

ἐλαύνω to drive, drive on, lead; to chase, expel; to vex, press; to strike, beat, hit, hurt, wound; to beat out (metal); to draw out; to build; to produce. — *intr.* to drive, ride, row, march, advance.

ἐλάφειος 2 of deer.

ἐλαφη-βολία, ἡ deer-hunt.

ἐλαφη-βολιών, ῶνος, ὁ ninth month of the Athenian calendar (March-April).

ἐλαφη-βόλος 2 deer-hunter.

ἔλαφος, ἡ and ὁ deer, stag, hind. [ness.]

ἐλαφρία, ἡ light-minded-)

ἐλαφρός 3 light, swift, nimble; active; light-armed; easy, without trouble.

ἐλαχίστερος 3 smaller, the smallest.

ἐλαχύς 3 little, small; comp. ἐλάσσων 2 smaller, less, worse, inferior; superl. ἐλάχιστος 3 (the) smallest, least, shortest.

ἐλάω = ἐλαύνω.

ἔλδομαι, ἐέλδομαι to wish, long for; to be wished for.

ἐλεαίρω, ἐλεάω = ἐλεέω.

ἐλεγεῖον, τό distich.

ἔλεγμός, ὁ and ἔλεγξις, ἡ a convincing, refuting; a blaming.

ἐλεγχείη, ἡ = ἔλεγχος, τό.

ἐλεγχής 2 shameful; cowardly; wretched.

ἔλεγχος[1], τό reproach, disgrace; coward.

ἔλεγχος[2], ὁ means of proving, proof, trial; conviction, refutation, reproach; test, examination; account; sentence, judgment.

ἐλέγχω to revile, blame, reproach; to put to shame; to despise, reject; to convince, refute; to prove, show; to examine, search, question.

ἐλεεινός 2 pitiable, pitied, miserable; pitiful.

ἐλεέω to have pity (upon), to pity. [mercy; alms.]

ἐλεημοσύνη, ἡ charity,] ἐλεήμων 2 pitiful.

ἐλεητύς, ύος, ἡ pity, mercy.

ἐλεινός 3 = ἐλεεινός.

ἔλειος 2 living in swamps.

ἐλελίζω[1] to raise the warcry.

ἐλελίζω[2] to cause to shake or tremble; to whirl round, to turn round quickly. — P. to tremble, shake; to turn oneself quickly. — M. to coil. [ing.]

ἐλελί-χθων 2 earth-shak-] ἐλεό-θρεπτος 2 swamp-bred. [dresser.]

ἐλεός, ὁ kitchen-table;] ἔλεος, ὁ (and τό) pity, mercy.

ἑλετός 3 to be caught.

ἐλευθερία, ἡ freedom, liberty; generosity.

ἐλευθέριος 3 like a free man, noble-minded, frank, liberal, noble; freeing, delivering; releaser.

ἐλεύθερος 3 free, freeborn, independent; free from; freed; liberal, free-spirited; noble, honest.

ἐλευθερόω to set free, release, acquit.

ἐλευθέρωσις, ἡ a setting free, release. [rival.]

ἔλευσις, ἡ a coming, ar-] ἐλεφαίρομαι M. to deceive.

ἐλεφάντινος 3 of ivory.

ἐλέφας, αντος, ὁ ivory; elephant. [medley.]

ἔλιγμα, τό what is rolled;] ἑλιγμός, ὁ a winding; a rolling. [of the ear.]

ἑλικτήρ, ῆρος, ὁ pendant] ἑλικτός 3 rolled, wreathed.

ἑλίκ-ωπ, ωπος and ἑλικῶπις, ιδος with bright eyes.

ἐλινύω to rest, repose.

ἕλιξ[1], ικος twisted; with twisted horns.

ἕλιξ[2], ικος, ἡ a winding, torsion, coil, curl; circle;

spiral line; bracelet, earring.

ἐλίσσω to turn about or round; to roll, whirl; swing; to wind, wrap round; to revolve, reflect. — P. and M. to turn round, coil; to move quickly, to spin round; to reflect.

ἑλκεσί-πεπλος 2, ἑλκεχίτων, ωνος with trailing robe.

ἑλκέω = ἕλκω.

ἑλκηθμός, ὁ a dragging away.

ἕλκος, τό wound; ulcer; evil. [to ulcerate.]

ἑλκόω to wound. — P.]

ἑλκυστάζω to drag along.

ἑλκύω, ἕλκω to draw, drag, pull, tear; to maltreat; to bend or draw (a bow, sail), to draw up or down; to weigh; to tear off (the hair); to draw out, stretch.

ἕλκωσις, ἡ ulceration.

ἑλ-λάμπομαι M. to shine forth. [hellebore.]

ἑλλέβορος, ὁ sneezewort,]

ἑλλεδανός, ὁ straw-rope.

ἔλ-λειμμα, τό a short-coming.

ἐλ-λείπω to leave behind; to leave out, omit, neglect intr. and P. to be left, to remain; to be inferior, to lack, to come short of; to be needed.

ἔλ-λειψις, ἡ deficiency.

ἔλ-λεσχος 2 subject to public talk.

ἑλληνίζω to speak Greek; to make Greek.

ἑλληνικῶς, ἑλληνιστί adv. in Greek fashion; in Greek.

ἐλ-λιπής 2 wanting, defective; inferior.

ἐλ-λογάω, -έω to impute.

ἐλ-λόγιμος 2 considerable, notable, excellent.

ἑλλός[1], ὁ young deer, fawn.

ἑλλός[2] 3 mute. [(for).]

ἐλ-λοχάω to lie in wait]

ἐλ-λύχνιον, τό lamp-wick.

ἕλος, τό marsh, swamp; meadow.

ἐλπίζω to hope, expect; to think; to fear.

ἐλπίς, ίδος, ἡ hope, expectation; opinion; fear.

ἔλπω to cause to hope. — M. = ἐλπίζω.

ἐλπωρή, ἡ = ἐλπίς.

ἔλυτρον, τό cover, case; cistern, reservoir.

ἐλύω = εἰλύω.

ἐλωΐ, ἐλωσί (Hebr.) my God!

ἔλωρ, ωρος and ἑλώριον, τό booty, prey, spoil; spoliation, murder.

ἐμ-βαδόν adv. on foot.

ἐμ-βαίνω to step in or into, to enter; to go on board, embark; to mount; to tread upon; to be fixed upon; to step on; to intervene. — trans. to bring into.

ἐμ-βάλλω to throw, put, or lay in; to throw upon; to inject, cause; intr. to make an inroad; to attack; to take in hand; to encounter, to rush against; to run out into

ἔμ-βαμμα, τό sauce, soup.

ἐμ-βάπτω to dip in.

ἐμ-βάς, άδος, ἡ shoe. slipper. [over.]

ἐμ-βασιλεύω to be king.

ἐμ-βατεύω to step along, in, or upon; to enter on possession; to persist in.

ἐμ-βάφιον, τό bowl, vessel.

ἐμ-βιβάζω to bring in; to put on board.

ἐμ-βλέπω to look at.

ἐμ-βοάω to shout aloud, to call to.

ἐμ-βολή, ἡ a throwing in, shot; attack, inroad; stroke (of a ship in battle); leak; head of a battering-ram; entrance, pass; mouth of a river. [tercalary.]

ἐμ-βόλιμος 2 inserted, in-

ἔμ-βολον, τό and ἔμ-βολος, ὁ wedge; tongue of land between two rivers; cuneiform order of battle; beak of a ship.

ἔμ-βραχυ adv. in short.

ἐμ-βρέμομαι M. to roar in.

ἐμ-βριθής 2 weighty, heavy; firm; grave.

ἐμ-βρῑμάομαι to snap one short, to be indignant.

ἐμ-βροντάω to thunder at; to stun.

ἐμ-βρόντητος 2 thunderstricken; frightened, stupid.

ἔμ-βρυον, τό little lamb.

ἔμετος, ὁ a vomiting.

ἐμέω to vomit; to spit out.

ἐμ-μαίνομαι P. to rave, to be mad.

ἐμ-μανής 2 raving, mad.

ἐμ-μαπέως adv. at once, quickly.

ἐμ-μάχομαι M. to fight in.

ἐμ-μέλεια, ἡ harmony; tune; dance.

ἐμ-μελής 2 harmonious, in tune; correct, regular, fit, agreeable; elegant, witty.

ἐμ-μεμαώς, υῖα, ός eager, hasty, ardent, impetuous.

ἐμ-μέμονα to be agitated.

ἐμ-μενής 2 steady, unceasing.

ἐμ-μένω to abide in; to remain steadfast, to keep to; to continue.

ἔμ-μετρος 2 in measure, moderate; metrical.

ἔμ-μηνος 2 happening every month. [involve in.]

ἐμ-μίγνῡμι to mix in; to

ἔμ-μισθος 2 in pay, hired; earning money.

ἐμ-μονή, ἡ an abiding in; continuance. [steadfast.]

ἔμ-μονος 2 abiding in,

ἔμ-μορος 2 partaking in.

ἐμός 3 my, mine.

ἐμ-πάζομαι to care for.

ἐμ-παιγμονή, ἡ and ἐμ-παιγμός, ὁ a jesting, mocking.

ἐμ-παίζω to mock, jest, trifle with; to deceive.

ἐμ-παίκτης, ου, ὁ mocker.

ἔμ-παιος 2 skilled, practised (in). [entangle.]

ἐμ-παίω to strike in; to

ἔμ-παλιν (τό) adv. backwards, back; contrary to, in the reverse order; on the other side or hand.

ἐμ-παρέχω to offer, to hand over; to abandon.

ἔμ-πᾶς adv. altogether, at

all events, on the whole, throughout; yet, in spite of; although. [embroider.]

ἐμ-πάσσω to strew in; to

ἐμ-πεδάω to bind with fetters, to check.

ἐμπεδ-ορκέω to abide by one's oath.

ἔμ-πεδος 2 steadfast, unmoved, firm; certain; continuous. [fastly.]

ἐμ-πεδόω to keep stead-

ἐμ-πειρία, ἡ experience, knowledge, skill, practise.

ἔμ-πειρος 2 experienced, skilful; proved by experience.

ἐμ-περιπατέω to walk about in. [thrust in.]

ἐμ-πήγνῡμι to fix in; to

ἐμ-πηρος 2 crippled.

ἔμπης = ἔμπας.

ἐμ-πικραίνομαι P. to be imbittered.

ἐμ-πί(μ)πλημι to fill full or up; to satiate. — P. and M. to fill oneself; to be satisfied or satiated; to get tired of.

ἐμ-πί(μ)πρημι to set on fire, burn; to blow into.

ἐμ-πίνω to drink in.

ἐμ-πίπτω to fall in or upon; to rush into, to throw oneself into; to attack, assault, to invade, burst in; to fall in with; to come over, to seize.

ἐμπίς, ίδος, ἡ gnat.

ἐμ-πίτνω = ἐμπίπτω.

ἐμ-πλάσσω to plaster up.

ἔμ-πλειος 3 = ἔμπλεος.

ἐμ-πλέκω to plait in; to entangle.

ἔμ-πλεος 2 full, filled up.

ἐμ-πλέω to sail in or on.

ἐμ-πλήγδην adv. rashly, at random.

ἐμ-πλήκτος 2 out of countenance, perplexed; rash; fickle.

ἔμ-πλην adv. close by.

ἐμ-πλήσσω to fall into.

ἐμ-πλοκή, ἡ a plaiting in.

ἐμ-πνέω to breathe in or on; to breathe, live; to inspire. — P. to recover oneself. [breathing, alive.]

ἔμ-πνοος, ἔμ-πνους 2]

ἐμ-ποδίζω to bind, fetter; to be in the way of, to hinder; to make doubtful; to cause to fall.

ἐμ-πόδιος 2 impeding.

ἐμ-πόδισμα, τό hindrance.

ἐμ-ποδών adv. before the feet, in the way, as a hindrance; what comes in one's way.

ἐμ-ποιέω to make or put in, insert; to cause, inspire, suggest.

ἐμ-πολάω to buy, purchase; to earn, gain by selling. — M. to acquire by trade; to bribe. [in war.]

ἐμ-πολέμιος 2 taking place]

ἐμ-πολή, ἡ traffic; merchandise. [sold.]

ἐμ-πολητός 3 bought and]

ἔμ-πολις, ὁ fellow-citizen.

ἐμ-πολῑτεύω to be a citizen.

ἐμ-πορεύομαι P. to travel to. — M. to trade, traffic; to overreach.

ἐμ-πορία, ἡ traffic, trade, commerce, business.

9*

ἐμ-πορικός 3 commercial.

ἐμ-πόριον, τό trading-place; pack-house.

ἔμ-πορος, ὁ passenger (on a ship); traveller; merchant, trader; furnisher.

ἐμ-πορπάομαι M. to fix on with a brooch.

ἐμ-πρέπω to excel.

ἐμ-πρήθω = ἐμπίπρημι.

ἔμ-πρησις, ἡ a setting on fire, ignition.

ἔμ-προσθεν adv. before, in front of, anterior, earlier.

ἐμ-πτύω to spit upon or at.

ἔμ-πυος 2 purulent.

ἐμ-πῦρι-βήτης, ου standing over the fire.

ἔμ-πῦρος 2 in or on the fire; τὰ -α burnt sacrifice. [low.]

ἐμ-φαγεῖν to eat up, swal-)

ἐμ-φαίνω to show, to make visible or conspicuous. — P. to show oneself, to appear.

ἐμ-φανής 2 conspicuous, visible; manifest, clear; known, public.

ἐμ-φανίζω = ἐμφαίνω.

ἐμ-φερής 2 equivalent, similar.

ἐμ-φέρω to hold up to, to object to. [tened.]

ἔμ-φοβος 2 fearful; frigh-)

ἐμ-φορέω to bear in; to object to. — P. to be borne about; to enjoy fully; to do to excess. [up.]

ἐμ-φράσσω to stop or block)

ἐμ-φρουρέω to keep guard in. [garrisoned.]

ἔμ-φρουρος on guard in;)

ἔμ-φρων 2 sensible; prudent.

ἔμ-φῦλιος 2, ἔμ-φῦλος 2 of the same tribe, native; kindred.

ἐμ-φῦσάω to breathe upon.

ἐμ-φυτεύω to (im)plant.

ἔμ-φῦτος 2 inborn, innate, implanted.

ἐμ-φύω to implant; intr. and M. to grow into; to be rooted in; to cling to; to be inborn or innate, to be in.

ἔμ-ψῦχος 2 souled, alive.

ἐν adv. within; with; upon; besides. — prp. with dat. in, at, on; between, among; during, within; by means of, with, through; from; upon, by dint of.

ἐν-αγής 2 guilty, polluted; bound by an oath. [dead.]

ἐν-αγίζω to sacrifice for the)

ἐν-αγκαλίζομαι M. to take in one's arms.

ἐν-αγκυλάω to provide with a leash.

ἔν-αγχος adv. just now, lately, the other day.

ἐν-άγω to lead in, on, or to; to urge, incite, promote.

ἐν-αγωνίζομαι M. to contend in, on, or among. to be one of the prize-fighters.

ἔν-αιμος 2 filled with blood. [undo, destroy.]

ἐν-αίρω and M. to kill; to)

ἐν-αίσιμος, ἐν-αίσιος 2 foreboding, auspicious, sent by fate; seemly, proper, fit; favourable.

ἐν-ακούω to listen to.

ἐν-αλείφω to anoint; to whitewash. [like.]

ἐν-αλίγκιος 2 resembling,)

ἐν-άλιος 2 (and 3) in or of the sea.

ἐν-αλλάξ adv. alternately.

ἐν-αλλάσσω to exchange; to change, alter. — P. to deal with, to have intercourse with. [rush upon.]

ἐν-άλλομαι M. to leap on,]

ἐν-αμέλγω to milk into.

ἐν-άμιλλος 2 a match for, equal to.

ἔν-αντα, ἔν-αντι adv. opposite, over against.

ἐναντί-βιον adv. against.

ἐν-αντίος 3 opposite, over against, facing; opposing, contrary, reverse, discordant, contradictory; hostile, adverse; enemy.

ἐναντιόω to place opposite. — P. to oppose oneself (to), to withstand, to be adverse to; to contradict; to forbid.

ἐναντίωμα, τό hindrance.

ἐναντίωσις, ἡ opposition.

ἐν-αποδείκνυμαι M. to distinguish oneself.

ἐν-αποθνήσκω to die in.

ἐν-αποκλάω to break off in.

ἐν-απόλλυμαι to perish in.

ἐν-απονίζομαι to wash oneself in.

ἐν-άπτω to fasten or bind to; to kindle. — M. to clothe oneself.

ἔναρα, τά armour; spoil.

ἐν-άργεια, ἡ distinctness.

ἐν-αργής 2 visible; distinct, bright, manifest.

ἐν-αρηρώς, υῖα, ός fastened in. [dite.]

ἐνάρης, ους, ὁ hermaphro-]

ἐναρίζω to strip of arms; to slay. [among.]

ἐν-ἀριθμέω to reckon]

ἐν-ἀρίθμιος 2, ἐν-ἀρίθ-μος 2 counted among; esteemed.

ἐν-άρχομαι M. to begin.

ἐναταῖος 3 on the ninth day.

ἔνατος 3 ninth.

ἐν-αυλίζω and P., M. to pass the night in; to stop for the night.

ἔν-αυλος[1], ὁ torrent; water-channel. [ears.]

ἔν-αυλος[2] 2 ringing in one's]

ἔν-αυλος[3] 2 dwelling in.

ἐν-αύω to kindle.

ἐν-αφίημι to put in.

ἐν-δατέομαι M. to distribute. — P. to be portioned out.

ἐν-δεής 2 needy, wanting, lacking; deficient, incomplete; inferior, worse, less.

ἔνδεια, ἡ want, need.

ἔν-δειγμα, τό proof.

ἐν-δείκνῡμι to mark out; to denounce. — M. to display, make known, prove; to declare oneself; to show, to hold out a prospect of.

ἔν-δειξις, ἡ a marking out, proof.

ἔν-δεκα, οἱ, αἱ eleven.

ἐνδεκά-πηχυς, υ eleven cubits long.

ἑνδέκατος 3 eleventh.

ἐν-δέκομαι = ἐνδέχομαι.

ἐνδελεχής 2 continual.

ἐν-δέμω to build in.

ἐν-δέξιος 3 on or to the right hand; propitious, favourable.

ἐν-δέχομαι *M.* to take upon oneself; to believe; to approve of, admit; ἐνδέχεται it is possible *or* allowed.

ἐν-δέω[1] to bind to.

ἐν-δέω[2] to be in want (of); to be wanting; ἐνδεῖ μοι I am in want of. — *M.* to be in want *or* need of.

ἔν-δηλος 2 = δῆλος.

ἐν-δημέω to be at home.

ἔν-δημος 2 at home, native; intestine.

ἐν-διαιτάομαι *P.* to live *or* dwell in; to sojourn.

ἐν-διατάσσω to arrange in.

ἐν-διατρίβω to pass *or* spend in; to dwell on.

ἐν-διδύσκω to put on.

ἐν-δίδωμι to surrender, give up; to betray; to offer; to exhibit, show, prove; to cause; to give way (to); to admit. — *intr.* to surrender oneself; to yield; to empty oneself.

ἐν-δίημι to chase. [just.]

ἔν-δικος 2 legal, right.

ἔνδῖνα, τά entrails.

ἔν-δῖος 2 at midday.

ἐν-δίφριος, ὁ companion *or* neighbour at table.

ἔνδοθεν *adv.* from within; within.

ἔνδοθι *adv.* = ἔνδον.

ἐν-δοιάζω to waver, hesitate. — *P.* to be thought possible.

ἐνδοιαστός 3 doubtful.

ἐν-δόμησις, ἡ building, structure.

ἐνδό-μυχος 2 hidden in the inmost part.

ἔνδον *adv.* and *prp.* with *gen.* within, at home, at heart.

ἐν-δοξάζω to glorify.

ἔν-δοξος 2 glorious, renowned; honoured.

ἐν-δουπέω to fall with a hollow sound.

ἐν-δυκέως *adv.* carefully, zealously, earnestly.

ἔν-δυμα, τό garment.

ἐν-δυναμόω to strengthen.

ἐν-δυναστεύω to rule in; to prevail (upon) by authority.

ἐν-δύνω, ἐν-δύνέω = ἐνδύομαι see ἐνδύω.

ἐν-δύω to put on; to clothe. — *intr.* and *M.* to put on; to wear; to enter, go in; to undergo, to engage (oneself) in. [ambush.]

ἐν-έδρα, ἡ a lying in wait;

ἐν-εδρεύω and *M.* to lie in wait *or* ambush.

ἔν-εδρος 2 inhabitant; τὸ ἔνεδρον = ἐνέδρα.

ἐν-ειλέω to press in; to wrap in.

ἐν-ειλίσσω = ἐνελίσσω.

ἐν-είλλω = ἐνειλέω.

ἔν-ειμι to be within, in, on, *or* at; to dwell in; to be present, extant; ἔνεστι *or* ἔνι it is possible.

ἐν-είρω to file on a string; to entwine; to join.

ἔνεκα, ἔνεκεν *prp.* with *gen.* on account of, for the sake of; with respect to, by force of.

ἐν-ελίσσω to wrap up in.

ἐν-εμέω to vomit in.

ἐνενήκοντα ninety.

ἐνενηκοστός 3 ninetieth.

ἐνεός 3 deaf and dumb; speechless.

ἐνέπω to speak, tell, relate; to address, accost.

ἐν-εργάζομαι M. to pursue one's calling at home; to make in; to create; to inject.

ἐν-έργεια, ἡ activity, efficacy, effect. [work.]

ἐν-εργέω to be active, to

ἐν-έργημα, τό = ἐνέργεια.

ἐν-εργής 2 and ἐν-εργός 2 active, busy, working; fertile; effective, energetic.

ἐν-ερείδω to thrust in.

ἔνερθεν adv. from beneath; beneath, in the nether world. — prp. with gen. beneath.

ἔνεροι, οἱ the dead, those beneath the earth; comp. ἐνέρτερος 3 lower.

ἔν-εσις, ἡ a putting in.

ἐν-ετή, ἡ pin, brooch.

ἐν-ετός 3 incited. [in.]

ἐν-ευδαιμονέω to be happy

ἐν-ευδοκιμέω to make the most of for one's glory.

ἐν-εύδω to sleep in or on.

ἐν-εύναιον, τό bed-clothes, bed.

ἐν-έχυρον, τό pledge.

ἐν-έχω to keep within, to entertain, cherish; to be angry. — M. and P. to be held fast, to be caught; to be affected with.

ἐν-ζεύγνυμι to bind together, to fasten.

ἐν-ηβητήριον, τό place of amusement.

ἐνηείη, ἡ kindness.

ἐν-ηής 2 kind, friendly.

ἔν-ημαι to sit in. [up in.]

ἐνήνοθα perf. to mount

ἔνθα adv. there; thither; where; then; when. [now.]

ἐνθάδε adv. thither; there;

ἐν-θᾱκέω to sit on or in.

ἐν-θάκησις, ἡ a sitting in or on.

ἔνθαπερ adv. just where.

ἐνθαῦτα = ἐνταῦθα.

ἐν-θεάζω to be inspired.

ἔνθεν adv. thence, from there; whence; after that, since, thereupon.

ἐνθένδε adv. hence, henceforward.

ἔνθενπερ adv. just whence.

ἔν-θεος 2 inspired.

ἐν-θερμαίνω to heat through.

ἐνθεῦτεν = ἐντεῦθεν.

ἔν-θηρος 2 savage, wild.

ἐν-θνῄσκω to die in; to die of.

ἐνθουσιάζω to be inspired.

ἐνθουσιασμός, ὁ inspiration, ecstasy. [upon.]

ἐν-θρῴσκω to leap into or

ἐν-θῡμέομαι P. to take to heart; to consider, ponder, deliberate; to devise.

ἐν-θῡμημα, τό, ἐν-θῡμησις, ἡ, ἐν-θῡμία, ἡ thought, consideration; device; advice, warning.

ἐν-θῡμιος 2 perceived; taken to heart, causing scruple or care.

ἐν-θῡμιστός = ἐνθύμιος.

ἐν-θωρᾱκίζω to arm with a coat of mail.

ἔνι = ἔνεστι.

ἐνί = ἐν.

ἐνταύσιος 3 and 2 one year old; for a year; year by year, yearly.

ἐνιαυτός, ὁ year.

ἐν-ιαύω to dwell in.

ἐνταχῆ, ἐνταχοῦ adv. in several places; sometimes.

ἐν-ιδρύω to set up in.

ἐν-ίζω, -ιζάνω to sit down in or on.

ἐν-ίημι to send, drive, or let into; to incite, cause; to inspire. [trate.]

ἐνι-κλάω to break, frus-]

ἔνιοι 3 some, several.

ἐνί-οτε adv. sometimes.

ἐνῑπή, ἡ a scolding, revile; reproach; threat.

ἐνι-πίμπλημι = ἐμπίπλημι.

ἐνί-πλειος 2 = ἔμπλειος.

ἐνι-πλήσσω = ἐμπλήσσω.

ἐν-ιππεύω to ride in or on.

ἐνι-πρήθω = ἐμπίμπρημι.

ἐνίπτω to rebuke, reprove, upbraid, blame; to tell.

ἐνι-σκίμπτω to stick in; to lower down.

ἐνίσπω = ἐνέπω.

ἐνίσσω = ἐνίπτω.

ἐν-ίστημι to put or place in or on; intr. and M. to undertake, begin; to stand in; to enter; to be present or extant; to be opposed (to), resist.

ἐν-ισχύω to strengthen.

ἐν-ίσχω = ἐνέχω.

ἐνι-χρίμπτω = ἐγχρίμπτω.

ἐννάετες = εἰνάετες.

ἐν-ναίω to dwell in.

ἐννάκις = ἐνάκις.

ἐν-ναυπηγέω to build ships in.

ἐννέα nine. [oxen.]

ἐννεά-βοιος 2 worth nine]

ἐννεα-καί-δεκα nineteen.

ἐννεά-κρουνος 2 with nine springs or water-pipes.

ἐννεά-μηνος 2 of nine months.

ἐννεά-πηχυς, υ nine cubits long.

ἐννεά-χῑλοι nine thousand.

ἐννε-όργυιος 2 nine fathoms long.

ἐννέπω = ἐνέπω.

ἐν-νεύω to nod to, to beckon.

ἐννέ-ωρος 2 nine years old.

ἐννήκοντα = ἐνενήκοντα.

ἐνν-ῆμαρ adv. for nine days.

ἐν-νοέω and M. P. to have in mind, to consider, think of; to contrive, devise; to plan, intend; to think, believe; to fear; to perceive, observe; to understand.

ἔν-νοια, ἡ thought, consideration; notion; intent, mind.

ἔν-νομος 2 legal, lawful; just, right. [shaker.]

ἐννοσί-γαιος, ὁ earth-]

ἔν-νους 2 sensible, prudent.

ἔννῡμι to put on. — P. and M. to clothe oneself; perf. to be clad.

ἐν-νυχεύω to pass the night in, to lurk in secret.

ἐν-νύχιος 3 and 2, ἔν-νυχος 2 at night, nightly.

ἐν-όδιος 3 and 2 by the road, on the road.

ἐν-οικέω to dwell in, to inhabit.

ἐν-οίκησις, ἡ a dwelling in.

ἐν-οικίζω to settle in a

place. — *M.* and *P.* to be settled, to dwell in.

ἐν-οικοδομέω to build in or on; — *M.* to build for oneself.

ἔν-οικος, ὁ inhabitant.

ἐν-οινο-χοέω to pour in wine.

ἐν-οπή, ἡ sound, voice; battle-cry; woeful cry.

ἐν-όπλιος 2, ἔν-οπλος in arms, armed.

ἐν-οράω to look at, see, observe; to understand.

ἔν-ορκος 2 bound by oath; included in a treaty; sworn.

ἐν-όρνῡμι to arouse in. — *M.* to arise. [assail.]

ἐν-ορούω to leap upon, to]

ἐν-όρχης, ου, ἔν-ορχις, ιδος, ἔν-ορχος, ου uncastrated. [one year old.]

ἔνος, ἔνος 3 last year's,]

ἐνοσί-χθων, ονος, ὁ earthshaker. [cord.]

ἑνότης, ητος, ἡ unity; con-]

ἐν-ουρέω to make water in.

ἐν-οχλέω to molest, trouble, to be in one's way.

ἔν-οχος 2 held in, liable to, subject to.

ἐν-ράπτω to sew in.

ἐν-σείω to shake, drive, or hurl into.

ἐν-σημαίνω to show or make known in, at, or through. — *M.* to make oneself known.

ἐν-σκευάζω to fit out, prepare, adorn. [to fall in.]

ἐν-σκήπτω to hurl into;]

ἔν-σπονδος 2 allied; ally.

ἐν-στάζω to instil.

ἐν-στάτης, ου, ὁ adversary.

ἐν-στέλλω to clothe, dress in. [in.]

ἐν-στηρίζω *P.* to be fixed]

ἐν-στρατοπεδεύω and *M.* to encamp in.

ἐν-στρέφομαι *P.* to turn in.

ἔν-ταλμα, τό = ἐντολή.

ἐν-τάμνω = ἐντέμνω.

ἐν-τανύω = ἐντείνω.

ἐν-τάσσω to range in, to enrol.

ἐνταῦθα *adv.* there; here; thither; hither; then; now; thereupon, in that case.

ἐν-ταυθοῖ *adv.* hither; thither; here. [bury.]

ἐν-ταφιάζω to embalm; to]

ἐν-ταφιασμός, ὁ an embalming. [a burial.]

ἐν-τάφιος 2 belonging to]

ἔντεα, εων, τά arms, armour; tools, appliances.

ἐν-τείνω to stretch or strain in; to bend; to versify; to set to music; to plait over; to strain, exert; to extend, stretch out.

ἐν-τειχίζω to fortify; to build in; — *M.* to wall in.

ἐν-τελευτάω to die in.

ἐν-τελής 2 complete; perfect, spotless. [command.]

ἐν-τέλλομαι *M.* to enjoin,]

ἐν-τέμνω to cut in, engrave; to kill, sacrifice.

ἔντερον, τό gut; *pl.* entrails. [harness.]

ἐντεσι-εργός 2 working in]

ἐν-τεταμένως *adv.* intensively, zealously.

ἐντεῦθεν *adv.* thence; hence; henceforward, then; thereupon; therefore.

ἔν-τευξις, ἡ encounter, meeting, visit; conversation; prayer, petition.

ἔν-τεχνος 2 artistical, ingenious.

ἐν-τήκω to melt in; to impress. intr. and P. to be impressed; to be molten.

ἐν-τίθημι to put in; to inspire; to put or lay over or on.

ἐν-τίκτω to engender in.

ἔν-τῑμος 2 honoured, noble, esteemed; costly, precious; honest. [injunction.]

ἐν-τολή, ἡ commandment,]

ἔν-τομος 2 cut up; τὰ ἔντομα sacrifices, victims.

ἔν-τονος 2 strained; earnest, vehement.

ἐν-τόπιος 2, ἔν-τοπος 2 native; inhabitant.

ἐντός adv. and prp. with gen. within, inside.

ἔντοσθεν = ἐντός.

ἐν-τρέπω to turn about or over; to put to shame. — P. to turn oneself round or towards; to give heed (to), to notice; to revere; to feel or be ashamed (of); to hesitate. [up in.]

ἐν-τρέφω to feed or bring]

ἐν-τρέχω to run in.

ἐν-τριβής 2 skilled, active.

ἔν-τριψις, ἡ a rubbing in.

ἔν-τρομος 2 trembling.

ἐν-τροπαλίζομαι M. to turn oneself repeatedly.

ἐν-τροπή, ἡ respect, regard; shame. [concerned in.]

ἔν-τροφος 2 brought up in;]

ἐν-τρυφάω to revel in; to be delicate; to mock.

ἐν-τυγχάνω to encounter, fall in with; to incur; to get; to meet; to visit; to converse; to entreat, accost.

ἐν-τυλίσσω to wrap up.

ἐντύνω to prepare, equip, make ready; to adorn.

ἐν-τυπάς, adv. enveloped tightly. [grave.]

ἐν-τυπόω to stamp in, en-]

ἐντύω = ἐντύνω.

ἐνῡάλιος 2 warlike.

ἐν-υβρίζω to insult (one) in (a thing).

ἔν-υδρις, ἡ otter.

ἔν-υδρος 2 living in water; watery. [dream.]

ἐν-υπνιάζω and M. to]

ἐν-ύπνιον, τό dream, vision.

ἐν-ύπνιος 2 in (one's) sleep, sleeping, in dreams.

ἐν-υφαίνω to weave in.

ἐνωμοτ-άρχης, ου, ὁ leader of an ἐνωμοτία.

ἐν-ωμοτίᾱ, ἡ a division of Spartan soldiers (25 or 30 men). [by oath]

ἐν-ώμοτος 2 sworn, bound]

ἐνωπαδίως adv. to one's face. [openly.]

ἐν-ωπή, ἡ face; ἐνωπῇ]

ἐν-ώπιος 2 to the face; τὰ ἐνώπια the front, outer or side-walls.

ἐν-ωτίζομαι to hear.

ἐξ = ἐκ.

ἕξ six.

ἐξ-αγγέλλω and M. to publish, tell, report, send word; to blab out; to promise.

ἐξ-άγγελος, ὁ messenger.

ἐξ-άγγελτος 2 told out.

ἐξ-αγῑνέω = ἐξάγω.

ἐξ-άγιστος 2 most holy; abominable.

ἐξ-άγνῡμι to break away.

ἐξ-αγοράζω and M. to buy off; to redeem.

ἐξ-αγορεύω to speak out, publish; to betray.

ἐξ-αγριαίνω, ἐξ-αγριόω to make wild; to exasperate.

ἐξ-άγω to lead out or away, to carry out, export; to lead to death; to expel; to bring forth; to lead on, excite, seduce; intr. to march out, go on.

ἐξ-αγωγή, ἡ a leading, carrying, drawing out; expulsion; way out.

ἐξ-ᾴδω to begin a song.

ἐξ-αείρω = ἐξαίρω.

ἐξά-ετες adv. for six years.

ἐξ-αιμάσσω to make bloody. [to rob.]

ἐξ-αίνυμαι to take away;]

ἐξ-αίρεσις, ἡ a taking out; an unbowelling.

ἐξ-αίρετος 2 taken out; picked out; chosen, excellent. [taken out.]

ἐξ-αιρετός 2 what can be]

ἐξ-αιρέω to take out; to unbowel; to disembark; to pick out, choose; to dedicate; to except; to take away, remove; to capture; to destroy; to confound; to drive away.— M. to take out for oneself; to unload; to rob; to set free.

ἐξ-αίρω to lift up; to extol, exalt, praise; to excite; to encourage; to make angry; to lead away, carry off,

remove. — M. to carry off for oneself, to win.

ἐξ-αίσιος 2 and 3 undue; immoderate. [out.]

ἐξ-αΐσσω and P. to rush]

ἐξ-αιτέω to demand from, to demand one's surrender. — M. to beg for oneself.

ἔξ-αιτος 2 chosen.

ἐξ-αίφνης adv. suddenly.

ἐξ-ακέομαι M. to heal thoroughly; to make up for; to appease.

ἑξάκις adv. six times.

ἑξακισ-μύριοι 3 six thousand.

ἐξ-ακολουθέω to follow.

ἐξ-ακοντίζω to throw a spear; to shoot.

ἑξακόσιοι 3 six hundred.

ἐξ-ακούω to hear, listen to.

ἐξ-ακρῑβόω to do exactly.

ἐξ-αλαόω to make quite blind. [unpeople, destroy.]

ἐξ-αλαπάζω to sack; to]

ἐξ-αλείφω to wipe out or off; to destroy; to besmear.

ἐξ-αλέομαι, -εύομαι M. to shun; to escape.

ἐξ-αλλάσσω to exchange; to alter; to turn away or aside.

ἐξ-άλλομαι M. to spring out of; to spring down or away, to rear (of horses).

ἐξ-αλύσκω = ἐξαλέομαι.

ἐξ-αμαρτάνω to mistake, err; transgress, sin.

ἐξ-αμαρτία, ἡ mistake, error. [destroy.]

ἐξ-αμάω to mow off; to]

ἐξ-αμελέω to neglect utterly or altogether.

ἐξά-μετρος 2 of six metres.

ἐξά-μηνος 2 lasting six months.

ἐξ-αναγκάζω to drive away by force; to compel.

ἐξ-ανάγομαι M. and P. to put to sea, to set sail.

ἐξ-αναδύομαι M. to rise out of, emerge.

ἐξ-ανακρούομαι M. to put to sea again.

ἐξ-αναλίσκω to consume or lavish utterly. [save.]

ἐξ-αναλύω to set free,

ἐξ-ανασπάω to draw out.

ἐξ-ανάστασις, ἡ resurrection.

ἐξ-ανατέλλω to rise from.

ἐξ-αναφανδόν adv. openly.

ἐξ-αναχωρέω to retreat, withdraw.

ἐξ-ανδραποδίζω and M. to reduce to slavery.

ἐξ-ανδραπόδισις, ἡ a reducing to slavery.

ἐξ-ανδρόομαι P. to grow up to be a man. [devise.]

ἐξ-ανευρίσκω to find out,

ἐξ-ανέχομαι M. to take upon oneself, to bear.

ἐξ-ανθέω to bloom forth; to burst forth; to fade.

ἐξ-ανίημι to send out, dismiss; intr. to slacken, relax.

ἐξ-ανίστημι to make rise from; to remove, expel; to unpeople, destroy; to lead out. — intr. and M. to rise; to depart, start, emigrate; to be driven out.

ἐξ-ανύ(τ)ω to accomplish, fulfil, perform, manage;

to kill; to finish one's way, to arrive.

ἐξά-πάλαιστος 2 of six handbreadths.

ἐξ-απαλλάσσω to make quite free. — P. to come off.

ἐξ-απατάω to deceive utterly, to cheat.

ἐξ-απάτη, ἡ deception.

ἐξ-απαφίσκω and M. = ἐξαπατάω.

ἐξά-πεδος 3 six feet long.

ἐξ-απεῖδον aor. to see from afar. [long.]

ἐξά-πηχυς, υ six cubits

ἐξ-απιναῖος 3 and 2 sudden.

ἐξά-πλεθρος 2 six plethra long.

ἐξα-πλήσιος 3 sixfold.

ἐξ-αποβαίνω to step out of.

ἐξ-αποδίεμαι to chase away. [off.]

ἐξ-αποδύνω to put or take

ἐξ-απόλλυμι to kill, destroy utterly. — intr. and M. to perish.

ἐξ-απονέομαι to return.

ἐξ-απονίζω to wash off.

ἐξ-απορέω and P. to be utterly at a loss, to despair. [or away.]

ἐξ-αποστέλλω to send out

ἐξ-αποτίνω to atone fully.

ἐξ-αποφθείρω to destroy utterly.

ἐξ-άπτω to fasten to, attach to; to kindle. — M. to hang from, cling to; to attack.

ἐξ-αραίρημαι see ἐξαιρέω.

ἐξ-αράομαι M. to curse.

ἐξ-αράσσω to knock out of.

ἐξ-αργέω to do carelessly

ἐξ-αργυρίζω, ἐξ-αργυρόω to turn into money.

ἐξ-αριθμέω to count; to number, reckon.

ἐξ-αρκέω to suffice, to be enough; to satisfy; to be able.

ἐξ-αρκής 2 sufficient, enough; in good order.

ἐξ-αρκούντως adv. enough.

ἐξ-αρνέομαι P. to deny; to refuse.

ἔξ-αρνος 2 denying.

ἐξ-αρπάζω to snatch away; to rob; to rescue.

ἐξ-αρτάω to hang on, to attach (to); to make depend. — P. to be fastened or attached to, to be hung upon.

ἐξ-αρτίζω to finish.

ἐξ-αρτύω to prepare, equip, fit out. — M. to fit out for oneself; to get ready.

ἔξ-αρχος 2 beginning; leader of the chorus.

ἐξ-άρχω and M. to begin (a song); to be beginner or author.

ἐξ-ασκέω to adorn.

ἐξ-ατῑμάζω not to care for. [up.

ἐξ-αυαίνω to dry or parch

ἐξ-αυδάω to speak out.

ἐξ-αυλίζομαι P. to start from an encampment.

ἐξ-αυτῆς adv. at once.

ἐξ-αὖτις adv. over again; back. [lieve firmly.

ἐξ-αυχέω to boast; to believe

ἐξ-αϋθω to cry aloud.

ἐξ-αφαιρέομαι M. to take out; to rob.

ἐξ-αφίημι to set free.

ἐξ-αφίσταμαι M. to step aside; to withdraw, to depart.

ἐξ-αφοράω to see from afar.

ἐξ-αφύω, ἐξ-αφύσσω to draw (water) out of.

ἐξ-εγγυάω to set free on bail, to bail out.

ἐξ-εγείρω to arouse, awake.

ἔξ-εδρος 2 away from home.

ἐξείης = ἑξῆς. [to copy.

ἐξ-εικάζω to make like,

ἔξ-ειμι[1] (-ιέναι) to go out, away, or forward; to march out; to come to an end.

ἔξ-ειμι[2] (-εἶναι) to come from; ἔξεστι it is allowed or possible; ἐξόν it being possible.

ἐξ-εῖπον aor. to speak out.

ἐξ-είργω to shut out, exclude, keep off; to chase, expel; to hinder, prevent; to press, urge, compel.

ἐξ-είρομαί τινα to inquire of a person.

ἐξ-είρω[1] to speak out (openly), publish, tell.

ἐξ-είρω[2] to thrust out.

ἐξ-έλασις, ἡ expulsion; departure; expedition.

ἐξ-ελαύνω, -ελάω to drive out, expel, chase, banish; to beat out, hammer out; intr. to set out, march out or on; to ride out or up.

ἐξ-ελέγχω to test, examine, search out; to convict, confute; to prove. — P. to be wrong.

ἐξ-ελευθερο-στομέω to speak out freely.

ἐξ-ελίσσω to unfold, develop, draw out.

ἐξ-έλκω, -ελκύω to draw out; to drag away; to entice.

ἐξ-εμέω to vomit.

ἐξ-εμπολάω, -έω to sell out; to gain by traffic; to betray. [arms; to slay.]

ἐξ-εναρίζω to strip of

ἐξ-επᾴδω to heal by incantation; to appease.

ἐξ-επεύχομαι M. to boast into the bargain.

ἐξ-επίσταμαι P. to know thoroughly, to understand fully. [pose.]

ἐξ-επίτηδες adv. on pur-

ἐξ-έραμα, τό vomit.

ἐξ-εργάζομαι M. to work out, to execute, finish, accomplish, make, do; to cause; to cultivate; to undo, destroy. [in work.]

ἐξ-εργαστικός 3 skilled

ἐξ-έργω = ἐξείργω.

ἐξ-ερεείνω and M. = ἐξ-ερέω[1]. [to tumble down.]

ἐξ-ερείπω to fall out of.

ἐξ-ερεύγω P. to empty oneself. [inquire after.]

ἐξ-ερευνάω to search out,

ἐξ-ερέω[1] and M. to search out; to examine; to question.

ἐξ-ερέω[2] fut. of ἐξ-είρω.

ἐξ-ερημόω to make empty or desolate. [είρομαι.]

ἐξ-έρομαι = ἐξερέω[1], ἐξ-

ἐξ-έρπω to creep out of; to come out or forth.

ἐξ-ερύκω to tear out.

ἐξ-έρχομαι to go or come out or away, to march out; to sally out; to come to one's turn; to come to an end, to elapse, expire; to come to pass, to come true; to turn out, to become.

ἐξ-ερωέω to shy, bolt.

ἐξ-εσία, ἡ a sending out, mission. [vorce.]

ἐξ-εσις, ἡ dismissal, di-

ἐξ-ετάζω to search out; to examine, test, question; to review, muster; to judge after, to compare with.

ἐξ-έτασις, ἡ examination, scrutiny, a searching out; review, inspection.

ἐξ-εταστικός 3 skilled in examining.

ἐξ-έτης 2 six years old.

ἐξ-έτι prp. with gen. since, from. [very cautious.]

ἐξ-ευλαβέομαι P. to be

ἐξ-ευπορ.ζω to convey to a place plentifully.

ἐξ-εύρεσις, ἡ, ἐξ-εύρημα, τό invention.

ἐξ-ευρίσκω to find out, discover, invent; to devise, decipher; to make possible, to cause. [command.]

ἐξ-εφίεμαι M. to enjoin,

ἐξ-έφω to boil thoroughly.

ἐξ-ηγέομαι M. to lead out or on; to be leader, to lead the way; to direct, govern, guide, teach; to explain, interpret; to describe, tell, narrate. [tion.]

ἐξ-ήγησις, ἡ interpreta-

ἐξ-ηγητής, οῦ, ὁ teacher, adviser, guide; interpreter.

ἐξήκοντα sixty.

ἐξηκοστός 3 sixtieth.

ἐξ-ήκω to have come out; to have arrived; to have

expired or elapsed; to come true. to come to pass.

ἐξ-ήλατος 2 beaten out.

ἐξ-ήλυσις, ἡ a going out, way out.

ἐξ-ῆμαρ adv. for six days.

ἐξ-ημερόω to tame, cultivate, civilize.

ἐξ-ημοιβός 2 for change.

ἑξῆς adv. in order, one after the other, successively; next: next to, further.

ἐξ-ηχέω to publish.

ἐξ-ιάομαι to heal thoroughly. [one's own.]

ἐξ-ιδιόομαι to make quite

ἐξ-ιδρύω to let repose.

ἐξ-ίημι to send out, away, or forth; to empty oneself. — M. to send from oneself.

ἐξ-ιθύνω to make quite straight. [earnestly.]

ἐξ-ικετεύω to entreat

ἐξ-ικνέομαι to come to, arrive at, reach; to meet; to obtain, attain; to be sufficient, to suffice.

ἐξ-ιλάσκομαι M. to propitiate.

ἕξις, ἡ condition, state; behaviour, habit, mode of life; faculty, skill.

ἐξ-ισόω to make equal or even. — intr. and P. to be equal, to resemble.

ἐξ-ίστημι to put out or away; to change, alter. — intr. and M. to step or stand aside from, to retire or remove from; to be far from; to be beside oneself, lose one's senses; to give up, abandon, leave; to

lose, forget; to be changed; to degenerate.

ἐξ-ιστορέω to inquire into.

ἐξ-ισχύω to be quite able.

ἐξ-ίσχω to put forth.

ἐξ-ίτηλος 2 destroyed, extinct. [track, trace out.]

ἐξ-ιχνο-σκοπέω and M. to

ἐξ-ογκόω to make swell up. — P. to be over-full, to be puffed (up).

ἐξ-οδεία, ἡ a marching out, expedition.

ἐξ-οδοιπορέω to go out of.

ἐξ-οδος, ἡ way out; gate; mouth; a going or marching out, start, sally, expedition; procession; end, close.

ἔξ-οιδα to know well.

ἐξ-οικέω to make the most of a dwelling.

ἐξ-οικήσιμος 2 habitable.

ἐξ-οικίζω to drive from home; to banish. — M. to go from home, emigrate.

ἐξ-οικοδομέω to build up.

ἐξ-οιμώζω to lament, wail.

ἐξ-οιχνέω to go out.

ἐξ-οίχομαι to have gone out or away.

ἐξ-οκέλλω to run aground; to go astray.

ἐξ-ολισθαίνω to slip off.

ἐξ-όλλῡμι to destroy wholly. — intr. and M. to perish utterly.

ἐξ-ολοθρεύω = ἐξόλλυμι.

ἐξ-ομνῡμι and M. to deny upon oath.

ἐξ-ομοιόω to make like. — P. to become like.

ἐξ-ομολογέω and M. to

confess, admit; to agree; to thank, praise.

ἐξ-ονειδίζω to revile.

ἐξ-ονομάζω, ἐξ-ονομαίνω to call by name; to speak out, to utter. [name.]

ἐξ-ονομα-κλήδην *adv.* by)

ἐξ-όπι(σ)θεν *adv.* and *prp.* with *gen.* behind, backward(s); from behind.

ἐξ-οπίσω *adv.* behind; hereafter. [completely.]

ἐξ-οπλίζω to arm or equip)

ἐξ-οπλισία, ἐξ-όπλισις, ἡ complete equipment; mustering under arms.

ἐξ-οπτάω to bake sufficiently.

ἐξ-οράω see ἐξεῖδον.

ἐξ-οργίζω to make very angry.

ἐξ-ορθόω to set upright.

ἐξ-ορίζω to banish.

ἐξ-ορκίζω, ἐξ-ορκόω to bind by oath; to conjure, exorcise. [exorcist.]

ἐξ-ορκιστής, οῦ.ὁ conjurer,)

ἐξ-όρκωσις, ἡ the binding by an oath.

ἐξ-ορμάω *trans.* to stir, start; to send out; to impel, excite; *intr.* and *P.* to set out, go away.

ἐξ-ορούω to leap out of.

ἐξ-ορύσσω to dig out or up.

ἐξ-οστρακίζω to banish by ostracism.

ἐξ-οτρύνω to excite.

ἐξ-ουδενέω, -όω, ἐξ-ου-θενέω to set at naught, to despise.

ἐξ-ουσία, ἡ means, fortune; right, power, per-mission, liberty; free will; authority, rule; magistrate, government; abundance.

ἐξ-ουσιάζω to have power or authority.

ἐξ-οφέλλω to increase abundantly. [minence.]

ἐξ-οχή, ἡ preference, pro-)

ἔξ-οχος 2 prominent; excellent; ἔξοχον *adv.* with *gen.* eminent among.

ἐξ-υβρίζω to become insolent; to do mischief; to revolt. [from under.]

ἐξ-υπανίσταμαι to rise)

ἐξ-ύπερθε *adv.* from above.

ἐξ-υπηρετέω to be quite at one's service. [sleep.]

ἐξ-υπνίζω to rouse from)

ἔξ-υπνος 2 awakened.

ἐξ-υφαίνω to weave to the end. [the way.]

ἐξ-υφηγέομαι *M.* to lead)

ἔξω *adv.* and *prp.* with *gen.* on the outside, without, outwards, outside of; beyond; far from, except.

ἔξωθεν *adv.* from without; without.

ἐξ-ωθέω to thrust out, to chase, drive, expel; to delay: to reject.

ἐξ-ώλεια, ἡ utter ruin.

ἐξ-ώλης 2 quite ruined.

ἐξωμιδο-ποιΐα, ἡ the making of ἐξωμίδες.

ἐξ-ωμίς, ίδος, ἡ short sleeveless coat.

ἐξ-ωνέομαι *M.* to buy off, to buy in advance; to ransom, redeem.

ἔξ-ωρος 2 untimely; inconvenient.

ἐξ-ώστης, ου, ὁ adverse.

ἐξωτάτω outermost.

ἐξώτερος 3 outer.

ἔοικα see εἴκω.

ἔολπα see ἔλπω.

ἔοργα see ἔρδω.

ἑορτάζω to keep a festival.

ἑορτή, ἡ feast, festival, holiday; amusement.

ἑός, ἑή, ἑόν his, hers, his or her own. [ult in.]

ἐπ-αγάλλομαι M. to ex-

ἐπ-αγγελίᾱ, ἡ announcement; promise.

ἐπ-αγγέλλω to announce, tell, proclaim, make known; to promise; to enjoin, command; to demand, ask. — M. to promise, offer; to profess (a calling); to claim; to command.

ἐπ-άγγελμα, τό promise; profession, business.

ἐπ-αγείρω to gather together. — M. to assemble in crowds. [thering.]

ἐπ-άγερσις, ιος, ἡ a ga-

ἐπ-αγῑνέω = ἐπάγω. [in.]

ἐπ-αγλαΐζομαι M. to exult

ἐπ-άγω to lead, bring, or drive to or on; to add; to apply; to impel, cause, instigate, seduce; intr. to march up, advance. — M. to bring or draw to oneself; to call to aid; to mention, quote; to procure; to bring on oneself.

ἐπ-αγωγή, ἡ a bringing on; an advancing, attack.

ἐπ-αγωγός 2 seductive.

ἐπ-αγωνίζομαι M. to contend for a thing.

ἐπ-ᾴδω to sing to; to lead the song; to charm by singing; to heal by incantations.

ἐπ-αείρω = ἐπαίρω.

ἐπ-αέξω to make thrive.

ἐπ-αθροίζομαι P. to assemble in crowds.

ἐπ-αιγίζω to rush upon.

ἐπ-αιδέομαι P. to be ashamed of.

ἐπ-αινέτης, ου, ὁ praiser, panegyrist.

ἐπ-αινέω to approve, sanction; to consent (to); to praise, commend; to thank, congratulate; to advise, persuade.

ἐπ-αίνημι = ἐπαινέω.

ἔπ-αινος, ὁ praise, eulogy; panegyric; reward.

ἐπ-αινός 3 awful.

ἐπ-αίρω to lift up, to set up; to excite, rouse, instigate; to seduce, induce; to exalt, to make haughty or wanton; intr. to raise oneself. — P. to be excited, induced, or impelled; to rise, to be roused, to be wanton or haughty; to exult in, to be proud.

ἐπ-αισθάνομαι M. to perceive, feel; to learn, hear.

ἐπ-αΐσσω to rush or dart upon, to assail. — M. to rush upon. [known.]

ἐπ-άϊστος 2 heard of,

ἐπ-αισχύνομαι P. to be ashamed of.

ἐπ-αιτέω to demand in addition; to solicit, beg.

ἐπ-αιτιάομαι M. to state

as a cause; to bring a charge against; to accuse.

ἐπ-αίτιος 2 guilty; blamed for.

ἐπ-αΐω to hear, listen to; to perceive, understand; to be expert (in).

ἐπ-ακολουθέω to follow, attend, join; to be attached (to); to yield; to understand.

ἐπ-ακούω to listen to; to obey.   [ken or listen to.

ἐπ-ακροάομαι M. to hear-

ἐπ-ακτήρ, ῆρος, ὁ huntsman.   [shore.

ἐπ-άκτιος 3 and 2 on the

ἐπ-ακτός 3 imported, foreign, alien.   [canoe.

ἐπ-ακτρίς, ίδος, ἡ boat.

ἐπ-αλαλάζω to raise the war-cry.   [about.

ἐπ-αλάομαι P. to wander

ἐπ-αλαστέω to be vexed or troubled at.

ἐπ-αλείφω to besmear.

ἐπ-αλέξω to defend; to assist.

ἐπ-αληθεύω to verify.

ἐπ-αλλαγή, ἡ mutual union, exchange. [interchange.

ἐπ-αλλάσσω to exchange,

ἐπ-άλληλος 2 mutual.

ἔπ-αλξις, ἡ parapet; defence.   [together.

ἐπ-αμάομαι M. to heap up

ἐπ-αμείβω to change; to exchange. [see ἐφάπτω.

ἐπ-αμμένος = ἐφημμένος,

ἐπ-αμοιβαδίς adv. alternately. [fender, helper.

ἐπ-αμύντωρ, ορος, ὁ de-

ἐπ-αμύνω to defend, help.

ἐπ-αμφοτερίζω to doubt,

hesitate. to be inclined to both sides.

ἐπ-άν, ἐπήν = ἐπειδάν.

ἐπ-αναβαίνω to go up; to mount (on horse-back).

ἐπ-αναβιβάζω to cause to mount. [thrown over.

ἐπ-αναβληδόν adv. being

ἐπ-αναγκάζω to force, compel.

ἐπ-ανάγκες adv. necessarily, on compulsion.

ἐπ-ανάγω to lead or bring up; to put to sea; to excite; to lead or bring back: intr. to return. — P. to put to sea; to set sail against; to be carried to.

ἐπ-αναγωγή a sailing out, attack.

ἐπ-αναίρω and M. to lift up against; to rise one or one against the other.

ἐπ-αναλαμβάνω to resume, repeat.

ἐπ-αναμένω to stay on.

ἐπ-αναμιμνήσκω to remind one again.

ἐπ-αναπαύομαι to repose upon; to rely on.

ἐπ-αναπλέω, -πλώω to sail up against; to sail back; to overflow.

ἐπ-ανάσεισις, ἡ a brandishing.

ἐπ-ανάστασις, ἡ subversion; a rising up, rebellion. [or wheel round.

ἐπ-αναστρέφω to turn

ἐπ-ανατείνω to hold up to.

ἐπ-ανατέλλω to rise.

ἐπ-ανατίθημι to put upon; to shut again.

ἐπ-αναφέρω to bring back; to refer to; to report; to return.

ἐπ-αναχωρέω to retreat.

ἐπ-αναχώρησις, ἡ retreat.

ἐπ-άνειμι to go up; to return, go back.

ἐπ-ανειπεῖν to proclaim in addition.

ἐπ-ανέρομαι, -είρομαι M. = ἐπανερωτάω.

ἐπ-ανέρχομαι = ἐπάνειμι.

ἐπ-ανερωτάω to question again. [again.]

ἐπ-ανήκω to come back

ἐπ-ανθέω to bloom; to appear on the surface.

ἐπ-ανίημι to let loose; to incite; to abandon.

ἐπ-ανισόω to make equal.

ἐπ-ανίσταμαι M. to stand upon; to rise, stand up; to revolt.

ἐπ-άνοδος, ἡ return.

ἐπ-ανορθόω and M. to set up, set upright; to re-establish; to amend, improve, correct.

ἐπ-ανόρθωμα, τό, ἐπ-ανόρθωσις, ἡ a correcting, improving.

ἐπ-άντης 2 steep, rugged.

ἐπ-αντλέω to draw (water); to pour over.

ἐπ-άνω adv. above; formerly; superior to.

ἐπ-άνωθεν adv. from above, from the inland.

ἐπ-άξιος 3 worthy, deserving; suitable.

ἐπ-αξιόω to appreciate, to think worthy, right, or meet.

ἐπ-αοιδή = ἐπῳδή.

ἐπ-απειλέω to threaten besides.

ἐπ-αρά, ἡ curse.

ἐπ-αράομαι M. to wish one an evil, to curse.

ἐπ-αραρίσκω to fasten to; to fit upon; intr. to be fit.

ἐπ-αράσσω to dash in(to) pieces.

ἐπ-άρατος 2 accursed.

ἐπ-άργυρος 2 overlaid with silver, silver-mounted.

ἐπ-αρήγω to help, assist.

ἐπ-άρκεια, ἡ, ἐπ-άρκεσις, ἡ help, aid, assistance.

ἐπ-αρκέω to suffice; to remain valid; to help, aid, assist; to supply, furnish; to hinder, prevent. [ciently.]

ἐπ-αρκούντως adv. suffi-

ἐπ-άρουρος, ὁ rustic serf.

ἐπ-αρτάομαι P. to impend.

ἐπ-αρτής 2 ready.

ἐπ-αρτύω, -ύνω to fix to.

ἐπ-αρχιά, ἡ prefecture, province. [vernor.]

ἔπ-αρχος, ὁ prefect, go-

ἐπ-άρχω to rule, govern. — M. to begin a libation.

ἐπ-αρωγός, ὁ helper.

ἐπ-ασκέω to work carefully, to practice.

ἐπ-ασσύτερος 3 crowded, one upon another.

ἐπ-άσσω = ἐπαΐσσω. [upon.]

ἐπ-αυδάω and M. to call

ἐπ-αυλίζομαι M. and P. to pass the night near.

ἔπ-αυλις, ἡ dwelling, quarters. [dwelling.]

ἔπ-αυλος, ὁ fold, stable;

ἐπ-αυξάνω, ἐπ-αύξω to increase, enlarge, augment.

10*

ἐπ-αύρεσις, ἡ enjoyment, fruit.

ἐπ-αύριον adv. to-morrow.

ἐπ-αυρίσκω to touch; to reach; to enjoy, taste, share. — M. to obtain; to involve oneself in; to enjoy, reap.

ἐπ-αυχέω to exult in, boast of.

ἐπ-αΰω to shout to.

ἐπ-αφρίζω to foam up.

ἐπ-αφρόδιτος 2 lovely, charming. [in addition.]

ἐπ αφύσσω to pour over}

ἐπ-αχθής 2 onerous; troublesome, grievous.

ἐπεάν = ἐπάν. [mock at.]

ἐπ-εγγελάω to laugh at,}

ἐπ-εγείρω to arouse, awaken; to excite. — P. to be roused; to awake.

ἐπ-έδρη, ἡ = ἐφέδρα.

ἐπεί conj. when, after that, since; as soon as; as often as; because, seeing that, for that; although; since really.

ἐπείγω to press, urge, pursue, drive, hasten, manage, forward, speed. — P. to be pressed upon; to hurry; to long for. ἐπεί.}

ἐπειδάν, ἐπειδή conj. =}

ἐπειδήπερ, ἐπειή conj. since really.

ἐπ-εικάζω to conjecture.

ἔπ-ειμι¹ (ἐπεῖναι) to be upon or at, to be fixed upon; to be existing, at hand, or forth-coming; to be set over; to be added; to live after, to be left.

ἔπ-ειμι² (ἐπιέναι) to go or come to or upon; to go through; to approach, to advance against, to attack; to befall, to enter one's mind; to impend.

ἐπ-ειπεῖν aor. to say besides, to add.

ἐπείπερ conj. since really.

ἐπ-είρομαι = ἐπέρομαι.

ἐπ-ειρύω = ἐπερύω.

ἐπ-ειρωτάω, -έω = ἐπερωτάω.

ἐπ-εισαγωγή, ἡ introduction, a bringing in besides; entrance.

ἐπ-εισαγώγιμος 2, ἐπ-είσακτος 2 brought in from abroad.

ἐπ-εισβαίνω to step in also. [again.]

ἐπ-εισβάλλω to invade}

ἐπ-είσειμι, ἐπεισέρχομαι to enter besides, likewise, or after; to come in or on; to appear. [entrance.}

ἐπ-είσοδος, ἡ intervention;}

ἐπ-εισπίπτω to fall in or to invade besides; to fall upon.

ἐπ-εισπλέω to sail in or on besides; to sail in against, to attack.

ἐπ-εισφέρω to bring in besides. — M. to bring in for oneself. — P. to intervene.

ἐπ-εισφρέω to let in after.

ἔπ-ειτα adv. thereupon, thereafter, then, thenceforward; further; therefore; nevertheless.

ἐπεί-τε = ἐπεί τε since, because.

ἔπειτεν = ἔπειτα.

ἐπ-εκβαίνω to disembark besides. [to aid.]

ἐπ-εκβοηθέω to come out to aid.

ἐπ-εκδιδάσκω to teach thoroughly in addition.

ἐπ-εκδιηγέομαι = ἐπεκδιδάσκω.

ἐπ-εκδρομή, ἡ excursion, expedition. [yond.]

ἐπ-έκεινα adv. yonder, beyond.

ἐπ-εκθέω = ἐπεκτρέχω.

ἐπ-εκπλέω to sail out against. [out against.]

ἐπ-έκπλους, ὁ a sailing

ἐπ-εκτρέχω to rush or sally out to attack.

ἐπ-ελαύνω to drive upon or over; to beat out on the surface; to lead on; intr. to come, march, or drive up, to approach.

ἐπ-ελπίζω to lead to hope.

ἐπ-εμβαίνω to step on or in; to stand upon; to tread down, insult.

ἐπ-εμβάλλω to put on besides; to add; to offer; to flow in besides. [man.]

ἐπ-εμβάτης, ου, ὁ horse-

ἐπ-εμπίπτω to fall in.

ἐπ-εναρίζω to slay besides.

ἐπ-ενδύνω, ἐπ-ενδύομαι to put on besides.

ἐπ-ενδύτης, ου, ὁ upper garment. [grown upon.]

ἐπ-ενήνοθα perf. to have

ἐπ-ενθρῴσκω to leap or rush upon.

ἐπ-εντανύω, ἐπ-εντείνω to stretch upon. — P. to lean upon. [sides.]

ἐπ-εντέλλω to enjoin be-

ἐπ-εντύνω, -τύω to prepare, equip. — P. to be ready.

ἐπ-εξάγω to lead out against; to lengthen a front line; intr. to march out. [ing.]

ἐπ-εξαγωγή, ἡ a lengthen-

ἐπ-έξειμι = ἐπεξέρχομαι.

ἐπ-εξελαύνω to drive on against.

ἐπ-εξεργάζομαι to do besides; to slay once more.

ἐπ-εξέρχομαι to go out against, to advance against; to march out, to sally forth, attack; to punish, proceed against, pursue; to go on, wander through; to go through, inspect; to execute.

ἐπ-εξέτασις, ἡ repeated inspection. [besides.]

ἐπ-εξευρίσκω to invent

ἐπ-εξῆς = ἐφεξῆς.

ἐπ-εξόδια, τά sacrifice at a departure. [against.]

ἐπ-έξοδος, ἡ a march out

ἐπ-έοικα perf. to be like; to be likely; to be convenient, fitting, or reasonable.

ἐπ-εργάζομαι M. to cultivate.

ἐπ-εργασίᾱ, ἡ unlawful cultivation of sacred land.

ἐπ-ερείδω to urge on, to apply vast strength to.

ἐπ-ερέφω to roof a building.

ἐπ-έρομαι M. = ἐπερωτάω.

ἐπ-ερύω to draw or pull on or up. — M. to draw on oneself.

ἐπ-έρχομαι to go or come up, towards, forward, or on,

to approach, attack; to occur, befall, come into one's mind; to go over; to visit; to go through, examine; to execute; to be at hand, impend.

ἐπ-ερωτάω to question, ask; to inquire of again; to consult.

ἐπ-ερώτημα, τό, ἐπ-ερώτησις, ἡ question, inquiry; demand.

ἐπεσ-βολία, ἡ forward talk.

ἐπεσ-βόλος 2 talking idly.

ἐπ-εσθίω to eat besides.

ἐπ-έτειος, ἐπ-έτεος 2 and 3 lasting the whole year; yearly.   [servant.

ἐπέτης, ου, ὁ attendant,

ἐπ-ετήσιος 2 = ἐπέτειος.

ἐπ-ευθύνω to direct upon.

ἐπ-ευφημέω to applaud; to demand aloud; to shout assent.

ἐπ-εύχομαι M. to pray at; to invoke; to wish; to accurse; to boast, exult, triumph.

ἐπ-έχω to have or hold upon; to place upon; to hold out, present, offer; to have opposite oneself; to keep shut; to hold fast, retain, hinder; to delay, retard; to reach to, extend; to have in one's power. — intr. to be intent upon, to turn one's mind to; to stop, stay, wait; to desist, hold back. — M. to aim at; to put (to the lips); to offer; to delay.

ἐπήβολος 2 partaking of, master of.

ἐπ-ηγκενίς, ίδος, ἡ plank of a ship.

ἐπ-ηγορεύω, -έω to reproach, upbraid.

ἐπηετανός 2 and 3 lasting; abundant, plentiful.

ἐπ-ήκοος 2 listening to; audible; within hearing.

ἐπ-ηλυγάζομαι M. to overshadow; to hide oneself.

ἔπ-ηλυς, υδος, ἐπ-ηλύτης, ου one coming, immigrant, foreigner.   [changing.

ἐπ-ημοιβός 2 in turn,

ἐπ-ημύω to drop or sink at.

ἐπήν = ἐπάν.   [plaud.

ἐπ-ηπύω to shout to, ap-

ἐπ-ήρατος 2 lovely, charming.

ἐπ-ηρεάζω to mortify; to revile, abuse, insult; to threaten.

ἐπ-ήρεια, ἡ insult, malice.

ἐπ-ήρετμος 2 rowing; furnished with oars.

ἐπ-ηρεφής 2 hanging over, covering; steep.

ἐπητής, οῦ considerate; kind.   [crowds.

ἐπ-ήτριμος 2 close, in

ἐπητύς, ύος, ἡ kindness.

ἐπ-ηχέω to re-echo.

ἐπί adv. on, at, or to it; afterwards, then; on the contrary; besides. — prp. with gen. on, upon, at, by, near, with; towards; in presence of; during, in the time of; over; with regard to, concerning; on the ground of. — with dat. on, in, at, near, beside; upon; after; towards; against;

during, in the time of; immediately after; in addition to; by reason of, on the ground of, for the purpose of, for the sake of, in respect to; in honour of, on condition of; in the power or under the rule of. — with *acc.* extending over, towards, up to; against; until; (with numbers) about, nearly; during; in quest of.

ἔπι = ἔπεστι it is there or at hand.

ἐπ-ιάλλω to send to; to lay on; to cause. [μαι.]

ἐπι-άλμενος see ἐφάλλο-)

ἐπι-ανδάνω = ἐφανδάνω.

ἐπ-ιάχω to shout to; to shout aloud. [fare.]

ἐπί-βαθρον, τό passenger's)

ἐπι-βαίνω to tread or walk upon; to go up, mount, ascend; to go over, to cross, to arrive at; to set on, attack, fall upon. — *trans.* to cause to mount, to bring, put, or send upon; to make arrive at.

ἐπι-βάλλω to throw, cast, or lay upon; to put on; *intr.* to go towards; to fall upon, to attack; to think of; to fall to, to be due. — *M.* to put upon oneself; to take upon oneself; to desire (earnestly), covet.

ἐπι-βαρέω to burden.

ἐπί-βασις, ἡ attack; approach; occasion, motive.

ἐπι-βάσκω to lead into.

ἐπι-βατεύω to be a sailor or passenger; to tread

upon; to mount; to lean upon.

ἐπι-βάτης, ου, ὁ horseman; sailor; naval soldier; passenger.

ἐπι-βατός 3 accessible.

ἐπι-βήτωρ, ορος, ὁ one who mounts; male animal, boar, bull. [cend.]

ἐπι-βιβάζω to cause to as-)

ἐπι-βιόω to live through; to survive; to live to see.

ἐπι-βλέπω to look at or upon, to regard.

ἐπί-βλημα, τό patch.

ἐπι-βλής, ῆτος, ὁ bar, bolt.

ἐπι-βοάω and *M.* to cry out to; to call to aid, invoke; to decry.

ἐπι-βοήθεια, ἡ succour, a coming to aid.

ἐπι-βοηθέω to come to aid.

ἐπι-βόημα, τό a call to.

ἐπι-βόητος 2 decried, ill spoken of.

ἐπι-βολή, ἡ a throwing or putting on; attack; attempt, project; cover; layer; penalty. [herdsman.]

ἐπι-βουκόλος, ὁ cowherd)

ἐπι-βουλευτής, οῦ, ὁ insidious foe.

ἐπι-βουλεύω to plot or plan against, to lay snares; to lie in wait for; to have a mind to, to intend, aim at.

ἐπι-βουλή, ἡ plot, plan against; treachery, deceit; wait, snare.

ἐπί-βουλος 2 plotting against, insidious. [into)

ἐπι-βρέμω to roar over or)

ἐπι-βρίθω to weigh down.

ἐπι-βρόντητος 2 stunned.

ἐπι-βώτωρ, ορος, ὁ shepherd.

ἐπί-γαιος 2 = ἐπίγειος.

ἐπι-γαμβρεύω to marry the brother's widow.

ἐπι-γαμίᾱ, ἡ intermarriage.

ἐπί-γαμος 2 marriageable.

ἐπι-γδουπέω to thunder at.

ἐπί-γειος 2 on the earth, earthly.

ἐπι-γελάω to laugh at or about.

ἐπι-γίγνομαι M. to be born, to come or live after; to follow, elapse; to approach, come, happen; to fall upon, attack.

ἐπι-γιγνώσκω to recognize, know exactly, observe; to discover, become conscious of; to contrive; to decide.

ἐπι-γνάμπτω to bend; to make one alter his intentions. [overseer.]

ἐπι-γνώμων 2 arbiter;}

ἐπί-γνωσις, ἡ knowledge.

ἐπί-γονος 3 born after.

ἐπι-γουνίς, ίδος, ἡ thigh.

ἐπι-γράβδην adv. scratching.

ἐπί-γραμμα, τό. ἐπι-γραφή, ἡ inscription, epigram.

ἐπι-γράφω to scratch (the surface), to graze; to write upon, inscribe; to order by letter; to enter in a register. — M. to paint on for oneself.

ἐπι-γρῡπος 2 with a crooked beak.

ἐπί-δαμος 2 = ἐπιδήμιος.

ἐπι-δαψιλεύομαι M. to give abundantly in addition. [of; less.]

ἐπι-δεής 2 needy, in want}

ἐπί-δειγμα, τό specimen, example, pattern.

ἐπι-δείκνῡμι, -ύω to show forth, exhibit, to show as a pattern; to represent; to demonstrate, prove. — M. to show oneself, to make oneself seen or heard.

ἐπι-δεικτικός 3 showy, for display.

ἐπί-δειξις, ἡ a showing, exhibition, display; review; specimen, pattern; panegyric; proof.

ἐπι-δέκατος 3 the tenth part; one and one tenth.

ἐπι-δέχομαι = ἐπιδέχομαι.

ἐπι-δέξιος 2 to the right.

ἐπί-δεξις, ἡ = ἐπιδειξις.

ἐπι-δέρκομαι to look at.

ἐπι-δευής 2 = ἐπιδεής.

ἐπι-δεύομαι = ἐπιδέομαι, see ἐπιδέω.

ἐπι-δέχομαι M. to receive or admit in addition.

ἐπι-δέω¹ to bind on; to bandage.

ἐπι-δέω² to want, lack. — P. to be in want of, to need; to fall short of, to be inferior (to).

ἐπί-δηλος 2 manifest, plain, conspicuous, known.

ἐπι-δημέω, -εύω to be at home; to return home; to be a stranger in a place.

ἐπι-δήμιος 2 living at home, native; spread among the people; living as a stranger.

ἐπι-δημιουργός, ὁ controller of magistrates.

ἐπί-δημος 2 = ἐπιδήμιος.

ἐπι-διαβαίνω to cross over in addition or one after the other. [sider anew.]

ἐπι-διαγινώσκω to con-)

ἐπι-διαιρέω to distribute. — M. to share among themselves. [finally.]

ἐπι-διακρίνω to decide)

ἐπι-διατάσσομαι to command besides.

ἐπι-διαφέρω to carry across after. [addition.]

ἐπι-διδάσκω to teach in)

ἐπι-δίδωμι to give besides; to give with; to deliver, yield. — intr. to increase, improve, grow. — M. to add; to present.

ἐπι-δίζημαι M. to seek or inquire for besides.

ἐπι-δῑνέω to swing round. — P. to move in a circle. — M. to reflect upon.

ἐπι-διορθόω to set fully in order.

ἐπι-διφριάς,άδος,ἡ chariot-rail. [chariot-seat.]

ἐπι-δίφριος 2 on the)

ἐπι-διώκω to pursue further.

ἐπί-δοξος 2 causing expectation; to be expected, likely.

ἐπί-δοσις, ἡ addition, contribution; increase, progress.

ἐπι-δοχή, ἡ reception after.

ἐπι-δρομή, ἡ inroad, raid.

ἐπί-δρομος 2 to be taken by storm, assailable.

ἐπι-δύω to go down or set upon.

ἐπι-είκεια, ἡ propriety, decency; equity, fairness; clemency.

ἐπι-είκελος 2 like.

ἐπι-εικής 2 fitting, suitable; fair, decent; moderate, kind; proper, fit; likely; ἐπιεικῶς properly, justly; in some respect, in a certain manner.

ἐπι-εικτός 3 yielding; to be conquered.

ἐπι-έλπομαι M. to hope for.

ἐπι-έννῡμι to put on over.

ἐπι-ζάφελος 2 vehement, furious.

ἐπι-ζάω = ἐπιβιόω.

ἐπι-ζεύγνῡμι,-ύω to fasten or join to.

ἐπι-ζεφύριος 2 towards the west, occidental.

ἐπι-ζέω to boil or flash up; to inflame.

ἐπι-ζήμιος 2 hurtful.

ἐπι-ζημιόω to punish.

ἐπι ζητέω to seek for or after; to long, wish, or crave for, covet.

ἐπι-ζώννῡμι to gird on.

ἐπι-ζώω = ἐπιζάω.

ἐπι-ήρανος 2, ἐπί-ηρος 2 pleasing, pleasant.

ἐπι-θαλασσίδιος 2, ἐπι-θαλάσσιος 2 and 3 lying on the sea. [to death.]

ἐπι-θανάτιος 2 condemned)

ἐπι-θαρσύνω to encourage.

ἐπι-θειάζω to invoke the gods; to adjure.

ἐπι-θειασμός, ὁ adjuration.

ἐπι-θεραπεύω to be compliant or courteous; to be intent on.

ἐπί-θεσις, ἡ a laying upon; attack.

ἐπι-θεσπίζω to pronounce oracles. [tack.]

ἐπι-θετικός 3 ready to at-

ἐπί-θετος 2 added; not natural, affected, studied.

ἐπι-θέω to run at or after.

ἐπί-θημα, τό cover, lid.

ἐπι-θορυβέω to make a noise at; to applaud.

ἐπι-θρῴσκω to leap upon.

ἐπι-θῡμέω to desire, long for, wish. covet.

ἐπι-θῡμητής,οῦ,ὁ desirous; lover, adherent.

ἐπι-θῡμητικός 3 desiring.

ἐπι-θῡμίᾱ, ἡ desire, longing. wish; lust.

ἐπι-θῡμίᾱμα, τό incense.

ἐπ-ῑθύνω to direct against.

ἐπι-θύω to sacrifice after.

ἐπ-ῑθύω to rush at.

ἐπι-θωΰσσω to ring to; to shout to.

ἐπι-ίστωρ, ορος acquainted with; accomplice.

ἐπι-καθαιρέω to demolish completely.

ἐπι-κάθημαι to sit upon; to weigh upon; to besiege.

ἐπι-καθίζω to set upon; to sit upon.

ἐπι-καθίσταμαι M. to put down for oneself.

ἐπι-καίριος 2 seasonable, fit, convenient; necessary; considerable, important, chief.

ἐπί-καιρος 2 seasonable, convenient, fit, proper.

ἐπι-καίω to kindle or burn at.

ἐπι-καλέω to summon, call in; to invoke; to give a surname; to accuse, reproach. — M. to call to oneself, to call to aid; to challenge.

ἐπι-κάλυμμα, τό covering, cloak. [hide.]

ἐπι-καλύπτω to cover up,]

ἐπι-καμπή, ἡ bend, curve, projection. [wheel round.]

ἐπι-κάμπτω to bend; to]

ἐπι-κάρσιος 2 head foremost; sideways, crosswise, at an angle. [against.]

ἐπι-καταβαίνω to go down]

ἐπι-κατάγομαι P. to come to land afterwards.

ἐπι-καταδαρθάνω to fall asleep at. [flow besides.]

ἐπι-κατακλύζω to over-]

ἐπι-κατακοιμάομαι P. to lie down to sleep upon.

ἐπι-καταλαμβάνω to overtake, to catch up. [longer.]

ἐπι-καταμένω to stay yet]

ἐπι-κατάρατος 2 accursed.

ἐπι-καταρριπτέω to throw down after.

ἐπι-κατασφάζω,-σφάττω to kill upon or at.

ἐπι-καταψεύδομαι M. to tell lies in addition.

ἐπι-κάτειμι to go down.

ἐπί-καυτος 2 burnt at the end.

ἐπί-κειμαι M. to be laid or to lie upon, in, at, or near; to entreat; to press upon, to attack; to impend; to be imposed.

ἐπι-κείρω to cut, mow off or down; to baffle.

ἐπι-κελαδέω to shout at.

ἐπι-κέλευσις, ἡ exhortation, cheer. [exhort.]

ἐπι-κελεύω and M. to cheer,

ἐπι-κέλλω to drive to the shore; to come ashore.

ἐπι-κέλομαι M. to call upon or to. [to mix after.]

ἐπι-κεράννυμι to mix in;

ἐπι-κερδία, ἡ profit in trade. [tease.]

ἐπι-κερτομέω to scoff; to

ἐπι-κεύθω to hide from.

ἐπι-κηρῡκείᾱ, ἡ negotiation through heralds.

ἐπι-κηρῡκεύομαι M. to send message by a herald; to treat, transact.

ἐπι-κηρύσσω to proclaim publicly.

ἐπι-κίδνημι to spread over.
— M. to be extended over.

ἐπι-κίνδῡνος 2 dangerous; in danger. [νυμι.]

ἐπι-κίρνημι = ἐπικεράν-

ἐπι-κλάω to break, bend, move; to dispirit. [more.]

ἐπι-κλείω to extol the

ἐπί-κλημα, τό reproach, accusation. [and heiress.]

ἐπί-κληρος, ἡ daughter

ἐπί-κλησις, ἡ surname; name.

ἐπί-κλητος 2 called, assembled; called to aid.

ἐπι-κλῑνής 2 sloping, steep.

ἐπι-κλίνω to bend towards, to lay upon; intr. to recline, to turn.

ἐπί-κλοπος 2 thievish: wily, cunning.

ἐπι-κλύζω to overflow.

ἐπί-κλυσις, ἡ flood, overflow.

ἐπι-κλύω to listen to.

ἐπι-κλώθω to spin to; to assign, allot.

ἐπί-κοινος 2 common.

ἐπι-κοινόω to communicate. [common with.]

ἐπι-κοινωνέω to have in

ἐπι-κομπέω to boast.

ἐπι-κόπτω to slay.

ἐπι-κοσμέω to adorn; to celebrate.

ἐπι-κουρέω to help, assist, to serve as a mercenary; to keep off from.

ἐπι-κούρημα, τό protection.

ἐπι-κουρία, ἡ help, auxiliary forces. [auxiliary.]

ἐπι-κουρικός 3 helping,

ἐπί-κουρος 2 helping, assisting. [to lift up.]

ἐπι-κουφίζω to relieve;

ἐπι-κραίνω, -κραιαίνω to accomplish, fulfil.

ἐπι-κράτεια, ἡ dominion, supremacy; reach.

ἐπι-κρατέω to prevail over, conquer, overcome; to obtain, achieve; to rule, govern. [torious, violent.]

ἐπι-κρατής 2 superior, vic-

ἐπι-κράτησις, ἡ an overcoming, overwhelming.

ἐπι-κρεμάννυμαι, -κρέμαμαι P. to impend over, to threaten.

ἐπι-κρίνω to decide.

ἐπ-ίκριον, τό sail-yard.

ἐπι-κρύπτω to hide, conceal. — M. to hide oneself.

ἐπι-κτάομαι M. to gain besides; to win; to enlarge.

ἐπι-κτείνω to kill anew.

ἐπί-κτησις, ἡ new gain.

ἐπί-κτητος 2 gained besides, acquired.

ἐπι-κῦδής 2 glorious, splendid; important.

ἐπι-κυΐσκομαι to become doubly pregnant. [upon.]

ἐπι-κυλινδέω to roll (down)

ἐπι-κύπτω to stoop down over. [to meet.]

ἐπι-κῦρέω to fall in with;

ἐπι-κῦρόω to confirm, ratify; determine.

ἐπι-κωκύω to lament at.

ἐπι-κωμῳδέω to mock at.

ἐπι-λαγχάνω to come last (by lot).

ἐπι-λαμβάνω to take or seize besides; to lay hold of, catch, oppress, attack; to retain; to prevent; to fall in with, to live to see; to reach to. — M. to seize, hold fast; to keep to; to attack; to blame, chide; to object to; to fall in with, get possession of.

ἐπί-λαμπτος 2 = ἐπιλημπτος. [to dawn.]

ἐπι-λάμπω to shine again;

ἐπι-λανθάνομαι M. to cause to forget; to forget; to conceal.

ἐπι-λεαίνω to smooth over; to make plausible.

ἐπι-λέγω to say at or besides; to add; to name; to select, pick out. — M. to collect, choose for one-

self; to read; to think over; to care for; to fear.

ἐπι-λείβω to pour upon.

ἐπι-λείπω to leave behind; to omit; intr. to fail, to be gone or wanting; to give out; to be dried up. — P. to be left.

ἐπι-λείχω to lick.

ἐπί-λειψις, ἡ failure.

ἐπί-λεκτος 2 chosen.

ἐπι-λεύσσω to look before one. [forget.]

ἐπί-ληθος 2 causing to

ἐπι-λήθω = ἐπιλανθάνομαι.

ἐπι-ληΐς, ΐδος, ἡ captured.

ἐπι-ληκέω to applaud by measure.

ἐπί-ληπτος 2 caught (at it).

ἐπι-λησμονή, ἡ forgetfulness. [unmindful.]

ἐπι-λήσμων 2 forgetful;

ἐπι-λίγδην adv. scratching.

ἐπ-ιλλίζω to wink at.

ἐπι-λογίζομαι M. and P. to reflect (upon), consider.

ἐπί-λογος, ὁ consideration; conclusion.

ἐπί-λοιπος 2 still left; future. [sides.]

ἐπι-λῦπέω to grieve be-

ἐπι-λύω to loose; to decide; to refute. — M. to release, protect.

ἐπι-λωβεύω to mock at.

ἐπι-μαίνομαι P. and M. to be mad after.

ἐπι-μαίομαι M. to touch, feel; to seize; to strive after, aim at.

ἐπι-μανθάνω to learn after.

ἐπι-μαρτύρέω to bear witness (to).

ἐπι-μαρτῠρίᾰ, ἡ a calling to witness.

ἐπι-μαρτύρομαι M. to call to witness; to conjure, implore.

ἐπι-μάρτῠρος 2 witness.

ἐπι-μάσσομαι fut. of ἐπιμαίομαι.

ἐπι-μαστος 2 dirty, squalid.

ἐπι-μαχέω to protect in arms.　[liance.]

ἐπι-μαχίᾱ, ἡ defensive al-

ἐπί-μαχος 2 assailable.

ἐπι-μειδάω, -μειδιάω to smile at.

ἐπι-μέλεια, ἡ care, diligence, attention; training, practice; direction, management; respect.

ἐπι-μελέομαι P. to take care of, pay attention to; to manage, superintend; to take pains, to toil; to respect.

ἐπι-μελής 2 caring for, careful, zealous; causing care, object of care.

ἐπι-μελητής, οῦ, ὁ provider, guardian; manager, superintendent.

ἐπι-μέλομαι = ἐπιμελέομαι.　[after.]

ἐπι-μέμονα perf. to strive]

ἐπι-μέμφομαι M. to find fault (with), to blame, grumble at, complain.

ἐπι-μένω to stay on; to adhere to; to tarry, wait; to expect. [send for after.]

ἐπι-μεταπέμπομαι M. to]

ἐπι-μετρέω to measure out to.　[against.]

ἐπι-μήδομαι M. to devise]

ἐπι-μήνιος 2 monthly.

ἐπι-μηνίω to be angry.

ἐπι-μηχανάομαι M. to devise against; to devise besides.

ἐπι-μήχανος 2 contriver.

ἐπι-μίγνῡμι (-μείγν.) and M. to mix in or with; to converse; to meet.

ἐπι-μιμνήσκομαι P. to remember, recall to mind; to mention.

ἐπι-μίμνω = ἐπιμένω.

ἐπι-μίξ adv. mixedly.

ἐπι-μιξίᾱ, ἡ intercourse.

ἐπι-μίσγω = ἐπιμίγνυμι.

ἐπι-μονή, ἡ delay.

ἐπι-μύζω to murmur at.

ἐπί-νειον, τό anchorage, dock, port; arsenal.

ἐπι-νέμω to allot, distribute; to lead to pasture. — M. to graze; to devastate.

ἐπι-νεύω to nod at or to; to assent; to grant.

ἐπι-νέφελος 2 clouded.

ἐπι-νεφρίδιος 2 upon the kidneys.

ἐπι-νέω[1] to spin to.

ἐπι-νέω[2] to load with; to heap or pile up.

ἐπι-νίκειος 2 victorious.

ἐπι-νίκιος 2 belonging to victory.

ἐπι-νίσσομαι to go or flow over, overflow.

ἐπι-νοέω to think of; to contrive, devise; to observe, perceive.

ἐπί-νοια, ἡ thought, intention, project; a thinking; after-thought.

ἐπι-νύμφειος 2 bridal.

ἐπι-νωμάω to allot, distribute.

ἐπί-ξῡνος 2 = ἐπίκοινος.

ἐπι-ορκέω to swear falsely, to forswear oneself.

ἐπί-ορκος 2 perjured, forsworn; τὸ -ον false oath.

ἐπι-όσσομαι to look at.

ἐπί-ουρος, ὁ guard; ruler.

ἐπ-ιοῦσα, ἡ the coming day.

ἐπι-τούσιος 2 sufficient for the day, daily.

ἐπί-πᾱν adv. on the whole, generally. [besides.]

ἐπι-παρανέω to heap up]

ἐπι-παρασκευάζομαι M. to prepare besides.

ἐπι-πάρειμι[1] (-εῖναι) to be present or near.

ἐπι-πάρειμι[2] (-ιέναι) to come on too; to advance against; to march back; to march on the height alongside of. [upon.]

ἐπι-πάσσω to sprinkle]

ἐπί-πεδος 2 level, flat.

ἐπι-πείθομαι P. to be persuaded; to obey.

ἐπι-πέλομαι M. to come near, approach.

ἐπι-πέμπω to send besides or after; to send to.

ἐπί-πεμψις, ἡ a sending to.

ἐπι-πέτομαι M. to fly to.

ἐπι-πίλναμαι to approach.

ἐπι-πίνω to drink besides.

ἐπι-πίπτω to fall upon or into; to attack; to befall; to put to shore.

ἔπιπλα, τά movables, goods and chattels, furniture.

ἐπι-πλάζομαι P. to be driven or wander over.

ἐπί-πλεος 3 full.

ἐπί-πλευσις, ἡ a sailing against, naval attack.

ἐπι-πλέω to sail upon or with; to sail against.

ἐπι-πληρόω to man (a ship) anew.

ἐπι-πλήσσω to strike at; to blame, revile, reproach.

ἐπίπλοα = ἔπιπλα.

ἐπί-πλοος[1], ὁ caul.

ἐπί-πλοος[2], ὁ a sailing upon or against, attack of a fleet, naval expedition.

ἐπι-πλώω = ἐπιπλέω.

ἐπι-πνέω, -πνείω to breathe or blow upon; to blow at or after

ἐπι-πόδιος 3 upon the feet.

ἐπι-ποθέω to long or yearn for. [θία, ἡ a longing.]

ἐπι-πόθησις, ἡ, ἐπι-πο-]

ἐπι-πόθητος 2 longed for.

ἐπι-ποιμήν, ένος, ὁ, ἡ shepherd, shepherdess.

ἐπι-πολάζω to be on the surface (of); to get to the top, to prevail.

ἐπι-πολή, ἡ surface, top.

ἐπί-πολος, ὁ servant.

ἐπι-πονέω to persevere in work.

ἐπί-πονος 2 toilsome; portending toil.

ἐπι-πορεύομαι P. to march or travel to or against.

ἐπι-πρέπω to be prominent at, to be conspicuous.

ἐπι-προϊάλλω to send out or place before one.

ἐπι-προΐημι to send forth towards; to send out; to steer towards.

ἐπί-προσθεν *adv.* before, near; in the way.

ἐπι-πταίρω to sneeze at.

ἐπι-πωλέομαι *M.* to go about, to inspect.

ἐπι-πώλησις, ἡ review.

ἐπι-ρράπτω to sew on.

ἐπι-ρράσσω = ἐπιρρήσσω.

ἐπι-ρρέζω to sacrifice upon.

ἐπι-ρρέπω to bend towards; to sink down.

ἐπι-ρρέω to flow on the surface (of); to stream to.

ἐπι-ρρήσσω to dash against, to push forward violently; *intr.* to burst forth.

ἐπι-ρρίπτέω, -ρρίπτω to throw upon.

ἐπι-ρροθος[1] 2 reviling, scolding.   [tector.]

ἐπι-ρροθος[2] 2 aiding; pro-)

ἐπί-ρρυτος 2 watered.

ἐπι-ρρώννῡμι to strengthen, encourage. — *P.* to recover strength, take heart.

ἐπι-ρρώομαι *M.* to be active; to flow down. [den.]

ἐπί-σαγμα, τό load, bur-)

ἐπι-σάσσω to heap or load upon; to saddle. [against.]

ἐπι-σείω to shake at or)

ἐπι-σεύω to put in motion against, to incite. — *P.* to be stirred; to hurry or hasten towards; to rush at, attack.

ἐπι-σημαίνω to mark; to announce; to give a sign of approval; to appear as a sign or omen. — *M.* to mark with a sign for oneself.

ἐπί-σημον, τό mark, device; symbol, emblem.

ἐπι-σῑμόω to cause to turn sideways.

ἐπι-σῑτίζομαι *M.* to provide oneself with food; to forage.

ἐπι-σῑτισμός, ὁ a victualling, supplying with provisions.   [σκοπέω.]

ἐπι-σκέπτομαι *M.* = ἐπι-)

ἐπι-σκευάζω to prepare, fit out, get ready; to restore; to pack upon. — *M.* to prepare for oneself.

ἐπι-σκευή, ἡ repair, restoration; a raising up.

ἐπί-σκεψις, ἡ inspection; inquiry.   [tent, openly.]

ἐπί-σκηνος 2 before the)

ἐπι-σκηνόω to live in, to be immanent or inherent.

ἐπι-σκήπτω to impose on, enjoin; to implore, entreat; to wish one something; to accuse. — *M.* to refuse; to indict, summon.

ἐπι-σκιάζω to overshadow; to hide.   [shadowed.]

ἐπί-σκιος 2 shading; over-)

ἐπι-σκοπέω to look upon or at; to regard, review, inspect, visit, examine, consider; to pay attention to, to take care of.

ἐπι-σκοπή, ἡ visitation, inspection; office of an overseer or bishop.

ἐπί-σκοπος[1], ὁ overseer, guardian; bishop.

ἐπί-σκοπος[2] 2 hitting the mark; convenient.

ἐπι-σκοτέω to darken, overshade.   [furious.]

ἐπι-σκύζομαι *M.* to grow)

ἐπι-σκυθίζω to cause to drink in Scythian manner.

ἐπι-σκύνιον, τό skin of the brows. [mock at; to jest.]

ἐπι-σκώπτω to laugh or

ἐπι-σμυγερῶς adv. shamefully, miserably.

ἐπι-σπαστήρ, ῆρος, ὁ handle of the door. [oneself.]

ἐπί-σπαστος 2 drawn upon

ἐπι-σπάω to draw upon; to drag on; to pull to; to seize; to gain; to draw along. — M. to draw to oneself, to induce, seduce; to obtain.

ἐπι-σπείρω to sow upon.

ἐπί-σπεισις, ἡ a pouring out on, libation.

ἐπι-σπένδω to pour upon, to offer a libation. — M. to make a new treaty.

ἐπι-σπέρχω to incite; intr. to rush on.

ἐπι-σπεύδω to urge, hasten; to hurry on.

ἐπι-σπονδαί, αἱ new treaty.

ἐπι-σσείω etc. see ἐπι-σείω.

ἐπί-σσωτρον, τό metal hoop of a wheel.

ἐπι-σταδόν adv. assistingly; earnestly.

ἐπί-σταθμος, ὁ commandant of a place.

ἐπίσταμαι P. to understand, know, to have insight (in), to be versed, skilled, or experienced (in); to be able; to think, believe.

ἐπι-στασία and ἐπί-στασις, ἡ a stopping, checking, halt; assembly; inspection; attention.

ἐπι-στατέω to be set over, to be prefect or overseer; to command, preside.

ἐπι-στάτης, ου, ὁ one who is present; one who stands upon something; the man behind; commander, overseer, prefect; master.

ἐπι-στείβω to tread on.

ἐπι-στέλλω to send to, to send message; to enjoin, command.

ἐπι-στενάζω, ἐπι-στενάχω, ἐπι-στένω to groan or lament at. [brim.]

ἐπι-στεφής 2 filled to the

ἐπι-στέφω to offer. — M. to fill to the brim.

ἐπι-στήμη, ἡ knowledge, intelligence, insight; skill; science, art.

ἐπι-στήμων 2 knowing, intelligent, skilful; learned.

ἐπι-στηρίζομαι to lean upon.

ἐπίστιον, τό dock for ships.

ἐπίστιος = ἐφέστιος.

ἐπι-στολεύς, ὁ vice-admiral; letter-carrier.

ἐπι-στολή, ἡ message, order; letter. [στολεύς.]

ἐπιστολᾱ-φόρος, ὁ = ἐπι-

ἐπιστολιμαῖος 2 existing only in papers.

ἐπι-στομίζω to bridle; to stop one's mouth.

ἐπι-στοναχέω to roar at.

ἐπι-στρατείᾱ, -στράτευσις, ἡ expedition against.

ἐπι-στρατεύω and M. to march against.

ἐπι-στρεφής 2 intense; attentive, careful; anxious.

ἐπι-στρέφω to turn to, direct to; to turn about or back; to force back; to correct. — *intr.*, *M.* and *P.* to turn oneself round, back, or forward(s); to visit; to care for.   [about.]

ἐπι-στροφάδην *adv.* round

ἐπι-στροφή, ἡ a turning to; a warning; punishment; care, regard; a turning back, wheeling round, return; change; conversion

ἐπί-στροφος 2 conversant with.

ἐπι-στρωφάω to frequent.

ἐπι-συνάγω to gather together.

ἐπι-συναγωγή, ἡ assembly.

ἐπι-συντρέχω to run together at.   [meeting.]

ἐπι-σύστασις, ἡ a riotous

ἐπι-σφάζω, ἐπι-σφάττω to slaughter or kill over.

ἐπι-σφαλής 2 unsteady; dangerous.

ἐπι-σφραγίζομαι *M.* to put a seal or mark upon.

ἐπι-σφύριον, τό clasp over the ankle.   [file.]

ἐπι-σχερώ *adv.* in single

ἐπι-σχεσίᾱ, ἡ pretext.

ἐπί-σχεσις, ἡ a stopping, checking; moderation, reluctance.   [to insist upon.]

ἐπ-ισχύω to press hard;

ἐπ-ίσχω = ἐπέχω.

ἐπι-σωρεύω to heap up.

ἐπί-ταγμα, τό, ἐπι-ταγή, ἡ order, command.

ἐπί-τακτοι, οἱ reserve, rear-guard.   [yet more.]

ἐπι-ταλαιπωρέω to labour

ἐπί-ταξις, ἡ = ἐπίταγμα.

ἐπι-ταράσσω to trouble yet more.   [assistant.]

ἐπιτάρροθος, ὁ, ἡ helper,

ἐπι-τάσσω and *M.* to arrange at; to place behind; to put in command; to command, order, enjoin, impose.

ἐπι-τάφιος 2 funeral.

ἐπι-ταχύνω to hasten on or forward.

ἐπι-τείνω to stretch upon or over; to strain, urge, heighten, increase; to excite.

ἐπι-τειχίζω to build a fortress or bulwark, to fortify.

ἐπι-τείχισις, ἡ, ἐπι-τειχισμός, ὁ the building a fortress; fort, bulwark.

ἐπι-τείχισμα, τό fortification, bulwark.

ἐπι-τελέω to finish, complete, accomplish, perform; to sacrifice; to pay. — *M.* to take upon oneself; to end.   [complete.]

ἐπι-τελής 2 accomplished,

ἐπι-τέλλω and *M.* to enjoin, command; to rise.

ἐπι-τέμνω to make a cut into, to cut off.

ἐπί-τεξ, εχος, ἡ about to bring forth.   [in.]

ἐπι-τέρπομαι *P.* to delight

ἐπι-τεχνάομαι *M.* to contrive besides.

ἐπι-τέχνησις, ἡ contrivance, additional improvement.

ἐπι-τήδειος 3 and 2 fit,

convenient, useful, serviceable; necessary; τὰ ἐπιτήδεια necessaries, victuals; ὁ ἐπ. relation. friend.

ἐπι-τηδές and ἐπίτηδες *adv.* for the purpose, purposely; sufficiently.

ἐπι-τήδευμα, τό and ἐπιτήδευσις, ἡ pursuit, business,practice;study;habits, manner of life.

ἐπι-τηδεύω to do on purpose, to pursue, practice; to invent.

ἐπι-τήκω to melt upon.

ἐπι-τηρέω to watch for, to wait attentively.

ἐπι-τίθημι to put or lay upon; to impose on, enjoin, cause; to grant; to add; to close by putting before. — *intr.* and *M.* to put on oneself or for oneself; to engage oneself in, to undertake; to attack, make an attempt upon.

ἐπι-τιμάω to honour or value after; to pronounce judgment; to punish, fine; to blame, reprove.

ἐπι-τίμησις, ἡ blame, reproach. [ger; protector.}

ἐπι-τιμήτωρ, ορος, ὁ aven-}

ἐπι-τιμίᾱ, ἡ enjoyment of civil rights; punishment, reproach. [rights.}

ἐπί-τιμος 2 enjoying civil}

ἐπι-τλῆναι *aor.* to bear patiently.

ἐπι-τολή, ἡ a rising.

ἐπι-τολμάω to endure at.

ἐπί-τονος, ὁ stretched rope; back stay (of the mast).

ἐπι-τοξάζομαι to shoot at.

ἐπι-τραπέω to give over.

ἐπι-τρέπω to turn to or towards; to give over, entrust, to put into one's hand; to leave; to admit, allow, permit; to enjoin, ordain; *intr.* to turn to; to entrust oneself to; to yield, succumb. — *M.* to turn oneself to, to incline to; to entrust oneself to.

ἐπι-τρέφω to feed, bring up. — *P.* to grow (up) after; to grow up.

ἐπι-τρέχω to run at, upon, after, or over; to attack, oppress, overrun.

ἐπι-τρίβω to rub on the surface; to weaken, afflict, destroy. [ning.}

ἐπί-τριπτος 2 crafty, cun-}

ἐπι-τροπαῖος 3 tutelar, pupillary.

ἐπι-τροπεύω to be guardian, tutor, trustee, or governor.

ἐπι-τροπή, ἡ an entrusting, charge, trust; decision, arbitration; guardianship.

ἐπί-τροπος, ὁ trustee, guardian, governor.

ἐπι-τροχάδην *adv.* fluently.

ἐπι-τυγχάνω to meet with, fall in with; to reach, attain, obtain, succeed.

ἐπι-τύμβιος 2 belonging to a tomb.

ἐπι-φαίνομαι *P.* and -φαίνω to appear, become conspicuous; to show oneself. [manifestation.}

ἐπι-φάνεια, ἡ appearance,}

ἐπι-φανής 2 conspicuous, manifest; excellent, famous, illustrious.

ἐπί-φαντος 2 conspicuous, still living.

ἐπι-φαύσκω to shine upon.

ἐπι-φέρω to bring, carry, or put upon or up; to cause, occasion; to add, increase; to throw or lay upon, to impose, inflict, impute, reproach. — M. to bring with oneself. — P. to rush on, attack, assail, rebuke; to pursue, follow.

ἐπι-φημίζω M. to foretel (bad) omens. [(bad) omen.]

ἐπι-φήμισμα, τό word of

ἐπι-φθέγγομαι M. to call out at; to sound a charge.

ἐπι-φθονέω to envy, grudge; to hate.

ἐπί-φθονος 2 envious, jealous, hostile; envied, hated.

ἐπι-φλέγω to burn; to consume.

ἐπι-φοιτάω, -έω to go or come repeatedly to, to visit frequently; to invade; to come after. [pay.]

ἐπι-φορά, ἡ addition to

ἐπι-φορέω = ἐπιφέρω.

ἐπι-φόρημα, τό dessert.

ἐπί-φορος 2 carrying towards: favourable.

ἐπι-φράζομαι M. to think of, reflect on, consider; to contrive; to discover.

ἐπι-φράσσω to fence in; to stop up.

ἐπι-φρονέω to be prudent.

ἐπι-φροσύνη, ἡ thoughtfulness, presence of mind.

ἐπί-φρων 2 thoughtful, prudent. [upon or at.]

ἐπί-φύομαι M. to grow

ἐπι-φωνέω to call at.

ἐπι-φώσκω to dawn.

ἐπι-χαίρω to rejoice at.

ἐπί-χαλκος 2 of brass or copper.

ἐπί-χαρις, ι pleasing, agreeable, engaging.

ἐπί-χαρτος 2 delightful.

ἐπι-χειμάζω to pass the winter at.

ἐπί-χειρα, τά wages; earnest-money.

ἐπι-χειρέω to put one's hand to; to attack, assail; to undertake, attempt, try, venture, manage.

ἐπι-χείρημα, τό, ἐπι-χείρησις, ἡ an undertaking, a beginning, attempt, project; attack.

ἐπι-χειρητής, οῦ. ὁ an enterprising man of action.

ἐπι-χειροτονέω to vote by show of hands.

ἐπι-χέω to pour or shed over, upon, or at. — M. and P. to flood in, befall.

ἐπι-χθόνιος 2 earthy.

ἐπί-χολος 2 producing bile.

ἐπι-χορηγέω to afford, procure in addition.

ἐπι-χορηγία, ἡ supply.

ἐπι-χράομαι M. to make use of; to converse with.

ἐπι-χράω, -χραύω to rush upon, attack.

ἐπι-χρίω to anoint, besmear. — M. to anoint oneself. [gold.]

ἐπί-χρūσος 2 overlaid with

11*

ἐπι-χωρέω to come up or on, to advance; to yield, concede.

ἐπι-χωριάζω to visit often.

ἐπι-χώριος 2 native, indigenous, in the fashion of the country. [surface.]

ἐπι-ψαύω to touch on the]

ἐπι-ψηλαφάω to grope for.

ἐπι-ψηφίζω to put to the vote. — M. to vote, decree, confirm by vote.

ἐπ-ιωγή, ἡ shelter, anchorage, landing-place.

ἐπ-οικέω to go or live as a settler or colonist; to dwell in: to be a neighbour.

ἐπ-οικοδομέω to build up, repair; to build upon.

ἔπ-οικος, ὁ settler, colonist; foreigner; inhabitant; (near) neighbour.

ἐπ-οικτείρω, ἐπ-οικτίζω to have compassion with.

ἐπ-οίχομαι M. to go or come towards, to approach; to attack; to go over, through, or along; to review, inspect; to set to work.

ἐπ-οκέλλω to run ashore (trans. and intr.), to be wrecked.

ἕπομαι M. to follow; to accompany, escort; to pursue. [upon or by.]

ἐπ-όμνυμι, -ύω to swear]

ἐπ-ομφάλιος 2 upon the navel. [to be reproached.]

ἐπ-ονείδιστος 2 shameful,]

ἐπ-ονομάζω to give a name, to surname; to call by name. [with awe.]

ἐπ-οπίζομαι M. to regard]

ἐπο-ποιΐα, ἡ epic poetry.

ἐπο-ποιός, ὁ epic poet.

ἐπ-οπτάω to roast upon.

ἐπ-οπτεύω to look on or at; to inspect, watch over.

ἐπ-όπτης, ου, ὁ watcher, guardian; witness.

ἐπ-ορέγω to hand to. — M. and P. to stretch oneself towards; to desire yet more.

ἐπ-ορθρεύομαι M. to rise early.

ἐπ-όρνυμι to arouse, stir up, excite; to send to. — P. to rise, rush on.

ἐπ-ορούω to rush at, to fall upon.

ἐπ-ορχέομαι M. to dance to.

ἔπος, τό word; speech, tale, saying; promise; oracle; maxim; advice, order; legend, report; song, epic poem; thing, story, something. [up, rouse.]

ἐπ-οτρύνω to incite, stir]

ἐπ-ουράνιος 2 heavenly.

ἔπ-ουρος 2 blowing favourably. [still.]

ἐπ-οφείλω to be indebted]

ἐπ-οχέομαι to ride upon.

ἐπ-οχετεύω to bring water by a channel to a place.

ἔπ-οχος riding or mounted upon; firm in the saddle.

ἔποψ, οπος, ὁ hoopoe.

ἐπ-όψιμος 2 that can be looked on or seen.

ἐπ-όψιος 3 visible, manifest; all-seeing.

ἔπ-οψις, ἡ view; range of vision, sight.

ἑπτά seven.

ἑπτά-βόειος 2, ἑπτά-βοιος 2
of seven bull's-hides.

ἑπτα-ετής, ἑπτα-έτης 2
seven years old, for seven
years.

ἑπτά-καί-δεκα seventeen.

ἑπτα-καὶ-δέκατος 3 se-
venteenth.

ἑπτάκις adv. seven times.

ἑπτάκισ-μύριοι 3 seventy
thousand.

ἑπτακισ-χίλιοι 3 seven
thousand.   [dred.]

ἑπτακόσιοι 3 seven hun-]

ἑπτά-λογχος 2 of seven
lances, under seven leaders.

ἑπτά-μηνος 2 of seven
months.

ἑπτά-πηχυς, υ seven cu-
bits long.   [long.]

ἑπτα-πόδης, ου seven feet]

ἑπτά-πυλος 2 seven-gated.

ἑπτά-τονος 2 seven-toned.

ἑπταχα adv. in seven parts.

ἑπτ-έτης 2 = ἑπταέτης.

ἕπω to be busy or engaged
with; to go; to come.

ἐπ-ῳδή, ἡ incantation, magic song; spell, charm.

ἐπ-ῳδός 2 acting as a
charm; enchanter, helper;
ἡ ἐ. concluding stanza.

ἐπ-ωμίς, ίδος, ἡ upper
part of the shoulder, arm
and shoulder.

ἐπ-ώμοτος 2 on oath;
sworn witness.   [name.]

ἐπ-ωνυμίᾱ, ἡ surname;]

ἐπ-ώνυμος, -ωνύμιος 2
named after, surnamed;
giving one's name to.

ἐπ-ωτίδες, αἱ battering
beams of a ship.

ἐπ-ωφελέω to aid, help.

ἐπ-ωφέλημα, τό help.

ἐπ-ώχατο they were shut
(from ἐπέχω).

ἔρᾱζε adv. to the earth.

ἔραμαι = ἐράω.

ἐραννός 3 lovely.

ἔρανος, ὁ common meal,
picnic; contribution; kindness.   [money, covetous.]

ἐρασι-χρήματος 2 loving]

ἐράσμιος 2, ἐραστός 3
lovely, charming, pleasant,
amiable; welcome.

ἐραστής, οῦ, ὁ lover, friend,
adherent.

ἐρατεινός 3 = ἐράσιμος.

ἐρατίζω to lust after or for.

ἐρατύω = ἐρητύω.

ἐράω and P. to love pas-
sionately, to fall in love
(with); to desire, long for.

ἐργάζομαι M. to work, be
busy; to do, perform, accomplish; to effect, cause; to
earn; to carry on a trade;
to do to, commit upon.

ἐργάθω = εἴργω.

ἐργαλεῖον, τό tool, instrument.   [to do.]

ἐργασείω to have a mind]

ἐργασίᾱ, ἡ work, business,
occupation;   husbandry;
trade; effect; a working at;
workmanship; gain, profit.

ἐργαστήριον, τό workshop,
factory.   [industrious.]

ἐργαστικός 3 laborious,]

ἐργάτης, ου, ὁ worker,
workman; husbandman.

ἐργατικός 3 = ἐργαστικός.

ἐργάτις, ιδος, ἡ fem. of
ἐργάτης.

ἔργμα, τό = ἔργον. [son.]

ἔργμα, τό confinement, pri-

ἐργο-λαβέω to enter upon work by contract.

ἔργον, τό work, deed, action, enterprise; fact, reality; business, occupation, employment, labour; husbandry; trade; war, combat; great or hard work; product of labour, building, cornfield; thing, matter, piece; circumstance.

ἔργω = εἴργω. [cult.]

ἐργώδης 2 toilsome, difficult.

ἔρδω, ἔρδω to do, make, act; to offer, sacrifice.

ἐρεβεννός 3 dark, gloomy.

ἐρέβινθος, ὁ chick-pea.

ἔρεβος, τό the dark nether world.

ἐρείνω and M. to ask.

ἐρεθίζω, ἐρέθω to provoke, irritate, tease, excite.

ἐρείδω to prop, stay, support; to press, urge, push; intr. to lean against; to rush on. — P. and M. to prop or support oneself, to lean upon; to be fixed in.

ἐρείκω to tear, break, crush; to pierce; to burst.

ἐρείπια, τά ruins.

ἐρείπω to pull down, dash down; intr. and P. to fall down in ruins.

ἔρεισμα, τό prop, support.

ἐρεμνός 3 dark, gloomy.

ἐρέπτομαι M. to pluck off.

ἐρέσσω to row; to move quickly, to ply.

ἐρέτης, ου, ὁ rower.

ἐρετμόν, τό oar.

ἐρεύγομαι[1] to spit out, vomit; to splash up, surge; to break out.

ἐρεύγομαι[2] to roar.

ἐρευθέδανον, τό madder.

ἐρεύθω to make red.

ἔρευνα, ἡ inquiry.

ἐρευνάω to search after, inquire (into), examine.

ἐρέφω to cover, roof in; to crown. [shatter.]

ἐρέχθω to rend; to dash.

ἐρέω[1] fut. I shall say.

ἐρέω[2], ἔρομαι M. εἴρομαι to ask, inquire, question.

ἐρημία, ἡ solitude, desert, loneliness; helplessness; absence, want.

ἐρῆμος and ἔρημος 3 and 2 lonely, solitary, desert, desolate, waste; helpless, abandoned, needy, destitute; ἡ ἐρήμη (δίκη) trial in default of appearance.

ἐρημόω to make solitary, to desolate, devastate, evacuate; to deprive, bereave; to abandon. [devastation.]

ἐρήμωσις, ἡ desolation.

ἐρητύω to keep back, to check, hinder, restrain.

ἐρι-αύχην, ενος with a strong neck. [thundering.]

ἐρι-βρεμέτης, ου loud-

ἐρι-βῶλαξ, ακος, ἐρί-βωλος 2 with large clods.

ἐρί-γδουπος 2 thundering, loud-roaring.

ἐριδαίνω = ἐρίζω.

ἐριδμαίνω to provoke, irritate. [πος.]

ἐρί-δουπος 2 = ἐρίγδου-

ἐρίζω to quarrel, wrangle, contend, rival; to be a match for, be equal to.

ἐρί-ηρος 2 dear, loving, beloved.

ἐριθεία, ἡ = ἔρις. [fertile.]

ἐρι-θηλής 2 luxurious,]

ἔριθος, ὁ, ἡ day-labourer; reaper. [mous.]

ἐρι-κῡδής 2 glorious, fa-]

ἐρί-μυκος 2 loud-bellowing.

ἐρινεός, ὁ wild fig-tree.

'Ερῑνύς, ύος, ἡ Erinys (avenging deity); revenge, punishment; curse; destruction.

ἔριον, τό wool.

ἐρι-ούνης, ἐρι-ούνιος, ὁ helper, bliss-bearer. [wool.]

ἐριουργέω to work in]

ἔρις, ιδος, ἡ quarrel, strife, discord, animosity; jealousy; combat; zeal, contention.

ἐρι-σθενής 2 very mighty.

ἔρισμα, τό cause of quarrel.

ἐρι-στάφυλος 2 with large clusters.

ἐριστός 3 to be disputed.

ἐρί-τῑμος 2 most honoured, highly prized.

ἐρίφειος 2 of a kid.

ἔριφος, ὁ, ἡ and ἐρίφιον, τό goat, kid.

ἑρκεῖος, ἕρκειος 2 belonging to a yard or enclosure; house-protecting.

ἑρκίον, τό, ἕρκος, τό fence, enclosure, hedge, wall; farm-yard; defence, protection: snare, net.

ἑρκτή, ἡ = εἱρκτή.

ἕρμα[1], τό prop, support, defence; reef, rock; hill.

ἕρμα[2], τό pendant of the ear; foundation, cause.

ἕρμαιον, τό godsend, windfall. [pretation.]

ἑρμηνεία, ἡ speech; inter-]

ἑρμηνεύς, ὁ, ἑρμηνευτής, οῦ, ὁ herald; interpreter, expounder.

ἑρμηνεύω to expound, interpret, translate, explain.

ἑρμίς, ῖνος, ὁ bed-post.

ἑρμο-γλυφεῖον, τό sculptor's workshop.

ἔρνος, τό shoot, scion, child.

ἔρξίης, ὁ worker.

ἔρομαι M. to ask, inquire.

ἑρπετόν, τό creeping animal, reptile: living being.

ἕρπω, ἑρπύζω to creep, crawl; to go; to come.

ἔρρω to walk slowly, to go away; to perish, be lost.

ἐρρωμένος 3 strong, stout; vigorous. [νυμι.]

ἔρρωσο fare-well; see ῥών-]

ἕρση, ἔρση, ἡ dew, dewdrop; new-born or late-born lamb.

ἐρσήεις 3 d'wy; fresh.

ἔρσην, ενος = ἄρρην.

ἐρύγμηλος ᾿ loud-bellowing.

ἐρυθαίνω to make red. — P. to become red, to blush.

ἐρύθημα, τ᾿ redness; inflammation. [to blush.]

ἐρυθραίνομαι, ἐρυθριάω]

ἐρυθρός 3 red.

ἐρύκω, ἐρῡκάνάω, ἐρῡκάνω to keep back, stop, restrain, check, hinder; to keep asunder. — M. and P. to be detained; to tarry.

ἔρυμα, τό fence, bulwark; fort; castle.   [tected.]

ἐρυμνός 3 fortified, pro-

ἐρύομαι *M.* to save, rescue, protect; to watch, observe; to lie in wait (for), to espy; to ward off, check.

ἐρυσ-άρματες, οἱ chariot-drawing.

ἐρυσίβη, ἡ mildew.

ἐρυσί-πτολις town-protecting.

ἐρυστός 3 drawn.

ἐρύω to draw, push; to bend (a bow); to tear off *or* away, to snatch from; to drag, pull, trail. — *M.* to draw to oneself, to snatch; to outweigh.   [up.]

ἐρχατάομαι *P.* to be shut]

ἔρχομαι *M.* to come, go, arrive at; to march, travel, drive; to flow, fly; to go away, march out; to be lost; to come back, return; to be about to do.

ἐρωδιός, ὁ heron.

ἐρωέω[1] to flow, stream.

ἐρωέω[2] to rest, repose, cease from; to stay behind; *trans.* to drive *or* push back.

ἐρωή[1], ἡ quick motion, force, impetus.

ἐρωή[2], ἡ rest.

ἔρως, ωτος, ὁ love; desire.

ἐρωτάω to ask, request; to inquire.

ἐρώτημα, τό, ἐρώτησις, ἡ question; questioning.

ἐρωτικός 3 of love; inclined to love, fond.

ἐς = εἰς.

ἐσθέω to clothe.

ἔσθημα, τό, ἐσθής, ῆτος, ἡ, ἔσθησις, ἡ garment, dress, clothing.

ἐσθίω = ἔδω.

ἐσθλός 3 good, kind; generous, noble; brave, valiant; valuable; lucky, favourable.

ἔσθος, τό = ἔσθημα.

ἔσθ' ὅτε sometimes.

ἔσθω = ἔδω, ἐσθίω.

ἐσμός, ὁ swarm, flock; plenty.

ἔσ-οπτρον, τό mirror.

ἑσπέρα, ἡ evening; west.

ἑσπέριος 3 and ἕσπερος 2 in the evening; western.

ἕσπερος, ὁ = ἑσπέρα.

ἔσπετε = εἴπετε see εἶπον.

ἑσσόομαι = ἡσσάομαι.

ἔσσυμαι see σεύω.

ἐσσύμενος 3 eager; hasty.

ἔσσων 2 = ἥσσων.

ἔστε *adv.* and *conj* till, until; as long as; even to.

ἑστίᾱ, ἡ hearth; house, home, family; altar; Hestia = Vesta.

ἑστίᾱμα, τό, ἑστίᾱσις, ἡ feast, banquet.   [tainer.]

ἑστιάτωρ, ορος, ὁ enter-]

ἑστιάω to receive hospitably, to feast, entertain. — *P.* to feast on.

ἑστιοῦχος 2 guarding the house; with holy altars.

ἑστιῶτις, ιδος belonging to the house.

ἕστωρ, ορος, ὁ pole-nail.

ἐσχάρᾱ, ἡ hearth; fireplace; coal-pan; altar.

ἐσχατιά, ἡ extreme part, remotest place, end, border.

ἔσχατος 3 the farthest, remotest, uttermost, extreme; latest; highest; last; worst; lowest.

ἐσχατόων 3 the farthest; lying on the edge or border.

ἔσω = εἴσω. [within.]

ἔσωθεν adv. from within;

ἐσώτερος 3 inner.

ἑταίρᾱ, ἡ female companion or friend; sweetheart, courtesan.

ἑταιρείᾱ, ἡ companionship, association, brotherhood; political club.

ἑταιρεῖος 3 of comrades or partisans.

ἑταιρίᾱ, ἡ = ἑταιρεία.

ἑταιρίζω to be a companion. — M. to choose for companion.

ἑταιρικός 3 = ἑταιρεῖος.

ἑταιρίς, ίδος, ἡ = ἑταίρα.

ἑταῖρος, ὁ companion, comrade, mate, friend.

ἑταρίζω = ἑταιρίζω.

ἕταρος, ὁ = ἑταῖρος.

ἐτεός 3 true, real.

ἑτερ - αλκής 2 giving strength to one of two, changing, doubtful.

ἑτερ-ήμερος 2 on alternate days.

ἑτέρηφι adv. with one or the other hand.

ἑτερό-γλωσσος 2 speaking a foreign language.

ἑτερο-διδασκαλέω to teach false doctrine.

ἑτερο-ζυγέω to be put to another yoke. [kind.]

ἑτεροῖος 3 of a different

ἕτερος 3 the other, one of two, another; the second; different, of another kind; at variance.

ἑτέρωθεν adv. from the other side; on the other side.

ἑτέρωθι adv. on the other side; elsewhere, to another place, sideways.

ἔτης, ου, ὁ kinsman, clansman, friend.

ἐτησίαι, οἱ periodical winds.

ἐτήσιος 2 for a year, yearly.

ἐτήτυμος 2 true, real, genuine.

ἔτι adv. yet, as yet, yet longer, still; besides.

ἑτοιμάζω to make ready, to prepare.

ἑτοιμασίᾱ, ἡ readiness.

ἑτοῖμος and ἕτοιμος 2 and 3 extant, ready, at hand, disposable; willing, quick, active, prompt; easy; real, confirmed.

ἔτος, τό year.

ἐτός adv. without reason.

ἔτυμος 2 real, true, actual.

ἐτώσιος 2 idle, useless.

εὖ, ἐΰ adv. well, properly, rightly; luckily.

εὖ = οὖ. [bring good news.]

εὐ - αγγελίζω and M. to

εὐ-αγγέλιον, τό good news, glad tidings, gospel; reward for good news.

εὐ-αγγελιστής, οῦ, ὁ evangelist.

εὐ-αγής 2 guiltless, pure, pious; purifying; shining, conspicuous. [ing.]

εὔ-αγρος 2 lucky in hunt-

εὐ-άγωγος 2 easily led.

εὔαδε aor. of ἁνδάνω.

εὐάζω to cry εὐά.

εὐ-αής 2 blowing fair; friendly.

εὐ-αίρετος 2 easy to be taken, chosen, or known.

εὐ-αίων, ωνος happy; making happy.

εὐ-άμερος 2 = εὐήμερος.

εὐ-ανδρίᾶ, ἡ plenty of good men.

εὐ-άνεμος 2 well aired.

εὐ-ανθής 2 blooming; flowery, gay. [described.]

εὐ-απήγητος 2 easy to be

εὐ-απόβατος 2 convenient for disembarking.

εὐ-αποτείχιστος 2 easy to be blockaded.

εὐ-αρεστέω to please well.

εὐ-άρεστος 2 well-pleasing; easily satisfied.

εὐ-αρίθμητος 2 easy to be counted. [chariots.]

εὐ-άρματος 2 famous for

εὐ-αρμοστίᾶ, ἡ harmony, evenness of temper.

εὐ-άρμοστος 2 well-adapted, harmonious, even.

εὐ-αυγής 2 far-seeing.

εὐ-βάστακτος 2 easy to be carried.

εὔ-βατος 2 accessible.

εὔ-βοτος 2 rich in pastures and cattle.

εὔ-βοτρυς, υ rich in grapes.

εὐ-βουλίᾶ, ἡ good counsel, prudence. [prudent.]

εὔ-βουλος 2 well-advised,

εὐ-γάθητος 2 joyous.

εὖγε = εὖ γε well done!

εὐ-γένεια, ἡ noble descent; generosity.

εὐ-γένειος 2 well-bearded.

εὐ-γενής 2 well-born, noble, generous. [vow.]

εὖγμα, τό boast; prayer,

εὐ-γναμπτος 2 well-bent.

εὐ-γνώμων 2 generous; kind; fair; sensible.

εὐ-γνωστος 2 well-known; visible. [or prosperous.]

εὐ-δαιμονέω to be happy

εὐ-δαιμονίᾶ, ἡ happiness, prosperity. [happy.]

εὐ-δαιμονίζω to consider

εὐ-δαιμονικός 3 of happiness; happy; making happy.

εὐ-δαίμων 2 happy; fortunate, lucky; prosperous, wealthy.

εὐ-δείελος 2 far-seen.

εὔ-δηλος 2 quite manifest.

εὐ-δίᾶ, ἡ fair weather; calm; security. [crossed.]

εὐ-διάβατος 2 easy to be

εὐ-διάβολος 2 exposed to misinterpretation.

εὐ-δικίᾶ, ἡ justice.

εὔ-διος 2 fair, clear, calm.

εὐ-δμητος 2 well-built.

εὐ-δοκέω to be pleased with; to consent to.

εὐ-δοκίᾶ, ἡ satisfaction, delight; wish.

εὐ-δοκιμέω to be of good repute, to be famous or distinguished.

εὐ-δόκιμος 2 honoured, esteemed, renowned.

εὐ-δοξέω = εὐδοκιμέω.

εὐ-δοξίᾶ, ἡ good repute, renown; approval.

εὔ-δοξος 2 = εὐδόκιμος.

εὐ-δρακής 2 sharp-sighted.

εὕδω to sleep; to fall asleep.

εὐ-ειδής 2 well-shaped.

εὐ-έλεγκτος 2 easy to be refuted or to be convinced.

εὔ-ελπις, ι hopeful.

εὐ-εξάλειπτος 2 easy to be blotted out.

εὐ-εξέλεγκτος 2 = εὐέλεγκτος. [being.]

εὐ-εξίᾱ, ἡ good state; well-

εὐ-έπεια, ἡ good wish.

εὐ-επής 2 well-speaking; well-spoken.

εὐ - ἐπιβούλευτος 2 open to snares. [attacked.]

εὐ-επίθετος 2 easy to be

εὐ-εργεσίᾱ, ἡ well-doing, kindness, good deed.

εὐ-εργετέω to do good, show kindness. — P. to receive a kindness.

εὐ-εργέτημα, τό = εὐεργεσία.

εὐ-εργέτης, ου, ὁ well-doer, benefactor; well-deserving man. [well-done.]

εὐ-εργής 2 well-wrought;

εὐ-εργός 2 doing good; easy to be wrought.

εὐ-ερκής 2 well-fenced.

εὔ-ερος 2 with good wool.

εὐ-εστώ, οῦς, ἡ well-being, happiness.

εὐ-ετηρίᾱ, ἡ good harvest.

εὐ-εύρετος 2 easy to find.

εὔ-εφοδος 2 easily accessible.

εὔ-ζυγος 2 well-joined.

εὔ-ζωνος 2 well-girt, girt up; active.

εὐ-ηγενής 2 = εὐγενής.

εὐ-ηγεσίᾱ, ἡ good government. [plicity.]

εὐ-ήθεια, ἡ goodness; sim-

εὐ-ήθης 2 good-natured; simple, silly.

εὐ-ηθικός 3 = εὐήθης.

εὐ-ήκης 2 well-pointed.

εὐ-ήλατος 2 easy to ride over.

εὐ-ημερέω to be happy or successful. [day.]

εὐ-ημερίᾱ, ἡ fine or happy

εὐ-ήμερος 2 bringing a fine day.

εὐ-ήνεμος 2 = εὐάνεμος.

εὐ-ήνωρ, ορος manly; giving manly strength.

εὐ-ήρατος 2 lovely.

εὐ-ήρετμος 2 rowing well; well-rowed.

εὐ-ήρης 2 manageable.

εὐ-ηφενής 2 wealthy.

εὐ-θάλασσος 2 of the mighty sea. [manly.]

εὐ-θαρσής 2 courageous,

εὐ-θενέω and P. to thrive, be prosperous. [win.]

εὐ-θεράπευτος 2 easy to

εὔ-θετος 2 convenient.

εὐθέως = εὐθύς.

εὐ-θηνέω = εὐθενέω.

εὔ-θριξ, τριχος having beautiful hair. [ful seat.]

εὔ-θρονος 2 on a beauti-

εὐθύ adv. = εὐθύς.

εὐθυ-δρομέω to run or come straight.

εὐ-θῡμέω and M. to be of good cheer. [gladness.]

εὐ-θῡμίᾱ, ἡ cheerfulness,

εὔ-θῡμος 2 well-disposed; cheerful, glad; eager.

εὐθύνη, εὔθῡνα, ἡ the giving an account; account, vindication; chastisement.

εὐθύνω and *M.* to make or direct straight, to guide; to correct; to blame; to accuse, call to account; to punish.

εὐθύς, εῖα, ὑ straight, direct; plain, honest. — *adv.* εὐθύς, εὐθύ, εὐθέως straightforward; forthwith, at once; without reserve; for instance.

εὐθύτης, ητος, ἡ straightness; justice.

εὐθύ - ωρον *adv.* = εὐθύς.

εὔιος 2 shouting; rejoicing; Bacchic.

εὔ-ιππος 2 with good horses; well-mounted.

εὐ-καθαίρετος 2 easy to overthrow.

εὐ-καιρέω to have leisure.

εὐ-καιρίᾱ, ἡ opportunity.

εὔ-καιρος 2 in time, seasonable, opportune.

εὐ-καμπής 2 well-bent.

εὐ-κάρδιος 2 stout-hearted.

εὔ-καρπος 2 fruitful.

εὐ-κατάλυτος 2 easy to destroy. [spicable.]

εὐ-καταφρόνητος 2 despicable.

εὐ-κατέργαστος 2 easy to work or to digest. [accuse.]

εὐ-κατηγόρητος 2 easy to accuse.

εὐ-κέατος 2 well-split.

εὔ-κερως, ων well-horned.

εὔκηλος 2 = ἔκηλος.

εὐ-κλεής 2 famous, glorious, noble. [renown.]

εὔ-κλεια, ἡ good fame, renown.

εὐ-κλεΐής = εὐκλεής.

εὐ-κλήΐς, ιδος well-closed.

εὐ-κνήμῑς, ιδος with good greaves.

εὔ-κολος 2 well-disposed; gay; easy; contented.

εὐ-κομιδής 2 well-cared for.

εὔ-κομος = ἠύκομος.

εὔ-κοπος 2 easy, without pains. [modesty, decency.]

εὐ-κοσμίᾱ, ἡ good order;]

εὔ-κοσμος 2 well-ordered; well-adorned, graceful; easy to arrange.

εὐ-κρινής 2 well-ordered; distinct, clear.

εὐ-κρότητος 2 well-hammered. [tive.]

εὐκταῖος 3 prayed for, votive.

εὐ-κτίμενος 3, εὔ-κτιτος well-built, well-made.

εὐκτός 3 wished for; desirable.

εὐλάβεια, ἡ caution, circumspection; awe, fear; piety.

εὐλαβέομαι *P.* to be cautious, circumspect, or careful; to fear, beware of; to reverence, worship; to care for.

εὐ-λαβής 2 cautious, circumspect, anxious; conscientious; devout.

εὐλάζω to plough.

εὐλάκα, ἡ ploughshare.

εὐ-λείμων 2 rich in meadows.

εὔ-λεκτρος 2 fit for marriage, bridal, lovely.

εὐλή, ἡ maggot, worm.

εὔ-ληπτος 2 easy to be taken or conquered.

εὔληρα, τά reins.

εὐ-λογέω to praise; to give thanks; to bless.

εὐ-λογητός 3 blessed.

εὐ-λογίᾱ, ἡ praise, eulogy; fair - speaking; blessing; kindness, bounty.

εὔ-λογος 2 sounding well; reasonable; probable.

εὔ-λοφος 2 with a fine plume.   [solve.]

εὔ-λυτος 2 easy to dis-

εὐ-μάθεια, ἡ docility.

εὐ-μαθής 2 docile; easy to be learned or understood.

εὐ-μάρεια, -ίᾱ, ἡ easiness; convenience; possibility; preventive; abundance; comfort; stool, privy.

εὐ - μαρής 2 easy; convenient.   [or great.]

εὐ-μεγέθης 2 very large

εὐ-μένεια, ἡ good will, kindness.

εὐ-μενής 2, εὐ-μενέτης, ου well - disposed, kind; favourable; convenient.

εὐ-μετάβολος 2 changeable, fickle.

εὐ-μετάδοτος 2 liberal.

εὐ-μεταχείριστος 2 easy to manage or to conquer.

εὔ-μηλος 2 rich in sheep.

εὐ-μήχανος 2 inventive; ingenious.   [threads.]

εὔ - μιτος 2 with fine

ἐΰ-μμελίης, ου skilled in thrusting spears. [bering.]

εὐ-μνάστος 2 well-remem-

εὔ-μορφος 2 well-shaped.

εὐ-μουσίᾱ, ἡ taste for the fine arts.

εὔ-μουσος 2 musical.

εὐνάζω to lay to sleep; to lay in ambush; to lull to sleep; to assuage. — P. and M. to lie down; to go asleep; to rest.

εὐ-ναιετάων, ουσα, ον and εὐ-ναιόμενος 3 well-inhabited or peopled.

εὐναῖος 3 of a couch; matrimonial; resting.

εὐνα(σ)τήριον, τό, εὐνή, ἡ bed, couch; marriage-bed; bed-chamber; stone used as an anchor.

εὐνῆθεν adv. out of bed.

εὐνήτρια, ἡ. εὐνίς[1], ιδος, ἡ wife.   [destitute.]

εὐνίς[2], ι(δ)ος, ὁ, ἡ bereft,

ἐΰ-ννητος 2 well-woven.

εὐ-νοέω to be well-disposed, favourable, or friendly.

εὔ-νοια, ἡ good will, kindness, favour.   [friendly.]

εὐ-νοϊκός 3 benevolent,

εὐ-νομέομαι P. to have good laws.

εὐ-νομίᾱ, ἡ the having good laws; order, legal constitution.

εὔ-νοος, εὔ-νους 2 well-disposed, kind, friendly, benevolent.

εὐνουχίζω to unman.

εὐνοῦχος, ὁ eunuch; chamberlain.

εὐ-νώμᾱς, ου quick moving.

εὔ-ξε(ι)νος 2 hospitable.

εὔ-ξεστος, εὔ-ξοος 2 well-polished.   [συμ-, -συν-.]

εὐ - ξυμ-, εὐ-ξυν- see εὐ-

εὔ-οδος 2 easy to travel in.

εὐοῖ int. Lat. evoe!

εὔ-οικος 2 convenient for dwelling in; economical.

εὔ-ολβος 2 very wealthy.

εὔ-οπλος 2 well-armed.

εὐ-όργητος 2 even-tempered. [oath.]

εὐ-ορκέω to keep one's/ εὔ-ορκος 2 true to one's oath; according to an oath. [chorage.]

εὔ-ορμος 2 with good an-/

εὐ-πάθεια, ἡ sensual enjoyment, luxury. [things.]

εὐ-παθέω to enjoy good/

εὐ-παιδίᾱ, ἡ the having good children.

εὔ-παις, -παιδος having good children.

εὐ-πάρεδρος 2 persevering.

εὐ-πατέρεια, ἡ daughter of a noble father.

εὐ-πατρίδης, ου, εὔ-πατρις, ιδος of a noble father; noble.

εὐ-πειθής 2, εὔ-πειστος 2 obedient, yielding.

εὔ-πεπλος 2 with a fine robe. [ensnaring.]

εὐ-περίστατος 2 easily/

εὐ-πέτεια, ἡ easiness, an easy getting.

εὐ-πετής 2 easy, convenient, without trouble.

εὐ-πηγής, εὔ-πηκτος 2 well put togéther, stout, compact.

εὔ-πιστος 2 trustworthy.

εὔ-πλαστος 2 plastic.

εὔ-πλειος 2 quite full.

εὐ-πλεκής, εὔ-πλεκτος 2 well-plaited.

εὔ-πλοια, ἡ good sailing.

εὐ-πλόκαμος 2, εὐ-πλοκαμίς, ιδος with fine locks.

εὐ-πλυνής 2 well-washed.

εὐ-ποίητος 2 well-wrought.

εὐ-ποιΐα, ἡ beneficence.

εὔ-πομπος 2 well-conducting.

εὐ-πορέω to have abundance or plenty (of); to be prosperous or successful; to find a way, to be able; trans. to supply abundantly.

εὐ-πορίᾱ, ἡ facility, opportunity; means, supply, resources; plenty, wealth.

εὔ-πορος 2 easy to pass over; convenient, easy; ready, ingenious, inventive; wealthy, rich.

εὐ-πρᾱγέω to be well off.

εὐ-πρᾱγίᾱ, ἡ, εὐ-πρᾱξίᾱ, ἡ well-doing, success, welfare; good action. [done.]

εὔ-πρᾱκτος 2 easy to be/

εὐ-πρέπεια, ἡ comely appearance, beauty; palliation, excuse.

εὐ-πρεπής 2 comely, well-looking, decent; distinguished, conspicuous; specious, shining.

εὔ-πρηστος 2 sparkling.

εὐ-πρόσδεκτος 2 acceptable. [affable.]

εὐ-πρόσοδος 2 accessible;/

εὐ-προσωπέω to please.

εὐ-πρόσωπος 2 with a fine face; cheerful.

εὐ-προφάσιστος 2 convincing, plausible. [stern.]

εὔ-πρυμνος 2 with a fine/

εὔ-πτερος 2 well-winged.

εὔ-πτυκτος 2 easy to be folded. [towers.]

εὔ-πυργος 2 with good/

εὔ-πωλος 2 with fine colts.

εὐρ-ακύλων, ωνος, ὁ northeast-wind.

εὐράξ *adv.* sideways.

εὐ-ραφής 2 well-sewed.

εὕρεσις, ἡ a finding.

εὑρετής, οῦ. ὁ inventor.

εὑρετικός 3 inventive.

εὑρετός 3 found, invented; to be found.

εὕρημα, τό a thing found; windfall, unexpected gain; foundling; invention.

εὔ-ρῑνος 2, εὔ-ρῑς, ῑνος 2 with a scenting nose.

εὔρῑπος, ὁ strait, narrow sea.

εὑρίσκω to find, find out, discover; to invent, contrive; to procure; to meet; to gain, obtain; to fetch money (of merchandise).

εὔ-ροος 2 fine-flowing.

εὗρος[1], ὁ south-east-wind.

εὗρος[2], τό breadth, width.

εὔ-ρραφής = εὐραφής.

εὔ-ρρεής 2, εὔ-ρρείτης, ου = εὔροος.

εὐρυ-άγυιος 3 with wide streets.

εὐρυ-εδής 2 spacious.

εὐ-ρυθμίᾱ, ἡ good time; proportion.

εὔ-ρυθμος 2 in good time or measure, fitting well; rhythmical; graceful.

εὐρυ-κρείων, οντος wide-ruling.

εὐρυ-μέτωπος 2 broad-fronted.   [broad.]

εὐρύνω to make wide or

εὐρύ-νωτος 2 broad-backed.

εὐρυ-όδειος 3 with broad ways.

εὐρύ-οπα, ὁ far-thundering; others: far-seeing

εὐρύ-πορος 2 with wide passage.   [gates.]

εὐρυ-πυλής 2 with wide

εὐρυ-ρέεθρος 2 and εὐρυ-ρέων 3 broad-flowing.

εὐρύς 3 broad, wide; widespread.   [ing.]

εὐρυ-σθενής 2 wide-rul-

εὐρυ-φυής 2 growing broad.

εὐρύ-χορος 2 with spacious places for dancing.

εὐρυ-χωρίᾱ, ἡ free space, open country.

εὐρώδης 2 = εὐρύς.

εὐρώεις 3 mouldy; dark.

εὐρώς, ῶτος, ὁ mould, must.

εὔ-ρωστος 2 stout, strong.

ἐΰς, ἐΰ good, brave.

εὐ-σέβεια, ἡ reverence, piety; filial love.

εὐ-σεβής 2 pious, religious, reverent.   [deck.]

εὔ-σελμος 2 with good

εὔ-σεπτος 2 most reverend.

εὔ-σημος 2 of good omen; clear, manifest.

εὔ-σκαρθμος 2 swift-springing.

εὐ-σκέπαστος 2 well-covered, protected.

εὐ-σκευέω to be well equipped.

εὐ-σκίαστος 2 well-shaded.

εὔ-σκοπος 2 sharp-glancing; shooting well.

εὔ-σοια, ἡ welfare.

εὔ-σπλαγχνος 2 compassionate.

ἐΰ-σσελμος 2 = εὔσελμος.

ἐΰ-σσωτρος 2 with good wheel-bands. [firmly built.]

εὐ-σταθής 2 steadfast,

εὐ-σταλής 2 well-equipped; happy, easy; decent, simple.

εὐ-στέφανος 2 well-crowned; well-walled.

εὔ-στολος 2 = εὐσταλής.

εὔ-στομος 2 speaking good words; keeping silence.

εὔ-στρεπτος 2, εὐ-στρεφής 2, εὔ-στροφος 2 well-twisted. [lars.]

εὐ-στῦλος 2 with fine pillars.

εὐ-σύμβλητος 2 easy to explain or guess.

εὐ-σύμβολος 2 sociable.

εὐ-σύνετος 2 intelligent.

εὐ-σχημοσύνη, ἡ good grace, decent behaviour.

εὐ-σχήμων 2 graceful, becoming; specious, shining.

εὐ-ταχτέω to keep order, to be subordinate.

εὔ-ταχτος 2 well-arranged; well-disciplined, orderly; modest.

εὐ-ταξίᾱ, ἡ good order, discipline, obedience.

εὖτε adv. at the time when, during that time; as often as; in the case that; just as.

εὐ-τειχής 2 well-walled.

εὐ-τέλεια, ἡ cheapness; frugality, economy.

εὐ-τελής 2 cheap; worthless, vile; frugal, plain.

εὔ-τμητος 2 well-cut.

εὔ-τολμος 2 daring, bold.

εὔ-τονος 2 sinewy, strong.

εὐ-τραπελίᾱ 2 versatility in jesting; politeness.

εὐ-τράπελος 2 versatile, witty, clever; cunning.

εὐ-τραφής 2 well-fed, fat.

εὐ-τρεπής 2 ready, prepared.

εὐ-τρεπίζω to make ready, prepare; to repair.

εὐ-τρεφής 2 = εὐτραφής.

εὔ-τρητος 2 well-bored.

εὔ-τριχος 2 = εὔθριξ.

εὐ-τροφίᾱ, ἡ good feeding; fatness. [wheels.]

εὔ-τροχος 2 with good wheels.

εὔ-τυχτος 2 well-wrought, well-made.

εὐ-τυχέω to be lucky, to meet with success; to turn out well.

εὐ-τύχημα, τό piece of good luck; success.

εὐ-τυχής 2 lucky, fortunate, happy; prosperous, successful.

εὐ-τυχίᾱ, ἡ = εὐτύχημα.

εὔ-υδρος 2 well-watered.

εὐ-υφής 2 well-woven.

εὐ-φαρέτρης, ου with beautiful quiver.

εὐ-φημέω to speak words of good omen; to observe solemn silence.

εὐ-φημίᾱ, ἡ solemn silence; good repute.

εὔ-φημος 2 speaking words of good omen; religiously silent; auspicious; of good sound.

εὐ-φιλής 2 well-beloved.

εὔ-φλεχτος 2 easy to set on fire. [fruit.]

εὐ-φορέω to bear good fruit.

εὔ-φορος 2 bearing well; patient; easily borne.

εὐ-φραδής 2 eloquent, considerate.

εὐ-φραίνω to cheer, gladden. — M. and P. to rejoice, to be glad or cheerful.

εὐ-φρονέων 3 well-meaning; sensible.

εὐ-φρόνη, ἡ night.

εὐ-φροσύνη, ἡ mirth, cheerfulness; joy.

εὔ-φρων 2 cheerful, joyous; well - minded, generous; cheering.

εὐ-φυής 2 well-grown, comely; well-gifted, clever; serviceable.   [guard; safe.]

εὐ-φύλακτος 2 easy to

εὐ-φωνίᾱ, ἡ good or loud voice.   [loud-voiced.]

εὔ-φωνος 2 well-voiced,]

εὔ-χαλκος 2 finely wrought of brass or copper.

εὔ-χαρις, ι graceful, lovely, pleasing; witty; decent.

εὐ-χαριστέω to be thankful; to return thanks.

εὐ-χαριστίᾱ, ἡ thankfulness; thanksgiving.

εὐ-χάρι(σ)τος 2 thankful; pleasant; witty.

εὔ-χειρ, ειρος dexterous.

εὐ-χείρωτος 2 easy to overcome.

εὐ-χέρεια, ἡ readiness, dexterity; inclination.

εὐ-χερής 2 placid; easy, without trouble; ready, quick; reckless, hasty.

εὐχετάομαι = εὔχομαι.

εὐχή, ἡ prayer; vow; wish; curse.

εὔ-χλοος 2 becoming green; making green.

εὔχομαι to boast; to assert, profess; to pray, beseech; to wish, vow.

εὖχος, τό boast; glory; vow; wish.   [serviceable.]

εὔ-χρηστος 2 fit for use,]

εὔ-χροος, εὔ-χρους 2, εὔ-χροής 2 of good complexion.

εὔ-χρῡσος 2 rich in gold.

εὐχωλή, ἡ boast, pride; shout; object of pride; prayer; vow; wish.

εὐχωλιμαῖος 3 bound by a vow.   [courage.]

εὐ-ψῡχέω to be of good]

εὐ-ψῡχίᾱ, ἡ courage.

εὔ-ψῡχος 2 courageous.

εὔω to singe.   [fragrant.]

εὐ-ώδης 2 sweet-scented,]

εὐ-ωδίᾱ, ἡ fragrance.

εὔ-ωνος 2 cheap.

εὐ-ώνυμος 2 of good name, of good omen; of the left hand.

εὐ-ῶπις, ιδος fair-faced.

εὐ-ωχέω to treat well, feast, entertain. — P. to be entertained; to make a hearty meal (of).   [fare.]

εὐ-ωχίᾱ, ἡ a feasting; good]

εὐ-ώψ, ῶπος = εὐῶπις.

ἐφ-αγιστεύω, ἐφ-αγνίζω to observe holy rites; to make offerings on a grave.

ἐφ-αιρέω to choose in addition   [upon or towards.]

ἐφ-άλλομαι M. to spring]

ἔφ-αλος 2 by the sea.

ἐφ-άμιλλος 2 disputed; rivalling; equal.

ἐφ-ανδάνω to please.

ἐφ-άπαξ adv. at once, once for all.

ἐφ-άπτω to fasten to, tie to; to decree, to cause. —

M. to touch, grasp; to undertake, partake of; to reach, attain.

ἐφ-αρμόζω to fit on, adapt, put on; to add; *intr.* to be fit.

ἐφ-έδρᾱ, ἡ siege.

ἐφ-εδρεύω to sit at or upon; to lie in wait.

ἔφ-εδρος 2 seated upon; lying in wait; lying in reserve; fresh enemy.

ἐφ-έζω to lay upon; to embark. — *M.* to sit upon, by, or near.

ἐφ-εῖσα *aor.* of ἐφέζω.

ἐφ-ελκύω, ἐφ-έλκω to draw on, attract; to drag, trail after. — *P.* ἐφελκόμενος straggler. — *M.* to draw to or after oneself.

ἐφ-έννῡμι = ἐπιέννυμι.

ἐφ-εξῆς = ἑξῆς.

ἐφ-έπω to follow; to pursue, press on, drive on; to run through; to strive after, to manage. — *M.* to follow, pursue; to yield, obey.

ἐφ-έσπερος 2 western.

ἐφ-έστιος 2 on the hearth, at the fireside; inmate, domestic; suppliant; protector of the household.

ἐφ-ετμή, ἡ order, injunction.

ἐφ-ευρετής, οῦ, ὁ inventor.

ἐφ-ευρίσκω to catch, to detect; to invent.

ἐφ-εφιάομαι *M.* to mock at.

ἐφ-ηβάω to grow to maturity.

ἔφ-ηβος, ὁ grown-up youth.

ἐφ-ηγέομαι *M.* to lead on.

ἐφ-ήδομαι to feel (mischievous) joy. [be present.]

ἐφ-ήκω to arrive at; to

ἔφ-ημαι to sit at, on, or by.

ἐφ-ημερίᾱ, ἡ daily service; section of priests on duty.

ἐφ-ημέριος 2, ἐφ-ήμερος 2 lasting one day, during the day, for one day, ephemeral.

ἐφ-ημοσύνη = ἐφετμή.

ἑφθός 3 boiled.

ἐφ-ιζάνω, ἐφ-ίζω to sit on, at, or by.

ἐφ-ίημι to send to, against, or at; to launch, to let go; to incite; to lay upon, impose, decree; to permit, abandon, yield; *intr.* to abandon oneself to. — *M.* to aim at, long after, desire; to enjoin, to allow.

ἐφ-ικνέομαι *M.* to reach to, arrive at; to hit, touch.

ἐφ-ίμερος 2 longed for.

ἔφ-ιππος 2 mounted, on horseback.

ἐφ-ίστημι to set or place upon, at, or near; to establish, set up, fix, appoint, order; to set over; to check, stop. — *intr.* and *M.* to stand upon, tread on; to stand near; to approach, impend, be at hand; to surprise; to stand against; to assist; to be set over, to be at the head, to direct; to set to, attend; to halt, stop.

ἐφ-οδεύω and *M.* to go the rounds, inspect.

ἐφ-οδιάζω to supply with money or stores for travelling. — M. to receive money for travelling.

ἐφ-όδιον, τό money or supplies for travelling.

ἔφ-οδος¹ 2 accessible.

ἔφ-οδος², ἡ way to, approach; intercourse, access; attack.

ἐφ-όλκαιον, τό rudder.

ἐφ-ολκός 2 attractive.

ἐφ-ομαρτέω to go along with. [ready, prepare.]

ἐφ-οπλίζω to equip, get]

ἐφ-οράω to look on, oversee, inspect, observe; to visit; to choose; to live to see.

ἐφ-ορεύω to be an ephor.

ἐφ-ορμάω to stir up against, rouse. — P. to be stirred up or roused; to set on, assail, attack.

ἐφ-ορμέω to lie at anchor; to blockade.

ἐφ-ορμή, ἡ access; attack.

ἐφ-όρμησις, ἡ anchorage; blockade.

ἐφ-ορμίζομαι P. to come to anchor. [chor.]

ἔφ-ορμος¹ 2 lying at an-]

ἔφ-ορμος², ὁ = ἐφόρμησις.

ἔφ-ορος, ὁ overseer, guardian; ephor.

ἐφ-υβρίζω to act insolently or wantonly; to insult; to illtreat. [ing rain.]

ἔφ-υδρος 2 watery, bring-]

ἐφ-υμνέω to sing at or over; to sing a funeral song; to wish one something; to curse.

ἐφ-ύπερθεν adv. from above, above; over along.

ἐφ-υστερίζω to be later.

ἐχ-έγγυος 2 trustworthy, secure; on security.

ἐχέ-θυμος 2 under self-control. [cing.]

ἐχε-πευκής 2 sharp, pier-]

ἐχέ-φρων 2 sensible, prudent.

ἐχθαίρω to hate.

ἐχθαρτέος 3 to be hated.

ἐχθές adv. yesterday, = χθές. [mity with.]

ἐχθοδοπέω to be at en-]

ἐχθοδοπός 3 hostile.

ἔχθος, τό, ἔχθρα, ἡ hatred, enmity.

ἐχθρός 3 hated, hateful; hating, hostile; ὁ ἐ. enemy, adversary.

ἔχθω to hate.

ἔχιδνα, ἡ adder, viper.

ἔχμα, τό hindrance, obstacle; bulwark; support, prop, holdfast. [cure, safe.]

ἐχυρός 3 firm, strong, se-]

ἔχω to have; to hold, to hold fast; to possess, to have wealth; to have to wife; to inhabit; to rule, govern; to suffer; to occupy; to obtain, to seize; to have put on; to contain, compass; to know, be able; to cause, imply, infer; to preserve; to detain; to protect; to retain, restrain, check, hinder; to direct to, to aim at. — intr. to behave, to be disposed, to be in a state; to stand fast, to keep one's ground, to hold out, endure; to reach to. — *M.* to have or hold for oneself. — *M.* and *P.* to hold oneself to, to cling to, to depend upon; to hold fast, to continue; to be attached or fixed to; to border on, to be next to; to concern, affect; to abstain, refrain.

ἔφημα, τό what can be boiled.

ἕφησις, ἡ a boiling.

ἑφητός 3 boiled. [oneself.]

ἐφιάομαι *M.* to jest, amuse)

ἕφω to boil.

ἔωθα = εἴωθα.

ἔωθεν *adv.* at dawn.

ἑωθινός 3 early in the morning. [mains.)

ἑωλο-κρᾱσίᾱ, ἡ dregs, re-)

ἔωμεν, ἐῶμεν *aor. conj.* we have enough.

ἑῷος 3 in the morning, at dawn; eastern.

ἑώρᾱ, ἡ suspension, string.

ἕως[1], ω, ἡ dawn (of day), day-break, morning; east.

ἕως[2] *conj.* as long as, while; till; in order that. — *adv.* for some time; till when.

ἕως-περ even till. [star.)

ἕως-φόρος, ὁ morning-)

Z

Z, ζ (ζῆτα) sixth letter of the alphabet; as a numeral ζ' = 7.

ζόγκλον, τό sickle.

ζαής 2 strong blowing.

ζά-θεος 3 most holy.

ζά-κοτος 2 wrathful.

ζάλη, ἡ surge, spray; storm.

ζα-μενής 2 very violent, raging, angry.

ζά-πλουτος 2 very rich or wealthy.

ζα-τρεφής 2 well-fed.

ζα-φλεγής 2 fiery, vigorous.

ζα-χρηής 2 vehement, impetuous, stormy.

ζά-χρῡσος 2 rich in gold.

ζάω to live, to be alive; to lead a life; to live on, to be strong.

ζειά, ἡ spelt, amel-corn.

ζεί-δωρος 2 corn-producing.

ζειρά, ἡ long cloak.

ζευγ-ηλατέω to drive a team; to plough.

ζευγ-ηλάτης, ου, ὁ driver of a team, ploughman.

ζεύγλη, ἡ collar of the yoke; rudder-band.

ζεῦγμα, τό band, bond; bar, impediment; bridge.

ζεύγνῡμι to join or link together; to yoke, harness, fetter; to marry, unite; to join by a bridge, to throw a bridge over, to close; to calk (ships).

ζεῦγος, τό yoke, team; carriage, vehicle; pair, couple.

ζευκτήριος 3 fit for joining.

ζεῦξις, ἡ a yoking, harnessing; a joining by a bridge.

ζέφυρος, ὁ west wind; west.

ζέω to boil, seethe; to be hot, to rage.

ζηλεύω = ζηλόω.

ζηλήμων 2 jealous.

ζῆλος, ὁ and τό eagerness, emulation, admiration, jealousy, envy, zeal, passion, anger; enviable happiness.

ζηλο-τυπέω to be jealous, to envy.

ζηλόω to rival, vie with; to admire, praise; to envy, to be jealous; to strive after.

ζήλωμα, τό emulation, pursuit; high fortune.

ζήλωσις, ἡ emulation.

ζηλωτής, οῦ, ὁ rival, admirer; zealot.

ζηλωτός 3 admired; envied; enviable.

ζημία, ἡ damage, loss; penalty, punishment; fine.

ζημιόω to damage, to punish, chastise; to fine. — P. to be hurt, to suffer damage.

ζημιώδης injurious.

ζημίωμα, τό punishment.

ζητέω to seek, seek for; to inquire into, examine; to endeavour, desire, demand.

ζήτημα, τό a seeking, inquiry, examination; question, problem.

ζήτησις, ἡ a seeking, seeking for, searching, inquiry, investigation; problem, dispute.   [searcher.]

ζητητής, οῦ, ὁ inquirer,

ζητητός 3 sought for.

ζιζάνιον, τό darnel.

ζόη, ζοή, ἡ = ζωή.

ζορκάς, ἡ = δορκάς.

ζόφος, ὁ darkness, gloom; reign of darkness; west.

ζύγαστρον, τό wooden chest or box.   [thong.]

ζυγό-δεσμον, τό yoke-

ζυγόν, τό, ζυγός, ὁ yoke, cross-bar; team, pair; bridge of a lyre; bank of oars; beam of the balance; balance; row, line.   [horses.]

ζυγωτός 3 drawn by good

ζύμη, ἡ leaven.

ζῡμίτης, ου leavened.

ζῡμόω to leaven, to cause to ferment.   [saving life.]

ζω-άγρια, τά reward for

ζω-γραφία, ἡ painting.

ζω-γράφος, ὁ painter.

ζωγρέω to catch alive; to give quarter to; to restore to life.

ζωγρία, ἡ a catching alive.

ζῴδιον, τό small animal, figure, image.

ζωή, ἡ life; lifetime; manner or mode of life; subsistence; property, goods.

ζῶμα, τό girdle, belt, apron; part of the armour.

ζώνη, ἡ belt, girdle; waist, loins.

ζώννῡμι, -ύω to gird. — M. to gird oneself (for battle or work).

ζωο-γονέω to produce living beings; to preserve alive.

ζῷον, ζῶον, τό living being, animal, creature, beast; figure, image, picture, painting, ornament ζωο-ποιέω to make alive, quicken.

ζωός, ζωός 3 alive.

ζωρός 2 strong, stout, unmixed.

ζώς, ζών = ζωός. [belt.]

ζωστήρ, ῆρος, ὁ girdle,

ζῶστρον, τό girdle.

ζωτικός 3 full of life, lively, animated.

H

H, η (ἦτα) seventh letter of the alphabet; as a numeral η' = 8.

ἦ adv. truly, verily; as an interr. particle = Lat. num, nonne.

ἤ conj. or, ἤ ... ἤ either ... or; if, whether, ἤ ... ἤ whether ... or; than.

ᾗ adv. where; whither; how, as, as far as; wherefore.

ἦ = ἦν I was (εἶναι); = ἔφη he said (from ἠμί = φημί).

ᾖα = ᾖειν (ἰέναι); = ᾔα, τά.

ἠ-βαιός 3 small, little, tiny. [estate.]

ἡβάσκω to come to man's

ἡβάω to be at man's estate, to be in the prime of youth.

ἥβη, ἡ youth, prime of youth; vigour; young men; manhood.

ἡβηδόν adv. in manhood.

ἡβητικός 3, ἡβός 3 youthful.

ἠγά-θεος 3 most holy.

ἡγεμονεύω to guide, lead the way; to be leader, to rule, command.

ἡγεμονία, ἡ the leading the way, leadership, command, chief place; sovereignty, supremacy.

ἡγεμονικός 3 fit for enterprising, for leading or commanding.

ἡγεμόσυνα, τά thank-offerings for safe-conduct.

ἡγεμών, όνος, ὁ, ἡ guide, leader; chief, ruler, commander; prince, governor.

ἡγέομαι M. to lead the way, to go before; to lead the van; to be leader, ruler, or chief; to think, mean, believe. [together.]

ἡγερέθομαι to be gathered

ἡγηλάζω to guide.

ἡγητήρ, ῆρος and ἡγήτωρ, ορος, ὁ = ἡγεμών.

ἠδέ and; ἠμέν ... ἠδέ as well as.

ἤδη adv. already, now; presently, forthwith; besides, further; therefore; even; yet.

ἥδομαι P. to rejoice, to be pleased or glad, to enjoy oneself. to delight.

ἡδονή, ἡ joy, pleasure, delight, enjoyment; lust; comfort; profit, gain; mischievous joy.

ἦδος, τό = ἡδονή.

ἡδυ-επής 2 sweet-speaking.

ἥδυμος 2 sweet, refreshing.

ἡδύ-οσμον, τό mint.

ἡδυ-παθέω to live pleasantly; to be luxurious.

ἡδύ-πνοος 2 sweet-breathing, auspicious.

ἡδύ-πολις, ὁ, ἡ agreeable to the city.

ἡδύ-ποτος 2 sweet to drink.

ἡδύς 3 sweet, pleasant, lovely, agreeable; joyous, amiable; dear; well-minded, kind.

ἥδυσμα, τό spice.

ἡέ or ἧε = ἤ.

ἠέλιος = ἥλιος.

ἠέπερ = ἤπερ.

ἠερέθομαι to float, to hang waving in the air; to be flighty.   [morning.]

ἠέριος 3 early in the

ἠερόεις 3, ἠερο-ειδής 2 aëriform; misty, dark.

ἠερο-φοῖτις, ιδος, ἡ walking in the dark.

ἠερό-φωνος 2 loud-voiced.

ἠήρ, ἠέρος = ἀήρ.

ἠθάς, άδος wont, accustomed; acquainted with.

ἠθεῖος 3 dear, beloved.

ἤθεος, ὁ = ἠίθεος.

ἠθικός 3 ethical, moral.

ἠθμός, ἤθμός, ὁ sieve, strainer.

ἦθος, τό accustomed place, seat, station, abode, stable; disposition, character, temper; custom; morality.

ἤϊα, τό provisions, food; prey.

ἠίθεος, ὁ youth, bachelor.

ἤϊκτο he was like (from ἔοικα)

ἠϊόεις 3 with high banks.

ἦϊος, ὁ shooting (or shining).

ἠϊών, όνος, ἡ shore, beach.

ἦκα adv. softly, gently; slowly.

ἤκεστος 3 ungoaded (or unmanageable).

ἥκιστα adv. least, not at all.

ἥκιστος 3 slowest, slackest

ἤκου = ἤπου.

ἥκω to have or be come, to be here; to be back; to have come to, to possess; to arrive, come to pass, occur.   [distaff.]

ἠλάκατα, τά wool on the

ἠλακάτη, ἡ distaff, spindle.

ἠλασκάζω, ἠλάσκω to wander, stray; to shun, flee from.

ἤλεκτρον, τό, ἤλεκτρος, ὁ, ἡ electron, alloy of gold and silver; amber.

ἠλέκτωρ, ορος beaming; the sun.

ἠλεός 3 distracted, befooled; befooling.

ἡλιαία, ἡ law-court, jury.

ἠλίβατος 2 steep, abrupt.

ἦλιθα adv. plentifully.

ἠλίθιος 3 silly; vain, idle.

ἠλιθιότης, ητος, ἡ silliness.

ἡλικία, ἡ time of life, age; prime of life, manhood; those of the same age; fit to bear arms, comrades; age, time, century; stature, bodily growth.

ἡλικιώτης, ου, ὁ of the same age; comrade.

ἡλίκος 3 as big or great as; how great, how old.

ἦλιξ, ικος = ἡλικιώτης.

ἥλιος, ὁ sun; sunlight, daylight, day; east; the sun-god.   [from the sun.]

ἡλιο-στεγής 2 protecting

ἠλιτό-μηνος 2 prematurely born. [the sun.]

ἠλιῶτις, ιδος belonging to] ἤλος, ὁ nail, stud.

ἤλυσις, ἡ a coming.

ἦμα, τό a throw.

ἠμαθόεις 3 sandy.

ἧμαι to sit; to be at leisure; to lie in wait; to tarry; to be built.

ἦμαρ, ατος, τό = ἡμέρα.

ἠμάτιος 3 by day; daily.

ἡμεῖς we. [ly.]

ἠμελημένως adv. careless-]

ἠμέν ... ἠδέ as well as.

ἡμέρα, ἡ day; daylight; time; time of life; fate.

ἡμερεύω to pass the day, to live on.

ἡμερήσιος 2 and 3, ἡμερινός 3, ἡμέριος 2 by day, daily; a day long; short-lived. [vine.]

ἡμερίς, ίδος, ἡ cultivated]

ἡμερο-δρόμος, ὁ day-runner, courier. [days.]

ἡμερο-λογέω to count by]

ἥμερος 2 tame; improved, cultivated; gentle.

ἡμερο-σκόπος, ὁ daywatcher. [ἡμεροσκόπος.]

ἡμερο-φύλαξ, ακος, ὁ =]

ἡμερόω to tame; to cultivate. — M. to subdue.

ἡμέτερος 3 our; ours.

ἠμί I say.

ἡμί-βρωτος 2 half-eaten.

ἡμι-δαής 2 half-burnt.

ἡμι-δαρεικόν, τό half-daric.

ἡμι-δεής 2 half-full.

ἡμί-εργος, ὁ half-done.

ἡμι-θανής 2 = ἡμιθνής.

ἡμί-θεος, ὁ demigod.

ἡμι-θνής, ῆτος half-dead.

ἡμι-μναῖον, τό a half-mine.

ἡμι-μόχθηρος 2 half-wretched.

ἡμι-όλιος 3 one and the half; half as large again.

ἡμιόνειος 3, ἡμιονικός 3 of mules.

ἡμί-ονος, ἡ, ὁ mule.

ἡμι-πέλεκκον, τό half-axe.

ἡμί-πλεθρον, τό halfplethron. [brick.]

ἡμι-πλίνθιον, τό half-]

ἥμισυς 3 half. [talent.]

ἡμι-τάλαντον, τό half-]

ἡμι-τέλεστος 2, ἡμι-τελής 2 half-finished. [through.]

ἡμί-τομος 2 half-cut]

ἡμι-ωβολιαῖος 3 as large as a half-obol.

ἡμι-ωβόλιον, τό half-obol.

ἡμι-ώριον, τό, ἡμι-ωρον, τό half-hour. [soon as.]

ἦμος conj. when, while; as]

ἡμύω to sink, droop.

ἥμων, ονος spear-throwing.

ἠνεμόεις 3 = ἀνεμόεις.

ἡνία, ἡ rein, bridle; pl. also τὰ ἡνία.

ἡνίκα conj. when, at the time when.

ἡνίον see ἡνία. [shop.]

ἡνιο-ποιεῖον, τό saddler's]

ἡνιο-στρόφος, ὁ = ἡνίοχος.

ἡνι-οχεία, ἡ a driving; a directing.

ἡνι-οχέω, -εύω to hold the reins, drive.

ἡνί-οχος, ἡνι-οχεύς, ὁ driver, charioteer.

ἦνις, ἦνῖς, ιος yearling (shining?) [ness.]

ἠνορέη, ἡ strength, manli-

ἤν-οφ, οπος shining.

ἠνώγεα see ἄνωγα.

ἠοίη, ἡ morning. [eastern.]

ἠοῖος 3 in the morning;

ἠός = ἕως.

ἧπαρ, ατος, τό liver; heart.

ἠπεδανός 3 feeble, infirm.

ἤπειρος, ὁ continent, mainland; inland. [mainland.]

ἠπειρόω to convert into

ἠπειρώτης, ου, ὁ, ἠπειρῶτις, ιδος, ἡ, ἠπειρωτικός 3 of the mainland, continental; Asiatic.

ἤπερ conj. even where; just as.

ἠπεροπεύς, ἠπεροπευτής, οῦ, ὁ deceiver. [cheat.]

ἠπεροπεύω to deceive,

ἠπιό-δωρος 2 kindly giving.

ἤπιος 3 gentle, mild, kind, friendly; soothing. [less.]

ἤπου adv. certainly, doubt-

ἤπου adv. or perhaps.

ἠπύτα, ὁ loud-calling; crier.

ἠπύω to cry aloud, to cry to; to sound, roar.

ἦρ, ἦρος, τό = ἔαρ. [ness]

ἦρα (φέρειν) favour, kind-

ἠρέμα adv. softly, gently, quietly; slowly; slightly.

ἠρεμαῖος 3 gentle, quiet.

ἠρεμέω to be or keep quiet or unchanged.

ἠρεμία, ἡ stillness, rest.

ἤρεμος 2 = ἠρεμαῖος.

ἦρι adv. early, in the morning.

ἠρι-γένεια, ἡ early-born.

ἠρινός 3 = ἐαρινός.

ἠρίον, τό mound. tomb.

ἡρωϊκός 3 heroic, of heroes.

ἡρῷος 3 = ἡρωικός; τό ἡρῷον temple of a hero.

ἥρως, ωος, ὁ hero; demigod.

ἧσσα, ἡ defeat.

ἡσσάομαι P. to be less, weaker, or inferior; to be defeated or beaten; to be subject, to be under the control of; to lose one's cause.

ἥσσων 2 less, weaker, inferior; defeated, subject, yielding; adv. ἧσσον less.

ἡσυχάζω to rest, be quiet; to stop, halt; to be silent; to give up resistance; trans. to calm, soothe.

ἡσυχαῖος 3 quiet, still, gentle; slow, cautious; peaceable; placid; untroubled, secure; secret.

ἡσυχῇ adv. = ἡσύχως.

ἡσυχία, ἡ stillness, quiet, silence; loneliness; rest, leisure; ease, content.

ἡσύχιος 2, ἥσυχος 2 = ἡσυχαῖος.

ἦτε adv. truly, verily, surely.

ἦτε conj. or, or also.

ἦτοι conj. surely, verily, indeed; now; therefore.

ἦτορ, ορος, τό heart, mind, soul; life, spirit, vigour.

ἦτρον, τό belly.

ἧττ- see ἧσσ-.

ἠϋ-γένειος 2 = εὐγένειος.

ἠΰ-ζωνος = εὔζωνος.

ἠΰ-κομος 2 = with fine locks.

ἠΰς, ἠΰ = ἐΰς.

ἠΰτε conj. as, like as, as if.

ἡφαιστό-τευκτος 2 made or wrought by Vulcane.

ἠχέω to sound, ring; to cause to sound, to utter.

ἠχή, ἡ sound, noise; cries; rumour.

ἠχήεις 3 sounding, roaring.

ἦχι adv. where.

ἦχος, ὁ and τό = ἠχή.

ἠχώ, οῦς, ἡ sound, echo; lament; report, rumour.

ἠῶθεν adv. from morning, at dawn.

ἠῶθι adv. early in the morning.

ἠών, όνος, ἡ = ἠϊών.

ἦφος 3 = ἑῷος.

ἠώς, ἠοῦς, ἡ = ἕως[1].

Θ

Θ, θ (θῆτα) eighth letter of the alphabet; as a numeral θ' = 9.

θαάσσω to sit.

θαιρός, ὁ hinge of a door.

θᾱκέω to sit.

θάκημα, τό, θάκησις, ἡ a sitting; seat; residence.

θαλάμη, ἡ = θάλαμος.

θαλαμη-πόλος 2 belonging to the bridal chamber; ὁ θ. bridegroom; ἡ θ. bridesmaid.

θαλαμίη, ἡ hole for an oar.

θαλάμιος, θαλαμιός, ὁ rower of the lowest bench.

θάλαμος, ὁ couch, chamber, apartment, bedroom; women's apartment; bridal chamber; store-room, treasury; palace.

θάλασσα, ἡ sea, sea-water.

θαλασσεύω to be at sea.

θαλάσσιος 3 of the sea, maritime, seafaring.

θαλασσο-κρατέω to be master of the sea.

θαλασσο-κράτωρ, ορος, ὁ master of the sea.

θάλεα, έων, τά good things, delights. [swelled (up).]

θαλέθω to bloom; to be

θαλερός 3 blooming, fresh,

young, vigorous; copious, abundant.

θαλίᾱ, ἡ bloom, happiness; good cheer, feast.

θαλλός, ὁ sprouting twig; olive-branch; foliage.

θάλλω to sprout, shoot, bloom, flourish; to be abundant, rich, or swelling; to grow; to prosper; to be esteemed.

θάλος, τό = θαλλός.

θαλπιάω to be warm.

θάλπος, τό warmth, heat.

θάλπω to warm, heat; to inflame; to be or become warm, to glow. [comfort.]

θαλπωρή, ἡ a warming,

θάλυς 3 blooming; θάλεια δαίς delicious feast.

θαλύσια, τά offering of first-fruits. [in crowds.]

θαμά adv. often, frequently;

θαμβέω to amaze; to be astonished or amazed; to shudder. [horror.]

θάμβος, τό astonishment;

θαμέες, οἱ, αἱ, θαμειός 3 frequent, thick, in crowds.

θαμίζω to come often, to frequent; to be frequent.

θαμινά adv. = θαμά.

θάμνος, ὁ bush, shrub.

θανάσιμος 2 belonging to death; deadly; mortal, dying; dead.

θανατάω to long for death.

θανατη-φόρος 2 death-bringing.

θανατόεις 3 = θανάσιμος.

θάνατος, ὁ death; murder; execution.

θανατόω to put to death, to kill, slay, execute.

θάομαι = θεάομαι.

θάπτω to bury, inter.

Θαργηλιών, ῶνος, ὁ the eleventh month of the Athenians (May to June).

θαρσαλέος, θαρραλέος 3 bold, daring, courageous; insolent, presumptious; encouraging, dangerless.

θαρσέω, θαρρέω to be bold, daring, courageous, confident, or presumptious; to believe confidently.

θάρσησις, ἡ confidence.

θάρσος, τό courage, boldness, confidence; daring, presumption.

θαρσύνω 2 confident, of good cheer. [θρασύνω.]

θαρσύνω, θαρρύνω = }

θάσσω to sit.

θάτερον = τὸ ἕτερον.

θαῦμα, τό wonder, marvel, wondrous thing; astonishment, admiration.

θαυμάζω to be astonished or amazed, to wonder; to admire, esteem; to wonder at; to be curious to learn.

θαυμαίνω = θαυμάζω.

θαυμάσιος 3 wondrous, wonderful, extraordinary;

marvellous, strange; admirable, excellent.

θαυμαστός 3 = θαυμάσιος.

θαυματο-ποιός, ὁ juggler, conjurer.

θάω to suckle, feed. — M. to suck; to milk.

θεά, θέαινα, ἡ goddess.

θέᾱ, ἡ a looking at, view; spectacle.

θέᾱμα, τό sight, spectacle.

θεάομαι M. to view, behold, observe; to reflect, know; to admire, gaze at.

θεᾱρός, ὁ = θεωρός.

θεᾱτής, οῦ, ὁ looker-on, spectator.

θεᾱτός 3 to be seen.

θεᾱτρίζω to expose to ridicule.

θέᾱτρον, τό theatre, stage; spectators, audience; play.

θέειον, τό = θεῖον.

θεειόω to fumigate with brimstone.

θε-ήλατος 2 sent by god; driven for the gods.

θειάζω to prophesy.

θειασμός, ὁ superstition.

θειλό-πεδον, τό sunny place.

θείνω to beat, strike, hit.

θεῖον, τό brimstone.

θεῖος[1], ὁ uncle.

θεῖος[2] 3 of gods, divine; holy, sacred; godlike, superhuman, sublime, august. τὸ θεῖον deity, divine being; τὰ θεῖα divine things; religion, oracles, worship.

θειότης, ητος, ἡ divinity, divine nature. [(τίθημι).]

θείω = θέω to run; = θῶ}

θειώδης 2 sulphurous.

θέλγω to charm, enchant; to blind, cheat, seduce; to fascinate, win.

θέλημα, τό, θέλησις, ἡ a willing, will.

θελκτήριος 2 charming, enchanting; τὸ θ. spell, charm; delight. [ριον.}

θέλκτρον, τό = θελκτή-}

θέλω = ἐθέλω.

θέμεθλα, τά, θεμείλια, τά see θεμέλιος.

θεμέλιος, ὁ and θεμέλιον, τό foundation-stone; base, bottom, foundation.

θεμελιόω to found; to make firm.

θέμις, ιστος, ἡ divine right, law, custom, prerogative, privilege; judicial sentence; tax.

θεμιστεύω to give law; to give oracles.

θεμιστός 3, **θεμιτός** 3 lawful, just.

θεμόω to cause. [hand.}

θέναρ, αρος, τό flat of the}

θεο-βλαβής 2 stricken with madness. [descent.}

θεο-γεννής 2 of divine}

θεο-γονία, ἡ genealogy of the gods. [God.}

θεο-δίδακτος 2 taught by}

θεό-δμητος 2 god-built.

θεο-ειδής 2, **θεο-είκελος** 2 godlike.

θεόθεν adv. from the gods.

θεο-λόγος, ὁ theologian.

θεό-μαντις, ὁ soothsayer.

θεο-μαχέω to fight against God. [gods.}

θεο-μαχία, ἡ battle of the}

θεο-μάχος 2 fighting against God.

θεο-προπέω to prophesy.

θεο-προπία, ἡ, θεο-πρόπιον, τό prophecy, oracle.

θεο-πρόπος 2 prophetic; prophet, soothsayer.

θεός, ὁ, ἡ god, goddess; deity, divine being.

θεο-σέβεια, ἡ fear of God.

θεο-σεβής 2 God-fearing, religious.

θεο-στυγής 2 hated by God; hating God.

θεότης, ητος, ἡ divinity.

θεουδής 2 fearing God.

θεο-φάνια, τά spring-festival at Delphi.

θεο-φιλής 2 beloved by God; blessed. [vant.}

θεράπαινα, ἡ maid-ser-}

θεραπεία, ἡ, θεράπευμα, τό service, attendance, a courting, deference, flattery; care, worship; a fostering, nurture, medical treatment, nursing, finery; servants, retinue. [ράπων.}

θεραπευτής, οῦ, ὁ = θε-}

θεραπευτικός 3 courteous, obedient. [fostered.}

θεραπευτός 3 to be}

θεραπεύω to serve, attend, wait on; to court, flatter, honour, win; to take care of, to treat carefully, to tend, nurse, heal; to cultivate; to pay attention to.

θεράπων, οντος, ὁ servant, attendant, waiter; companion in arms, comrade.

θερεία, ἡ summer-time.

θερίζω to pass the summer; to reap; to cut off; to destroy.

θερινός 3 in summer.

θερισμός, ὁ a reaping; harvest-time; crop.

θεριστής, οῦ, ὁ reaper.

θερμαίνω to warm, heat; to burn. — P. to become warm or hot.

θερμασίᾱ, ἡ warmth, heat.

θέρμη, ἡ warmth; fever; hot spring.

θερμός 3 warm, hot; rash.

θερμότης, ητος, ἡ = θερμασία. [ing, rash.]

θερμουργός 2 hot in act-)

θέρμω = θερμαίνω.

θέρομαι P. to become warm or hot; to be burnt.

θέρος, τό summer; harvest.

θέσις, ἡ a setting, placing; condition, situation; proposition.

θέσκελος 2 marvellous.

θέσμιος 2 according to law.

θεσμο-θέτης, ου, ὁ lawgiver; Athenian magistrate.

θεσμός, ὁ place; statute, law, rule; institution, custom.

θεσμο-φόρια, τά a festival of the Athenian women.

θεσμο-φοριάζω to keep the Thesmophoria.

θεσμο-φόρος 2 lawgiving.

θεσμο-φύλαξ, ακος, ὁ guardian of the law.

θεσπέσιος 3 and 2 divinely sounding or singing; divine, august, unspeakable.

θεσπι-δαής 2 blazing prodigiously.

θεσπι-έπεια, ἡ prophetic.

θεσπίζω to prophesy.

θέσπις, ιος, ὁ, ἡ inspired (by God), divine.

θέσπισμα, τό oracle.

θέσ-φατος 2 announced or decreed by God; made by God.

θετός 3 adopted.

θέω to run, hasten.

θεωρέω to look at, view, behold, observe; to be a spectator; to consider, contemplate, examine; to perceive. [tacle.]

θεώρημα, τό sight, spec-)

θεωρίᾱ, ἡ a looking at, beholding, viewing; curiosity, presence at a festival; examination, contemplation, theory; festival, spectacle; sending of ambassadors on an oracle.

θεωρικός 3 belonging to a spectacle or festival; τὰ θεωρικά money for spectacles.

θεωρίς, ίδος, ἡ sacred ship for carrying ambassadors.

θεωρός, ὁ spectator; ambassador sent to a festival or oracle.

θεώτερος 3 = θειότερος.

θηγάνη, ἡ whetstone.

θήγω to whet, sharpen; to incite, encourage.

θηέομαι = θεάομαι.

θηητήρ, ῆρος, ὁ = θεατής.

θηκαῖος 3 belonging to a sepulchre.

θήκη, ἡ box, chest; tomb, coffin; sheath. [to suck.]

θηλάζω and M. to suckle;)

θηλέω to flourish.

θηλυδρίας, ου, ὁ effeminate man. [prolific.

θῆλυς 3 female; effeminate;

θημών, ῶνος, ὁ heap.

θήν adv. certainly, surely.

θήρ, θηρός, ὁ wild beast, beast of prey; monster.

θήρᾱ, ἡ a hunting, chase; game. [or won.

θηρᾱτέος 3 to be hunted

θηρᾱτικός 3 belonging or pertaining to hunting.

θήρᾱτρον, τό hunting-equipage.

θηράω and M. to hunt, chase, pursue; to catch.

θήρειος 2 of wild beasts.

θηρευτής, οῦ, ὁ hunter.

θηρευτικός 3 belonging or pertaining to the chase.

θηρεύω = θηράω.

θηρητήρ, ῆρος and θηρήτωρ, ορος, ὁ = θηρευτής.

θηριο-μαχέω to fight with wild beasts.

θηρίον, τό = θήρ.

θηριώδης 2 full of wild beasts; beastly, brutal.

θηροβολέω to kill wild beasts. [journeyman.

θής, θητός, ὁ labourer,

θησαυρίζω to treasure up, lay in.

θησαύρισμα, τό store.

θησαυρός, ὁ store-room, treasure-house; store, treasure.

θητεία, ἡ hired service.

θητεύω to work for pay.

θίασος, ὁ band of revellers in honour of Bacchus; procession; dance; company.

θιγγάνω to touch, handle, take hold of; to reach, gain.

θίς, θῑνός, ὁ, ἡ heap (of sand), sand; beach, strand; sand-bank, sandy desert.

θλάω to crush, bruise.

θλίβω to press; to rub; to oppress, confine.

θλῖψις and θλίψις, ἡ oppression, affliction, distress.

θνήσκω, θνῄσκω to die, perish; to be killed.

θνητο-γενής 2 of mortal race. [nature.

θνητο-ειδής 2 of mortal

θνητός 3 mortal; human.

θοάζω to hurry along; to move quickly; = θάσσω.

θοινάω to feast, entertain; to eat. [enjoyment.

θοίνη, ἡ banquet, feast;

θολερός 3 muddy, dirty; troubled.

θόλος, ἡ dome-shaped roof; vaulted building.

θοός[1] 3 quick, swift.

θοός[2] 3 sharp, pointed.

θοόω to make pointed.

θορή, ἡ, θορός, ὁ seed of the male, semen.

θόρνυμαι to copulate.

θορυβάζω to trouble.

θορυβέω to make a noise; to applaud; to murmur; to trouble, disturb.

θόρυβος, ὁ noise; uproar, confusion.

θοῦρος 3 and θοῦρος 2, fem. θοῦρις, ιδος rushing on, impetuous.

θόωκος, ὁ = θῶκος, θᾶκος.

θρᾶνίτης, ου, ὁ rower of the uppermost bench.

θράσος, τό = θάρσος.

θράσσω to trouble.

θράσσω to trouble.

θρχσυ-κάρδιος 2 stout-hearted. [bold.]

θρασυ-μέμνων 2 enduring,

θρασύνω to encourage. — intr., P. and M. to take comfort; to be bold.

θρασύς 3 = θαρσαλέος.

θρασυ-στομέω to speak boldly.

θρασύτης, ητος, ἡ boldness, audaciousness. [crush.]

θραύω to break, shiver,

θρέμμα, τό nursling, child; cattle for breeding; breed.

θρέομαι to cry, lament.

θρεπτήρια, θρέπτρα, τά food; reward for bringing up.

θρηνέω to wail, lament.

θρῆνος, ὁ a wailing, la-menting; dirge.

θρῆνυς, υος, ὁ footstool.

θρησκεία, ἡ worship, re-ligious observance.

θρησκεύω to observe re-ligiously.

θρῆσκος 2 religious.

θριαμβεύω to triumph; to cause to triumph.

θρίαμβος, ὁ hymn; pro-cession, triumph.

θριγκός, ὁ cornice, pro-jection of a wall.

θριγκόω to surround with a cornice, to fence in, to finish.

θρῖδαξ, ακος, ἡ lettuce.

θρίξ, τριχός, ἡ hair; wool, bristle.

θροέω to cry aloud, shreak; to utter, tell, speak; to frighten. — P. to be afraid.

θρόμβος, ὁ lump.

θρομβώδης 2 clotty.

θρόνα, τά flowers (in em-broidery). [throne.]

θρόνος, ὁ seat, chair;

θρόος, θροῦς, ὁ cry, shout; murmur; report.

θρυλέω to babble; to dis-cuss, to make a great talk of.

θρυλίσσω to shiver.

θρύον, τό rush.

θρυπτικός 3 exhausted; effeminate.

θρύπτω to grind, crush. — P. to be or become en-feebled or enervated; to boast. [fly; to assault.]

θρῴσκω to spring, leap,

θρωσμός, ὁ height; hill.

θυγάτηρ, τρός, ἡ daughter.

θυγατριδέος, ὁ grandson.

θυγατριδῆ, ἡ grand-daugh-ter. [ter.]

θυγάτριον, τό little daugh-

θύελλα, ἡ whirlwind, storm.

θυήεις 3 fragrant.

θυηλή, ἡ burnt-offering.

θυία, θυϊάς, άδος, ἡ Bac-chante. [wood.]

θύϊνος 3 made of cedar

θύλακος, ὁ, θυλάκιον, τό bag, pouch. [fice.]

θῦμα, τό offering, sacri-

θυμαίνω to be angry.

θυμ-αλγής 2 aggrieving.

θυμ-ἄρής 2 well-pleasing, dear. [one's spirit.]

θυμ-ηγερέω to collect

θυμ-ηδής 2 well-pleasing.

θυμ-ήρης = θυμαρής.

θυμίαμα, τό incense.

θυμιατήριον, τό censer.

θυμιάω to burn as incense.

θυμο-βόρος 2, θυμο-δακής aggrieving, mortifying.

θυμο-ειδής 2 courageous; angry, hot, wild. [hearted.]

θυμο-λέων, οντος lion-]

θυμο-μαχέω to fight with all one's heart.

θυμο-ραϊστής, οῦ life-destroying.

θυμός, ὁ soul, life; will, desire; appetite; resolution; thought; mind, heart, sense; courage, spirit, passion, anger, wrath.

θυμο-φθορέω to fret.

θυμο-φθόρος 2 life-destroying; mortifying.

θυμόω to make angry. — P. to become angry, wroth, or excited.

θύννος, ὁ tunny(-fish).

θύνω = θύω.

θυόεις 3 fragrant.

θύον, τό cypress; cedar or lemon-tree.

θύος, τό incense; offering.

θυο-σκόος, ὁ sacrificer.

θυόω to make fragrant.

θύρα, ἡ fold of a door; door, gate; palace, royal court; entrance, threshold; table, board, raft.

θύραζε adv. to the door; outside the door, outdoors.

θύραθεν, θύρηθε adv. from without; outside.

θυραῖος 3 outside the door, outdoor(s), abroad; alien, stranger.

θύρασι adv. outside, out of doors; abroad. [shield.]

θυρεός, ὁ door-stone; large]

θύρετρα, τά = θύρα.

θυρίς, ίδος, ἡ small door.

θυρόω to furnish with doors. [staff of Bacchantes).]

θύρσος, ὁ thyrsus (wreathed)

θύρωμα, τό door with frame, portal. [vestibule.]

θυρών, ῶνος, ὁ anteroom,]

θυρωρός, ὁ, ἡ door-keeper.

θυσανόεις 3 tasselled, fringed.

θύσανος, ὁ tassel, tuft.

θυσανωτός 3 = θυσανόεις.

θύσθλα, τά sacred implements. [sacrifice.]

θυσία, ἡ a sacrificing;]

θυσιαστήριον, τό altar.

θύσιμος 2 fit for sacrifice.

θυσσανόεις 3 = θυσανόεις.

θυστάς, άδος, ἡ sacrificial.

θυτήρ, ῆρος, ὁ sacrificer.

θύω¹ to move oneself quickly, to rush on or along; to roar, rage.

θύω² to burn (incense), to offer burnt-sacrifice; to slay, kill; intr. to smoke. — M. to sacrifice for oneself.

θυ-ώδης 2 fragrant.

θύωμα, τό incense.

θωή, ἡ penalty [θᾶκος.]

θωκέω, θῶκος see θᾶκος.]

θῶμα, θωμάζω, θωμάσιος see θαῦμα. [string.]

θῶμιγξ, ιγγος, ὁ cord,]

θωπεύω to flatter; to serve.

θωρακίζω to arm with a breast-plate.

θωρακο-ποιός, ὁ maker of breast-plates.

θωρᾱκο-φόρος 2 wearing a breast-plate.

θώρᾱξ, ᾱκος, ὁ breast-plate, cuirass.

θωρηκτής, οῦ, ὁ = θωρακοφόρος.

θωρήσσω to arm with a breast-plate. to equip, arm.

θώς, θωός, ὁ jackal.

θωῦμα etc. see θαῦμα.

θωΰσσω to cry aloud, shout.

θώψ, θωπός, ὁ flatterer.

I

I, ι (ἰῶτα) ninth letter of the alphabet, as a numeral ιʹ = 10.

ἰά, ἡ sound, voice, cry.

ἴα, ἰῆς one; see ἴος.

ἰά, τά pl. of ἴος.

ἰαίνω to warm, heat; to refresh, cheer.

ἰαχάζω, ἰαχέω to raise the cry of Bacchus.

ἴακχος, ὁ the cry of Bacchus.

ἰάλλω to send, throw, or put forth; to assail.

ἴᾱμα, τό remedy, healing.

ἰαμβεῖον, τό iambic verse.

ἰαμβο-φάγος, ὁ bad reciter of iambic verses.

ἰάομαι to heal, cure.

ἰάπτω to move, stir; to send, thrust; to hit, wound, hurt.

ἰάσιμος 2 healable.

ἴᾱσις, ἡ a healing.

ἴασπις, ιδος, ἡ jasper.

ἰαστί adv. in Ionic fashion.

ἰᾱτήρ, ῆρος, ὁ = ἰατρός.

ἰᾱτορίᾱ, ἡ art of healing.

ἰᾱτρείᾱ, ἡ = ἴασις.

ἰᾱτρεῖον, τό infirmary.

ἰᾱτρεύω to be a physician, to heal.

ἰᾱτρικός 3 medical.

ἰᾱτρός, ὁ physician, surgeon.

ἰαύω to pass the night, to sleep.

ἰαχέω, ἰάχω to cry aloud, to shout.

ἴβις, ιος, ἡ ibis. [knee.]

ἰγνύᾱ, ἡ hollow of the

ἰδέ¹, ἴδε lo! behold!

ἰδέ² = ἠδέ and.

ἰδέᾱ, ἡ appearance, form; way, manner, nature; opinion, notion, idea.

ἴδη, ἡ woody mountain; wood, timber.

ἰδιο-βουλέω to act according to one's own will.

ἴδιος 3 one's own, personal, private; peculiar, strange; adv. ἰδίᾳ separately, privately, for oneself.

ἰδιότης, ητος, ἡ peculiarity.

ἰδιο-τρόφος 2 feeding separately.

ἰδίω to sweat.

ἰδιωτεύω to live as a private man; to know nothing of a certain art.

ἰδιώτης, ου, ὁ private man, single citizen; private soldier; bungler.

ἰδιωτικός 3 belonging to a private man or to a single person; common, trivial; ignorant, unlearned.

ἰδνόομαι P. to writhe.

ἰδού lo! behold! there! well, up!

ἰδρεία, ἡ knowledge, skill.
ἴδρις, ι knowing, skilful, experienced.
ἰδρόω to sweat, perspire.
ἴδρῡμα, τό foundation; building; statue, image.
ἱδρύω to make sit down; to fix, settle, establish. — P. to be established, settled, or seated; to sit still; to be placed or situated. — M. to establish, found for oneself, build, erect.
ἱδρώς, ῶτος, ὁ sweat, perspiration. [sible.]
ἰδυῖα, ἡ knowing, sen-
ἱέραξ, ᾱκος, ὁ hawk, falcon.
ἱεράομαι M. to be a priest or priestess.
ἱερᾱτεία, ἡ, ἱεράτευμα, τό priesthood, body of priests.
ἱερατεύω to be a priest.
ἱέρεια, ἡ priestess.
ἱερεῖον, τό victim; cattle to be killed.
ἱερεύς, ὁ priest.
ἱερεύω to sacrifice; to slaughter. [flesh.]
ἱερό-θυτον, τό offered
ἱερο-μηνίᾱ, ἡ, ἱερο-μήνια, τά festive month; festivity.
ἱερο-μνήμων, ονος, ὁ ambassador to the Amphictyons; chief magistrate.
ἱερο-ποιός, ὁ overseer of sacrifices.
ἱερο-πρεπής 2 becoming a sacred matter.
ἱερός 3 vigorous, strong, fresh; holy, sacred; τὸ ἱερόν, τὰ ἱερά victim, sacrifice, offering, dedica-

tion; holy place, temple, oracle; omen, auspices, mystery, sacred rite, worship.
ἱερο-σῡλέω to rob a temple.
ἱερο-σῡλίᾱ, ἡ temple-robbery. [temple.]
ἱερό-σῡλος, ὁ robbing a
ἱερουργέω to perform sacred rites.
ἱερουργίᾱ, ἡ worship.
ἱερο-φάντης, ου, ὁ initiating priest.
ἱερόω to dedicate.
ἱερωσύνη, ἡ office of a priest; priest's living.
ἱζάνω, ἵζω to cause to sit; intr. and M. to sit down, to place oneself; to encamp; to sink in.
ἰή, ἡ = ἰά.
ἰήιος 2 wailing, mournful; helper (in need).
ἴημα, τό = ἴαμα.
ἵημι to send (off), let go; to utter; to cast, throw, shoot; to let down; intr. to flow. — M. to be driven; to hasten, hurry; to long for, desire.
ἴησις etc. see ἴασις.
ἰθα-γενής 2, ἰθαι-γενής 2 of good birth, legitimate; genuine; natural.
ἰθεῖα, ἰθέως see εὐθύς.
ἴθμα, τό gait, step.
ἰθύ-θριξ, τριχος with straight hair.
ἰθυ-μαχίᾱ, ἡ direct battle.
ἰθύντατα adv. most rightly.
ἰθύνω = εὐθύνω.
ἰθυ-πτίων, ωνος flying straight on.

ἐθύς[1] 3 = εὐθύς.

ἐθύς[2], ύος, ἡ direct course; undertaking; bent of mind, endeavour.

ἰθύω to go straight on, to rush (up)on; to strive after, desire.

ἱκανός 3 sufficient, enough, copious; fit, serviceable, becoming; empowered; considerable, respectable, trustworthy. [ciency; ability.]

ἱκανότης, ητος, ἡ suffi-}

ἱκανόω to make able or sufficient.

ἱκάνω and M. = ἵκω.

ἵκελος 3 like, similar.

ἱκέσιος 3 = ἱκετήριος.

ἱκετεία, ἡ, ἱκέτευμα, τό supplication.

ἱκετεύω to supplicate.

ἱκετήριος 3 suppliant, entreating; ἡ ἱκετηρία olive branch of suppliants; entreaty.

ἱκέτης, ου, ὁ suppliant, entreating; one protected.

ἱκετήσιος 3 = ἱκετήριος.

ἱκέτις, ιδος. ἡ fem. of ἱκέτης.

ἰκμάς, άδος moisture.

ἵκμενος 2 favourable.

ἱκνέομαι M. = ἵκω.

ἴκρια, τά props of a ship; deck; board; scaffold.

ἰκτήρ, ῆρος suppliant.

ἱκτήριος 3 = ἱκετήριος.

ἰκτῖνος, ὁ kite.

ἵκω, ἱκάνω, ἱκνέομαι to come; to arrive at, reach; to come upon or over; to come as a suppliant, to implore; to be due.

ἰλαδόν adv. in troops.

ἱλάομαι = ἱλάσκομαι.

ἵλαος 2 gracious; propitious; gentle, cheerful.

ἱλαρός 3 cheerful, gay.

ἱλαρότης, ητος, ἡ gaiety.

ἱλάσκομαι M. to propitiate, reconcile; to appease; to atone for.

ἱλασμός, ὁ atonement.

ἱλαστήριον, τό means of propitiation, mercy-seat.

ἵλεως 2 = ἵλαος.

ἵλη, ἡ troop, band; squadron of horse.

ἵλημι, ἱλήκω to be propitious. [giddy.}

ἱλιγγιάω to be or become}

ἴλιγγος, ὁ giddiness, swoon.

ἱλλάς, άδος, ἡ rope, band, noose.

ἵλλω to roll; to force together, shut up. — P. to turn round.

ἰλύς, ύος, ἡ mud, slime.

ἱμάντινος 3 of leather thongs.

ἱμάς, άντος, ὁ thong, strap; rein; shoe-string; doorlatch; girdle of Venus.

ἱμάσθλη, ἡ whip.

ἱμάσσω to whip, scourge.

ἱματίζω to clothe.

ἱμάτιον, τό garment; upper garment, cloak; piece of cloth.

ἱματισμός, ὁ clothing.

ἱμείρω and M. and P. to long for, desire.

ἱμερόεις 3 exciting desire; lovely, charming; longing.

ἵμερος, ὁ a longing, yearning; love; charm.

ἱμερτός 3 lovely.

ἴνα adv. there; where; to what place, whither. — conj. that, in order that.

ἰνδάλλομαι P. to appear.

ἴνιον, τό neck, nape.

ἴξαλος αἴξ wild goat, stone-buck.

ἰξῦς, ὑος, ἡ groin, waist.

ἰο-δνεφής 2 violet.

ἰο-δόκος 2 holding arrows.

ἰο-ειδής 2 violet-coloured.

ἰόεις 3 = ἰοειδής.

ἰό-μωρος 2 arrow-shooting; braggart.

ἴον, τό a violet.

ἰονθάς, άδος shaggy.

ἰός[1], ὁ arrow.

ἰός[2], ὁ poison; rust.

ἴος, ἴα, ἴον one, the same.

ἰότης, ητος, ἡ will, desire.

ἰού oh! woe! hey-day!

ἰουδαΐζω to live in the Jewish fashion.

ἰουδαϊσμός, ὁ Judaism.

ἴουλος, ὁ down of the cheek. [rows.]

ἰο-χέαιρα, ἡ shooting ar-]

ἰπνός, ὁ oven, furnace.

ἱππ-αγρέτης, ου, ὁ leader of Spartan horse-guards.

ἱππ-αγωγός 2 transporting horses.

ἱππάζομαι M. to guide horses; to drive; to ride.

ἱππ-αρμοστής, οῦ, ὁ = ἵππαρχος.

ἱππ-αρχέω to command the cavalry. [of cavalry.]

ἵππ-αρχος, ὁ commander]

ἱππάς, άδος, ἡ riding-coat.

ἱππασία, ἡ = ἱππεία.

ἱππάσιμος 2 fit for horses.

ἱππεία, ἡ a riding, driving, horsemanship; cavalry.

ἵππειος 3 = ἱππικός.

ἱππεύς, ὁ horseman, rider, charioteer, knight.

ἱππεύω to ride, to be a horseman.

ἱππ-ηλάσιος 2 fit for riding or driving. [knight.]

ἱππ-ηλάτα, ὁ horseman,]

ἱππ-ήλατος 2 = ἱππηλάσιος. [milker.]

ἱππ-ημολγός, ὁ mare-]

ἱππικός 3 of a horse, belonging to horses, for riding or driving; for horsemen; skilled in riding; ἡ ἱππική horsemanship, τὸ ἱππικόν cavalry.

ἵππιος 3 rich in horses; chivalrous.

ἱππιο-χαίτης, ου with horse-hair. [fighter.]

ἱππιο-χάρμης, ου chariot-]

ἱππο-βότης, ου breeder of horses, knight.

ἱππό-βοτος 2 fed on by horses. [horses.]

ἱππό-δαμος 2 tamer of]

ἱππό-δασυς 3 thick with horse-hair. [horses.]

ἱππο-δέτης, ου bridling]

ἱππο-δρομιά, ἡ horse-race.

ἱππό-δρομος, ὁ race-course.

ἱππο-δρόμος, ὁ light horse-man.

ἱππόθεν from the horse.

ἱππο-κέλευθος 2 driving horses. [dier's boy.]

ἱππο-κόμος, ὁ groom; sol-]

ἱππό-κομος 2 of horse-hair. [teer, knight.]

ἱππο-κορυστής, οῦ chario-]

ἱππο-κρατέω to be superior in cavalry. — P. to be inferior in cavalry.

ἱππο-μανής 2 swarming with horses; what makes horses mad. [horseback.]

ἱππο-μαχέω to fight on[

ἱππο-μαχία, ἡ combat of horsemen. [horseback.]

ἱππό-μαχος 2 fighting on[

ἱππο-νώμᾶς, ου guiding horses. [horses.]

ἱππο-πόλος 2 breeding[

ἵππος, ὁ, ἡ horse; chariot; charioteers; ἡ ἱ. cavalry.

ἱπποσύνη, ἡ horsemanship; cavalry.

ἱππότης, ου, ἱππότα, ὁ on horseback, mounted; horseman, knight. [ed archer.]

ἱππο-τοξότης, ου, ὁ mount-[

ἱππο-τροφέω to feed or keep horses. [of horses.]

ἱππο-τροφία, ἡ the feeding[

ἱππο-τρόφος 2 feeding or keeping horses.

ἵππ-ουρις = ἱππόκομος.

ἱππο-φόρβιον, τό troop of horses; stable. [to punish.]

ἵπτομαι M. to press hard;[

ἱράομαι, etc. see ἱεράομαι.

ἱρήϊον, τό = ἱερεῖον.

ἱρήν, ένος, ὁ Spartan young man.

ἵρηξ, ηκος, ὁ = ἱέραξ.

ἶρις, ιδος, ἡ rainbow.

ἱρός, ἱρόν see ἱερός.

ἴς, ἰνός, ἡ sinew, nerve, muscle; strength, force.

ἰσ-άγγελος 2 angel-like.

ἰσάζω to make equal. — M. to hold oneself equal.

ἰσ-ηγορία, ἡ equal freedom of speech; equality in rights.

ἴσθμιον, τό necklace.

ἰσθμός, ὁ neck of land.

ἰσθμώδης 2 isthmus-like.

ἴσκε he said.

ἴσκω to make like or equal; to think or hold like; to suppose, think.

ἰσο-δίαιτος 2 equal in mode of life.

ἰσό-θεος 2 godlike.

ἰσο-κίνδῡνος 2 equal to the danger. [power.]

ἰσο-κρατής 2 equal in[

ἰσο-κρατίᾱ, ἡ equal right of citizens, democracy.

ἰσο-μέτρητος 2 equal in measure. [front.]

ἰσο-μέτωπος 2 with equal[

ἰσο-μοιρέω to have equal share or rights.

ἰσο-μοιρίᾱ, ἡ equal share; partnership.

ἰσό-μοιρος 2, ἰσό-μορος 2 having (an) equal share; enjoying the same right.

ἰσο-νομέομαι M. to have equal rights.

ἰσο-νομίᾱ, ἡ equality of rights, democracy.

ἰσο-νομικός 2 democratical.

ἰσο-παλής 2 equal in fight.

ἰσό-πεδος 2 level, even.

ἰσο-πλατής 2 equal in breadth.

ἰσό-πλευρος 2 equilateral.

ἰσο-πληθής 2 equal in number.

ἰσο-ρροπίᾱ, ἡ equipoise.

ἰσό-ρροπος 2 equally balanced; equivalent; equally matched.

ἴσος, ἴσος, εἶσος 3 equal; the same; proportionable, equally distributed, reasonable, due, fair, impartial; ἡ ἴση, τὸ ἴσον, τὰ ἴσα equality, equilibrium, equal share or proportion, right, equity, compensation. — adv. ἴσον, ἴσα equally; ἴσως perhaps, probably; fairly; about.

ἰσο-σκελής 2 with equal legs.   [taxation.)

ἰσο-τέλεια, ἡ equality in)

ἰσο-τέλεστος 2 making all equal at last.

ἰσότης, ητος, ἡ equality.

ἰσό-τῑμος 2 equally honoured.

ἰσο-φαρίζω to cope with.

ἰσο-φόρος 2 equal in strength.   [the edge.)

ἰσο-χειλής 2 level with)

ἰσό-ψηφος 2 having an equal vote. [same mind.)

ἰσό-ψῡχος 2 having the)

ἰσόω to make equal. — M. and P. to be equal.

ἰστάω, ἰστάνω = ἴστημι.

ἴστημι to cause to stand; to set, place, establish, fix; to set up, to raise up; to stir, to begin; to stop, check; to balance, weigh; to appoint. — intr. to stand, be placed; to place oneself; to rise, arise, begin; to lie, be situated; to stand firm, be fixed; to be inactive; to continue.

ἱστιάω, ἱστίη, ἡ = ἑστ.

ἱστιητόριον, τό public inn.

ἱστίον, τό sail.

ἱστο-δόκη, ἡ mast-holder.

ἱστο-πέδη, ἡ hole for fixing the mast in.

ἱστορέω and M. to inquire, question, search; to know by inquiry; to narrate.

ἱστορίᾱ, ἡ inquiry, knowledge, information; science; narration; history.

ἱστός, ὁ ship's mast; yarn-beam; loom; warp; web.

ἱστουργέω to weave.

ἴστωρ, ορος knowing; judge.

ἰσχαλέος 3 dry.

ἰσχανάω, ἰσχάνω to hold back, to check; to cling to.

ἰσχίον, τό socket of the hip-bone.

ἰσχναίνω to make dry, withered, or thin.

ἰσχνός 3 dry; thin; lean.

ἰσχνό-φωνος 2 with a weak voice, stammering.

ἰσχῡρίζομαι to exert oneself; to insist strongly (upon); to affirm; to persist in.

ἰσχῡρός 3 strong, mighty, powerful; firm, fortified; safe, lasting; resolute; violent.

ἰσχῡς, ύος, ἡ strength, power, firmness, force; troops.

ἰσχύω to be strong, mighty, powerful.

ἴσχω = ἔχω.

ἰτέα, ἡ willow.

ἰτεΐνος 3 of willows.

ἴτης, ου, ὁ bold, impetuous; insolent, impudent.

ἴττω = ἴστω (οἶδα).

ἴτυς, υος, ἡ rim or felloe of a wheel; edge of a shield.

ἰυγή, ἡ, ἰυγμός, ὁ cry, howling, shout, yelling.

ἰύζω to yell, shout, shriek.

ἴφθιμος 3 and 2 strong, stout, stalwart.

ἶφι adv. valiantly.

ἶφιος 3 strong; fat.

ἰχθυάω to fish.

ἰχθύδιον, τό little fish.

ἰχθυο-ειδής 2 fish-like; swarming with fish.

ἰχθυο-φάγος, ὁ fish-eating.

ἰχθύς, ύος, ὁ fish.

ἰχθυώδης 2 = ἰχθυοειδής.

ἰχνευτής, οῦ, ὁ ichneumon.

ἰχνεύω to track, trace out, find out.

ἴχνος, τό, ἴχνιον, τό footstep, track, trace; pl. movement, gait. [gods; lymph.]

ἰχώρ, ῶρος, ὁ blood of the

ἴψ, ἰπός, ὁ worm that bores through wood.

ἰώ oh! woe! hey-day!

ἰωγή, ἡ defence, shelter.

ἰωή, ἡ a roaring, whistling, sounding.

ἰῶκα = ἰωκήν.

ἰωκή, ἡ battle-din.

ἰῶτα, τό iota.

ἰωχμός, ὁ = ἰωκή.

K

K, κ (κάππα) tenth letter of the alphabet; as a numeral κ' = 20.

κά = κέ (see ἄν).

καβ-βάλλω = καταβ.

κάγ = κατὰ γε.

κάγκανος 2 dry.

καγχάζω, καγχαλάω to laugh aloud; to shout.

κάδ = κατὰ δέ.

καδίσκος, ὁ balloting-urn.

κάδος, ὁ pitcher, jar, pail.

καθά (καθ' ἅ) according as.

καθ-αγίζω, καθ-αγνίζω to dedicate, devote, offer; to burn; to bury.

καθ-αίρεσις, ἡ a taking down, destruction. [down.]

καθ-αιρετέος 3 to be put

καθ-αιρέω to take or pull down; to close (the eyes of the dead); to demolish, destroy, kill; to overpower; to take away, carry off, seize; to achieve; to con-

demn; to obtain; to catch, surprise.

καθαίρω to clean, cleanse, purify; to atone; to wash off.

καθ-άλλομαι M. to spring down. [μέριος.]

καθ-αμέριος 2 = καθη-

καθ-ανύω = κατανύω.

καθ-άπαξ adv. once for all.

καθ-άπερ adv. just as.

καθ-άπτω to tie to, fasten on, attach to, to take hold of. — M. to lay hold of, seize, attack, scold; to call to witness.

καθαρεύω to keep oneself clean; to keep clean.

καθαρίζω to make clean, purify.

καθαριότης, ητος, ἡ purity, cleanliness. [μός.]

καθαρισμός, ὁ = καθαρ-

κάθαρμα, τό off-scourings, rubbish, filth; outcast.

καθ-αρμόζω to fit to.

καθαρμός, ὁ a cleansing, purifying; atonement.

καθαρός 3 pure, clean, unsoiled; sound; undisturbed; unmixed, unalloyed, genuine; guiltless, innocent, chaste; honest; perfect.

καθαρότης, ητος, ἡ purity.

καθάρσιος 2 purifying, cleansing, atoning.

κάθαρσις, ἡ = καθαρμός.

καθαρτής, οῦ, ὁ purifier, atoner.

καθ-έδρᾱ, ἡ seat, couch, chair; a sitting still.

καθ-έζω to place, set down, establish. — M. to sit down, sit still, tarry.

καθ-είργνῡμι = κατείργω.

καθείς = καθ' εἷς one by one. [back.]

καθ-εκτός 3 to be held/

καθ-έλκω, -ύω to draw down; to launch.

καθ-εξῆς adv. in succession, one after the other.

κάθ-εξις, ἡ a holding fast.

καθ-εύδω to sleep, be at rest.

καθ-ευρίσκω to find out.

καθ-εσφιάομαι to mock at.

καθ-ηγεμών, όνος, ὁ guide.

καθ-ηγέομαι M. to lead the way, to guide, to show the way; to do first.

καθ-ηγητής, οῦ, ὁ leader, guide; teacher. [der.]

καθ-ηδυπαθέω to squan-/

καθ-ήκω to come down; to reach to; to arrive; to be meet, proper, or sufficient.

κάθ-ημαι to be seated; to sit in court; to sit still or idle; to stop; to be encamped.

καθ-ημερινός 3 daily.

καθ-ημέριος 3 of to-day.

καθ-ιδρύω to make sit down; to set down, establish, settle.

καθ-ιερεύω, -όω to dedicate, vow, offer.

καθ-ίζω, καθ-ιζάνω to make sit down; to set down; to place, establish, appoint, constitute; to place in a certain condition. — intr. and M. to sit down, to be settled or seated.

καθ-ίημι to send down; to let down; to let return. — intr. and M. to come down; to reach to; to move on.

καθ-ικετεύω to implore.

καθ-ικνέομαι M. to come to, arrive at.

καθ-ιππάζομαι M. to ride down, to overrun with horse.

καθ-ίστημι trans. to set down, put down, place; to establish, appoint, constitute, ordain; to place in a certain condition. — intr. to be placed, set down, established, or appointed; to stand; to appear; to come to; to be in a certain condition, to become or have become; to stand still, be fixed, ordained; to exist; to be in value. — M. (also = intr.)

to set down or place for oneself.

καθό = καθ' ὅ in so far as.

κάθ-οδος, ἡ way down or back.

καθ-ολικός 3 universal.

καθ-όλου *adv.* on the whole, generally.

καθ-ομολογέω to grant, consent (to). [to overcome.]

καθ-οπλίζω to arm, equip;]

καθ-οράω and *M.* to look down; to see from afar; to behold, view; to perceive, know.

καθ-ορμίζω to bring to anchor. — *M.* and *P.* to come into harbour.

καθ-ότι *adv.* in so far as, in what manner.

καθ-υβρίζω to be insolent, haughty, or wicked; to insult, treat with contempt.

κάθ-υδρος 2 full of water.

καθ-υπάρχω to exist, to fall to one's lot.

καθ-ύπερθεν *adv.* from above; above, on high; yonder; before.

καθ-υπέρτερος 3 upper, higher, superior; **καθ-υπέρτατος** 3 highest.

καθ-υπνόω and *M.* to fall asleep; to sleep sound.

καθ-υφίημι and *M.* to let go, abandon, betray; to yield.

καθ-ώς *adv.* as.

καθ-ώσπερ *adv.* just as.

καί *conj.* and, also, even, though; especially; **καί ... καί** as well as, both ... and. [verns or chasms.]

καιετάεις 3 rich in ca-]

καινίζω to make new.

καινο-παθής 2 never before suffered.

καινο-ποιέω to make new.

καινός 3 new; unheard of, strange. [ness.]

καινότης, ητος, ἡ new-]

καινο-τομέω to begin something new, to make innovations. [new way.]

καινουργέω to act in a]

καινόω to make new; to consecrate anew. [pass.]

καίνυμαι to excel; to sur-]

καίνω to kill.

καί-περ *conj.* although.

καίριος 3 happening at the right time and place, seasonable; vital, deadly.

καιρός, ὁ right proportion, due measure; right place; right time or season, opportunity; time, circumstances; critical moment; embarrassment; importance, influence; profit, success.

καιροσσέων *gen. pl. fem.* of **καιρόεις** 3 close-woven.

καί-τοι *adv.* and yet, and indeed; however; although.

καίω to kindle, set on fire, burn, waste. — *P.* to be set on fire, to be burnt; to burn. [evil tidings.]

κακ-αγγελέω to bring]

κακ-άγγελτος 2 caused by bad news.

κακ-ανδρία, ἡ unmanliness.

κάκη, ἡ = κακία.

κακ-ηγορέω to abuse, revile, slander.

κακία, ἡ badness, wickedness, vice, cowardice, shame; disgrace; reproach.

κακίζω to make bad; to abuse, blame. — *P.* to be reproached or blamed; to play the coward.

κακ-κεῖαι, κακκῆαι see κατακαίω. [κεῖοντες.]

κακ-κείοντες = κατα-

κακό-βιος 2 living wretchedly. [bour of misery.]

κακο-γείτων, ονος neigh-

κακο-δαιμονάω, -έω to be possessed by an evil spirit.

κακο-δαιμονίᾱ, ἡ misfortune; infatuation; raving madness.

κακο-δαίμων 2 unhappy, wretched. [repute.]

κακο-δοξέω to be in ill

κακο-είμων 2 badly clad.

κακο-εργίᾱ, ἡ = κακουργία.

κακο-ήθεια, ἡ malignity.

κακο-ήθης 2 malicious.

κακό-θροος, -θρους 2 slanderous. [Ilios.]

κακο-ίλιος ἡ unhappy

κακο-λογέω to abuse, slander, accurse.

κακο-λογίᾱ, ἡ slander.

κακο-μήχανος 2 contriving evil, mischievous.

κακό-νοια, ἡ ill will, enmity. [laws.]

κακό-νομος 2 with bad

κακό-νοος 2 ill-disposed, hostile. [guests.]

κακό-ξεινος 2 having ill

κακό-ξύνετος 2 guileful.

κακο-πάθεια, ἡ suffering, distress. [be distressed.]

κακο-παθέω to suffer evil,

κακο-πινής 2 foul.

κακο-ποιέω to do ill; to hurt, spoil.

κακο-ποιός, ὁ wrong-doer.

κακό-πους, ποδος with bad feet.

κακο-πρᾱγέω to be unfortunate, to fail in one's enterprise.

κακο-πρᾱγίᾱ, ἡ ill condition; failure. [vous.]

κακο-πράγμων 2 mischie-

κακός 3 bad, ill, evil; useless, unfit; mean, vile; foul, unfair, wicked, mischievous, shameful; injurious, hurtful; miserable, wretched. τὸ κακόν evil, ill, mischief, distress, suffering; damage; vice.

κακο-σκελής 2 with bad legs. [language.]

κακο-στομέω to use bad

κακο-τεχνέω to act maliciously.

κακό-τεχνος 2 artful.

κακότης, ητος, ἡ badness; cowardice; misfortune, distress; defeat.

κακο-τροπίᾱ, ἡ bad habits.

κακο-τυχέω to be unfortunate.

κακουργέω to do evil, to act badly; to hurt, damage; to ravage.

κακούργημα, τό, κακουργίᾱ, ἡ bad or wicked deed, wickedness.

κακοῦργος, ὁ doing evil, mischievous, artful; damaging; wrong-doer, criminal, knave.

κακουχέω to treat ill.

κᾰκο-φρᾰδής 2 devising ill.

κᾰκό-φρων 2 ill-minded; foolish.

κᾰκόω to treat ill, to maltreat, vex, hurt, destroy; to make angry, exasperate.

κάκτανε see κατακτείνω.

κάκωσις, ἡ ill-treatment; humiliation; suffering, distress. [reed; stubble.]

κᾰλάμη, ἡ stalk of corn,)

κᾰλᾰμη-φόρος 2 carrying reeds. [cane.]

κᾰλάμῐνος 3 of reed or)

κάλᾰμος, ὁ reed, cane; writing-reed.

κᾰλᾰσῑρις, ἡ long garment of females.

κᾰλαῦροψ, οπος, ἡ shepherd's staff.

κᾰλέω to call, call by name (P. to be called, ὁ καλούμενος the so-called); to summon, to call to aid; to invoke, implore; to summon before the court; to invite.

κᾰλήτωρ, ορος, ὁ crier.

κᾰλινδέομαι P. to roll, wallow; to be busied with.

κᾰλλείπω = καταλείπω.

κᾰλλι-βόᾱς, ου beautiful-sounding.

κᾰλλί-βοτρυς, υος with beautiful grapes.

κᾰλλῐ-γύναιξ, αικος with beautiful women.

κᾰλλῐ-έλαιος, ἡ cultivated olive. [speech.]

κᾰλλῐ-επέω to use flowery)

κᾰλλῐ-ερέω to sacrifice with good omens, to give good omens.

κᾰλλί-ζωνος 2 with beautiful girdles.

κᾰλλί-θριξ, τριχος with beautiful hair or mane.

κᾰλλί-κομος 2 with fine hair. [fine hair-bands.]

κᾰλλι-κρήδεμνος 2 with)

κάλλῐμος 2 = καλός.

κᾰλλῐ-πάρῃος 2 with beautiful cheeks.

κᾰλλῐ-πλόκαμος 2 with beautiful locks or braids.

κᾰλλῐ-ρέεθρος 2, κᾰλλί-ρροος 2 beautifully flowing.

κᾰλλιστεῖον, τό prize of beauty or valour.

κᾰλλιστεύω and M. to be the most beautiful.

κᾰλλί-σφυρος 2 with beautiful ankles.

κᾰλλί-φθογγος 2 sounding beautifully.

κᾰλλί-χορος 2 with beautiful dancing-places.

κᾰλλονή, ἡ, κάλλος, τό beauty; ornament; excellence; beautiful thing.

κᾰλλύνω to beautify, embellish. — M. to boast, pride oneself (up)on.

κᾰλλ-ωπίζω to beautify, embellish, adorn. — M. to adorn oneself; to boast, pride oneself (up)on; to be affected or coy.

κᾰλλ-ώπισμα, τό, κᾰλλωπισμός, ὁ embellishment, ornament, finery.

κᾰλο-διδάσκαλος, ὁ, ἡ teacher of virtue.

κᾰλοκἀγᾰθία, ἡ nobleness and goodness.

κᾶλον, τό wood; ship.

καλο-ποιέω to do good.

καλό-πους, ποδος, ὁ shoemaker's last.

κᾶλός 3 beautiful, fair, charming, lovely, pretty; honest, noble, good, right, virtuous; agreeable, auspicious, favourable, dear.

καλὸς κᾰγαθός honest man, gentleman, aristocrat. τὸ καλόν the beautiful, beauty; virtue, honesty, honour; joy, happiness.

κάλος, ὁ = κάλως.

κάλπις, ιδος, ἡ pitcher, urn.

καλύβη, ἡ hut, cabin.

κάλυμμα, τό covering, veil.

κάλυξ, υκος, ἡ husk, shell; cup; bud; pendant of the ear.

καλυπτός 3 enveloping.

καλύπτρᾱ, ἡ covering, cover; veil. [conceal.]

καλύπτω to cover, envelop,

καλχαίνω to be agitated in mind, to consider deeply.

καλώδιον, τό rope, cord.

κάλως, ω, ὁ rope, cable.

κάμαξ, ακος, ἡ pole for vines. [coach.]

καμάρα, ἡ chamber, vault;

καματηρός 3 wearisome; sick. [labour; distress.]

κάματος, ὁ weariness; toil,

κάμηλος, ὁ, ἡ camel.

κάμῑλος, ὁ anchor-cable.

κάμῑνος, ἡ furnace, kiln.

καμῑνώ, οῦς, ἡ furnace-woman. [victory.]

καμ-μονίη, ἡ endurance;

κάμ-μορος 2 unfortunate.

κάμνω to work hard; to toil, exert oneself; to be

weary, exhausted, or tired; to be sick or ill; to feel trouble. — M. to work out; to gain by toil. [turning.]

καμπή, ἡ a bending, curve,

κάμπτω to bend, bow, turn round; to make one alter his sentiments.

καμπύλος 3 curved, bent.

κἄν = καὶ ἄν, καὶ ἐάν.

καναναῖος, κανανίτης, ου, ὁ zealot.

καναχέω to clash, clang.

καναχή, ἡ ringing sound, clash, gnashing, noise.

καναχίζω = καναχέω.

κάνδυς, υος. ὁ caftan.

κάνεον, κάνειον, τό basket; dish.

κάνθαρος, ὁ beetle.

κανθήλιος, ὁ pack-ass.

κάνναβις, ἡ hemp; hempen garment.

καννεύσας = κατανεύσας.

κανοῦν, τό = κάνεον.

κανών, όνος, ὁ rod, bar; weaving-staff; handle of the shield; rule, ruler, level; precept, law; model, standard; district.

κάπετος, ἡ ditch, trench; hole, grave.

κάπη, ἡ manger. [vern.]

καπηλεῖον, τό shop; ta-

καπηλεύω to be a retail-dealer, to hawk, sell; to adulterate.

κάπηλος, ὁ retailer, shopkeeper; innkeeper.

καπίθη, ἡ a Persian measure.

καπνίζω to light a fire.

καπνο-δόκη, ἡ smoke-hole.

καπνός, ὁ smoke, steam, vapour.

κάπριος 2 like a wild boar; = κάπρος.

κάπρος, ὁ wild boar.

κ . ρ¹ = κάρα head.

κάρ², καρός, τό chip; ἐν καρὸς αἴσῃ for nothing.

κάρᾱ, τό head; top, summit; mountain-castle.

κᾱρᾰ-δοκέω to watch, expect eagerly.

κᾱρᾱ-δοκίᾱ, ἡ expectation.

κάρᾱνος, ὁ chief, lord.

κᾱρᾱ-τομος 2 cut off from the head. [shoe.|

καρβατίνη, ἡ peasant's|

καρδίᾱ, ἡ heart, mind, soul, interior; stomach.

καρδιο-γνώστης, ου, ὁ knower of hearts.

κάρδοπος, ἡ trough.

κάρη, τό = κάρα.

καρη-κομόωντες, οἱ with hair on the head.

κάρηνον, τό = κάρα.

καρκαίρω to ring; to quake.

καρκίνος, ὁ cancer, crab.

καρπαία, ἡ a mimic dance.

καρπάλιμος 2 swift, quick, hasty.

καρπός¹, ὁ fruit, corn, harvest, produce; profit, success.

καρπός², ὁ wrist.

καρπο-φορέω to bear fruit.

καρπο-φόρος 2 fruit-bearing.

καρπόω to bear fruit. — *M.* to gather fruit, to reap; to have the usufruct or enjoyment of; to plunder.

καρ-ρέζω = καταρέζω.

κάρτα *adv.* very, very much.

καρτερέω to be firm, steadfast, or patient; to endure, bear, persist in.

καρτέρησις, **καρτερίᾱ**, ἡ patience, endurance; abstinence. self-control.

καρτερικός 3 enduring, patient. [hearted.|

καρτερό-θῡμος 2 stout-|

καρτερός 3 strong, firm, staunch; enduring, steadfast; mighty, master, valiant, courageous, brave; violent, obstinate, cruel.

κάρτιστος 3 = κράτιστος.

κάρτος, τό = κράτος.

καρτύνω = κρατύνω.

κάρυον, τό nut. [(sound).|

καρφαλέος 3 dry; hollow|

κάρφη, ἡ, **κάρφος**, τό dry stalk, hay, straw, chaff, dry stick; mote.

κάρφω to make dry or withered. [dry.|

καρχαλέος 3 rough, hoarse,|

καρχαρ-όδους, -όδοντος with sharp teeth.

κασίᾱ, ἡ cassia.

κασι-γνήτη, ἡ sister.

κασί-γνητος 3 brotherly, sisterly; ὁ κ. brother.

κάσις, ὁ, ἡ brother, sister.

κασσίτερος, ὁ tin.

κάστωρ, ορος, ὁ beaver.

κατά *adv.* downwards, down; entirely. — *prp.* with *gen.* from above, down from; down upon; opposite to, against. — with *acc.* downwards, down; over; among, throughout, along; near, opposite, at; during, about;

because of; in search of; in relation to, concerning. according to, answering to; after; κατὰ τρεῖς three at a time; κατὰ φῦλα by tribes; κατ' ἐνιαυτόν year by year.

κᾱτα = καὶ εἶτα.

κατα-βαίνω to go or come down, to go down to the sea; to go into the arena (as a fighter); to fall down; to condescend; to come to; to enter into.

κατα-βάλλω to throw or cast down, to overthrow; to let fall, drop, lay down; to slay, destroy; to put down, pay off; to bring or carry down, to store up; to throw away, reject, disparage.

κατα-βαρέω, -βαρύνω to weigh down, burden, molest.

κατά-βασις, ἡ a going down, way or march down, descent, return.

κατα-βιβάζω to cause to go down, to lead or bring down.

κατα-βιβρώσκω to eat up.

κατα-βιόω to live through.

κατα-βλακεύω to spoil by carelessness. [through.]

κατα-βλώσκω to go)

κατα-βοάω to cry aloud, to cry out against, to complain of.

κατα-βοή, ἡ outcry against; report; accusation.

κατα-βολή, ἡ attack, payment, foundation.

κατα-βραβεύω to decide against. [down.]

κατα-βρόχω to swallow)

κατα-βυρσόω to cover over with hides.

κατά-γαιος 2 = κατάγειος.

κατ-αγγελεύς, ὁ announcer.

κατ-αγγέλλω to announce, proclaim.

κατ-άγγελτος 2 betrayed.

κατά-γειος 2 underground; on the ground.

κατά-γέλαστος 2 ridiculous. [mock.]

κατα-γελάω to laugh at,)

κατά-γελως, ωτος, ὁ mockery, ridiculousness.

κατα-γηράσκω, -γηράω to grow old.

κατα-γιγνώσκω to observe, discover, perceive; to think ill of; to charge with, to condemn, to give judgment against.

κατ-αγῑνέω = κατάγω.

κάτ-αγμα, τό flock of wool.

κατ-άγνῡμι to break in or to pieces, shatter, shiver. — *intr.* and *P.* to be broken, to burst.

κατά-γνωσις, ἡ disregard, contempt; condemnation.

κατα-γοητεύω to bewitch, enchant; to impose upon.

κατ-αγορεύω to denounce.

κατα-γράφω to scratch; to write down.

κατ-άγω to lead, bring, or carry down; to lead to a place; to bring down from the sea to the land; to lead or bring back or home.

— *M.* to come to land, put in; to return.

κατ-αγωγή, ἡ a landing, putting in; harbour, quarters. [abode.]

κατ-αγώγιον, τό quarters,]

κατ-αγωνίζομαι *M.* to overpower. [rend asunder.]

κατα-δαίομαι to divide.]

κατα-δακρύω to weep, lament. [due.]

κατα-δαμάζομαι to sub-]

κατα-δαπανάω to use up, spend entirely.

κατα-δάπτω to rend to pieces. [asleep.]

κατα-δαρθάνω to fall]

κατα-δεής 2 needy; καταδεέστερος inferior, weaker, less.

κατα-δείδω to fear much.

κατα-δείκνυμι to show, make known; to teach.

κατα-δειλιάω to neglect from fear or cowardice.

κατα-δέομαι *P.* to entreat earnestly. [down upon.]

κατα-δέρχομαι *P.* to look]

κατα-δεύω to wet.

κατα-δέχομαι *M.* to admit, receive back.

κατα-δέω[1] to bind to; to fetter, imprison; to tie up, close, shut up; to check; to convict, condemn.

κατα-δέω[2] to want, lack, need.

κατά-δηλος 2 quite manifest or conspicuous.

κατα-δημοβορέω to consume public goods.

κατα-διαιτάω to decide against (as an arbiter).

κατα-δίδωμι to flow into.

κατα-δικάζω to give judgment against, to condemn. — *M.* to obtain judgment against another, to gain one's lawsuit.

κατα-δίκη, ἡ condemnation; fine. [chase.]

κατα-διώκω to pursue,]

κατα-δοκέω, κατα-δοξάζω to think ill of one, to suspect; to think, suppose. judge.

κατα-δουλόω to enslave, subdue. [slaving.]

κατα-δούλωσις, ἡ an en-]

κατα-δρέπω to pluck off.

κατα-δρομή, ἡ raid, inroad.

κατα-δυναστεύω = καταδουλόω. [μαι *M.*]

κατα-δύνω = καταδύο-]

κατα-δύω *trans.* to dive, submerge, dip; to cause to sink. — *intr.* and *M.* to go under water, to sink; to enter; to go down, set; to creep into; to hide oneself; to put on (garments, arms).

κατ-άδω to annoy one by singing; to sing to; to sing a spell; to conjure.

κατα-έννυμι to clothe, cover.

κατ-αζαίνω to dry up.

κατα-ζεύγνυμι to yoke together, harness; to bind, tie, fetter, imprison.

κατα-θάπτω to bury, inter.

κατα-θεάομαι *M.* to look down upon, to behold, watch, view.

κατα-θέλγω to subdue by charms.

κατά-θεμα, τό curse; accursed thing.

κατα-θεματίζω to curse.

κατα-θέω to run down; to make an inroad or raid, to overrun, attack.

κατα-θεωρέω = καταθεάομαι.

κατα-θνήσκω to die(away).

κατα-θνητός 3 mortal.

κατα-θορυβέω to silence by noise.

κατα-θρῴσκω to leap down or over. [heart.]

κατ-αθūμέω to lose all]

κατα-θῡμιος 3 being in or upon the mind.

κατα-θύω to slaughter, sacrifice; to dedicate.

καται-βατός 2 accessible.

κατ-αιδέομαι to feel or be ashamed; to reverence.

κατ-αικίζω to disfigure.

κατ-αινέω to agree, assent to, approve of; to grant, promise.

κατ-αίρω to come to land.

κατ-αισθάνομαι M. to perceive or understand fully.

κατ-αισχύνω to disgrace, dishonour; to shame, put to the blush; to deceive. — P. to feel ashamed.

κατ-ίσχω to possess.

κατ-αιτιάομαι M. to accuse, lay to one's charge.

καταῖτυξ, υγος, ἡ steel-cap.

κατα-καίνω = κατακτείνω.

κατα-καίριος 2 deadly.

κατα-καίω to burn down.

κατα-καλέω to summon.

κατα-καλύπτω to envelop, cover up.

κατα-καυχάομαι M. to boast against; to treat with contempt.

κατά-κειμαι M. to lie down; to lie at table; to lie hid, still, or sick.

κατα-κείρω to cut down; to consume, waste.

κατα-κείω to go asleep.

κατα-κερτομέω to mock at.

κατα-κηλέω to enchant.

κατα-κηρόω to cover with wax.

κατα-κηρύσσω to proclaim by a herald. [wail.]

κατα-κλαίω and M. to be-]

κατα-κλάω to break off, to break in or to pieces; to move or shake one's heart.

κατα-κλείω to shut up or in, blockade; to decree, stipulate.

κατα-κληροδοτέω to distribute by lot.

κατα-κλήω = κατακλείω.

κατα-κλίνω to lay down; to make lie down (at table). — P. to lie down.

κατά-κλισις, ἡ a making to lie down.

κατα-κλύζω to inundate.

κατα-κλυσμός, ὁ inundation, flood.

κατα-κοιμάω, -κοιμίζω to put to sleep; to lull to sleep; to let fall into oblivion; to sleep through. — P. to fall asleep.

κατ-ακολουθέω to follow.

κατα-κολπίζω to run into a bay.

κατα-κολυμβάω to dive.

κατα-κομιδή, ἡ exportation.

κατα-κομίζω to bring down to the sea; to import. — *P.* to arrive, come into harbour.

κατ-ακοντίζω to strike down with a spear.

κατα-κόπτω to strike down, slay, kill; to coin money; to rend, tear to pieces.

κατά-κορος 2 excessive.

κατα-κοσμέω to arrange, set in order; to adorn.

κατ-ακούω to hear, hearken to; to obey.

κατ-άκρας *adv.* thoroughly.

κατα-κρατέω to prevail, to be superior. [upon.]

κατα-κρεμάννῦμι to hang]

κατα-κρεουργέω to cut to pieces, lacerate.

κατά-κρηθεν *adv.* from the head downwards; entirely.

κατα-κρημνίζω to throw down a precipice. [κρίσις.]

κατά-κρῖμα, τό = κατά-)

κατα-κρίνω to give judgment against, to condemn.

κατά-κρισις, ἡ judgment, condemnation. [ceal.]

κατα-κρύπτω to hide, con-)

κατα-κρυφή, ἡ pretext, evasion. [possess.]

κατα-κτάομαι *M.* to gain,)

κατα-κτείνω to kill, destroy, execute.

κατα-κυλίομαι *P.* to roll or fall down.

κατα-κύπτω to bend down, stoop. [mand.]

κατα-κῡρισύω to com-)

κατα-κῡρόω to ratify. — *P.* to be fulfilled or realised.

κατα-κωλΰω to keep back.

κατα-λαλέω to slander.

κατα-λαλία, ἡ slander, calumny.

κατά-λαλος, ὁ slanderer.

κατα-λαμβάνω to seize, lay hold of, take possession of, take away, occupy; to catch, overtake, surprise, discover, find out, meet; *intr.* to happen, come to pass, befal; to hold fast or back; to check; to bind by oath; to oblige. — *M.* to seize for oneself, to occupy, conquer; to understand, apprehend.

κατα-λάμπω to shine upon.

κατ-αλγέω to suffer pain.

κατα-λέγω[1] to recite, count up, relate, tell, explain, mention; to pick out, choose; to enlist, enrol.

κατα-λέγω[2] = καταλέχω.

κατα-λείβομαι *P.* to trickle or drop down. [residue.]

κατά-λειμμα, τό remnant,)

κατα-λείπω to leave behind, bequeath; to spare one's life; to forsake, abandon; to lose. — *P.* to remain behind; to be impending. — *M.* to leave behind for oneself, to retain, reserve to oneself.

κατα-λεύω to stone to death.

κατα-λέχω to lay down.

— *M.* to lie down, to sleep.

κατ-αλέω to grind down.

κατα-λήϑομαι *M.* to forget wholly.

κατα-ληπτός 3 to be seized.

κατά-ληψις, ἡ a seizing, catching, capture; assault.

κατα-λιϑόω, -λιϑάζω to stone to death. [λείπω.]

κατα-λιμπάνω = κατα-)

κατα-λῑπαρέω to entreat earnestly. [tion.]

κατ-αλλαγή, ἡ reconcilia-)

κατ-αλλάσσω to change, exchange; to reconcile. — *P.* to become reconciled. — *M.* to exchange for oneself. [prose.]

κατα-λογάδην *adv* in)

κατ-αλογέω to despise.

κατα-λογίζομαι *M.* to count among; to reckon; to consider.

κατά-λογος, ὁ a counting up; catalogue, list.

κατά-λοιπος 2 remaining.

κατα-λοφάδεια *adv.* on the neck.

κατά-λυμα, τό inn.

κατα-λύσιμος 2 to be repaired.

κατά-λυσις, ἡ a dissolving, disbanding; destruction, end, overthrow, expulsion; resting-place, inn.

κατα-λύω to dissolve; to destroy, end, abolish, depose, dismiss, disband. — *intr.* and *M.* to make peace, become reconciled; to make halt, to repose, to alight; to cease.

κατα-λωφάω to rest, recover.

κατα-μανϑάνω to learn exactly; to know well; to search out; to perceive; to consider; to understand.

κατα-μαργέω to turn or go mad. [hold of.]

κατα-μάρπτω to catch)

κατα-μαρτυρέω to bear witness against.

κατ-αμάω to mow down. — *M.* to pile or heap up.

κατ-αμβλύνω to make blunt.

κατα-μεϑύσκω to make drunk. [μίγνυμι.]

κατα-μείγνῡμι = κατα-)

κατ-αμελέω to neglect.

κατά-μεμπτος 2 blamable.

κατα-μέμφομαι *M.* to blame, accuse, reproach.

κατά-μεμψις, ἡ a blaming.

κατα-μένω to stay behind, remain; to sojourn.

κατα-μερίζω to distribute.

κατα-μετρέω to measure out to.

κατα-μηνύω to give information; to bear witness against; to convict.

κατα-μιαίνω *P.* to wear mourning-dress.

κατα-μίγνῡμι to mix up. — *M.* to be mixed with, to intrude oneself.

κατα-μόνας *adv.* alone, apart. [rend.]

κατ-αμύσσω to scratch)

κατα-μύω to close the eyes. [velop fully.]

κατ-αμφικαλύπτω to en-)

κατ-αναγκάζω to obtain

by force; to constrain, fetter.

κατ-ανάϑεμα, τό curse.

κατ-αναϑεματίζω to curse.

κατ-αναλίσκω to consume, spend; to waste.

κατα-ναρκάω to be burdensome to.

κατα-νάσσω to beat down.

κατα-ναυμαχέω to conquer at sea.

κατα-νέμω to distribute; to divide. — M. to divide among themselves.

κατα-νεύω to nod assent; to consent, grant.

κατα-νέω[1] to impart by spinning.

κατα-νέω[2] to heap or pile up.

κατ-ανϑρακόω to burn to coal.

κατα-νοέω to perceive, observe, watch, to learn (to know); take to heart; to consider.   [arrive at.]

κατ-αντάω to come to; to

κατ-άντης 2 and κάτ-αντα adv. down-hill, downwards.

κατ-άντησιν adv. just opposite.

κατ-αντικρύ, -αντίον, κατ-αντιπέρας adv. just opposite; over against; downwards.

κατά-νυξις, ἡ stupefaction.

κατα-νύσσω to prick; to aggrieve.

κατ-ανύω, -ανύτω to finish; to arrive at; to alight; to accomplish, fulfil, grant.

κατα-ξαίνω to scratch; to tear to pieces; to stone to death.

κατ-άξιος 2 quite worthy.

κατ-αξιόω to think worthy, esteem; to desire.

κατα-πακτός 3 fastened downwards.   [down.]

κατα-πάλλομαι M. to leap

κατα-πατέω to tread or trample down.   [fort.]

κατά-παυμα τό rest, com-

κατά-παυσις, ἡ a stopping; a deposing.

κατα-παύω to put to rest, stop, finish, assuage; to check, hinder; to depose. — intr. to rest.

κατα-πεδάω to fetter.

κατ-απειλέω to threaten.

κατα-πειράζω to try, put to the test.

κατα-πειρητηρίη, ἡ sounding-line.

κατα-πέμπω to send down.

κατάπερ adv. = καϑάπερ.

κατα-πέσσω to digest; to swallow, suppress.

κατα-πετάννῡμι to spread out over.   [veil.]

κατα-πέτασμα, τό curtain,

κατα-πέτομαι M. to fly down.   [death.]

κατα-πετρόω to stone to

κατα-πεφνεῖν to kill.

κατα-πήγνῡμι to stick fast, to fix. — intr. and P. to be firmly fixed, stand fast.

κατα-πηδάω to leap down.

κατα-πίμπλημι to fill quite full.   [down.]

κατα-πίνω to swallow

κατα-πίπτω to fall down; to subside, sink.

κατα-πισσόω to cover with pitch.

14*

κατα-πλάσσω to besmear, plaster. [plaster.]

κατά-πλαστύς, ύος, ἡ

κατα-πλέκω to entwine; to unroll, unweave; to finish.

κατα-πλέω to sail down; to put to shore; to sail back. [nation, terror.]

κατά-πληξις, ἡ conster-

κατα-πλήσσω to strike down; to terrify, confound. — P. to be frightened or amazed.

κατά-πλους, ὁ a sailing down; a landing; course, passage, return.

κατα-πλουτίζω to enrich.

κατα-πλώω = καταπλέω.

κατα-πολεμέω to conquer in war; to overcome.

κατα-πολῑτεύομαι M. to ruin by one's policy. [toil.]

κατα-πονέω to vex with

κατα-ποντίζω, κατα-ποντίεω to throw into the sea; to drown.

κατα-ποντιστής, οῦ, ὁ pirate. [tute.]

κατα-πορνεύω to prosti-

κατα-πράσσω to effect, accomplish, achieve. — M. to achieve for oneself, to obtain.

κατα-πραΰνω to appease.

κατα-πρηνής 2 head foremost (downwards).

κατα-πρίω to saw to pieces.

κατα-προδίδωμι to betray.

κατα-προΐσσομαι to do with impunity.

κατα-πτήσσω to cower down, creep away; to be timid.

κατά-πτυστος 2 despicable.

κατα-πτύω to spit upon; to abhor. [πτήσσω.]

κατα-πτώσσω = κατα-

κατα-πύθομαι P. to become rotten.

κατ-άρα, ἡ curse.

κατ-άράομαι M. to curse, utter imprecations; to wish one evil.

κατ-αράσσω to dash down, smash; to push back.

κατ-άρατος 2 cursed; abominable.

κατ-αργέω to make inactive or barren; to undo, abolish, remove, release.

κάτ-αργμα, τό introductory offering; firstlings.

κατ-αργυρόω to overlay with silver; to bribe.

κατα-ρέζω to stroke, caress.

κατ-αρέομαι = καταράομαι.

κατα-ρῑγηλός 2 horrible.

κατ-αριθμέω and M. to count up or among.

κατ-αρκέω to be quite sufficient.

κατ-αρνέομαι P. to deny.

κατα-ρρᾳθῡμέω to be careless; to lose by carelessness. [rags.]

κατα-ρρακόω to tear to

κατα-ρράκτης, ου, ὁ, κατα-ρρακτός 3 precipitous, gushing down; waterfall.

κατα-ρράπτω to stitch up.

κατα-ρρέπω to fall down.

κατα-ρρέω to flow down; to fall down; to collapse.

κατα-ρρήγνῡμι to break or

tear down; to tear to or in pieces. — *intr.* and *P.* to fall down; to burst out.

κατα-ρροφέω to swallow down. [down.]

κατα-ρρυής 2 flowing)

κατα-ρρυπαίνω to soil, dirty.

κατά-ρρυτος 2 alluvial.

κατ-αρρωδέω to be afraid.

κατα-ρρώξ, ῶγος precipitous, broken.

κάτ-αρσις, ἡ landing-place.

κατ-αρτάω, -αρτίζω to adjust fitly, prepare, restore, repair, equip.

κατ-άρτισις, ἡ, -αρτισμός, ὁ restoration, perfection.

κατ-αρτύω to prepare, adjust, arrange; to train, master.

κατ-άρχω to begin, do first. — *M.* to begin the rites.

κατα-σβέννῡμι to quench, extinguish. — *intr.* and *P.* to be quenched.

κατα-σείω to shake down; to beckon. [down.]

κατα-σεύομαι *M.* to rush)

κατα-σημαίνω to mark. — *M.* to seal.

κατα-σήπω to let rot. — *intr.* to rot away.

κατα-σῑγάω to keep secret.

κατα-σῑτέομαι *M.* to eat up.

κατα-σιωπάω to keep secret; to silence. — *M.* to impose silence.

κατα-σκάπτω to dig down, demolish. [lishing; tomb]

κατα-σκαφή, ἡ a demo-)

κατα-σκαφής 2 underground.

κατα-σκεδάννῡμι to scatter about. [κατασκοπέω.]

κατα-σκέπτομαι *M.* =)

κατα-σκευάζω to prepare, equip, adjust, furnish, adorn; to get ready; to make, build, found; to provide, supply, contrive. — *M.* to prepare oneself or for oneself.

κατα-σκευή, ἡ preparation, equipment, furniture; a building; state, condition; furniture; baggage.

κατα-σκηνάω, -όω to take up one's quarters; to pitch a tent, encamp.

κατα-σκήνωσις, ἡ an encamping, rest(ing place).

κατα-σκήπτω to rush down upon; to be hurled down upon; to assail, attack.

κατα-σκιάζω, -σκιάω to overshadow; to bury.

κατά-σκιος 2 overshadowed.

κατα-σκοπέω to inspect, view, examine; to spy out, explore.

κατά-σκοπος, ὁ spy, scout.

κατα-σκώπτω to mock.

κατα-σμύχω to burn slowly.

κατα-σοφίζομαι *M.* to circumvent, cheat. [down.]

κατα-σπάω to draw or pull)

κατα-σπείρω to sow; to spread out; to cause.

κατα-σπένδω to pour out as a libation; to pour out upon; = σπένδω.

κατα-σπέρχω to press or urge upon.

κατα-σπουδάζομαι to be earnest about.

κατα-στάζω to trickle down, to drop.

κατα-στασιάζω to overthrow by a counter-party.

κατά-στασις, ἡ an establishing, appointing, arragement, presentation, equipment; state, condition; surety; constitution, nature.

κατα-στάτης, ου, ὁ arranger, establisher.

κατα-στεγάζω to cover.

κατα-στέγασμα, τό a covering, roof. [vered.]

κατά-στεγος 2 roofed, co-

κατα-στείβω to tread or step on. [to check.]

κατα-στέλλω to arrange;

κατα-στένω to sigh over.

κατα-στεφής 2 wreathed.

κατά-στημα, τό condition, state, bearing.

κατα-στολή, ἡ dress.

κατα-στόρνῡμι = καταστρώννῡμι. [lightning.]

κατ-αστράπτω to flash

κατα-στρατοπεδεύω to cause to encamp. — intr. and M. to encamp.

κατα-στρέφω to turn over, overturn, bring to an end. — M. to subdue.

κατα-στρηνιάω to behave greedily towards.

κατα-στροφή, ἡ an overturning, overthrowing, sudden turn, end, death, perdition; a subduing.

κατά-στρωμα, τό deck of a ship.

κατα-στρώννῡμι to spread over, to strow to the ground; to kill, overthrow; to cover.

κατα-στυγέω to shudder at.

κατα-σύρω to drag away; to plunder. [kill.]

κατα-σφάζω to slaughter,

κατα-σφραγίζω to seal up.

κατά-σχεσις, ἡ occupation, possession.

κατά-σχετος 2 held back.

κατα-σχίζω to cleave asunder, to break or burst open.

κατα-σχολάζω to linger, tarry.

κατα-σώχω to rub or grind to powder, to pound, bruise.

κατα-τάσσω to arrange, draw up in order; to classify; to appoint.

κατα-τείνω to stretch out, to strain, force; intr. to exert oneself; to reach to.

κατα-τέμνω to cut into pieces, mutilate; to cut (trenches).

κατα-τήκω to cause to melt, to dissolve. — intr. and P. to melt, to pine away.

κατα-τίθημι to place or put down, to lay down, propose (a prize); to lay in, preserve; to pay. — M. to lay down for oneself, to deposit, lay up in store; to put away, lay aside; to neglect; to put an end to.

κατα-τιτρώσκω to wound.

κατα-τομή, ἡ a cutting into pieces, mutilation.

κατα-τοξεύω to shoot down.

κατα-τραυματίζω to in-jure, wound; to make leaky.

κατα-τρέχω to run down; to attack, rush on against; to run over, overrun.

κατα-τρίβω to rub down or in pieces; to wear away or out; to waste, exhaust. — P. to be worn out or exhausted; to be weary.

κατα-τρύχω to rub down; to wear out, exhaust.

κατα-τρωματίζω = κατα-τραυματίζω.

κατα-τυγχάνω to reach, obtain; to be successful.

κατ-αυδάω to declare aloud.

κατ-αυλέω to play on the flute. — M. to listen to flute-playing.

κατ-αυλίζομαι P. to en-camp, pass the night.

κατα-φαίνομαι P. to ap-pear, become visible.

κατα-φανής 2 visible; con-spicuous, manifest.

κατά-φαρκτος 2 = κατά-φρακτος.

κατα-φαρμάσσω to poison, enchant. [protest.]

κατα-φατίζω to assure,]

κατα-φερής 2 inclining, inclined, setting.

κατα-φέρω to carry or bring down. — P. to be driven down; to be car-ried to.

κατα-φεύγω to flee down; to take to flight; to re-sort to. [fuge; evasion.]

κατά-φευξις, ἡ flight; re-]

κατά-φημι to assent to.

κατα-φθείρω to ruin.

κατα-φθίνω to perish.

κατα-φθίω to ruin, de-stroy, kill. — P. to pe-rish, waste away, be ruined or destroyed.

κατ-αφίημι to let glide down. [derly.]

κατα-φιλέω to kiss ten-]

κατα-φλέγω to burn down.

κατα-φοβέω to frighten.

κατα-φοιτάω to use to come down.

κατα-φονεύω to slay, kill.

κατα-φορέω = καταφέρω.

κατα-φράζομαι M. and P. to observe, see.

κατά-φρακτος 2 fenced in; covered, decked.

κατα-φρονέω to despise, disdain, scorn; to think of, suppose.

κατα-φρόνημα, τό, κατα-φρόνησις, ἡ contempt; haughtiness.

κατα-φρονητής, οῦ, ὁ des-piser. [scornfully.]

κατα-φρονητικῶς adv.]

κατα-φυγγάνω = κατα-φεύγω.

κατα-φυγή, ἡ = κατά-φευξις. [by tribes.]

κατα-φῦλαδόν adv. in or]

κατα-φωράω to catch in the act, discover; to be-tray; to convict.

κατα-χαίρω to feel mis-chievous joy. [with brass.]

κατα-χαλκόω to cover]

κατα-χαρίζομαι M. to do a favour; to flatter; to abandon to. [against.]

κατα-χειροτονέω to vote]

κατα-χέω to pour down

upon or over, to shed; to let fall; to throw down; to spread out. — *P.* to fall down; to flow out. — *M.* to cause to be melted down.

κατα-χθόνιος 2 underground, infernal.

κατα-χορδεύω to split up.

κατα-χορηγέω to spend.

κατα-χόω = καταχώννῡμι.

κατα-χράω to suffice, be enough. — *M.* to make use of, to use up, consume; to misuse; to destroy, murder.

κατα-χρῡσόω to overlay with gold, to gild.

κατα-χώννῡμι to cover with earth, to inter.

κατα-χωρίζω to place properly.

κατα-ψάω to stroke.

κατα-ψεύδομαι *M.* to invent, feign.

κατα-ψευδομαρτυρέομαι *P.* to be condemned by false witness. [feigned.]

κατα-ψευστός 2 invented,]

κατα-ψηφίζομαι *M.* to vote against.

κατα-ψήχω to rub down. — *P.* to crumble away.

κατα-ψύχω to cool.

κάτ-έαται = κάθηνται.

κατ-έδω = κατεσθίω.

κατ-είβω to let flow down, to shed. — *M.* to flow down; to elapse. [idols.]

κατ-είδωλον 2 full of]

κατ-εικάζω to make (a)like; to guess. — *P.* to be (a)like.

κατ-ειλέω to force together, enclose.

κατ-ειλίσσω to wrap round, enfold.

κατ-ειλύω to cover up.

κάτ-ειμι (-ιέναι) to go or come down, to fall or flow down; to come back.

κατ-εῖπον to speak against, accuse; to speak out, tell, denounce.

κατ-είργω, -είργνῡμι to press hard; to confine; to force; to hinder.

κατ-ειρύω = κατερύω.

κατ-ελεέω to have pity.

κατ-ελπίζω to hope confidently. [kill, destroy.)

κατ-εναίρω, -εναρίζω to]

κατ-εναντίον, κατ-έναντι *adv.* over against, opposite.

κατ-ένωπα, -ενώπιον *adv.* right opposite.

κατ-εξουσιάζω to exercise authority over. [against.)

κατ-επάδω to use charms]

κατ-επείγω to press hard, oppress, urge, hasten.

κατ-εργάζομαι *M.* to accomplish, achieve, effect; to acquire, gain; to overcome, oppress; to kill.

κατ-έργνῡμι, κατ-έργω = κατείργω.

κατ-ερείκω to tear, rend.

κατ-ερείπω to demolish, destroy, to cast down. — *intr.* to fall down, perish.

κατ-ερητύω, -ερῡκάνω, -ερῡκω to hold back, detain, hinder. [to launch.)

κατ-ερύω to draw down;]

κατ-έρχομαι = κάτειμι.

κατ-εσθίω, -έσθω to eat up, consume.

κάτ-ευγμα, τό vow, wish, prayer; votive offering.

κατ-ευθύνω to make straight; to direct.

κατ-ευλογέω to bless.

κατ-ευνάζω, -ευνάω to lull to sleep; to soothe. — P. to lie down to sleep.

κατ-εύχομαι M. to wish, pray, vow; to curse.

κατ-ευωχέομαι to feast, make merry.

κατ-σφάλλομαι M. to spring down upon.

κατ-εφίσταμαι to rise up against.

κατ-έχω to keep down or back; to direct to; to check, restrain, withhold, delay; to occupy, possess, keep; to bear, suffer. — intr. to come to pass, happen, befal; to dwell, sojourn; to continue; to stop, cease. — M. to keep for oneself, retain; to stop, to make a halt.

κατ-ηγορέω to speak against; to accuse, blame, reproach; to assert, state, signify, indicate, prove.

κατ-ηγόρημα, τό, κατ-ηγορίᾱ, ἡ accusation, reproach, charge.

κατ-ήγορος, ὁ, κατ-ήγωρ, ορος accuser.

κατ-ήκοος 2 obedient, subject; listener, spy.

κατ-ηπιάω to assuage.

κατ-ηρεμίζω, -μέω to calm, soothe.

κατ-ηρεφής 2 covered; roofed; overshadowed.

κατ-ήρης 2 well-supplied.

κατ-ηρτημένως adv. most deliberately. [shame.]

κατήφεια, ἡ dejection;

κατηφέω to be dejected or dismayed.

κατηφής 2 dejected, downcast, despised. [reprobate.]

κατηφών, όνος, ὁ knave,

κατ-ηχέω to resound; to teach; to inform.

κατ-ιάπτω to hurt, disfigure. [against.]

κατ-ιθύ adv. just over

κατ-ιόομαι P. to grow rusty. [or lean.]

κατ-ισχναίνω to make thin

κατ-ισχόω to gather strength; to have power; to prevail over.

κατ-ίσχω = κατέχω.

κάτ-οιδα to know exactly.

κατ-οικέω to inhabit; to regulate by laws. — intr. and M. to settle down; to dwell. [dwelling-place.]

κατ-οίκησις, ἡ a settling;

κατ-οικητήριον, τό, κατ-οικία, ἡ dwelling, habitation.

κατ-οικίζω to remove to a colony, to settle; to colonize, found or establish a colony in. — P. to be or become a colonist, to be colonized. [colonization.]

κατ-οίκισις, ἡ settlement,

κατ-οικτείρω to have compassion; to pity.

κατ-οικτίζω = κατοικτείρω; to excite pity. — M. to lament. [tate.]

κατ-οκνέω to doubt, hesi-

κατ-ολοφύρομαι *M.* to bewail, lament.

κατ-όμνῡμι and *M.* to confirm by oath; to accuse.

κατ-όνομαι *P.* to depre-
ciate, disdain.

κατ-όπιν, κατ-όπισθεν
adv. behind, after; afterwards. [discover.]

κατ-οπτεύω to spy out,

κατ-όπτης, ου, ὁ spy.

κάτ-οπτος 2 visible.

κάτ-οπτρον, τό mirror.

κατ-ορθόω to set right,
make straight, manage
well; to mend; to erect:
to keep sound. — *intr.* and
P. to be successful, prosperous. [emendation.]

κατ-όρθωμα, τό success,

κατ-ορύσσω to bury, inter.

κατ-ορχέομαι *M.* to insult,
mock. [destination.]

κατ-ουρίζω to reach one's

κατ-οχή, ἡ a holding fast;
detention.

κάτ-οχος 2 constrained.

κατ-τάδε = κατὰ τάδε.

κάτω *adv.* down, down-
wards; beneath, below; in
the nether world; down
to the coast. [below.]

κάτωθεν *adv.* from below;

κατ-ωθέω to thrust down.

κατ-ωμάδιος down from
the shoulder. [shoulder.]

κατ-ωμαδόν *adv.* from the

κατ-ωμοσίᾱ, ἡ accusation
on oath.

κατ-ῶρυξ, υχος imbedded
in the earth, underground;
ἡ κ. pit, cavern.

κατώτατος 3 nethermost.

κατώτερος 3 lower.

καυλός, ὁ stalk, stem;
shaft; hilt.

καῦμα, τό heat. [heat.]

καυματίζω to consume by

καύσιμος 2 combustible.

καῦσις, ἡ a burning.

καυσόομαι *P.* to perish
from heat.

καύστειρα, ἡ burning, hot.

καύσων, ωνος, ὁ = καῦμα.

καυ(σ)τηριάζω to cast a
brand upon, stigmatize.

καυχάομαι *M.* to boast.

καύχημα, τό, καύχησις, ἡ
object of boasting; a boast.

καχ-εξίᾱ, ἡ neglected state.

κάχληξ, ηκος, ὁ pebble,
gravel.

κάω, κάω = καίω.

κέ, κέν = ἄν.

κεάζω to split, shiver.

κέαρ, τό = κῆρ heart.

κέγχρος, ὁ millet; spawn
of fish.

κεδάννῡμι = σκεδάννυμι.

κεδνός 3 careful; able, excellent; dear, valued; respectable; modest.

κεδρίᾱ, ἡ cedar-resin.

κέδρινος 2 of cedar-wood.

κέδρος, ἡ cedar-tree.

κεῖθεν, κεῖθι = ἐκεῖθεν,
ἐκεῖθι.

κεῖμαι to be laid down, to
lie; to lie inactive, idle,
still, sick, despised, dead,
or unburied; to be situated;
to be ready, present, *or* extant; to be in value; to
be fixed *or* proposed.

κειμήλιον, τό treasure, ornament.

κεῖνος 3 = ἐκεῖνος.

κεινός 3 = κενός.

κειρία, ἡ bandage; bed-girth.

κείρω to cut off, clip, shear; to hew off; to eat off, consume entirely; to waste, ravage. — M. to cut off one's hair.

κεῖσε = ἐκεῖσε.

κείω[1] to split, cleave.

κείω[2] to wish to sleep.

κεκαφηώς see χάζομαι.

κεκαφηώς 3 weak, gasping.

κέκονα see καίνω.

κεκρύφαλος, ὁ woman's hood; hair-net.

κελαδεινός 3 noisy, roaring.

κέλαδος, ὁ noise, tumult, sound, clap. [δεινός.]

κελάδων, οντος = κελαδεινός.

κελαι-νεφής 2 with dark clouds; dark. [black.]

κελαινός 3 dark, gloomy, κελαιν-ώπης 2 black-faced, gloomy. [mur.]

κελαρύζω to ripple, murmur.

κέλευθος, ἡ way, road, path; gait; journey.

κέλευ(σ)μα, τό, κελευσμοσύνη, ἡ order, command; call. [mander of rowers.]

κελευστής, οῦ, ὁ commander.

κελευτιάω to exhort repeatedly.

κελεύω to exhort, command, bid, order; to beseech, desire; to grant, permit.

κέλης, ητος, ὁ courser, race-horse; swift-sailing yacht. [horse.]

κελητίζω to ride a race-horse.

κελήτιον, τό yacht.

κέλλω to drive on, push ashore; to run ashore.

κέλομαι M. = κελεύω and καλέω.

κέλωρ, ὁ son.

κεμάς, άδος, ἡ young deer.

κέν = κέ (ἄν).

κεν-ανδρος 2 empty of men. [ous.]

κενε-αυχής 2 vain-glorious.

κενεός 3 = κενός. [groins.]

κενεών, ῶνος, ὁ flank, groins.

κενο-δοξία, ἡ vain-glory.

κενό-δοξος 2 vain-glorious.

κενός 3 empty, hollow, void; destitute, bereft; vain, idle, fruitless. [tomb.]

κενο-τάφιον, τό empty tomb.

κενο-φωνία, ἡ idle talk.

κενόω to empty; to unpeople; to bereave, bare.

κεντέω, -όω to prick, sting, goad, stab, pierce; to incite; to scourge, beat, torture.

κεντρ-ηνεκής 2 goaded on.

κέντρον, τό sting, prick, goad, spur; pain.

κεντρόω to furnish with stings; to pierce. [turion.]

κεντυρίων, ωνος, ὁ centurion.

κέντωρ, ορος, ὁ goader.

κέομαι = κεῖμαι.

κεραΐα, ἡ sail-yard; beam, pole; stroke, tittle.

κεραΐζω to destroy, plunder, ravage; to kill, exterminate; to sink (a ship).

κεραίω = κεράννυμι.

κεραμεία, ἡ pottery.

κεραμεοῦς, ᾶ, οῦν earthen, of clay.

κεραμεύς, ὁ potter.

κεραμεύω to be a potter.

κεραμικός 3, κεράμι(ν)ος 3 = κεραμεοῦς.

κεράμιον, τό earthenware vessel. [tile.]

κεραμίς, ίδος or ῖδος, ἡ

κέραμος¹, ὁ potter's earth, clay; pot, jar, earthenware; tile.

κέραμος², ὁ prison.

κεράννῡμι to mix, mix up; to temper, blend together.

κεραο-ξόος 2 polishing horn.

κεραός 3 horned.

κέρᾱς, ᾱτος and ως, τό horn, antlers; bow; horn for blowing or drinking; mountain-peak, branch of a river; wing of an army or fleet, flank. ἐπὶ κέρως in single file, in column.

κεράστης, ου horned.

κεράτινος 3 of horn.

κεράτιον, τό fruit. of the carob-tree. [struck.]

κεραύνιος 3 and 2 thunder-

κεραυνός, ὁ lightning, thunderbolt.

κεραυνόω to strike with the thunderbolt.

κεράω = κεράννῡμι.

κερδαίνω to win, gain, profit, to be benefited (by); to spare, save trouble.

κερδαλέος 3 profitable; crafty, cunning. [of gain.]

κερδαλεό-φρων 2 greedy

κερδίων 2 more profitable.

κέρδιστος 3 most profitable or useful; most cunning.

κέρδος, τό gain, profit, advantage, wages, pay;

greediness of gain; pl. cunning arts, tricks.

κερδοσύνη, ἡ cunning.

κερκίς, ίδος, ἡ weaver's shuttle

κέρκουρος, ὁ cutter.

κέρμα, τό small coin, change. [scoff, mortify.]

κερτομέω to mock, deride,

κερτόμησις, κερτομία, ἡ mockery.

κερτόμιος 2, κέρτομος 2 stinging, mocking.

κέσκετο = ἔκειτο (κεῖμαι).

κεστός 3 embroidered.

κευθάνω = κεύθω.

κευθμός, ὁ, κευθμών, ῶνος, ὁ, κεῦθος, τό hiding-place; hole, den, dwelling; abyss, depth.

κεύθω to hide, conceal, to keep secret. — intr. and P. to be hidden.

κεφάλαιον, τό chief point, main thing; summary, sum, chief result; capital.

κεφαλαιόω to sum up, to bring under heads; to beat on the head. [total.]

κεφαλαίωμα, τό sum, the

κεφαλ-αλγής 2 causing a headache.

κεφαλή, ἡ head; front; end, point; source, top; chief person.

κεφαλίς, ίδος, ἡ little head.

κέω = κείω.

κῇ, κή = πῇ, πή.

κηδεία, ἡ affinity, connexion by marriage.

κήδειος 2 dear, beloved; sepulchral.

κηδεμών, όνος, ὁ tutor,

guardian, protector; relation; chief mourner.

κήδεος 2 = κήδειος.

κηδεστής, οῦ, ὁ allied by marriage. [marriage.]

κηδεστίᾱ, ἡ connexion by

κήδευμα, τό affinity.

κηδεύω to care for, tend; to bury; intr. to ally oneself in marriage.

κήδιστος 3 dearest.

κῆδος, τό care, concern, mourning; burial; distress, sorrow, misery; affinity; marriage.

κήδω to grieve, distress, mortify; to hurt, damage. — M. to be troubled, anxious, or distressed; to care for, favour.

κηκίς, ίδος, ἡ grease, juice.

κηκίω and P. to gush forth.

κήλεος, κήλειος 2 blazing.

κηλέω to charm, fascinate, delight; to beguile, seduce; to soothe.

κηληθμός, ὁ fascination.

κηλητήριον, τό charm.

κηλίς, ίδος, ἡ burn; stain; blemish.

κῆλον, τό arrow.

κηλώνειον, -ήϊον, τό pump, machine for drawing water.

κημόω to muzzle.

κῆνσος, ὁ capitation-tax.

κήξ, κηκός, ἡ sea-gull.

κηπίον, τό little garden.

κῆπος, ὁ garden, orchard.

κηπ-ουρός, ὁ gardener.

κῆρ, κῆρος, τό heart, breast.

κήρ, κηρός, ἡ fate, death; goddess of death; doom, destruction, mischief, evil.

κηρεσσι-φόρητος 2 driven on by the goddesses of fate.

κηρίον, τό honeycomb.

κηρο-δέτης, ου bound together by wax.

κηρόθι adv. heartily.

κηρός, ὁ wax.

κήρυγμα, τό a herald's proclamation, order; sermon, teaching.

κηρύκειον, κηρυκήιον, κηρύκειον, τό herald's staff.

κηρυκήτη, ἡ herald's office.

κῆρυξ, ῦκος, ὁ herald, town-crier; ambassador; preacher.

κηρύσσω to be a herald, to proclaim or summon as a herald; to order publicly; to announce; to praise; to preach. [ster.]

κῆτος, τό abyss; sea-mon-

κητώεις 2 rich in caverns.

κηφήν, ῆνος, ὁ drone.

κηώδης 2, κηώεις 3 fragrant.

κίβδηλος 2 adulterated, spurious, ambiguous, bastard.

κῑβωτός, ἡ, κῑβώτιον, τό chest, box; ark; ark of the covenant.

κιγχάνω = κιχάνω.

κίδναμαι = σκεδάννυμαι.

κιθάρᾱ, κίθαρις, ἡ lyre; lyre-playing.

κιθαρίζω to play the lyre.

κιθάρισις, ἡ lyre-playing.

κιθάρισμα, τό piece for the lyre.

κιθαριστής, οῦ, ὁ player on the lyre. [playing.]

κιθαριστικός 3 for lyre-

κιθαριστύς, ύος, ἡ art of playing the lyre.

κιθαρ-ῳδέω to sing to the lyre. [lyre.

κιθαρ-ῳδός player on the lyre.

κιθών, ῶνος, ὁ = χιτών.

κίκι, εως, τό castor-oil; castor-plant.

κικλήσκω = καλέω.

κίκυς, υος, ἡ strength, vigour.

κίναδος, τό fox.

κίναιδος, ὁ voluptuary.

κινάμωμον, τό = κιννάμωμον.

κινδύνευμα, τό = κίνδυνος.

κινδυνευτής, οῦ, ὁ rash, foolhardy man.

κινδυνεύω to get into danger, to run a risk, to be in danger; to be bold, daring; to be likely or possible; to be feared. — P. to be exposed to danger, to be hazarded.

κίνδυνος, ὁ danger, risk, hazard, venture, experiment; law-suit; battle.

κινέω to move, set in motion, to urge on, advance; to shake, stir, arouse, trouble, excite; to turn, change. — P. to be put in motion, to be moved; to march on; to be shaken.

κίνησις, ἡ motion; tumult, disturbance.

κιννάμωμον, τό cinnamom.

κίνυμαι P. to be moved, to move. [ing.

κινυρός 3 whining, wail-

κιό-κρανον, τό capital of a column.

κίρκος, ὁ hawk. [ράννυμι.

κιρνάω, κίρνημι = κε-

κισσ-ήρης 2 ivy-clad.

κισσός, ὁ ivy. [with ivy.

κισσο-φόρος 2 crowned

κισσύβιον, τό bowl, cup.

κίστη, ἡ chest, box.

κιττός, ὁ = κισσός.

κιχάνω and M. to arrive at; to catch, meet, find.

κίχλη, ἡ thrush. [borrow.

κίχρημι to lend. — M. to

κίω to go (away).

κίων, ονος, ὁ, ἡ column,

κλαγγή, ἡ sound; song; scream, noise. [noise.

κλαγγηδόν adv. with a

κλάδος, ὁ branch; shoot.

κλάζω to sound, clash, clang; to scream, make a noise.

κλαίω to weep, wail, lament, to have cause to repent; to bewail.

κλάσις, ἡ a breaking.

κλάσμα,τό fragment,morsel.

κλαυθμός, ὁ, κλαῦμα, τό a weeping, wailing; woe.

κλαυσί-γελως, ωτος, ὁ smiles and tears.

κλαυστός 3 to be bewailed.

κλάω[1] to break off; to break to pieces.

κλάω[2], κλάω = κλαίω.

κληηδών, ἡ = κληδών.

κλεῖθρον, τό bolt, bar, lock. [ous; noble.

κλεινός 3 renowned, fam-

κλείς, κλειδός, ἡ bar; bolt; key; hook; tongue of a clasp; thole; collar-bone.

κλεισιάς, άδος, ἡ = κλισιάς.

κλείσιον, τό servants' hall.

κλεισίον, τό hut, stable.

κλειστός 3 = κληστός.

κλειτός 3 = κλεινός.

κλείω¹ = κλέω.

κλείω² to shut, close; to confine; to block up.

κλέμμα, τό theft; trick.

κλέος, τό report, fame, rumour; glory, good repute, honour.

κλέπτης, ου, ὁ thief; cheat, rogue.

κλεπτικός 3 thievish.

κλεπτοσύνη, ἡ thievishness; roguery.

κλέπτω to steal, purloin; to do stealthily or secretly; to cheat, deceive; to conceal, hide.

κλεψ-ύδρα, ἡ water-clock.

κλέω to make famous, praise, extol. — P. to become famous.

κλήδην adv. by name.

κλῃδ-οῦχος, ὁ, ἡ priest, priestess.

κληδών, κληηδών, όνος, ἡ = κλέος; omen, presage; favourable cry.

κλῄζω to praise, extol; to call, name. — P. to be called.

κλήθρη, ἡ alder.

κλῆθρον, τό = κλεῖθρον.

κληΐζω = κλῄζω.

κληΐς, ῖδος, ἡ = κλείς.

κληϊστός 3 = κληστός.

κληΐω = κλείω².

κλῆμα, τό, κληματίς, ίδος, ἡ shoot, branch; vine-twig; faggot-wood.

κληρο-νομέω to inherit, to obtain by inheritance.

κληρο-νομία, ἡ inheritance, patrimony, property.

κληρο-νόμος 2 getting a share; heir, heiress.

κλῆρος, ὁ lot, allotment; share, portion, inheritance; estate, piece of land.

κληρ-ουχέω to possess by allotment.

κληρ-οῦχος 2 possessing an allotment, colonist.

κληρόω to choose by lot, to allot, assign. — P. to be allotted to. — M. to draw lots; to obtain by lot.

κλήρωσις, ἡ a choosing by lots.

κλής, κλῆδος = κλείς.

κλῆσις, ἡ a calling, shouting; invitation; summons.

κλῇσις, ἡ a blockading.

κλητεύω to summon into court.   [welcome.

κλητός 3 called; chosen;

κλήτωρ, ορος, ὁ witness for a legal summons.

κλήω = κλείω².   [oven.

κλίβανος, ὁ pan, baking

κλίμα, κλῖμα, τό region, district; climate.

κλῖμαξ, ακος, ἡ ladder, staircase; a clasping in one's arms.

κλίνη, ἡ, κλινάριον, τό couch, bed; bier; litter; dining-sopha.

κλινο-πετής 2 bedridden.

κλιντήρ, ῆρος, ὁ arm-chair, couch, bed.

κλίνω to incline, bend; to turn; to put to flight; to make recline; intr. to lean, sink, be sloping; to lie down at table.— *M.* to lie against, recline. — *P.* to be bent, to lean; to rest, support oneself against; to stoop, sink, fall down; to lie down; to be situated.

κλισία, ἡ hut, tent, cabin; couch; company of guests.

κλισιάς, άδος, ἡ *pl.* door, gate.   [tent.]

κλισίηθεν *adv.* out of the tent.

κλισίηνδε *adv* to the tent.

κλισίηφι *adv.* in the tent.

κλίσιον, τό = κλείσιον.

κλισμός, ὁ reclining-chair.

κλιτύς, ύος, ἡ slope, hillside.   [lory.]

κλοιός, ὁ iron collar, pillory.

κλονέω to press hard, drive on; to confound, agitate. — *P.* to flee in confusion; to be chased wildly.

κλόνος, ὁ press of battle, bustle, throng.

κλοπεύς, ὁ thief; secret wrong-doer.

κλοπή, ἡ theft, fraud; secret flight; trick.

κλόπιος 3 thievish.

κλοτοπεύω to use idle talk.

κλύδων, ωνος. ὁ wave, billow, surge; tempest, throng.

κλυδωνίζομαι *P.* to be tossed (about) by the waves.

κλυδώνιον, τό little wave.

κλύζω to wash, splash; to ripple over; to rinse, wash out *or* away. — *P.* to surge.

κλύσμα, τό clyster, drench.

κλυστήρ, ῆρος, ὁ clysterpipe.

κλυτο-εργός 2 famous for work.

κλυτό-πωλος 2 famous for horses.   [loud, noisy.]

κλυτός 3 = κλεινός; audible,]

κλυτο-τέχνης, ου famous artist.   [cher.]

κλυτό-τοξος 2 famous archer.]

κλύω to hear, listen to; to learn by hearing; to perceive; to know; to obey; to be spoken of.   [ners.]

κλῶθες, αἱ (female) spinners.]

κλώθω to spin.

κλωμακόεις 3 rocky.

κλών, κλωνός, ὁ shoot, sprout, twig.

κλωπεύω to steal.

κλώψ, κλωπός, ὁ thief, robber.

κνάπτω to scratch; to full.

κναφεῖον, τό fuller's shop.

κναφεύς, ὁ fuller.

κνάφος, ὁ instrument of torture.

κνάω to scrape, grate.

κνέφας, αος, τό darkness, dusk, twilight.'

κνήθομαι *P.* to itch.

κνήμη, ἡ shin-bone, leg.

κνημῖδο-φόρος wearing greaves.   [legging.]

κνημίς, ῖδος, ἡ greave;]

κνημός, ὁ wooded valley.

κνησιάω to itch.   [grater.]

κνῆστις, ἡ scraping-knife,]

κνίζω to scrape, scratch; to itch; to vex, tease.

κνῖσα, κνίση, ἡ steam of burnt-offerings; fat.

κνισήεις 3 steaming of burnt fat.

κνυζέομαι *M.* to gnarl, whine, whimper.

κνυζηθμός, ὁ a whining.

κνύζημα, τό a stammering.
κνυζόω to make dim.
κνώδαλον, τό dangerous animal, monster.
κνώδων, οντος, ὁ sword; sword-hook.
κνώσσω to sleep.
κόγχη, ἡ muscle(-shell).
κογχυλιάτης, ου, ὁ shell-limestone. [cockle, shell.]
κογχύλιον, τό muscle,]
κοδράντης, ου, ὁ quarter of a Roman as (halfpenny).
κόθεν = πόθεν.
κόθορνος, ὁ cothurn, buskin (high boot worn by tragic actors).
κοιλαίνω to hollow out.
κοιλία, ἡ hollow of the belly; belly; womb.
κοῖλος 3 hollow, hollowed; lying in a vale.
κοιμάω, -έω to lull to sleep; to calm, soothe, assuage. — P. and M. to go to bed; to fall asleep; to rest, cease.
κοίμημα, τό sleep; bed-rite.
κοίμησις, ἡ a sleeping, sleep.
κοιμίζω = κοιμάω.
κοινανέω = κοινωνέω.
κοινο-λεχής 2 bedfellow.
κοινο-λογέομαι M. to consult together. [gether.]
κοινό-πλους 2 sailing to-]
κοινό-πους, ποδος walking together.
κοινός 3 common, public, belonging to the state; kindred; affable, popular, impartial; profane; τὸ κοινόν community, state, republic; common weal, pub-

lic affair, administration; state authorities, public treasury; κοινῇ, κοινῶς in common, publicly.
κοινό-τοκος 2 brotherly.
κοινόω to make common; to communicate; to make unclean, to pollute, profane. — M. to have communion; to consult or act in common; to make public.
κοινωνέω to have a share in, partake of.
κοινωνία, ἡ communion; share; company, society; intercourse; charity.
κοινωνικός 3 communicative, liberal. [ner, fellow.]
κοινωνός 2 common; part-]
κοῖος 3 = ποῖος.
κοιρανέω to be master or lord; to rule, command.
κοιρανίδης, ου. ὁ = κοίρανος. [master.]
κοίρανος, ὁ ruler; lord,]
κοιταῖος 3 lying in bed.
κοίτη, ἡ, κοῖτος, ὁ a going to bed; sleep; couch, bed; marriage-bed; embryo; offspring. [ber.]
κοιτών, ῶνος, ὁ bed-cham-]
κόκκινος 3 scarlet.
κόκκος, ὁ kernel; scarlet-berry.
κολάζω and M. to hold in check, tame; to chastise, punish; to correct.
κολακεία, ἡ flattery.
κολακευτικός 3 flattering.
κολακεύω to flatter, deceive. [τικός.]
κολακικός 3 = κολακευ-]
κόλαξ, ακος, ὁ flatterer.

κόλασις, ἡ a punishing; correction. [ment, prison.]

κολαστήριον, τό punish-

κολαστής, οῦ. ὁ chastiser, punisher. [a p.'s ears.]

κολαφίζω to cuff; to box

κολεός, ὁ sheath of a sword.

κόλλα, ἡ glue.

κολλάω to glue (together), cement. — P. to attach oneself to, cleave to.

κολλήσεις 3, κολλητός 3 glued together, cemented; welded. [gether; welding.]

κόλλησις, ἡ a gluing to-

κολλ(ο)ύριον, τό eye-salve.

κόλλοψ, οπος, ὁ screw of the lyre. [changer.]

κολλυβιστής, οῦ, ὁ money-

κολοβόω to shorten.

κολοιός, ὁ jackdaw.

κόλος 2 curtailed.

κολοσσός, ὁ gigantic statue.

κολοσυρτός, ὁ noise, up-roar. [lessen, abridge.]

κολούω to curtail, shorten,

κόλπος, ὁ bosom; womb; fold of a garment; bay; hollow, depth.

κολυμβάω to dive.

κολυμβήθρᾱ, ἡ swimming-bath; pond. [swimmer.]

κολυμβητής, οῦ, ὁ diver,

κολῳάω to croak, brawl, scold. [hill; mound, tomb.]

κολώνη, ἡ, κολωνός, ὁ

κολωνίᾱ, ἡ colony.

κολῳός, ὁ screaming, noise, altercation.

κομάω, -έω to wear long hair; to be proud or haughty.

κομέω to tend, take care of.

κόμη, ἡ the hair, foliage.

κομήτης, ου, ὁ long-haired; feathered; comet.

κομιδή, ἡ care, attendance; a carrying of supplies, transport, stores; recovery; a going and coming; pas-sage; return.

κομιδῇ adv. with care, wholly, altogether, very much so, just so, indeed.

κομίζω to take care of, tend, mind; to mention; to receive hospitably; to man-age; to carry away, con-vey; to store up; to fetch, bring back. — P. to be carried or conveyed; to tra-vel, betake oneself to; to return. — M. to shelter, entertain; to get, gain, procure; to keep, save, preserve; to bring to, to rescue, recover.

κόμμι, ιδος and εως, τό gum. [finery.]

κομμωτικός 3 given to

κομπάζω, κομπέω to clat-ter, clank; to vaunt, boast.

κόμπος, ὁ noise, rattling; boasting, vaunt.

κομπώδης 2 boastful.

κομφεία, ἡ refinement, subtlety.

κομφεύω and M. to refine; to make a display of wit.

κομφός 3 refined, well-dressed; pretty; elegant; witty, clever, exquisite.

κοναβέω to sound, clash, resound. [ing.]

κόναβος, ὁ noise, a clash-

κονίᾱ, ἡ dust; sand; cinders; ashes; limestone; plaster.

κονιᾱτός 3 whitewashed.

κονιάω to whitewash.

κονι-ορτός, ὁ cloud of dust, dust.

κόνις, ἡ = κονία.

κονί-σαλος, ὁ = κονιορτός.

κονίω to cover, fill, or sprinkle with dust; to raise dust; to speed.

κοντός, ὁ pole.   [weary.]

κοπάζω to grow tired or axe.

κοπίς, ίδος, ἡ knife, sword; axe.

κόπος, ὁ a striking, beating; wailing; weariness, trouble, pain.

κοπρέω to manure.

κοπρίᾱ, ἡ, κόπριον, τό, κόπρος, ὁ dung, manure; filth, dirt; dung-yard, stable.   [dung.]

κοπρο-φόρος 2 carrying]

κόπτω to strike, cut, slay, fell; to lay waste, damage, hurt, wound, weary; to hammer, forge, coin; to knock, peck. — M. to beat oneself; to mourn; to get coined.

κόραξ, ακος, ὁ raven.

κοράσιον, τό little girl.

κόρδαξ, ακος. κορδακισμός, ὁ an obscene dance.

κορέννῡμι, κορέω[1] to satisfy; to glut, surfeit. — P. and M. to have one's fill; to grow weary of.

κορέω[2] to sweep, brush.

κόρη, ἡ girl, maid; newly-married woman; daughter; doll, puppet; eye-ball; long sleeve.   [to rise.]

κορθύω to lift up. — P.]

κορμός, ὁ trunk of a tree.

κόρος[1], ὁ lad, youth; warrior; boy, son; youthful, noble.   [insolence.]

κόρος[2], ὁ satiety, surfeit;]

κόρρη, κόρση, ἡ side of the forehead; temples.

κορυβαντιάω to be in ecstasy like a 'Corybant.

κορυθ-άϊξ, ικος, κορυθ-αίολος 2 helmet-shaking.

κόρυμβος, ὁ top, peak; cluster of flowers.

κορύνη, ἡ club, staff.

κορυνήτης, ου. κορυνηφόρος, ὁ club-bearer.

κόρυς, υθος, ἡ helmet.

κορύσσω to rear; to stir; to arm, equip, array. — P. to rise, swell; to arm oneself.

κορυστής, οῦ armed.

κορυφαῖος 3 at the head; leader, chief, first man.

κορυφή, ἡ top, summit; crown of the head.

κορυφόω to bring to a head. — P. to rise high.

κορώνη[1], ἡ crow, raven.

κορώνη[2], ἡ handle of a door; tip of a bow.

κορωνίς, ίδος curved.

κόσκινον, τό sieve.

κοσμέω to order, arrange; to equip; to keep in order; to rule, govern; to adorn, deck, embellish; to honour, extol.   [ornament.]

κόσμησις, ἡ an adorning;]

κοσμητός 3 well-arranged.

κοσμήτωρ, ορος, ὁ arranger, ruler.   [earthly.]

κοσμικός 3 of the world,]

κόσμιος 3 orderly, modest,

15*

chaste, decent, obedient; regular, well-arranged.

κοσμιότης, ητος, ἡ decency.

κοσμο-κράτωρ, ορος, ὁ ruler of the world.

κόσμος, ὁ order, arrangement; decency, good behaviour; regularity, good government, constitution; world, universe; ornament, decoration, finery; glory, honour.

κόσος 3 = πόσος.

κότε, κοτέ = πότε, ποτέ.

κότερος = πότερος.

κοτέω and M. to bear a grudge, to be angry.

κοτήεις 3 angry. [hatred.]

κότος, ὁ grudge, anger.

κοτύλη, ὁ small cup; socket of the hip-bone.

κοτυληδῶν, όνος, ὁ sucker of the ink-fish.

κοτυλ-ήρυτος 2 flowing abundantly.

κουλεός = κολεός. [ping.]

κουρά, ἡ a shearing, clipping.

κουρεῖον, τό barber's shop.

κουρεύς, ὁ barber.

κούρη, ἡ = κόρη.

κούρητες, ων, οἱ young men. [ded.]

κουρίδιος 3 lawfully wed-

κουρίζω to be youthful or vigorous.

κουρίξ adv. by the hair.

κοῦρος, ὁ = κόρος.

κουρο-τρόφος 2 rearing or bringing up boys.

κουφίζω to make light, lift up; to relieve, help, assuage; to bury. — intr.

and P. to be light; to rise; to be relieved. [relief.]

κούφισις, ἡ a lightening,

κουφο-λογία, ἡ light talk.

κουφό-νοος 2 light-minded, silly, gay.

κοῦφος 3 light, unloaded; nimble, dexterous; indifferent, little; soft; digestible; easy, light-minded; vain.

κόφινος, ὁ basket.

κόχλος, ὁ muscle. shell.

κράββατος, ὁ couch, bed.

κραγγάνομαι M. to cry aloud. [swing, brandish.]

κραδαίνω, κραδάω to

κραδίᾱ, ἡ = καρδία.

κράζω to croak; to scream.

κραίνω, κραιαίνω to accomplish, fulfil, execute; to rule, command. [debauch.]

κραιπάλη, ἡ intoxication;

κραιπνός 3 rapid, swift, sweeping, rushing; rash, hot.

κρανᾱός 3 rocky, stony.

κράνεια, κρανείη, ἡ cornel-tree. [wood.]

κρανέϊνος 3 made of cornel-

κρανίον, τό skull.

κράνος, τό helmet.

κρᾶσις, ἡ a mixing, blending; temperature.

κράσ-πεδον, τό border, edge; fringe.

κράτα, τό = κάρα.

κραται-γύαλος 2 with strong breast-plates.

κραταιΐς, ἡ force, bulk.

κραταιός 3 strong, mighty.

κραταιόω to strengthen. — P. to become strong.

κραταί-πεδος 2 with hard ground.

κραταί-ρῑνος 2 with a hard hide or shell.

κρατερός 3 = καρτερός.

κρατερό-φρων 2 stout-hearted.

κρατερ-ῶνυξ, υχος with strong hoofs or claws.

κρατευταί, οἱ forked frame of a spit.

κρατέω to be strong or mighty, to have power, be lord, rule; to conquer, subdue, prevail over; to obtain by force; to surpass; to hold fast, seize; to check, hinder.

κρᾱτήρ, ῆρος, ὁ mixing vessel, bowl, b sin.

κρᾱτηρίζω to pour out a libation. [excel.]

κρατιστεύω to be best, to/
κράτιστος 3 strongest, mightiest; most excellent, best; bravest; noblest.

κράτος, τό strength, might, power, force; violence; dominion, rule, superiority, ascendency, victory.

κρατύνω and M. to strengthen, fortify, secure; to rule, govern; to possess.

κρατύς, ὁ strong. mighty.

κραυγάζω, κραυγανάομαι = κράζω. [ing.]

κραυγή, ἡ crying, scream-/
κρέας, ως, τό flesh, meat.

κρεῖον, τό dresser.

κρείσσων, κρείττων 2 stronger, mightier, better; braver; superior, surpassing. lord, master, victor; nobler; worse, more dangerous.

κρείων, οντος, ὁ, κρείουσα, ἡ lord, master, ruler; mistress.

κρεμάννῡμι to hang, hang up. — P. (κρέμαμαι) to be hung up or suspended, to be in suspense.

κρεμαστός 3 hung up, hanging. [bird.]

κρέξ, κρεκός, ἡ an unknown/
κρεουργηδόν adv. cut up in butcher's fashion.

κρεο-φάγος 2 eating flesh.

κρέσσων 2 = κρείσσων.

κρήγυος 2 agreeable, delighting.

κρή-δεμνον, τό head-dress, veil; battlements; lid, cover.

κρῆθεν adv. from the head, from above.

κρημνός, ὁ steep precipice, slope, steep bank or edge.

κρημνώδης 2 precipitous, steep.

κρηναῖος 3 of a spring or fountain. [well.]

κρήνη, ἡ spring, fountain,/
κρηπίς, ῖδος, ἡ shoe, boot; foundation, base; enclosing wall. [refuge.]

κρησφύγετον, τό place of/
κρητήρ, ὁ = κρατήρ.

κρῑ, τό = κριθή.

κρίζω to creak, screech.

κρῑθή, ἡ barley.

κρῑθινος 3 of barley.

κρίκος, ὁ ring, circle, bracelet.

κρῖμα, κρίμα, τό sentence, judgment; accusation, condemnation.

κρίνον, τό, κρίνος, τό lily.

κρίνω to separate, divide; to pick out, choose, prefer, approve; to judge, decide, explain, think, believe, accuse, bring to trial, examine, question; condemn. — M. to choose for oneself. — P. to be chosen, judged, or decided; to be accused, tried, or condemned; to contend, fight.

κριο-πρόσωπος 2 ramfaced. [ram.]

κριός, ὁ ram; battering-]

κρίσις, ἡ separation; discord, dispute; a choosing, deciding, judgment, sentence; trial, examination, law-suit, court of justice, condemnation, justice, punishment; issue, event.

κριτήριον, τό means for judging, test; court of justice; law-suit.

κριτής, οῦ, ὁ judge.

κριτικός 3 able to judge.

κριτός 3 chosen, picked out.

κροαίνω = κρούω.

κρόκη, ἡ woof, thread.

κροκόδειλος, ἡ lizard; crocodile. [robed.]

κροκό-πεπλος 2 saffron-]

κρόκος, ὁ saffron.

κροκύς, ύδος, ἡ flock of wool. [onion.]

κρόμμυον, κρόμυον, τό]

κρόσσαι, αἱ battlements; steps. [cause to rattle.]

κροταλίζω to rattle; to]

κρόταλον, τό rattle, castanet. [forehead, temple.]

κρόταφος, ὁ side of the]

κροτέω to knock, strike; to clap the hands.

κροτητός 3 rattling.

κρότος, ὁ a clapping, applause; rattling noise.

κρουνός, ὁ spring, well.

κρούω to knock, strike; to beat; to clap. — M. πρύμναν κρούεσθαι to row back stern foremost.

κρύβδα, κρύβδην = κρύφα.

κρυερός 3 chilly; awful.

κρυμός, ὁ frost; wintertime.

κρυόεις 3 = κρυερός.

κρύος, τό frost, ice.

κρυπτάδιος 3 = κρυπτός.

κρυπτή, ἡ vault, crypt.

κρυπτός 3 hidden, covered; secret.

κρύπτω to hide, cover, conceal; to keep secret; to be hidden, conceal oneself.

κρυσταλλίζω to shine like crystal. [crystal.]

κρύσταλλος, ὁ ice; rock-]

κρύφα, κρυφῇ, κρυφηδόν adv. secretly. [κρυπτός]

κρυφαῖος 3, κρύφιος 3 =]

κρωβύλος, ὁ tuft of hair; crest. [urn.]

κρωσσός, ὁ pitcher, jar,]

κτάομαι M. to gain, get for oneself, acquire; perf. κέκτημαι to possess, have.

κτέαρ, ατος, τό = κτῆμα.

κτεατίζω = κτάομαι and κέκτημαι.

κτείνω to slay, kill, murder.

κτείς, κτενός, ὁ comb.

κτενίζω to comb.

κτέρας, τό, pl. κτέρεα, ἐων gifts for the dead, funeral. [funeral honours.]

κτερίζω, κτερεΐζω to pay]

κτερίσματα, τά = κτέρεα.

κτῆμα, τό possession, property, goods, treasure.

κτηνηδόν *adv.* like beasts.

κτῆνος, τό possession, property; cattle, sheep.

κτήσιος 3 of one's property.

κτῆσις, ἡ a getting, an acquiring; possession, property, goods.

κτητός 3 gained, acquired.

κτήτωρ, ορος, ὁ owner.

κτίδεος 3 made of the skin of a fitchet or marten.

κτίζω to people, colonize; to found, establish, institute; to create.

κτίλος, ὁ ram.

κτιλόω to tame. — *M.* to win one's affections.

κτίννυμι, κτιννύω = κτείνω.

κτίσις, ἡ, **κτίσμα,** τό a founding, foundation, establishing; creation; creature. [creator.]

κτίστης, ου, ὁ founder,

κτιστύς, ύος, ἡ = κτίσις.

κτυπέω to crash, ring, resound; to thunder.

κτύπος, ὁ crash, sound, noise, rattling clash; cries.

κύαθος, ὁ dipper, cup.

κυαμευτός 3 chosen by beans. [beans; election.]

κύαμος, ὁ bean; vote by

κυάνεος 3 dark-blue; dark.

κυανό-πεζα, ἡ dark-footed.

κυανό-πρῳρος 2, -πρῴρειος 2 with dark prow.

κύανος, ὁ azure-stone, blue steel; smalt-blue.

κυανο-χαίτης, ου, -χαίτα dark-haired.

κύαν-ῶπις, ιδος dark-eyed.

κυβεία, ἡ dice-playing; deceit.

κυβερνάω to be a steersman; to steer; to direct, guide, govern.

κυβέρνησις, ἡ a steering; governing.

κυβερνήτης, ου, **κυβερνητήρ,** ῆρος, ὁ steersman; governor.

κυβερνητικός 3 skilled in steering or governing.

κυβευτής, οῦ, dice-player.

κυβευτικός 3 skilled in dicing.

κυβεύω to play at dice.

κυβιστάω to turn a somersault, to turn over.

κυβιστητήρ, ῆρος, ὁ mountebank; diver.

κύβος, ὁ cube.

κυδάζω to revile.

κυδαίνω to praise, glorify, honour, adorn.

κυδάλιμος 2 glorious.

κυδάνω = κυδαίνω; to boast.

κῦδι-άνειρα, ἡ men-honouring. [boast.]

κυδιάω to be proud, to

κύδιστος 3 most glorious, noblest.

κυδοιμέω to rave, rage; to drive in confusion.

κυδοιμός, ὁ tumult, confusion, uproar.

κῦδος, τό glory, fame, renown; pride; bliss, luck.

κυδρός 3 = κυδάλιμος.

κυέω, κυΐσκομαι *P.* to be pregnant.

κυκάω to stir up, mix, confound. — *P.* to get into confusion. [drink.]

κυκεών, ῶνος, ὁ mixed

κυκλεύω to surround, beset.

κυκλέω to wheel along; to turn in a circle; to surround. — *intr.* and *M.* to form a circle; to move in a circle, to turn round.

κύκλιος 3 and 2, κυκλόεις 3 circular. [all around.]

κυκλόθεν *adv.* in a circle,

κύκλος, ὁ circle, circular body; circular motion; ring, wheel, disk, eye, shield; town-wall. [all around.]

κυκλόσε *adv.* in a circle,

κυκλο-τερής 2 circular.

κυκλόω to make round or circular; to turn in a circle; to encircle. — *M.* to form into a circle. to form a circle; to enclose.

κύκλωσις, ἡ an encircling, enclosing.

κύκνος, ὁ swan.

κυλίνδω, κυλινδέω to roll (on or along). — *P.* to be rolled; to roll along; to wallow.

κύλιξ, ικος, ἡ drinking-cup.

κύλισμα, τό, κυλισμός, ὁ a rolling; stirred-up dirt.

κυλίω = κυλίνδω. [bread.]

κυλλῆστις, ιος, ὁ Egyptian

κυλλο-ποδίων, ονος crook-legged, halting.

κυλλός 3 crooked; maimed.

κῦμα, τό wave, billow, surge.

κῦμαίνω and *P.* to swell or rise in waves.

κῦματίας, ου surging; causing waves.

κῦματο-ᾱγής 2 breaking like waves. [beaten.]

κῦματο-πλήξ, ῆγος wave-

κῦματόομαι *P.* to rise in waves. [beach.]

κῦματ-ωγή, ἡ strand,

κύμβαλον, τό cymbal.

κύμβαχος[1], ὁ crown of the helmet.

κύμβαχος[2] 2 head foremost.

κύμινδις, ιδος, ὁ night-hawk.

κύμῑνον, τό cumin.

κυνά-μυια, ἡ dog-fly.

κυνάριον, τό little dog.

κυνέη, κυνῆ, ἡ cap. bonnet; helmet. [less.]

κύνεος 3 like a dog, shame-

κυνέω to kiss.

κυν-ηγέσιον, τό chase, hunt; hunting expedition; pack of hounds; game. [sue.]

κυν-ηγετέω to chase, pur-

κυν-ηγέτης, ου, ὁ, κυνηγός, ὁ, ἡ, huntsman, huntress.

κυν-ηγετικός 3 of hunting.

κυν-ηγία, ἡ = κυνηγέσιον.

κυνίδιον, τό little dog.

κυνικός 3 like a dog.

κυνίσκος, ὁ little dog. [ed.]

κυνο-κέφαλος 2 dog-head-

κυνό-μυια, ἡ = κυνάμυια.

κυνο-ραιστής, οῦ, ὁ dog-tick. [by dogs.]

κυνο-σπάρακτος 2 torn

κύντατος 3 most shameless.

κύντερος 3 more shameless.

κυν-ώπης, ου, κυν-ῶπις, ιδος dog-eyed.

κυπαρίσσινος 3 of cypress wood.

κυπάρισσος, ἡ cypress.

κύπειρον, τό, κύπειρος, ὁ cyperus.

κύπελλον, τό goblet.

κύπερος, ὁ = κύπειρος.

κύπτω to bend forward, stoop. [net, turban.]

κυρβασία, ἡ Persian bon-/

κύρβις, ὁ, ἡ movable pillar with inscriptions.

κῠρέω to hit or light upon, reach, meet with, arrive at; to gain, obtain; = τυγχάνω to happen, come to pass.

κῠριακός 3 belonging to a lord or master.

κῠριεύω to rule, be lord.

κύριος 3 having power, ruling; valid, legal, entitled, capable: appointed, regular, authorized, principal; ὁ κ. lord, master, ruler, owner; ἡ κυρία mistress, lady; τὸ κύριον legal power; statute; appointed time.

κῠριότης, ητος, ἡ dominion; ruler.

κυρίσσω to butt, strike against. [prey.]

κύρμα, τό godsend, booty,/

κῦρος, τό power, authority; decision; ratification; validity.

κῡρόω and M. to make valid, confirm, ratify; to decide; to accomplish.

κύρτη, ἡ, κύρτος, ὁ fishing-basket.

κυρτός 3 curved, arched.

κυρτόω to curve, bend, arch.

κῦρω and M. = κῠρέω.

κύρωσις, ἡ = κῦρος. [der.]

κύστις, εως or ιδος, ἡ blad-/

κύτος, τό hollow, vessel, urn; skin; shield, cuirass.

κῡφός 3 bent, curved, stooping.

κυφέλη, ἡ chest, box.

κύω = κυέω.

κύων, κυνός, ὁ, ἡ dog, bitch; monster; dog-star; sea-dog.

κώ = πώ.

κῶας, τό fleece, sheep-skin.

κώδεια, ἡ head of a poppy.

κώδιον, τό = κῶας.

κώδων, ωνος, ὁ and ἡ bell; patrol; trumpet.

κώκῡμα, τό, κωκῡτός, ὁ a shrieking, wailing.

κωκύω to wail, lament; to bewail. [the knee.]

κώληψ, ηπος, ἡ hollow of/

κῶλον, τό limb, member; foot, leg, knee; part; story, side, wall.

κωλῡτής, οῦ, ὁ hinderer.

κωλῡτικός 3 hindering.

κωλύω to hinder, prevent, check, forbid.

κῶμα, τό deep sleep, trance.

κωμάζω to revel, to go in a festal procession, to celebrate a feast; to be wanton or playful. [a village.]

κωμάρχης, ου, ὁ head of/

κωμαστής, οῦ, ὁ reveller.

κώμη, ἡ village.

κωμήτης, ου, ὁ villager.

κωμικός 3 belonging to comedy, comic.

κωμό-πολις ἡ village-town, borough.

κῶμος, ὁ festal procession, revel, merry-making; band of revellers; feast, banquet.

κωμ-ῳδέω to ridicule.

κωμ-ῳδία, ἡ comedy.

κωμῳδ(ι)ο-ποιός ὁ comic poet. [poet.]

κωμ-ῳδός comic actor or/

κώνειον, τό hemlock.
κών-ωφ, ωπος, ὁ gnat.
κωπεύς, ὁ wood for oars.
κώπη, ἡ handle of an oar
or sword or key; oar.
κωπήεις 3 with a handle.
κωπ-ήρης 2 furnished with
oars.

κώρυκος, ὁ leather(n) bag.
κῶς, κώς = πῶς. πώς.
κωτίλλω to talk over, to
wheedle.
κωφός 3 blunt, dumb, deaf
and dumb, mute, speech-
less; dull, weak, stupid;
insensate.

Λ

Λ, λ (λάμβδα, λάβδα) eleventh
letter of the alphabet; as a
numeral λʹ = 30.
λᾶας, ὁ stone; rock; crag.
λαβή, ἡ handle, haft, hilt,
hold; weak side.
λαβρ-αγόρης, ου, ὁ bold
prattler.   [boldly.]
λαβρεύομαι M. to talk]
λάβρος 2 rapid, furious,
vehement, boisterous.
λαβύρινθος, ὁ labyrinth,
maze.
λαγνεία, ἡ lust.
λαγός, ὁ = λαγῶς.
λαγχάνω to obtain by lot
or fate; to draw lots; to be
chosen by lot; to receive
a share; to give a share.
λαγῶς, λαγώς, ῶ, λαγωός,
ὁ hare.
λάδανον, τό = λήδανον.
λάζομαι = λαμβάνω.
λάθα, ἡ = λήθη.
λάθι-κηδής 2 banishing
care.   [sorrow.]
λαθί-πονος 2 forgetful of]
λάθρα, λάθρα adv. secretly,
stealthily; without one's
knowledge.
λαθραῖος 3 secret, stealthy.
λάϊγξ, ιγγος, ἡ pebble.

λαῖλαψ, απος, ἡ storm,
hurricane.
λαιμός, ὁ throat, gullet.
λάϊνεος 3, λάϊνος 2 of stone.
λαιός 3 left (hand).
λαισήϊον, τό light shield.
λαῖτμα, τό depth, abyss.
λαῖφος, τό piece of cloth,
sail; ragged garment.
λαιφηρός 3 swift, quick.
λᾱκέω = ληκέω = λάσκω.
λάκκος, ὁ hole, pit; cistern;
pond.   [down.]
λακ-πάτητος 2 trodden]
λακτίζω to kick with the
foot, trample (up)on; to
move in convulsions.
λακτιστής, οῦ kicking,
trampling.
λακωνίζω to imitate or
side with the Laconians.
λακωνισμός, ὁ a siding
with the Lacedæmonians.
λακωνιστής, οῦ imitating
the Laconians.
λαλέω to talk, prate, chat-
ter; to speak, teach, praise.
λάλημα, τό talk, prattling;
prater.   [dialect.]
λαλιά, ἡ a talking, chat;]
λάλος 2 talkative.
λαμβάνω to take, seize,

grasp, catch. capture, obtain; to meet with, incur, suffer; to receive, take in; to choose, select; to take away, steal; to receive hospitably; to comprehend, understand, perceive; to come upon, overtake, find out, detect, convict. — M. to keep hold of, grasp, touch; to get possession of, win, gain, obtain.

λαμπαδη - δρομία, λαμπαδη-φορία, ἡ torch-race.

λαμπάδιον, τό small torch.

λαμπάς, άδος, ἡ torch; sun, light; lamp; torch-race; adj. lighted by torches.

λαμπετάω = λάμπω.

λαμπρός 3 bright, shining, beaming, brilliant; limpid; clear, sonorous, keen; fresh; manifest, evident; splendid, magnificent; noble.

λαμπρότης, ητος, ἡ brilliancy, splendour; glory, honour.   [voice.

λαμπρο - φωνία, ἡ clear
λαμπρό - φωνος 2 clear-voiced.

λαμπρύνω to make bright, polish. — M. to be liberal.

λαμπτήρ, ῆρος, ὁ stand for torches; torch; beacon-light.   [brilliant.

λάμπω and M. to shine, be

λανθάνω to escape a p.'s notice, to be hidden, unnoticed; to cause to forget. — M. to forget.

λάξ, adv. with the heel or foot.   [in stone.

λαξευτός 3 cut or hewn

λάξις, ιος, ἡ district.

λᾱός, ὁ people, crowd, host, army; pl. men, soldiers, fellows.   [men.

λᾱοσ-σόος 2 stirring the

λᾱο-φόρος 2 = λεωφόρος.

λαπάρη, ἡ flank, loins.

λάπτω to lick, lap.

λάρναξ, ακος, ἡ receptacle; chest, urn, coffin.

λάρος, ὁ gull.   [licious.

λᾱρός 3 dainty, sweet, de-

λαρυγγίζω to shout with all one's lungs.   [gullet.

λάρυγξ, υγγος, ὁ throat,

λάσθη, ἡ mockery, insult.

λασι-αύχην, ενος maned.

λάσιος 3 shaggy, woolly; grown with bushes.

λάσκω to crash, cry, ring, shriek; to speak loud, shout.

λᾱ-τομέω to hew stones.

λατρεία, ἡ, λάτρευμα, τό service, servitude, hired labour; worship.

λάτρις, ιος, ὁ servant, slave.

λαυκανίη, ἡ throat.

λαύρα, ἡ lane, passage, defile.

λάφυρον, τό booty, spoil.

λαφυρο - πωλέω to sell booty.

λαφυρο-πώλης, ου, ὁ seller of booty.   [vour.

λαφύσσω to swallow, de-

λαχανισμός, ὁ a gathering of vegetables.   [getables.

λάχανον, τό greens, ve-

λάχεια fem. level, flat.

λάχεσις, ἡ = λάχος.

λάχνη, ἡ wool; woolly hair; downy beard.

λαχνήεις 3 woolly; hairy.

λάχνος, ὁ = λάχνη.

λάχος, τό lot, share; section; fate.

λάω to seize, grasp; to wish.

λέαινα, ἡ lioness

λεαίνω to polish, smooth; to make agreeable; to bray or pound.

λέβης, ητος, ὁ kettle, caldron; basin; urn.

λεγεών, λεγιών, ῶνος, ὁ, ἡ legion.

λέγω[1] = λέχω to lay down or asleep. — M. to lie down to sleep.

λέγω[2] to pick, gather; to reckon among; to tell, relate, speak, say, declare, assert, promise; to call, name; to order, request; to recite, read. — M. to gather for oneself, to count up; to converse, discourse. — P. to be told, related, or said; ὁ λεγόμενος the so-called.

λεηλατέω to drive away booty, to plunder.

λεία, ἡ booty, plunder.

λειαίνω = λεαίνω.

λείβω to pour out; to pour a libation.

λεῖμμα, τό = λείψανον.

λειμών, ῶνος, ὁ meadow, pasture.

λειμώνιος 3, λειμωνιάς, άδος, ἡ of a meadow.

λειμωνόθεν adv. from a meadow. [chinned.]

λειο-γένειος 2 smooth-

λεῖος 3 smooth, polished; level, flat; bald. [ness.]

λειότης, ητος, ἡ smooth-

λειπο-στρατία, ἡ, λειπο-στράτιον, τό desertion.

λειπο-ψῡχέω to swoon; to be dejected.

λειπο-ψῡχία, ἡ swoon.

λείπω to leave, leave remaining or behind; to abandon, desert; intr. to be gone; to fail, come short of. — M. to leave behind, bequeath. — P. and M. to be left, left behind, remain; to be inferior or weaker; to be abandoned; to be far from; to want, lack. [cate.]

λειριόεις 3 lily-like; deli-

λεϊστός 3 = λῃστός.

λειτουργέω to perform public duties; to bear the charges of public duties; to officiate.

λειτουργία, ἡ public service; expenditure for the state; divine service.

λείχω to lick.

λε.φανον, τό remnant.

λεκτικός 3 eloquent.

λεκτός 3 picked out; said; to be spoken.

λέκτρον, τό couch, bed; bed-clothes; marriage-bed; marriage.

λελιημένος 3 longing for.

λελογισμένως adv. deliberately.

λέντιον, τό linen cloth.

λέξις, ἡ speech, mode of speech, style.

λεοντέη, λεοντῆ, ἡ lion's skin. [ion, yoke.]

λέπαδνον, τό leather cush-

λέπας, τό bare rock or hill.

λεπιδωτός 3 scaly, scaled.

λεπίς, ίδος, ἡ scale, shell.

λέπρᾱ, ἡ leprosy.

λεπρός 3 leprous.

λεπταλέος 3 fine, delicate.

λεπτό-γεως 2 with poor soil.

λεπτός 3 cleaned of the husks; thin, fine, slender, delicate, lean, narrow, small, weak; subtle, clever.

λεπτουργέω to do fine work.

λέπω to peel or bark.

λέσχη, ἡ town-hall; place of public resort; assembly; conversation, talk.

λευγαλέος 3 sad, wretched, miserable, pitiful; mischievous.

λευΐτης, ου, ὁ Levite.

λευΐτικός 3 Levitical.

λευκαίνω to make white.

λευκ-ανθής 2 white-blossoming, white.

λευκ-ανθίζω to be white.

λεύκ-ασπις, ιδος white-shielded.

λεύκη, ἡ white poplar; white leprosy.   [horses.)

λεύκ-ιππος 2 with white/

λευκο-θώραξ, ᾱκος with white cuirass.

λευκό-λινον, τό white flax.

λευκό-πωλος 2 = λεύκ-ιππος.

λευκός 3 bright, brilliant, clear; white, pale.

λεύκ-οφρυς, υος with white eyebrows.   [white.)

λευκόω to whiten, paint/

λευκ-ώλενος 2 white-armed.   [wide.)

λευρός 3 smooth, level,/

λεύσσω to gaze, look (at), behold, see.

λευστήρ, ῆρος, ὁ one who stones, executioner.

λεύω to stone.   [grassy.)

λεχε-ποίης, ου meadowy,)

λέχος, τό couch, bed; bier; marriage-bed; marriage.

λέχοσδε adv. to bed.

λέχριος 3 slanting, oblique.

λέχω see λέγω[1].

λέων, οντος, ὁ lion.

λεωργός, ὁ offender.

λεώς, ώ, ὁ = λᾱός.

λεω-σφέτερος 2 one of their own people.

λεω-φόρος 2 frequented; high-way.

λήγω to cease, leave off; to abate, assuage; to keep back.

λήδανον, τό gum.

λήζω = ληΐζω.

λήθη, ἡ a forgetting, forgetfulness.

λήθω = λανθάνω.

ληΐάς, άδος, ἡ captive.

ληΐ-βότειρα, ἡ crop-devouring.

ληΐζω and M. to make plunder or spoil; to rob, ravage.

ληΐη, ἡ = λεία.

λήΐον, τό cornfield, crop.

ληΐς, ίδος, ἡ = λεία.

ληϊστήρ, ῆρος, ὁ robber, plunderer.   [booty.)

ληϊστός 3 to be seized as/

ληϊστύς, ύος, ἡ a plundering, robbing.   [booty.)

λήϊτις, ιδος, ἡ dispenser of/

λήκυθος, ἡ oil-flask.

λῆμα, τό will, purpose; courage; arrogance, pride.

λῆμμα, τό income; profit, gain; gratification.

ληνός, ἡ, ὁ wine-press; trough. [share.]

λῆξις, ἡ allotment, lot,|

ληρέω to talk idly; to be foolish or silly.

λήρημα, τό, **λῆρος**, ὁ idle talk, nonsense, frivolousness; swaggerer.

λησμοσύνη, ἡ = λήθη.

λῃστείᾱ, ἡ robbery, piracy, plundering expedition.

λῃστεύω = λῄζομαι. [bers.]

λῃστήριον, τό band of rob-|

λῃστής, οῦ, ὁ robber, pirate, free-booter.

λῃστικός 3 inclined to rob, piratical. [receiving.]

λῆψις, ἡ a taking, seizing,|

λιάζομαι P. to bend sideways; to withdraw, recede; to fall.

λίᾱν adv. very much; too much; καὶ λ. certainly, of course.

λιᾱρός 3 warm, tepid; soft.

λίβανος, ὁ frankincense (-tree). [censer.]

λιβανωτός, ὁ frankincense;|

λιβανωτο-φόρος 2 bearing incense. [stream.]

λιβάς, άδος, ἡ drop; water;|

λιβερτῖνος, ὁ freedman.

λίγα adv. of λιγύς.

λιγαίνω to cry aloud with clear voice.

λίγγω to sound, twang.

λίγδην adv. scrapingly.

λιγνύς, ύος, ἡ smoke.

λιγυ-πνείων, οντος shrill-blowing, whistling.

λιγυρός 3, **λιγύς** 3 shrill, clear, sharp, piercing, clear-toned. [voiced.]

λιγύ - φθογγος 2 clear-|

λίζω = λίγγω.

λίην = λίαν.

λιθάζω to stone.

λίθαξ, ακος. **λίθεος** 2, **λίθινος** of stone, stony, rocky.

λιθίδιον, τό small stone.

λιθο-βολέω to stone.

λιθο - κόλλητος 2 inlaid with precious stones.

λιθό-λευστος 2 stoned to death.

λιθο-λόγος, ὁ mason.

λίθος, ὁ stone, marble.

λιθο-σπαδής 2 made by tearing out a stone.

λιθό-στρωτος 2 paved with stones.

λιθο-τομίᾱ, ἡ quarry.

λιθουργός 2 working in stone; stone-mason.

λιθο-φορέω to carry stones.

λικμάω to winnow; to scatter.

λικμητήρ, ῆρος, ὁ winnower.

λίκνον, τό basket; cradle.

λικνο - φόρος, ὁ basket-bearer.

λικριφίς adv. sideways.

λιλαίομαι to long for, desire, crave.

λῖμαίνω to hunger, starve.

λιμήν, ένος, ὁ harbour, haven, port, bay; refuge; gathering-place. [nant.]

λιμνατος 3 marshy, stag-|

λίμνη, ἡ lake, pool, pond; basin; swamp; sea.

λιμνώδης 2 like a lake.

λῑμο-κτονίᾱ, ἡ a hungering, fasting.

λῖμός, ὁ hunger; famine.
λίνεος, λινοῦς 3 of flax, linen. [linen cuirass.]
λινο-θώρηξ, ηκος with a
λίνον, τό flax, linen: thread; fishing-net, fishing-line; linen cloth; wick.
λίνος, ὁ song of Linos.
λίπα adv. unctuously.
λῖπαρέω to persist, persevere; to entreat, beg earnestly.
λῖπαρής 2 persisting, persevering; entreating; liberal, lavishing.
λῖπαρίᾱ, ἡ perseverance.
λῖπαρο-κρήδεμνος 2 with bright head-band.
λῖπαρο-πλόκαμος 2 with shining locks.
λῖπαρός 3 oily, shining, fat, greasy; bright, brilliant; rich, blessed, copious. ample; comfortable, easy; splendid; fresh, gay.
λῖπαρῶς adv. of λιπαρής and λιπαρός. [guents.]
λῖπάω to shine with un-
λίπος, τό fat, oil.
λῖπο-στρατίᾱ, ἡ = λειποστρατία.
λιπόω = λιπάω.
λῖς[1], ὁ lion.
λῖς[2] smooth. [cloth.]
λῖς[3], λῖτός, ὁ linen, linen
λίσσομαι M. to beg, pray, entreat, beseech, implore.
λισσός 3 smooth. [prayer.]
λιστός 3 to be won by
λιστρεύω to dig round.
λίστρον, τό shovel; spade.
λιτανεύω = λίσσομαι.
λιτή, ἡ prayer, entreaty.

λίτομαι = λίσσομαι.
λιτότης, ητος, ἡ plainness, simplicity.
λίτρᾱ, ἡ pound.
λίτρον, τό soda. [greedy]
λίχνος, 3 and 2 lickerish;
λίψ, λιβός, ὁ south-west wind. [of the liver.]
λοβός, ὁ lobe of the ear or
λογάδην adv. picked out.
λογάς, άδος gathered, picked.
λογίᾱ, ἡ collection.
λογίζομαι M. to count, reckon, calculate; to reckon among; to consider, reason, reflect; to conclude, infer, judge, think.
λογικός 3 rational, fit for reasoning. [markable.]
λόγιμος 3 considerable, re-
λόγιος 3 eloquent; learned; λόγιον. τό oracle.
λογισμός, ὁ reckoning, computation, arithmetics; consideration, thought, reasoning, reflection; cause, conclusion, judgment; project; reason, insight.
λογιστής, οῦ. ὁ calculator, auditor, judge.
λογιστικός 3 skilled in calculating; arguing, sensible.
λογο-γράφος, ὁ historian, annalist; writer of speeches.
λογο-μαχέω to dispute about words.
λογο-μαχίᾱ, ἡ dispute about words.
λογο-ποιέω to invent words or news.
λογο-ποιός, ὁ historian;

writer of fables; inventor of stories.

λόγος, ὁ a saying, speaking, speech, mode of speaking; eloquence, discourse; conversation, talk; word, expression; assertion; principle, maxim; proverb; oracle; promise; order, command; proposal; condition, agreement; stipulation, decision; pretext: fable, news, story, report, legend; prose-writing, history, book, essay, oration; affair, incident; thought, reason, reckoning, computation, reflection, deliberation, account, consideration, opinion; cause, end; argument, demonstration; meaning, value; proportion; Christ.

λόγχη, ἡ spear-head, lance.

λοέω = λούω.

λοετρόν, τό = λουτρόν.

λοιβή, ἡ libation, drink-offering. [nicious.]

λοίγιος 2 destructive, per-]

λοιγός, ὁ ruin, mischief, destruction, death.

λοιδορέω and M. to revile, abuse; to blame.

λοιδορία, ἡ a reviling, abuse, reproach.

λοίδορος 2 reviling, abusive. [lence.]

λοιμός, ὁ plague, pesti-]

λοιμώδης 2 pestilential.

λοιπός 3 remaining, surviving, future.

λοισθήιος 2, **λοίσθιος** 3 and 2, **λοῖσθος** 2 left behind; last.

λεξός 3 slanting, oblique.

λ.πός, ὁ husk, peel, bark.

λουτρόν, τό bath, bathing-place; ablution, baptism; libation.

λουτρο-χόος 2 pouring water for a bath.

λούω to wash, bathe. — M. to wash oneself. [hill.]

λοφιά, ὁ mane, bristles;]

λόφος, ὁ neck, crest of a helmet, tuft of hair; ridge of a hill, hill.

λοχ-αγέω to lead a λόχος.

λοχ-αγία, ἡ office of a λοχαγός.

λοχ-αγός, ὁ captain, leader of a λόχος.

λοχάω and M. to lie in wait or ambush; to set a trap for.

λοχεία, ἡ child-birth; child.

λοχεῖος 3 of child-birth.

λοχεύω to bring forth. — P. to be born.

λοχ-ηγέω = λοχαγέω.

λοχίζω to arrange men in companies; = λοχάω.

λοχίτης, ου, ὁ soldier of the same company; fellow-soldier; life-guard.

λόχμη, ἡ lair, thicket.

λοχμώδης 2 overgrown with bushes.

λόχος, ὁ ambush, ambuscade; company of soldiers, band.

λόω = λούω.

λύγδην adv. with sobs.

λυγίζω to bend, twist. — P. to writhe.

λύγξ¹, λυγκός. ὁ lynx.

λύγξ², λυγγός, ἡ hiccough.

λύγος, ὁ willow-twig.
λῠγρός 3 sad, mournful, miserable; mischievous; cowardly.
λύθρον, τό, λύθρος, ὁ gore, blood; filth.
λυκά-βᾱς, αντος, ὁ sun's course, year.
λυκέη, ἡ a wolf's skin.
λυκη-γενής 2 born from light.
λυκιο-εργής 2 of Lycian workmanship. [ing.]
λυκο-κτόνος 2 wolf-slay-
λύκος, ὁ wolf.
λῦμα, τό dirty water, filth; disgrace.
λῡμαίνομαι M. to disgrace, outrage; to maltreat; to destroy, spoil; to hurt.
λῡμαντής, οῦ. λῡμεών, ῶνος, ὁ destroyer, spoiler.
λῡμη, ἡ disgrace, outrage; maltreatment, mutilation; ruin.
λῡπέω to afflict, grieve, annoy, trouble. — P. to be grieved, sad or mournful.
λύπη, ἡ, λύπημα, τό sorrow, grief, pain. distress.
λῡπηρός, λῡπρός 3 sad, painful, wretched, distressed.
λύρᾱ, ἡ lyre.
λῠσι-μελής 2 limb-relaxing.
λύσις, ἡ a loosing, release, ransoming, deliverance; dissolution, separation; departure; divorce.
λῠσι-τελέω to be useful or advantageous.
λῠσι-τελής 2 useful, advantageous.

λύσσα, ἡ rage, fury.
λυσσαίνω, λυσσάω to be raving mad, to rage; to be angry.
λυσσητήρ, ῆρος, λυσσώδης 2 raving. raging.
λῠτήριος 2 releasing.
λύτρον, τό ransom.
λυτρόω and M. to release on receipt of ransom; to redeem.
λύτρωσις, ἡ redemption.
λυτρωτής, οῦ. ὁ redeemer.
λυχνίᾱ, ἡ lamp-stand.
λυχνο-καΐη, ἡ feast of lamps.
λύχνος, ὁ light, lamp, torch.
λύω to loosen, untie, slacken, unbend; to set free, release, redeem; to dissolve, sever; to destroy; to abrogate, annul; to atone, amend; to profit; to be useful. — M. to loosen for oneself; to redeem, ransom, relieve, release.
λωβάομαι M., λωβεύω to act shamefully; to insult, maltreat, disgrace; to mutilate, hurt; to seduce.
λώβη, ἡ outrage, disgrace, shame; maltreatment, mutilation; ruin.
λωβητήρ, ῆρος, ὁ slanderer; destroyer; murderer.
λωβητός 3 ill-treated, outraged, insulted; insulting.
λωΐων 2, λωΐτερος 3 better, more profitable.
λώπη, ἡ jerkin, mantle.
λωπο-δυτέω to steal clothes.

λωπο-δύτης, ου, ὁ clothes-stealer, thief, rogue.

λῷστος 3 the best, dearest.

λωτόεις 3 rich in lotus.

λωτός, ὁ lotus; clover; lo-tus-tree and fruit; lily of the Nile.

λωτο-φάγος, ὁ lotus-eater.

λώφησις, ἡ cessation.

λώων 2 = λωΐων.

M

M, μ (μῦ) twelfth letter of the alphabet; as a numeral μ' = 40.

μᾶ Particle of affirmation and protestation.

μάγαδις, ιδος, ἡ string-instrument, harp.

μαγγάνευμα, τό = μαγεία.

μαγγανεύω to cheat, put a trick upon.

μαγεία, ἡ magic, delusion, juggling tricks.

μαγειρική, ἡ cookery.

μάγειρος, ὁ cook.

μαγεύω to enchant, charm; to be a magician.

μαγία, ἡ = μαγεία.

μάγος, ὁ soothsayer, astro-loger, magus: enchanter, wizard. [of the Magi.]

μαγο-φόνια, τά slaughter]

μάζα, μᾶζα, ἡ barley-bread.

μαζός, ὁ = μαστός.

μάθημα, τό, μάθησις, ἡ the act of learning; know-ledge, learning, science, art, doctrine.

μαθητεύω to be a scholar; to teach, instruct. [ciple.]

μαθητής, οῦ, ὁ pupil, dis-]

μαθητός 3 to be learned.

μαθήτρια, ἡ female pupil.

μαῖα, ἡ good mother, foster-mother.

μαιμακτηριών, ῶνος, ὁ fifth Attic month (November).

μαιμάω to strive after, to be eager for; to rave.

μαινάς, άδος, ἡ raving; Mænad.

μαίνω to make mad. — P. to be mad, to rave, rage, to be furious or frenzied.

μαίομαι M. to strive, en-deavour; to seek.

μάκαρ, αρος, ὁ (fem. μά-καιρα) blessed, happy, for-tunate: rich.

μακαρίζω to call happy.

μακάριος 3 and 2 = μά-καρ. [cing happy.]

μακαρισμός, ὁ a pronoun-]

μακαριστός 3 to be pro-nounced happy, enviable; welcome.

μακεδνός 3 tall, slender.

μάκελλα, ἡ pick-axe, sho-vel.

μάκελλον, τό meat-market.

μάκιστος 3 = μήκιστος.

μακρ-αίων 2 long-lived, lasting. [with prolixity.]

μακρ-ηγορέω to speak]

μακρ-ημερία, ἡ season of the long days.

μακρό-βιος 2 long-lived.

μακρόθεν adv. from afar.

μακρο-θυμέω to be for-bearing: to be patient.

μακρο-θυμία, ἡ forbear-ance, patience.

μακρο-λογέω to speak at length. [at length.]

μακρο-λογία a speaking.

μακρός 3 long; tall, high, deep, far; long-lasting; tedious, prolix, circumstantial. [lived.]

μακρο-χρόνιος 2 long-

μάλα adv. much, very much, quite, wholly, particularly, exceedingly; certainly, verily.

μαλακία, ἡ softness, weakness; illness; slackness, cowardice.

μαλακίζομαι P. and M. to become weak, effeminate, lazy, cowardly, or timid; to be appeased.

μαλακός 3 soft, tender, sickly; mild, gentle; tender, delicate; effeminate, cowardly; careless, remiss; luxurious, wanton.

μαλάσσω to soften, appease. — P. to be softened by entreaties; to be relieved.

μαλερός 3 strong, mighty, terrible, vehement, raging; greedy.

μάλη, ἡ arm-pit.

μαλθακ- see μαλακ-.

μάλιστα adv. most, most strongly; especially, mostly; even, most certainly; by far; at most.

μᾶλλον adv. more, more strongly, rather, the more, yet, far; too much; by all means. [fleece.]

μαλλός, ὁ flock of wool,

μάμμη, ἡ grandmother.

μαμωνᾶς, ᾶ, ὁ mammon.

μάν = μήν. [mandrake.]

μανδραγόρας, ου or ᾶ, ὁ

μανθάνω to learn, have learnt, know; to ask, inquire, hear, perceive; to understand. [enthusiasm.]

μανία, ἡ madness. frenzy;

μανικός 3 (μανιάς, αδος, ἡ), μανιώδης 2 mad, frantic, raving; revelling.

μάννα, τό manna.

μᾱνός 3 thin, scanty, slack.

μαντεία, ἡ. μαντεῖον, τό, μάντευμα, τό gift of prophesying, divination, prophecy, oracle.

μαντεῖος 3 = μαντικός.

μαντευτός 3 foretold by an oracle.

μαντεύω and M. to prophesy, divine; to presage, forebode; to consult an oracle. [τεία, -τεῖον.]

μαντηίη, μαντήιον = μαν-

μαντικός 3 prophetic, prophesying; ἡ -ή art of divination.

μάντις, ὁ, ἡ soothsayer, diviner, seer. prophet.

μαντοσύνη, ὁ = μαντεία.

μάομαι = μαίομαι; to rush on, hasten.

μάραθον, τό fennel.

μαραίνω to undo, destroy, quench. — P. to die away, disappear.

μαρὰν ἀθά our Lord comes.

μαργαίνω to rage.

μαργαρίτης, ου, ὁ pearl.

μάργος 3 and 2 raving, mad, frantic; lustful.

μαρμαίρω to sparkle, glisten, gleam.

μαρμάρεος 3, μαρμαρόεις, 3 sparkling, glistening.

μάρμαρος 2 sparkling; ὁ, ἡ stone, rock; marble.

μαρμαρυγή, ἡ dazzling brightness; trembling motion.

μάρναμαι = μάχομαι.

μάρπτω to grasp, seize, hold, touch, reach, clasp.

μάρσιπος, ὁ bag, pouch.

μαρτυρέω to be a witness, to bear witness; to agree to, confirm; to confess, praise. — P. to obtain a (good) testimony.

μαρτυρία, ἡ, μαρτύριον, τό witness, testimony, evidence, proof; sermon.

μαρτύρομαι M. to call to witness; to testify, confirm by oath, protest.

μάρτυρος, ὁ, ἡ, μάρτυς, υρος, ὁ, ἡ witness; martyr.

μασάομαι M. to chew.

μάσασθαι see ἐπιμαίομαι.

μασθός, ὁ = μαστός.

μάσσω and M. to knead, handle.

μάσσων 2 comp. of μακρός.

μάσταξ, ακος, ἡ mouth, cavity of the mouth; mouthful, morsel.

μαστεύω to seek, inquire after; to endeavour, strive.

μαστήρ, ῆρος, ὁ seeker, investigator.

μαστιγέω = μαστιγόω.

μαστιγίας, ου, ὁ one who is frequently whipped; good-for-nothing.

μαστιγο-φόρος, ὁ whipbearer, constable.

μαστιγόω, μαστίζω to whip, scourge.

μάστιξ, ῑγος. μάστις, ιος, ἡ whip, scourge; plague.

μαστίω = μαστιγόω.

μαστός, ὁ teat; breast, woman's breast; hill, knoll.

μασχαλίζω to mutilate.

μασχαλιστήρ, ῆρος, ὁ shoulder-strap.

ματάζω to act foolishly.

ματαιο-λογία, ἡ idle talk.

ματαιο-λόγος 2 talking idly.

μάταιος 3 and 2 idle, foolish, vain, inefficient; unmeaning, unfounded; thoughtless, wanton, untrue, wicked. [vanity.]

ματαιότης, ητος, ἡ folly,

ματαιόω to make foolish.

ματάω to miss, do in vain; to loiter, linger.

ματεύω = μαστεύω.

μάτηρ, μᾱτρός, ἡ = μήτηρ.

ματίη, ἡ folly; vain attempt.

μαδρος = ἀμαυρός.

μάχαιρα, ἡ large knife; dagger; sword.

μαχαιρο-φόρος 2 swordbearing.

μάχη, ἡ combat, fight, battle; battle-field; single combat; quarrel.

μαχήμων 2 = μάχιμος.

μαχητής, οῦ, ὁ fighter, warrior; warlike.

μαχητός 3 conquerable.

μάχιμος 3 and 2 warlike.

μαχλοσύνη, ἡ lust, lewdness.

μάχομαι M. to fight, make

war; to resist, withstand; to quarrel. dispute.

μάφ, μαφιδίως *adv.* rashly, thoughtlessly, at random; fruitlessly, falsely; indecorously.

μάω see μάομαι.

μέγαθος, τό see μέγεθος.

μεγά-θῡμος 2 high-minded, magnanimous.

μεγαίρω to grudge, envy, refuse, forbid.

μεγα-κήτης 2 with huge sea-animals.

μεγαλ-αυχέω and *M.* to boast highly.

μεγαλεῖος 3 magnificent, splendid; haughty

μεγαλειότης, ητος, ἡ magnificence, majesty.

μεγαλ-ηγορέω to boast.

μεγαλ-ήτωρ, ορος high-minded, héroic; over-weening. [proud.\

μεγαλίζομαι *P.* to be\

μεγαλο-πράγμων 2 forming great designs.

μεγαλο-πρέπεια, ἡ magnificence, splendour; love of splendour.

μεγαλο-πρεπής 2 magnificent, splendid; magnanimous, liberal; fond of pomp.

μεγαλο-φρονέω to be hopeful; to be proud.

μεγαλο-φροσύνη, ἡ greatness of mind; haughtiness.

μεγαλό-φρων 2 high-minded; haughty.

μεγαλο-φῡχία, ἡ magnanimity; boldness.

μεγαλύνω to make great or powerful; to praise. ex-

tol. — *M.* to be exalted; to boast. [praised.\

μεγαλ-ώνυμος 2 much\

μεγάλως, μεγαλωστί *adv.* of μέγας. [λειότης.\

μεγαλωσύνη, ἡ = μεγα-\

μέγαρον, τό chamber, hall, apartment for men or for women, bed-chamber; house, mansion; inner room of a temple, sanctuary.

μέγας, μεγάλη, μέγα, *comp.* μείζων 2, *sup.* μέγιστος 3 large, great, big, grand; spacious, long, high, wide; powerful, mighty, strong, violent; arrogant, proud; illustrious. *adv.* μεγάλως (μεγαλωστί), μέγα, μεγάλα much, very much, exceedingly.

μέγεθος, τό greatness, bulk, size; might, power, excellence; importance. [men.\

μεγιστᾶνες, οἱ the chief\

μέδιμνος, ὁ a dry measure containing 48 χοίνικες.

μέδω, μεδέω to think of, give heed to, attend to; to devise; to rule; ὁ μέδων ruler, guardian. [turn.\

μεθ-αιρέω to catch in\

μεθ-άλλομαι *M.* to leap upon; to rush after.

μεθ-αρμόζω to alter; to correct.

μέθ-εξις, ἡ a partaking.

μέθ-έπω and *M.* to follow after; to obey; to call upon, visit; to pursue; to drive on in pursuit of; to manage. [late.\

μεθ-ερμηνεύω to trans-

μέθη, ἡ drunkenness.

μεθ-ημαι to sit among.

μεθ-ημερινός 3 happening by day; daily.

μεθ-ημοσύνη, ἡ carelessness, remissness.

μεθ-ήμων 2 careless, lazy.

μεθ-ίημι to let loose, let go; to release, set free; to forgive, pardon; to lay in, bring to; to send away; to abandon; to neglect; to permit, allow. — intr. to cease, slacken, be careless. — M. to loose oneself from, let go, abandon.

μεθ-ιστάνω, μεθ-ίστημι to transpose, place in another way; to substitute, change, remove. — intr. and P. to appear in a crowd; to withdraw, retire; to change one's place, to go over to another party, to revolt. — M. to send away, remove.

μεθό = μεθ' ὅ.

μεθ-οδεία, ἡ craft, trick.

μέθ-οδος, ἡ way of inquiring; method. [with.]

μεθ-ομιλέω to converse

μεθ-όριος 3 bordering on; τὰ μεθόρια border, frontier.

μεθ-ορμάομαι P. to rush after; to follow closely.

μεθ-ορμίζω to bring to another anchorage — intr. and M. to sail to another place.

μέθυ, υος, τό wine.

μεθύσκω to make drunk. — P. to get drunk.

μέθυσος 3 drunk(en).

μεθ-ύστερος 3 later.

μεθύω to be drunk; to be drenched.

μείγνῡμι = μίγνῡμι.

μειδάω, μειδιάω to smile.

μειζότερος, μείζων comp. of μέγας.

μεικτός 3 = μικτός.

μείλᾱς = μέλας.

μείλιγμα, τό sedative, means of appeasing; propitiation.

μείλινος 3 = μέλινος.

μείλιον, τό love-gift.

μειλίσσω to make mild, soothe, propitiate. — M. to extenuate.

μειλιχίη, ἡ mildness.

μειλίχιος 3, μείλιχος 2 mild, gentle, sweet, soft, kind, gracious, bland.

μειον-εκτέω to have too little, to be at a disadvantage.

μειόω to lessen; to degrade. — P. to decrease. — M. to be inferior.

μειράκιον, τό boy, lad, young man. [boyish.]

μειρακιώδης 2 youthful;/

μείρομαι to receive as one's share; perf. ἔμμορα to have one's share; εἵμαρται it is decreed by fate; εἱμαρμένη fate, destiny.

μείς, μηνός, ὁ month.

μείωμα, τό deficiency.

μείων 2 comp. of μικρός.

μελάγ-γαιος 2 with black soil.

μελαγ-χαίτης, ου black-haired. [bile.]

μελάγ-χολος 2 with black/

μελάγ-χροος 2, μελαγ-χροιής 2 black-skinned, swarthy.

μέλαθρον, τό rafters of a roof; roof; house.

μελαίνω to blacken, dye black. — intr. and M. to grow black.

μελάμ-φυλλος 2 with dark foliage. [black.]

μελάν-δετος 2 bound with

μελανία, ἡ dark cloud.

μελανό-χροος, -χρως, οος 2 = μελάγχροος. [water.]

μελάν-υδρος 2 with black

μελάνω = μελαίνω.

μέλας, αινα, ἄν black; dark, dusky, gloomy; τὸ μέλαν black dye; ink.

μέλδομαι M. to melt out.

μελεδαίνω to care for, tend; to be anxious.

μελεδών, ῶνος, ἡ, μελεδώνη, ἡ, μελέδημα, τό care, sorrow.

μελεδωνός, ὁ, ἡ attendant, guardian, nurse.

μελεϊστί adv. limb by limb.

μέλεος 3 fruitless, vain; careless, foolish; miserable, wretched.

μελετάω to take care of, to care for; to study, to prosecute earnestly, to practise, exercise; to exert oneself; to project, plan; to study; to declaim.

μελέτη, ἡ, μελέτημα, τό care, attention; study, practice, exercise; employment; pursuit; exercise of speaking. [diligently.]

μελετηρός 3 practising

μελέτωρ, ορος, ὁ guardian: avenger.

μέλημα, τό object of care.

μέλι, τος, τό honey.

μελί-γηρυς, υος sweet-sounding.

μελίη, ἡ ash-tree; lance.

μελι-ηδής 2 honey-sweet.

μελί-κρᾱτος, -κρητος 2 mixed with honey.

μελίνη, ἡ millet.

μέλινος 3 ashen.

μέλισσα, ἡ bee; honey.

μελίσσιος 3 made by bees.

μελιτόεις 3 rich in honey; made of honey.

μελιτόω to mix with honey. [er.]

μελιττουργός, ὁ bee-keep-

μελί-φρων 2 honey-sweet.

μέλλησις, ἡ a being about, intention; a threatening, impending; delay.

μελλητής, οῦ, ὁ delayer.

μελλό-γαμος 2, μελλό-νυμφος 2 betrothed, about to be wedded.

μέλλω to be about, to be going, to intend, purpose; μέλλων future; to be destined; to be likely, probable, or certain; to be meaning to do; to delay, hesitate, scruple.

μελο-ποιός, ὁ lyric poet.

μέλος, τό limb; song, strain, melody.

μέλπηθρον, τό delight, amusement; sport, toy.

μέλπω and M. to sing and dance; to celebrate, praise.

μέλω and M. to be an object of care, to be a care

to; μέλει μοί, μέλομαί
τινος I care for, take care
of, tend.
μελ-ῳδός 2 singing.
μέμαα perf. of μάομαι with
pres. sense.
μέμβλεται from μέλω.
μεμβράνᾱ, ἡ parchment.
μεμελημένως adv. care-
fully.   [(μεθίημι).]
μεμετιμένος = μεθειμένος]
μέμηλα perf. of μέλω with
pres. sense.   [pres. sense.]
μέμονα perf. of μάομαι with]
μεμπτός 3 to be blamed,
despisable; blaming.
μέμφομαι M. to blame, re-
proach, reject, find fault
with, despise.   [μαι.]
μεμφι-μοιρέω = μέμφο-]
μεμφί-μοιρος 2 discon-
tented.   [discontent.]
μέμψις, ἡ blame, reproach;]
μέν conj. indeed, rather,
certainly; μέν ... δέ on
the one hand ... on the
other; as well as.
μενεαίνω to long for ar-
dently, to desire; to be
angry.
μενε-δήϊος 2, μενε-πτό-
λεμος 2 steadfast, staunch,
brave.   [fast. patient.]
μενετός 3 lasting. stead-]
μενε-χάρμης, ου, μενέ-
χαρμος 2 = μενε-δήϊος.
μενο-εικής 2 plentiful;
satisfying, heart-pleasing.
μενοινάω, -έω to have a
mind, to intend, purpose;
to reflect.
μένος, τό desire, ardour,
wish, purpose; anger;

courage, spirit, vigour;
power, strength; violence.
μὲν οὖν conj. indeed,
rather; yet.
μενοῦνγε conj. rather.
μεντᾶν = μέντοι ἄν.
μέντοι conj. indeed, rather,
certainly. of course; yet,
however, nevertheless.
μένω to abide, stay, stay
behind, linger; to remain,
continue; to stand one's
ground; trans. to await,
expect, wait for.
μερίζω to divide into parts,
attribute. — M. to be at
variance.
μέριμνα, ἡ care, trouble.
μεριμνάω to care, to be
anxious or thoughtful.
μερίμνημα, τό = μέριμνα.
μερίς, ίδος, ἡ part, por-
tion, share; party; class,
company.
μερισμός, ὁ a dividing,
distributing; separation.
μεριστής, οῦ, ὁ divider.
μέρμερος 2 startling, horrible, dreadful.
μερμηρίζω to be anxious or
thoughtful, to ponder; to
devise.
μέρμις, ῑθος, ἡ string, cord.
μέρος, τό part, portion,
share, lot; class; turn; station, rank; piece, section;
party; district, place.
μέροψ, οπος mortal; others:
endowed with speech.
μεσαι-πόλιος 2 half-gray.
μεσᾰμβρίη, ἡ = μεσημβρία.
μέσ-αυλος = μέσσαυλος.
μεσεύω to be neutral.

μεσηγύ'ς) *adv.* in the middle, between; meanwhile.

μεσήεις 3 middling.

μεσ-ημβρίᾱ, ἡ midday, south.   [southern.]

μεσ-ημβρινός 3 at noon;

μεσῑτεύω to be a mediator.

μεσό-γαια, -γεια, ἡ inland, midland.

μεσό-γαιος 2 interior.

μεσό-δμη, ἡ cross-beam, cross-plank with a hole for the mast.

μεσ-όμφαλος 2 from the centre of the earth, central.

μεσο-ποτάμιος 2 between two rivers.

μέσος 3 middle, in the middle; moderate, middling, indifferent; impartial, neutral. τὸ μέσον the middle, centre; space between; interval; difference; distance; middle number; moderation; impartiality, neutrality; public(ity).   [wall.]

μεσό-τοιχον, τό partition;

μεσο-τομέω to cut through the middle. [mid-heaven.]

μεσ-ουράνημα, τό zenith,

μεσόω to be in the middle, to be half over. [middle.]

μέσσατος 3 quite in the

μέσσ-αυλος, ὁ. μέσσαυλον, τό inner court, farm, stable.

μεσσηγύ = μεσηγύ.

μεσσίας, ου, ὁ the Messiah.

μεσσο-παγής 2 driven in to the middle.

μέσσος 3 = μέσος. [sated.]

μεστός 3 full, filled up;

μεστόω to fill up.

μέσφα *adv.* = μέχρι till.

μετά *adv.* among them; besides; afterwards. — *prp.* with *gen.* among, between; with, together with; at; according to. — with *dat.* among, in company with. — with *acc.* into the middle (of); in quest or pursuit of, after, behind; next to, next after; according to.

μετα-βαίνω to pass to another place, to pass over or on.

μετα-βάλλω to turn over, to turn about; to change, alter; to exchange. — *intr.*, *M.* and *P.* to be changed. undergo a change; to change one's mind, fall off to; to exchange, traffic; to change one's clothes; to turn oneself; to take on one's back.

μετά-βασις, ἡ a passing over, shifting.

μετα-βιβάζω to carry over or away; to alter.

μετα-βολή, ἡ exchange, traffic; change; mutability.

μετα-βουλεύω and *M.* to decree after; to change one's mind.

μετ-άγγελος, ὁ, ἡ messenger, go-between.

μετα-γειτνιών, ῶνος, ὁ second Attic month (August to September).

μετα-γιγνώσκω to change one's mind; to repeal; to repent. [σις, ἡ repentance.]

μετά-γνοια, μετά-γνω-

μετα-γράφω to alter something written. — *M.* to have something translated.

μετ-άγω to convey to another place; to march after.

μετα-δαίνυμαι M. to partake of a feast.

μετα-δήμιος 2 native; at home. [share of.]

μετα-δίδωμι to give a]

μετα-δίωκτος 2 overtaken.

μετα-διώκω to pursue, overtake; to follow close upon.

μετα-δοκεῖ τινι one changes one's mind, one repents. [per.]

μετα-δόρπιος 2 after sup-]

μετά-δοσις, ἡ the giving a share. [ning after.]

μετα-δρομάδην adv. run-]

μετα-δρομή, ἡ pursuit.

μετά-δρομος 2 pursuing; punishing. [tion; change.]

μετά-θεσις, ἡ transposi-]

μετα-θέω to run after.

μετα-ίζω to take one's seat beside. [to set out.]

μετ-αίρω to carry away;]

μετ-αΐσσω to rush after.

μετ-αιτέω to demand one's share. [complice.]

μετ-αίτιος 2 accessory; ac-]

μετ-αίχμιον, τό space between two armies; disputed frontier. [to call in.]

μετα-καλέω to call back;]

μετα-κιάθω to follow after; to pursue; to visit; to march over.

μετα-κινέω to remove. — M. to depart. [changed.]

μετα-κίνητος 3 to be]

μετα-κίω = μετακιάθω.

μετα-κλαίω to weep afterwards.

μετα-κλίνομαι P. to turn to the other side.

μετα-λαγχάνω to get a share of.

μετα-λαμβάνω to get a share, partake; to take in exchange. — M. to claim to oneself, assume.

μετα-λήγω to leave off.

μετά-ληψις, ἡ a partaking; changing.

μετ-αλλαγή, ἡ change.

μετ-αλλάσσω to exchange; to alter; to undergo a change.

μεταλλάω to question, inquire, search after.

μέταλλον, τό pit, mine; quarry. [breasts.]

μετα-μάζιος 2 between the]

μετα-μανθάνω to learn differently: to unlearn.

μετα-μέλεια, ἡ, μετάμελος, ὁ change of mind, repentance.

μετα-μέλει μοι, μεταμέλομαι P. I repent.

μετα-μίγνῦμι, -μίσγω to mix among, confound.

μετα-μορφόω to transform.

μετα-μώνιος 2 idle, vain; useless.

μετ-αναγιγνώσκω to make one alter his mind.

μετ-ανάστασις, ἡ migration. [derer, alien.]

μετανάστης, ου, ὁ wan-]

μετα-νίσσομαι to pass over.

μετ-ανίσταμαι M. to change one's abode, to emigrate.

μετα-νοέω to change one's mind; to repent.

μετά-νοια, ἡ = μετάγνοια.

μεταξύ adv. and prp. with gen. between; meanwhile; afterwards; during.

μετα-παύομαι to rest in the mean time.

μετα-παυσωλή, ἡ rest, repose between.

μετα-πείθω to persuade to another opinion.

μετα-πέμπω and M. to send for, summon; to recall.

μετα-πίπτω to undergo a change; to fall differently; to be altered.

μετα-ποιέω to alter. — M. to lay claim to.

μετα-πορεύομαι P. to go after, to avenge.

μετα-πρεπής 2 excellent.

μετα-πρέπω to be conspicuous or excellent.

μετα-πύργιον, τό wall between two towers. [form.]

μετα-ρρυθμίζω to transform

μετ-άρσιος 2 lifted up; high in the air; on the high sea.

μετ-αρσιόω to lift up.

μετα-σεύομαι M. to rush after; to rush up to.

μετα-σπάω to draw to the other side.

μέτασσαι, αἱ lambs of middle age.

μετά-στασις, ἡ a changing of place, removal; banishment; migration; change of government, revolution.

μετα-στένω to bewail afterwards.

μετα-στοιχί adv. in a line one after another.

μετα-στρέφω to turn about or round, to change one's

course; to alter. — intr. and P. to turn oneself to, to regard.

μετά-σχεσις, ἡ a partaking.

μετα-σχηματίζω to transform, remodel; to refer or apply to.

μετα-τάσσω to arrange differently. — M. to change one's opinion.

μετα-τίθημι to place among; to place differently; to alter, change. — M. to change one's opinion, to retract; to fall off; to impute, ascribe.

μετα-τρέπομαι M. to turn oneself round; to regard.

μετα-τροπαλίζομαι M. to turn frequently round (intr.).

μετ-αυδάω to speak among or to others.

μετ-αυτίκα adv. forthwith.

μετ-αῦτις adv. afterwards.

μετα-φέρω to carry to another place, to transfer; to change, alter; to change by mistake.

μετά-φημι to speak among or to others; to accost.

μετα-φορέω = μεταφέρω.

μετα-φράζομαι M. to consider after. [of the back.]

μετά-φρενον, τό upper part

μετα-φωνέω = μετάφημι.

μετα-χειρίζω and M. to have in one's hands, to handle, manage, treat; to administer, govern; to pursue, practise. [migrate.]

μετα-χωρέω to go away,

μέτ-ειμι[1] (-εῖναι) to be among, between, or near;

μέτεστί μοί τινος I have a claim or share of.

μέτ-ειμι² (-ιέναι) to go between or among; to go away; to come up to; to go after, follow, pursue, avenge; to visit; to strive after; to practise, manage.

μετ-εῖπον see μετάφημι.

μετ-εκβαίνω to step over into.

μετ-εμβιβάζω to put on board another ship.

μετ-ενδύω to put other clothes on. [others.]

μετ-εξ-έτεροι 3 some

μετ-έπειτα adv. afterwards, thereupon. [(ιέναι).]

μετ-έρχομαι = μέτειμι

μετ-εύχομαι M. to change one's wish.

μετ-έχω to have a share of, partake (of), to enjoy with others.

μετ-εωρίζω to lift up, raise; to excite, buoy up, encourage. — P. to rise; to come to the high sea; to be excited.

μετ-έωρος 2 lifted up, raised on high, suspended in the air, aloft; on the high sea; being in suspense, anxious, excited; fluctuating, doubtful; τὸ μετέωρον the high sea; τὰ μετέωρα things on high, high places, heavenly bodies, phenomena of the sky.

μετ-ίσχω = μετέχω.

μετ-οικεσία, ἡ emigration; captivity.

μετ-οικέω to change one's abode; to be a μέτοικος.

μετ-οίκησις, μετ-οικία, ἡ a living with; change of abode, migration.

μετ-οικίζω to bring to another abode, to settle as colonists.

μετ-οίκιον, τό tax paid by a μέτοικος.

μέτ-οικος 2 living with; foreigner, alien suffered to settle at Athens.

μετ-οίχομαι M. to have gone through; to be in pursuit of, to go after.

μετ-οκλάζω to squat timidly. [new name.]

μετ-ονομάζω to call by a

μετ-οπάζω to give to companion.

μετ-όπιν, μετ-όπισθεν adv. behind, backwards, from behind; after(wards).

μετ-οπωρινός 3 autumnal.

μετ-όπωρον, τό autumn.

μετ-ουσία, ἡ, μετοχή, ἡ a partaking, communion, share.

μετ-οχλίζω to remove out of the way by a lever or by force. [partner.]

μέτ-οχος 2 partaking;

μετρέω to measure; to pass over; to estimate, compute.

μέτρημα, τό measure.

μέτρησις, ἡ a measuring.

μετρητής, οῦ, ὁ a liquid measure = 9 gallons.

μετρητικός 3 belonging to measuring.

μετριάζω to be moderate.

μετριο-παθέω to be lenient.

μέτριος 3 moderate, within measure; ordinary, convenient, sufficient, tolerable; fair, just, temperate, simple, orderly, honest, modest; indifferent, little.

μετριότης, ητος, ἡ moderation, modesty; average measure.

μέτρον, τό measure, rule, standard; vessel for measuring; size, measured space; full measure; prime of life; metre.

μετ-ωπηδόν adv. in front-line.   [head.]

μετ-ώπιος 2 on the fore-]

μέτ-ωπον, τό forehead; front, fore part.

μέχρι adv. and prp. with gen. until, unto, as far as; within, during; as long as.

μή adv. not, that not.

μηδαμά, μηδαμῇ adv. not at all; nowhere; never.

μηδαμόθεν adv. from no place.

μηδαμός 3 = μηδείς.

μηδαμοῦ adv. nowhere; not at all.

μηδαμῶς = μηδαμά.

μηδέ adv. and not, but not; nor.

μηδ-είς, μηδε-μία, μηδ-έν no one, none, not even one; nothing.   [at any time.]

μηδέ-ποτε adv. never, not]

μηδέ-πω adv. not as yet.

μηδ-έτερος 3 neither of the two.   [side.]

μηδετέρωσε adv. to neither]

μηδίζω to side with the Persians.

μηδισμός, ὁ a siding with the Persians.

μήδομαι to devise, counsel, advise; to plot, contrive, decree.

μῆδος[1], τό thought, plan, scheme, counsel.

μῆδος[2], τό a man's yard.

μηθείς = μηδείς. [shriek.]

μηκάομαι M. to bleat; to]

μηκάς, άδος bleating.

μηκ-έτι adv. no more, no longer.

μήκιστος 3 longest; tallest; greatest.   [greatness.]

μῆκος, τό length; tallness.]

μή-κοτε = μήποτε.

μηκύνω to lengthen, prolong, extend.

μήκων, ωνος. ἡ poppy; head of a poppy; poppy-juice.

μηλέα, ἡ apple-tree.

μήλειος 2 of a sheep.

μηλο-βοτήρ, ῆρος, ὁ shepherd.   [sheep.]

μηλό-βοτος 2 grazed by]

μῆλον[1], τό apple; tree-fruit.

μῆλον[2], τό sheep; goat.

μηλο-σφαγέω to kill sheep.

μηλ-οφ, οπος like apples, golden.

μηλωτή, ἡ a sheep's skin.

μήν adv. truly, verily, indeed; yet, however; οὐ μὴν ἀλλά not but.

μήν, μηνός, ὁ month, new moon.

μήνη, ἡ moon.

μηνιθμός, ὁ = μῆνις.

μήνιμα, τό cause of anger.

μῆνις, ιος, ἡ anger, wrath.
μηνίω to be angry or wroth.
μηνο-ειδής 2 crescent-shaped.
μήνυμα, τό information.
μηνῡτής, οῦ, ὁ informer, denouncer.
μήνῡτρον, τό reward for information.
μηνύω to make known. denounce, betray; to inform, announce.   [ever.
μή-ποτε adv. never; lest}
μή-που adv. lest anywhere.
μή-πω adv. not yet.
μή-πως adv. lest anyhow.
μῆρα, τά, pl. of μῆρος.
μήρινθος, ἡ cord, string.
μηρίον, τό, μηρός, ὁ thigh-bone, thigh.
μηρύομαι M. to furl the sails.   [causer.}
μήστωρ, ωρος, ὁ counsellor;}
μή-τε adv. and not; μήτε ... μήτε neither ... nor.
μήτηρ, μητρός, ἡ mother.
μητιάω and M. to meditate, consider; to devise, contrive, invent.
μητί-ετα, ὁ adviser.
μητιόεις 3 ingenious.
μητίομαι = μητιάω.
μή-τις, τι none, no one, nothing; lest any one, lest anything.
μῆτις, ιος and ιδος, ἡ counsel, wisdom; device, project.   [(up)on no account.}
μή-τοι adv. in no wise,}
μήτρα, ἡ womb.   [cide.}
μητρ-αλοίας, ᾱ, ὁ matri-}
μητρόθεν adv. from the mother's side.

μητρο-πάτωρ, ορος, ὁ one's mother's father.
μητρό-πολις, ἡ mother-city, mother-country, mother-state; capital.
μητρυιά, ἡ stepmother.
μητρῷος, μητρώϊος 3 of a mother, maternal.
μήτρως, ωος, ὁ maternal uncle.
μηχανάω and M. to make by art, to construct, devise, contrive, prepare.
μηχανή, ἡ, μηχάνημα, τό artificial implement, instrument, machine; engine of war; contrivance, artificial means, device, mode, way.
μηχανητικός 3, μηχανικός 3, μηχανόεις 3 ingenious, inventive, clever.
μηχανο-ποιός, ὁ maker of war-engines.   [cunning.}
μηχανο-ρράφος 2 crafty,}
μῆχος, τό = μηχανή.
μιαίνω to dye; to stain, soil. pollute.
μιαι-φονέω to slay.
μιαι-φόνος 2 blood-stained; murderer.
μιαρία, ἡ wickedness.
μιαρός 3 stained, polluted; wicked.
μίασμα, τό, μιασμός, ὁ stain, defilement, pollution, abomination.
μιάστωρ, ορος, ὁ wicked person, defiler; avenger.
μιγάζομαι M. = μίγνυμαι.
μιγάς, άδος mixed, confused.
μίγδα adv. promiscuously.

μῖγμα, τό mixture.

μίγνῡμι, μιγνύω to mix, mix up, mingle, bring together. — P. and M. to be mingled or brought together; to meet with; to lie with.

μῑκρο-λογέομαι M. to be a pedant, to be given to trifles. [ness, pedantry.]

μῑκρο-λογία, ἡ minute-

μῑκρο-λόγος 2 narrow-minded. pedantic; stingy.

μῑκρο-πολίτης, ου, ὁ citizen of a small town or state.

μῑκρός 3 small, little, short; petty, mean; poor, trivial; young.

μῑκρότης, ητος, ἡ smallness, littleness.

μῑκρο-φῡχία, ἡ meanness of mind. [minded.]

μῑκρό-φῡχος 2 narrow-

μῑκτός 3 mixed.

μίλιον, τό Roman mile.

μιλτ-ηλιφής 2 painted red.

μιλτο-πάρῃος 2 red-cheeked. [nium.]

μίλτος, ἡ red chalk; mi-

μιλτόω to paint red.

μῑμέομαι M. to imitate, copy; to represent.

μίμημα, τό, μίμησις, ἡ an imitating, imitation; copy.

μιμητικός 3 imitative.

μιμητός 3 worth to be imitated.

μιμνάζω to stay, remain.

μιμνήσκω, μιμνίσκω to remind (of), put in mind (of), admonish. — P. to remember, recall to one's me-

mory; to mention; to be mindful of.

μίμνω = μένω. [player.]

μῖμος, ὁ imitator, actor,

μίν him, her, it; himself.

μινύθω to diminish, lessen, weaken; to decrease, decay, perish.

μίνυνθα adv. a short time.

μινυνθάδιος 2 lasting a short time.

μινυρίζω and M. to whimper, whine. [lation.]

μῖξις, ἡ a mixing; copu-

μιξο-βάρβαρος 2 half barbarian half Greek.

μιξο-πάρθενος 2 half maiden (half serpent).

μῑσ-ανθρωπία, ἡ man-hatred.

μῑσ-άνθρωπος, ἡ man-hater. [of glens.]

μισγ-άγκεια, ἡ meeting

μίσγω = μίγνυμι.

μῑσέω to hate.

μίσημα, τό = μῖσος.

μῑσητός 3 hated; to be hated.

μισθ-αποδοσία, ἡ payment of wages, recompense.

μισθ-αποδότης, ου, ὁ recompenser. [pay.]

μισθ-αρνέω to serve for

μισθ-αρνίᾱ, ἡ hired service. [τός.]

μίσθιος 3 and 2 = μισθω-

μισθο-δοσίᾱ, ἡ payment of wages.

μισθο-δοτέω to pay wages.

μισθο-δότης, ου, ὁ payer of wages.

μισθός, ὁ wages, pay, hire, rent, salary; reward; punishment.

μισθο-φορά, ἡ receipt of wages; pay.

μισθο-φορέω to receive wages; to serve for hire.

μισθο-φορίᾱ, ἡ hired service.

μισθο-φόρος 2 serving for hire; mercenary, hireling.

μισθόω to let out for hire, farm out. — *P.* to be hired for pay. — *M.* to engage on hire, to farm.

μίσθωμα, τό stipulated pay, rent; hired dwelling.

μίσθωσις, ἡ a letting for hire; = μίσθωμα.

μισθωτός 3 hired, to be hired; mercenary, hireling. [mocracy.]

μῑσό-δημος 2 hating de-

μῖσο-λογίᾱ, ἡ hatred of letters.

μῖσό-λογος 2 hating argument. [bad.]

μῖσο-πονηρέω to hate the

μῖσος, τό hatred, enmity; hateful thing or person.

μῖσο-τύραννος 2 tyrant-hating.

μῖσό-χρηστος 2 hating the good. [pieces.]

μιστύλλω to cut into little

μίτος, ἡ thread; web.

μίτρα, ἡ girdle; head-dress.

μιτρη-φόρος 2 wearing a μίτρα.

μιτώδης 2 thread-like.

μνᾶ, ᾶς, ἡ mine (= 100 drachms).

μνάομαι *M.* = μιμνήσκο-μαι; to covet, strive after; to woo, court.

μνείᾱ, ἡ = μνήμη.

μνῆμα, τό, μνημεῖον, τό memorial, remembrance; monument; sepulchre.

μνήμη, ἡ memory, remembrance; faculty of memory; monument; mention, relation; renown.

μνημονεύω to remember, recollect; to mention.

μνημονικός 3 of good memory.

μνημοσύνη, ἡ = μνήμη.

μνημόσυνον, τό = μνῆμα.

μνήμων 2 mindful, remembering, unforgetting.

μνησι-κακέω to remember old wrongs, to be resentful.

μνηστεύω and *M.* to woo, court, seek in marriage. — *P.* to be betrothed.

μνηστήρ, ῆρος, ὁ wooer, suitor.

μνῆστις, ἡ = μνήμη.

μνηστός 3 wooed, wedded.

μνηστύς, ύος, ἡ a wooing, seeking in marriage.

μογέω to toil, labour; to suffer, be in distress.

μογι-λάλος 2 stammering.

μογερός 3 distressed, wretched.

μόγις *adv.* with toil, hardly.

μογοσ-τόκος 2 causing throes in child-birth.

μόδιος, ὁ a corn-measure.

μόθος, ὁ noise or throng of battle.

μοῖρα, ἡ part, portion, division; portion of land; party; share; the due, due reverence; rank; lot, destiny, fate; death. [fortune.]

μοιρη-γενής 2 favourite of

μοιρίδιος 3 destined, fated.

μοιχ-άγρια, τά fine of one taken in adultery.

μοιχαλίς, ίδος, ἡ adulterous. [tery.\

μοιχάω to commit adul-/ μοιχεία, ἡ adultery.

μοιχεύω to commit adultery, to seduce to adultery. [adultery.\

μοιχίδιος 3 begotten in/ μοιχός, ὁ adulterer.

μολεῖν inf. aor. of βλώσκω

μόλιβος, ὁ = μόλυβδος.

μόλις adv. with difficulty, hardly. [beggar.\

μολοβρός, ὁ dirty fellow,/ μολπή, ἡ song, dance, music; play, amusement.

μολύβδαινα, ἡ, μολυβδίς, ίδος, ἡ leaden bullet.

μόλυβδος, ὁ lead.

μολύνω to stain, sully.

μολυσμός, ὁ defilement. pollution.

μομφή, ἡ blame. complaint.

μον-αρχέω to be a monarch.

μον-αρχία, ἡ monarchy, sovereignty.

μόν-αρχος, ὁ monarch.

μονάς, άδος, ἡ a unit.

μοναχῇ, -ῆ adv. single, alone.

μονή, ἡ a staying; an abiding; sojourn, dwelling; tarrying.

μόνιμος 2 staying; steadfast, constant; faithful.

μονο-γενής 2 only child.

μονο-ειδής 2 of one kind, simple.

μονό-κροτος 2 with one bench of oars.

μονο-μαχέω to fight in single combat. [bat.\

μονο-μαχία, ἡ single com-/ μονό-ξυλος 2 made of one piece of wood.

μόνος 3 alone, only; forsaken, left alone; adv. μόνως, μόνον only, merely.

μον-όφθαλμος 2 one-eyed.

μονόω to leave alone; to make single. — P. to be forsaken; to be taken apart.

μόρα, ἡ division of Spartan infantry. [tree.\

μορία, ἡ the sacred olive-/ μόρσιμος 2 = μόρσιμος.

μόριον, τό part; division; limb. [spectre. phantom.\

μορμολύκειον, τό bugbear,/ μορμολύττομαι M. to frighten (children)

μορμύρω to roar.

μορμώ, οῦς, μορμών, ὁ ος, ἡ bugbear, spectre.

μόρεις, 3 mulberry-like.

μόρος, ὁ fate, destiny, death.

μόρσιμος 2 destined, fatal.

μορύσσω to blacken, soil.

μορφή, ἡ form, shape, figure, appearance, fashion. image; beauty, grace.

μόρφνος 3 dark-coloured.

μορφόω to form, shape.

μόρφωσις, ἡ a shaping; form, semblance.

μόσσυν, υνος, ὁ wooden tower or house.

μόσχειος 2 of a calf.

μοσχο-ποιέω to make a calf.

μόσχος, ὁ shoot, sprout; descendant; calf, young bull.

μουν- see μον-.

μουνάξ *adv.* alone, singly.

μουνόθεν *adv.* = μουνάξ.

μουνό-λιθος 2 made of one stone.

μοῦνος 3 = μόνος. [one.]

μουνο-φυής 2 grown in

μουνυχιών, ῶνος, ὁ tenth Attic month (April to May).

μουσικός 3 of the Muses, devoted to the Muses, musical; musician; (lyric) poet; scholar, man of letters; ἡ μουσική, τὰ μουσικά art of the Muses, music, song, poetry, dancing, arts, letters, accomplishments.

μουσο-ποιός 2 poet, singer.

μοχθέω to toil, to weary oneself, to be troubled or distressed, to suffer.

μόχθημα, τό, μοχθηρία, ἡ toil, hardship; wretchedness; badness, wickedness.

μοχθηρός 3 toilsome, miserable, wretched; bad, wicked, villainous.

μοχθίζω to suffer.

μόχθος, ὁ toil, hardship; distress, misery.

μοχλεύω, μοχλέω to move by a lever.

μοχλός, ὁ lever; bar; pole.

μῦ-γαλῆ, ἡ shrew-mouse.

μυδαλέος 3 dripping, wet.

μυδάω to be dripping or wet; to decay, rot.

μύδρος, ὁ red-hot metal; lump of metal.

μυελόεις 3 full of marrow.

μυελός, ὁ marrow; brain.

μυέω to initiate into the mysteries; to instruct.

μύζω, μυζέω to suck.

μυθέομαι *M.* to speak, say, tell; to name, explain; to consider.

μυθο-λογεύω, -λογέω to tell tales, fables, or legends; to converse fully.

μυθο-λογικός 3 fabulist.

μῦθος, ὁ word, speech, public speech; narration, news, intelligence; conversation, talk; thought, project, plan; advice, order; report, tale, story; affair, occurrence.

μυθώδης 2 legendary.

μυῖα, ἡ fly.

μυκάομαι *M.* to bellow, low, bray; to roar.

μυκηθμός, ὁ a bellowing.

μύκης, ητος, ὁ mushroom; end of a scabbard.

μυκτήρ, ῆρος, ὁ nostril; nose; snout.

μυκτηρίζω to mock.

μύλαξ, ακος millstone.

μύλη, ἡ mill. [ground.]

μύλη-φατος 2 bruised;

μυλικός, μύλινος 3 λίθος millstone. [stone.]

μυλο-ειδής 2 like a mill-

μύλος, ὁ = μύλη; μύλαξ.

μυλών, ῶνος, ὁ mill-house.

μύνη, ἡ pretext. [τήρ.]

μυξωτήρ, ῆρος, ὁ = μυκ-

μῡριάκις *adv.* ten thousand times.

μῡρι-άρχης, ου, μῡρί-αρχος, ὁ commander of ten thousand men.

μυριάς, άδος, ἡ myriad (10 000).

μυρίζω to anoint.

μυρίκη, ἡ tamarisk. [risk.]
μυρίκινος 3 of the tama-
μύριοι 3 ten thousand.
μυριό-καρπος 2 with countless fruit.
μυριό-λεκτος 2 said ten
thousand times.
μύριος 3 countless, num-
berless, immense, endless.
μύριο-φόρος 2 ναῦς big
transport-ship.
μύρμηξ, ηκος, ὁ ant.
μύρομαι M. to flow; to
melt into tears.
μύρον, τό fragrant oil, unguent, balsam.
μυρρίνη, μυρσίνη, ἡ myrtle,
myrtle-twig.
μύρτον, τό myrtle-berry.
μῦς, μυός, ὁ mouse.
μυσαρός 3 foul, loathsome.
μύσος, τό abomination;
atrocity. [mystery.]
μυστήριον, τό secret rite,
μύστης, ου, ὁ one ini-
tiated. [cret.]
μυστικός 3 mystical; se-
μυχμός, ὁ a groaning, sighing. [most corner.]
μυχοίτατος 3 in the in-

μυχόνδε adv. to the in-
terior.
μυχός, ὁ inmost corner.
interior, recess.
μύω to be shut or closed;
to cease; to shut the eyes.
μυών, ῶνος, ὁ knot of
muscles. [sighted.]
μυωπάζω to be short-
μύ-ωψ¹, ωπος short-sighted.
μύωψ², ωπος, ὁ gad-fly;
goad, spur. [din.]
μῶλος, ὁ toil; battle, battle-
μῶλυ, υος, τό a magic herb.
μώλ-ωψ, ωπος stripe, mark,
bruise.
μῶμαι = μάομαι.
μωμάομαι M., μωμεύω to
blame, revile. [shame.]
μῶμος, ὁ blame; disgrace,
μῶν = μὴ οὖν is it not?
μῶνυξ, υχος soliped.
μωραίνω to be silly or
foolish; to make foolish.
— P. to become a fool; to
become insipid.
μωρία, ἡ folly.
μωρο-λογία, ἡ silly speech.
μωρός, μῶρος 3 foolish,
stupid; insipid, tasteless.

N

N, ν (νῦ) thirteenth letter of the
alphabet; as a numeral ν' = 50.
ναί adv. verily, truly, yes.
ναΐάς, άδος, ἡ water-nymph,
Naiad.
ναιετάω = ναίω. [ship.]
ναΐος 3 belonging to a
ναῖς, ιδος, ἡ = ναΐάς.
ναίχι = ναί.
ναίω¹ to dwell, abide, in-

habit; to settle one in. —
P. to be inhabited; to settle.
ναίω² = νάω.
νάκη, ἡ, νάκος, τό fleece.
νᾶμα, τό fountain, stream.
νᾱμέρτεια, ἡ = νημέρτεια.
νᾱός, ὁ temple.
ναπαῖος 3 of a wooded
vale. [vale, dell, glen.]
νάπη, ἡ, νάπος, τό wooded

17*

νάρδος, ἡ nard; nard-oil.

ναρθηκο-φόρος, ὁ staff-bearer, thyrsus-bearer.

νάρθηξ, ηκος, ὁ reed, cane, rod. [benumbed.]

ναρκάω to grow stiff or

νάρκισσος, ὁ narcissus, daffodil.

νᾶσιῶτις, ιδος = νησιῶτις.

νᾶσος, ἡ = νῆσος.

νάσσω to stamp down.

ναυ-αγέω to be shipwrecked.

ναυ-αγία, ἡ shipwreck.

ναυ-άγιον, τό (piece of a) wreck.

ναυ-αγός 2 shipwrecked.

ναυ-αρχέω to be a sea-captain or admiral.

ναυ-αρχία, ἡ office of an admiral. [admiral.]

ναύ-αρχος, ὁ sea-captain,

ναυ-βάτης, ου, ὁ sailor, seaman; sea-soldier.

ναυηγέω etc. = ναυαγ-.

ναυ-κληρέω to be a ship-owner; to steer, govern.

ναυ-κληρία, ἡ a seafaring, voyage. [captain.]

ναύ-κληρος, ὁ shipowner,

ναύ-κραρος, ὁ captain; president of a division of citizens. [the sea.]

ναυ-κρατέω to be lord of

ναυ-κρατής 2, ναυ-κράτωρ, ορος shipowner; commanding the sea. [money.]

ναῦλον, τό fare, passage-

ναυ-λοχέω to lie in a harbour, at anchor, or in wait.

ναύ-λοχος 2 affording safe anchorage.

ναυ-μαχέω to fight at sea.

ναυ-μαχησείω to long for a sea-fight.

ναυ-μαχία, ἡ battle at sea.

ναύ-μαχος 2 suited to a sea-fight.

ναυ-πηγέω to build ships.

ναυ-πηγήσιμος 2 fit for shipbuilding.

ναυ-πηγία, ἡ shipbuilding.

ναυ-πηγός, ὁ shipbuilder.

ναῦς, νεώς, ἡ ship.

ναῦσθλον, τό = ναῦλον.

ναυσί-κλειτος 2, ναυσί-κλυτος 2 famous for ships.

ναυσι-πέρᾱτος 2 to be crossed by ships.

ναυσί-πορος 2 navigable.

ναυ-σταθμον, τό, ναύ-σταθμος, ὁ harbour, anchorage, naval station.

ναυ-στολέω to convey by sea; to go by sea, to voyage.

ναύτης, ου, ὁ = ναυβάτης.

ναυτικός 3 of or for a ship; naval; seafaring; τὸ ναυτικόν fleet, navy.

ναυτιλία, ἡ a seafaring, navigation, voyage.

ναυτίλλομαι to go by ship, to sail. [man.]

ναυτίλος, ὁ sailor, ship-

ναυτο-δίκαι, οἱ judges in commercial law-suits.

νάω to flow (over).

νεάζω to be young or younger, to grow up.

νεᾱκόνητος 2 newly or lately whetted.

νεάλής 2 young, fresh.

νεᾱνίᾱς, ου youthful; young man, youth.

νεᾱνιεύομαι M. to be youthful, vigorous, wanton, or boastful.

νεᾱνικός 3 youthful, fresh, vigorous; wanton, insolent; hasty.

νεᾱνίς, ιδος, ἡ girl, maiden, young woman.

νεᾱνίσκος, ὁ = νεανίας.

νεᾱρός 3 youthful, fresh: = νέος. [extreme.

νέατος 3 last, uttermost,]

νεβρίζω to wear a fawn's skin. [fawn.]

νεβρός, ὁ, ἡ young deer,]

νεη-γενής 2 new-born.

νε-ήκης 2, νε-ηκονής 2 = νεακόνητος.

νε-ήλατον, τό honey-cake.

νέ-ηλυς, υδος newly come

νεηνίης etc. = νεανίας.

νείαιρα and νείατος 3 = νέατος.

νεικέω, νεικείω to quarrel, dispute; to scold, revile, insult.

νεῖκος, τό quarrel, dispute; a scolding, blaming, reproach; cause of quarrel; dispute before a judge; battle, fight. [tom.]

νειόθεν adv. from the bottom]

νειόθι adv. at the bottom.

νειός, ἡ new or fallow land.

νείφω, νίφω to snow.

νεκάς, άδος, ἡ heap of slain men. [corpse.]

νεκρός 3 dead; dead body.]

νεκρόω to kill, to make dead.

νέκρωσις, ἡ a making dead; deadness.

νέκταρ, αρος, τό nectar.

νεκτάρεος 3 like nectar; divine.

νέκυια, ἡ sacrifice for the dead. [of the dead.]

νεκυο-μαντήϊον, τό oracle]

νέκυς, υος = νεκρός.

νεμέθω M. to graze.

νεμεσάω to be indignant, angry, or wroth; to find fault with, to blame. — M. and P. to be indignant; to be ashamed.

νεμεσητός 3 causing indignation; awful.

νεμεσίζομαι M. = νεμεσάω.

νέμεσις, ἡ indignation, anger, resentment; vengeance, punishment; wrong; remorse; sense of honour.

νέμος, τό pasture; grove, wood.

νέμω to divide; to distribute, assign, allot, grant; to possess, enjoy; to inhabit; to manage, control; to esteem, consider; to drive to pasture; to graze; to consume. — M. to distribute among themselves; to occupy; to control, manage; to enjoy; to graze, feed; to consume; to spread.

νεο-άλωτος 2 newly caught.

νεο-αρδής 2 newly watered.

νεό-γαμος 2 newly wedded.

νεό-γιλός 3, νεο-γνός 2 new-born.

νεο-δαμώδης, ους, ὁ new citizen, one newly enfranchised.

νεό-δαρτος 2 newly flayed.

νεόθεν adv. anew, of late.

νεο-θηλής 2 fresh-sprouting.

νεοίη, ἡ youthful spirit.

νεο-κατάστατος 2 newly settled. [founded.]

νεό-κτιστος 2 newly founded.

νέομαι to go; to come; to go away; to return.

νεο-μηνίᾰ, ἡ = νουμηνία.

νεο-πενθής 2 fresh-mourning.

νεό-πλυτος 2 newly washed.

νεό-ποκος 2 newly shorn.

νεό-πριστος 2 newly sawn.

νεό-ρραντος 2 newly sprinkled.

νεό-ρρῠτος 2 fresh-flowing.

νέ-ορτος 2 newly risen.

νέος 3 young, youthful, early; thoughtless; new, fresh; unheard of, strange, unexpected; νεώτερόν τι novation; revolution; news, bad things; adv. νέον newly, anew, afresh; lately, just now. [cleaned.]

νεό-σμηκτος 2 newly cleaned.

νεο-σπάς, άδος newly plucked.

νεοσσεύω = νοσσεύω.

νεοσσιά, ἡ nest with young birds. [child.]

νεοσσός, ὁ a young one;

νεό-στροφος 2 newly twisted.

νεο-σφαγής 2 newly killed.

νεό-τευκτος 2, νεο-τευχής 2 newly made.

νεότης, ητος, ἡ youth, youthfulness; body of young men.

νεό-τομος 2 newly cut.

νεουργός = νεότευκτος.

νε-ούτατος 2 newly wounded.

νεό-φυτος 2 newly converted.

νεο-χάρακτος 2 newly imprinted.

νεοχμός 2 = νέος.

νεοχμόω = νεωτερίζω.

νέποδες, ων, οἱ children.

νέρθεν = ἔνερθεν.

νέρτερος 3 lower, nether; infernal.

νεῦμα, τό nod, sign.

νεῦμαι = νέομαι.

νευρά, ἡ, νεῦρον, τό sinew, tendon; cord; bow-string; cord of a sling; strength, vigour.

νευρο-σπαδής 2, νευρό-σπαστος 2 drawn back, driven from the bow-string.

νευστάζω, νεύω to nod, beckon, bow; to promise.

νεφέλη, ἡ cloud, darkness; multitude.

νεφελ-ηγερέτης, -έτα, ὁ cloud-gatherer.

νέφος, τό = νεφέλη.

νεφρῖτις, ιδος, ἡ disease in the kidneys.

νεφρός, ὁ kidney.

νέω[1] to swim.

νέω[2] to spin. [to load.]

νέω[3] to heap up, pile up;

νέω[4] = νέομαι.

νεω-κόρος, ὁ, ἡ sweeper in a temple, temple-servant.

νε-ώρης 2 new, young.

νεώριον, τό dock-yard.

νεώρος 3 = νεώρης.

νεώς, ώ, ὁ = ναός (also gen. of ναῦς).

νεώς-οικοι, οἱ ship's houses, docks. [cently.]

νεωστί adv. lately, re-

νεωτερίζω to make changes

or innovations; to revolutionize.

νεωτερικός 3 youthful.

νεωτερισμός, ὁ. νεωτεροποιία̅, ἡ innovation, revolution.

νεωτερο-ποιός 2 innovating, revolutionary.

νή adv. yea, truly.

νηγάτεος 3 newly made, splendid.

νήγρετος 2 unwaking, sleeping soundly.

νήδυια, τά bowels.

νήδυμος 2 sweet, refreshing.

νηδύς, ύος, ἡ belly; stomach; womb.

νηέω = νέω³ to heap up.

νήθω = νέω² to spin.

νηϊάς, ἡ = ναϊάς.

νήϊος 3 = νάϊος.

νηΐς, ίδος = ναΐς.

νῆϊς, ιδος not knowing.

νηΐτης, ου = νάϊος.

νη-κερδής 2 useless, without gain.

νηκουστέω to disobey.

νηλεής 2 pitiless; unpitied. [ιδος = νηλιτής.]

νηλειτής 2, fem. **νηλεῖτις**,

νηλής 2 = νηλεής.

νηλίπους, ποδος barefooted.

νηλιτής 2, fem. **νηλῖτις**, ιδος guiltless.

νῆμα, τό thread, yarn.

νημερτής 2 infallible, unerring.

νηνεμίᾱ, ἡ calm.

νήνεμος 2 breezeless, calm.

νηός, ὁ = νεώς; = νηός νεώς (ναῦς). [row.]

νη-πενθής 2 soothing sor-

νηπιάζω to be a child.

νηπιαχεύω to play like a child.

νηπίαχος 2 = νήπιος.

νηπιέη, ἡ childishness.

νήπιος 3 infant, childish, foolish, harmless; weak.

νή-ποινος 2 without recompense; unavenged.

νηπύτιος 3 = νήπιος.

νήριτος 2 numberless.

νησίδιον, τό, νησίον, τό.

νησίς, ίδος, ἡ small island.

νησιώτης, ου, ὁ islander.

νησιῶτις, ιδος insular.

νῆσος, ἡ island; peninsula.

νῆσσα, ἡ duck.

νηστείᾱ, ἡ a fasting.

νηστεύω to fast.

νῆστις, ιδος and ιος fasting.

νησύδριον, τό = νησίδιον.

νητός 3 heaped up.

νηῦς, ἡ = ναῦς.

νηυσι-πέρητος 2 = ναυσιπέρητος.

νηφάλιος 3 sober.

νήφω to be sober.

νήχω and M. to swim.

νίζω to wash; to wash off, clean; to atone. — M. to wash oneself.

νικάω to conquer, prevail; to be superior or better; to win in court; to be victorious, carry the day; to vanquish, overcome, surpass.

νίκη, ἡ victory, conquest.

νικητήριον, τό prize of victory. [victory.]

νικητικός 3 conducing to

νίκη-φόρος bringing victory; victorious.

νῖκος, τό = νίκη.

νίν = αὐτόν, -ήν, -ό him, her, it. [basin.]

νιπτήρ, ῆρος, ὁ washing-

νίπτω = νίζω.

νίσσομαι, νίσομαι to go (away); to return.

νιφάς, άδος, ἡ snow-flake; snow-storm; snowy.

νιφετός, ὁ shower of snow.

νιφόεις 3 snow-covered.

νιφο-στιβής 2 passing over snow.

νίφω = νείφω.

νοέω to perceive, remark, notice, see; to think, consider; to devise, contrive; to intend, have a mind.

νόημα, τό thought; purpose, design; understanding; mind.

νοήμων 2 sensible.

νοητός 3 intelligible. [ous.]

νόθος 3 illegitimate; spuri-]

νόμαιον, τό custom, usage.

νομ-άρχης, ου, ὁ chief of a district.

νομάς, άδος, ὁ, ἡ roaming, wondering on pasture-grounds; nomad.

νομεύς, ὁ herdsman; rib of a ship. [tend a flock.]

νομεύω to drive afield; to]

νομή, ἡ pasture; field; grazing flock; division. distribution.

νομίζω to hold or acknowledge as a custom or usage; to be wont; to adopt as a law; to use; to think. believe, acknowledge, take for; to be persuaded, judge. — P. to be in esteem; to be customary.

νομικός 3 legal; learned in the law; scribe.

νόμιμος 2 customary; legal, lawful; honest, righteous; τὰ νόμιμα custom, usage, law.

νόμισις, ἡ usage.

νόμισμα, τό usage, institution; current coin, money.

νομο-διδάσκαλος, ὁ teacher of the law.

νομο-θεσία, ἡ legislation.

νομο-θετέω to give laws, ordain by law.

νομο-θέτης, ου, ὁ law-giver.

νομο-θετικός 3 law-giving.

νομός, ὁ = νομή; dwelling, residence; district; region.

νόμος, ὁ custom, usage; law, ordinance, statute; principle, rule, maxim; tune, mode of singing, song, melody.

νομο-φύλαξ, ακος, ὁ guardian of the laws.

νόος, νοῦς, ὁ mind, understanding, reason; thought, insight; purpose, intention; meaning, sense.

νοσέω to be sick.

νοσηλεία, ἡ, νόσημα, τό = νόσος. [sickly.]

νοσηρός 3 unhealthy;]

νόσος, ἡ sickness, disease, plague; insanity, madness; evil, distress; defect.

νοσσεύω to hatch.

νοσσιά, ἡ etc. = νεοσσιά etc.

νοστέω to return, come home; to travel.

νόστιμος 2 belonging to a return; returning.

νόστος, ὁ return home; travel, journey.

νόσφι(ν) *adv.* far, remote, apart; with *gen.* far from, away from; without, besides.

νοσφίζω to remove, put or take away; to rob. — *M.* to withdraw, retire; to forsake, abandon; to embezzle.

νοσώδης 2 = νοσηρός.

νοτερός 3 wet, moist; southern.

νοτίη, ἡ moisture, rain.

νότιος 3 and 2 = νοτερός.

νοτίς, ίδος, ἡ = νοτίη.

νότος, ὁ south or southwest wind; the south.

νου-θεσίᾱ, ἡ = νουθέτησις.

νου-θετέω to bring to mind, to warn, admonish, reprimand, chastise.

νου-θέτημα, τό, **νου-θέτησις**, ἡ admonition, warning.

νου-θετικός 3 admonitory.

νου-μηνίᾱ, ἡ new moon, first of the month.

νουν-εχής 2 sensible.

νοῦς, ὁ = νόος.

νοῦσος, ἡ = νόσος.

νύ = νύν.

νυκτερευτικός 3 fit for hunting by night.

νυκτερεύω to pass the night; to watch by night.

νυκτερινός 3 nightly; northern.

νυκτερίς, ίδος, ἡ bat.

νύκτερος 2 = νυκτερινός.

νυκτο-θήρᾱς, ου, ὁ hunting by night.

νυκτο-μαχίᾱ, ἡ night-battle. [watch.]

νυκτο-φύλαξ, ὁ night-)

νύκτωρ *adv.* by night.

νυμφεῖος 3 bridal, nuptial; τὸ νυμφεῖον bride-chamber; marriage. [bride.)

νύμφευμα, τό marriage;)

νυμφεύω and *M.* to wed, marry; to be married.

νύμφη, ἡ bride; young wife; maiden; nymph.

νυμφίδιος, **νυμφικός** 3 bridal, nuptial.

νυμφίος, ὁ bridegroom; husband. [chamber.)

νυμφών, ῶνος, ὁ bride-)

νῦν, **νῦνί** *adv.* now. just now, at present; then, thereupon; therefore.

νύν, **νύ** *adv.* now, then; therefore.

νύξ, νυκτός, ἡ night.

νυός, ἡ daughter-in-law.

νύσσα, ἡ turning-stone, pillar on the race-course; winning-post; lists. [wound.)

νύσσω to prick, pierce,)

νυστάζω to nod; to fall asleep; to slumber.

νυχθ-ήμερον, τό a day and night.

νύχιος 3 = νυκτερινός.

νώ = νῶι.

νώδυνος 2 soothing pain.

νωθής 2, **νωθρός** 3 lazy, sluggish; stupid.

νῶι, **νώ** we two. [us two.)

νωίτερος 3 belonging to)

νωλεμές, **νωλεμέως** *adv.* incessantly; steadfastly.

νωμάω to distribute, portion out; to move to and

fro, brandish, wield, ply; to direct, guide, govern; to consider, observe, perceive.   [or fame.]

νώνυμ(ν)ος 2 without name]

νῶροψ, οπος flashing.

νωτίζω to turn one's back.

νῶτον, τό; **νῶτος**, ὁ the back.

νωχελίη, ἡ laziness.

Ξ

Ξ, ξ (ξῖ) fourteenth letter of the alphabet; as a numeral ξ΄ = 60.

ξαίνω to scratch.

ξανθός 3 yellow; red-yellow.

ξειν- see ξεν-.

ξεν-αγέω to lead mercenary soldiers.   [cenaries.]

ξεν-αγός, ὁ leader of mer-]

ξεν-ηλασία, ἡ banishment of foreigners.

ξενία, ἡ hospitality; hospitable reception or entertainment; usurpation of civic rights.

ξενίζω to receive hospitably; to entertain; to be like a foreigner. — P. to be astonished.

ξενικός 3 foreign, of a stranger; mercenary.

ξένιος 3 and 2 hospitable; τὸ ξένιον a guest's gift.

ξένισις, ἡ hospitable entertainment.   [ξενίζω.]

ξενο-δοκέω, -δοχέω =] **ξενο-δόκος** 2 entertaining guests.   [or strangers]

ξενο-κτονέω to slay guests]

ξενο-λογέω to engage mercenaries.

ξένος 3 foreign, strange; unacquainted with. ὁ ξ. foreigner, stranger; mercenary; guest, friend; ἡ ξένη foreign country.

ξενό-στασις, ἡ lodging for strangers.

ξενοσύνη, ἡ = ξενία.

ξενο-τροφέω to maintain mercenary troops.

ξενόω = ξενίζω; to be abroad; to be (lodged as) a guest, to be entertained.

ξερός 3 = ξηρός.

ξέστης, ου, ὁ a measure; jar.

ξέω to scrape; to polish (by scraping); to carve.

ξηραίνω to parch up, dry up. — P. to become dry.

ξηρός 3 dry, parched; ἡ ξηρά dry land.

ξηρότης, ητος, ἡ dryness.

ξιφίδιον, τό dagger.

ξιφο-κτόνος 2 slaying with the sword.

ξίφος, τό sword.

ξόανον, τό carved image; wooden statue of a god.

ξυήλη, ἡ curved sword.

ξυλίζομαι M. to gather wood.

ξύλινος 3 wooden.

ξύλον, τό wood, timber; piece of wood; tree, beam; wooden ware; stick, cudgel; shaft; spear; bench; cross; wooden collar, pillory.

ξυλουργέω to work wood.

ξύλ-οχος, ὁ thicket.

ξύλωσις, ἡ wood-work.

ξῠνήϊος 3 public, common.

ξῡνός 3 = κοινός.

ξῠρέω, ξῠράω to shear, shave.

ξῠρόν, τό razor.

ξυστόν, τό shaft; spear, lance; pole.

ξυστός 3 polished.

ξύω to scrape, smooth, polish.

O

Ο, ο (ὃ μικρόν) fifteenth letter of the alphabet; as a numeral ο' = 70.

ὁ, ἡ, τό demonstrative Pronoun this; definite Article the.

ὄαρ, ὄαρος, ἡ consort; wife. [liarly.)

ὀαρίζω to converse fami-)

ὀαριστής, οῦ, ὁ confidential friend.

ὀαριστύς, ύος, ἡ friendly converse, intimacy; company.

ὀβελίσκος, ὁ small spit.

ὀβελός, ὁ spit; pointed pillar.

ὀβολός, ὁ obol (6th part of a drachm).

ὀβριμο-εργός forcible.

ὀβριμο-πάτρη, ἡ daughter of a mighty father.

ὄβριμος 2 strong, mighty.

ὀγδόατος 3 = ὄγδοος.

ὀγδοήκοντα eighty.

ὄγδοος 3 eighth.

ὀγδώκοντα = ὀγδοήκοντα.

ὀγκηρός 3 pompous.

ὄγκιον, τό chest for iron tools. [hook.)

ὄγκος¹, ὁ barb, grapple-)

ὄγκος², ὁ bulk, mass, heap, size, weight; molestation; dignity; importance, pride.

ὀγκόω to puff, swell. — P. to be swollen or proud.

ὀγμεύω to make furrows, to trace a straight line.

ὄγμος, ὁ furrow; swath.

ὄγχνη, ἡ pear-tree; pear.

ὁδαῖος 3 belonging to a way or journey; τὰ ὁδαῖα merchandise.

ὀδάξ adv. with the teeth.

ὅ-δε, ἥ-δε, τό-δε this, that.

ὁδεύω to go, travel, journey.

ὁδ-ηγέω to show the way, to guide.

ὁδ-ηγός, ὁ guide.

ὁδίτης, ου, ὁ traveller.

ὀδμή, ἡ scent, odour.

ὁδοι-πορέω = ὁδεύω.

ὁδοι-πορίᾱ, ἡ journey, way.

ὁδοι-πόριον, τό reward for a journey.

ὁδοι-πόρος, ὁ = ὁδίτης.

ὁδο-ποιέω to make a road.

ὁδός, ἡ way, street, road, path; journey, voyage, march, expedition; departure, return; way, means, manner, occasion, method.

ὀδός, ὁ threshold.

ὀδούς, όντος, ὁ tooth, tusk.

ὁδο-φύλαξ, ακος, ὁ watcher of the roads.

ὁδόω to lead the right way, to guide. — P. to succeed.

ὀδυνάω to cause pain. — P. to feel pain, suffer.

ὀδύνη, ἡ pain, grief.

ὀδυνηρός 3 painful.

ὀδυνή-φατος 2 killing pain.

ὄδυρμα, τό, ὀδυρμός, ὁ wailing, lamentation.

ὀδύρομαι M. to wail, lament; to bewail.

ὀδύσσομαι M. to be angry.

ὀδών, όντος, ὁ = ὀδούς.

ὀδωτός 3 practicable.

ὄζος, ὁ branch, twig; servant.

ὄζω to smell, savour.

ὅθεν adv. whence, from whom or which, wherefore.

ὅθι adv. where.

ὀθνεῖος 3 foreign, strange.

ὄθομαι to give or pay heed to, to regard, care for.

ὀθόνη, ἡ linen; linen garment; veil.

ὀθόνιον, τό linen bandage.

ὀθούνεκα = ὅτου ἕνεκα because.   [hair.

ὅ-θριξ, ὅτριχος with like

οἴ woe, oh!

οἵ adv. whither.

οἴαξ, ακος, ὁ handle of the rudder; helm; ring.

οἴγνῡμι, οἴγω to open.

οἶδα see εἴδω.

οἰδάω, -έω, -άνω to cause to swell. — intr. and P. to swell.

οἴδμα, τό a swelling, waves.

οἰέτης 2 of the same age.

ὀϊζῡρός 3 miserable, poor, wretched.

ὀϊζύς, ύος, ἡ woe, misery.

ὀϊζύω to wail; to toil; to suffer.

οἰήϊον, τό = οἴαξ.

οἰηχίζω to steer, manage.

οἴησις, ἡ opinion.

οἶκα = ἔοικα.   [home.

οἴκαδε adv. homeward(s),

οἰκεῖος 3 belonging to a home, a household, or a family; cognate, akin; intimate, familiar; proper, one's own; private, personal; home(-grown), native; fit, suited.

οἰκειότης, ητος, ἡ relationship; friendship.

οἰκειόω to make one's own; to make a person one's friend. — P. to become an intimate friend (of).

οἰκείωσις, ἡ appropriation.

οἰκετεία, οἰκέτεια, ἡ the servants.

οἰκέτης, ου, ὁ member of the household; servant, slave.

οἰκετικός 3 of slaves.

οἰκεύς, ὁ = οἰκέτης.

οἰκέω to inhabit, occupy; to settle; to dwell, live; to manage, govern; to be situated; to be governed. — P. to be inhabited, situated; to be settled or governed; ἡ οἰκουμένη the civilized world.

οἰκήϊος, οἰκηΐόω = οἰκεῖος, οἰκειόω.

οἴκημα, τό dwelling, house; chamber; story; cage; prison; temple; workshop.

οἴκησις, ἡ an inhabiting; house, dwelling.

οἰκητήρ, ῆρος, ὁ, οἰκητής, οῦ, ὁ inhabitant.

οἰκητήριον, τό a dwelling.

οἰκητός 3 inhabited; habitable.   [κητήρ.

οἰκήτωρ, ορος, ὁ = οἰ-

οἰκία, ἡ = οἶκος.

οἰκιακός of a household; domestic.

οἰκίδιον, τό = οἰκίσκος.

οἰκίζω to build, establish, found; to settle, colonize, people; transplant. — M. to settle oneself; to dwell.

οἰκίον, τό = οἶκος.

οἴκισις, ἡ settlement, colonization.

οἰκίσκος, ὁ small house, hut.

οἰκιστήρ, ῆρος, οἰκιστής, οῦ, ὁ founder of a colony, settler. [ter of a house.]

οἰκο-δεσποτέω to be mas-/

οἰκο-δεσπότης, ου, ὁ master of a house.

οἰκο-δομέω to build a house: to build; to found; to edify

οἰκο-δόμησις, ἡ, οἰκο-δόμημα, τό, οἰκο-δομία, ἡ, οἰκο-δομή, ἡ the act of building; building, edifice, house.

οἰκο-δόμος, ὁ architect.

οἴκοθεν adv. from one's house or home; from one's own means, of oneself; from the beginning.

οἴκοθι, οἴκοι adv. in the house, at home.

οἴκονδε adv. = οἴκαδε.

οἰκο-νομέω to be a steward; to manage, order.

οἰκο-νομικός 3 of a household; economical.

οἰκο-νόμος, ὁ householder, steward.

οἰκό-πεδον, τό ruins of a house. [bitable.]

οἰκο-ποιός 2 making ha-/

οἶκος, ὁ house, habitation, dwelling; chamber, hall; temple; camp, nest; household; household property; family, race; servants; home.

οἰκός, οἰκότως = εἰκός.

οἰκουμένη, ἡ see οἰκέω.

οἰκουρέω to keep or guard a house; to stay at home.

οἰκούρημα, τό, οἰκουριά, ἡ watch of a house; guard, protection. [housekeeping.]

οἰκούρια, τά wages for/

οἰκουρός 2 keeping the house, domestic.

οἰκο-φθορέομαι P. to be ruined in one's household.

οἰκο-φθορία, ἡ loss of fortune.

οἰκτείρω, οἰκτίζω and M. to pity, to bewail.

οἰκτιρμός, ὁ = οἶκτος.

οἰκτίρμων 2 compassionate.

οἰκτίρω = οἰκτείρω.

οἴκτιστος 3 superl. of οἰκτρός. [compassion.]

οἶκτος, ὁ a wailing; pity;

οἰκτρός 3 pitiable, lamentable; mournful.

οἰκ-ωφελίη, ἡ thrift in household affairs.

οἶμα, τό attack, rage.

οἰμάω to attack violently.

οἴμη, ἡ heroic tale; song, lay.

οἴμοι int. woe to me!

οἶμος, ὁ way, road, course; strip of land. [wailing.]

οἰμωγή, ἡ lamentation.

οἰμώζω to wail, lament; to bewail. [full of wine.]

οἰνηρός 3 rich in vines;/

οἰνίζομαι to procure wine.

οἰνο-βαρής 2, οἰνο-βα-ρείων 3 drunk(en) with wine.

οἰνό-πεδος 2 bearing vine; τὸ -ον vineyard. [in wine.]

οἰνο-πληθής 2 abounding]

οἰνο-ποτάζω to drink wine.

οἰνο-ποτήρ, ῆρος, ὁ, οἰνο-πότης, ου, ὁ wine-drinker.

οἶνος, ὁ wine. [ness.]

οἰνο-φλυγία, ἡ drunken-]

οἰνο-χοέω, -χοεύω to pour out wine. [ing wine.]

οἰνο-χόη, ἡ cup for draw-]

οἰνο-χόος, ὁ cup-bearer.

οἰνό-χυτος 2 of poured-out wine.

οἶν-οφ, οπος = οἰνώφ.

οἰνών, ῶνος, ὁ wine-cellar.

οἰν-ώψ, ῶπος wine-coloured.

οἰο-βώτης feeding alone.

οἰό-ζωνος 3 single wanderer.

οἰόθεν adv. alone.

οἴομαι see οἴω.

οἰο-πόλος 2 lonely, solitary. [tary.]

οἶος 3 alone, only, soli-]

οἷος 3 of what manner or kind; such as; οἷός τέ εἰμι I am able, I can; οἷον, οἷα adv. how, as, like (as), just as, for instance.

οἰο-χίτων, ωνος dressed in a tunic only.

οἰόω to leave alone.

ὄϊς, οἷς, οἰός, ὁ, ἡ sheep.

οἴσπη, ἡ unwashed wool.

οἰστέος 3 to be borne, bearable.

ὀϊστεύω to shoot arrows.

ὀϊστός, οἰστός, ὁ arrow.

οἰστράω, -έω to goad, sting; intr. to rage.

οἴστρημα, τό sting.

οἰστρο-πλήξ, ῆγος stung to madness.

οἶστρος, ὁ gadfly; sting, pain; madness.

οἰσύϊνος 3 made of wicker-work. [death.]

οἶτος, ὁ lot, fate, ruin,]

οἰχνέω, οἴχομαι M. to go, come, fly; to go away; to be gone, to be absent, lost, or dead.

οἴω, ὀΐω, οἴομαι, ὀΐομαι P. to suppose, fear, think, believe; to intend, purpose, mean.

οἰωνίζομαι M. to forebode, prophesy. [divining.]

οἰωνιστής, οῦ auguring.]

οἰωνο-θέτης, ου, ὁ, οἰωνο-πόλος, ὁ augur, diviner.

οἰωνός, ὁ bird of prey; bird of omen; omen, presage.

ὀκέλλω to run aground.

ὀκλάζω to bend the knees, to bend, sink down.

ὀκνέω, -είω to shrink from, scruple, hesitate, fear.

ὀκνηρός 3 shrinking, hesitating; fearful, troublesome.

ὄκνος, ὁ hesitation, unreadiness, disinclination.

ὀκριάω to exasperate.

ὀκριόεις 3 awful. [days.]

ὀκτα-ήμερος 2 for eight]

ὀκτακισ-χίλιοι 3 eight thousand.

ὀκτά-κνημος 2 with eight spokes. [dred.]

ὀκτα-κόσιοι 3 eight hun-]

ὀκτώ eight.

ὀκτω-καί-δεκα eighteen.

ὀκτω-καί-δέκατος 3 the eighteenth.

ὀλβίζω to pronounce happy.

ὀλβιο-δαίμων 2 blessed by a god.

ὄλβιος 3 prosperous, happy, fortunate, blessed; rich.

ὄλβος, ὁ happiness, bliss; wealth, power.

ὀλέθριος 3 and 2 destructive; undone.

ὄλεθρος, ὁ destruction, ruin, loss; defeat; rogue. rascal.

ὀλέκω = ὄλλυμι.

ὀλετήρ, ῆρος, ὁ destroyer.

ὀλιγάκις adv. seldom.

ὀλιγ-ανθρωπία, ἡ scantiness of people.

ὀλιγ-αρχέομαι P. to live in an oligarchy.

ὀλιγ-αρχία, ἡ oligarchy, government by a few.

ὀλιγ-αρχικός 3 oligarchical. [parts.]

ὀλιγαχόθεν adv. from few

ὀλιγ-ηπελέω to be weak.

ὀλιγ-ηπελία, ἡ weakness.

ὀλιγο-γονία, ἡ scanty procreation. [ful.]

ὀλιγό-γονος 2 little fruit-

ὀλιγο-δρανέω = ὀλιγηπελέω. [little faith.]

ὀλιγό-πιστος 2 having

ὀλίγος 3 few, little; small, short, weak, indifferent; οἱ ὀλίγοι: the few, aristocrats; ὀλίγον a little, little, a short time. [part.]

ὀλιγοστός 3 only a little

ὀλιγο-χρόνιος 2 and 3 of short duration.

ὀλιγό-ψῡχος 2 faint-hearted.

ὀλιγ-ωρέω to regard lightly, neglect.

ὀλιγ-ωρία, ἡ a regarding lightly, neglect.

ὀλίγ-ωρος 2 disregardful, neglecting.

ὀλίζων 2 lesser (ὀλίγος).

ὀλισθάνω to slip, slide.

ὀλισθηρός 3 slippery.

ὁλκάς, άδος, ἡ trading vessel.

ὁλκός, ὁ strap; lifting-engine, hauling-machine; track, trail.

ὄλλῡμι to destroy, ruin, kill; to lose; pf. ὄλωλα I am undone or ruined. — M. to perish, die, to be undone or lost.

ὅλμος, ὁ roller; mortar.

ὁλόεις 3 = ὁλοός.

ὀλοθρευτής, οῦ, ὁ destroyer.

ὀλοθρεύω = ὄλλυμι.

ὁλοιός = ὁλοός.

ὀλοί-τροχος, ὀλοί-τροχος, ὁ rolling stone, piece of rock.

ὁλο-καυτέω to bring a burnt-offering. [offering.]

ὁλο-καύτωμα, τό burnt-

ὁλο-κληρία, ἡ soundness, entireness. [fect.]

ὁλό-κληρος 2 entire, per-

ὀλολυγή, ἡ a loud crying, wailing, lamentation.

ὀλολύζω to cry aloud, to wail; to shout.

ὀλοοί-τροχος, ὁ = ὀλοί-.

ὀλοός 3 destructive; hurtful, painful.

ὀλοό-φρων 2 meaning mischief, pernicious.

ὅλος 3 whole, complete, entire, all.

ὀλο-τελής 2 perfect.

ὀλοφυδνός 3 wailing, lamenting. miserable.

ὀλοφυρμός, ὁ lamentation.

ὀλοφύρομαι M. and P. to wail, lament; to feel pity or compassion.

ὀλόφυρσις, ἡ = ὀλοφυρμός.

ὀλοφώϊος 2 malicious, artful.

ὄλυνθος, ὁ winter fig.

ὄλυρα, ἡ spelt.

ὁμαδέω to make a noise.

ὅμαδος, ὁ noise, din: throng, crowd.

ὅμ-αιμος 2, ὁμ-αίμων 2 related by blood; brother; sister. [of arms, alliance.]

ὁμ-αιχμία, ἡ brotherhood/

ὅμ-αιχμος, ὁ companion in arms. [level; average.]

ὁμαλής 2, ὁμαλός 3 even./

ὁμ-αρτέω to walk together; to follow; to meet.

ὁμαρτῆ, ὁμαρτήδην adv. together, jointly.

ὅμ-αυλος 2 united.

ὄμβριος 3 of rain, rainy.

ὄμβρος, ὁ water, moisture; rain, shower of rain or snow.

ὀμείρομαι to long for.

ὁμ-ευνέτις, ιδος, ἡ consort. [together.]

ὁμ-ηγερής 2 assembled/

ὁμ-ηγυρίζομαι M. to call together.

ὁμ-ήγυρις, ἡ assembly.

ὁμ-ηλικίᾱ, ἡ equality of age: = ὁμῆλιξ.

ὁμ-ῆλιξ, ικος of the same age; comrade.

ὁμηρείᾱ, ἡ the giving a pledge.

ὁμηρέω to meet.

ὅμ-ηρος, ὁ, ὅμ-ηρον, τό pledge, security; hostage.

ὁμῑλαδόν adv. in crowds.

ὁμῑλέω to be together, to associate, converse, to be friends; to live with; to meet, encounter; to negotiate, to be engaged in.

ὁμίλημα, τό = ὁμιλία.

ὁμῑλητής, οῦ, ὁ friend; scholar.

ὁμῑλίᾱ, ἡ a living together, intercourse, company; conversation; instruction; assembly, meeting.

ὅμῑλος, ὁ crowd, throng of people, mob; troop of warriors; tumult of battle.

ὁμίχλη, ἡ, ὀμίχλη, ἡ mist, fog; cloud.

ὅμμα, τό eye, look; face; sight, image, spectacle.

ὀμματο-στερής 2 eyeless.

ὄμνῡμι, ὀμνύω to swear, affirm by oath; to swear by.

ὁμο-βώμιος 2 having one common altar.

ὁμο-γάστριος 2 of the same mother.

ὁμο-γενής 2 kindred.

ὁμό-γλωσσος 2 speaking the same language.

ὁμό-γνιος 2 protecting the same race. [one mind.]

ὁμο-γνωμονέω to be of/

ὁμο-γνώμων 2 having the same mind.

ὁμο-δοξέω = ὁμογνωμονέω.

ὁμό-δουλος, ὁ, ἡ fellow-slave.

ὁμο-εθνής 2 of the same tribe. [character.]

ὁμο-ήθης 2 of the same]

ὁμόθεν *adv.* from the same place or origin.

ὁμο-θῡμαδόν *adv.* unanimously.

ὁμοιάζω to be like.

ὁμοίϊος 3 = ὅμοιος.

ὁμοιο-παθής 2 being similarly affected.

ὅμοῖος, ὅμοιος 3 like, similar, resembling; the same, of the same rank; equal citizen; equal; common, mutual; a match for; agreeing, convenient.

ὁμοιότης, ητος, ἡ likeness, resemblance.

ὁμοιό-τροπος 2 agreeing, similar.

ὁμοιόω to make (a)like, to liken, compare. — *P.* to be or become (a)like.

ὁμοίωμα, τό, ὁμοίωσις, ἡ likeness, image; a likening; simile.

ὁμο-κλέω, -κλάω to cry aloud; to cheer on; to upbraid.

ὁμο-κλή, ἡ loud cry, shout; command; menace.

ὁμο-κλητήρ, ῆρος, ἡ a cheerer on, encourager.

ὁμό-κλῑνος 2 neighbour at table.

ὁμο-λογέω to agree with; to grant, concede, allow, admit, confess; to promise; to assent (to), come to an agreement, make a treaty; ὁμολογεῖται it is allowed, granted. — *M.* to come to

an understanding or agreement.

ὁμο-λογίᾱ, ἡ, ὁμο-λόγημα, τό agreement; confession; assent; terms, treaty; capitulation.

ὁμο-λογουμένως *adv.* confessedly; agreeably to, conformably to. [mother.]

ὁμο-μήτριος 3 of the same]

ὁμο-νοέω to be of one mind. [cord.]

ὁμό-νοια, ἡ unity, concord]

ὁμο-πάτριος 2 of the same father. [same city.]

ὁμό-πτολις, εως of the]

ὁμόργνῡμι to wipe off.

ὁμ-ορέω to border on.

ὅμ-ορος 2 bordering on.

ὁμο-ρροθέω to agree with.

ὁμός 3 common; one and the same; *adv.* ὁμῶς together; equally, alike.

ὁμό-σε *adv.* straight on; to the same place.

ὁμο-σῑτέω to eat together.

ὁμό-σῑτος 2 eating together. [alike.]

ὁμό-σκευος 2 equipped]

ὁμό-σπλαγχνος 2 kindred; brother. [at table.]

ὁμό-σπονδος 2 companion]

ὁμό-σπορος 2 kindred.

ὁμο-σπόρος 2 married to the same wife. [side.]

ὁμο-στιχάω to walk be-]

ὁμό-στολος 2 companion.

ὁμό-τεχνος 2 of the same craft or trade. [oured.]

ὁμό-τῑμος 2 equally hon-]

ὁμο-τράπεζος 2 companion at table. [τροπος.]

ὁμό-τροπος 2 = ὁμοιό-]

ὁμό-τροφος 2 brought up together.

ὁμοῦ adv. together, at the same place; at once; near.

ὁμ-ουρέω see ὁμορέω.

ὁμο-φρονέω to have the same mind.

ὁμο-φροσύνη, ἡ concord.

ὁμό-φρων 2 of one mind.

ὁμο-φυής 2 of the same nature. [tribe.]

ὁμό-φῦλος 2 of the same

ὁμο-φωνέω to speak the same language.

ὁμό-φωνος 2 speaking the same language.

ὁμό-χροιη, ἡ skin.

ὁμό-ψηφος 2 having an equal vote; of one mind.

ὁμόω to unite.

ὀμφαλόεις 3 having a boss.

ὀμφαλός, ὁ navel; knob or boss of a shield; centre.

ὄμφαξ, ακος, ἡ unripe grape. [speech; oracle.]

ὀμφή, ἡ (divine) voice;

ὁμ-ώνυμος 2 of the same name.

ὁμ-ωρόφιος 2 living under the same roof.

ὅμως adv. nevertheless, yet.

ὁμῶς adv. see ὁμός.

ὁμ-ωχέτης, ου worshipped together.

ὄναρ, τό dream, vision.

ὀνάριον, τό little ass.

ὄνᾱσις, ἡ = ὄνησις.

ὄνειαρ, ατος, τό help, assistance; refreshment; food, victuals.

ὀνείδειος 2 reproachful.

ὀνειδίζω to reproach, upbraid, blame.

ὄνειδος, τό, ὀνείδισμα, τό, ὀνειδισμός, ὁ reproach, blame; disgrace.

ὀνείρειος 3 of dreams.

ὄνειρον, τό = ὄνειρος.

ὀνειρο-πολέω to dream.

ὀνειρο-πόλος ὁ interpreter of dreams.

ὄνειρος, ὁ dream, vision.

ὀνεύω to haul up.

ὀνήσιμος 2 useful.

ὀνησί-πολις, εως benefiting the state.

ὄνησις, ἡ profit, help; bliss, delight.

ὄνθος, ὁ dung, dirt.

ὀνικός 3 μύλος upper millstone.

ὀνίνημι to benefit, help; to gratify, delight. — M. and P. to have profit, advantage, delight, or enjoyment.

ὄνομα, τό name, word, term; title; fame, report; pretence, pretext.

ὀνομάζω to name, call by name; to speak of; to pronounce, enumerate; to promise. — P. to be called.

ὄνομαι to blame, revile, find fault with; to reject, despise.

ὀνομαίνω = ὀνομάζω.

ὀνομα-κλήδην = ἐξονομακλήδην.

ὀνομά-κλυτος 2 famous.

ὀνομαστί adv. by name.

ὀνομαστός 3 to be named; named, renowned.

ὄνος, ὁ, ἡ ass; windlass, crane; upper millstone.

ὀνοστός 3 blamable.

ὀνο-φορβός, ὁ ass-keeper.

ὄντως *adv.* really, actually, indeed. [claw, hoof.]

ὄνυξ, υχος, ὁ nail, talon,

ὄξος, τό vinegar.

ὀξυ-βελής 2 sharp-pointed.

ὀξυ-δερκής 2 sharp-sighted.

ὀξύ-θηκτος 2 sharp-edged.

ὀξύ-κώκῦτος 2 loudly bewailed.

ὀξυ-λαβέω to be quick.

ὀξύνω to sharpen; to provoke.

ὀξυόεις 3 sharp-pointed.

ὀξύς 3 sharp, keen, pointed; pungent; piercing, shrill, clear; quick, swift; passionate, fiery; bold; active; clever.

ὀξύτης, ητος, ἡ sharpness; quickness; hotness, passion.

ὀξύ-τονος 2 sharp-sounding, piercing.

ὀξύ-φωνος 2 with clear voice.

ὀξύ-χολος 2 given to anger.

ὀπᾱδέω to follow, accompany. [attendant.]

ὀπᾱδός, ὁ, ἡ companion,

ὀπάζω to give as a companion or follower; to add, attach; to pursue, press hard. — *M.* to take as a companion.

ὀπαῖον, τό hole in the roof (for the smoke).

ὅ-πατρος 2 of the same father. [ὀπαδός.]

ὀπάων, ονος, ὁ (= ὀπέων =)

ὀπή, ἡ hole, opening; cave.

ὅπη, ὅπη *adv.* where; whither; how, in what way.

ὀπηδέω = ὀπᾱδέω.

ὁ-πηνίκα *adv.* when; since.

ὀπίζομαι *M.* to care for, regard; to honour; to dread.

ὄπιθεν = ὄπισθεν.

ὀπῑπεύω to gaze at; to observe, watch.

ὄπις, ιδος, ἡ regard, respect; punishment, vengeance.

ὄπισθε(ν) *adv.* behind, after, hereafter; *prp.* with *gen.* behind.

ὀπίσθιος 3 hinder.

ὀπισθο-νόμος 2 grazing backwards. [guard.]

ὀπισθο-φύλακες, οἱ rear-

ὀπισθο-φυλακέω to guard the rear.

ὀπισθο-φυλακία, ἡ (command of the) rear.

ὀπίστατος 3 hindmost.

ὀπίσω *adv.* behind, backwards; in future; back; *prp.* with *gen.* after, behind.

ὁπλέω to make ready.

ὁπλή, ἡ hoof.

ὁπλίζω to prepare, equip, make ready, harness; to arm; to train. — *M.* to prepare for oneself. — *P.* and *M.* to get or be ready; to be going. [ing.]

ὅπλισις, ἡ equipment; arm-

ὁπλῑτ-ἀγωγός 2 leading the heavy-armed.

ὁπλῑτεύω to serve as a heavy-armed soldier.

ὁπλίτης, ου, ὁ heavy-armed (foot-)soldier.

ὁπλῑτικός 3 belonging to a ὁπλίτης. [oneself.]

ὅπλομαι to prepare for

ὁπλο-μαχία, ἡ art of using heavy arms, tactics.

18*

ὅπλον, τό toil, implement: furniture of a ship; arms, harness, armour, weapon; camp, quarter; = ὁπλῖται.

ὁπλότατος 3 youngest.

ὁπλότερος 3 younger, fresh. [try.]

ὁποδαπός 3 of what coun-

ὁπόθεν adv. whence.

ὅποι adv. whither, thither where.

ὁποῖος 3 of what sort, kind, or quality.

ὀπός, ὁ juice of plants, especially: of the fig-tree.

ὁπόσε adv. = ὅποι.

ὁπόσος 3 as many, as many as; as large as.

ὁπότε, ὁπόταν adv. when, whensoever: because, since.

ὁπότερος 3 which of the two; one of the two.

ὁποτέρωθεν adv. from which of the two sides.

ὁποτέρωσε adv. to which of the two sides.

ὅπου adv. where; when; how; because, since.

ὀπταλέος 3 = ὀπτός.

ὀπτάνομαι to be seen.

ὀπτασία, ἡ sight, appearance.

ὀπτάω to roast; to bake.

ὀπτήρ, ῆρος, ὁ spy.

ὀπτός 3 roasted; baked.

ὀπυίω to marry, wed; to be married. — P. to become a wife. [sight]

ὀπωπή, ἡ sight; (faculty of)

ὀπώρα, ἡ late summer and early autumn; fruit-time; tree-fruit.

ὀπωρίζω to gather fruit(s).

ὀπωρινός 3 of early autumn.

ὀπωρ-ώνης, ου, ὁ fruiterer.

ὅπως adv. how, in what manner; as, when, as soon as; that, in order to.

ὅραμα, τό, ὅρασις, ἡ sense of sight; sight; view.

ὁρατός 3 visible.

ὁράω to see, to look; to have sight; to look to, to take heed (of), beware (of); to look at, behold, perceive, observe; to see again; to visit; to understand; conceive; to know. — P. to be seen, to appear, become visible.

ὀργάζω to knead; tan.

ὀργαίνω to make angry: to be angry.

ὄργανον, τό instrument, implement, tool.

ὀργάω to teem, swell; to be wanton; to long for.

ὀργή, ἡ impulse; feeling, disposition, temper; passion, eagerness; anger, wrath; punishment.

ὄργια, τά secret rites or worship, mysteries.

ὀργίζω to make angry. — P. to become angry.

ὀργίλος 3 given to anger.

ὀργυιά, ὄργυιά, ἡ fathom.

ὀρέγω, ὀρέγνῦμι and M. to reach, stretch out, extend; to hand, offer, give. — M. and P. to stretch oneself out; to reach to; to aim at, grasp at; to long for, desire. [ranging.]

ὀρει-βάτης, ου mountain-

ὀρεινός 3, ὄρειος 3 and 2

mountainous, hilly; living on the mountains, mountaineer.

ὀρεκτός 3 stretched out.

ὄρεξις, ἡ desire, longing.

ὀρέομαι to hasten.

ὀρεσί-τροφος 2 mountain-bred. [βάτης.

ὀρεσσι-βάτης, ου = ὀρει-

ὀρέστερος 3 = ὀρεινός.

ὀρεστιάς, άδος mountain-nymph.

ὀρεύς, ὁ mule.

ὀρεχθέω to pant, quiver.

ὀρέω = ὁράω.

ὀρεω-κόμος, ὁ muleteer.

ὄρθιος 3 and 2 straight up, rising upwards, upright, uphill, straight on, in a column or file; shrill, loud, clear.

ὀρθό-κραιρος 3 with straight horns; with upright beaks. [top.

ὀρθό-κρᾱνος 2 with high

ὀρθο-ποδέω to walk or go straight. [steep.

ὀρθό-πους, ποδος uphill,

ὀρθός 3 straight, upright, erect; straight forward, in a straight line; unharmed, safe, prosperous; anxious, attentive, expecting; right, just, righteous, upright; true, exact, convenient, decent.

ὀρθότης, ητος, ἡ upright standing; rightness, right sense. [aright.

ὀρθο-τομέω to handle

ὀρθόω to set upright, raise; to erect, build; to maintain; to make straight; to improve, repair; to extol, exalt; to bring to a happy end. — P. to stand or sit upright; to succeed, prosper, flourish; to be right or true.

ὀρθρίζω to rise early.

ὄρθριος 3, ὀρθρινός 3 early in the morning.

ὄρθρος, ὁ early morning, daybreak.

ὁρίζω to divide, confine, define, limit; to mark out by boundaries. — M. to mark out for oneself; to assign; to determine; to define (a word).

ὀρίνω = ὄρνυμι.

ὅριον, τό boundary, frontier; dock. [adjure.

ὁρκίζω to make swear; to

ὅρκιον, τό oath; pledge, surety; treaty, covenant; victim sacrificed at a treaty. [of oaths.

ὅρκιος 2 sworn; guardian

ὅρκος, ὁ oath; vow; sworn stipulation; form of oath; cojurer, witness.

ὀρκόω to make swear.

ὀρκ-ωμοσίᾱ, ἡ a swearing.

ὀρκ-ωμοτέω to take an oath.

ὀρκωτής, οῦ, ὁ one who administers an oath.

ὁρμαθός, ὁ row, chain; flight (of bats).

ὁρμαίνω = ὁρμάω to set in quick motion; to rouse, stir up; to consider, ponder, contrive, devise. — intr., M. and P. to start, set out, proceed, depart; to proceed or begin from; to hurry or rush on, make an attack; to be about, to be eager, to purpose; to begin.

ὁρμέω and *M.* to lie at anchor; to depend upon.

ὁρμή, ἡ assault, attack, onset; start, setting out, march; impulse, intention, eagerness.

ὅρμημα, τό passionate desire; attack.   [place.]

ὁρμητήριον, τό starting-[

ὁρμίζω to bring into harbour, to anchor. — *M.* and *P.* to come to anchor, to lie at anchor, to reach the harbour.

ὅρμος¹, ὁ chain; necklace.

ὅρμος², ὁ anchorage, harbour.

ὄρνεον, τό bird.

ὀρνίθειος 2 of fowl.

ὀρνῑθο-σκόπος 2 observing the flight of birds.

ὄρνις, ῑθος, ὁ, ἡ bird; fowl, cock, hen; bird of augury; augury, prophecy.

ὄρνῡμι, -ύω to stir (up), rouse, move; to incite, chase; to encourage, cheer on; to cause, excite. — *intr.* and *M.* to stir oneself, start up, arise; to be roused, excited, or troubled; to rush or hurry on, hasten; to rise to do, to begin.

ὁρο-θεσία, ἡ boundary.

ὁροθύνω to stir up, rouse.

ὅρομαι to watch, be on guard.   [tain-range.]

ὄρος, τό mountain, moun-[

ὀρός, ὁ whey.

ὅρος, ὁ boundary, limit,

frontier; land-mark; standard; definition.

ὀροσάγγαι, οἱ benefactors of the king.

ὀρούω to start up or forward, to rush on, hasten.

ὀροφή, ἡ roof, ceiling.

ὄροφος, ὁ reed for thatching; roof.   [twig.]

ὄρπηξ, ηκος, ἡ branch,[

ὀρρωδέω to be afraid, fear, dread.

ὀρρωδία, ἡ affright, fear.

ὀρσο-θύρη, ἡ back-door; *others:* raised door.

ὀρτάζω = ἑορτάζω.

ὀρτάλιχος, ὁ young bird, chicken.

ὀρτή, ἡ = ἑορτή.

ὄρτυξ, υγος, ὁ quail.

ὄρυγμα, τό pit, hole, trench; mine, tunnel.

ὀρυκτός 3 dug (out).

ὀρυμαγδός, ὁ noise, tumult, roaring. [(gazelle?).]

ὄρυς, υος, ὁ wild animal[

ὀρύσσω to dig, dig up; to cover with earth, bury; to dig through.

ὀρφανία, ἡ bereavement.

ὀρφανίζω to make orphan.

ὀρφανός 3 left orphan; destitute, bereft.

ὀρφανιστής, οῦ, ὁ guardian.

ὀρφναῖος 3 dark, dusky.

ὄρχαμος, ὁ leader, lord, master.

ὄρχατος, ὁ garden.

ὀρχέομαι *M.* to dance.

ὀρχηδόν *adv.* one after another.

ὀρχηθμός, ὁ, ὄρχημα, τό, ὄρχησις, ἡ dance, dancing;

ὀρχηστήρ, ῆρος, ὀρχηστής, οῦ, ὁ dancer.

ὀρχήστρα, ἡ place for dancing; orchestra. [girl.]

ὀρχηστρίς, ίδος, ἡ dancing]

ὀρχηστύς, ύος, ἡ = ὄρχησις.

ὄρχις, εως and ιος, ὁ testicle.

ὄρχος, ὁ row of vines.

ὅς, ἥ, ὅ relat. pron. who, which, that; demonstr. pron. this, that; he, she, it: possess. pron. his, her, one's own.

ὁσάκις adv. as many times as.

ὁσ-ημέραι adv. daily.

ὁσία, ἡ divine law; sacred duty.

ὅσιος 3 and 2 sanctioned by divine law or by the law of nature, sacred, approved by the gods; holy, pious; chaste, pure; atoning.

ὁσιότης, ητος, ἡ piety, religiousness. [to atone.]

ὁσιόω to hallow; to purify;]

ὀσμή, ἡ = ὀδμή.

ὅσος 3 as great as, how great, as much, far, long as.

ὅσ-περ, ἥ-περ, ὅ-περ who or which indeed.

ὄσπριον, τό pulse, legumes.

ὄσσα, ἡ rumour; voice.

ὀσσάκι = ὁσάκις.

ὀσσάτιος 3 = ὅσος.

ὄσσε, τὼ the eyes.

ὄσσομαι M. to see; to see in one's mind; to forebode, foretell.

ὀστέϊνος 3 of bone, bony.

ὀστέον = ὀστοῦν, τό bone.

ὅσ-τις, ἥ-τις, ὅ τι whosoever; whichsoever; who, which, that.

ὀστρακίζω to banish by potsherds, ostracize.

ὀστρακισμός, ὁ banishment by potsherds, ostracism.

ὄστρακον, τό potsherd.

ὀσφραίνομαι to smell, to track by scent. [smelling.]

ὄσφρησις, ἡ (sense of)]

ὀσφύς, ύος, ἡ hip.

ὅτ-αν adv. whenever.

ὅτε adv. when, whenever; before that; since.

ὁτέ adv. sometimes.

ὅτι conj. that; because; with sup. of adj. as ... as possible.

ὅτλος, ὁ suffering, distress

ὅτοβος, ὁ noise, din, sound

ὀτοτοῖ int. ah! woe!

ὀτραλέος 3, ὀτηρός 3 nimble, quick.

ὄτριχες pl. of ὄθριξ.

ὀτρυντύς, ύος, ἡ encouragement.

ὀτρύνω to stir up, rouse, encourage, wake; to send; to speed. — M. to hasten.

οὐ, οὐκ, οὐχ not.

οὗ adv. where; when.

οὐά, οὐᾶ for shame!

οὐαί ah! woe!

οὖας, ατος, τό = οὖς.

οὐδαμά, οὐδαμῇ, -ῆ adv. nowhere; to no place; never; in no way, not at all.

οὐδαμόθεν adv. from no place.

οὐδαμόθι = οὐδαμοῦ.

οὐδαμοῖ, οὐδαμόσε adv. to no place. [δαμά.]

οὐδαμοῦ, οὐδαμῶς = οὐ-]

οὖδας, εος, τό ground, surface of the earth.

οὐδέ *conj.* but not; and not; nor; not even.

οὐδείς, οὐδεμία, οὐδέν no one, none, nobody, nothing; good-for-nothing, worthless, powerless.

οὐδενός-ωρος 2 worth no notice.

οὐδέ-ποτε *adv.* never.

οὐδέ-πω *adv.* not yet; not at all.

οὐδε-πώποτε = οὐδέποτε.

οὐδέτερος 3 neither of the two. [of the two sides.]

οὐδετέρωσε *adv.* to neither/

οὐδός[1], ὁ = ὁδός.

οὐδός[2], ἡ = ὁδός.

οὖθαρ, ατος, τό udder.

οὐθ-είς, οὐθ-έν = οὐδείς, οὐδέν.

οὐκ-έτι *adv.* no longer, no more, no further.

οὔκ-ουν *adv.* not therefore? not then? is it not?; not therefore, so not; indeed not.

οὐκ-οῦν *adv.* is it not? not then?; therefore, accordingly.

οὐλαί, αἱ (bruised) barley for a sacrifice. [band.]

οὐλαμός, ὁ throng, tumult,/

οὖλε hail to thee!

οὐλή, ἡ scar.

οὔλιος 3 pernicious.

οὐλό-θριξ, τριχος with curly hair. [headed.]

οὐλο-κάρηνος 2 curly-/

οὐλόμενος 3 pernicious, destructive.

οὖλος[1] 3 whole, entire.

οὖλος[2] 3 woolly, fleecy, thick; matted.

οὖλος[3] = οὔλιος.

οὐλό-χυται, αἱ = οὐλαί.

οὖν *adv.* indeed, really, certainly; therefore, accordingly, consequently.

οὔνεκα *conj.* wherefore; because. — *prp.* with *gen.* for, on account of.

οὔνομα etc. see ὄνομα.

οὔνομαι = ὄνομαι.

οὔ-περ *adv.* by no means.

οὔ-περ *adv.* just where.

οὔ-πη, οὔ-πῃ *adv.* nowhere; in no wise.

οὔ-ποθι *adv.* nowhere.

οὔ-ποτε *adv.* never.

οὔ-πω, οὐ-πώποτε not yet, never yet.

οὔ-πως *adv.* in no wise, not at all.

οὐρά, ἡ tail; after-part, rear, rear-rank. [rear.]

οὐρ-αγός, ὁ leader of the/

οὐραῖος 3 of the tail.

οὐράνιος 3 heavenly, in or from heaven.

οὐρανίωνες, οἱ the heavenly gods. [ven.]

οὐρανόθεν *adv.* from hea-/

οὐρανόθι *adv.* in heaven.

οὐρανο-μήκης 2 as high as heaven. [ment.]

οὐρανός, ὁ heaven; firma-/

οὔρειος 3 = ὄρειος.

οὐρεσι-βώτης, ου feeding on the mountains. [guard.]

οὐρεύς, ὁ mule; watcher,/

οὐρέω to make water.

οὐρία, ἡ fair wind.

οὐρίαχος, ὁ lowest end.

οὐρίζω[1] to sail with a fair wind.

οὐρίζω[2] = ὁρίζω.

οὔριος 3 fair, prosperous.

οὔρισμα, τό boundary line.

οὖρον[1], τό urine.

οὖρον[2], τό boundary, distance (of throwing), stretch.

οὖρος[1], ὁ fair wind; fair time.

οὖρος[2], ὁ watcher, guard.

οὖρος[3], ὁ = ὄρος.

οὐρός, ὁ trench, channel.

οὖς, ὠτός the ear; handle.

οὐσία, ἡ the being, essence, substance; property.

οὐτάζω, οὐτάω to hit, strike, wound, hurt.

οὔ-τε adv. and not; οὔτε ... οὔτε neither ... nor.

οὐτιδανός 3 worthless.

οὔ-τις, οὔ-τι no one, nobody, nothing.

οὔ-τοι adv. indeed not.

οὗτος, αὗτη, τοῦτο this, this one.

οὕτω, οὕτως, οὕτωσί adv. thus, in this way or manner, only so.

οὐχί adv. no, not.

ὀφειλέτης, ου, ὁ debtor.

ὀφείλημα, τό, ὀφειλή, ἡ debt.

ὀφείλω to owe, be indebted; ὀφειλόμενος 3 due; τὸ ὀφειλόμενον one's due; to be bound, to be under an obligation; ὤφελον I ought, o that I!

ὀφέλλω[1] = ὀφείλω.

ὀφέλλω[2] to increase, augment, strengthen; to promote, help.

ὄφελος, τό profit, advantage; usefulness.   [eyes.)

ὀφθαλμία, ἡ disease of the[

ὀφθαλμιάω to have bad eyes or a disease of the eyes.   [service.)

ὀφθαλμο-δουλεία, ἡ eye-)

ὀφθαλμός, ὁ the eye; face; the dearest, choicest, best, help, delight.

ὄφις, ὁ serpent, snake.

ὀφλισκάνω to incur a debt or punishment, to lose one's cause, to be found guilty; to incur a charge.

ὄφρα conj. as long as, while; until; that, in order that; adv. some time.

ὀφρύη, ἡ = ὀφρύς.

ὀφρυόεις 3 hilly.

ὀφρύς, ύος, ὁ eyebrow; forehead; pride, dignity; edge, brow of a hill.

ὄχα adv. by far.

ὄχανον, τό handle. [canal.)

ὀχετεύω to divert by a)

ὀχετ-ηγός 2 drawing a canal.   [ditch.)

ὀχετός, ὁ conduit, canal,)

ὀχεύς, ὁ handle, band, strap; clasp; bolt.

ὀχεύω to cover.

ὀχέω to bear, endure. — P. and M. to be carried or borne; to drive, ride.

ὄχημα, τό carriage, chariot; vessel.

ὀχθέω to be vexed.

ὄχθη, ἡ, ὄχθος, ὁ height, hill; high bank of a river; edge.

ὀχλέω to move by a lever, to roll; to molest, trouble.

ὀχληρός 3 troublesome.

ὀχλίζω = ὀχλέω.

ὀχλικός 3 = ὀχλώδης.

ὀχλο-ποιέω to make a riot.

ὄχλος, ὁ molestation, disturbance, trouble; throng, crowd, the common people, mob. [common, turbulent.]

ὀχλώδης 2 like a mob,

ὀχμάζω to hold fast; to rein in.

ὄχος, ὁ receptacle, support; carriage, chariot. [tenable.]

ὀχυρός 3 firm, strong,

ὀχυρόω and M. to fortify.

ὀχύρωμα, τό fort, stronghold, fortress. [saying.]

ὄψ, ὀπός, ἡ voice; speech,

ὀψάριον, τό = ὄψον.

ὀψέ adv. long after; late, too late; in the evening.

ὀψείω to wish to see.

ὀψία, ἡ evening; afternoon.

ὀψί-γονος 2 late-born, afterborn.

ὀψίζω and P. to be (too) late. [tardy.]

ὄψιμος 2, ὄψιος 3 late,

ὄψις, ἡ faculty of sight, a seeing, viewing; sight, appearance; view, vision; perception; eye; face.

ὀψι-τέλεστος 2 of late fulfilment.

ὄψον, τό by-meat, anything eaten with bread; meat, fish, dainty food, sauce.

ὀψο-ποιέω and M. to dress or season meat.

ὀψο-ποιΐα, ἡ, ὀψο-ποιϊκή, ἡ cookery.

ὀψο-ποιός, ὁ cook.

ὀψο-φάγος 2 eater of meat; dainty feeder. [dainties.]

ὀψ-ωνέω to buy victuals or

ὀψ-ώνιον, τό = ὄψον; provisions; wages.

Π

Π, π (πῖ) sixteenth letter of the alphabet; as a numeral π' = 80.

πᾶ, πά = πῇ, πή.

πᾱγά, ἡ = πηγή.

παγετώδης 2 icy, chilly.

πάγη, ἡ snare; trap.

παγιδεύω to entrap.

παγίς, ίδος, ἡ = πάγη.

πάγ-κακος 2 utterly bad, nefarious.

πάγ-καλος 2 and 3 most beautiful or good.

πάγ-καρπος 2 rich in all sorts of fruit. [cealing.]

παγ-κευθής 2 all-con-

πάγ-κλαυτος 2 ever weeping, all tearful; all-lamented.

πάγ-κοινος 2 common to all. [rest to all.]

παγ-κοίτης, ου giving

παγ-κόνιτος 2 quite covered with dust. [ful.]

παγ-κρατής 2 all-power-

παγ-κρατιάζω to practise the παγκράτιον.

παγ-κρατιαστής, οῦ, ὁ wrestler and boxer.

παγ-κράτιον, τό combined wrestling and boxing.

πάγος, ὁ ice; frost; rock, peak, hill, crag.

παγ-χάλεπος 2 most difficult.

παγ-χάλκεος 2, πάγ-χαλκος 2 all-brazen.

πάγ-χρηστος 2 good for all things.

πάγ-χριστος 2 all-anointed.

παγ-χρύσεος 2 all golden.

πάγχυ adv. quite, wholly.

πάθη, ή, πάθημα, τό, πάθος, τό occurrence, accident; misfortune, suffering, loss; grief; passion, affection.

παιάν, ᾶνος, ὁ saviour, physician; pæan, choral song (of triumph). [pæan.]

παιᾱνίζω to chant the pæan.

παιγνιά, ή play, sport.

παιγνιήμων 2, παιγνιώδης 2 sportive, jocose.

παιδ-αγωγέω to lead, train, or educate boys.

παιδ-αγωγός, ὁ trainer of boys, tutor, master, teacher.

παιδάριον, τό little child, boy, or girl.

παιδείᾱ, ή education, teaching, training, discipline, correction; letters, knowledge, science; school.

παιδεῖος 2 = παιδικός.

παιδ-εραστέω to love boys.

παιδ-εραστής, οῦ, ὁ lover of boys. [boys.]

παιδ-εραστίᾱ, ή love of

παίδευμα, τό, παίδευσις, ή = παιδεία.

παιδευτής, οῦ, ὁ instructor, teacher, corrector.

παιδεύω to bring up, train, teach, instruct, educate; to accustom.

παιδιά, ή = παιδεία.

παιδιά, ή child's play; sport, game.

παιδικός 3 belonging to children, childish, young; τὰ παιδικά darling. [child.]

παιδιόθεν adv. from a

παιδίον, τό = παιδάριον.

παιδίσκη, ή girl, damsel, young female slave.

παιδίσκος, ὁ = παιδάριον.

παιδνός 3 and 2 = παιδικός.

παιδο-κτόνος 2 child-slaying. [children.]

παιδο-ποιέω to beget

παιδο-ποιΐα, ή the begetting of children.

παιδο-ποιός 2 begetting children.

παιδο-τρίβης, ου, ὁ training-master for boys.

παιδο-τρόφος 2 rearing children.

παιδουργία, ή mother.

παιδο-φόνος 2 = παιδοκτόνος.

παίζω to sport, play, jest; to invent in jest.

παιήων, ονος, ὁ = παιάν.

παιπαλόεις 3 steep, rocky, cragged.

παῖς, παιδός, ὁ, ή child, son, daughter, descendant; boy, girl, young man or woman; servant, slave.

παιφάσσω to quiver, to move like lightning.

παίω to strike, smite; to hit, wound; intr. to dash against.

παιών, ῶνος, ὁ = παιάν.

παιωνίζω = παιανίζω.

παιώνιος 3 healing, saving.

παιωνισμός, ὁ the chanting of the pæan. [stop.]

πᾱκτόω to close fast; to

παλάζω = πάλλω.

παλάθη, ἡ fruit-cake.

πάλαι *adv.* of old, formerly, before; just past.

παλαι-γενής 2 aged. [old.]

παλαιό-πλουτος 2 rich of]

παλαιός 3 old, aged; ancient; antiquated.

παλαιότης, ητος, ἡ age, antiquity.

παλαιόω to make old; to abrogate. — *P.* to become obsolete.

πάλαισμα, τό a wrestling; trick, artifice; struggle.

παλαισμοσύνη, ἡ art of wrestling.

παλαιστής, οῦ, ὁ wrestler.

παλαιστιαῖος 3 a palm long or broad. [legendary.]

παλαί-φατος 2 ancient,]

παλαίω to wrestle, struggle; to succumb.

παλάμη, ἡ palm; hand; power, force; device, method, means.

παλαμναῖος, ὁ murderer; avenger. [defile.]

παλάσσω[1] to besprinkle,]

παλάσσω[2] = πάλλω.

παλέω = παλαίω.

πάλη, ἡ a wrestling, struggle. [birth.]

παλιγ-γενεσία, ἡ new]

παλίγ-κοτος 2 relapsing; malignant.

παλιλ-λογέω to say again.

παλίλ-λογος 2 collected again.

παλιμ-πετές *adv.* back.

παλιμ-πλάζω to drive back.

πάλιν *adv.* back, backwards; reversely; again, once more.

παλιν-άγρετος 2 revocable.

παλιν-αυτόμολος, ὁ deserter for a second time.

παλιν-όρμενος 3, παλίν-ορσος 2 hastening back.

παλίν-τιτος 2 requited.

παλίν-τονος 2 elastic.

παλιν-τριβής 2 crafty, obdurate. [back.]

παλίν-τροπος 2 turning]

παλιν-ῳδία, ἡ recantation.

παλιρ-ρόθιος 2 flowing back. [back, ebb.]

παλίρ-ροια, ἡ a flowing]

παλίρ-ρυτος 2 flowing in requital. [back.]

παλίσ-συτος 2 rushing]

παλ-ίωξις, ἡ pursuit in turn. [as a concubine.]

παλλακεύομαι *M.* to keep]

παλλακή, παλλακίς, ίδος, ἡ concubine.

πάλλω to swing, wield, whirl, brandish, shake. — *M.* to move quickly, quiver, tremble.

πάλος, ὁ lot.

παλτόν, τό dart, javelin.

παλτός 3 hurled.

παλύνω to strew, scatter; to besprinkle.

παμ-βῶτις, ιδος all-feeding.

πάμ-μαχος 2 all-conquering. [θης 2 enormous.]

πάμ-μεγας 3, παμ-μεγέ-]

παμ-μέλᾱς 3 all black.

παμ-μήκης 2 of enormous length. [month.]

πάμ"-μηνος 2 through every]

παμ-μήτωρ, ορος, ἡ true mother.

πάμ-μορος 2 quite unhappy.

πάμ - παν, παμ - πήδην wholly, quite.

παμ-πληθεί *adv.* with the whole multitude. [πολύς.

παμ - πληθής 2 = πάμ-

πάμ-πληκτος 2 beaten all over. [varied.

παμ-ποίκιλος 2 quite

πάμ-πολις, εως prevailing in all cities. [very great.

πάμ-πολυς 3 very much;

παμ-πόνηρος 2 utterly bad.

πάμ-πρωτος 3 the very first.

παμ-φαής 2 all-shining.

παμφαίνω, παμφανάω to shine brightly.

παμ-φεγγής 2 = παμφαής.

πάμ-φλεκτος 2 all-blazing.

παμ-φόρος 2 all-productive.

πάμ-φῠχος 2 in full vigour.

πάν-αγρος 2 catching all.

παν-άθλιος 3 quite unhappy.

πᾶν-αιθος 2 all-blazing.

παν-αίολος 2 all-shining, variegated. [ἥμερος.

παν-άμερος 2 = παν-

παν-άμωμος 2 quite blameless.

παν-άπαλος 2 quite tender or young. [happy.

παν-άποτμος 2 quite un-

παν-άργυρος 2 all of silver.

πάν-αρχος 2 all-ruling.

παν-αφηλιξ, ικος quite without one's early friends.

παν-αώριος 2 all-untimely.

παν-δαισία, ἡ complete banquet.

παν-δάκρῠτος 2 most lamented; all in tears.

παν - δαμάτωρ, ορος all-subduing.

παν-δημεί *adv.* with the whole people or force.

πάν-δημος 2, παν-δήμιος 2 of the whole people, public, universal; common.

πάν-δικος 2 quite just.

παν-δοκεύω to receive or entertain all.

παν-δοχεῖον, τό inn.

παν-δοχεύς, ὁ inn-keeper.

πάν-δυρτος 2 ever-lamenting.

παν - ηγυρίζω to keep or attend a festival.

παν-ήγυρις, ἡ public festival. [long.

παν-ῆμαρ *adv.* all day

παν-ημέριος 3, παν-ήμερος 2 lasting the whole day, all day.

πάνθηρ, ηρος, ὁ panther.

παν-θῡμαδόν *adv.* in high wrath. [ped.

πάν-θυτος 2 all-worship-

παν-ίμερος 2 all-desired.

παν-νύχιος 3 all night long. [festival, vigil.

παν-νυχίς, ἰδος, ἡ night-

πάν-νυχος 2 = παννύχιος

παν-οικησίᾳ, παν-οικίᾳ *adv.* with the whole house.

παν-ομφαῖος 2 author of all oracles.

παν-οπλίᾱ, ἡ full armour.

πάν-ορμος 2 quite fit for landing.

παν-ουργέω to act wickedly.

παν-ούργημα, τό wickedness.

παν-ουργίᾱ, ἡ fraud, villany, knavery.

παν-οῦργος 2 crafty, cunning, villanous, knavish, wicked; knave, rogue, villain.

παν-όψιος 2 visible to all.

παν-σαγία, ἡ = πανοπλία.

παν-σέληνος 2 of the full moon.

πάν-σοφος 2 very wise.

παν-στρατία, ἡ the whole army.

παν-συδίη, παν-συδί adv. with all speed, in a hurry.

πάν-συρτος 2 accumulated.

παντᾷ, παντᾷ = πάντη.

παντά-πᾶσιν adv. = πάνυ.

πάντ-αρχος 2 all-ruling.

πανταχῇ, πανταχῆ adv. everywhere, in every direction, in every way; wholly.   [sides.

πανταχόθεν adv. from all

πανταχοῖ, πανταχόσε adv. in all directions.

πανταχοῦ = πανταχῇ.

παν-τελής 2 all complete, entire.   [ταχῇ.

πάντη, πάντη adv. = παν-

πάν-τιμος 2 all-honoured.

παν-τλήμων 2 quite unhappy.   [ing all.

παντο-γήρως, ων enfeebl-

παντοδαπός 3 = παντοῖος.

πάντοθεν = πανταχόθεν.

παντοῖος 3 of all kinds, manifold.   [mighty.

παντο-κράτωρ, ορος all-

παντο-πόρος 2 versatile.

παντ-όπτης, ου all-seeing.

πάντοσε = πανταχόσε.

παντουργός 2 = πανοῦργος.

πάντως, πάνυ adv. wholly, entirely, altogether; at any rate; at least; very much; certainly, indeed.

παν-υπέρτατος 3 the very uppermost.

παν-ύστατος 3 last of all.

παν-ωλεθρία, ἡ utter ruin.

παν-ώλεθρος 2, παν-ώλης 2 utterly ruined, destroyed; all-destructive.

πάομαι M. to acquire; perf. to possess.

παπαῖ woe! ah!

παπάζω to call papa.

πάππας, ου, ὁ papa.

πάππος, ὁ grandfather.

παππῷος 3 of one's grandfather.

παπταίνω to look timidly or cautiously; to peer about.

πάρ = παρά.

παρά adv. near, beside, along. — prp. with gen. from beside; from alongside of, from; with dat. by the side of, beside, near, in the presence of; according to; with acc. along; beside; towards; during; beyond, except; against, in comparison with.

παρα-βαίνω to go by the side of; to go beyond, transgress; to pass over, omit, neglect.

παρα-βάλλω to throw beside, to put before; to put side by side, to compare; intr. to come near, approach; to pass over. — M. to expose oneself; to stake; to rival; to compare; to omit, neglect; to deceive, betray.

παρά - βασις, ἡ transgression, crime. [ραβάτης.]

παρα-βάσκω to be a πα-]

παρα-βάτης, ου, ὁ warrior standing beside the charioteer; transgressor.

παρα - βατός to be transgressed. [one.]

παραβιάζομαι M. to urge]

παρα-βλήδην adv. with a side stroke or indirect cut.

παρά - βλημα, τό screen, cover.

παρα-βλώσκω to assist.

παρα-βλώψ, ῶπος looking sideways. [help.]

παρα-βοηθέω to come to]

παρα - βολεύομαι M. to stake, risk.

παρα-βολή, ἡ comparison, simile; proverb, parable; venture.

παρά-βολος 2 risking, reckless; perilous.

παρ-αγγελίᾱ, ἡ announcement, proclamation; command, order; doctrine, teaching.

παρ-αγγέλλω to announce; to pass the watchword, to give the word of command; to exhort, encourage; to command, to summon.

παρ-άγγελμα, τό, παρ-άγγελσις, ἡ = παραγγελία.

παρα-γίγνομαι M. to be present or at hand; to arrive at, to happen; to assist, help.

παρα-γιγνώσκω to decide wrong, to err in one's judgment.

παρ-αγκάλισμα, τό embrace.

παρ-άγορος 2 consoling.

παρα-γράφω to write beside, add in writing.

παρα-γυμνόω to disclose, reveal.

παρ-άγω to lead beside, by, or past; to lead up or along, to introduce, to bring forward; to make march sideways; to delay, keep in suspense; to lead astray, mislead, deceive; intr. to pass by, on, or away.

παρ - αγωγή, ἡ passage along the coast; sliding motions of the oars; variety in speech; fallacy, misleading. [beside.]

παρα-δαρθάνω to sleep]

παρά-δειγμα, τό pattern, model, example; warning.

παρα - δειγματίζω to expose to shame.

παρα - δείκνῡμι to show, exhibit, represent, assign.

παράδεισος, ὁ park; paradise.

παρα-δέχομαι M. to take or receive from; to charge oneself with; to admit, allow. [occupation.]

παρα-διατριβή, ἡ useless]

παρα-δίδωμι to give over, consign, deliver, transmit; to entrust; to abandon, betray; to grant, allow.

παρά-δοξος 2 unexpected; incredible, marvellous; strange, startling.

παρά-δοσις, ἡ a handing

over, transmission, surrender; tradition.

παρα-δράω to serve.

παρα-δυναστεύω to rule beside one.

παρα-δύομαι *M.* to steal or creep in or past.

παρα-δωσείω to be ready to deliver up.

παρ-αείδω to sing to.

παρ-αείρομαι *M.* to hang down on one side.

παρα-ζηλόω to provoke to jealousy or anger.

παρα-θαλασσίδιος 2, παρα-θαλάσσιος 2 on the seaside. [age.]

παρα-θαρσύνω to encourage.

παρα-θέω to run beside or past; to outrun.

παρα-θεωρέω to compare; to overlook, despise.

παρα-θήκη, ἡ = παρακαταθήκη.

παραί = παρά. [βάτης.]

παραι-βάτης = παραιβάτης.

παρ-αίνεσις, ἡ consolation, exhortation, advice, warning.

παρ-αινέω to exhort, counsel, warn, recommend.

παρ-αίρεσις, ἡ a taking away; lessening.

παρ-αιρέω to take away from; to lessen; to divert on. — *M.* to draw over to one's own side; to take away. [band.]

παρ-αίρημα, τό strip,]

παρ-αίσιος 2 fatal, ominous.

παρ-αΐσσω to rush on past.

παρ-αιτέομαι *M.* to beg from, to obtain by entreaty,

to intercede, plead for; to avert by entreaty, beg off; to decline, reject.

παρ-αίτησις, ἡ an obtaining by prayer; deprecation.

παρ-αίτιος 2 = αἴτιος.

παραί-φασις, ἡ exhortation, encouragement.

παρ-αιωρέομαι *P.* to hang down on one side.

παρα-καθέζομαι *M.*, παρα-κάθημαι, παρα-καθίζω and *M.* to sit down beside.

παρα-καθίστημι to put or place down beside.

παρα-καίομαι *P.* to be burnt beside.

παρα-καλέω to call to, summon, send for, call to aid; exhort, encourage, excite; to invite; to comfort. [veil.]

παρα-καλύπτω to cover,]

παρα-καταβάλλω to throw down beside; to put on.

παρα-καταθήκη, ἡ deposit, trust, pledge.

παρα-καταλείπω to leave behind for protection.

παρα-καταλέχομαι to lie down beside.

παρα-καταπήγνῦμι to drive in beside.

παρα-κατατίθεμαι *M.* to give in trust, deposit.

παρα-κατέχω to keep back.

παρά-κειμαι to lie beside; to be ready, at hand.

παρα-κελεύομαι *M.* to exhort, encourage; to advise.

παρα-κέλευσις, ἡ, παρα-κελευσμός, ὁ an exhorting, cheering on.

παρα-κελευστός 3 summoned; helper. [venture.]

παρακινδύνευσις, ἡ risk;
παρα-κινδῡνεύω to venture, hazard, risk.

παρα-κῑνέω to move aside; intr. to be mad, beside oneself.

παρα-κίω to pass by.

παρα-κληΐω to shut out.

παρά-κλησις, ἡ a calling to, summons; exhortation, imploring, comforting; encouraging. [aside.]

παρα-κλῐδόν adv. turning]

παρα-κλίνω to turn or bend aside; to open; intr. to slip away, escape.

παρ-ακμάζω to be faded or withered.

παρ-ακοή, ἡ disobedience.

παρα-κοίτης, ου, ὁ husband.

παρά-κοιτις, ἡ wife.

παρ-ακολουθέω to follow close; to attach oneself to; to understand.

παρα-κομιδή, ἡ a transporting, passage.

παρα-κομίζω to carry along or across, to convey. — M. to procure for oneself. — P. to sail beside or along.

παρ-ακούω to hear by the way; to hear wrong, misunderstand; to disobey.

παρα-κρεμάννῡμι to let hang down.

παρα-κρίνομαι P. to be drawn up along.

παρα-κρούω and M. to strike beside; to strike

the scale of a balance; to cheat, deceive.

παρα-κτάομαι M. to acquire beside. [shore.]

παρ-άκτιος 3 on the sea-]

παρα-κύπτω to stoop aside; to take a side glance at; to look at.

παρα-λαμβάνω to receive from another, to succeed to an office, to take possession of; to capture, seize; to light upon; to hear, learn; to take with one, to intercept; to invite.

παρα-λέγομαι to sail along.

παρα-λείπω to leave remaining; to leave unnoticed, to neglect.

παρα-λέχομαι M. to lie beside. [αλος.]

παρ-άλιος 2 and 3 = πάρ-]

παρ-αλλαγή, ἡ change, transfer; relief, relay.

παρ-αλλάξ adv. alternately; crosswise.

παρ-αλλάσσω to change, alter; to exchange; to pervert, seduce; to pass by; intr. to escape; to deviate, vary; to miss.

παρα-λογίζομαι M. to reckon wrong; to cheat.

παρά-λογος 2 unexpected; ὁ π. wrong reckoning, miscalculation; disappointment. [sea, maritime.]

πάραλος 2 lying by the]

παρα-λῡπέω to grieve, vex in surplus.

παρα-λυτικός 3 paralytic.

παρα-λύω to loosen from the side, to detach from;

to relieve, release, set free, dismiss: to affect with palsy, to enfeeble.

παρ-αμείβω to change, alter; to pass by; to exceed, surpass. — *M.* to change for oneself; to pass by, outrun.   [less of.]

παρ-αμελέω to be heed-

παρα-μένω to stay beside, to stand fast, hold out; to survive.   [for the legs.]

παρα-μηρίδια, τά armour

παρα-μίγνῡμι to mix with.

παρα-μιμνήσκομαι *M.* to mention by the way.

παρα-μίμνω = παραμένω.

παρα-μίσγω = παραμίγνυμι.

παρα-μόνιμος 2, παρά-μονος 2 steadfast, faithful.

παρα-μῡθέομαι *M.* to exhort, cheer, encourage; to advise; to console, soothe.

παρα-μῡθία, ἡ, παρα-μύθιον, τό exhortation, persuasion; consolation, soothing.   [beside.]

παρ-αναγιγνώσκω to read

παρα-ναιετάω to dwell beside.   [beside.]

παρα-νηνέω to heap up

παρα-νήχομαι *M.* to swim by or along the coast.

παρ-ανίσχω to hold up beside.

παρά-νοια, ἡ madness.

παρα-νομέω to transgress the law, to offend.

παρα-νόμημα, τό, παρα-νομία, ἡ transgression, law-breaking.   [wrong.]

παρα-νομίζω to judge

παρά-νομος 2 contrary to law, unlawful; lawless, unjust.

παρά-νους 2 mad.

πάρ-αντα *adv.* sideways.

παρα-παίω to be mad or crazy.

παρά-πᾶν *adv.* on the whole, altogether.

παρ-απαφίσκω to befool.

παρα-πειθω to win by persuasion, to prevail upon; to seduce.

παρα-πέμπω to send by or along; to escort; to leave unnoticed, be heedless of; to convey, transport.

παρα-πέτασμα, τό curtain; veil.

παρα-πέτομαι *M.* to fly by.

παρα-πήγνῡμι to fix beside or near. — *P.* to be fixed to.   [bitter.]

παρα-πικραίνω to em-

παρα-πικρασμός, ὁ exasperation.

παρα-πίπτω to fall in with; to befal, happen, offer itself; to commit a fault, to err; to fall off.

παρα-πλάζω to make wander from the right way, to mislead. — *P.* to go astray.

παρα-πλέω to sail along or by; to sail up.

παρα-πληξ, ῆγος, παρά-πληκτος 2 sloping; mad.

παρα-πλήσιος 3 and 2 nearly like, resembling, about equal.

παρά-πλους, ὁ a sailing beside or by; passage.

παρα-πλώω = παραπλέω.

παρα-πνέω to blow by the side. [terleit.]

παρα-ποιέω to copy, coun-

παρα-πομπή, ἡ escort; transport supply.

παρα-πορεύομαι P. to go beside or past. [a river.]

παρα-ποτάμιος 3 beside]

παρα-πράσσω to do beside, to help in doing.

παρα-πρεσβείᾱ, ἡ fraudulent embassy.

παρα-πρεσβεύω and M. to act fraudulently as an ambassador. [grasped.]

παρ-άπτομαι P. to be]

παρά-πτωμα, τό trespass, sin. [as a border.]

παρα-ρράπτω to sow to]

παρα-ρρέω to flow by or down; to slip from memory; to be lost or missing; to steal in.

παρα-ρρήγνῡμι to break, rend; intr. to burst.

παρα-ρρητός 3 to be persuaded.

παρα-ρρίπτω to throw aside; to run the risk.

παρά-ρρῠμα, τό protecting cover.

παρ-αρτάω, -έω to prepare, make ready; to be ready. [mile.]

παρασάγγης, ου, ὁ Persian]

παρα-σάσσω to stuff or cram beside.

παρά-σημος 2 marked; stamped falsely, counterfeit, base.

παρα-σῑτέω to eat with one; to be a parasite.

παρα-σκευάζω to get rea-

dy, prepare, equip, provide, procure, furnish; to make, render; to make willing; to manage. — M. to prepare for oneself; to prepare oneself, get ready, prepared. [preparing.]

παρα-σκευαστής, οῦ, ὁ]

παρα-σκευαστικός 3 fit for procuring a thing.

παρα-σκευή, ἡ preparation, a getting ready, equipment, provision, furniture, pomp; force, power, armament; means, resources; scheme, plot, intrigue; Friday. [camp beside.]

παρα-σκηνέω, -όω to en-]

παρα-σκοπέω to look at.

παρα-σπάω and M. to draw aside or over; to detach from a party.

παρα-σπονδέω to act contrary to a treaty.

παρά-σπονδος 2 contrary to a treaty. faithless.

παρα-σταδόν adv. standing beside. [pl. portic.]

παρα-στάς, άδος, ἡ pillar;]

παρα-στατέω to stand by.

παρα-στάτης, ου, ὁ next man; comrade, compeer, helper. [sistant.]

παρα-στάτις, ιδος, ἡ as-]

παρα-στείχω to step by; to pass into.

παρα-στρατηγέω to outwit by stratagems.

παρα-σφάλλω to push off sideways.

παρα-σχίζω to make a cut beside. [side.]

παρα-τανύω to spread be-]

παρά-ταξις, ἡ an arranging; army in array.

παρα-τάσσω to put beside others; to draw up in order of battle. — M. to meet in battle; to arrange one's men.

παρα-τείνω to stretch out beside; to stretch or draw out; to protract, prolong; to torture, put to the rack. — intr. and P. to run along; to be stretched; to be tortured.

παρα-τείχισμα, τό wall built beside.

παρα-τεκταίνομαι M. to transform; to falsify.

παρα-τηρέω and M. to watch, observe. [tion.)

παρα-τήρησις, ἡ observa-

παρα-τίθημι to place beside or before; to supply, provide; to compare; to declare, explain. — M. to set before oneself; to be provided with; to call in to aid; to deposit; to entrust; to stake, hazard.

παρα-τρέπω to turn aside, divert, mislead; to make one alter one's mind; to pervert, falsify.

παρα-τρέχω to run by or past; to outrun, run down; to escape; to run up to.

παρα-τρέω to start aside from fear.

παρα-τρίβω to rub beside.

παρα-τροπέω to turn aside. [τρέπω.)

παρα-τρωπάω = παρα-

παρα-τυγχάνω to be present by chance, to happen; to offer itself; ὁ παρατυχών any chance person.

παρ-αυδάω to speak to, to console; to colour, palliate. [near.)

πάρ-αυλος 2 neighbouring,)

παρ-αυτίκα = παραχρῆμα.

παρα-φαίνομαι P. to show oneself.

παρα-φέρω to bear or carry by or along; to bring forward, produce, serve up; to mention, allege; to carry away, avert, lead away, remove; intr. to differ.

παρα-φεύγω to flee by or past. [to; to persuade.)

παρά-φημι and M. to speak)

παρα-φθάνω and M. to be beforehand; to overtake.

παρα-φορέω to present.

παρά-φορος 2 staggering.

παρά-φραγμα, τό breastwork; bulwark. [oneself.)

παρα-φρονέω to be beside)

παρα-φρονίᾱ, ἡ, παρα-φροσύνη, ἡ madness.

παρα-φρόνιμος 2, παρά-φρων 2 mad.

παρα-φρυκτωρεύομαι M. to make fire-signals to the enemy. [take care.)

παρα-φυλάσσω to watch,)

παρα-φύομαι M. to grow at the side.

παρα-χειμάζω to pass the winter. [tering.)

παρα-χειμασίᾱ, ἡ a win-)

παρα-χέω to heap up beside; to pour in beside.

παρα-χόω to throw up beside.

παρα-χράομαι M. to depreciate, undervalue, disregard; to misuse.

παρα-χρῆμα adv. on the spot, instantly, at once, immediately, straightway.

παρα-χωρέω to go aside, to make room; to concede, grant, yield.

παρδαλέη, ἡ panther's skin.

παρδαλίς, ὁ, ἡ panther.

παρ-εγγυάω to hand on, recommend; to pass on the watchword or word of command; to exhort, encourage, command.

παρ-εγγύη, ἡ call, exhortation; watchword.

παρ-εδρεύω to sit beside.

πάρ-εδρος 2 sitting beside; companion at table; assessor, assistant.

παρ-έζομαι M. to sit beside. [piece.]

παρειά, ἡ cheek; cheek-

παρειάς, ου, ὁ serpent sacred to Aesculapius.

παρ-είκω to yield, give way; to permit, allow; παρείκει it is allowed or practicable. [ἔρχομαι.]

πάρ-ειμι[1] (-ιέναι) = παρ-

πάρ-ειμι[2] (-εῖναι) to be by, present, or near; to stand by, help, assist; to have arrived; to be extant, at hand, or possible; τὰ παρόντα present circumstances.

παρ-ειπεῖν see παράφημι.

παρ-ειρύω to draw along the side.

παρ-εισάγω to introduce secretly.

παρ-είσακτος 2 introduced secretly. [in besides.]

παρ-εισδέχομαι M. to take

παρ-εισδύομαι to come in secretly, to slip in.

παρ-εισφέρω to bring in beside.

παρ-έκ, παρ-έξ, πάρ-εξ adv. out beside, along, past, or beyond; senselessly, foolishly. — prp. with gen. outside, before, except; with acc. beyond, alongside of, without. [κειμαι.]

παρ-εκέσκετο see παρά-

παρεκ-προφεύγω to flee away from before.

παρ-εκτός adv. besides.

παρ-ελαύνω to drive by or along; intr. to drive, ride, march, sail, or run by, past, or along.

παρ-έλκω, -ελκύω to draw to the side; to delay. — M. to draw to oneself.

παρ-εμβάλλω to throw up (a wall).

παρ-εμβολή, ἡ a drawing up in battle-order; fort, camp, barracks.

παρ-ενθήκη, ἡ insertion, addition; digression.

παρ-ενοχλέω to trouble or annoy besides.

παρ-έξ see παρέκ.

παρ-εξάγω to delude.

παρ-έξειμι = παρεξέρχομαι. [stern of a ship.]

παρεξ-ειρεσία, ἡ prow or

παρ-εξελαύνω, -ελάω to drive out past; intr. to go, ride, or drive out past.

παρ-εξέρχομαι M. to go

out beside; to transgress, elude.

παρ-εξευρίσκω to find out besides. [side.]

παρ-εξίημι to let pass be-)

παρ-επίδημος 2 immigrant, stranger. [close.]

παρ-έπομαι M. to follow)

πάρ-εργον, τό by-work, by-matter, addition.

πάρ-εργος 2 secondary, subordinate, by the way.

παρ-έρχομαι M. to go by, beside, past, or beyond; to pass; to escape notice; to neglect, slight; to surpass, overreach, delude; to overtake, outrun; to come to, pass to; to come forward, make one's appearance.

πάρ-εσις, ή forgiveness.

παρ-έστιος 2 by the hearth, domestic.

παρ-ευθύνω to direct aside.

παρ-ευνάζομαι P. to sleep beside.

παρ-εύρεσις, ή pretext.

παρ-ευρίσκω to find out, invent.

παρ-έχω to hold in readiness; to offer, furnish, supply, afford; allow, grant; to cause, render; to show, exhibit, represent, produce. — M. to offer, supply, produce or display from one's own means or on one's own part.

παρ-ηβάω to grow old.

παρ-ηγορέω and M. to exhort, encourage.

παρ-ηγορίᾱ, ή exhortation; consolation.

παρήϊον, τό, παρηΐς, ίδος, ή = παρειά.

παρ-ήκω to reach or extend to; to come forth.

πάρ-ημαι M. to sit by or beside; to be present or near.

παρ-ηορίαι, αἱ reins of the by-horse.

παρ-ήορος 2 by-horse; sprawling; silly.

παρθενεύω M. to remain a maiden.

παρθενίᾱ, ή maidenhead.

παρθένιος 3, παρθενικός 3 of a maiden, maidenly; son of an unmarried woman.

παρθεν-οπίπης, ου, ὁ one who looks at maidens.

παρθένος, ή maiden, virgin, young woman.

παρθενών, ῶνος, ὁ maiden's chamber; temple of Athena.

παρ-ιαύω to sleep beside.

παρ-ίζω to place beside; (and M.) to be seated beside.

παρ-ίημι to let fall at the side, to let by, past, or through; to relax, yield, give way; to remit, to let pass, allow, permit; to forgive, pardon; to neglect, abandon, refuse; to let in. — M. to beg to be excused; to beg off; to grant.

παρ-ιππεύω to ride along; to ride up to.

παρ-ισόω to make like. — M. to vie with.

παρ-ίστημι to place by, beside, near, or before; to present, offer; to bring to one's side, win over, persuade; to make ready; to explain, describe, prove; to cause. — *intr.* and *P.* to stand beside, by, or near, to be near, at hand, or present; to help, assist; to surrender, submit; to come to one's mind, to suggest itself.— *M.* to place at one's side; to produce; to win over, to overcome, subdue. [to offer.]

παρ-ίσχω to keep ready;)

πάρ-οδος, ἡ way past, passage, passing by; entrance.

πάροιθεν *adv.* before; with *gen.* in front of, in the presence of.

παρ-οικέω to dwell by or along; to be a neighbour or stranger. [hood.]

παρ-οίκησις, ἡ neighbour-)

παρ-οικία, ἡ a dwelling abroad. [near.]

παρ-οικίζομαι *P.* to settle)

παρ-οικοδομέω to build beside. [foreigner.]

πάρ-οικος 2 neighbouring;)

παρ-οιμία, ἡ proverb; parable. [to maltreat.]

παρ-οινέω to be drunken;)

παροίτερος 3 fore, front.

παρ-οίχομαι *M.* to have passed by.

παρ-οκωχή, ἡ = παροχή.

παρ-ολιγωρέω to be careless.

παρ-ομοιάζω to be like.

παρ-όμοιος 2 and 3 nearly like or equal.

παρ-οξυντικός 3 inciting.

παρ-οξύνω to sharpen, incite, spur on, irritate.

παρ-οξυσμός, ὁ an inciting, provoking.

παρ-οράω to look at, notice; to look past, overlook. [anger.]

παρ-οργίζω to provoke to)

παρ-ορμάω to stir up, set in motion.

παρ-ορμίζω to bring to anchor beside. [side.]

παρ-ορύσσω to dig be-)

πάρος *adv.* before, formerly, in front; *conj.* = πρίν before. — *prp.* with *gen.* before, rather than.

παρ-οτρύνω = παρορμάω.

παρ-ουσία, ἡ presence; arrival, return; assistance; right time.

παρ-οχή, ἡ a supplying, offering. [dish.]

παρ-οψίς, ίδος, ἡ small)

παρ-ρησία, ἡ freedom of speech, licence of speech; courage.

παρρησιάζομαι to speak freely. [φασις.]

πάρ-φασις, ἡ = παραί-)

παρ-ωθέω to push aside, drive away, displace; to conceal. [cornice.]

παρ-ωροφίς, ίδος, ἡ eaves,)

πᾶς, πᾶσα, πᾶν all, whole, entire; every; τὸ πᾶν, τὰ πάντα the whole, everything; the universe. [all.]

πᾶσι-μέλουσα, ἡ a care to)

πάσσαλος, ὁ peg.

πάσ-σοφος 2 = πάνσοφος.

πασ-συδί see πανσυδί.

πάσσω to sprinkle upon; to interweave.

πάσσων 2 *comp.* of παχύς

παστάς, άδος, ἡ porch, colonnade, portico; bridal chamber; dining-room; tomb. [Passover.]

πάσχα, τό the paschal lamb,

πάσχω to suffer, to be affected by; to be liable to.

παταγέω and M. to clatter, make a noise.

πάταγος, ὁ noise, clattering, chattering (of the teeth).

πατάσσω to beat, knock; to kill. [consume.]

πατέομαι M. to eat, taste,

πατέω to tread, walk; to tread on, trample on.

πατήρ, τρός, ὁ father; forefather, ancestor; founder.

πάτος, ὁ tread, path.

πάτρᾱ, ἡ = πατρίς.

πατρ-αλοίᾱς, ᾱ, -φᾱς, ου, ὁ parricide.

πατριά, ἡ descent, lineage; people, tribe, family.

πατρι-άρχης, ου, ὁ patriarch.

πατρικός 3, πάτριος 3 and 2 of one's father or forefathers; hereditary, customary, native, national.

πατρίς, ίδος, ἡ one's country, fatherland, native city; race. [countryman.]

πατριώτης, ου, ὁ fellow-

πατρόθεν adv. from the father's side.

πατρο-κασίγνητος, ὁ father's brother, uncle.

πατρο-κτόνος 2 parricidal.

πατρο-παράδοτος 2 handed down from one's fathers.

πατροῆχος, ἡ sole heiress.

πατρο-φόνος 2, πατρο-

φονεύς, ὁ, πατρο-φόντης, ου = πατροκτόνος.

πατρῷος 3, πατρώϊος 3 = πάτριος.

πάτρως, ωος, ὁ father's brother, uncle.

παῦλα, ἡ rest, repose, pause, end. [short.]

παῦρος 2 very little, small,

παυστήρ, ῆρος, ὁ, παυστήριος 2 allaying; reliever.

παυσωλή, ἡ = παῦλα.

παύω to cause to cease, to stop, bring to an end; to check, hinder; to depose. — P. and M. to come to an end, leave off, cease, rest; to be deposed.

παφλάζω to bubble, foam.

πάχετος 2, πάχιστος 3 see παχύς.

πάχνη, ἡ hoar-frost.

παχνόομαι P. to be frozen.

πάχος, τό thickness.

παχύνω to thicken, fatten; to make dull.

παχύς 3 (πάσσων, παχίων, πάχιστος) thick, fat, stout, great, large; rich, wealthy; stupid, dull.

παχύτης, ητος, ἡ = πάχος.

πεδάω to bind, fetter, check, constrain; to entangle.

πέδη, ἡ fetter.

πεδιάς, άδος, ἡ level, even; plain country. [boot.]

πέδῑλον, τό sandal; shoe;

πεδῑνός 3 even, level, flat.

πεδίον, τό a plain, field, open country; πεδίονδε adv. to the plain.

πέδον, τό ground, soil;

πέδονδε *adv.* to the ground; πεδόθεν *adv.* from the bottom of the heart.

πέζα, ἡ foot; end, top.

πεξ-έταιροι, οἱ foot-guards in Macedonia.

πεζεύω to go on foot; to travel by land.

πεζῇ *adv.* on foot; by land.

πεζικός 3 = πεζός.

πεζο-μαχέω to fight by land. [land.]

πεζο-μαχίᾱ, ἡ fight by]

πεζός 3 on foot; by land; ὁ π. walker; foot-soldier, infantry.

πειθ-αρχέω and *M.* to obey.

πειθός 3 persuasive.

πείθω to persuade, prevail upon, win over; to appease, propitiate, win by entreaty; to bribe; to cause, impel; to mislead, cheat. — *intr.* and *P.* to be won over or persuaded; to believe, trust, rely on; to listen to, obey, comply with, yield.

πειθώ, οὖς, ἡ persuasion, eloquence.

πείκω to pick, card.

πεῖνα, πείνη, ἡ hunger; famine. [famished.]

πεινάω to be hungry or]

πεῖρα, ἡ trial, attempt, proof; experience; enterprise; plot, design.

πειράζω = πειράω.

πειραίνω to tie to, fasten by a knot; to finish, complete.

πεῖραρ[1], ατος, τό end, farthest point; issue; instrument.

πεῖραρ[2], ατος, τό rope; snare.

πείρασις, ἡ, πειρασμός, ὁ temptation. [deal.]

πειρατήριον, τό trial, or-]

πειράω, -έω *M.* and *P.* to try, attempt, undertake; to make a trial (of), to test, experience, examine; to try one's skill; to try to persuade; to lead into temptation; to know by experience.

πειρητίζω = πειράω.

πείρινς, ινθος, ἡ wicker-basket in a carriage.

πείρω to pierce through, to spit; to stud with nails; to cleave, pass through.

πεῖσα, ἡ obedience.

πεῖσμα, τό rope, cable.

πεισμονή, ἡ = πειθώ.

πειστικός 3 = πειστήριος.

πέκω to comb, card.

πελαγίζω to form a sea.

πελάγιος 3 of or on the sea. [open sea.]

πέλαγος, τό the high sea,]

πελάζω to bring near. — *intr.* and *P.* to approach, draw near, to be brought near; to reach to, meet.

πέλανος, ὁ offering-cake.

πέλας *adv.* near; ὁ π. neighbour, fellow-man. — *prp.* with *gen.* near to.

πελάτης, ου, ὁ neighbour; day-labourer.

πελάω = πελάζω.

πέλεθρον, τό = πλέθρον.

πέλεια, πελειάς, άδος, ἡ rock-pigeon. [axe.]

πελεκάω to hew with an]

πελεκίζω to behead.

πέλεκκον, τό axe-handle.

πέλεκυς, εως, ὁ axe.

πελεμίζω to swing, shake; to make tremble. — P. to be shaken, to tremble; to flee trembling.

πελιτνός 3 livid, fallow.

πέλλα, ἡ milk-pail.

πέλομαι see πέλω.   [tast.]

πελτάζω to serve as a pel-

πελταστής, οῦ, ὁ a light-armed soldier, peltast.

πελταστικός 3 armed with a light shield.

πέλτη, ἡ light shield; shaft, spear.   [στής.]

πελτο-φόρος 2 = πελτα-

πέλω and M. to be in motion; to go, come; to behave; to be; to become; to happen.

πέλωρ, τό monster.

πελώριος 3 and 2, πέλωρος 3 huge, immense.

πέμμα, τό cakes, baker's ware.

πεμπάζω and M. to count by fives.   [ber five.]

πεμπάς, άδος, ἡ the num-

πεμπταῖος 3 in five days.

πέμπτος 3 the fifth.

πεμπτός 3 sent.

πέμπω to send, send away or home, dismiss; to send word; to throw, shoot; to escort, convoy, attend; to conduct a procession. — M. to send for.

πεμπ-ώβολον, τό five-pronged fork.

πέμψις, ἡ a sending.

πενέστης, ου, ὁ labourer; bondsman.

πένης, ητος poor, needy.

πενθερά, ἡ mother-in-law.

πενθερός, ὁ father-in-law.

πένθος, τό grief, sorrow; misfortune.

πενία, ἡ poverty, need.

πενιχρός 3 = πένης.

πένομαι to toil, work; to be poor; to prepare, be busy with.   [five drachms.]

πεντα-δραχμος 2 worth

πεντα-έτης, -ετής 2, πεντα-έτηρος 2 five years old.

πέντ-αθλον, τό contest of the five exercises.

πέντ-αθλος, ὁ practising (or winning) the five exercises.

πεντάκις adv. five times.

πεντακισ-μύριοι 3 fifty thousand.

πεντακισ-χίλιοι 3 five thousand.   [dred.]

πεντα-κόσιοι 3 five hun-

πεντακοσιο-μέδιμνος 2 reaping 500 μέδιμνοι.

πεντά-πηχυς, υ, εως of five cubits.

πεντα-πλάσιος 3 fivefold.

πεντά-πολις, ἡ union of five cities.

πεντά-στομος 2 with five mouths.   [in five parts.]

πένταχα, πενταχοῦ adv.

πέντε five.   [drachms.]

πεντε-δραχμία, ἡ five

πεντε-καὶ-δεκα fifteen.

πεντε-καὶ-δέκατος 3 fifteenth.   [five talents.]

πεντε-τάλαντος 2 worth

πεντ-ετηρίς, ίδος, ἡ space of five years; festival celebrated every five years.

πεντήκοντα fifty.

πεντηκοντήρ, ῆρος, ὁ leader of fifty men. [acres.]

πεντηκοντό-γυος 2 of fifty

πεντηκοντ-όργυιος 2 of fifty fathoms.

πεντηκόντ-ορος 2 ship with fifty oars.

πεντηκοντούτης 2 lasting fifty years. [κόσιοι.]

πεντηκόσιοι 3 = πεντα-)

πεντηκοστός 3. fiftieth; ἡ -ή Pentecost.

πεντηκοστύς, ύος, ἡ division of fifty men.

πεντ-ήρης, ἡ quinquereme.

πεπαίνω to make ripe. — P. to be softened.

πέπλος, ὁ, πέπλωμα, τό garment, robe, cloak, long dress; curtain.

πεποίθησις, ἡ trust.

πέπων[1] 2 ripe; soft, gentle; weakling.

πέπων[2] 2 dear; friend.

πέρ enclitic particle much, very; even; however, at any rate.

πέρᾱ adv. beyond; farther; over; longer. — prp. with gen. beyond, more than. (comp. περαιτέρω still farther, beyond).

πέραθεν adv. from beyond.

περαίνω to bring to an end, finish, complete, accomplish. — P. to be accomplished.

περαῖος 3 being beyond.

περαιόω to carry across. — P. to pass over.

πέρᾱν adv. on the other side, across, beyond; over against. — Prp. with gen. over against, beyond.

πέρας, ατος, τό end, extremity, issue, goal; accomplishment; adv. at last.

πέρᾱσις, ἡ end; passage from life.

πέρᾱτος 3 last, extreme.

περᾱτός 3 to be passed over.

περάω to carry across; to sell beyond the sea; to pass through, traverse; intr. to come through, to penetrate, to come over, across, or beyond; to exceed.

πέργαμον, τό, πέργαμα, τά, περγαμός, ὁ castle, citadel. [tridge.]

πέρδιξ, ικος, ὁ and ἡ par-)

πέρηθεν, πέρην = πέραθεν, πέραν.

πέρθω to destroy, ravage; to get by plunder.

περί adv. around, about; exceedingly. — Prp. with gen. around, about; on account of, for, for the sake of; above, beyond, more than; περὶ πολλοῦ of much consequence. — with dat. around, about; hard by, near; for, on account of. — with acc. about, around; near, by; in relation to, with regard to.

περι-αγγέλλω to announce around, to send a message round; to send round orders.

περι-άγνυμι, P. to be echoed all round.

περι-άγω and M. to lead (drive, or turn) round or about; intr. to go round.

περι-αιρετός 3 able to be taken off.

περι-αιρέω to take off all round; to pull down; to abrogate, to take away. — *M.* to take away from oneself; to strip off; to rob.

περι-αλγέω to feel heavy pain. [ingly.]

περί-αλλα *adv.* exceed-

περι-αμπέχω to put round about.

περι-άπτω to attach to, to fasten round; to inflict; to kindle round about.

περι-αστράπτω to flash all round.

περι-αυχένιος 2 running round the neck.

περι-βαίνω to go round; to sound round; to sit astride on; to protect, defend.

περι-βάλλω to throw round, about, or over; to put round, to embrace, surround; to invest, attribute, ascribe; to sail round, double; to surpass. — *M.* to throw round oneself, to put on; to aim at, take possession of; to put round oneself for defence; to encompass, surround, enclose.

περί-βλεπτος 2 gazed at or on; notable, famous.

περι-βλέπω and *M.* to look round about, to gaze on.

περι-βόητος 2 notorious, of good or evil fame; surrounded by noise.

περι-βόλαιον, τό, περι-βολή, ἡ, περί-βολος, ὁ wall, enclosure; circum-

ference, circuit, compass; curve; an aiming at; cover, garment, sheath, veil.

περι-βρύχιος 2 surging around.

περι-γίγνομαι to be superior, prevail (over), overcome; to result, proceed; to survive, escape, remain.

περι-γλαγής 2 full of milk.

περι-γνάμπτω to sail round, double.

περι-γραπτός 2 circumscribed, enclosed.

περι-γράφω to circumscribe; to define, determine.

περι-δεής 2 very timid or fearful.

περι-δείδω to fear very much. [repast.]

περί-δειπνον, τό funeral

περι-δέξιος 2 (equally) skilful with both hands.

περι-δέω to bind round.

περι-δίδομαι *M.* to wager, stake.

περι-δῑνέω to whirl round. — *P.* to spin round.

περι-δίω = περιδείδω.

περί-δρομος 2 running round, circular; standing detached. [round.]

περι-δρύπτω to scratch

περι-δύω to put off around.

περι-ειλέω to wrap round.

περι-ειλίσσω = περιελίσσω.

περί-ειμι[1] (-ιέναι) = περιέρχομαι.

περί-ειμι[2] (-εῖναι) to be around; to be superior, to surpass; to result, ensue; to remain, survive, be extant.

περι - είργω to enclose round, fence in, confine.

περι-είρω to file, put together.

περι-έλασις, ἡ a driving round; way round.

περι-ελαύνω to drive or ride round; to push round; to press hard, distress.

περι-ελίσσω to wind or roll round. — M. to wind round oneself.   [or about.]

περι-έλκω to drag round]

περι-έπω to be busy about, to attend to, take care of; to honour, treat (well).

περι-εργάζομαι M. to waste one's labour; to intermeddle.

περί-εργος 2 wasting one's labour; over-careful, over-officious, forward; petty, paltry; interfering.

περι-έργω = περιείργω.

περι-έρχομαι to go round or about, to execute a wheel; to take a round-about way; to travel about or through; to come round to; to come in turn; to elapse; to enclose, surround; to overreach, cheat.

περι-έσχατα, τά outside; circuit.

περι-έχω to hold around, encompass, embrace, surround; to surpass, be superior; to comprehend, hold. — M. to hold fast by, cling to, insist on, protect; to entreat earnestly; to strive after.

περι-ζώννῡμι to gird round.

περι-ηγέομαι M. to lead round.

περι-ήγησις, ἡ outline.

περι-ήκω to have come round; to have arrived at.

περι-ήλυσις, ἡ a coming round; revolution.

περι-ημεκτέω to be much aggrieved or disconcerted.

περι-ηχέω to sound all round.

περί-θεσις, ἡ a putting on.

περι-θέω to run round.

περί-θῡμος 2 very angry.

περι-ίζομαι M. to sit round about.

περι-ίστημι to place or set round; to bring to a certain state; to alter; intr. and M. to stand round about, encircle, surround; to turn out, be changed into, devolve upon; to avoid, shun.

περι-ίσχω to surpass.

περι-κάθαρμα, τό offscouring, offscum.

περι-κάθημαι M., περι-καθίζω to sit down round about; to beleaguer.

περι-καίω to set on fire round about.

περι-καλλής 2 very beautiful.   [round.]

περι-καλύπτω to cover all]

περι-καταρρέω to fall down all round.

περί-κειμαι to lie round, to embrace; to be put round; to be clothed.   [round.]

περι-κείρω to shear all]

περι-κεφαλαίᾱ, ἡ helmet.

περι-κήδομαι M. to be very anxious.

περί-κηλος 2 quite dry.

περι-κλείω, -κλήω, -κλῄω and M. to shut in all round. [round.]

περι-κλύζω to wash all]

περι-κλυτός 3 far-famed, renowned.

περι-κομίζω to carry round. — P. to go round.

περι-κοπή, ἡ mutilation.

περι-κόπτω to cut off, mutilate; to waste, plunder.

περι-κρατής 2 mastering.

περι-κρύπτω to conceal wholly. [about.]

περι-κτείνω to kill round]

περι-κτίων, ονος, περι-κτίτης, ου, ὁ neighbour.

περι-κυκλόω, -έω to encircle. [circling.]

περι-κύκλωσις, ἡ an en-]

περι-λαμβάνω to seize around, embrace; to surround; to comprehend.

περι-λάμπω to shine round about. [περικλυτός.]

περι-λεσχήνευτος 2 =]

περι-λιμνάζω to surround with a marsh.

περί-λοιπος 2 left remaining. [ful.]

περί-λῦπος 2 very sorrow-]

περι-μαιμάω to search thoroughly.

περι-μάρναμαι to fight for or round about.

περι-μάχητος 2 fought for; much desired. [around.]

περι-μάχομαι M. to fight]

περι-μένω to wait, wait for.

περί-μετρος 2 exceedingly large, immense; τὸ περίμετρον circumference.

περι-μήκης 2, -μήκετος 2 very long or high.

περι-μηχανάομαι M. to devise cunningly. [round.]

περι-ναιετάω to dwell]

περι-ναιέτης, ου, ὁ neighbour. [up round.]

περι-νέω, -νηέω to heap]

περι-νεώς, ω, ὁ passenger.

περί-νοια, ἡ overwiseness.

πέριξ adv. and prp. with gen. or acc. round about, all round.

περί-ξεστος 3 polished all round. [round.]

περι-ξυρέω to shear all]

περί-οδος, ἡ a going round, way round, circuit, circumference; periodical return; cycle; period; circuitous way. [περίοικος.]

περί-οικίς, ίδος, fem. of]

περι-οικοδομέω to build round about, to enclose.

περί-οικος 2 dwelling round about, neighbouring; free inhabitant in Laconia.

περι-οπτέος 3 to be regarded, overlooked, or suffered.

περι-οράω to look around for, wait for; to overlook, neglect; to suffer, allow. — M. to wait for; to be anxious (about); to avoid, shun.

περι-οργής 2 very wrathful.

περί-ορθρον, τό dawn.

περι-ορμέω, -ορμίζομαι M. to anchor round.

περι-ορύσσω to dig round.

περι-ουσία, ἡ overplus, residue; abundance, plenty; advantage; superiority.

περι-ούσιος 2 exceeding, excellent.

περι-οχή, ἡ contents.

περι-πατέω to walk about; to lead a life.

περί-πατος, ὁ walk, a walking about; colonnade, hall.

περι-πείρω to pierce or bore through.

περι-πέλομαι M. to move round, revolve; to surround.

περι-πέμπω to send round or about.

περι-πετής 2 falling round, clasping, embracing; piercing; falling in with; reversed.   [(a)round.]

περι-πέτομαι M. to fly)

περι-πευκής very sharp.

περι-πήγνυμαι P. to grow stiff round.

περι-πίμπλημι to fill full.

περι-πίμπρημι to set on fire round about.

περι-πίπτω to fall around, upon, or into; to incur; to fall in with, to meet.

περι-πλανάομαι P. to roam about.

περι-πλέκω to twist round about. — P. to fold oneself round, to cling to.

περι-πλευμονία, ἡ inflammation of the lungs.

περι-πλέω to sail about; to sail round, double.

περι-πλεως 2, περι-πλη-θής 2 quite full; populous.

περίπλοος, -πλους, ὁ a sailing round, circumnavigation.

περι-πλώω = περιπλέω.

περι-ποιέω to make to remain over and above; to save, preserve, protect; to

procure. — M. to save for oneself; to acquire.

περι-ποίησις, ἡ a saving; an acquiring; possession.

περιπόλ-αρχος, ὁ commander of the boundary-watch.   [or about.]

περι-πολέω to go round)

περιπόλιον, τό fort, garrison.

περί-πολος, ὁ, ἡ patrol; boundary-guard; attendant.

περι-ποτάομαι M. = περι-πέτομαι.

περι-πρό adv. advancing (or pushing forward) round about. [poured out round.]

περι-προχέομαι P. to be)

περι-πτύσσω and M. to enfold, enwrap; to surround.

περι-πτυχής 2 enfolding; fallen round.   [cident.]

περί-πτωμα, τό chance, in-)

περι-ρραίνω to besprinkle round. [water vessel.]

περι-ρραντήριον, τό holy-)

περι-ρρέω to flow round; to fall down; to flow abundantly.

περι-ρρήγνυμι to break off round. — P. to be broken or parted all round.

περι-ρρηδής 2 stumbling or reeling over. [round.]

περι-ρροή, ἡ a flowing)

περί-ρροος 2, -ρρυτος 2 surrounded with water, sea-girt.

περι-σθενέω to be overpotent.   [rigid.]

περι-σκελής 2 very hard,)

περι-σκέπτομαι M. to look round; to consider well.

περί-σκεπτος 2 protected around. [σκέπτομαι.]

περι - σκοπέω = περι-

περι-σπάω to draw off from around. — M. to be distracted.

περι-σπερχέω to become alarmed or excited.

περι-σπερχής 2 hasty.

περι-σσαίνω to wag the tail round one.

περισσεϊά, ἡ = περίσσευμα.

περι-σσείομαι P. to wave or float about.

περίσσευμα, τό abundance, plenty; remnant.

περισσεύω to be over and above; to be too many for; to have more than enough; to grow, excel; to shower upon, enrich.

περισσός 3 above measure, more than enough; extraordinary, unusual, strange, monstrous; excellent; superfluous, excessive; useless; exaggerated; remaining, over; odd (numbers). τὸ περισσόν surplus, residue.

περισσότης, ητος, ἡ oddness (of numbers).

περι-σταδόν adv. standing round about.

περι-σταυρόω to palisade around. — M. to fortify oneself with a palisade.

περι-στείχω to step around.

περι-στέλλω to dress, manage, perform round; to take care of, protect; to clothe and bury a corpse; to cover, wrap in.

περι-στεναχίζομαι M. to resound around.

περι-στένω to cram full all around.

περιστερά, ἡ pigeon, dove.

περι-στεφανόω to surround with a crown.

περι-στεφής 2 crowned round. [φανόω.]

περι-στέφω = περιστε-

περι-στίζω to stick round with; to place round in a row.

περι-στοιχίζω and M. to net in, surround with snares.

περι-στρατοπεδεύω and M. to encamp about, beleaguer.

περι-στρέφω to whirl or spin round. — P. to be turned round.

περι-στρωφάομαι M. to go round. [all round.]

περί-στῦλος 2 with pillars

περι-σῦλάω to rob entirely.

περι-σφύριον, τό anklet.

περι-σχίζω to cleave all round. — P. to be split or divided. [death.]

περι-σῴζω to save from

περι-τάμνω = -τέμνω.

περι-τείνω to stretch all round.

περι-τειχίζω to wall all round, fortify; to beleaguer.

περι - τείχισις, ἡ, περιτείχισμα, τό, περι-τειχισμός, ὁ a walling round, circumvallation, blockade.

περι-τέλλομαι M. to run round, revolve.

περι-τέμνω to cut round, to cut off, to intercept; to rob. — M. to rob. — P. to be cut off.

περι-τέχνησις, ἡ cunning.

περι-τίθημι to put or place round about; to put on; to confer upon, invest with. — M. to put round oneself.

περι-τίλλω to pluck round.

περι-τομή, ἡ circumcision.

περι-τρέπω to turn round about or upside down, destroy. *intr.* and *P.* to go round. [geal round about.]

περι-τρέφομαι *P.* to con-

περι-τρέχω to run round; to run round about; to run through, to discuss.

περι-τρέω, περι-τρομέομαι *M.* to tremble round about.

περι-τροπέω = περιτρέπω.

περι-τροπή, ἡ total change, revolution.

περι-τρόχαλος 2, περί-τροχος 2 round.

περι-τυγχάνω to fall in with, meet by chance, encounter, light upon.

περι-υβρίζω to insult wantonly, to ill-treat.

περι-φαίνομαι *P.* to be visible all round. [ledge.]

περι-φάνεια, ἡ full know-

περι-φανής 2, περι-φαντος 2 seen all round, manifest; famous, excellent.

περι-φέρω to carry round or about; to move or drive round in a circle; to carry or bring to; to divulge; to endure.— *P.* to move round, revolve; to wander about.

περι-φεύγω to flee from.

περι-φλεύω to burn all round. [fied.]

περί-φοβος 2 much terri-

περι-φορά, ἡ a carrying round; revolution, circuit.

περι-φορητός 3 carried round.

περι-φραδής 2 very thoughtful, cautious.

περι-φράζομαι *M.* to consider carefully.

περι-φρονέω to despise.

περι-φρουρέω to guard on all sides.

περί-φρων 2 = περιφραδής.

περι-φύομαι *M.* to grow all round; to cling to.

περι-χαρής 2 highly rejoiced, exceedingly glad.

περι-χέω to pour round about, over, or upon.— *P.* to surround, be spread all round. [over.]

περι-χρῡσόω to gild all

περι-χώομαι *M.* to be in high wrath.

περι-χωρέω to go round; to pass over to.

περί-χωρος 2 surrounding, neighbouring.

περί-ψημα, τό an offscouring, offscum. [all round.]

περι-ψιλόω to make bald

περι-ώδυνος 2 very painful.

περι-ωθέω to thrust about; to expel; to vex.

περι-ωπή, ἡ circumspection, look-out, caution.

περι-ώσιος 2 immense.

περκνός 3 dark-coloured.

πέρνημι to sell.

περονάω to pierce. — *M.* to pin with a brooch.

περόνη, περονίς, ίδος, ἡ brooch, clasp. [boast.]

περπερεύομαι to brag,

περσίζω — — πῖαρ

περσίζω to imitate the Persians.

περσιστί *adv.* in the Persian language, in Persian.

πέρυσι *adv.* last year.

περυσινός 3 of last year.

περ-φερέες, οἱ escorters.

πέσημα, τό a falling.

πεσσεία, ἡ game at draughts.

πεσσεύω to play at draughts.

πεσσός, ὁ game at draughts, and stone for it.

πέσσω to make soft or ripe; to boil, cook; to digest.

πέταλον, τό leaf; tablet.

πετάννῡμι to spread out, unfold.　　[= πτηνός.]

πετεεινός 3, πετεηνός 3]

πέτομαι *M.* to fly, dart, rush; to escape.

πέτρᾱ, ἡ rock, crag; stone.

πετραῖος 3, πετρήεις 3, πετρήρης 2, πέτρινος 3 rocky; living among the rocks.

πετρο-βολία, ἡ a stoning.

πετρο-βόλος 2 throwing stones.

πέτρος, ὁ = πέτρα.

πετρώδης 2 = πετραῖος.

πεύθομαι *M.* = πυνθάνομαι.　　[prudent.]

πευκάλιμος 3 sensible,]

πευκεδανός 3 bitter, destructive.

πεύκη, ἡ fir; torch.

πευκήεις 3, πεύκινος 3 of fir-wood.

πῇ, πῆ *adv.* which way? where? how? why?

πή, πή *adv.* anyway; somewhere; somehow.

πήγανον, τό rue.　[fleeced.]

πηγεσί-μαλλος 2 thick-]

πηγή, ἡ spring, well, source; fount.

πήγνῡμι to stick, fix, make firm, plant; to harden, to cause to congeal or freeze. *intr.* and *P.* to be fixed, stiff, or frozen, to congeal.

πηγός 3 strong, stout.

πηγυλίς, ίδος icy.

πηδάλιον, τό rudder.

πηδάω to spring, leap, dart, rush, fly; to throb.

πήδημα, τό a leaping.

πηδόν, τό blade of an oar.

πηκτίς, ίδος, ἡ Lydian harp.

πηκτός fixed in; compact.

πήληξ, ηκος, ἡ helmet.

πηλίκος 3 how great, much, or old?　　[doll.]

πήλινος 3 of clay; earthen]

πηλός, ὁ clay, loam; mud.

πηλώδης 2 like clay; muddy.

πῆμα, τό a suffering; misery, harm.

πημαίνω to make suffer, to hurt, grieve, ruin, injure.

πημονή, ἡ = πῆμα.　[time?]

πηνίκα *adv.* at what day-]

πηνίον, τό shuttle.

πηός, ὁ related by marriage.

πήρᾱ, ἡ wallet.　[blind.]

πηρός 3 maimed, lame;]

πηρόω to maim, lame.

πηχυαῖος 3, πήχυιος 3 a cubit long.

πῆχυς, εως, ὁ fore-arm; cubit; middle of a bow; side of a lyre.

πιάζω = πιέζω.

πιαίνω to fatten.

πῖαρ, τό fat, tallow.

πίδαξ, ακος, ἡ spring, fountain.

πῖδήεις 3 rich in springs.

πιεζέω, πιέζω to press, squeeze; to apprehend, arrest; to trouble.

πίειρα *fem.* of πίων.

πιθανο-λογία, ἡ gift of persuasion.

πιθανός 3 persuading, persuasive, winning; plausible, credible, likely; obedient, true.

πιθέω to obey.

πίθηκος, ὁ ape.

πιθηκο-φαγέω to eat ape's flesh.   [vessel.]

πίθος, ὁ tub, cask; earthen

πικραίνω to make bitter. — *P.* to grow angry.

πικρία, ἡ bitterness; irritation, malice.   [married.]

πικρό-γαμος 2 unhappily

πικρός 3 piercing, keen; sharp, bitter; harsh, cruel, severe, stern; morose; repugnant, odious, hateful.

πικρότης, ητος, ἡ = πικρία.

πίλναμαι to approach.

πίλος, ὁ felt; felt-hat; felt-covering; felt-cuirass.

πιμελή, ἡ fat.

πιμπλάνω, πίμπλημι to fill (up). — *P.* to be or become full, to be filled or satisfied.

πίμπρημι = πρήθω.

πινάκιον, τό, πίναξ, ακος, ὁ board; trencher; plate; table; tablet; map; painting; drawing.

πίνος, ὁ dirt, filth.

πινύσκω to make prudent.

πινυτή, ἡ prudence.

πινυτός 3 prudent, wise.

πίνω to drink.

πιότης, ητος, ἡ fatness.

πιπράσκω, πιπρήσκω to sell; to betray.

πίπτω to fall, fall down; to be thrown down; to fail, err, sin; to rush upon, attack; to sink down; to be killed; to turn out, happen.

πῖσος, τό meadow.

πίσσα, ἡ pitch.   [lief.]

πιστευτικός deserving be-

πιστεύω to believe, trust in, put faith in, confide in; to entrust, to give one credit for. — *P.* to be believed or trusted.

πιστικός 3 = πιθανός.

πίστις, ἡ trust, faith, belief; faithfulness, honesty; credit, trust, security, assurance, pledge of faith, warrant, oath; treaty; hostage; argument, proof.

πιστός 3 faithful, trusty, sure, trustworthy, credible; believing, relying on; τὸ πιστόν = πίστις.

πιστότης, ητος, ἡ faithfulness.

πιστόω to make faithful or trustworthy. — *P.* to have confidence, to trust in; to pledge oneself. — *M.* to give one another pledges; to bind one by oaths.

πίσυνος 2 confiding in.

πίσυρες, α four.   [τάννυμι.]

πιτνάω, πίτνημι = πε-

πίτνω = πίπτω.

πίτῦρα, τά bran.

20*

πίτυς, υος, ἡ pine-tree.

πιφαύσκω and M. to let appear; to show, make known, declare.

πίων, πῖον, πίονος fat, plump; fertile; rich, wealthy; plentiful.

πλᾱγά, ἡ = πληγή.

πλάγιος 3 slanting, sideways; τὸ πλάγιον side, flank.

πλαγκτός 3 wandering, roaming; mad, insane; striking. [ing.)

πλαγκτοσύνη, ἡ a wander-)

πλάζω to strike; to beat back; to drive away, out of the course; to mislead. — P. to wander, go astray; to glance off.

πλάϑω to approach.

πλαίσιον, τό square.

πλακοῦς, οῦντος, ὁ cake.

πλανάω, -έω to lead astray; to deceive. — P. to go astray, wander; to wander in mind, be at a loss.

πλάνη, ἡ, πλάνημα, τό a wandering, going astray; error; perverseness.

πλάνης, ητος, πλανήτης, ου wandering, roaming; vagabond.

πλάνησις, ἡ = πλάνη.

πλάνος 2 wandering; deceiving; vagabond.

πλάξ, ακός, ἡ table, plain; table-land, flat land.

πλάσμα, τό image, figure, plastic work, imagery; fiction, forgery.

πλάσσω to form, mould, shape, fabricate; to forge.

— M. to invent for oneself; to feign. [sculptor.)

πλάστης, ου, ὁ modeller;)

πλαστός 3 formed, moulded; forged, invented.

πλάτανος, πλατάνιστος, ἡ plane-tree.

πλατεῖα, ἡ street.

πλάτη, ἡ blade of an oar, oar; ship.

πλάτος, τό breadth; plain.

πλατύνω to make broad, widen. [broad.)

πλατύς[1] 3 flat, level; wide,)

πλατύς[2] 3 salt, brackish.

πλέγμα, τό plaited work.

πλεϑριαῖος 3 of the size of a plethron.

πλέϑρον, τό a measure of length (100 feet); square measure, acre.

πλεῖος 3 = πλέως.

πλειστάκις adv. most times.

πλεκτός 3 plaited, twisted.

πλέκω to plait, twist; to devise, contrive.

πλεονάζω to be more than enough; to claim too much, to presume on; to grow, increase; to exaggerate.

πλεονάκις adv. more frequently.

πλεον-εκτέω to have more, to claim more, be greedy; to be superior, gain some advantage, overreach.

πλεονέκτημα, τό = πλεονεξία.

πλεον-έκτης, ου, πλεον-εκτικός 3 greedy, grasping; selfish.

πλεον-εξία, ἡ advantage, gain; superiority; greediness, grasping temper, arrogance.

πλέος 3 = πλέως or πλήρης.

πλεύμων, ονος, ὁ = πνεύμων.

πλευρά, ἡ rib; side; flank.

πλευρο-κοπέω to smite or break the ribs.

πλευρόν, τό = πλευρά.

πλέω to sail, go by sea; to swim.

πλέως, ᾶ, ων = πλήρης.

πληγή, ἡ, πλῆγμα, τό blow, stroke; wound; a drubbing; shock.

πλῆθος, τό mass, throng, crowd; the greater part, multitude; the people, mob; army; democracy; size, length, magnitude.

πληθύνω to make full, increase; intr. = πληθύω.

πληθύς ύος, ἡ = πλῆθος.

πληθύω and P., πλήθω to be or become full, to abound, spread, swell.   [satiety.)

πληθώρη, ἡ abundance;)

πλήκτης, ου, ὁ a striker; an abuser.   [scuffle.)

πληκτίζομαι M. to fight,)

πλῆκτρον, τό plectrum (instrument for striking the lyre); punting-pole.

πλημ-μέλεια, ἡ mistake, fault; offence.   [fend.)

πλημ-μελέω to err; to of-)

πλημ-μελής 2 making a false note; erring; offending.

πλημμυρίς, ἡ, πλημυρίς, ίδος, ἡ flood.

πλήμνη, ἡ nave of a wheel.

πλήν adv. and prp. with gen. more than; except; besides, however.

πλήξ-ιππος 2 driving or working horses.

πλήρης 2 full, filled with; well provided; satisfied, satiated; complete.

πληρο-φορέω to fill up, to fulfil; to assure, persuade fully.

πληρο-φορία, ἡ fulness; full conviction.

πληρόω to make full, fill; to man; to complete, supply; to satiate; to perform.

πλήρωμα, τό, πλήρωσις, ἡ a filling up; manning; complement; crew, equipment; satiety, fulness; whole sum.

πλησιάζω to approach; to converse, associate with.

πλησίος 3 near, close by; ὁ πλ. neighbour, fellow-man; adv. πλησίον near, hard by.

πλησιό-χωρος 2 neighbouring; neighbour.

πλησ-ίστιος 2 swelling the sails.   [pletion.)

πλησμονή, ἡ satiety, re-)

πλήσσω to strike, smite, beat, hit; to wound; to strike back, drive away; to frighten, trouble. — M. to beat oneself.

πλινθεύω to make into bricks; to make bricks; to build of bricks.

πλινθηδόν, adv. in the shape of bricks.

πλίνθινος 3 of bricks.

πλινθίον, τό small brick.

πλίνθος, ἡ brick.

πλίσσομαι M. to stride.

πλοῖον, τό ship, vessel.

πλόκαμος, ὁ, πλόκος, ὁ braid, lock of hair.

πλόος, πλοῦς, ὁ voyage; time or wind for sailing.

πλούσιος 3 rich, wealthy; noble.

πλουτέω to be rich.

πλουτίζω to enrich.

πλουτο-κρατίᾱ, ἡ government of the wealthy.

πλοῦτος, ὁ wealth, riches; treasure, plenty; power.

πλοχμός, ὁ = πλόκαμος.

πλυνός, ὁ washing-pit.

Πλυντήρια, τά washing-festival.

πλύνω to wash, cleanse.

πλωΐζω to sail on the sea.

πλώϊμος 2, πλώσιμος 2, πλωτός 3 navigable; sea-worthy; floating.

πλώω = πλέω.

πνείω = πνέω.

πνεῦμα, τό wind, air; breath; life, spirit, mind; inspiration; ghost, spiritual being, Holy Ghost. [divine.]

πνευματικός 3 spiritual;/

πνεύμων, ονος, ὁ the lungs.

πνέω to blow, breathe; to exhale, smell; to pant. — P. to be prudent or wise; to be souled.

πνιγηρός 3 stifling, hot.

πνῖγος, τό stifling heat.

πνίγω to stifle, choke, throttle; to stew. — P. to be drowned.

πνικτός 3 stifled, strangled.

πνοή, πνοιή, ἡ = πνεῦμα.

πόα, ἡ grass, fodder; meadow; summer.

ποδ-αβρός 2 tender-footed.

ποδ-ᾱγός, ὁ guide.

ποδα-νιπτήρ, ῆρος, ὁ basin for washing the feet.

ποδά-νιπτρον, τό water for washing the feet.

ποδ-απός 3 of what country?

ποδ-άρκης 2 swift-footed.

ποδεών, ῶνος, ὁ end, extremity.

ποδ-ηγός 2 = ποδαγός.

ποδ-ηνεκής 2 reaching to the feet. [wind.)

ποδ-ήνεμος 2 swift as the/

ποδ-ήρης 2 = ποδηνεκής.

ποδίζω to bind the feet (of).

ποδ-ώκεια, ἡ swiftness of foot.

ποδ-ώκης 2 quick of foot.

ποθεινός 3 longed for, desired.

πόθεν adv. whence? from what place? why? how? where?

ποθέν adv. from anywhere.

ποθέω to long for, desire; to miss.

ποθή, ἡ = πόθος.

πόθι, ποθί = ποῦ, πού.

πόθος, ὁ desire, longing for; regret; want.

ποῖ, ποί = πῇ, πή.

ποίᾱ, ἡ = πόα.

ποιέω to make, do, produce, bring about, effect, cause; to perform, build, accomplish, execute; to create, beget; to compose, write, represent in poetry; to be active. — M. to make for oneself; to hold, reckon, esteem.

ποίη, ἡ = πόα. [grass.)

ποιήεις 3 grassy, rich in/

ποίημα, τό work, piece of workmanship; instrument; poem. book.

ποίησις, ἡ a making. creating; poetry, poem.

ποιητής, οῦ, ὁ maker, creator; poet.

ποιητικός 3 capable of making, productive; poetical. [well made.]

ποιητός 3 made, fabricated;

ποιη-φαγέω to eat grass.

ποικιλία, ἡ a being party-coloured or variegated; embroidery.

ποικίλλω to variegate, colour; to embroider; to work artificially; to be captious.

ποίκιλμα, τό = ποικιλία.

ποικιλο-μήτης, ου full of various devices.

ποικίλος 3 party-coloured, pied, dappled. worked in various colours; changeful, various, varying, variegated; intricate, ambiguous; cunning.

ποικιλό-στολος 2 with variegated robe. [riddles.]

ποικιλ-φδός 2 singing

ποιμαίνω to be a shepherd; to keep or feed a flock; to guide, govern; to tend. — P. to graze. [ruler.]

ποιμήν, ένος, ὁ shepherd;

ποίμνη, ἡ flock, herd.

ποιμνήϊος 3 of a flock or herd.

ποίμνιον, τό = ποίμνη.

ποινή, ἡ ransom, wergild; requital, vengeance; penalty, punishment. [punishing.]

ποίνιμος 2 avenging,

ποῖος 3 of what nature? of what kind?

ποιπνύω to pant, gasp; to hasten, bustle.

ποιώδης 2 = ποιήεις.

πόκος, ὁ shorn-off wool, fleece, tuft of wool.

πολεμαρχεῖον, τό residence of a polemarch. [march.]

πολεμαρχέω to be a pole-

πολεμ-αρχίᾱ, ἡ office of a polemarch.

πολέμ-αρχος, ὁ leader in war, polemarch.

πολεμέω to make war; to wage war with.

πολεμήϊος 3 = πολεμικός.

πολεμησείω to wish for war.

πολεμίζω = πολεμέω.

πολεμικός 3, πολέμιος 3 of or for war, warlike, hostile; ὁ π. enemy, adversary; ἡ πολεμική art of war; τὸ πολεμικόν signal for battle; τὰ πολεμικά, πολέμια matters of war, hostilities.

πολεμιστής, οῦ, ὁ warrior.

πολεμόνδε adv. to the war.

πολεμο-ποιέω to cause war.

πόλεμος, ὁ war, fight, battle.

πολεμόω to make hostile. — M. to make one an enemy. — P. to be made an enemy.

πολεύω to turn up; to wander about. [the city.]

πολιάς, άδος, ἡ guardian of

πολίζω to found, build a city.

πολιήτης, ου, ὁ = πολίτης.

πόλιν-δε adv. to the city.

πολιο-κρόταφος 2 with gray hair on the temples.

πολιορκέω to besiege, beleaguer; to harrass, vex.

πολιορκία, ἡ siege.

πολιός 3 gray, white.

πολιοῦχος 2 town-protecting.

πόλις, ἡ city, town; citadel; country, state, republic; body of citizens.

πόλισμα, τό = πόλις.

πολίτ-άρχης, ου, ὁ ruler of the city or state.

πολιτεία, ἡ, πολίτευμα, τό right of a citizen, citizenship; life of a citizen; government, administration; policy, constitution; democracy; commonwealth.

πολιτεύω to be a citizen, live in a free state, to have a certain form of government; to administer public affairs — M. and P. to govern, administer; to be a statesman; = Akt. — P. to be governed.

πολίτης, ου, ὁ citizen; fellow-citizen.

πολιτικός 3 of or for a citizen; constitutional, civil, politic, public; ὁ. π. statesman; ἡ -ή science of politics. [tizen.]

πολῖτις, ιδος, ἡ female citizen.

πολίχνη, ἡ small town.

πολλάκις adv. many times, often.

πολλα-πλάσιος 3, πολλαπλασίων 2 many times as many. [many ways.]

πολλαχῇ, -ῆ adv. often;

πολλαχόθεν adv. from many places. [sides.]

πολλαχόσε adv. to many

πολλαχοῦ = πολλαχῇ.

πολλός 2 = πολύς.

πολλοστός 3 little, slight.

πόλος, ὁ axis, pole; firmament; sundial.

πολυ-αινος 2 much-praised;

πολυ-άϊξ, ικος impetuous.

πολυ-ανδρέω to be populous. [soming.]

πολυ-ανθής 2 much-blos-

πολυ-ανθρωπία, ἡ multitude of people.

πολυ-άνθρωπος 2 populous. [silver.]

πολυ-άργυρος 2 rich in

πολυ-άρητος 2 much prayed for.

πολυ-αρκής 2 sufficient.

πολυ-άρματος 2 with many chariots. [flocks.]

πολύ-αρνι (dat.) with many

πολυ-αρχία, ἡ polyarchy, government of many.

πολυ-βενθής 2 very deep.

πολύ-βουλος 2 rich in counsel. [cattle.]

πολυ-βούτης, ου rich in

πολυ-γηθής 2 very glad.

πολύ-γλωσσος 2 with many tongues; slanderous.

πολυ-γονία, ἡ prolificacy.

πολύ-γονος 2 prolific.

πολυ-δαίδαλος 2 very skilful.

πολυ-δάκρυος, -δάκρυτος, πολύδακρυς 2 muchwept; much-weeping.

πολυ-δειράς, άδος with many summits. [trees.]

πολύ-δενδρος 2 with many

πολύ-δεσμος 2 with many bands.

πολυ-δίψιος 2 waterless.

πολυ-δωρος 2 well-dowered.

πολύ-ειδής 2 of many shapes. [sired.]

πολύ-ευκτος 2 much desired.

πολύ-ζηλος 2 much beloved; full of envy.

πολύ-ζυγος 2 with many benches. [in crowds.]

πολυ-ηγερής 2 assembled

πολυ-ήρατος 2 lovely.

πολυ-ηχής 2 much resounding.

πολυ-θαρσής 2 very bold.

πολυ-θρύλητος 2 much spoken of, notorious.

πολύ-θυτος 2 with many sacrifices. [knowledge.]

πολυ-ιδρείη, ἡ extensive

πολυ-ίδρις, ιος rich in knowledge, knowing much.

πολύ-ιππος 2 rich in horses.

πολυ-καγχής 3 very dry or parched.

πολυ-καρπίᾱ, ἡ rich crop.

πολύ-καρπος 2 rich in fruit. [ning.]

πολυ-κέρδεια, ἡ much cun-

πολυ-κερδής 2 crafty.

πολύ-κερως, ων of many horned beasts.

πολύ-κεστος 2 richly embroidered. [ful.]

πολυ-κηδής 2 very sorrow-

πολυ-κλήϊς, ῐδος, -κληΐς, ῐδος with many oars.

πολύ-κληρος 2 with large inheritance.

πολύ-κλητος 2 called from many sides. [washed.]

πολύ-κλυστος 2 much

πολύ-κμητος 2 wrought with much toil.

πολύ-κνημος - with many glens. [many.]

πολύ-κοινος 2 common to

πολυ-κοιρανίᾱ, ἡ rule of many. [thy.]

πολυ-κτήμων 2 very weal-

πολύ-κωπος 2 with many oars. [cornfields.]

πολυ-λήϊος 2 with many

πολύ-λλιστος 2 much implored. [ing.]

πολυ-λογίᾱ, ἡ much speak-

πολυ-λόγος 2 talkative.

πολυ-μαθής 2 knowing much. [ways.]

πολυ-μερῶς adv. in many

πολυ-μηκάς, άδος muchbleating.

πολύ-μηλος 2 rich in flocks.

πολύ-μητις, ιος of many counsels. [tiveness.]

πολυ-μηχανίᾱ, ἡ inven-

πολυ-μήχανος 2 inventive.

πολύ-μνηστος 2 much wooed. [toil.]

πολύ-μοχθος 2 with much

πολύ-μῦθος 2 talkative.

πολύ-ξενος 2 very hospitable; visited by many.

πολύ-ξεστος 2 much polished.

πολύ-οινος 2 rich in wine.

πολυ-οφίᾱ, ἡ abundance of meat or food. [cunning.]

πολύ-παιπαλος 2 crafty,

πολυ-πάμων 2 wealthy; much suffering. [perience.]

πολυ-πειρίᾱ, ἡ much ex-

πολυ-πενθής 2 very mournful. [many springs.]

πολυ-πῐδαξ, ακος with

πολύ-πικρος 2 very bitter or keen.

πολύ-πλαγκτος 2, πολυπλάνητος much-wandering. [intricate.]

πολύ-πλοκος 2 tangled,]

πολύ-ποίκιλος 2 much-variegated. [painful.]

πολύ-πονος 2 laborious,]

πολύ-πους, -ποδος many-footed; sea-polypus.

πολύ-πραγμονέω to be very busy; to be meddlesome or officious; to intrigue.

πολυ-πραγμοσύνη, ή a being busy with many things; a meddling, over-curiousness; quarrelsomeness.

πολύ-πράγμων 2 busy with many things; meddling, officious, curious; quarrelsome. [sheep.]

πολυ πρόβατος 2 rich in]

πολύ-πτυχος 2 with many valleys.

πολύ-πῡρος 2 rich in wheat.

πολύ-ρραφος 2 much-stitched.

πολύ-ρρην, ηνος, -ρρηνος 2 rich in flocks. [ing.]

πολύ-ρρυτος 2 much-flow-]

πολύς, πολλή, πολύ much, many, frequent; large, ample, spacious, long: heavy, strong, mighty; οἱ πολλοί the majority, the many. — Adv. πολύ, πολλά much, very; often; far, by far; very much. — Comp. πλείων, πλέων 2 more, more numerous; larger, stronger; οἱ πλείονες the greater part, majority; the democrats; τὸ πλέον to greater part, advantage, profit.— Superl. πλεῖστος 3 most, very much, οἱ πλεῖστοι the greatest number.

πολυ-σαρκία, ή fleshiness.

πολυ-σῑτίᾱ, ή abundance of corn.

πολύ-σκαρθμος 2 much-springing, swift. [spread.]

πολυ-σπερής 2 widely]

πολύ-σπλαγχνος 2 very compassionate. [grapes.]

πολυ-στάφυλος 2 rich in]

πολυ-στεφής 2 with many wreaths. [ing.]

πολύ-στονος 2 much sigh-]

πολύ-σχιστος 2 much-split.

πολυ-τέλεια, ή great expense, sumptiousness.

πολυ-τελής 2 costly, expensive, sumptuous.

πολυ-τίμητος, πολύ-τῑμος, πολύ-τῑτος 2 much valued, costly.

πολύ-τλᾱς, αντος, πολυτλήμων 2 much-enduring, persevering.

πολύ-τλητος 2 unfortunate.

πολυ-τρήρων 2 with many doves. [porous.]

πολύ-τρητος 2 full of holes,]

πολυ-τροπίᾱ, ή versatility.

πολύ-τροπος 2 versatile, ingenious; crafty; manifold; much wandering.

πολυ-φάρμακος 2 knowing many drugs.

πολύ-φημος 2 with many voices; much talked of.

πολύ-φθορος 2 full of destruction.

πολύ-φλοισβος 2 loud-roaring. [many.]

πολύ-φορβος nourishing.

πολυ-φροσύνη, ἡ great understanding. [ingenious.]

πολύ-φρων 2 very wise,

πολύ-χαλκος 2 rich in copper. [handed.]

πολύ-χειρ, ειρος many-

πολυ-χειρία, ἡ plenty of hands. [long.]

πολυ-χρόνιος 2 lasting.

πολύ-χρῦσος 2 rich in gold.

πολυ-ψηφία, ἡ majority of votes.

πολυ-ψήφῐς, ῐδος with many pebbles. [names; famous.]

πολυ-ώνυμος 2 with many

πολυ-ωπός 2 close-meshed.

πόμα, τό drink.

πομπαῖος 3 escorting.

πομπεία, ἡ jeering, buffoonery.

πομπεύς, ὁ = πομπός.

πομπεύω to conduct, escort, attend; to lead a procession; to jeer.

πομπή, ἡ a sending, an escorting, conduct, escort; a sending home; solemn procession; intervention.

πόμπιμος 2 = πομπαῖος; sent.

πομπός, ὁ, ἡ one who escorts, guide; mess nger.

πονέω and M. to toil, work hard, to be busy; to be worn out, to suffer, be distressed, feel pain; trans. to work at, perform zealously; to gain by toil.

πονηρία, ἡ badness, wickedness

πονηρός 3 bad, wicked, villanous; useless, ill, distressed, painful, dangerous.

πόνος, ὁ toil, drudgery, hard work, hardship: battle; distress, pain, suffering, grief, misery; result of labour, work.

ποντίζω to plunge into the sea. [lord of the sea.]

πόντιος 3 of or in the sea;

ποντόθεν adv. from the sea.

πόντονδε adv. into the sea.

ποντο-πορεύω, -έω to pass over the sea.

ποντο-πόρος 2 sea-faring.

πόντος, ὁ open sea.

πόποι int. ah! woe! shame!

πόρδαλις = πάρδαλις.

πορεία, ἡ journey, march, way, expedition; a walking, gait; manner of life.

πορεῖν aor. (of πόρω) to bring, give, offer, bestow, grant; πέπρωται it has been fated, or allotted.

πορεύω to bring, carry, convey, furnish. — P. to be carried; to go, walk, march, travel; to pass over, traverse. [plunder.]

πορθέω to destroy, waste,

πορθμεῖον, τό ferry, ford; passenger's fare.

πορθμεύς, ὁ ferryman.

πορθμεύω to carry or ferry over; intr. and P. to be carried over. [strait; ferry.]

πορθμός, ὁ passage; ford,

πορίζω to bring, conduct, convey; to furnish, provide, supply; to contrive, fabricate. — M. to get for oneself, procure; to provide from one's own means.

πόριμος 2 rich in resources; inventive.

πόρις = πόρτις.

πορισμός, ὁ means of acquiring.

ποριστής, οῦ, ὁ provider, purveyor; adviser. [cure.]

ποριστικός 3 able to procure.

πόρκης, ου, ὁ ring, ferrule.

πορνεία, ἡ fornication; idolatry.

πορνεύω and M. to fornicate.

πόρνη, ἡ harlot.

πόρνος, ὁ fornicator.

πόρος, ὁ passage; ford, strait, bridge, thoroughfare, way for ships; sea, river; means of achieving, resource, income, revenue.

πόρπαξ, ἄκος, ὁ handle.

πόρπη, ἡ pin, clasp, brooch.

πόρρω, adv. and prp. with gen. forwards, onwards, further; far off, afar; before, in future; far towards; far from; far into.

πόρρωθεν adv. from afar; from long ago.

πορσαίνω, πορσύνω to make ready, provide, procure; to offer, present, give.

πόρσω = πόρρω.

πόρταξ, ακος, ἡ, πόρτις, ἡ heifer, calf.

πορφύρα, ἡ purple, purplefish; purple cloth.

πορφύρεος, -οῦς 3 purple, purple-coloured; dark-red, bloody; bright, shining.

πορφυρεύς, ὁ fisher for purple-fish; purple-dyer.

πορφυρό-πωλις, ιδος, ἡ dealer in purple.

πορφύρω to wave, heave, be agitated.

ποσάκις adv. how often?

πόσε adv. whither?

πόσις[1], ἡ a drinking; drink; drinking-bout.

πόσις[2], ὁ husband.

πόσος 3 how much? how great?

ποσσ-ῆμαρ, adv. how many days? [the feet.]

ποσσί-κροτος 2 beaten by]

πόστος 3 which of a number? [unheard of.]

ποταίνιος 2 new, fresh;]

ποτάμιος 3 of or on a river.

ποταμόνδε adv. into the river. [canal.]

ποταμός, ὁ river, stream;]

ποταμο-φόρητος 2 carried away by a river.

ποτάομαι P. to fly, flit.

ποταπός 3 = ποδαπός.

πότε adv. when?

ποτέ adv. at any time, once; sometimes; perhaps.

ποτέομαι = πέτομαι.

πότερος 3 which of the two? either of the two; πότερον... ἤ whether ... or.

ποτέρωθι adv. on which of two sides? [two ways?]

ποτέρως adv. in which of]

ποτέρωσε adv. to which of two sides?

ποτή, ἡ a flying, flight.

ποτήριον, τό drinking-cup.

πότης, ητος, ἡ drink.

ποτητός 3 winged; τὸ π. bird.

ποτί = πρός.

ποτι-βάλλω = προσβάλλω.

ποτίζω to give to drink; to water.   [sweet.]

πότιμος 2 fit to drink;

πότμος, ὁ lot, destiny, fate; misfortune; death.

πότνα, πότνια, ἡ mistress; revered, august.

ποτόν, τό drink, beverage; liquid, water. [ing-bout.]

πότος, ὁ a drinking; drink-

ποτός 3 for drinking.

ποττώς = ποτὶ τώς, πρὸς τούς.   [manner?]

ποῦ adv. where? in what

πού adv. anywhere; at any time; perhaps.

πουλυ-βότειρα, ἡ nourishing many.

πουλύ-πους = πολύπους.

πουλύς, ύ = πολύς.

πούς, ποδός, ὁ foot, hoof, talon; lower corner of a sail, tightening rope; gait, course; race; foot (as a measure).

πρᾶγμα, τό, πρᾶξις, ἡ a doing, deed, execution, transaction; action; fact, occurrence, matter, circumstance; business, task, enterprise; affair, object; condition; difficulty, annoyance, intrigue; reality; public or private affairs, state-affairs, public business, government, politics; matter of consequence; effect, issue, success, profit.

πραγματεία, ἡ employment, business; pursuit, diligent study, diligence; written work, history.

πραγματεύομαι M. and P.

to be busy, pursue a business; to take in hand, to carry on; to execute, accomplish, work out.

πρᾶγος, τό = πρᾶγμα.

πραιτώριον, τό hall of the prætor or governor; encampment of the imperial body-guard.

πρακτικός 3 fit for action or business; active, busy, able, energetic.

πράκτωρ, ορος, ὁ doer, worker; tradesman; tax-collector; beadle; avenger.

πρᾱνής 2 bent forward, head-foremost; down-hill, steep.

πρᾶξις, ἡ = πρᾶγμα.

πρᾶος, πρᾶος, πραεῖα, πρᾶον, πρᾶον soft, mild; gentle, kind, even-tempered; regardless of.

πρᾳότης, ητος, ἡ meekness, mildness, gentleness, patience.

πραπίς, ίδος, ἡ midriff, diaphragm; mind, heart.

πρασιά, ἡ bed in a garden.

πράσιμος 2 for sale.

πράσις, ἡ sale.

πράσσω to pass through; to effect, achieve, do, work; to win, gain; to manage, practise, administer, transact; to mind, intend; to demand, exact (money). — intr. to be in a certain state or condition; to fare. — M. to do or exact for oneself, to earn (money).

πρᾱτός 3 sold.

πραΰνω to soften, soothe.

πραϋ - πάθεια, πραϋτης,
ητος, ἡ = πραότης.
πραῢς 3 = πρᾷος.
πρέμνον, τό butt-end of a
tree, trunk, stump.
πρεπόντως *adv.* fitly, de-
cently, beseemingly.
πρέπω to be conspicuous,
distinguished, or seen, to be
manifest; to resemble; πρέ-
πει it is fitting, it suits or
becomes. [decent, proper.]
πρεπώδης 2 beseeming,
πρέσβα, ἡ aged; august.
πρεσβεία, ἡ primogeniture;
embassy.
πρεσβεῖον, τό privilege;
gift of honour.
πρέσβευσις, ἡ = πρεσβεία.
πρεσβευτής, οῦ, ὁ ambas-
sador.
πρεσβεύω to be older or the
eldest; to take precedence,
be superior, rule over; to
be an ambassador; to send
ambassadors; to honour,
revere, worship; to mediate
as an ambassador. — *M.*
to send ambassadors; to be
an ambassador.
πρεσβυ-γένεια, ἡ the being
first-born.
πρεσβυ-γενής 2 first-born.
πρέσβυς, ὁ old; old man; revered, honoured, mighty;
οἱ πρεσβύτεροι elders, chiefs,
ancestors; οἱ πρέσβεις
ambassadors. [of elders.]
πρεσβυτέριον, τό council
πρεσβύτης, ου, ὁ = πρέσβυς.
πρεσβῦτις, ιδος, ἡ old woman.
πρῆγμα etc. see πρᾶγμα.

πρήθω to sparkle; to blow
out; to swell out; to kindle,
burn.
πρηκτήρ = πράκτωρ.
πρηνής = πρανής.
πρῆξις = πρᾶξις.
πρῆσις = πρᾶσις.
πρήσσω = πράσσω.
πρηστήρ, ῆρος, ὁ flash of
lightning. [place.]
πρητήριον, τό trading-
πρηῦνω, πρηῢς = πρα...
πρίασθαι to buy, purchase.
πρίζω = πρίω.
πρίν *adv.* before, formerly,
first, sooner; ὁ πρίν an-
cient, preceding. *Conj.* before that.
πρῑστός 3 sawn.
πρίω to saw, saw up or asunder; to seize with the teeth,
hold fast.
πρίων, ονος, ὁ saw.
πρό *adv.* and *prp.* with *gen.*
before, in front; beforehand,
sooner; outside; in defence
of, in favour of, for; instead of, in lieu of; in comparison to. [summons.]
προ-άγγελσις, ἡ early
προ-αγορεύω to tell be-
forehand, prophesy, fore-
warn; to publish, proclaim
publicly; to ordain in advance, order, command.
προ-άγω to lead on or forward; to carry forward,
bring on; to induce, per-
suade; to promote, advance;
to go on, advance, proceed,
lead the way.
προ-άγων, ωνος, ὁ preliminary contest; introduction.

προ-αγωνίζομαι *M.* to fight before.

προ-αδικέω to wrong first.

προ-αιδέομαι *P.* to be indebted to or under obligations to one for a favour.

προ-αίρεσις, ἡ free choice; purpose; plan, mode; party, sect.

προ-αιρέω to bring forward; to prefer. — *M.* to choose for oneself, prefer; to intend, purpose

προ-αισθάνομαι *M.* to perceive before, to know beforehand. [beforehand.]

προ-αιτιάομαι *M.* to accuse

προ-ακούω to hear before.

προ-αλής 2 abrupt. [fore.]

προ-αμαρτάνω to sin be-

προ-αμύνομαι *M.* to defend oneself beforehand.

προ-αναβαίνω to go up before. [to sea before.]

προ-ανάγομαι *M.* to put

προ-αναισιμόω, προ-αναλίσκω to spend or use up before.

προ-αναχώρησις, ἡ a going away before. [fore.]

προ-απαντάω to meet be-

προ-απέρχομαι to depart first. [fore.]

προ-αποθνήσκω to die be-

προ-απόλλυμι to destroy before. — *P.* to perish before.

προ-αποπέμπω, προ-αποστέλλω to send away first or before.

προ-αποτρέπομαι *M.* to desist before. [show first.]

προ-αποφαίνομαι *M.* to

προ-αποχωρέω to go away before. [first.]

προ-αρπάζω to snatch up

προ-άστειον, -άστιον, τό suburb, environs.

προ-αύλιον, τό vestibule.

προ-αφικνέομαι *M.* to arrive first or before.

προ-αφίσταμαι *M.* to revolt or fall off before.

προ-βαίνω to step forward, advance, make progress, to go on; to elapse; to grow older; to go before, be superior (to).

προ-βάλλω to throw before, down, or away; to put forward, propose, oppose; to stake, pledge, venture. — *M.* to put before oneself, to hold before oneself as a defence; to use a pretence, allege; to throw away, abandon; to propose for election; to surpass.

πρό-βασις, ἡ cattle.

προβατικός 3 of or for sheep.

προβάτιον, τό little sheep.

πρό-βατον, τό cattle; flock, sheep.

προ-βιβάζω to bring forward; to lead on; to incite beforehand. [vide for.]

προ-βλέπομαι *M.* to pro-

πρό-βλημα, τό projection, cape; guard, defence, shelter, bulwark; armour, spear; excuse, pretext; problem.

προ-βλής, ῆτος projecting; foreland.

πρό-βλητος 2 thrown away.

προ-βλώσκω to come forth (from), go out of.

προ-βοάω to shout before, cry out.

προ-βόλαιος, ὁ spear.

προ-βολή, ἡ, πρό-βολος, ὁ = πρόβλημα; a putting forward (of arms), defence, attack; preliminary impeachment.

προ-βοσκός, ὁ herdsman.

προ-βούλευμα, τό preliminary decree.

προ-βουλεύω to consult, consider before; to form a preliminary decree; to provide for. — M. to consider first.

πρό-βουλος, ὁ preliminary counsellor.   [before.]

προ-βωθέω to come to aid]

προ-γενής 2 born before, old, ancient, aged.

προ-γίγνομαι M. to be born before; to happen before; to come forward, appear.

προ-γιγνώσκω to know or learn beforehand; to decide beforehand.   [ledge.]

πρό-γνωσις, ἡ foreknow-]

πρό-γονος 2 born before, elder; ancestor, forefather.

προ-γράφω to write before; to write in public.

προ-δαῆναι to know before.

προ-δείδω to fear before-hand.

προ-δείκνυμι to show forth, point out; to point before one; to publish beforehand.

προ-δειμαίνω to fear before-hand.   [signifier.]

προ-δέκτωρ, ορος, ὁ pre-]

πρό-δηλος 2 manifest, known to all.

προ-δηλόω to show future things.

προ-διαβαίνω to go across before.   [beforehand.]

προ-διαβάλλω to slander]

προ-διαγιγνώσκω to consider before.

προ-διαφθείρω to destroy or ruin beforehand.

προ-διδάσκω to teach beforehand.

προ-δίδωμι to give or pay in advance; to give up, betray, forsake, abandon; intr. to flee, turn traitor; to fail.

προ-διηγέομαι M. to relate beforehand.

πρό-δικος, ὁ advocate, guardian.   [ther.]

προ-διώκω to pursue fur-]

προ-δοκεῖ, pf. προδέδοκται it was resolved before.

προ-δοκή, ἡ (shooting-) stand, ambush.

πρό-δομος, ὁ fore-house.

προ-δοσιά, ἡ treachery.

προ-δότης, ου, ὁ traitor; runaway.

προ-δοτικός 3 traitorous.

πρό-δοτος 2 betrayed, abandoned.   [ward.]

προ-δρομή, ἡ a running for-]

πρό-δρομος 2 running before, forerunner: scout, vanguard; skirmisher.

προ-εδρίᾱ, ἡ presidency, precedence; first place.

πρό-εδρος, ὁ president.

προ-έργω to obstruct by stepping in the way.

προ-εθίζω to accustom beforehand.   [έρχομαι.]

πρό-ειμι¹ (-ιέναι) = προ-]

πρό-ειμι² (-εῖναι) to be before.

προ-εῖπον see προαγορεύω.

προ-εισάγω to bring in before. [fore.]

προ-εκθέω to run out before.

προ-εκκομίζω to carry out before. [ney in advance.]

προ-εκλέγω to collect mo-

προ-εκφόβησις, ἡ an intimidating beforehand.

προ-ελαύνω intr. and P. to ride forward, advance.

προ-ελπίζω to hope before.

προ-εμβάλλω to make an inroad, attack before.

προ-ενάρχομαι to begin before. [aloud.]

προ-εννέπω to pronounce

προ-ενοίκησις, ἡ a dwelling in before.

προ-εξαγγέλλω to announce beforehand. [first.]

προ-εξάγω to bring out

προ-εξαΐσσω, -ᾴσσω to rush out before.

προ-εξανίστημι intr. and M. to rise before others or too soon: to start first.

προ-εξέδρα, ἡ high seat.

προ-έξειμι, προ-εξέρχομαι to go out before.

προ-εξορμάω to start before.

προ-επαγγέλλω and M. to promise before. [fore.]

προ-επαινέω to praise be-

προ-επανασείω to menace before. [first.]

προ-επιχειρέω to attack

προ-εργάζομαι M. to do or work before; to earn before.

προ-ερέσσω to row forward. [forward.]

προ-ερύω to draw on or

προ-έρχομαι to go forth, on, or forward, advance; to appear in public; to pass; to proceed, start; to go first.

προ-ετικός 3 prodigal.

προ-ετοιμάζω to prepare.

προ-ευαγγελίζομαι M. to bring glad tidings beforehand.

προ-έχω to hold before; to have before; to know beforehand; to have in preference to. intr. to project, jut out; to be before, be the first, superior, eminent; οὐ προέχει it is not better. — M. to hold before oneself, hold out as a pretext; to offer.

προ-ηγεμών, όνος, ὁ guide.

προ-ηγέομαι M. to go before or forward, lead the way; to be the leader.

προ-ηγητής, οῦ, ὁ = προηγεμών. [others.]

προ-ηγορέω to speak for

προ-ήκης 2 pointed in front.

προ-ήκω to have advanced; to be the first or superior.

προ-θέλυμνος 2 having several layers; from the root.

πρό-θεσις, ἡ exhibition, show; purpose, design.

προ-θέσμιος 3 appointed, fixed before; ἡ προθεσμία term, period, limitation.

προ-θέω¹ to run forward.

προ-θέω² = -τίθημι.

προ-θνήσκω to die before.

προ-θρῴσκω to leap forward.

προ-θῡμέομαι P. to be willing, ready, eager, or zealous; to desire, endeavour.

προ-θῡμίᾱ, ἡ willingness, readiness; zeal, wish, desire; good will.

πρό-θῡμος 2 ready, willing; eager, earnest, zealous; well-disposed.

πρό-θυρον, τό front door; space before a door; porch, entry.   [before.]

προ-θύω and M. to sacrifice

προ-ῐάλλω, προ-ῐάπτω to send forth. [first seat.]

προ-ῐζομαι M. to take the

προ-ῐημι to send before, on, or forward; to dismiss, let go; to forsake, abandon, throw away; to deliver over; to allow. — M. to utter, pronounce; to devote oneself (to); to offer, present; to entrust; to allow, suffer; to abandon, throw away, neglect.

προ-ΐκτης, ου, ὁ beggar.

προΐξ, προίξ, προικός, ἡ gift, present; dower: adv. προῖκα, προικός freely, without return.

προ-ΐστημι to place before or in front. — intr. and P. to place oneself before, to stand before; to be opposed to; to protect, guard; to approach, entreat; to be at the head (of), to be set over, be the chief, manage, govern; to place before oneself; to prefer.

προ-ῐσχω = προέχω.

πρόκα adv. at once, suddenly.

προ-κάθημαι M. to sit before; to protect, defend.

προ-καθίζω and M. to sit down before, in front, or in public.

προ-καθίστημι, pf. and M. to be placed before.

προ-καθοράω to view beforehand.

προ-καίω to burn before.

προ-καλέω, προ-καλίζω to call forth. — M. to challenge; to summon, incite, invite; to offer, propose; to cause, effect.

προ-καλινδέομαι = προκυλίνδομαι.

προ-κάλυμμα, τό curtain, covering; screen; pretext.

προ-καλύπτω to hang before as a covering. — M. to veil or screen oneself; to pretend.

προ-κάμνω to toil before; to grow weary beforehand; to work for another.

προ-καταγγέλλω to announce beforehand.

προ-καταγιγνώσκω to accuse or condemn beforehand.   [fore.]

προ-κατακαίω to burn be-

προ-καταλαμβάνω to seize or occupy beforehand, anticipate; to prevent.

προ-καταλέγω to describe beforehand.

προ-καταλύω to break up or annul before.

προ-καταρτίζω to make ready before.

προ-κατάρχομαι *M.* to begin first. [before.]

προ-καταφεύγω to escape]

προ-κατέχω to occupy or take possession of before.

προ-κατηγορέω to accuse beforehand.

προ-κατηγορία, ἡ previous accusation.

πρό-κειμαι *M.* to lie before; to lie exposed; to jut out; to be set before or in front of; to be proposed.

προ-κήδομαι *M.* to take care of.

προ-κηραίνω to be anxious.

προ-κηρύσσω to proclaim publicly.

προ-κινδυνεύω to run the first risk; to fight as a champion; to defend.

προ-κινέω to move forward.

προ-κλαίω to weep beforehand or aloud.

πρό-κλησις, ἡ challenge; summons, proposal.

προ-κλίνω to lean forward.

πρό-κλυτος 2 far-famed.

προ-κομίζω to bring forward. [growth.]

προ-κοπή, ἡ progress,]

προ-κόπτω to promote; *intr.* and *P.* to advance, thrive.

πρό-κριμα, τό preference.

προ-κρίνω to choose before, prefer; to judge, decide. — *P.* to be preferred or thought superior. [in rows.]

πρό-κροσσος 2 and 3 ranged]

προ-κυλίνδομαι, -δέομαι *M.* to be rolled forward; to prostrate oneself.

προ-λαμβάνω to take (away) beforehand, before, or first; to obtain first, anticipate; to claim before, prefer; to apprehend, surprise.

προ-λέγω to foretell, prophesy; to tell publicly, proclaim; to choose before.

προ-λείπω — to leave, forsake; to omit. — *intr.* to cease, disappear.

προ-λεσχηνεύομαι *M.* to discuss orally before.

προ-λεύσσω to see at a distance, foresee.

προ-λοχίζω to lay an ambush before, to beset with an ambush.

προ-μανθάνω to learn before; to continue learning.

προ-μαντεία, ἡ precedence in consulting an oracle.

πρό-μαντις, ὁ, ἡ prophetic; prophet, priest.

προ-μαρτύρομαι *M.* to witness beforehand.

προ-μαχέω, προ-μαχίζω and *M.*, προ-μάχομαι to fight in front or as a champion. [part; bulwark.]

προ-μαχεών, ῶνος, ὁ ram-]

πρό-μαχος fighting before or in front; fighting for.

προ-μελετάω to practise beforehand. [ful before.]

προ-μεριμνάω to be care-]

προ-μετωπίδιον, τό skin of the forehead; front-piece.

προμήθεια, ἡ foresight; care.

προμηθέομαι *P.* to consider or take care (of) beforehand.

21*

προ-μηθής 2 cautious, caring.

προμηθία, ἡ = προμήθεια.

προ-μηνύω to inform beforehand. [beforehand.]

προ-μίγνῦμαι P. to lie with

προ-μνάομαι M. to woo for another; to advise; to presage.

προ-μνηστῖνοι 3 one by one.

προ-μνήστρια, -μνηστρίς, ίδος, ἡ match-maker.

προ-μολεῖν see προβλώσκω.

πρόμος, ὁ foremost, leader, prince; champion.

πρό-νᾶος 2 = προνήϊος.

προ-ναυμαχέω to fight at sea for. [ground.]

προ-νέμομαι M. to gain

προ-νήϊος 3 before a temple; ὁ πρ. vestibule.

προ-νηστεύω to fast beforehand. [forehand.]

προ-νῑκάω to conquer be-

προ-νοέω and P. to perceive beforehand, to presage; to consider, care, or think beforehand; to provide.

προ-νοητικός 3 provident, cautious.

πρό-νοια, ἡ foresight, forethought; providence; purpose, intention; care.

προ-νομή, ἡ a foraging.

πρό-νοος, πρό-νους 2 cautious, prudent. [fawn.]

πρόξ, προκός, ἡ hind-calf,

πρό-ξεινος, ὁ = πρόξενος.

προ-ξενέω to be a public guest; to be a protector or patron; to negotiate, manage, procure; to recommend.

προ-ξενία, ἡ the being a πρόξενος.

πρό-ξενος, ὁ, ἡ public guest or host, agent of a foreign state; patron.

προ-ξυγγίγνομαι M. to meet with beforehand.

πρό-οδος, ἡ a going on, advance.

πρό-οιδα to know before.

προ-οιμιάζομαι M. to make a preamble.

προ-οίμιον, τό prelude, preamble, preface, introduction; hymn; false show.

προ-ομνῦμι to swear before.

προ-ομολογέω to agree beforehand. [manifest.]

πρό-οπτος 2 seen from afar,

προ-οράω to look forward; to see before or from afar; to foresee; to provide for, consider beforehand; to take care, be cautious.

προ-ορίζω to determine beforehand.

προ-ορμάω and P. to start forward or in advance.

προ-ορμίζω to moor in front.

προ-οφείλω to owe from a former time. — P. to be in arrear. [ing.]

πρό-οψις, ἡ a previous see-

πρό-παππος, ὁ greatgrandfather.

προ-παραβάλλομαι M. to put in rows beforehand.

προ-παρασκευάζω to make ready beforehand.

προ-παρέχω to offer before. — M. to provide oneself before.

προ-πάροιθεν adv. and prp. with gen. in front of, before, forward(s); along.

πρό-πᾶς, ᾶσα, ᾶν all; altogether.

προ-πάσχω to suffer before.

προ-πάτωρ, ορος, ὁ forefather, ancestor.

πρό-πειρα, ἡ previous trial.

προ-πέμπω to send before, in advance, on, or forth; to afford, offer; to send away, dismiss; to conduct, escort; to pursue. [impetuosity.]

προ-πέτεια, ἡ rashness,

προ-πετής 2 falling forward(s), prostrate; ready; rash, prone, hasty.

προ-πηλακίζω to cover with mud; to maltreat, abuse, reproach.

προ-πηλακισμός, ὁ insult.

προ-πίνω to drink to; to give or trifle away.

προ-πίπτω, -πίτνω to fall forward; to rush forward; to prostrate oneself.

προ-πλέω to sail before.

πρό-πλοος, -πλους 2 sailing before.

προ-ποδίζω to step forward.

προ-ποιέω to do beforehand; to prepare.

προ-πολεμέω to fight for.

πρό-πολος, ὁ, ἡ servant in a temple, priest, priestess.

προ-πομπός, ὁ, ἡ conductor.

προ-πονέω to work beforehand; to work or toil for. — M. to suffer on.

πρό-πονος, ὁ previous toil.

προ-πορεύομαι P. to go forward.

προ-πρηνής 2 bent forward; lying on one's face.

προπρο-κυλίνδομαι to roll on and on or to and fro.

προ-πύλαιον, πρό-πυλον, τό entry, porch, vestibule.

προ-πυνθάνομαι to learn or hear before.

προ-ρέω to flow forward.

πρό-ῤῥησις, ἡ previous announcement; order.

πρό-ῤῥητος 2 foretold, ordered. [radical.]

πρό-ῤῥιζος 2 by the roots;

πρός adv. besides, over and above. — Prep. with gen. from, from forth, from the side of; on the side of, against, towards; on the part of, in presence of, before; with a passive verb = ὑπό; according to; suiting. — with dat. at, on, near, hard by, in presence of; in addition to, besides. — with acc. towards, to, upon; against, in answer to; in regard to; according to; in proportion to; in comparison of. [the Sabbath.]

προ-σάββατον, τό eve of

προσ-αγορεύω to address, accost, greet; to call by name; to speak, utter.

προσ-άγω to bring on; to lead on, induce; to add, supply, introduce; intr. to advance, approach. — M. to attach to oneself, win over; to induce.

προσ-αγωγή, ἡ a bringing on; admission, access; solemn procession.

προσ-αγωγός 2 attractive.

προσ-ᾴδω to sing to; to agree, consent.

προσ-αιρέομαι *M.* to choose in addition to.

προσ-αΐσσω to rush to.

προσ-αιτέω to ask besides; to beg of. [sides.]

προσ-ακούω to hear be-]

προσ-αλείφω to smear upon. [come to aid.]

προσ-αμύνω to defend,]

προσ-αναβαίνω to mount besides.

προσ-αναγκάζω to force]

προσ-αναιρέομαι *M.* to undertake besides.

προσ-αναισιμόω, προσ-αναλίσκω to spend or consume besides.

προσ-αναπληρόω to fill up by addition.

προσ-ανατίθεμαι *M.* to take on oneself in addition; to consult with; to un-bosom oneself.

προσ-άνειμι to go up to.

προσ-ανειπεῖν to announce besides.

προσ-ανέχω to approach.

προσ-άντης 2 up-hill, steep; arduous, adverse, hostile.

προσ-απαγγέλλω to re-port besides.

προσ-απειλέω to threaten besides.

προσ-αποβάλλω to lose besides. [nounce besides.]

προσ-απογράφω to de-]

προσ-αποδείκνυμι to prove besides.

προσ-απόλλυμι, -ύω to destroy or kill besides. —

intr. and *M.* to perish be-sides. [off besides.]

προσ-αποστέλλω to send]

προσ-άπτω to attach or fasten to; to add, attri-bute, grant; *intr.* to be added. — *M.* to touch, lay hold on. [fit to.]

προσ-αραρίσκω to join,]

προσ-αρκέω to lend aid; to grant, afford.

προσ-αρμόζω to attach, fit to. [join to.]

προσ-αρτάω to fasten,]

προ-σάττω to equip be-forehand. [by name.]

προσ-αυδάω to accost, call]

προσ-αύω to burn partly.

προσ-αφικνέομαι *M.* to arrive besides.

προσ-αφίστημι to cause to revolt besides.

προσ-βαίνω to go towards, up, or to: to come near, to step on: to attack.

προσ-βάλλω to throw to or upon; to apply to, affix; to add, assign; to thrust, hit, shine upon; to offer, pre-sent. — *intr.* and *M.* to throw oneself upon; to ap-proach, attack; to come to land; to strike against; to contribute. [cent.]

πρόσ-βασις, ἡ access, as-]

προσ-βατός 3 accessible.

προσ-βιάζομαι *P.* to be pressed towards.

προσ-βιβάζω to bring or convey to.

προσ-βλέπω to look at or on.

προσ-βοάομαι *M.* to call to oneself.

προσ-βοηθέω to come to aid.

προσ-βολή, ἡ a throwing upon; a coming on, attack, assault; landing; harbour.

προσ-βωθέω = -βοηθέω.

προσ-γελάω to smile upon.

προσ-γίγνομαι M. to come to; attach oneself to; to be present; to arrive; to happen to. [writing.]

προσ-γράφω to add in]

προσ-δανείζω to lend in addition.

πρόσ-δεγμα, τό reception.

προσ-δεῖ there is still wanting.

προσ-δέομαι P. to want besides; to beg, ask besides.

προσ-δέρχομαι P. to look at; to look around.

προσ-δέχομαι M. to receive, accept; to admit; to wait for, expect; to, suppose.

προσ-δέω[1] to tie to.

προσ-δέω[2] see προσ-δεῖ, -δέομαι. [besides.]

προσ-δηλέομαι M. to ruin]

προσ-διαλέγομαι P. to converse with besides.

προσ-διαφθείρω to destroy besides. [sides.]

προσ-δίδωμι to give be-]

προσ-δοκάω = -δέχομαι.

προσ-δοκέω to seem besides. [anticipation.]

προσ-δοκία, ἡ expectation,]

προσ-δόκιμος 2 expected.

προσ-εάω to let approach.

προσ-εγγίζω to approach.

προσ-εγγράφω to inscribe besides

προσ-εδρεία, ἡ blockade, siege.

προσ-εδρεύω to sit near; to adhere, keep to.

πρόσ-εδρος 2 enclosing.

προσ-εικάζω to make like, to liken.

προσ-είκελος 3 resembling.

προσ-ειλέω to press against.

πρόσ-ειμι[1] = προσέρχομαι.

πρόσ-ειμι[2] (-εῖναι) to be near, by, or at; to be added or attached; to be there, belong to.

προσ-σείω to hold out.

προσ-εκβάλλω to expel besides.

προσ-εκτικός 3 attentive.

προσ-ελαύνω to drive or ride towards. [upon.]

προσ-εμβαίνω to trample]

προσ-εμπικραίνομαι P. to be angry all the more.

προσ-εμφερής 2 resembling. [greet.]

προσ-εννέπω to accost,]

προσ-εξαιρέομαι M. to select for oneself besides.

προσ-έοικα to resemble, be like; to be fit.

προσ-επεξευρίσκω to invent besides

προσ-επικτάομαι M. to acquire besides. [join in.]

προσ-επιλαμβάνω M. to]

προσ-επιστέλλω to charge besides.

προσ-εργάζομαι M. to effect or acquire besides.

προσ-ερεύγομαι M. to vomit forth against.

προσ-έρπω to creep on, approach.

προσ-έρχομαι *M.* to go or come up, to, or forward, to approach; to mount; to visit; to advance, attack; to come in (of money).

προσ-ερωτάω to question besides.

προσ-εταιρίζομαι *M.* to take as a comrade.

προσ-εταιριστός 3 taken as a comrade.

προσ-έτι *adv.* besides.

προσ-ευρίσκω to find besides.

προσ-ευχή, ἡ prayer; place of prayer.

προσ-εύχομαι *M.* to pray to or for. [close to.

προσ-εχής 2 adjoining,

προσ-έχω to hold to, bring to, direct to; to bring to land; πρ. τινί (τὸν νοῦν) to turn one's mind or attention to, to attend, give heed; to devote oneself to, to be attached to; to have besides. — *M.* to attach oneself to, cling to; to be implicated in.

προσ-ζημιόω to punish into the bargain. [greet.

προσ-ηγορέω to accost,

προσ-ηγορίᾱ, ἡ an addressing; a naming, title.

προσ-ήγορος 2 accosting, imploring; accosted.

προσ-ήκω to have arrived, be near; to reach to; to concern, affect. προσήκει it belongs to or concerns; it befits or beseems.

προσ-ήκων 3 belonging to; befitting, seemly; related, akin.

προσ-ηλόω to nail to.

προσ-ήλυτος, ὁ a new comer, stranger, proselyte.

πρόσ-ημαι to sit close to.

προ-σημαίνω to announce before, to order.

προσ-ηνής 2 kind, gentle; suitable.

προσ-θᾱκέω to sit beside.

πρόσθεν *adv.* (and *prp.* with *gen.*) in front of, before, to the front, forwards, further; in defence of; formerly, of old; ὁ πρ. front man; τὸ πρ., τὰ πρ. the front, vanguard, place in front; day before.

πρόσ-θεσις, ἡ an adding; a putting on.

προσ-θέω to run to.

προσ-θήκη, ἡ addition, supplement, appendix; assistance.

προσ-θιγγάνω to touch.

πρόσθιος 3 the foremost.

προσ-ιζάνω, -ίζω to sit on or by.

προσ-ίημι to admit. — *M.* to suffer to approach; to admit, allow, approve, accept.

προσ-ίκελος 2 = προσείκελος.

προσ-ιππεύω to ride up to.

προσ-ίστημι to place near. *intr.* and *M.* to stand near or beside; to arrive at; to enter one's mind.

προσ-ίσχω = προσέχω.

προσ-καθέζομαι, -κάθημαι, -καθίζω to sit near or beside; to besiege; to keep to; to be hard upon one.

πρόσ-καιρος 2 transitory.

προσ-καλέω to call to or

on, summon. — *M.* to call to aid; to call into court.

προσ - καρτερέω to persevere still longer; to adhere to.

προσ-καταλείπω to leave behind; to lose besides.

προσ-κατηγορέω to accuse besides.

πρόσ-κειμαι to lie near or upon; to be joined with, involved in, added, or imposed; to belong to; to be attached or devoted to; to be hard upon one.

προ-σκέπτομαι *M.* = προ-σκοπέω.

προσ-κεφάλαιον, τό pillow. [allied to.]

προσ-κηδής 2 affectionate;]

προσ-κηρῡκεύομαι *M.* to send a herald to.

προσ-κληρόομαι *P.* to be associated with.

πρόσ-κλησις, ἡ citation, summons.

προσ-κλίνω to lean against. — *P.* to attach oneself to.

πρόσ-κλισις, ἡ inclination.

προσ-κνάομαι *M.* to rub oneself against.

προσ-κολλάω to glue to. — *P.* to cleave to.

προσ-κομίζω to carry, convey to.

πρόσ-κομμα, τό stumble; offence, fault; scandal.

προ-σκοπέω and *M.* to see or consider beforehand; to provide against.

προ-σκοπή, ἡ a spying beforehand. [κομμα.]

προσ-κοπή, ἡ = πρόσ-]

προσ-κόπτω to stumble; to take offence.

προσ-κρούω to strike against; to offend; to take offence.

προσ-κτάομαι *M.* to gain or acquire besides.

προσ-κυλίω to roll to.

προσ-κυνέω to prostrate oneself before; to worship.

προσ-κυνητής, οῦ, ὁ worshipper.

προσ-κύρω to befal, meet with. [rower.]

πρόσ-κωπος 2 rowing;]

προσ-λαλέω to speak to.

προσ-λαμβάνω and *M.* to take hold of; to take with one or to oneself; to receive besides or in addition; to win besides. [or on.]

προσ-λεύσσω to look at]

προσ-λέχομαι *M.* to lie near.

πρόσ-ληψις, ἡ reception.

προσ-λογίζομαι *M.* to reckon in addition to.

προσ-μάσσω to knead to.

προσ-μάχομαι *M.* to assail.

προσ-μένω to abide, remain; to wait for.

προσ-μεταπέμπομαι *M.* to send for besides.

προσ-μίγνῡμι, -ύω to mix to; to join to; *intr.* to unite oneself to; to approach, arrive at, land; to meet in battle. [assault.]

πρόσ-μιξις, ἡ approach,]

προσ-μίσγω = -μίγνυμι.

προσ-μισθόομαι to hire besides.

προσ-ναυπηγέω to build still more ships.

προσ-νέμω and *M.* to attribute; to devote, assign.

προσ-νέω to swim towards.

προσ-νίσσομαι *M.* to go to, come near.

προσ-νωμάω to move to.

πρόσ-οδος, ή an approaching, advance, attack; public appearance; solemn procession; path; income, revenue; return, profit.

πρόσ-οιδα to know besides.

προσ-οικέω to dwell by or near. [in addition.]

προσ-οικοδομέω to build)

πρόσ-οικος 2 dwelling near to; neighbour.

προσ-ολοφύρομαι *M.* to complain to.

προσ-ομιλέω to converse with; to busy oneself with

προσ-όμνῡμι to swear in addition.

προσ-ομολογέω to concede, grant, or agree to besides; to surrender.

προσ-όμουρος 2 neighbouring. [at, behold.]

προσ-οράω and *M.* to look)

προσ-ορέγομαι *P.* to entreat earnestly.

προσ-ορμίζω to anchor near. — *P.* and *M.* to put to shore.

προσ-όρμισις, ή a landing.

πρόσ-ορος, -ουρος 2 adjoining; neighbour.

προσ-ουδίζω to dash to the earth.

προσ-οφείλω,-οφλισκάνω to owe besides; to incur or deserve besides. [dignant.]

προσ-οχθίζω to be in-)

πρόσ-οψιος 2 visible.

πρόσ-οψις, ή sight; view; appearance. [or jest with.]

προσ-παίζω to sport, play,)

προσ-παίω to knock at, to strike against. [in besides.]

προσ-παρακαλέω to call)

προσ-παρασκευάζω to prepare besides. [besides.]

προσ-παρέχω to furnish)

προσ-πασσαλεύω to nail to. [sides.]

προσ-πάσχω to suffer be-)

πρόσ-πεινος 2 very hungry.

προσ-πελάζω to bring near (to). — *intr.* and *P.* to approach.

προσ-πέμπω to send to.

προσ-περιβάλλω to put around besides. — *M.* to seek to obtain still more.

προσ-περονάω to fix to.

προσ-πέτομαι *M.* to fly, rush to. [πυνθάνομαι.]

προσ-πεύθομαι *M.* = προσ-)

προσ-πήγνῡμι to fix to.

προσ-πίλναμαι *M.* = προσπελάζω.

προσ-πίπτω to fall against or upon; to run up to; to attack, assault; to attach oneself to; to fall in with, encounter; to happen, occur; to fall down before one, supplicate.

προσ-πίτνω = προσπίπτω.

προσ-πλάζω to strike against.

προσ-πλάσσω to form upon.

προσ-πλέω to sail against.

προσ-πληρόω to fill up, complete; to man besides.

προσ-πλωτός 3 navigable.

προσ-πλώω = -πλέω.

προσ-ποιέω to add to. — M. to add to oneself; to take to oneself, pretend, lay claim to; to appropriate, arrogate; to feign. allege.

προσ-ποίησις, ἡ acquisition, addition; claim, pretence.

προσ-πολεμέω to make war against.

προσ-πολεμόομαι M. to make an enemy of one.

προσ-πολέομαι to come near. [vant, attendant.]

πρόσ-πολος 2 serving; ser-

προσ-πορεύομαι P. to go near. [besides.]

προσ-πορίζω to procure

προσ-πταίω to strike against; to stumble; to fail, suffer defeat or loss.

προσ-πτύσσω M. to fold oneself close to, to cling close round; to entreat, solicit; to embrace, treat kindly, greet.

προσ-πυνθάνομαι M. to inquire besides.

προσ-ρέω to flow up to.

προσ-ρήγνῡμι to dash against.

πρόσ-ρησις, ἡ an addressing; a naming.

πρόσσοθεν adv. forwards.

προσσταυρόω = προ-σταυρόω. [wards.]

προσ-στείχω to step to-

προσ-στέλλω to fit to; προσεσταλμένος tight; plain, modest.

προσ-συμβάλλομαι M. to contribute to besides.

πρόσσω = πόρρω.

πρόσ-ταγμα, τό, πρόσ-ταξις, ἡ command, order.

προσ-ταλαιπωρέω to suffer or persist still longer.

προ-στασία, ἡ a leading, governing, presidency; administration.

προσ-τάσσω to place to or beside; to assign, appoint, ascribe; to array; to order, ordain, enjoin. [στασία.]

προ-στατεία, ἡ = προ-

προ-στατεύω, -έω to be at the head (of), govern; to manage; to be forthcoming.

προ-στατήριος 3 protecting.

προ-στάτης, ου, ὁ front man; protector, defender, patron; leader, chief, ruler, head; suppliant. [tectress.]

προ-στάτις, ιδος, ἡ pro-

προ-σταυρόω to palisade in front. [within a wall.]

προσ-τειχίζω to include

προ-στείχω to go forward, advance. [spend besides.]

προσ-τελέω to pay or

προ-στέλλω to send forward. — P. to go forward.

προ-στερνίδιον, τό breastplate of horses. [fast to.]

προσ-τήκω intr. to stick

προσ-τίθημι to put to, upon, or in front; to enjoin, command, impose; to attribute, impute, deliver, procure, apply to; to add; join to. — M. to associate oneself, join; to agree to: to take to oneself; to add for oneself. [plicate.]

προσ-τρέπω and M. to sup-

προσ-τρέχω to run to.
προσ-τρόπαιος 2 suppliant.
προσ-τροπή, ἡ entreaty, prayer. [τρόπαιος.]
πρόσ-τροπος 2 = προσ-)
προσ-τυγχάνω to meet with by chance; to obtain.
προ-στῷον, τό corridor.
προ-συγγίγνομαι = προ-ξυγγ. [mix first.]
προ-συμμίσγω to inter-)
προ-συνοικέω to dwell together before. [tional food.]
προσ-φάγιον, τό addi-)
πρόσφατος 2 fresh, new.
προσ-φερής 2 resembling; serviceable.
προσ-φέρω to bring or carry to, upon, or near, to set before one; to offer, furnish, provide; to add, increase; to apply to. — M. and P. to approach, to come near; to converse; to rush against, attack; to deal with, treat; to behave oneself; to take to oneself, eat; to give besides. [to.]
πρόσ-φημι and M. to speak)
προσ-φθέγγομαι M. to speak to, address.
πρόσ-φθεγκτος 2 addressed. [salutation.]
πρόσ-φθεγμα, τό address,)
προσ-φιλής 2 dear, beloved; pleasing; kind, friendly. [larly to.]
προσ-φοιτάω to go regu-)
προσ-φορά, ἡ gift, present, offering; addition, increase.
προσ-φορέω = προσφέρω.
προσ-φυής 2 growing upon; natural; fitted.

προσ-φύω intr. and M. to grow upon; to cling to.
προσ-φωνέω to call in; to address, greet.
προσ-φώνημα, τό address, salutation.
πρό-σχημα, τό outward show, ornament; pretence, screen, pretext.
προσ-χόω to heap up besides; to choke up with earth, throw earth against; to form by alluvion.
προσ-χράομαι M. to employ besides.
προσ-χρῄζω, -χρῃζω to require or desire besides.
πρόσ-χυσις, ἡ a sprinkling.
προσ-χωρέω to approach; to be like; to accede, consent, agree to; to yield, surrender. [neighbour.]
πρόσ-χωρος 2 adjoining;)
πρόσ-χωσις, ἡ a heaping up, mound; alluvion.
προσ-ψαύω to touch.
πρόσω = πόρρω.
πρόσωθεν adv. from afar.
προσωπο-ληπτέω to be a respecter of persons.
προσωπο-λήπτης, ου, ὁ respector of persons.
προσωπο-ληψία, ἡ respect of persons.
πρόσ-ωπον, τό face, countenance, mien; look, appearance, figure; mask; person. [sist.]
προσ-ωφελέω to help, as-)
προσ-ωφέλησις, ἡ assistance, help. [beforehand.]
προ-ταλαιπωρέω to suffer)

προ-ταμιεῖον, τό ante-room of a magazine.

προ-τάμνω = -τέμνω.

προ-ταρβέω to fear beforehand. [forehand.]

προ-ταρῑχεύω to salt beforehand.

προ-τάσσω to place in front; to determine beforehand.

προ-τείνω to stretch out or forth, put forward; to offer, expose; to pretend, promise, feign. — M. to claim, demand; to pretend.

προ-τείχισμα, τό outwork.

προ-τελέω to pay in advance.

προ-τεμένισμα, τό place in front of a sacred ground.

προ-τέμνω to cut beforehand; to cut off in front.

προτεραῖος 3 on the day before.

προτερέω to be before, in front, or beforehand.

πρότερος 3 before, forward, in front; sooner, earlier; former, older; higher, superior; adv. πρότερον formerly, before, sooner; προτέρω further, forward. [beforehand.]

προ-τεύχω to make or do

προτί = πρός.

προ-τίθημι to place before, prefer; to set out, propose, expose, put forth, present; to fix; to permit, allow; to impose, lay to one's charge; to exhibit, show, publish, ordain; to bring under discussion. — M. to put before oneself;

to put forth on one's own part; to pretend, feign; to purpose; to put out publicly, proclaim, announce; to prefer, to offer.

προ-τῑμάω and M. to honour more or above, to prefer, distinguish. — P. to be preferred in honour.

προ-τίμησις, ἡ preference.

προτι-μῡθέομαι M. to speak to.

προ-τῑμωρέω to help beforehand. — M. to revenge oneself before.

προτι-όσσομαι to look at; to presage.

προ-τίω = προ-τιμάω.

πρό-τμησις, ἡ belly.

προ-τολμάω to venture before. [stay-sail.]

πρό-τονος, ὁ rope of the

προ-τρεπτικός 3 admonishing, persuasive.

προ-τρέπω to turn or urge forward; to impel, exhort, persuade, compel. — M. to turn oneself to, to devote oneself to; to exhort.

προ-τρέχω to run forward; to outrun. [before.]

πρό-τριτα adv. three days

προ-τροπάδην adv. turned forward(s), headlong.

προ-τύπτω to burst forward.

προὐννέπω = προεννέπω.

προὐξεφίεμαι to enjoin beforehand.

προ-ὑπάρχω to be beforehand, begin with; to exist before.

πρόὑπτος 2 = πρόοπτος.

προυσελέω to maltreat.

προ-φαίνω to show forth, bring to light, display; to predict, foreshow, promise. — *P.* to appear from afar, to come to light; to appear before.

πρό-φαντος 2 foreshown, foretold.

προ-φασίζομαι *M.* to use a pretence, allege, prevaricate.

πρό-φασις, ἡ pretence, pretext, evasion, excuse; cause. motive; prediction.

προ-φερής 2 preferred, excellent; older.

προ-φέρω to bring to, before, or forward; to produce; to declare, proclaim; to present, propose; to object, reproach; *intr.* to surpass, exceed, be beforehand.

προ-φεύγω to flee forward(s); to escape.

προφητεία, ἡ prophecy.

προφητεύω to be a prophet or interpreter of oracles; to prophesy.

προ-φήτης, ου, ὁ prophet, interpreter of oracles, seer, foreteller.

προφητικός 3 prophetic.

προφῆτις, ιδος, ἡ prophetess.   [hand.]

προ-φθάνω to be before-]

προ-φράζω to foretell; to say openly.

πρόφρασσα *fem.* of πρόφρων.

πρό-φρων 2 kindly, willing; hearty; earnest.

προ-φυλακή, ἡ guard in front, out-post.

προ-φυλακίς, ιδος, ἡ guardship.   [vanced guard.]

προ-φύλαξ, ακος, ὁ ad-]

προ-φυλάσσω to keep guard before or in front, to be on guard. — *M.* to guard oneself, ward off. [before.]

προ-φύω *intr.* to be born]

προ-φυτεύω to beget.

προ-φωνέω to proclaim publicly.

προ-χειρίζομαι *M.* to take into one's hand, to choose, appoint, decree; to make ready. — *P.* to be arranged or ready before.

πρό-χειρος 2 at hand, ready; easily procured; common; cheap.   [before.]

προ-χειροτονέω to choose]

προ-χέω to pour forth or out. — *P.* to be poured out, to stream forth.

πρόχνυ *adv.* kneeling; precipitously.

προ-χοή, ἡ a pouring out; mouth of a river.

πρό-χοος, -χους, ὁ pitcher, jug.

προ-χρίω to smear before.

πρό-χυσις, ἡ a pouring or spreading out; alluvion.

προ-χωρέω to go forward, advance; to make progress, succeed.   [push forward.]

προ-ωθέω to thrust or]

προ-ωλής 2 wholly ruined.

πρυλέες, έων, οἱ foot-soldiers, champions.   [poop.]

πρύμνα, πρύμνη, ἡ stern,]

πρύμνη-θεν *adv.* from the stern.   [a ship's stern.]

πρυμνήσια, τά ropes from]

πρυμνός 3 hindmost, endmost. [mountain.]

πρυμν-ώρεια, ἡ foot of a[

πρυτανεία, ἡ presidency, office of a Prytanis; chief command of the day.

πρυτανεῖον, τό town-hall, hall of the Prytanes.

πρυτανεύω to be a Prytanis; to manage, administer.

πρύτανις, ὁ Prytanis, president, ruler, chairman, master.

πρῴ = πρωί. [see πρώιος.]

πρῴαίτερος, πρῴαίτατος]

πρῴην adv. lately, just now; the day before yesterday.

πρωθ-ήβης, ου, fem. πρωθήβη in the first bloom of youth. [too early.]

πρωί adv. early in the day;]

πρωιζά = πρῴην.

πρώιμος 2, πρωινός 3, πρώιος 3 early, early in the day. [height.]

πρών, πρῶνος, ὁ foreland;]

πρῷρα, ἡ fore-part of a ship. [front.]

πρῷρᾱ-θεν adv. from the]

πρῳρεύς, ὁ look-out man in a ship. [first rank.]

πρωτεῖον, τό first prize;]

πρωτεύω to be the first, have precedence.

πρώτιστος 3 first of all.

πρωτό-γονος 2 first-born; high-born.

πρωτο-καθεδρίᾱ, πρωτοκλισίᾱ, ἡ first seat.

πρωτο-παγής 2 newly built.

πρωτο-πλόος, -πλους 2

sailing for the first time; sailing foremost.

πρῶτος 3 first, foremost, earliest, highest, noblest; τὰ πρῶτα the first prize or rank, highest degree, chief part.

πρωτο-στάτης, ου, ὁ frontrank man; file-leader; chief. [right.]

πρωτο-τόκια, τά birth-]

πρωτο-τόκος 2 giving birth for the first time.

πρωτό-τοκος 2 first-born.

πταίρω = πτάρνυμαι.

πταῖσμα, τό stumble, false step; accident, failure, defeat.

πταίω to stumble (against); to fail, make a mistake, undergo a mishap.

πτᾱνός 3 = πτηνός.

πταρμός, ὁ a sneezing.

πτάρνυμαι to sneeze.

πτελέᾱ, ἡ elm-tree.

πτέρνα, ἡ heel; ham.

πτερόεις 3 feathered, winged.

πτερόν, τό feather, wing; soaring, flight; augury, omen; anything like wings.

πτερόω to feather.

πτερύγιον, τό little wing; pinnacle.

πτέρυξ, υγος, ἡ = πτερόν.

πτερωτός 2 = πτερόεις.

πτηνός 3 feathered, winged; fledged; fleeting, swift; coy, bashful.

πτήσσω intr. to crouch, cower; to be frightened, to tremble; to flee; trans. to frighten, alarm, terrify.

πτίλον, τό feather; wing.

πτίσσω to husk; to pound.

πτοέω, πτοιέω = πτήσσω.

πτόησις, πτοίησις, ἡ fear; passion.

πτολεμίζω etc. = πολ.

πτολι - πόρθιος, πτολί- πορθος, ὁ destroyer of cities.

πτόρθος, ὁ shoot, branch.

πτύγμα, τό a folding, fold.

πτυκτός 3 folded.

πτύξ, πτυχός fold; layer, plate; cleft; dell.

πτύον, τό winnowing-shovel.

πτύρω to frighten, scare.

πτύσμα, τό spittle.

πτύσσω to fold, double up. — M. to be bent.

πτυχή, ἡ = πτύξ.

πτύω to spit, spit out.

πτωκάς, άδος, ἡ = πτώξ. [hare.]

πτῶμα, τό fall, ruin, dis- aster; corpse.

πτώξ, πτωκός shy; ὁ, ἡ

πτῶσις, ἡ = πτῶμα.

πτωσκάζω, πτώσσω = πτήσσω. [beggary.]

πτωχεία, ἡ a begging,

πτωχεύω to be a beggar, to be poor.

πτωχός 3 beggarly, beggar.

πῦγ-αργος, ὁ white-rump.

πῦγή, ἡ rump, buttocks.

πυγμαῖος 3 of the size of a fist; pigmy.

πυγ-μαχέω = πυκτεύω.

πυγ-μαχίη, ἡ a boxing.

πυγ-μάχος, ὁ = πύκτης.

πυγμή, ἡ fist; a boxing.

πυγούσιος 3 one cubit long.

πυγών, όνος, ἡ elbow - cubit

πύελος, ἡ bathing-tub; trough; coffin.

πυθμήν, ένος, ὁ bottom, stand, base, foundation, root. [P. to rot, decay.]

πύθω to cause to rot. —

πύθων, ωνος ventriloquist.

πύκα adv. thickly; fre- quently; wisely.

πυκάζω to make thick or close; to press together, shut up; to cover thick, shelter; intr. to enwrap one- self. [cautious.]

πυκι - μήδης 2 sensible,

πυκινός 3 = πυκνός.

πυκνί dat. of πνύξ.

πυκνο - πτερος 2 thick- feathered.

πυκνός 3 thick, close, com- pact, well-guarded; crowd- ed; frequent; strong, well made, great, mighty; care- ful, cautious, discreet.

πυκνο - στικτος 2 thick- spotted.

πυκνότης, ητος, ἡ thick- ness, closeness, compact- ness; crowd.

πυκτεύω to be a boxer.

πύκτης, ου, ὁ boxer. [ing.]

πυκτικός 3 skilled in box-

πυλ - αγόρας, ου, πυλ- άγορος, ὁ orator at the Amphictyonic council.

πυλ - αγορέω to be a πυ- λαγόρας. [keeper.]

πυλ - άρτης, ου, ὁ gate-

πυλα - ωρός, ὁ = πυλωρός.

πύλη, ἡ gate, door, en- trance, inlet; mountain- pass.

πυλίς, ιδος, ὁ little gate.

πύλος, ὁ gateway.

πυλ-ουρός, ὁ = πυλωρός.

πυλόω to · enclose with gates. [vestibule.]

πυλών, ῶνος, ὁ porch;

πυλ-ωρός, ὁ, ἡ gate-keeper; guard.

πύματος 3 uttermost, last.

πυνθάνομαι M. to inquire, ask; to hear, learn; to understand, know.

πύξ adv. with the fist.

πύξινος 3 of boxwood.

πῦρ, πυρός, τό fire; lightning; fire-sign; fever-heat; blaze.

πυρά, ἡ place where fire is kindled, funeral-pile, burial-place.

πυρ-άγρα, ἡ a pair of fire-tongs. [hot.]

πυρ-ακτέω to make red-

πῡραμίς, ίδος, ἡ pyramid.

πυργηδόν adv. in masses.

πυργο-μαχέω to assail a tower.

πύργος, ὁ tower, towered wall; castle, fortress, bulwark; division or column of soldiers.

πυργόω M. to furnish with towers; to raise on high.

πυργώδης 2 like a tower.

πύργωμα, τό = πύργος.

πυρεῖα, τά contrivance to light a fire.

πυρέσσω to have a fever.

πυρετός, ὁ fever-heat.

πυρή, ἡ = πυρά.

πῡρήν, ῆνος, ὁ stone of a fruit. [φόρος.]

πύρη-φόρος 2 = πυρο-

πυρίᾱ, ἡ vapour-bath.

πῠρι-ήκης 2 pointed in the fire. [the fire.]

πυρί-καυστος 2 burnt in

πύρινος[1] 3 of wheat.

πύρινος[2] 3 fiery.

πυρι-φλεγής 2 blazing with fire.

πυρ-καϊά, ἡ stake, funeral-pile; conflagration; stump of an olive-tree.

πύρνον, τό wheaten bread.

πῡρός, ὁ wheat.

πῡρο-φόρος 2 wheat-bearing.

πῠρόω to burn, waste with fire. [breathing.]

πύρ-πνοος, -πνους 2 fire-

πυρ-πολέω to keep up a fire; to waste with fire.

πυρράζω to be fiery-red.

πυρρίχη, ἡ war-dance.

πυρρός 3 fire-coloured, red.

πυρσεύω to make fire-signs. [con.]

πυρσός[1], ὁ fire-brand; bea-

πυρσός[2] 3 = πυρρός.

πυρ-φόρος 2 fire-bearing, torch-bearing. [tion.]

πύρωσις, ἡ fire, conflagra-

πύστις, ἡ an inquiring, asking; question, trial; report.

πώ adv. yet, ever, anyhow.

πώγων, ωνος, ὁ beard.

πωλέομαι M. to frequent, wander about.

πωλέω to sell. [horses.]

πωλικός 3 drawn by (young)

πωλο-δαμνέω to break young horses. [foal.]

πῶλος, ὁ a young one;

πῶμα[1], τό cover, lid.

πῶμα[2], τό drink, potion.

πώ-ποτε *adv.* ever yet.

πώρινος 3 made of tuff-stone.

πῶρος, ὁ tuff-stone.

πωρόω to petrify, harden, obdurate.

πώρωσις, ἡ a hardening, callousness.

πῶς *adv.* how? in what way or manner? how much!

πωτάομαι = πέτομαι.

πῶυ, εος, τό flock of sheep.

P

P, ρ (ῥῶ) seventeenth letter of the alphabet; as a numeral ρ' = 100.

ῥά, ῥ' = ἄρα.   [Rabbi.

ῥαββί, ῥαββεί master,

ῥαββουνί = ῥαββί.

ῥαβδίζω to cudgel, flog.

ῥαβδο-νομέω to be an umpire.   [staff.

ῥάβδος, ἡ rod, stick, wand,

ῥαβδ-οῦχος, ὁ staff-bearer; umpire; lictor.

ῥαδινάκη, ἡ petroleum.

ῥαδινός 3 slender, tender; swift.

ῥάδιος 3 easy; ready, willing, complaisant; heedless, reckless.

ῥᾳδιούργημα,τό, ῥᾳδιουρ-γία, ἡ recklessness; laziness, indolence; wickedness, roguery.   [grain.

ῥαθαμιγξ, ιγγος, ἡ drop;

ῥᾳ-θῡμέω to be reckless or idle.

ῥᾳ-θῡμία, ἡ thoughtlessness, carelessness; laziness; easiness; pastime.

ῥᾴ-θῡμος 2 light-minded, careless; lazy; pleasure-seeking.   [cover.

ῥᾴζω to grow easy, re-

ῥαίνω to sprinkle, besprinkle.

ῥαιστήρ, ῆρος, ὁ hammer.

ῥαίω to smash, shiver, shatter. — *P.* to be shattered; to burst; to be maltreated.

ῥακά worthless fellow.

ῥάκος, τό rag, tatter; patch.

ῥαντίζω to sprinkle; to cleanse.

ῥαντισμός, ὁ a sprinkling.

ῥαπίζω to cudgel, whip, box on the ear.   [cheek.

ῥάπισμα, τό slap on the

ῥαπτός 3 sewed, stitched.

ῥάπτω to sew, stitch (together); to contrive, plot.

ῥαστώνη, ἡ easiness, facility; readiness, cessation; relief, rest, ease; laziness.

ῥαφή, ἡ seam.

ῥαφίς, ίδος, ἡ needle.

ῥάχία, ἡ surf, surge, breakers; coast.

ῥαχίζω to cut in pieces.

ῥάχις, ἡ back; backbone.

ῥαψ-ῳδέω to recite poems.

ῥαψ-ῳδός, ὁ singing, reciting; reciter of poems.

ῥέγκω, ῥέγχω to snort.

ῥέδη, ἡ wagon.

ῥέεθρον, τό = ῥεῖθρον.

ῥέζω to do, act, work, make, effect, accomplish; to sacrifice.

ῥέθος, τό limb; face.

ῥεῖα adv. easily, lightly.

ῥεῖθρον, τό river, stream; bed of a river.

ῥέπω to incline downwards; to preponderate, prevail; to incline towards.

ῥεῦμα, τό flow, stream, river, flood; a bleeding; volcanic eruption.

ῥέω and P. to flow, stream, run, gush; to fall or drop off, melt away.

ῥῆγμα, τό a breaking, fracture; downfall.

ῥηγμίν, ῖνος, ἡ = ῥαχία.

ῥήγνῡμι to break, break in pieces, rend, smash; to let break loose.

ῥῆγος, τό carpet, blanket, coverlet.

ῥηΐδιος 3 = ῥᾴδιος.

ῥηκτός 3 to be broken or rent.

ῥῆμα, τό word, saying, phrase; sentence, speech; thing.

ῥηξ-ηνορίη, ἡ a breaking through ranks of warriors.

ῥηξ-ήνωρ, ορος breaking through ranks of warriors.

ῥῆσις, ἡ a saying, speaking, mode of speech; = ῥῆμα.

ῥήσσω to tear, rend, break; to beat with the feet, dance.

ῥητήρ, ῆρος = ῥήτωρ.

ῥητορεύω to be a public speaker.

ῥητορικός 3 oratorical, rhetorical.

ῥητός 3 said, spoken; settled, determined, concerted; to be told.

ῥήτρα, ἡ speech; agree-

ment, treaty; maxim, law, statute.

ῥήτωρ, ορος, ὁ orator, public speaker; statesman; politician; rhetorician.

ῥῑγεδανός 3 causing shudder.

ῥῑγέω to shudder with cold, to be chill; to shudder at, shrink from.

ῥίγιον, ῥίγιστος see ῥῖγος.

ῥῖγος, τό frost, cold; comp. ῥίγιον worse, more horribly; sup. ῥίγιστος.

ῥῑγόω to be cold or chill.

ῥίζα, ἡ root; stem, origin; family.

ῥιζόω to let strike root; to plant. — P. to be firmly rooted.

ῥίμφα adv. lightly, swiftly.

ῥιμφ-άρματος 2 with a swift chariot.

ῥῑνόν, τό, ῥῑνός, ἡ skin, hide, leather; shield.

ῥῑνο-τόρος 2 piercing shields.

ῥίον, τό peak, promontory.

ῥῑπή, ἡ throw, flight, swing; rushing motion; impetus.

ῥῑπίζω to blow up a flame.

ῥίπος, τό reed mat, wicker hurdle.

ῥῑπτάζω to throw to and fro.

ῥίπτω, ῥιπτέω to throw, cast, or hurl down, out, away, forth, or to and fro.

ῥίς, ῥινός, ἡ nose; pl. nostrils.

ῥίψ, ῥῑπός, ἡ wand, rod; reed, bulrush; mat, hurdle.

ῥίψο-κίνδῡνος 2 foolhardy.

ῥοδανός 3 waving.

22*

ῥοδο-δάκτυλος 2 rosy-fingered.

ῥοδόεις 3 of roses.

ῥόδον, τό rose.

ῥοή, ἡ = ῥόος. [murmur.]

ῥοθέω to roar, rush, buzz,]

ῥόθιος 2 roaring, rushing.

ῥόθος, ὁ a roaring, rushing noise.

ῥοιά, ἡ pomegranate-tree.

ῥοιβδέω to swallow down.

ῥοῖβδος, ὁ a roaring, hissing, whizzing.

ῥοιζέω to whistle, whizz.

ῥοιζηδόν adv. with a rushing noise.

ῥοῖζος, ὁ = ῥοῖβδος.

ῥομφαία, ἡ large sword.

ῥόος, ὁ stream, current; flood, wave.

ῥόπαλον, τό club, stick, cudgel, mace; knocker of a door.

ῥοπή, ἡ inclination downwards, turn of the scale; turning-point, crisis, decision, result; weight, momentum, push, impetus.

ῥόπτρον, τό = ῥόπαλον.

ῥοῦς, ὁ = ῥόος. [down.]

ῥοφέω to sip; to swallow]

ῥοχθέω to roar.

ῥοώδης 2 flowing, surging.

ῥύαξ, ἄκος, ὁ stream that bursts forth; stream of lava. [undantly.]

ῥυδόν adv. in streams; ab-]

ῥυθμίζω to bring into proportion; to order, arrange; to govern, educate.

ῥυθμός, ὁ measure, rhythm; proportion, harmony, symmetry; form, shape.

ῥῦμα, τό string of a bow; bow-shot; protection, deliverance.

ῥύμη, ἡ swing, impetus; attack, force; street.

ῥυμός, ὁ pole of a carriage.

ῥύομαι M. to save, deliver, protect, redeem; to cure, heal; to shield, cover; to check, hold back.

ῥύπα, τά, pl. of ὁ ῥύπος.

ῥυπαίνω, ῥυπαρεύω to sully.

ῥυπαρία, ἡ dirt; sordidness.

ῥυπαρός 3 dirty.

ῥυπάω, -όω to be dirty; to dirty.

ῥύπος, ὁ dirt, filth.

ῥύσιον, τό booty, prey; pledge, restitution, amends.

ῥυσί-πολις, ὁ, ἡ saving the city. [course.]

ῥύσις, ἡ stream, river,]

ῥυσός 3 wrinkled.

ῥυστάζω to drag to and fro, to maltreat.

ῥυστακτύς, ύος, ἡ ill-treatment.

ῥυτήρ[1], ῆρος, ὁ one who draws a bow, archer; rope, thong; rein. [fender.]

ῥυτήρ[2], ῆρος, ὁ saver, de-]

ῥυτίς, ίδος, ἡ wrinkle; stain, taint.

ῥυτόν, τό drinking-horn.

ῥυτός[1] 3 dragged along.

ῥυτός[2] 3 flowing.

ῥωγαλέος 3 rent, ragged.

ῥωμαλέος 3 strong, mighty.

ῥώμη, ἡ strength, force; might; army; energy.

ῥώννυμι to strengthen, confirm. — *P.* to exert one-self; to be resolved. — *pf.* ἐρρῶσθαι to be strong, vigorous; ἔρρωσο farewell.

ῥώξ, ῥωγός, ἡ chink, fissure, narrow passage.

ῥώομαι *M.* to move swiftly, to rush on; to dance.

ῥωπήιον, τό = ῥώψ.

ῥωχμός, ὁ = ῥώξ.

ῥώψ, ῥωπός, ἡ shrub, bush, underwood.

Σ

Σ, σ, ς (σίγμα) eighteenth letter of the alphabet; as a numeral σ' = 200.

σαβαχθανί thou hast forsaken me.

σαβαώθ hosts, armies.

σαββατισμός, ὁ the keeping of the Sabbath. [week.]

σάββατον, τό sabbath; *pl.*

σάγαρις, ἡ double-axe, battle-axe.

σαγηνεύω to catch in a net.

σαγήνη, ἡ drag-net.

σαθρός 3 rotten, decayed, unsound, sick, perishable.

σαίνω to wag the tail; fawn, wheedle, caress; to shake.

σαίρω to sweep clean.

σακέσ-παλος 2 brandishing a shield. [bearer.]

σακεσ-φόρος 2 shield-)

σακίον, τό small bag.

σακκέω to strain, filter.

σάκκος, σάκος, ὁ bag, sack; sack-cloth; mourning-dress.

σάκος, τό large shield.

σαλεύω to swing, shake; to incite. — *intr.* and *P.* to totter, move to and fro, toss, roll.

σάλος, ὁ tottering, rolling, surging; surge; disquiet.

σαλπιγκτής, οῦ, ὁ = σαλπικτής. [trumpet-signal.]

σάλπιγξ, ιγγος, ἡ trumpet;)

σαλπίζω to sound the trumpet, to give a trumpet-signal.

σαλπικτής, σαλπιστής, οῦ, ὁ trumpeter. [sandal.]

σάνδαλον, σανδάλιον, τό)

σανδαράκινος 3 minium-coloured. [catalogue.]

σανίδιον, τό writing-tablet,)

σανίς, ίδος, ἡ board, plank; wooden frame-work; writing-tablet; fold of a door; pole; pillory.

σάος = σῶς.

σαό-φρων 2 = σώφρων.

σαόω = σῴζω.

σαπρός 3 rotten, decayed; putrid; worthless.

σαργάνη, ἡ wickerwork; basket. [castic.]

σαρδάνιος 3 scornful, sar-)

σάρδιον, τό, σάρδιος, ὁ carnelian, sardoin. [νυξ.]

σαρδ-όνυξ, υχος, ὁ sardo-)

σαρκίζω to strip off the flesh.

σαρκικός 3, σάρκινος 3 of flesh, fleshy; fleshly, carnal, sensual.

σαρκο-φάγος 2 eating flesh; limestone coffin.

σαρκώδης 2 fleshy.

σάρξ, σαρκός, ἡ flesh, piece of flesh; body.

σαρόω to sweep clean.

σατᾶν, σατανᾶς, ᾶ, ὁ satan, devil.

σάτον, τό a corn-measure.

σατραπεία, ἡ satrapy.

σατραπεύω to be a satrap.

σατράπης, ου, ὁ satrap, Persian governor.

σάττω to fill, stuff, cram; to load; to equip.

σαύρα, ἡ, σαῦρος, ὁ lizard.

σαυρωτήρ, ῆρος, ὁ butt-end of a spear.

σάφα, σαφέως see σαφής.

σαφηνής, σαφής 2 clear, plain, manifest; distinct; true, certain, real.

σαφηνίζω to make clear or plain; to announce.

σάω to strain, sift.

σβέννῡμι to quench, put out, quell. — intr. and P. to be quenched, go out, die.

σβεστήριος 3 fit for quenching.

σεβάζομαι M. = σέβω.

σέβας, τό awe, reverence, worship, respect; astonishment; wonder; majesty; pride, glory. [or worship.)

σέβασμα, τό object of awe)

σεβαστός 3 venerable, awful, august.

σέβω and P. to feel awe, fear, shame, or respect; to honour, revere, worship; to wonder.

σειρά, ἡ rope, string, chain.

σειραῖος 3, σειρη-φόρος 2 fastened by a rope; near horse.

σειρός, ὁ = σιρός.

σεισ-άχθεια, ἡ a shaking off of burdens.

σεισμός, ὁ earthquake.

σείω to shake, brandish; σείει there is an earthquake. — M. and P. to be shaken, to move to and fro.

σέλας, τό brightness, light, beam; fire, flame.

σεληναῖος 3 moon-lit.

σελήνη, ἡ moon, moon-shine.

σεληνιάζομαι to be lunatic.

σέλῑνον, τό parsley.

σέλμα, τό rowing-bench; deck.

σεμίδᾱλις, ἡ finest wheaten flour.

σεμνο-λόγος, ὁ speaking solemnly. [seer.)

σεμνό-μαντις, ὁ reverend)

σεμνός 3 august, sacred, solemn, dignified, holy; majestic, noble, stately; grave, honest; haughty, arrogant; pompous.

σεμνότης, ητος, ἡ solemnity, dignity, majesty; pomposity.

σεμνόω, σεμνύνω to dignify, make solemn, pompous, or stately; to magnify, amplify. — M. to boast, be proud.

σεύω to put in quick motion; to drive or chase away; to bring forth; to throw, hurl, shake. — M. and P. to rush, run, start, dart or spout forth; to strive (for), desire.

σηκάζω to pen, coop up.

σηκο-κόρος, ὁ stableman.

σηκός, ὁ pen, fold, enclosure, stable; sacred precinct, shrine; enclosed trunk of an olive-tree.

σῆμα, τό sign, mark, token; omen; trace; signal, word of command; image, seal, written character, device, emblem; mound, tomb.

σημαίνω to signify, mark, seal; to give a sign or signal, to command, rule; to show a sign, point out, announce, prove. — *M.* to mark for oneself, note down; to infer, conclude.

σημαντρίς, ίδος, ἡ sealed earth.

σήμαντρον, τό seal.

σημάντωρ, ορος, ὁ leader, commander; messenger.

σημεῖον, τό = σῆμα.

σημειόω to mark. — *M.* to mark for oneself.

σήμερον *adv.* to-day.

σηπεδών, όνος, ἡ putrefaction.

σήπω to make rotten. — *intr.* and *P.* to rot, decay.

σῆραγξ, αγγος, ἡ cleft, hollow.

σηρικός 3 silken.

σής, σεός, σητός, ὁ moth.

σησάμινος 3 made of sesame.

σήσαμον, τό sesame.

σητό-βρωτος 2 moth-eaten.

σθεναρός 3 strong, mighty.

σθένος, τό strength, might; courage; power, force; army.

σθενόω to strengthen.

σθένω to be strong or

mighty; to rule, have power; to be able.

σιαγών, όνος, ἡ jaw-bone.

σίαλον, τό spittle.

σίαλος 2 fat; fat hog.

σῖγα *adv.* silently; secretly.

σιγάζω to silence. [tering.]

σιγαλόεις 3 shining, glit-

σιγάω to be silent, keep silence; to conceal. [quiet.]

σιγή, ἡ silence, stillness,

σιγηλός 3 silent, still, mute.

σίγλος, ὁ shekel.

σιγύννης, ου, ὁ javelin; retail-dealer.

σιδηρεία, ἡ a working in iron.

σιδήρειος 3, σιδήρεος 3 of iron or steel; hard, unfeeling. [weapon.]

σιδήριον, τό iron tool or

σιδηρο-βρώς, ῶτος iron-eating, whetting. [iron.]

σιδηρό-δετος 2 clad with

σιδηρο-κμής, ῆτος slain by the sword.

σίδηρος, ὁ iron, steel; iron tool, sword, knife, sickle, axe; ironmonger's shop.

σιδηροῦς 3 = σιδήρεος.

σιδηρο-φορέω and *M.* to wear arms. [with iron.]

σιδηρόω to overlay or cover

σίζω to hiss.

σικάριος, ὁ assassin.

σίκερα, τό strong drink.

σιλλικύπριον, τό wonder-tree (ricinus).

σίλφιον, τό a kind of plant.

σιμικίνθιον, τό apron.

σιμός 3 flat-nosed, flat; up-hill. [waste.]

σινα-μωρέω to damage,

σινά-μωρος 2 hurtful.

σίνᾱπι, ιδος, εως, τό mustard.

σινδών, όνος, ἡ fine linen; linen cloth or shirt.

σινέομαι = σίνομαι.

σινιάζω to sift, winnow.

σίνομαι to damage, hurt; to rob, plunder, ravage.

σίνος, τό damage, harm; mischief. [cious.]

σίντης, ου robbing, rapacious.

σιός, ὁ = θεός.

σῑρός, ὁ pit, hole.

σισύρᾱ, σίσυρνα, ἡ rough or furred coat.

σῖτα, τά pl. of σῖτος. [corn.]

σῑτ-αγωγός 2 conveying corn.

σιτευτός 3 fatted.

σιτεύω, σιτέω to feed, fatten. — P. to be fed, to eat.

σῑτ-ηγός = σιταγωγός.

σιτηρέσιον, τό food, provisions; pay for maintenance.

σίτησις, ἡ a feeding; public maintenance.

σῑτίζω = σιτεύω.

σίτιον, τό = σῖτος.

σίτιστός = σιτευτός.

σῑτο-δείᾱ, ἡ want of food, dearth.

σῑτο-δοτέω to deal out corn. — P. to be furnished with corn. [sions.]

σῖτο-μέτριον, τό provisions.

σῖτο-νόμος 2 dealing out food. [food; baker.]

σῖτο-ποιός 2 preparing food; baker.

σῖτο-πομπίᾱ, ἡ transport of corn. [merchant.]

σῑτο-πώλης, ου, ὁ corn-merchant.

σῖτος, ὁ wheat, corn; flour, bread; food, provisions.

σῑτο-φάγος 2 eating bread.

σῖτο-φόρος 2 conveying provisions.

σῖτο-φύλακες, οἱ corn-inspectors. [corn.]

σῑτ-ώνης, ου, ὁ buyer of corn.

σιφλόω to maim; to hurt.

σιωπάω = σιγάω.

σιωπή, ἡ = σιγή.

σκάζω to halt, limp.

σκαιός 3 left, on the left hand or side; western; awkward, clumsy, silly; unlucky.

σκαιοσύνη, σκαιότης, ητος, ἡ awkwardness, stupidity; coarseness.

σκαίρω to bound, dance.

σκάλλω to dig, hoe.

σκαλμός, ὁ thole of an oar.

σκανδαλίζω to give offence, scandalize. — P. to take offence. [scandal.]

σκάνδαλον, τό offence.

σκαπτός 3 dug.

σκάπτω to dig, hoe.

σκάφη, ἡ, σκάφος, τό hollow vessel, trough, tub; ship, boat, canoe.

σκαφίς, ιδος, ἡ tub, bowl.

σκεδάννῡμι to scatter, disperse, spread abroad. — P. and M. to be scattered, to be spread about.

σκέδασις, ἡ a scattering.

σκέλλω to dry up, parch. — intr. and P. to be parched.

σκέλος, τό leg.

σκέμμα, τό = σκέψις.

σκεπάζω = σκεπάω.

σκέπαρνον, τό carpenter's axe.

σκέπας, αος, τό = σκέπη.

σκέπασμα, τό a covering, shelter; dress.

σκεπάω to cover; to shelter, protect. [protection.]

σκέπη, ἡ covering; shelter,

σκέπτομαι M. = σκοπέω.

σκευ-αγωγέω to secure one's goods.

σκευάζω to prepare, make ready, make; to provide, equip; to dress up.

σκευή, ἡ, σκεῦος, τό dress, attire; ornament; equipment; disguise; vessel, implement, tool; pl. utensils, tools, baggage; tacklings, riggings. [gage.]

σκευο-φορέω to carry bag-

σκευο-φόρος 2 carrying baggage; carrier, porter, baggage-boy.

σκευ-ωρέομαι M. to contrive cunningly.

σκέψις, ἡ an examining, observation, consideration.

σκηνάω, -έω, -όω to dwell in a tent; to dwell, live, be encamped. — M. to dwell; to build for oneself.

σκηνή, ἡ, σκήνημα, τό tent, hut, house; tabernacle, temple; stage, theatre; arbour, bower; banquet.

σκηνίδιον, τό small tent.

σκηνο-πηγία, ἡ feast of the tabernacles.

σκηνο-ποιός, ὁ tent-maker.

σκῆνος, τό = σκηνή.

σκηνο-φύλαξ, ακος, ὁ guard of tents.

σκηνόω = σκηνάω.

σκήνωμα, τό = σκηνή.

σκηπάνιον, τό = σκῆπτρον.

σκηπτός, ὁ storm, gale; thunderbolt.

σκηπτοῦχος 2 bearing a staff or sceptre.

σκῆπτρον, τό staff, stick; sceptre; kingly power.

σκήπτω to prop; to hurl, let fall upon; intr. to fall upon or down. — M. and P. to support oneself; to pretend, allege as an excuse.

σκηρίπτομαι M. to support oneself, to lean against.

σκῆψις, ἡ pretence, excuse, reason.

σκιά, ἡ shadow, shade, darkness; outline; ghost, phantom, spectre.

σκιᾱ-γραφία, ἡ outline; phantom. [cover, veil.]

σκιάζω to overshadow; to

σκιᾱ-μαχέω to fight in the shade; to fight with a shadow.

σκιᾱ-τροφέω to rear in the shade or at home. — intr. and P. to be reared in the shade or effeminately.

σκιάω = σκιάζω.

σκίδνημι = σκεδάννυμι.

σκιερός 3 shady, shaded.

σκίμ-πους, ποδος, ὁ couch, low bed.

σκιο-ειδής 2 shadowy.

σκιόεις 3 = σκιερός.

σκίπων, ωνος, ὁ staff.

σκιρτάω to bound, leap.

σκληρο-καρδία, ἡ hardness of heart.

σκληρός 3 dry, hard, harsh, rough, inflexible; stiff; tough; stern, stubborn; cruel, unyielding.

σκληρότης, ητος, ἡ hardness, stubbornness.

σκληρο-τράχηλος 2 stiffnecked.

σκληρύνω to harden.

σκολιόν, σκόλιον, τό drinking-song.

σκολιός 3 crooked, bent, slanting; tortuous, unjust.

σκόλοψ, οπος, ὁ pale, stake; thorn.

σκόπελος, ὁ rock, crag.

σκοπέω and M. to look at, about, or out; to behold, survey, view; to consider, regard, observe; to spy out; to examine, inquire (into), ascertain; to pay regard to, to heed.

σκοπή, σκοπιά, ἡ a spying, looking out, watch; watchtower, look-out.

σκοπιάζω and M. to keep watch, spy.

σκοπός, ὁ spy; guardian, watcher; mark, aim; object, scope.

σκόροδον, τό garlic.

σκορπίζω to scatter.

σκορπίος, ὁ scorpion.

σκοταῖος 3, σκοτεινός 3 dark, shady; in the dark; blind; secret.

σκοτία, ἡ = σκότος.

σκοτίζω to make dark.

σκότιος 3 and 2 = σκοταῖος.

σκοτο-μήνιος 2 moonless.

σκότος, ὁ and τό darkness, gloom; night; blindness; swoon; nether world; place of concealment; derangement of mind; unclearness.

σκοτόω to make dark.

σκοτώδης 2 dark.

σκύβαλον, τό dirt, filth.

σκυδμαίνω, σκύζομαι to be angry or wroth.

σκυθρωπάζω to look angry or sullen.

σκυθρ-ωπός 2 angry-looking, sullen.

σκύλαξ, ακος, ὁ, ἡ young dog, whelp.

σκύλευμα, τό = σκῦλον.

σκυλεύω to spoil a slain enemy; to rob. [to annoy.]

σκύλλω to rend, mangle;]

σκῦλον, σκύλον, τό spoils, booty, prey. [whelp.]

σκύμνος, ὁ young animal,]

σκυτάλη, ἡ stick, staff; letter-staff, despatch, message. [staff.]

σκυταλίς, ίδος, ἡ small]

σκύταλον, τό = σκυτάλη.

σκυτεύς, ὁ shoemaker, saddler. [maker.]

σκυτεύω to be a shoe-]

σκύτηνος, σκύτινος 3 leathern.

σκῦτος, τό hide, leather.

σκυτο-τομεῖον, τό shoemaker's shop.

σκυτο-τόμος, ὁ = σκυτεύς.

σκύφος, ὁ cup, beaker.

σκωληκό-βρωτος 2 worm-eaten.

σκώληξ, ηκος. ὁ worm.

σκῶλος, ὁ pointed pale.

σκῶμμα, τό jest, joke.

σκώπτω to jest; to jeer, mock.

σκώψ, ωπός, ὁ owl.

σμαράγδινος 3 of emerald.

σμάραγδος, ἡ emerald.

σμαραγέω to sound hollow, to resound; to crash.

σμάω to rub or wipe off. — *M.* to wipe off; to smear oneself.

σμερδαλέος 3, σμερδνός 3 terrible, awful.

σμῆνος, τό swarm of bees, bee-hive; crowd.

σμήχω to rub off.

σμιχρός 3 = μιχρός.

σμυγερός 3 toilsome.

σμύρνα, ἡ myrrh.

σμυρνίζω to season with myrrh.   [smoulder:)

σμύχω to burn, make)

σμῶδιξ, ιγγος, ἡ weal, bloody stripe.   [μαι.)

σοέομαι, σοῦμαι = σεύο-)

σολοικίζω to speak incorrectly.

σόλοικος 2 speaking incorrectly; boorish.

σόλος, ὁ iron disc.

σόος = σῶς.

σορός, ἡ urn; coffin.

σός, σή, σόν thy, thine.

σουδάριον, τό handkerchief.

σοφίᾶ, ἡ cleverness, skill; prudence; craft; knowledge; wisdom; philosophy.

σοφίζω to make wise, instruct, teach. — *M.* to devise, contrive shrewdly.

σόφισμα, τό device, cunning contrivance, craft, trick, artifice, deceit.

σοφιστής, οῦ, ὁ crafty man, artist, master; prudent man, philosopher; teacher of wisdom or eloquence; sophist, shamphilosopher.

σοφιστικός 3 sophistical.

σοφός 3 clever, skilful; prudent; cunning; learned; wise.

σόω = σῴζω.

σπαδίζω to draw off.

σπάθη, ἡ spattle; broad sword.

σπάκα = κύνα. [want of.)

σπανίζω and *P.* to be in)

σπάνιος 3 needy; scarce, scanty; rare.

σπανιότης, ητος, σπάνις, ἡ need, scarcity.

σπανιστός 3 = σπάνιος.

σπανο-σῖτίᾶ, ἡ want of food.   [off; torn body.)

σπάραγμα, τό piece torn)

σπαραγμός, ὁ convulsion.

σπαράσσω and *M.* to tear, rend in pieces.   [cloth.)

σπάργανον, τό swaddling-)

σπαργανόω to swaddle.

σπαργάω to teem, be full.

σπάρτον, τό rope, cable.

σπαρτός 3 scattered, sown.

σπάσμα, τό, σπασμός, ὁ convulsion.   [ously.)

σπαταλάω to live luxuri-)

σπάω to draw, pull, drag; to tear, rend; to drain.

σπεῖος, τό = σπέος.

σπεῖρα, ἡ twisted fold; coil, net; body of soldiers.

σπειρίον, τό light garment.

σπεῖρον, τό wrapper, garment, shroud; sail.

σπείρω to sow, engender; to scatter, spread. — *P.* to be scattered.

σπεχουλάτωρ, ορος, ὁ guard; executioner.

σπένδω to pour out a drink-offering. — *M.* to make a treaty or truce, conclude a peace; to stipulate by treaty.

σπέος, τό cave, grot.

σπέρμα, τό seed, germ; race, family; descent, origin; issue, offspring.

σπερμο-λόγος, ὁ babbler.

σπέρχω to drive or press on. *intr.* and *P.* to haste, hurry; to be hot or angry.

σπεύδω = σπουδάζω.

σπήλαιον, τό cave. [wide.]

σπιδής 2 far-stretched,

σπιθάμη, ἡ span (a measure).

σπιλάς¹, άδος, ἡ crag, rock.

σπιλάς², άδος, ἡ, σπίλος, ὁ, σπίλος, ὁ lime-floor; stain, blemish. [nate.]

σπιλόω to stain, contami-

σπινθήρ, ῆρος, ὁ spark.

σπλαγχνίζομαι *P.* to have compassion or pity.

σπλάγχνον, τό inward parts, bowels; heart, inward nature.

σπλήν, ηνός, ὁ milt.

σπογγίζω to wipe with a sponge.

σπόγγος, ὁ sponge.

σποδιά, ἡ, σποδός, ὁ ashes; heap of ashes; dust.

σπολάς, άδος, ἡ leather bodkin; jerkin.

σπονδ-αρχίαι, αἱ right of beginning a libation.

σπονδή, ἡ drink-offering, libation; *plur.* treaty of peace, truce, covenant.

σπορά, ἡ = σπόρος.

σποράδην *adv.* of σποράς.

σποράς, άδος scattered, detached.

σπορητός, ὁ = σπόρος.

σπόριμος 2 sown; fit for sowing.

σπόρος, ὁ a sowing; seed; birth, descent; produce, crop, offspring.

σπουδάζω *intr.* to make haste, to be zealous, busy, or earnest. — *trans.* to do hastily or earnestly, pursue zealously.

σπουδαιο-λογέομαι *M.* to speak on serious objects.

σπουδαῖος 3 hasty, swift; earnest, zealous; busy, serious; honest, good, grave; excellent, esteemed, costly; serviceable, weighty.

σπουδή, ἡ haste, speed; zeal, earnestness, seriousness, regard, pains, trouble, rivalry.

σπυρίς, ίδος, ἡ basket.

σταγών, όνος, ἡ drop.

στάδιον, τό stadium (a measure of length); racecourse.

στάδιος 3 standing, standing fast; ἡ σταδία close fight. [drop, destil, drip.]

στάζω *trans.* and *intr.* to

σταθμάω and *M.* to measure out, calculate; to estimate, judge.

στάθμη, ἡ chalk-line, rule.

σταθμός, ὁ standing-place; stable, fold, dwelling, quarters; resting-place, station, stage, day's march; standing-post, door-post; balance, weight.

σταῖς, σταιτός, τό wheaten dough.

σταίτινος 3 of dough.

στάλαγμα, τό drop.

σταμίς, ῖνος, ὁ pillar, rib of a ship.

στάμνος, ὁ, ἡ jar, pot.

στασιάζω to rise in rebellion, revolt, quarrel, dispute; to be divided into factions.

στασιασμός, ὁ = στάσις.

στασιαστής, οῦ, ὁ = στασιώτης. [σιώδης.]

στασιαστικός 3 = στα-]

στάσιμος 2 standing.

στάσις, ἡ a standing; position, station, condition; standing-place; a rising, revolt, sedition, party-strife; discord, quarrel; party, faction.

στασιώδης 2 seditious; divided into factions.

στασιώτης, ου, ὁ partisan; insurgent. [ώδης.]

στασιωτικός 3 = στασι-]

στατήρ, ῆρος, ὁ stater, a gold or silver coin.

στατός 3 standing, placed.

σταυρός, ὁ palisade; cross.

σταυρόω to palisade; to crucify.

σταύρωμα, τό, σταύρωσις, ἡ palisade, stockade.

σταφυλή, ἡ bunch of grapes.

στάχυς, υος, ὁ ear of corn.

στέαρ, ατος, τό fat, tallow; fish-oil.

στεγάζω = στέγω.

στεγανός 3 covering; tight; covered, roofed. [the house.]

στέγ-αρχος, ὁ master of]

στέγασμα, τό, στέγη, ἡ covering, roof; ceiling; shelter, house, dwelling.

στεγνός 3 covering, sheltering; covered.

στέγος, τό = στέγη.

στέγω to cover, shelter; to protect, keep off; to contain, hold; to conceal, hide, keep secret; to bear, endure.

στείβω to tread; to tread on; to tread under food.

στειλειή, ἡ, στειλειόν, τό handle.

στεινο- etc. see στενο-.

στειπτός 3 trodden on.

στεῖρα, ἡ stem, cut-water.

στεῖρος 3 barren.

στείχω to walk, step, go, march; to approach; to go away.

στέλεχος, τό stump, trunk.

στέλλω to arrange; to make ready, equip; to furnish, fit out, clothe, adorn; to invite, fetch, summon; to send, despatch. — intr. and P. to equip oneself, make oneself ready; to start, set off, depart; to go, come, travel. — M. to put on (one's clothes), to send for; to retire from, avoid.

στέμμα, τό fillet, wreath, chaplet; olive-branch.

στέναγμα, τό, στεναγμός. ὁ = στόνος.

στενάζω = στένω.

στενακτός 3 to be sighed for; sighing.

στεναχίζω and M. στενάχω and M. = στένω. [στ. defile.]

στενό-πορος 2 narrow; τὰ]

στενός 3 narrow, strait; scanty; τὸ στενόν, τὰ στενά strait, narrows; limited means, embarrassment.

στενότης, ητος, ἡ narrowness, straitness.

στενο-χωρέω to straiten; to be straitened. — P. to be distressed.

στενο-χωρία, ἡ narrowness; defile; distress, anguish.

στένω[1] to make narrow. — P. to be compressed; to be crammed or full.

στένω[2] to sigh, moan, groan; to sound, ring; trans. to bemoan, bewail, lament.

στεν-ωπός 2 narrow; ὁ στ. narrow way, strait.

στέργημα, τό love-charm.

στέργω to love, like, be fond of; to be pleased with; to be content or satisfied; to pray.

στερεός 3 stiff, stark, solid; strong; stubborn, constant; cruel, unrelenting.

στερεό-φρων 2 stubborn.

στερεόω to make firm or strong.

στερέω to deprive, bereave. — P. to be deprived (of), to lose.   [ment.]
στερέωμα, τό firmness; firμ-

στέρησις, ἡ privation, loss.

στερίσκω = στερέω.

στέρίφος 3 = στερεός; = στεῖρος.   [loved.]
στερκτός 3 beloved, to be

στέρνον, τό breast; heart.

στερνοῦχος 2 far-stretched.

στέρομαι P. to be deprived.

στεροπή, ἡ flash of lightning; glare.

στεροπ-ηγερέτα, ὁ sender of lightning.

στέροψ, οπος flashing, dazzling.

στερρός 3 = στερεός.

στεῦμαι to make gestures; to take on as if, show signs as if; to promise, threaten.

στεφάνη, ἡ = στέφανος.

στεφανη-φορέω to wear a wreath.

στεφανη-φόρος 2, στεφανίτης, ου wearing a wreath, crowned, wreathed; giving a wreath as prize.

στέφανος, ὁ circlet, crown, wreath; circle, ring; crown of victory, prize, reward.

στεφανόω to encircle, surround, put round as a crown; to crown, wreath, adorn, distinguish, reward. — M. to crown oneself.

στεφάνωμα, τό, στέφος, τό = στέφανος.

στέφω = στεφανόω.

στῆθος, τό breast; heart, feelings; understanding.

στήκω to stand.

στήλη, ἡ pillar, post; boundary-post; upright stone.

στηλίτης, ου inscribed on a pillar as infamous.

στήμων, ονος, ὁ warp in the loom; thread.

στηριγμός, ὁ prop, support, firmness.

στηρίζω to set fast, prop, confirm. — intr. and M. to stand fast; to lean against; to have a footing.

στιβαρός 3 compact, stout, sturdy.

στιβάς, άδος, ή bed of straw, litter; tuft of leaves.

στιβέω to search through.

στίβη, ή rime, hoar-frost.

στίβος, δ path, footstep, track, trail.

στίβω = στείβω. [matiser.]

στιγεύς, δ brander, stig-/

στίγμα, τό prick, point; brandmark, blemish, stain.

στιγματίας, ου, δ one who has been branded.

στιγμή, ή = στίγμα.

στίζω to prick, sting; to tattoo; to brand.

στικτός 3 spotted.

στίλβω to shine, glitter.

στιλπνός 3 glittering.

στίξ, στιχός, ή = στίχος.

στίφος, τό dense crowd, column of warriors.

στιχάομαι M. to march in rows.

στίχος, δ row, line; battle-array; line of writing, verse.

στλεγγίς, ίδος, ή scraper; comb.

στοά, ή colonnade, portico.

στοιβάς, άδος, ή = στιβάς.

στοιχεῖον, τό first principle, element, primary matter; elements of knowledge; letter of the alphabet.

στοιχέω = στιχάομαι.

στοῖχος, δ = στίχος.

στολάς, άδος, ή = σπολάς.

στολή, ή dress, garment, clothing; equipment; state-dress.

στόλος, δ equipment, sending, expedition, journey;

army, fleet, armament; troop, people; ship's beak.

στόμα, τό mouth; tongue, speech, language, words; face; outlet; chasm, cleft; point, edge; front.

στόμ-αργος 2 talkative, obtrusive in speech.

στόμ-αχος, δ throat; stomach; mouth. [bridle-bit.]

στόμιον, τό mouth, opening;/

στομόω to stop the mouth; to prepare an attack.

στόμωσις, ή a sharpening; sharp speech.

στοναχέω = στένω.

στοναχή, ή = στόνος.

στοναχίζω = στεναχίζω.

στονόεις 3 roaring; moaning; mournful.

στόνος, δ a roaring, sighing, groaning.

στόρνῡμι to spread out, stretch out; to cover with blankets; to spread smooth, to level; to calm; to strew over.

στοχάζομαι M. to aim at, shoot at, look at; to hit the mark; to guess, conjecture.

στοχαστικός 3 sagacious.

στόχος, δ aim, guess.

στράπτω to lighten.

στρατάομαι P. to be encamped.

στρατ-άρχης, ου, δ general.

στρατεία, ή expedition, campaign; army; military service.

στράτευμα, τό expedition; army; camp; soldiers.

στρατεύω and M. to serve

as a soldier; to take the field, march, fight.

στρατηγέω to be a general; to command, lead, manage.

στρατήγημα, τό stratagem, strategy.

στρατηγίᾱ, ἡ office of a general, command; strategy.

στρατηγιάω to wish to be general.

στρατηγικός 3 fit for a general, skilled in command. [tent.]

στρατήγιον, τό general's]

στρατηγίς, ίδος, ἡ of a general.

στρατ-ηγός, ὁ general, leader, commander of an army; admiral; governor; consul; a military magistrate at Athens.

στρατηλασίη, ἡ = στρατεία.

στρατ-ηλατέω = στρατηγέω. [στρατηγός.]

στρατ-ηλάτης, ου, ὁ =]

στρατιά, ἡ army, force; band, company; campaign.

στράτιος 3 military, warlike.

στρατιώτης, ου, ὁ soldier, warrior, mercenary.

στρατιωτικός 3 of or for soldiers; fit for military service.

στρτιῶτις, ιδος, fem. (ναῦς) troop-ship.

στρατο-λογέω to levy an army. [τάομαι.]

στρατόομαι P. = στρα-]

στρατοπεδ-άρχης, ου, ὁ commander of the imperial guard.

στρατοπεδείᾱ, στρατοπέ-

δευσις, ἡ an encamping; station; encamped army.

στρατοπεδεύομαι M. to encamp; to lie at anchor.

στρατό-πεδον, τό encampment, camp; army; fleet.

στρατός, ὁ camp; army, body of soldiers; people.

στρεβλόω to twist, distort; to sprain, wrench; to rack, torture.

στρέμμα, τό sprain.

στρεπτός 3 twisted, plaited; pliant, flexible; ὁ στ. neckchain; cracknel.

στρεπτο-φόρος 2 wearing a necklace. [hausted.]

στρεύγομαι P. to be ex-]

στρεφο-δῑνέομαι P. to be whirled or giddy.

στρέφω to twist, turn, bend; to turn about, wheel round, alter, twist back, sprain. — intr. and P. to be twisted, twist oneself, turn oneself (round about, to and fro); to turn back, flee; to roam about; to attach oneself (to); to be changed; to evade.

στρηνιάω to be wanton.

στρῆνος, τό vigour; wantonness.

στρογγύλος 3 round(ed); στρογγύλη ναῦς merchantship.

στρόμβος, ὁ whirl-gig.

στρουθίον, τό, στρουθός, ὁ sparrow; ostrich. [eddy.]

στροφάλιγξ, ιγγος.ἡ whirl,]

στροφάς, άδος whirling.

στροφο-δῑνέομαι P. = στρεφοδ.

στρόφος, ὁ rope, cord, band.

στρυφνός 3 sour; morose.

στρῶμα, τό = στρωμνή.

στρωματό-δεσμον, τό sack for packing beds in.

στρωμνή, ἡ couch, bed; mattress; bedding.

στρώννῦμι = στόρνυμι.

στρωτός 3 spread.

στρωφάω to turn, spin. — P. to roam about; to stay, dwell.

στυγερός = στυγνός.

στυγέω to hate, abhor, detest; to fear; to make horrid.

στυγητός 3 abominated.

Στύγιος 3 Stygian.

στυγνάζω to be sad or gloomy.

στυγνός 3 hated, abominated; horrible, terrible; gloomy, morose, sad; mournful, miserable.

στῦλος, ὁ pillar, prop.

στυππεῖον, τό tow.

στυπτηρία, ἡ alum.

στυράκιον, τό, στύραξ[1], ακος, ὁ end of a spearshaft. [tree.]

στύραξ[2], ακος, ὁ, ἡ storax-

στυφελίζω to thrust, push; to shake; to drive; to beat; to maltreat.

στυφελός 3 and 2 close, dense, solid, rough, harsh.

σύ thou. [herd of swine.]

σύ-βόσιον, -βόσειον, τό

σύ-βώτης, ου, ὁ swineherd.

συγ-γένεια, ἡ relationship; kinsfolk, family.

συγ-γενής 2 born with one, inborn; connected by birth, related; kinsman; resembling, natural.

συγ-γενίς, ιδος, ἡ fem. of συγγενής. [together.]

συγγενής. [together.]

συγ-γηράσκω to grow old

συγ-γίγνομαι M. to come together, meet; to converse with; to come to assist; to live with.

συγ-γιγνώσκω to concur in opinion, agree, consent; to acknowledge, concede, yield; to know with; to excuse, pardon. — M. to grant, allow, yield.

σύγ-γνοια, ἡ, συγ-γνώμη, ἡ, συγ-γνωμοσύνη, ἡ pardon, forgiveness, excuse; permission.

συγ-γνώμων 2 forgiving, indulgent, allowing; pardonable.

σύγ-γονος 2 = συγ-γενής.

σύγ-γραμμα, ὁ written paper, essay; (prose-)book.

συγ-γραφεύς, ὁ writer, author; historian; prosewriter; writer of laws and statutes

συγ-γραφή, ἡ a writing down = σύγγραμμα.

συγ-γραφικῶς adv. exactly.

συγ-γράφω to write or note down; to describe, compose; to write history; to draw up a contract or resolution.

συγ-γυμνάζομαι P. to train oneself together.

συγ-καθαιρέω to pull down or overthrow together. [together.]

συγ-καθαρμόζω to inter-

συγ-καθέζομαι P., συγ-κάθημαι to sit with.

συγ-καθίζω and *M.* to sit together; to place together.

συγ-καθίημι to let down; *intr.* to stoop, condescend.

συγ-καθίστημι to establish together or with.

συγ-κακοπαθέω, συγ-κακουχέομαι *P.* to suffer together.

συγ-καλέω to call together, summon. — *M.* to call to oneself. [veil completely.]

συγ-καλύπτω to cover,]

συγ-κάμνω to work, labour, or suffer together or with.

συγ-κάμπτω to bend together. [down together.]

συγ-καταβαίνω to go]

συγ-κατάγω to lead down with. [together.]

συγ-καταδιώκω to pursue]

συγ-καταδουλόω and *M.* to subdue together.

συγ-καταζεύγνυμι to entangle. [jointly.]

συγ-καταθάπτω to bury]

συγ-κατάθεσις, ἡ agreement. [gether.]

συγ-καταίθω to burn to-]

συγ-κάταινος 2 agreeing.

συγ-κατακαίω, -κάω to burn at once. [down with.]

συγ-κατάκειμαι *M.* to lie]

συγ-κατακλείω, -κληίω to shut in together.

συγ-κατακτάομαι *M.* to acquire together.

συγ-κατακτείνω to slay together.

συγ-καταλαμβάνω to seize or capture together.

συγ-καταλείπω to leave behind together.

συγ-καταλύω to overthrow jointly.

συγ-κατανέμομαι *M.* to possess in company.

συγ-καταπράττω and *M.* to effect together.

συγ-κατασκεδάννυμι to pour over at once.

συγ-κατασκευάζω to make ready or prepare together.

συγ-καταστρέφομαι *M.* to help in subduing.

συγ-κατατίθεμαι *M.* to lay down at the same time; to consent to.

συγ-καταψηφίζω to choose in addition. — *M.* to condemn together.

συγ-κατεργάζομαι *M.* to accomplish together; to help in procuring; to assist.

συγ-κατέρχομαι to return together. [for together.]

συγ-κατεύχομαι *M.* to pray]

συγ-κατηγορέω to accuse together. [together.]

συγ-κατοικέω to dwell]

συγ-κατοικίζω to colonize jointly; to help in restoring.

σύγ-κειμαι to lie with, be together; to be composed or agreed (upon).

συγ-κελεύω to join in bidding. [or to the ground.]

συγ-κεντέω to stab down]

συγ-κεράννυμι to mix or blend together.

συγ-κεφαλαιόω to sum up.

συγ-κινδυνεύω to be partners in danger.

συγ-κινέω to raise up.

σύγ-κλεισις, ἡ a shutting up; tightness.

συγ-κλείω, -κλήω, συγ-κληίω to shut up, enclose, compress; to encompass, surround; to close, shut. — *intr.* and *M.* to be joined, concentrated, united, or shut in.

συγ-κληρονόμος, ὁ co-heir.

σύγ-κληρος 2 assigned by the same lot.

συγ-κληρόω to assign by the same lot.

σύγ-κλητος 2 called together; ἡ σ. senate.

συγ-κλίνομαι *P.* to lie with.

συγ-κλονέω to confound.

σύγ-κλυς, υδος flocked together. [or sleep with.]

συγ-κοιμάομαι *P.* to lie

συγ-κοινόομαι *M.* to make common with, give a share.

συγ-κοινωνέω to get a share.

συγ-κοινωνός 2 partaking.

συγ-κομιδή, ἡ a bringing together, gathering in; concourse.

συγ-κομίζω to bring together, gather in; to afford together; to bury together. — *M.* to gather in for oneself, to procure for oneself; to send for.

συγ-κόπτω to beat together; to knock to pieces; to beat soundly, slay.

σύγ-κρασις, ἡ a mixing together, blending.

συγ-κρίνω to put together; to compare; to judge.

συγ-κροτέω to beat, strike, or hammer together; to drill, train well.

συγ-κρούω to strike together; to set at variance, make enemies; — *intr.* to collide.

συγ-κρύπτω to help in hiding; to conceal completely.

συγ-κτάομαι *M.* to acquire jointly, to help to acquire.

συγ-κτίζω to found together. [founder.]

συγ-κτίστης, ου, ὁ fellow-

συγ-κυβεύω to play at dice with.

συγ-κύπτω to bend forward or stoop so as to meet; to draw nearer; to conspire; to be bent or curved.

συγ-κυρέω and *M.* to encounter, meet; to happen, come to pass. [chance.]

συγ-κυρία, ἡ coincidence,

συγ-χαίρω to rejoice with.

συγ-χέω to pour together, mix by pouring, mingle; to confound, trouble, disturb; to frustrate, spoil, break up.

σύγ-χορευτής, οῦ, ὁ partner in a dance.

συγ-χόω to cover over with earth; to demolish.

συγ-χράομαι *M.* to have intercourse with.

συγ-χύννω = συγχέω.

σύγ-χυσις, ἡ a mixing, confounding; disturbing; overthrow, revolt.

συγ-χώννῡμι = συγχόω.

συγ-χωρέω to go together; to agree, accede, assent to; to give way, yield, acquiesce in, concede; συγχωρεῖ it is allowed or possible.

σύειος 3 of swine.

συ-ζάω to live with or together.

συ-ζεύγνῡμι to yoke together, couple, unite.

συ-ζητέω to debate.

συ-ζήτησις, ἡ disputation.

συ-ζητητής, οῦ, ὁ disputer.

συ-ζυγία, ἡ union; pair.

σύ-ζυγος 2 yoked together; consort, mate.

συ-ζωοποιέω to quicken at the same time.

σῡκάμῑνος, ἡ, σῡκο-μορέα, ἡ fig-mulberry.

σῡκῆ, σῡκέη, ἡ fig-tree.

σῦκον, τό fig.

σῡκο-φαντέω to be a false accuser, slanderer or extorter.

σῡκο-φάντης, ου, ὁ fig-informer, false accuser, slanderer, extorter.

σῡκο-φαντία, ἡ false accusation, slander.

σῡλ-αγωγέω to carry off as booty.

σῡλάω, σῡλεύω to take away; to strip off, despoil, pillage, plunder.

σῡλη, ἡ = σῦλον pl.

σῡλ-λαβή, ἡ syllable.

σῡλ-λαλέω to talk with.

σῡλ-λαμβάνω M. to put or bring together; to collect; to comprehend; to take away, carry away; to lay hold of, seize, arrest; to receive; to perceive, understand; to take part (in), assist, help.

σῡλ-λέγω to collect, gather, call together, levy (an army).

— P. to assemble, meet. M. to collect for oneself.

συλ-λήβδην, adv. taken together, in short.

συλ-λήπτρια, ἡ, -λήπτωρ, ορος, ὁ partner, assistant.

σύλ-ληψις, ἡ a seizing, comprehension.

συλ-λογή, ἡ a gathering, collecting, assembly, concourse; a levying of soldiers.

συλ-λογίζομαι M. to reckon, consider, think, reflect; to infer, conclude.

σύλ-λογος, ὁ = συλλογή.

συλ-λοχίτης, ου, ὁ soldier of the same company.

συλ-λῡπέομαι P. to feel compassion.

συλ-λύω to help in loosing.

σῦλον, τό seizure of a cargo; privateering.

σῦμα, τό = θῦμα.

συμ-βαίνω to go or come together, meet; to agree, make an agreement, make friends, reconcile; to suit, fit, correspond, be like; to coincide, happen, fall out, come to pass, turn out, result, succeed. συμ-βαίνει it happens, it is possible.

συμ-βάλλω and M. to throw together, bring together, unite, mix, join closely; to engage in, begin; to set together, incite; to compare, compute, guess; to interpret, understand; to come together, meet, join, encounter, fight. — M. to agree, make a treaty; to contribute, furnish, be useful; to put forth, produce, offer; to judge, consider.

συμ-βασείω to wish to make a treaty.

συμ-βασιλεύω to reign jointly. [ment.]

σύμ-βασις, ἡ treaty, agree-]

συμ-βατήριος 2, συμβατικός 3 tending to agreement, conciliatory.

συμ-βιάζω to oppress all together.

συμ-βιβάζω to bring or put together; to reconcile; to compare, contrast; to guess; to perceive; to prove; to teach.

συμ-βιόω to live with.

συμ-βοάω to cry aloud or shout together with; to call to.

συμ-βοήθεια, ἡ joint aid

συμ-βοηθέω to render joint aid.

συμβόλαιος 3 stipulated. τὸ συμβόλαιον intercourse; bargain; contract; debenture; debt, money lent; symptom, token.

συμ-βολή, ἡ a meeting; encountering, engagement, battle; joint, end, joining; contribution.

σύμ-βολον, τό treaty (of commerce); mark, sign, token, signal, symbol; ticket, badge.

συμ-βουλεύω to advise, counsel; to propose. — M. to take counsel with, deliberate, consult.

συμ-βουλή, -βουλία, ἡ,

συμ-βούλιον, τό advice, counsel, consultation; senate, council.

συμ-βούλομαι P. to wish too, agree. [counsellor.]

συμ-βουλος, ὁ, ἡ adviser,]

συμ-μαθητής, οῦ, ὁ schoolfellow, fellow-disciple.

συμ-μανθάνω to learn together; aor. to be used to.

συμ-μάρπτω to grasp together.

συμ-μαρτυρέω and M. to bear witness with, corroborate. [ness.]

σύμ-μαρτυς, υρος, ὁ wit-]

συμ-μαχέω to fight jointly, to be allied in war; to help.

συμ-μαχία, ἡ alliance in war; allies; assistance.

συμ-μαχικός 3 of or for alliance; τὸ συμμαχικόν auxiliaries, allied forces; treaty of alliance; treasury of allies.

συμ-μαχίς, ίδος, fem. of σύμμαχος; allied state; body of allies. [μαχέω.]

συμ-μάχομαι M. = συμ-]

σύμ-μαχος 2 allied, fighting jointly; ally; assistant, helper.

συμ-μένω to stay together; to abide, continue.

συμ-μερίζομαι M.. συμμετέχω, συμ-μετίσχω to receive a share along with.

σύμ-μετοχος 2 partaking in jointly.

συμ-μετρέω and M. to measure, compute, measure out. — P. to be commensurate, correspond.

συμ-μέτρησις, ἡ admeasurement. [symmetry.]

συμ-μετρίᾱ, ἡ proportion,]

σύμ-μετρος 3 measured with, commensurate with, in due proportion, symmetrical, fitting, fitted.

συμ-μητιάομαι M. to take counsel with.

συμ-μιγής 2 = σύμμικτος, adv. σύμμιγα along with.

συμ-μίγνῡμι to mix with, mingle with; to unite; to communicate to.— intr. and P. to be mingled, blended, or united; to have intercourse; to converse with; to encounter, engage in battle, come to blows; to befall.

σύμ-μικτος 2 intermingled, promiscuous, confounded; common. [imitator.]

συμ-μῑμητής, οῦ, ὁ fellow-]

σύμ-μῑξις, ἡ a mixing together; marriage.

συμ-μίσγω = -μίγνῡμι.

συμ-μορίᾱ, ἡ class of taxpayers; division of the fleet.

σύμ-μορος 2 paying taxes along with.

συμ-μορφίζω to form alike

σύμ-μορφος 2 of like shape.

συμ-μορφόω = συμμορφίζω.

συμ-παθέω to feel with, sympathize. [nate.]

συμ-παθής 2 compassio-]

συμ-παίζω to play with.

συμ-παίω to beat or strike together or against one another.

συμ-παραγίγνομαι M. to arrive at the same time, be present, assist.

συμ-παραθέω to run along with.

συμ-παρακαλέω to call upon, invite, comfort, or exhort at the same time.

συμ-παρακομίζω to conduct (together).

συμ-παραλαμβάνω to take along with. [along with.]

συμ-παραμένω to stay]

συμ-παρασκευάζω to join in preparing, to make ready or provide jointly. [helper.]

συμ-παραστάτης, ου, ὁ]

συμ-παρατάσσομαι M. to be drawn up in battle-array with, to fight along with.

συμ-πάρειμι[1](-ιέναι) to go along at the same time.

συμ-πάρειμι[2](-εῖναι) to be present with or at the same time. [along with.]

συμ-παρέχω to present]

συμ-παρίσταμαι M. to stand beside one at the same time.

σύμ-πᾱς, ᾱσα, ᾱν all together, all at once; the whole, in sum.

συμ-πάσχω to suffer with, sympathize. [suading.]

συμ-πείθω to join in per-]

συμ-πέμπω to send along with; to join in a procession.

συμ-περαίνω and M. to finish along with; to achieve entirely.

συμ-περιλαμβάνω to comprehend together with.

συμ-περιπατέω to walk to and fro with. [congeal.]

συμ-πήγνῡμι to fasten; to]

σύμ-πηκτος 2 compact.

συμ-πιέζω to press together.

συμ-πίνω to drink with.

συμ-πίπτω to fall down; to fall in with, meet with; to come to blows; to coincide; to happen, come to pass; to fall into.

συμ-πλαταγέω to clap together.

συμ-πλέκω to plait together. — P. to be plaited or entangled; to come to close quarters.

συμ-πλέω to sail together.

σύμ-πλεως, ων quite full.

συμ-πληθύω -πληρόω to fill or man completely; to complete.

σύμ-πλοος, -πλους, ὁ, ἡ fellow-passenger, comrade.

συμ-πνέω to be of the same mind.

συμ-πνίγω to choke up.

συμ-ποδίζω to fetter (the feet); to entangle.

συμ-πολεμέω to make war along with. [jointly.]

συμ-πολιορκέω to besiege.

συμ-πολῑτεύω and M. to live in the same state, be a fellow-citizen.

συμ-πονέω to partake in work or misery.

συμ-πορεύομαι P. to go or travel together. [ther.]

συμ-πορίζω to bring together.

συμποσί-αρχος, ὁ president of a drinking-party.

συμ-πόσιον, τό drinking-bout, entertainment; banquet. [drinker, guest.]

συμ-πότης, ου, ὁ fellow-

συμ-πράκτωρ, ορος. ὁ helper, assistant.

συμ-πράσσω to help in doing, assist. — M. to join in avenging.

συμ-πρεσβεύω and M. to be a fellow-ambassador.

σύμ-πρεσβυς, εως, ὁ fellow-ambassador.

συμ-πρεσβύτερος, ὁ fellow-elder. [ωνέομαι.]

συμ-πρίασθαι, aor. of συν-

συμ-προθῡμέομαι P. to have equal zeal or eagerness.

συμ-προπέμπω to join in escorting. [ther.]

συμ-πτύσσω to fold together.

σύμ-πτωμα, τό chance; accident, misfortune.

συμ-φερόντως adv. profitably.

συμ-φερτός 3 united.

συμ-φέρω to bring together, collect; to contribute; to bear jointly. — intr. to be useful, profitable, advantageous, or expedient; συμφέρει it is profitable; it is advantageous; to agree with; to assist, be serviceable. — P. to come together; to agree together, assent to; to converse with, have intercourse; to encounter; to happen, come to pass.

συμ-φεύγω to flee along with; to be a fellow-exile.

σύμ-φημι to assent, say yes, approve; to promise.

συμ-φιλέω to join in loving.

συμ-φιλονῑκέω to take sides. [frightening.]

συμ-φοβέω to join in

συμ-φοιτάω to go regular-
ly to together.

συμ-φοιτητής, οῦ, ὁ schoolfellow.

συμ-φορά, ἡ event, chance,
good luck; misfortune,
disaster, calamity; defeat;
success, result. [camp.]

συμ-φορεύς, ὁ aide-de-
συμ-φορέω = συμφέρω.

σύμ-φορος 2 useful, profitable, favourable; conve-
nient.

συμ-φρ δμων 2 counsellor.

συμ-φράζομαι to take counsel with; to consider.

συμ-φράσσω to press toge-
ther.

σύμ-φρουρος 2 protecting.

συμ-φυγάς, άδος, ὁ fellow-
exile. [watchman.]

συμ-φύλαξ, ακος, ὁ fellow-
συμ-φυλάσσω to watch to-
gether. [same tribe.]

συμ-φῡλέτης, ου, ὁ of the
συμ-φύρω to knead or mix
together.

συμ-φυτεύω to plant in
together; to contrive together.

σύμ-φυτος 2 grown toge-
ther; innate, cognate.

συμ-φύω to let grow toge-
ther. — intr. and P. to grow
together or into one.

συμ-φωνέω to agree in
sound, be in unison; to
make an agreement.

συμ-φώνησις, ἡ, συμ-
φωνίᾱ, ἡ harmony; music.

σύμ-φωνος 2 harmonious,
agreeing in sound; con-
cordant.

συμ-φάω to sweep away.

συμ-ψηφίζω to reckon to-
gether. — M. to vote with.

σύμ-ψῡχος 2 unanimous.

σύν, ξύν adv. together, at
once. — prp. with dat. with,
in company with, together
with, in connexion with;
in accordance with; fur-
nished with, by means of;
under the command of.

συν-άγγελος, ὁ fellow-
messenger.

συν-αγείρω to gather to-
gether, assemble, collect.

συν-άγνῡμι to break in or
to pieces, shiver.

συν-αγορεύω to agree to,
join in recommending.

συν-άγω to lead or bring together, collect, assemble; to
summon, admit; to contract,
draw together, straiten. —
P. to be assembled; to be
admitted. [cruiter.]

συν-αγωγεύς, ὁ uniter; re-
συν-αγωγή, ἡ a collecting,
gathering, uniting; place
of meeting, synagogue; preparation.

συν-αγωνίζομαι M. to con-
tend along with; to assist,
help.

συν-αγωνιστής, οῦ, ὁ fel-
low-combatant; helper.

συν-άδελφος 2 having bro-
ther or sister. [wrong.]

συν-αδικέω to join in doing
συν-ᾄδω to accord with.

συν-αείρω[1] = συναίρω.

συν-αείρω[2] to yoke together.

συν-αθλέω = συναγωνίζο-
μαι.

συν-αθροίζω to gather together. [blood.]

σύν-αιμος 2 related by

συν-αινέω to join in approving; to assent, agree.

συν-αίνυμαι to take together.

συν-αιρέω to seize together, comprise, comprehend; to seize wholly; to snatch away, destroy; to help in taking.

συν-αίρω and M. to raise or lift up together. — M. to undertake jointly.

συν-αίτιος 2 and 3 accessory, accomplice. [captive.]

συν-αιχμάλωτος, ὁ fellow-

συν-αιωρέομαι to be held in suspense with.

συν-ακολουθέω to follow along with. [same time.]

συν-ακούω to hear at the

συν-αλγέω to suffer pain with; to feel pity.

συν-αλίζω to assemble. — P. to come together.

συν-αλλαγή, ἡ change, interchange; intercourse, conversation; reconciliation, intervention; lot, vicissitude.

συν-αλλάσσω to associate; to reconcile, settle; intr. to have intercourse or to deal with. — P. to be united or reconciled.

συν-αμφότερος 3 both together; both in the same manner. [along with.]

συν-αναβαίνω to go up

συν-αναγκάζω to enforce at the same time.

συν-αναιρέω to destroy at the same time.

συν-ανάκειμαι to recline at table with.

συν-αναλίσκω to spend or waste along with.

συν-αναμίγνυμαι P. to have intercourse with.

συν-αναπαύομαι M. to refresh oneself together with.

συν-αναπείθω to join in persuading. [exacting.]

συν-αναπράσσω to join in

συν-αναχωρέω to go back together.

συν-ανίστημι to help in restoring; intr. and M. to rise together.

συν-αντάω and M. to meet with; to happen.

συν-άντησις, ἡ a meeting.

συν-αντιάζω = συναντάω.

συν-αντιλαμβάνομαι M. to lay hold of along with, to help.

συν-άντομαι = -αντάω.

συν-αορέω to be joined to.

συν-άορος 2 united, linked with; consort.

συν-απάγω to lead away with.

συν-άπας 3 = σύμπας.

συν-άπειμι (-ιέναι) to go away with.

συν-αποβαίνω to disembark along with.

συν-αποθνῄσκω to die together with.

συν-απολαμβάνω to receive at once.

συν-απόλλυμι to destroy, lose together. — M. to perish together.

συν-απονεύω to bend away according to.

συν-αποπέμπω, συν-αποστέλλω to send away together.

συν-άπτω and M. to tie or join together, unite. — intr. to join, attach oneself (to), to partake in; to border on; to take counsel together; to come to blows.

συν-αράσσω to strike together, dash to pieces.

συν-αρέσκει μοί τι it pleases me too.

συν-αρμόζω and M. to fit together, to join; to agree together.

συν-αρμολογέομαι to be joined exactly.

συν-αρμόττω = -αρμόζω.

συν-αρπάζω to seize abruptly; to snatch or carry away.

συν-αρτάω to knit together. — P. pf. to be caught by.

συν-άρχω to rule jointly with, be a colleague.

συν-ασπιδόω to keep the shields close together.

συν-ασπιστής, οῦ, ὁ fellow-soldier.

συν-αυδάω to agree to.

σύν-αυλος 2 dwelling together.

συν-αυξάνω, -αύξω to let grow or increase together. — P. to grow larger together.

συν-αφαιρέω and M. to assist in delivering.

συν-αφίστημι to make revolt together. — intr and M. to revolt along with.

συν-άχθομαι P. to mourn with. [with.]

συν-δαΐζω to kill together]

συν-δακρύω to weep with.

συν-δειπνέω to dine together.

σύν-δειπνον, τό banquet.

σύν-δειπνος 2 dining together. [fetter; bundle.]

σύν-δεσμος, ὁ band, union;]

συν-δεσμώτης, ου, ὁ fellow-prisoner. [ther.]

συν-δέω to bind together, fetter; to join, unite.

συν-διαβάλλω to slander or accuse jointly; to cross over together. [over with.]

συν-διαβιβάζω to carry]

συν-διαγιγνώσκω to decide jointly. [together.]

συν-διαιτάομαι P. to live]

συν-διακινδῡνεύω to incur danger jointly.

συν-διαλύω to break up or abolish jointly.

συν-διαπεραίνω to help in finishing.

συν-διαπολεμέω to join in making war to the end.

συν-διαπράσσω to effect together — M. to help in negotiating.

συν-διασκέπτομαι M., συν-διασκοπέω to examine together with.

συν-διασῴζω to help in preserving.

συν-διαταλαιπωρέω to endure hardship with.

συν-διατελέω to continue with. [time with.]

συν-διατρίβω to pass one's]

συν-διαφέρω and M. to bear with to the end.

συν-διαχειρίζω to manage jointly.

συν-διέξειμι (-ιέναι) to go through along with.

συν-δικάζω to assist in judging. [vocate.]

συν-δικέω to act as an ad-]

σύν-δικος 2 helping · in court; advocate; attorney; assistant.

συν-διώκω to help in pursuing. [to me too.]

συν-δοκεῖ μοι it seems good]

συν-δοκιμάζω to test along with.

συν-δοξάζω to join in approving of or in extolling.

συν-δούλη, ἡ, σύν-δουλος, ὁ, ἡ fellow-slave.

συν-δράω to do together.

συν-δρομή, ἡ concourse.

σύν-δυο two and two, two together.

σύν-εγγυς adv. quite near.

συν-εδρία, ἡ, -εδριον, τό a sitting together or in council; senate; senate-house.

σύν-εδρος 2 sitting together; sitting in council.

συν-εθέλω to wish likewise.

συν-εθίζω to accustom. — P. to become used to.

συν-είδησις, ἡ joint knowledge; consciousness; conscience.

συν-ειλέω to press or bind together. [χομαι.]

σύν-ειμι[1] (-ιέναι) = συνέρ-]

σύν-ειμι[2] (-εῖναι) to be or live together, to be joined,

united, or associated; to have intercourse (with); to assist.

συν-είργω to shut in together; to enclose or bind together, gird; to unite.

συν-είρω to string together; to unite. [with.]

συν-εισάγω to bring in]

συν-εισβάλλω to invade together. [together.]

συν-εισέρχομαι to go in]

συν-εισπίπτω to fall into along with; to invade together. [together.]

συν-εισπλέω to sail into]

συν-εισφέρω to join in contributing. [gether.]

συν-εκβαίνω to go up to-]

συν-εκβάλλω to cast out together. [bringing out.]

συν-εκβιβάζω to help in]

συν-έκδημος, ὁ travelling companion.

συν-εκδίδωμι to help in portioning out.

συν-εκδύομαι M. to put off clothes together.

συν-εκκομίζω to help in burying. [cutting off.]

συν-εκκόπτω to help in]

συν-εκλεκτός 3 chosen along with.

συν-εκπέμπω to assist in sending out or escorting.

συν-εκπίνω to drink off together.

συν-εκπίπτω to fall out; to be thrown out together.

συν-εκπλέω, -πλώω to sail out together.

συν-εκπορίζω to help in procuring.

συν-εκπράσσομαι *M.* to help in avenging.

συν-εκσᾐζω to help in preserving.

συν-εκτρέφω to rear up jointly. [funeral.]

συν-εκφέρω to attend a/

συν-ελαύνω to drive or bring together; to clench (the teeth); to exhort. — *intr.* to meet in quarrel.

συν-ελευθερόω to help in freeing.

συν-εμβάλλω to join in making an inroad.

συν-έμπορος, ὁ fellow-traveller, companion.

συν-εξαιρέω to help in destroying or capturing.

συν-εξακούω to hear exactly with one.

συν-εξαμαρτάνω to err or commit a fault along with.

συν-εξαπατάω to deceive or cheat along with.

συν-έξειμι (-ιέναι) = συν-εξέρχομαι to go out together.

συν-εξορμάω to help to urge on.

συν-εοχμός, ὁ junction.

συν-επάγω to help in leading against or in inciting.

συν-επαινέω to join in praising; to approve, recommend.

συν-έπαινος 2 approving.

συν-επαιτιάομαι *M.* to accuse together.

συν-επακολουθέω to follow along with.

συν-επαμύνω to help in warding off.

συν-επανίσταμαι *M.* to join in a revolt.

συν-έπειμι (-ιέναι) to join in attacking.

συν-επελαφρύνω to help in relieving.

συν-επεύχομαι *M.* to join in a prayer or vow.

συν-επιβουλεύω to plot against jointly.

συν-επιλαμβάνω and *M.* to support, assist.

συν-επιμαρτυρέω to bear witness along with.

συν-επιμελέομαι *P.* to join in taking care of.

συν-επισκέπτομαι *M.* and συν-επισκοπέω to examine along with.

συν-επισπάομαι *M.* to draw to oneself; to win for oneself. [speeding.]

συν-επισπεύδω to join in/

συν-επίσταμαι *P.* to know along with.

συν-επιστρατεύω to make war together with.

συν-επισχύω to help in assisting.

συν-επιτελέω to join in accomplishing.

συν-επιτίθεμαι *M.* to join in attacking.

συν-επιτρίβω to destroy together. [close upon.]

συν-έπομαι *M.* to follow/

συν-επόμνῡμι to swear at the same time.

συν-εργάζομαι *M.* to work together. [ἔργος.]

συν-εργάτης, ου, ὁ = σύν-/

συν-εργέω to help in work.

σύν-εργος, συν-εργός 2

helping in work, cooperating.

συν-έργω = -είργω.

συν-έρδω to work together.

συν-ερείδω to fasten, bind, or press together.

συν-έριθος, ὁ, ἡ fellow-worker.

συν-έρχομαι M. to go together or with; to meet; to make an appointment or an agreement; to encounter, meet in battle; to have intercourse (with); to come in (money), be gathered. [with.]

συν-εσθίω to eat together.

σύν-εσις, ἡ a joining; understanding, intelligence.

συν-εστιάομαι P. to feast together.

συν-εστίη, ἡ banquet.

συν-έστιος, ἡ sharing one's hearth, inmate.

συν-εστώ, οῦς, ὁ a being together. [friend.]

συν-έταιρος, ὁ companion.

συν-ετός 3 intelligent, sensible, sagacious; intelligible. [in happiness with.]

συν-ευδαιμονέω to share

συν-ευδοκέω to be pleased with, agree to, consent (to).

συν-εύδω, συν-ευνάζομαι P. to sleep with.

σύν-ευνος, ὁ, ἡ bedfellow.

συν-ευ-πάσχω to be benefited with.

συν-ευπορέω to join in providing or assisting.

συν-εύχομαι M. to pray together. [together.]

συν-ευωχέομαι P. to feast

συν-εφάπτομαι M. to lay hold of together.

συν-εφέλκω to draw after along with. [together.]

συν-εφέπομαι M. to follow

συν-εφίστημι intr. and M. to superintend together; to rise together with.

συν-έχεια, ἡ perseverance.

συν-εχής 2 holding together, continuous, unbroken; contiguous, adjacent; frequent, unceasing.

συν-έχθω to hate along with.

συν-έχω to hold or keep together; to contain, comprise; to constrain, compress, vex. — intr. and P. to be joined or united; to be affected by; to be busy.

συν-ηγορέω to be an advocate.

συν-ήγορος 2 advocate, interceder; agreeing with.

συν-ήδομαι P. to rejoice with; to congratulate.

συν-ήθεια, ἡ intercourse; habit, usage.

συν-ήθης 2 familiar, intimate; of like mind and habits; costumary, habitual.

συν-ήκω to come together.

συν-ηλικιώτης, ου, ὁ of equal age. [day with.]

συν-ημερεύω to pass the

συν-ημοσύνη, ἡ agreement.

συν-ήορος 2 = συναόρος.

συν-ηρετέω to be a friend to. [vered.]

συν-ηρεφής 2 thickly co-

σύν-θακος 2 sitting with.

συν-θάπτω to help to bury.

συν-θεάομαι M. to view or behold together.

συν-θεσίη, ἡ = συνθήκη.

σύν-θεσις, ἡ composition, combination.

σύν-θετος 2 compound, combined, complex; settled; agreed upon. [to succeed.]

συν-θέω to run along with; [

συν-θήκη, ἡ = σύνθεσις; agreement, treaty, covenant, peace; commandment, order.

σύν-θημα, τό = συνθήκη; preconcerted signal, token; watch-word. [hunter.]

συν-θηρᾱτής, οῦ, ὁ fellow-[

συν-θηράω, -εύω to hunt or catch together. [τῆς.]

σύν-θηρος, ὁ = συνθηρα-[

συν-θλάω to crush, shatter.

συν-θλίβω to press together.

συν-θνῄσκω to die with.

συν-θρύπτω to break in or to pieces.

συν-θύω to sacrifice with.

συν-ίζω to sit together.

συν-ίημι to seat or bring together; to perceive, hear; to understand, know exactly. — M. to come to an agreement; to perceive.

συν-ίππαρχος, ὁ joint commander of horse.

συν-ιστάνω, συν-ίστημι to place, bring, or set together, to unite; to bring together in dispute or battle; to introduce or recommend to; to compose, create, found, cause; to prove, show. — M. to put

together, to produce or create for oneself. — intr. and M. to come or stand together; to league together, conspire; to encounter, meet in battle, be engaged or implicated in; to be composed; to begin; to be combined; to stand fast; to continue, live, exist; to stand still, make a halt.

συν-ίστωρ, ορος 2 knowing together with.

συν-ίσχω = συνέχω.

συν-ναίω to dwell together.

συν-νάσσω to cram together.

συν - ναυβάτης, ου, συν-ναύτης, ου, ὁ shipmate.

συν - ναυμαχέω to fight at sea along with.

συν-ναυστολέω to go in the same ship.

συν-νεύω to nod assent.

συν - νέω, -νηέω to heap up together. [tory.]

συν-νῑκάω to join in vic-[

συν-νοέω and M. to consider, reflect ([up]on).

σύν-νοια, ἡ meditation; trouble.

σύν-νομος 2 feeding together; companion, friend, consort, mate.

σύν-νους 2 meditating, thoughtful. [with.]

συν-οδεύω to travel along[

συν-οδίᾱ, ἡ company of travellers. [traveller.]

συν-οδοιπόρος, ὁ fellow-[

σύν-οδος, ἡ assembly, meeting, company; council; encounter, attack, battle.

σύνοιδα — 367 — συντεκνοποιέω

σύν-οιδα to know together with; to know thoroughly; to be conscious.

συν-οικέω to dwell or live together; to wed; *trans.* to inhabit together.

συν-οίκημα, τό a dwelling together; cohabitant.

συν-οίκησις, ἡ, συν-οικία, ἡ cohabitation; marriage; house let out to tenants.

σύν-οικια, τά festival of union.

συν-οικίζω to make dwell together, to join in one state, concentrate; to people, colonize; to give to wife.

συν-οίκισις, ἡ a joining in one state; colony.

συν-οικοδομέω to build together; to build jointly.

σύν-οικος 2 dwelling or living together; house-mate, companion.

συν-ολολύζω to scream or shout together. [with.]

συν-ομιλέω to converse

συν-όμνυμι to swear along with or together; to join in conspiracy.

συν-ομολογέω and *M.* to agree with or to; to concede, promise; to make a treaty.

συν-ομορέω to border on.

συν-οράω to see together or at once.

συν-οργίζομαι *P.* to grow angry along with.

συν-ορίνω to stir up, excite; to rush on against each other. [anchor together.]

συν-ορμίζω to bring to

σύν-ορος, -ουρος 2 bordering on.

συν-ουσία, ἡ a being or living together, intercourse; society, party; conversation; banquet.

συν-ουσιαστής, οῦ, ὁ companion, friend, disciple.

συν-οφρυόομαι *M.* to frown.

συν-οχή, ἡ connection, meeting: straitness; anguish.

σύν-οψις, ἡ survey.

σύν-ταγμα, τό. σύν-ταξις, ἡ a putting together in order; order, arrangement; array of battle; body of troops, contingent; contribution, tax, rate, pay.

συν-ταράσσω to stir up together; to disturb utterly, trouble, disquiet, confound, vex. — *P.* to be drawn into confusion.

συν-τάσσω to put together in order; to put in array; to arrange, organize, systematize; to command, ordain; to assign. — *P.* to collect one's thoughts. — *M.* to put in order for oneself; to draw up in a line.

συν-ταχύνω to hasten (*trans.* and *intr.*).

συν-τείνω to stretch, strain, exert; to direct to; *intr.* to tend towards.

συν-τειχίζω to help in fortification.

συν-τεκμαίρομαι *M.* to infer from, conjecture, estimate.

συν-τεκνοποιέω to breed children with.

συν-τεκταίνομαι *M.* to help in building or framing.

συν-τέλεια, ἡ joint payment or contribution; union of tax-payers; completion, end.

συν-τελέω to accomplish or complete together, bring quite to an end; to pay joint taxes, contribute; to belong to a certain class.

συν-τελής 2 paying joint taxes; tributary to.

συν-τέμνω to cut down; to cut short, abridge, curtail; to make a short cut; to rush on to.

συν-τήκω to melt together. — *intr.* and *P.* to melt away, fade, disappear.

συν-τηρέω to help in preserving, watching, or protecting.

συν-τίθημι to put or place together, compose, construct; to contrive, devise; to unite, comprehend, sum up. — *M.* to put together for oneself; to perceive, observe, hear; to agree on, concert, make a treaty or covenant; to set in order.

συν-τῑμάω to honour along with. [in many places.⟩

συν-τιτρώσκω to wound⟩

σύν-τομος 2 cut short, abridged, shortened, concise, brief.

σύν-τονος 2 stretched, strait, intense; earnest; vehement.

συν-τράπεζος, ὁ companion at table. [three.⟩

σύν-τρεις, -τρια three and⟩

συν-τρέφω to rear up together.

συν-τρέχω to run together or along with; to come together, assemble; to rush together, encounter; to agree; to meet.

συν-τρίβω to rub together; to crush, shiver; to wear away, undo.

σύν-τριμμα, τό destruction.

σύν-τροφος 2 reared up together; foster-brother: living with; familiar, common; natural.

συν-τυγχάνω to meet with, fall in with; ὁ συντυχών any one; to happen, come to pass; chance

συν-τυχία, ἡ incident, occurrence, chance; accident; happy event.

συν-υποκρίνομαι to simulate along with.

συν-υπουργέω to join in assisting. [gether.⟩

συν-υφαίνω to contrive to-⟩

συν-ωδίνω to be in travail or labour together.

συν-ῳδός 2 = σύμφωνος.

συν-ωθέω to thrust together. [political club.⟩

συν-ωμοσία, ἡ conspiracy:⟩

συν-ωμότης, ου, ὁ fellow-conspirator. [by oath.⟩

συν-ώμοτος 2 confirmed⟩

συν-ωνέομαι *M.* to buy together; to take into one's pay. [team: pair.⟩

συν-ωρίς, ίδος, ἡ double⟩

συν-ωφελέω to join in helping, to be of use.

σῦριγξ, ιγγος, ἡ shepherd's

συρμαία, ἡ purging oil; radish.

συρμαΐζω to purge.

συρ-ράπτω to sew or stitch together.

συρ-ράσσω to clash together; to rush on.

συρ-ρέω to flow together; to come together.

συρ-ρήγνῦμι to break in pieces; *intr.* to rush or run together; to clash together; to break down, fall in or to pieces. — *P.* to be broken.

συρφετός, ὁ offscum, rubbish; mob, crowd.

σύρω to drag, draw, trail.

σῦς, σύός, ὁ, ἡ swine, pig; boar.

συ-σκευάζω to pack up; to make ready, prepare; to contrive. — *M.* to pack up, to get ready for marching off; to prepare, equip, contrive for oneself; to win over. [in devising.]

συ-σκευωρέομαι *M.* to help]

συ-σκηνέω, -όω to live in the same tent; to dine with. [gether.]

συ-σκηνία, ἡ a dining to-]

σύ-σκηνος, ὁ comrade.

συ-σκιάζω to overshadow or cover thickly.

σύ-σκιος 2 shady. [jointly.]

συ-σκοπέω to observe]

συ-σκοτάζει it grows dark.

συ-σπαράσσω to dishevel or distort utterly.

συ-σπάω to draw together.

συ-σπειράω to press to-

gether; to form in close order.

συ-σπεύδω, συ-σπουδάζω to join in speeding, to be busy along with.

σύσ-σημος 2 concerted.

συσ-σιτέω to dine together.

συσ-σίτιον, τό common meal.

σύσ-σιτος, ὁ mess-mate.

συσ-σῴζω to help to save.

σύσ-σωμος 2 belonging to the same body. [combat.]

συ-σταδόν *adv.* in near]

συ-στασιάζω to join in sedition, be factious.

συ-στασιαστής, οῦ, ὁ, συ-στασιώτης, ου, ὁ partisan; fellow-rioter.

σύ-στασις, ἡ association, arrangement; a standing together, union, meeting; hardness, rigour; riot; conspiracy; close combat, conflict; emotion. [tory.]

συ-στατικός 3 commenda-]

συ-σταυρόω to crucify along with.

συ-στέλλω to draw together, contract; to abridge, condense, lessen, shorten; to put together; to wrap; to humble. — *P.* to restrict oneself.

συ-στενάζω to sigh with.

σύ-στημα, τό composition.

συ-στοιχέω to correspond to. [paign.]

συ-στρατεία, ἡ joint cam-]

συ-στρατεύω and *M.* to join in an expedition, to serve along with. [mander.]

συ-στράτηγος, ὁ joint com-]

συ-στρατιώτης, ου, ὁ fellow-soldier.

συ-στρατοπεδεύομαι M. to encamp along with.

συ-στρέφω to twist together; to combine, contract, compress. — P. to form one body or crowd; to conspire.

συ-στροφή, ἡ body of men, crowd; revolt, plot.

συ-σχηματίζομαι M. to accommodate oneself to.

σύφε(ι)ός, ὁ pig-sty.

σύ-φορβός, ὁ swineherd.

συχνός 3 frequent, often; numerous, copious; long; far. [derer; sword.]

σφαγεύς, ὁ butcher, mur-]

σφαγή, ἡ slaughter, butchery; sacrifice; murder; wound; throat.

σφαγιάζω = σφάττω. [fice.]

σφάγιον, τό victim; sacri-]

σφάγιος 3 killing.

σφαδάζω to struggle in convulsions.

σφάζω = σφάττω.

σφαίρα, ἡ ball; globe.

σφαιρηδόν adv. like a ball.

σφαιρο-ειδής 2 ball-like.

σφακελίζω to become gangrenous.

σφάκελος, ὁ gangrene.

σφαλερός 3 slippery, smooth; precarious, fallacious, delusive; perilous.

σφάλλω to make fall or stumble; to destroy, ruin, undo; to baffle, disconcert. — P. and M. to totter, stagger, reel, fall, perish; to be defeated, disappointed,

or baffled; to be unsuccessful; to fail; be deceived; to err, transgress.

σφάλμα, τό stumble, fall; failure, disaster, defeat; trespass; blunder.

σφαραγέομαι M. to be full to bursting; to hiss.

σφάττω to slaughter, kill, slay; to sacrifice. [ger.]

σφεδανός 3 vehement, ea-]

σφεῖς, σφέα they.

σφέλας, τό footstool.

σφενδονάω to sling.

σφενδόνη, ἡ sling; hoop of a ring; stone of the sling.

σφενδονήτης, ου, ὁ slinger.

σφενδονητική, ἡ art of slinging. [priate.]

σφετερίζομαι to appro-]

σφέτερος 3 their (own).

σφηκόω to pinch in at the waist; to bind tight.

σφήξ, σφηκός, ὁ wasp.

σφοδρός 3 vehement, violent; impetuous, eager, zealous; mighty. — adv. σφόδρα, σφοδρῶς very much, vehemently. [tuosity.]

σφοδρότης, ητος, ἡ impe-]

σφονδύλιος, ὁ vertebra; vertebral column.

σφραγίζω to seal up, shut up; to confirm; to mark, sign.

σφραγίς, ῖδος, ἡ seal; signet-ring; sign, token; authorization.

σφράγισμα, τό seal.

σφρηγίς = σφραγίς.

σφῦρα, ἡ hammer.

σφυρ-ήλατος 2 beaten out with the hammer.

σφυρίς, ίδος, ή little basket.
σφυρόν, τό ankle.
σφωέ both of them; *gen.* and *dat.* σφωίν.
σφῶϊ, σφώ both of you; *gen.* and *dat.* σφῶϊν, σφῶν.
σφωΐτερος 3 belonging to you two. [(a vein).]
σχάζω to slit; to cut open]
σχεδία, ή raft, float; boat; pontoon-bridge.
σχεδίην *adv.* near, in close combat. [near.]
σχεδόθεν *adv.* from nigh,]
σχεδόν *adv.* near, nigh, close; impending, at hand; nearly, almost, pretty well.
σχέσις, ή = σχῆμα.
σχετλιάζω to wail. [tion.]
σχετλιασμός, ὁ indigna-]
σχέτλιος 3 bold; insolent; wicked; cruel, savage; shocking, horrid; miserable, wretched; strange, astonishing.
σχῆμα, τό a bearing, mien, behaviour; figure, form, shape, outward appearance; constitution, nature; dress; manner, fashion; stateliness, dignity.
σχηματίζω to form, fashion, shape, dress; to adorn. — *M.* to pretend. [dancing.]
σχημάτιον, τό figure in]
σχίζα, ή cleft piece of wood. [parate.]
σχίζω to split, cleave, se-]
σχῖνος, ἡ mastich-tree.
σχίσις, ἡ division; by-road.
σχίσμα, τό division, schism.
σχιστός 3 parted, divided.
σχοινίον, τό rope, cord.

σχοῖνος, ὁ rush, reed; thicket of rushes; rope, cord, cable; measuring-line.
σχοινο-τενής 2 straight.
σχολάζω to be at leisure, have spare time; to have leisure or time for; to devote oneself to; to linger, delay.
σχολαῖος 3 at leisure; slow.
σχολαιότης, ητος, ή slowness.
σχολή, ή leisure, spare time, rest, ease; peace; work of leisure, disputation, discussion; school; delay, slowness; idleness. — *adv.* σχολῇ at leisure, slowly; hardly, scarcely.
σώζω, σῴζω to save, keep safe, preserve, protect, spare, bring back safe and sound; to observe, keep secret; to remember. — *M.* to keep or save for oneself.
σωκέω to be able.
σῶκος 2 strong.
σωλήν, ῆνος, ὁ pipe.
σῶμα, τό body; dead body; corpse; person, individual; slave; life, existence; sensual pleasures; main point.
σωμ-ασκέω to train one's body. [cise.]
σωμ-ασκία, ἡ bodily exer-]
σωματικός 3, σωματο-ειδής 2 bodily.
σῶος 3 = σῶς. [heap with.]
σωρεύω to heap up; to]
σωρός, ὁ heap.
σῶς, σῶν safe and sound, healthy, entire; sure.
σῶστρον, τό reward for

24*

saving one's life, for bringing back a runaway slave.
σωτήρ, ῆρος, ὁ, σώτειρα,
ἡ saviour, preserver, deli-
verer.
σωτηρίᾱ, ἡ a saving, deliverance, means of pre-
serving; safe existence;
well-being, ease.
σωτήριος 2 saving, delivering; saved; τὰ -α =
σωτηρία, offering for preservation.
σωφρονέω to be sensible,
reasonable, discreet, or moderate.

σωφρονίζω to bring to
reason, to make wise; to
admonish; to correct, chastise.
σωφρονισμός, ὁ a warning;
= σωφροσύνη.
σωφρονιστής, οῦ, ὁ chastiser, censor.
σωφροσύνη, ἡ prudence,
moderation, discretion; self-
control; chastity, decent
behaviour.
σώφρων 2 sensible, discreet, prudent; moderate,
temperate, sober; modest.
σώω = σώζω.

T

T, τ (ταῦ) nineteenth letter of the
alphabet; as a numeral τ' = 300.
ταβέρνα, ἡ inn.
τᾱγείᾱ, ἡ command, rule.
τᾱγεύω to command, rule.
τάγμα, τό body of soldiers,
division; command.
τᾱγός, ὁ commander, ruler;
chief of a confederacy.
ταινίᾱ, ἡ riband; fillet.
ταινιόω to adorn with a
head-band.
τακτικός 3 fit for arranging or for tactics.
τακτός 3 ordered, arranged, fixed.
τάκω = τήκω.
ταλα-εργός 2 able to work.
ταλαιπωρέω to suffer hardship or distress, to do hard
work, to toil, drudge.
ταλαιπωρίᾱ, ἡ hardship,
hard work, distress; affliction, suffering.

ταλαί-πωρος 2 toilsome,
wretched, miserable.
ταλαί-φρων 2, **ταλαι-
κάρδιος** 2 wretched; bold,
daring.
ταλαντιαῖος 3 worth a
talent; weighing a talent.
τάλαντον, τό, *pl.* pair of
scales; talent.
ταλα-πείριος 2 suffering
much, severely tried by
fate.   [pain, miserable.]
ταλα-πενθής 2 enduring)
τό λαρος, ὁ basket.
τάλᾱς, τάλαινα, τάλᾰν
enduring, patient, suffering, wretched; audacious.
ταλασίᾱ, ἡ wool-spinning.
ταλασιουργέω to spin wool.
ταλασί-φρων 2 = ταλαι-
φρων.
ταλαύρῑνος 2 shield-bearing.   [φρων.]
ταλά-φρων 2 = ταλαί-)

ταλιθά girl, maiden.

τάλις, ιδος, ἡ maiden.

ταμεῖον, τό = ταμιεῖον.

ταμεσί-χρως, οος cutting the skin. [housewife.]

ταμία, ἡ housekeeper,
ταμίας, ου, ὁ housekeeper, dispenser, steward; treasurer.

ταμιεῖον, τό storehouse; treasury; chamber.

ταμιεύω and M. to be a housekeeper, steward, or manager; to manage.

τάμνω = τέμνω.

τάν, τᾶν thou; ὦ τᾶν my good friend!

τανα-ήκης 2 with a long point or edge. [long.]

ταναός 3 and 2 stretched,
ταναύ-πους, ποδος stretching the feet, long-striding.

τανηλεγής 2 grieving much (others: stretching at full length). [down.]

τανταλόω to swing, hurl,
τανύ-γλωσσος 2 long-tongued. [long point.]

τανυ-γλώχιν, ῑνος with,
τανυ-ήκης 2 = ταναήκης.

τανῦν = τὰ νῦν. [robe.]

τανύ-πεπλος 2 with long,
τανύ-πους = ταναύπους.

τανυ-πτέρυξ, υγος, ταναυσί-πτερος 2 with outstretched wing. [ing.]

τανυστύς, ύος, ἡ a stretch-,
τανύ-φλοιος 2 with thin bark. [leaves.]

τανύφυλλος 2 with long,
τανύω = τείνω.

ταξιαρχέω to be a taxiarch.

ταξι-άρχης, ου, ταξί-αρχος, ὁ taxiarch, commander of a division; captain.

τάξις, ἡ an arranging, putting in order, disposition; order, arrangement; class, post, rank, office, duty; military arrangement, line of soldiers, battle-array, order of battle; body of troops, division of an army, band, company.

ταπεινός 3 low, level; small, narrow; trifling, insignificant, poor; humble, lowly; humiliated, downcast, mean.

ταπεινότης, ητος, ἡ lowness; lowliness, weakness; baseness, poorness; dejection, humiliation; humility.

ταπεινο-φροσύνη, ἡ humility, meekness.

ταπεινό-φρων 2 humble.

ταπεινόω to make low; to humble, bring down.

ταπείνωσις, ἡ = ταπεινότης. [ιδος, ἡ carpet.]

τάπης, ητος, ὁ, ταπίς,
ταράσσω to stir up, disturb, trouble, confound; to rouse alarm, agitate, raise up; perf. τέτρηχα to be in uproar or confusion.

ταραχή, ἡ, τάραχος, ὁ disorder, confusion, tumult, noise, uproar, sedition.

ταραχώδης 2 confused, troubled, disordered; fickle, angry; troubling.

ταρβαλέος 3 frightened.

ταρβέω to be afraid or alarmed.

τάρβος, τό, **ταρβοσύνη**, ἡ fear, fright, awe.

ταρίχευσις, ἡ an embalming. [balmer.]

ταριχευτής, οῦ, ὁ embalmer.

ταριχεύω to preserve by smoking or salting; to embalm. [salting fish.]

ταριχήϊαι, αἱ places for salting fish.

τάριχος, ὁ, τό salted meat; mummy.

ταρσός, ταρρός, ὁ frame of wicker-work; crate; mat of reeds; gabion; blade or flat of the foot; oar.

ταρταρόω to hurl into Tartarus.

τάρφος, τό thicket.

ταρφύς 3 thick, frequent, numerous.

ταρχύω to bury, inter.

τάσσω to arrange, put in order; to draw up in line or in order of battle; to post, station, appoint; to assign to a class; to order, command, give instructions; to fix, settle. — *M.* to order, arrange for oneself; to agree upon among themselves; to bind oneself to paying by instalments.

ταύρειος 3 of oxen or cows; of bullock's hide.

ταυρηδόν *adv.* like a bull, staringly.

ταυρο-κτονέω to kill bulls.

ταυρο-κτόνος 2 bull-slaying. [ing bulls.]

ταυρο-πόλος 3 and 2 hunt-

ταῦρος, ὁ bull, ox.

ταυρο-σφάγος 2 bull-slaughtering.

ταύτῃ *adv.* on this side, here; hither; in this way or manner.

τάφε, ταφεῖν see τέθηπα.

ταφεύς, ὁ burier.

ταφή, ἡ = τάφος[1].

ταφήιος 3 of a burial.

τάφος[1], ὁ burial; grave, tomb; funeral-feast.

τάφος[2], τό astonishment.

ταφρεία, ἡ the making a ditch.

ταφρεύω to make a ditch.

τάφρος, ἡ ditch, trench.

τάχα *adv.* quickly, soon; perhaps.

ταχινός 3 quick, swift.

τάχος, τό quickness, swiftness, speed. [quickly.]

ταχυ-άλωτος 2 captured

ταχυ-ναυτέω to sail fast.

ταχύνω to hasten, make quick, be quick.

ταχύ-πωλος 2 with swift horses. [moving.]

ταχύ-ρρωστος 2 swift-

ταχύς 3 swift, quick, fast, fleet. — *adv.* ταχέως, ταχύ quickly, soon; at once; perhaps.

ταχυτής, ῆτος, ἡ = τάχος.

ταώς, ώ, ταῶς, ῶ, ὁ peacock.

τέ *enclit. part.* and. [cock.]

τέγγω to wet, moisten; to shed. — *P.* to be poured (forth), to be softened.

τέγεος 2 roofed. [room.]

τέγος, τό roof; chamber,

τέθηπα *perf. aor.* ἔταφον to be amazed or astonished; to wonder at.

τεθριππο - βάτης, ου, ὁ driving in a four-horse chariot.

τέθρ - ιππον, τό team of four horses, four-in-hand.

τεθριππο-τροφέω to keep a four-horse chariot.

τεθριππο-τρόφος 2 keeping a four-horse chariot.

τείν = σοί, dat. of σύ.

τείνω to stretch, strain, extend, draw tight; to stretch out, lay prostrate, lengthen; intr. to tend to, aim at, strive; to extend to; to refer or belong to. — P. to be stretched tight; to rush, run with full speed; to be spread. — M. to stretch oneself or for oneself.

τεῖος adv. = τέως. [star.]

τεῖρος, τό constellation,

τείρω to rub; to rub away, wear out; to distress.

τειχεσι - πλήτης, ου, ὁ stormer of walls.

τειχέω, τειχίζω to build a wall or fort; to fortify, to wall in; to build.

τειχ-ήρης 2 besieged.

τειχιόεις 3 walled.

τειχίον, τό wall.

τείχισις, ἡ the building a wall; fortress.

τείχισμα, τό = τεῖχος.

τειχισμός, ὁ = τείχισις.

τειχο-μαχέω to attack the walls. [walls.]

τειχο-μαχία, ἡ attack of

τειχο - ποιός, ὁ officer of the board of works.

τεῖχος, τό wall; fortification, fortress, castle.

τειχο - σκοπιά, ἡ review from the walls.

τειχο-φύλαξ, ακος, ὁ guard of the walls.

τειχύδριον, τό small fortified place.

τείως = τέως.

τεκμαίρομαι M. to know from certain signs, to infer, conclude, judge; to decree, ordain, appoint, show by a sign.

τέκμαρ[1], τό end, goal, mark, boundary; just cause.

τέκμαρ[2], τεκμήριον, τό sign, token, mark; proof, demonstration.

τεκμηριόω to prove.

τέκμωρ, τό = τέκμαρ[1] and [2].

τεκνίον, τό little child.

τεκνο - γονέω to bear children.

τεκνο-γονία, ἡ a child-bearing. [dren.]

τεκνόεις 3 rich in chil-

τεκν - ολέτειρα, ἡ bereft of children. [one.]

τέκνον, τό child; a young

τεκνο-ποιέομαι M. to beget children.

τεκνο-ποιία, ἡ the begetting or bearing of children.

τεκνο - ποιός 2 begetting or bearing children.

τεκνο - τροφέω to rear children.

τεκνόω and M. to beget or bear children. [ποιία.]

τέκνωσις, ἡ = τεκνο-

τέκος, τό = τέκνον.

τεκταίνομαι M. to make, build, frame, construct; to contrive, devise.

τεκτονικός 3 belonging to the art of building; carpenter, builder.

τεκτοσύνη, ἡ carpentry.

τέκτων, ονος, ὁ carpenter, joiner, builder; master workman.

τελαμών, ῶνος, ὁ strap for supporting a thing; baldrick, shoulder-belt; surgeon's bandage.

τελέθω to be there; to come forth; to become.

τέλειος 3 and 2 complete, finished, fulfilled, accomplished; perfect, entire, full-grown, full in number; spotless; definite, fixed; accomplishing, able to do.

τελειότης, ητος, ἡ perfection, full growth.

τελειόω to make perfect or successful.

τελείω = τελέω.

τελείωσις, ἡ completion; perfection.

τελειωτής, οῦ, ὁ finisher.

τελεό-μηνος 2 with full months.

τέλεος = τέλειος.

τελεσ-φορέω to bring (or come) to ripeness.

τελεσ-φόρος 2 bringing to an end, accomplishing; brought to an end, complete, fulfilled.

τελετή, ἡ initiation, celebration; pl. mysteries.

τελευταῖος 3 last, highest, extreme.

τελευτάω to complete, accomplish, finish, fulfil; intr. to end, come to an

end, die, be fulfilled; part. τελευτῶν at last.

τελευτή, ἡ end, death; issue, event; success; accomplishment.

τελέω to end, bring to an end, complete, finish, perform, execute, fulfil; to pay one's dues or taxes, to spend money; to pay; to consecrate, initiate (in the mysteries). — intr. and P. to be fulfilled, to come to an end, turn out.

τελήεις 3 perfect, complete; promising success.

τέλλω to accomplish. — intr. and P. to rise, arise.

τέλμα, τό pool; mortar, clay.

τέλος, τό end, issue; death; term, fulfilment, accomplishment; complete state, result, event; highest or ideal station, full power, magistrate, government (τὰ τέλη); tax, duty, toll; cost, expense; present, offering; initiation, celebration, mysteries; body of soldiers, division, squadron. [end.)

τέλοσ-δε adv. towards the)

τέλσον, τό boundary.

τελ-ώνης, ου, ὁ toll-gatherer; publican.

τελ-ώνιον, τό toll-house.

τεμάχιον, τό, τέμαχος, τό slice, morsel.

τεμένιος 3 belonging to sacred land.

τέμενος, τό piece of land cut off for a certain purpose, crown-estate; sacred land, precincts of a temple.

τέμνω to cut, hew; to use the knife; to cut up, slaughter, sacrifice; to wound; to carve; to cut off or down, to sever; to lay waste; to fell trees; to cut or draw a line.

τέμω = τέμνω.

τέναγος, τό shallow water; swamp.

τένων, οντος, ὁ sinew; tendon (of the nape).

τέρας, α(τ)ος, τό sign, omen, prodigy; wonder, monster.

τερα-σκόπος, τερατοσκόπος, ὁ soothsayer.

τερατώδης 2 marvellous, prodigious.

τερεβίνθινος 3 of the turpentine-tree.

τέρετρον, τό gimlet.

τέρην, εινα, εν, gen. ενος smooth, soft, delicate.

τέρμα, τό end, boundary; goal, mark.   [bordered.]

τερμιόεις 3 tasselled; long-

τέρμιος 3 last, extreme.

τερπι-κέραυνος 2 delighting in thunder.   [sant.]

τερπνός 3 delightful, plea-

τέρπω to refresh; to cheer, delight, please.

τερπωλή, ἡ = τέρψις.

τερσαίνω, τέρσω to wipe up, dry up. — P. to become dry.

τερψί-μβροτος 2 pleasing the heart of man.

τέρψις, ἡ enjoyment, delight.   [four oxen.]

τεσσαρα-βοιός 2 worth

τεσσαράκοντα forty.

τεσσαρακοντα-ετής 2 forty years old.

τεσσαρακοστός 3 fortieth.

τέσσαρες, α four.

τεσσαρεσ-καί-δεκα fourteen.   [fourteenth.]

τεσσαρεσ-και-δέκατος 3

τεσσεραχοντ-όργυιος 2 of forty fathoms.

τέσσερες = τέσσαρες.

τεταγών taking, seizing.

τεταρταῖος 3 on the fourth day.   [fourth part.]

τεταρτη-μόριον, τό the

τέταρτος 3 fourth.

τετίημαι to be grieved;

τετιηώς grieved.

τετμεῖν aor. to arrive at, overtake.   [four acres.]

τετρά-γυος 2 as large as

τετράγωνο - πρόσωπος 2 square-faced.

τετρά-γωνος 2 with four angles, square; perfect, complete.   [soldiers.]

τετράδιον, τό body of four

τετρα-έτης 2 four years old.

τετρα-θέλυμνος 2 of four layers.   [perforate.]

τετραίνω to bore through,

τετράκις adv. four times.

τετρακισ-μύριοι 2 forty thousand.   [thousand.]

τετρακισ-χίλιοι 3 four

τετρακόσιοι 3 four hundred.   [wheeled.]

τετρά-κυκλος 2 four-

τετρά-μετρος 2 consisting of four metres or eight feet.   [months.]

τετρά-μηνος 2 lasting four

τετρα-μοιρίᾱ, ἡ fourfold pay.

τετρ-άορος 2 drawn by four horses.

τετρα-πάλαιστος 2 of four handbreadths. [cubits.]

τετρά-πηχυς, υ of four

τετρα-πλάσιος 3, τετρα-πλοῦς 3 fourfold. [cities.]

τετρά-πολις, εως of four

τετρά-πους, πουν four-footed. [tra͂rch.]

τετρ-αρχέω to be a te-

τετρ-άρχης, ου, ὁ one of four princes.

τετράς, άδος, ἡ the number four; fourth day.

τετρα-φάληρος 2, τετρά-φαλος 2 with four ridges or bosses.

τετρά-φῦλος 2 divided into four tribes.

τέτραχα, τετραχῆ, τε-τραχθά adv. fourfold, in four parts. [stories.]

τετρ-ώροφος 2 with four

τέττα dear father.

τέττιξ, ῑγος, ὁ grass-hopper; hair pin. [τοῦ (τινός).]

τεῦ = τοῦ (τίνος); τεὐ =

τεῦχος, τό tool, implement, utensil; armour, arms; ship's implements; vessel, urn.

τεύχω to make, build, construct, work, form; to cause, create.

τέφρα, ἡ ashes.

τεφρόω to reduce to ashes.

τεχνάζω, τεχνάω and M. to devise, work, make by art; to execute skilfully; to use tricks, to devise cunningly. [artifice, trick.]

τέχνασμα, τό work of art;

τέχνη, ἡ art, skill, craft, trade, science; artifice, cunning, trick; work of art.

τεχνήεις 3 made by art, ingenious.

τέχνημα, τό work of art; tool; artifice, trick; cunning person.

τεχνικός 3 artistic, skilful.

τεχνίτης, ου, ὁ artist, craftsman, expert; workman, master; deceiver.

τέως adv. so long, meanwhile; hitherto, till now; ere this; for a time.

τῇ adv. there! take!

τῇ adv. here, there, thither; in this way; where; how, as.

τῇδε adv. here, there; in this way; therefore.

τήθη, ἡ grandmother.

τῆθος, τό oyster. [tion.]

τηκεδών, όνος, ἡ consump-

τήκω to melt; to make pine, consume. — intr. and P. to melt; to pine away; to vanish, decay.

τηλ-αυγής 2 far-shining.

τῆλε = τηλοῦ.

τηλεδαπός 3 coming from afar, foreign, distant.

τηλεθάω to bloom, flourish.

τηλε-κλειτός 3, τελε-κλυτός far-famed.

τηλέ-πορος 2 far, distant.

τηλε-φανής 2 seen or heard from afar.

τηλίκος 3, τηλικόσδε 3, τηλικοῦτος 3 so great; so much; so old or young.

τηλόθεν adv. from afar.

τηλόθι = τηλοῦ.

τηλόσε adv. to a distance.

τηλοῦ *adv.* far away, at a distance.

τηλύγετος 3 youthful, late-born; spoiled child.

τηλ-ωπός 2 seen or heard from afar, far off. [tend.]

τημελέω to take care of,

τήμερον *adv.* to-day.

τῆμος *adv.* at that time, then; thereupon.

τηνίκα, τηνικάδε, τηνικαῦτα = τῆμος.

τῆος = τέως.

τῇπερ *adv.* in which way.

τηρέω to watch, observe, take care of, guard; to keep, preserve; to keep in prison.

τήρησις, ἡ a watching, guarding, preserving; prison. [to be in want.]

τητάω to deprive. — P.

τήσιος 3 useless, vain.

τιάρα, ἡ, τιάρης, ου, ὁ tiara, turban.

τιαρο-ειδής 2 like a tiara.

τιέω see τετίημαι.

τίη *adv.* why?

τιθαιβώσσω to make a nest, to make honey.

τιθασεύω to tame, make tractable.

τιθασός 2 tamed, tame.

τίθημι to put, place, set, lay; to inter; to ordain, establish, order, fix; to reckon, count; to estimate, esteem, consider; to suppose; to make, cause, create, effect, appoint. — *M.* ὅπλα τίθεσθαι to put on arms, to fight; to take up one's quarters, to bivouac; to

lay down one's arms, to surrender. [foster.]

τιθηνέομαι to tend, nurse,

τιθήνη, ἡ nurse. [beget.]

τίκτω to bring forth, bear,

τίλλω to pluck, pull, tear. — *M.* to mourn, bewail.

τίλων, ωνος, ὁ a kind of fish.

τιμά-ορος = τιμωρός.

τιμάω to estimate; to judge, condemn; to esteem, honour, respect, revere, value, cherish, love; to reward, honour with; to estimate the amount of punishment.

τιμή, ἡ estimate, valuation, census; price, worth; penalty, punishment, damages, reward; honour, esteem, distinction; place of honour, dignity, magistracy, privilege.

τιμήεις 3 = τίμιος.

τίμημα, τό valuation, estimate; census, rate of assessment; property; penalty, fine.

τίμιος 3 valued, esteemed, honoured; costly, precious.

τιμιότης, ητος, ἡ worth, value, preciousness.

τιμωρέω and *M.* to avenge, revenge; to help, succour; to punish, chastise.

τιμωρητήρ, ῆρος, ὁ helper, avenger.

τιμώρημα, τό, τιμωρία, ἡ vengeance, punishment; help, aid, succour. [ing.]

τιμωρός 2 avenging, help-

τινάσσω and *M.* to swing, shake; to disturb, upset.

τίνυμαι *M.* = τίνομαι.

τίνω (ῑ or ῖ) to pay; to pay a penalty or debt; to reward; to atone. — *M.* to avenge, punish, make suffer, take vengeance.

τίπτε *adv.* why then?

τίς, τί, *gen.* τίνος, who? which? what? τί why? wherefore? how?

τὶς, τὶ, *gen.* τινός, any one, some one, a certain; anything, something; many a one, each, every one; *pl.* many, several.

τίσις, ἡ payment; penalty, punishment, atonement, retribution, reward; vengeance.

τιταίνω to stretch, spread out, extend, draw, strain. — *M.* to stretch oneself or for oneself, exert oneself.

τίτθη, ἡ nurse.

τίτλος, ὁ superscription.

τιτός 3 requited.

τιτράω, τίτρημι = τετραίνω.

τιτρώσκω to pierce; to wound, hurt; to overpower.

τιτύσκομαι to make ready, prepare; t aim at; to intend, design.

τίω = τιμάω.

τλάμων 2, τλήμων 2 enduring, persevering, steadfast, bold; suffering, wretched.

τλῆναι to suffer, endure, bear; to dare, risk.

τλητός 3 suffering, patient; pliant; endurable.

τμήγω to cut, hew. — *P.* to be severed or dispersed.

τμήδην *adv.* by cutting, scratching.

τμῆμα, τό, τμῆσις, ἡ cut, incision; section, piece.

τμητός 3 cut, hewn.

τόθι *adv.* there.

τοί[1] = οἱ, οἵ; = σοί.

τοί[2] *adv.* in truth, certainly, verily.

τοι-γάρ, τοιγαρ-οῦν, τοι-γάρ-τοι *adv.* so then, therefore, accordingly; therefore indeed.

τοί-νυν *adv.* yet, so then, therefore; further, moreover.

τοῖος 3, τοιόσ-δε 3, τοι-οῦτος 3 of such kind or quality, quite such.

τοιουτό-τροπος 2 of such kind. [side of a ship.]

τοῖχος, ὁ wall of a house; τοιχωρυχέω to be a house-breaker, burglar.

τοιχ-ώρυχος, ὁ house-breaker, burglar, thief.

τοκάς, άδος, ἡ one who has brought forth.

τοκεύς, ὁ begetter; *pl.* parents.

τόκος, ὁ a bringing forth, birth; offspring, child, son; descent; use-money, interest. [daring; venture.]

τόλμα, ἡ courage, boldness,

τολμάω to bear, endure, undergo; to take heart, to dare.

τολμήεις 3, τολμηρός 3 enduring, steadfast; bold; daring.

τόλμημα, τό adventure, enterprise.

τολμητής, οῦ, ὁ bold or fool-hardy man.

τολμητός 3 ventured, to be ventured.

τολυπεύω to devise, invent; to toil through.

τομάω to need cutting.

τομή, ἡ a cutting, hewing; cut, stroke; hewn surface or corner; stump of a tree, end of a beam.

τομός 3 cutting, sharp.

τόνος, ὁ rope, cord; chord; a stretching, tension; tone, note; metre.

τοξάζομαι M. = τοξεύω.

τόξ-αρχος, ὁ captain of the archers.

τόξευμα, τό missile, arrow, bolt; body of archers; bowshot.

τοξευτής, οῦ, ὁ = τοξότης.

τοξευτός 3 struck by an arrow.

τοξεύω to shoot with the bow, to strike with an arrow; to aim at; to hit.

τοξικός 3 belonging to archery. [arrow; archery.]

τόξον, τό bow; missile,/

τοξοσύνη, ἡ archery.

τοξότης, ου, ὁ bowman, archer; policeman.

τοξο - φόρος 2 bearing a bow; archer.

τοπάζιον, τό topaz.

τοπάζω to guess, divine.

τόπος, ὁ place, spot; passage in a book; region, district; space, locality; position, rank, opportunity.

τορεύω to enchase, engrave.

τορέω to bore through.

τόρμος, ὁ hole.

τορνεύω to turn on a lathe.

τόρνος, ὁ compasses.

τορνόω to make round.

τόρος 3 piercing, shrill; clear, distinct, sharp.

τόσος 3, τοσόσδε 3, τοσοῦτος 3 so great, so wide, so long, so much, so little, so strong.

τοσσάκι adv. so often.

τόσσος 3 = τόσος.

τότε adv. then, at that time; formerly; just then.

τοτέ adv. at times, now and then.

το-τηνίκα adv. then.

τοτοτοῖ woe!

τοὔνεκα adv. therefore.

τόφρα adv. so long, till then, meanwhile.

τραγ-έλαφος, ὁ goat-stag, antelope.

τραγήματα, τά sweetmeats.

τραγικός 3 tragic; majestic, pompous.

τράγος, ὁ he-goat.

τραγο-σκελής 2 goat-footed.

τραγ - ῳδέω to declaim pathetically.

τραγ - ῳδία, ἡ tragedy.

τραγ - ῳδός, ὁ tragic poet or actor.

τρᾱνής 2 clear, distinct.

τράπεζα, ἡ table; dining-table, board; dinner, meal; money - changer's table; shop. [to a table.]

τραπεζεύς, έως belonging/

τραπεζίτης, ου, ὁ money-changer, banker.

τραπέω to tread grapes.

τραυλός 3 stammering.

τραῦμα, τό wound, hurt; loss, defeat. [man.]

τραυματίας, ου, ὁ wounded]

τραυματίζω to wound.

τραφερός 3 firm, dry (land) [to expose to view.]

τραχηλίζω to lay bare;]

τράχηλος, ὁ neck, throat.

τραχύνω to make rough or rugged. [harsh, angry.]

τραχύς 3 rough, rugged;]

τραχύτης, ητος, ἡ roughness, ruggedness; hardness.

τρεῖς, τρία three.

τρέμω to tremble, quiver.

τρέπω to turn, turn round, away or about; to divert, alter, change, direct; to turn to flight; to hinder, prevent. — intr., P. and M. to turn oneself; to be changed.

τρέφω to make solid, congeal, curdle; to feed, nourish, rear, bring up, nurse, tend; intr. to become solid, grow up. — P. to be fed; to grow (up); to live; to be brought up.

τρέχω to run.

τρέω to tremble, quiver; to fear; to flee.

τρῆμα, τό hole, aperture.

τρήρων, ωνος timid, shy.

τρητός 3 bored through.

τρηχύς 3 = τραχύς.

τρίαινα, ἡ trident.

τριᾱκάς, άδος, ἡ the number thirty. [thirty days.]

τριᾱκονθ-ήμερος 2 of]

τριάκοντα thirty.

τριᾱκοντα-έτης 2, τριᾱ-

κοντα-έτις, ιδος, fem. lasting thirty years.

τριᾱκοντ-αρχίᾱ, ἡ rule of thirty men. [κονθήμερος.]

τριᾱκοντ-ήμερος 2 = τρια-]

τριᾱκόντ-ορος, ἡ vessel with thirty oars.

τριᾱκοντούτης, fem. τριᾱκοντοῦτις, ιδος = τριακονταέτης.

τριᾱκόσιοι 3 three hundred.

τριᾱκοστός 3 thirtieth.

τριάς, άδος, ἡ the number three, triad.

τρΐβή, ἡ a rubbing, wearing away, spending; a practising, practice, skill; delay, evasion; pastime.

τρί-βολος 2 three-pointed; thistle. [= τριβή.]

τρίβος, ὁ, ἡ path, road;]

τρίβω to rub, thrash, grind, pound, bruise; to wear away, spend, consume; to damage, weaken, waste; to delay, tarry. — P. to be busied with.

τρίβων, ωνος, ὁ worn cloak; adj. practised, versed, or skilled. [pearls.]

τρί-γληνος 2 with three]

τρι-γλώχῑν, ῑνος three-forked. [ration.]

τρι-γονία, ἡ third gene-]

τρί-γωνον, τό triangle.

τρί-δουλος, ὁ thrice a slave.

τρι-έλικτος 2 thrice wound.

τρι-ετηρίς, ίδος, ἡ triennial festival. [ennial.]

τρι-έτης, -ετής 2 tri-]

τρι-ετία, ἡ space of three years.

τρίζω to chirp, twitter, squeak, crack.

τριηκάς etc. see τριακάς etc.

τριηραρχέω to be captain of a trireme; to fit out a trireme.

τριηρ-αρχία, ἡ the fitting out of a trireme.

τριηραρχικός 3 belonging to a τριηραρχία.

τριήρ-αρχος, ὁ trierarch: commander of a trireme; one who has to fit out a trireme.

τριηρ-αύλης, ου, ὁ flute-player of a trireme.

τριήρης, ους, ἡ trireme, ship with three banks of oars.

τριηρίτης, ου, ὁ serving on board a trireme.

τρι-κάρηνος 2, τρί-κρα-νος 2 three-headed.

τρί-λλιστος 2 thrice prayed for. [tres.]

τρί-μετρος 2 of three me-

τρί-μηνος 2 lasting three months.

τρι-μοιρία, ἡ triple pay.

τριξός = τρισσός.

τρί-οδος, ἡ the meeting of three roads.

τρι-πάλαιστος 2 three hands broad. [long.]

τρί-πηχυς, υ three cubits

τρί-πλαξ, ακος threefold.

τρι-πλάσιος 3 thrice as great or as much.

τρί-πλεθρος 2 three ple-thra long. [triple.]

τρι-πλοῦς 3 threefold,

τρι-πόλιστος 2, τρί-πολος 2 thrice ploughed; much talked of.

τρίπος, ὁ, τρί-πους, ποδος, ὁ three-footed; tripod.

τρί-πτυχος 2 of three layers; threefold.

τρίς adv. thrice.

τρισ-άθλιος 3 thrice-un-happy. [pleased.]

τρισ-άσμενος 3 thrice-

τρισ-καί-δεκα thirteen.

τρισκαιδεκα-στάσιος 2 of thirteen times the weight.

τρισ-και-δέκατος 3 thir-teenth. [blessed.]

τρισ-μάκαρ, αρος thrice

τρισ-μύριοι 3 thirty thou-sand. [poured.]

τρί-σπονδος 2 thrice-

τρισσός 3 threefold.

τρί-στεγος 2 with three stories. [rows.]

τρί-στοιχος 2 in three

τρισ-χίλιοι 2 three thou-sand. [the third part.]

τριτ-αγωνιστέω to act

τριτ-αγωνιστής, οῦ, ὁ player who acts the third part. [on the third day.]

τριταῖος 3 in three days;

τρίτατος 3 = τρίτος.

τριτη-μόριος 3 forming a third part. [third part.]

τριτη-μορίς, ίδος. ἡ the

τρίτος 3 third.

τρι-φάσιος 3 threefold, three. [clover.]

τρί-φυλλον, τό trefoil,

τρί-φῦλος 2 consisting of three tribes.

τρίχα adv. in three parts.

τριχά-ϊκες, οἱ in three tribes. [τρίχα.]

τριχῇ, τριχῆ, τριχθά =

τρίχῐνος 3 of hair.

τρι-χοίνικος 2 holding three χοίνικες.

τριχοῦ *adv.* in three places.

τρίχωμα, τό growth of hair.

τρῖψις, ἡ a rubbing, touching; resistance, elasticity.

τρι-ώβολον, τό three-obol piece. [stories.]

τρι-ώροφος 2 of three

τρομέω and M. to tremble, quiver; to fear.

τρόμος, ὁ a trembling; fear.

τροπαῖον, τρόπαιον, τό sign of victory, trophy.

τροπαῖος, τρόπαιος 3 giving victory.

τροπέω to turn.

τροπή, ἡ a turning, turn; solstice; flight; defeat; victory; change.

τρόπις, ἡ ship's keel.

τρόπος, ὁ turn, direction: manner, way, fashion, custom, mode of life; character, temper. [for oars.]

τροπός, ὁ leathern thong

τροπο-φορέω to bear with one's manners. [πός.]

τροπωτήρ, ῆρος. ὁ = τρο-

τροφεῖα, τά reward for rearing, wages of a nurse; food, sustenance.

τροφεύς, ὁ = τροφός.

τροφέω = τρέφω.

τροφή, ἡ food, nourishment; maintenance; rearing, nursing; means or mode of living; offspring, brood.

τρόφιμος 2 nourished, reared up; foster-child.

τρόφις, ι, τροφόεις 3 well-fed.

τροφός, ὁ, ἡ feeder, nurse.

τροφο-φορέω to bear like a nurse.

τροχάζω to run along.

τροχ-ηλάτης, ου, ὁ charioteer. [wheels.]

τροχ-ήλατος 2 moved on

τροχιά, ἡ track; way.

τροχίλος, ὁ plover.

τροχο-ειδής 2 circular.

τροχός, ὁ wheel, potter's wheel, disc; wheel of torture. [tion.]

τρόχος, ὁ course, revolu-

τρύβλιον, τό cup, bowl.

τρυγάω to gather in.

τρύγητος, ὁ the gathering of fruits, harvest. [dove.]

τρυγών, όνος, ἡ turtle-

τρύζω to coo: to mutter.

τρύμαλιά, ἡ hole or eye of the needle. [refuse.]

τρύξ, υγός. ἡ must; dregs;

τρύπανον, τό borer, gimlet.

τρυπάω to bore, pierce through.

τρύπημα, τό hole.

τρυσ-άνωρ, ορος harrassing men.

τρυ-φάλεια, ἡ helmet.

τρυφάω to live delicately or in luxury, be effeminate or licentious; to be insolent or haughty.

τρυφερός 3 delicate, effeminate, luxurious.

τρυφή, ἡ delicacy, luxury; pride. insolence.

τρῦφος, τό piece, morsel, fragment.

τρύχόω, τρύχω to wear out, consume, waste; to vex, distress, afflict. [haust.]

τρύω to wear out, ex-

τρωγλο-δύτης, ου, ὁ dwelling in caves.

τρώγω to gnaw, chew, eat.

τρώκτης, ου, ὁ knave, cheat.

τρώμα etc. see τραῦμα.

τρωπάω to change. — M. to turn oneself.

τρωτός 3 vulnerable.

τρωχάω to run.

τρώω = τιτρώσκω.

τύ = σύ.

τυγχάνω to hit (a mark), to hit upon; to fall in with, meet; to reach, gain, get, gain one's end. — intr. to happen, be at a place; to come to pass, fall out, occur by chance. [axe.]

τύκος, ὁ hammer; battle-

τυκτός 3 made, well-made, wrought by art, artificial; made ready.

τύλος, ὁ, τύλη, ἡ a swelling, hard swelling, callosity; nail, peg.

τυλόω to knob with iron.

τύμβευμα, τό = τύμβος.

τυμβεύω to bury; intr. to be buried.

τυμβ-ήρης 2 buried; tomblike. [grave.]

τύμβος, ὁ mound; tomb,

τυμβο-χοέω to throw up a mound over a grave.

τυμβο-χόη, ἡ the throwing up a mound.

τυμβο-χωστος 2 thrown up into a mound. [a stick.]

τυμπανίζω to beat with

τυμπανίστρια, ἡ a woman that beats a drum.

τύμπανον, τό drum.

τύνη = σύ.

τυπή, ἡ = τύπος.

τυπικός 3 typical.

τύπος, ὁ stroke, blow; impress, stamp, mark; figure, image, statue; outline, sketch, model, type; system, character. [model.]

τυπόω to stamp, form,

τύπτω to strike, beat, smite, hit; to wound. — M. to mourn for. [urn.]

τύπωμα, τό figure; vessel,

τυραννεύω, -έω to be a tyrant or absolute ruler. — P. to be ruled with absolute power.

τυραννικός 3 fit for a τύραννος, royal, princely; tyrannical.

τυραννίς, ίδος, ἡ absolute power, monarchy, royalty.

τύραννος, ὁ absolute monarch, sovereign, lord, master; tyrant; adj. princely, imperious, despotic.

τυρβάζομαι M. to be concerned; to be in disorder.

τύρβη, ἡ crowd, disorder.

τῦρός, ὁ cheese. [castle.]

τύρσις, εως, ιος, ἡ tower,

τυτθός 2 small, young; adv. τυτθόν a little.

τυφλός 3 blind; dull; unseen, dim, invisible, secret. [blind or dull.]

τυφλόω to blind, make

τῦφος, ὁ smoke, mist; conceit, vanity.

τυφόω to make dull or foolish.

τύφω to raise smoke, make a cloud. — P. to smoke.

τῦφῶς, ῶ, τῦφῶν, ῶνος, ὁ hurricane. [wind.]

τῦφωνικός 3 like a whirl-[wind.]

τύχη, ἡ chance; fortune, luck, hap; accident.

τῷ adv. therefore, then, in this wise or case.

τωθάζω to scoff at.

τώς, τῶς adv. so, thus.

τωυτό = ταὐτό.

Υ

Υ, υ (ὗ ψιλόν) twentieth letter of the alphabet; as a numeral υ′ = 400.

ὕαινα, ἡ hyena.

ὑακίνθινος 3 dark-blue.

ὑάκινθος, ὁ, ἡ hyacinth; jacinth (sapphire).

ὑάλινος 3 of glass.

ὕαλος, ὁ crystal; glass.

ὑβ-βάλλω = ὑποβάλλω.

ὑβρίζω to be or become wanton, insolent, licentious, or extravagant; to outrage, insult, affront, maltreat.

ὕβρις, ἡ, ὕβρισμα, τό wantonness, insolence, licentiousness; violence, outrage, insult.

ὑβριστής, οῦ, ὁ wanton, insolent, licentious, or wicked man.

ὑβριστικός 3 given to wantonness or insolence; luxurious, wicked, violent.

ὑγιαίνω to be or become sound or healthy; to be of mind; to be wholesome.

ὑγίεια, ἡ health, soundness.

ὑγιεινός 3, ὑγιηρός 3, ὑγιής 2 healthy, sound; wholesome; sound in mind, true, genuine.

ὑγρός 3 wet, moist, liquid, flowing; pliant, supple; languid, languishing.

ὑγρότης, ητος, ἡ wetness, moisture; suppleness.

ὑδατο-τρεφής 2 growing in or by the water.

ὑδατώδης 2 watery.

ὕδρα, ἡ water-serpent.

ὑδραίνω to wet; to wash.

ὑδρεία, ἡ a fetching water.

ὑδρεύω to draw or fetch water.

ὑδρήϊον, τό = ὑδρία.

ὑδρηλός 3 watered, moist.

ὑδρία, ἡ water-pot, bucket; urn.

ὑδρο-ποτέω to drink water.

ὑδρο-πότης, ου, ὁ water-drinker.

ὕδρος, ὁ = ὕδρα.

ὑδρο-φορέω to carry water.

ὑδρο-φόρος 2 carrying water; water-carrier.

ὑδρωπικός 2 dropsical.

ὕδωρ, ατος, τό water, rain, sweat; water of the water-clock.

ὕελος, ὁ = ὕαλος.

ὑέτιος 3 bringing rain.

ὑετός, ὁ rain.

ὕθλος, ὁ fun, buffoonery.

ὕΐδιον, τό little pig.

ὑϊδοῦς, οῦ, ὁ grandson.

ὑϊκός 3 swinish. [a son.]

υἱο-θεσία, ἡ adoption as

υἱός, ὁ son, grandson.
υἰωνός, ὁ grandson.
ὑλαγμός, ὁ a barking.
ὑλάεις 3 = ὑλήεις. [ing.]
ὑλακό-μωρος 2 ever bark-
ὑλακτέω, ὑλάω and M. to bark, howl; to bark at.
ὕλη, ἡ wood, forest, woodland; timber; fuel; brushwood; matter, stuff, raw material; ballast; stock, plenty.
ὑλήεις 3 wooded.
ὑλο-τόμος 2 woodcutter.
ὑλώδης 2 woody.
ὑμεῖς you.
ὑμέναιος, ὁ wedding-song; wedding; Hymen, the god of marriage.
ὑμέτερος 3 your, yours.
ὑμνέω to sing; to praise; to keep talking about a thing.
ὕμνος, ὁ song, hymn; melody.
ὑμός 3 = ὑμέτερος.
ὑπ-αγκάλισμα, τό embrace; wife.
ὑπ-άγω to lead or bring under; to yoke; to summon before a court; to draw from under; to seduce, deceive; intr. to withdraw, retire slowly or secretly; to advance, go on slowly. — M. to bring under one's power; to draw to oneself. [down; retreat.]
ὑπ-αγωγή, ἡ a leading
ὑπ-αείδω to accompany with the voice.
ὑπαί = ὑπό.
ὑπ-αιδέομαι P. to have awe or respect.

ὕπαιθα adv. out under; escaping to one side.
ὑπ-αίθρειος, -αίθριος, ὑπ-αίθρος 2 in the open air.
ὑπ-αίθω to set on fire.
ὑπ-αΐσσω to dart from under; to rush on.
ὑπ-αισχύνομαι P. to feel somewhat ashamed.
ὑπ-αίτιος 2 accused, guilty, responsible.
ὑπ-ακοή, ἡ obedience.
ὑπ-ακούω to listen, hearken; to answer; to obey, submit to; to appear in court.
ὑπ-αλείφω to anoint, besmear.
ὑπ-αλεύομαι M., ὑπ-αλύσκω to avoid, escape.
ὑπ-άλυξις, ἡ an escaping.
ὑπ-αναλίσκω to spend gradually. [degrees.]
ὑπ-αναχωρέω to retire by]
ὑπ-ανδρος 2 subject to a man, married. [stand up.]
ὑπ-ανίσταμαι M. to rise,]
ὑπ-αντάω to go to meet, to meet. [meet.]
ὑπ-άντησις, ἡ a going to]
ὑπ-αντιάζω = ὑπαντάω.
ὑπ-απειλέω to threaten indirectly.
ὑπ-άπειμι (-ιέναι) to go away secretly.
ὕπαρ, τό reality; adv. really; in a waking state. [good.]
ὕπ-αρξις, ἡ subsistence,]
ὑπ-αρχή, ἡ the beginning.
ὕπ-αρχος, ὁ vice-commander; governor.
ὑπ-άρχω to begin, to be the first; to lie under; to

25*

come into being, arise; to exist, be ready, at hand; to belong to, fall to; to be possible, sufficient, or useful; ὑπάρχων extant, present; τὰ ὑπάρχοντα property, means, present circumstances; ὑπάρχει it is possible or in one's power.

ὑπ-ασπίδιος 2 covered by a shield.

ὑπ-ασπιστής, οῦ, ὁ shield-bearer; life-guardsman.

ὑπ-άσσω = ὑπαΐσσω.

ὑπ-άτοπος 2 somewhat absurd. [consul.]

ὕπατος 3 highest; last;]

ὕπ-αυλος 2 under cover of a house or tent.

ὑπ-άφρων 2 somewhat silly.

ὕπεαρ, ατος, τό cobbler's awl.

ὑπ-έγγυος 2 responsible.

ὑπ-εικάθω, -είκω to retire, withdraw, escape; to yield, give way, obey, submit to.

ὕπ-ειμι[1] (-εῖναι) to be or lie under or underneath; to lie at the bottom; to be at hand.

ὕπ-ειμι[2] (-ιέναι) to come on secretly; to retire gradually.

ὑπείρ = ὑπέρ.

ὑπ-εισᾶς part. aor. of ὑφέζω.

ὑπ-εισδύομαι M. to steal in.

ὑπ-έκ, ὑπ-έξ adv. and prp. with gen. out from under or from beneath.

ὑπ-εκδύομαι M. to slip out of, escape, steal out.

ὑπ-έκκειμαι to be brought secretly into a safe place.

ὑπ-εκκομίζω to carry away secretly.

ὑπ-εκπέμπω to send away or escort secretly.

ὑπ-εκπροθέω to run out before; to outrun.

ὑπ-εκπρολύω to put out, unyoke (horses).

ὑπ-εκπρορέω to flow forth from under.

ὑπ-εκπροφεύγω to escape secretly. [under.]

ὑπ-εκσαόω to save from]

ὑπ-εκτίθεμαι M. to remove secretly; to carry away safely.

ὑπ-εκτρέπω to turn secretly. — M. to avoid.

ὑπ-εκτρέχω to run away, escape; to run beyond.

ὑπ-εκφέρω to carry away secretly; to remove a little; intr. to run away; to have the start. [cretly.]

ὑπ-εκφεύγω to escape se-]

ὑπ-εκχωρέω to retire secretly, withdraw.

ὑπ-ελαύνω to ride up to.

ὑπ-εναντίος 3 opposite; hostile; adversary.

ὑπ-ενδίδωμι to give way a little.

ὑπ-ένερθεν adv. and prp. with gen. underneath; beneath; in the nether world.

ὑπ-εξάγω to lead or carry out secretly; intr. to retire secretly.

ὑπ-εξαιρέω and M. to take away, remove by stealth; to take out privily.

ὑπ-εξαλέομαι M. to escape.

ὑπ-εξανάγομαι *P.* to put to sea secretly.

ὑπ-εξαναδύομαι *M.* to come up from under gradually.

ὑπ-έξειμι = ὑπεξέρχομαι.

ὑπ-εξειρύω to draw out from under.

ὑπ-εξελαύνω to drive away secretly; *intr.* to march away secretly.

ὑπ-εξέρχομαι to go away secretly *or* slowly; to withdraw, emigrate.

ὑπ-εξέχω to withdraw secretly, escape.

ὑπ-εξίσταμαι *M.* to stand up; to give way (to), avoid, shun; to desist.

ὑπέρ *prp.* with *gen.* over; above; across; beyond; for, in behalf of, in defence of, for the sake of, because of, by reason of; in the name of. [yards.]

ὑπέρᾱ, ἡ brace of the

ὑπερ-αγαπάω to love exceedingly. [hard.]

ὑπερ-αής 2 blowing very

ὑπερ-αίρω to surpass, outdo. — *intr.* and *M.* to rise above.

ὑπερ-αιωρέομαι *P.* to be suspended over, project over; to come off a place at sea.

ὑπέρ-ακμος 2 over-ripe.

ὑπερ-άκριος 2 over the heights. [exceedingly.]

ὑπερ-αλγέω to be grieved

ὑπερ-αλγής 2 grieving exceedingly.

ὑπερ-άλλομαι *M.* to leap over.

ὑπερ-ανατείνω to stretch over.

ὑπερ-άνω *adv.* above on high. [for.]

ὑπερ-αποθνήσκω to die

ὑπερ-απολογέομαι *M.* to speak for, defend.

ὑπερ-αρρωδέω to fear excessively.

ὑπερ-αυξάνω *intr.* to grow excessively. [proud.]

ὑπερ-αυχέω to be over-

ὑπέρ-αυχος 2 over-proud.

ὑπερ-άχθομαι *P.* to be vexed *or* grieved beyond measure.

ὑπερ-βαίνω to step over; to transgress, trespass, offend; to pass over, take no notice of; to go beyond.

ὑπερ-βαλλόντως *adv.* exceedingly, beyond measure.

ὑπερ-βάλλω to throw over *or* beyond, to throw farther; to exceed the right measure, to overflow, surpass, outdo, excel, exaggerate, overrun; to go beyond, pass over, cross, traverse, double. — *M.* to surpass, excel, exceed; to put off, delay.

ὑπερ-βασίᾱ, ἡ transgression, trespass, offence; wantonness.

ὑπερ-βατός 3 to be passed over; transposed. [whelm.]

ὑπερ-βιάζομαι *M.* to over-

ὑπέρ-βιος 2 overwhelming; overweening, excessive; passionate, wanton.

ὑπερ-βολή, ἡ a passing over, passage, mountain-pass, height; excess, highest degree; preeminence, preponderance; delay, putting off. [heavy.]

ὑπερ-βριθής 2 exceedingly.

ὑπερ-δεής 2 much inferior in number.

ὑπερ-δείδω, ὑπερ-δειμαίνω to fear exceedingly.

ὑπερ-δέξιος 2 situated above one.

ὑπερ-δικέω to plead for.

ὑπέρ-δικος 2 most just.

ὑπ-ερείδω to prop, support. [down.]

ὑπ-ερείπω aor. to fall]

ὑπερ-έκεινα adv. beyond.

ὑπερ-εκπερισσοῦ, -ῶς adv. more than superabundantly.

ὑπερ-εκπλήσσομαι P. to be frightened or astonished excessively.

ὑπερ-εκτείνω to stretch beyond measure.

ὑπερ-εκχύνομαι P. to overflow. [intercession for.]

ὑπερ-εντυγχάνω to make]

ὑπερ-επαινέω to praise exceedingly. [from below.]

ὑπ-ερέπτω to take away]

ὑπερ-έρχομαι to go beyond.

ὑπερ-εσθίω to eat immoderately. [well.]

ὑπέρ-ευ adv. exceedingly]

ὑπερ-εχθαίρω to hate exceedingly.

ὑπερ-έχω to hold over; intr. to rise above, be above, stand out; to be superior or more powerful, to excel.

ὑπερ-ήδομαι P. to rejoice exceedingly. [half.]

ὑπερ-ήμισυς, υ more than]

ὑπερ-ηνορέων, οντος overbearing, overmanly.

ὑπερηφανέω to be proud or overweening.

ὑπερηφανίᾱ, ἡ arrogance, haughtiness.

ὑπερή-φανος 2 excellent, splendid; arrogant, overweening.

ὑπερ-θαλασσίδιος 2 above the sea. [exceedingly.]

ὑπερ-θαυμάζω to wonder]

ὑπέρθεν adv. from above; above; over; beyond.

ὑπερ-θρῴσκω to leap over.

ὑπέρ-θῡμος 2 high-spirited; generous.

ὑπερ-θύριον, ὑπέρ-θυρον, τό l¹intel.

ὑπερ-ίημι to throw beyond. [hurriedly.]

ὑπερ-ικταίνομαι to run]

ὑπερ-ίσταμαι M. to stand over, to protect.

ὑπερ-ίστωρ, ορος knowing but too well.

ὑπερ-ίσχω = ὑπερέχω.

ὑπερ-κάθημαι M. to sit over or above; to lie in wait.

ὑπερ-καταβαίνω to step down over.

ὑπέρ-κειμαι M. to lie over or beyond. [wanton.]

ὑπέρ-κοπος 2 overbearing.]

ὑπερ-κτάομαι M. to acquire through one's own fault.

ὑπερ-κύδᾱς, αντος triumphant.

ὑπερ-λίᾱν adv. beyond all measure.

ὑπερ-λῡπέομαι P. to be grieved beyond measure.

ὑπερ-μαχέω, -μάχομαι to fight for.

ὑπερ-μεγέθης, -μεγάθης 2 exceedingly large.

ὑπερ-μεθύσκομαι P. to be excessively drunk.

ὑπερ-μενέων, οντος, ὑπερμενής 2 high-spirited; excessively mighty.

ὑπερ-μήκης 2 exceedingly long or mighty.

ὑπερ-μῑσέω to hate excessively.

ὑπέρ-μορον adv. beyond destiny. [far.]

ὑπερ-νῑκάω to surpass by]

ὑπερ-νοέω to think on still more. [south wind.]

ὑπερ-νότιος 2 beyond the]

ὑπέρ-ογκος 2 of excessive size or bulk; overgrown; overweening. [or beyond.]

ὑπερ-οικέω to dwell above]

ὑπέρ-οικος 2 dwelling above or beyond.

ὕπερον, τό pestle, club.

ὑπερ-οπλίᾱ, ἡ presumption, defiance.

ὑπερ-οπλίζομαι M. to despise wantonly.

ὑπέρ-οπλος 2 overweening, arrogant. [disdainful.]

ὑπερ-όπτης, ου despiser;]

ὑπερ-οπτικός 3, ὑπέροπτος 2 haughty, overweening, proud, disdainful.

ὑπερ-οράω to look over, survey; to overlook, disregard, slight, despise, disdain; to let pass, indulge.

ὑπερ-όριος 3 and 2 outlandish, foreign.

ὑπερ-οχή, ἡ superiority, excess; preeminence, excellence.

ὑπέρ-οχος 2 prominent; distinguished. [disdain.]

ὑπερ-οφίᾱ, ἡ haughtiness;]

ὑπερ-περισσεύω to become excessively abundant.

ὑπερ-περισσῶς adv. beyond all measure. [over.]

ὑπερ-πέτομαι M. to fly]

ὑπερ-πίμπλημι to overfill.

ὑπερ-πίπτω to be gone by, to elapse.

ὑπερ-πλεονάζω to be superabundant.

ὑπέρ-πολυς 3 overmuch.

ὑπερ-πονέω to toil exceedingly; to endure for another.

ὑπερ-πόντιος 2 beyond the sea; across the sea.

ὑπέρτατος 3 uppermost, highest.

ὑπερ-τείνω to stretch over; to extend beyond; intr. to project beyond.[the mark.]

ὑπερ-τελής 2 going beyond]

ὑπερ-τέλλω to rise over.

ὑπερτερίᾱ, ἡ upper frame of a carriage.

ὑπέρτερος 3 upper, higher; superior, better, more excellent, stronger; further, more.

ὑπερ-τίθημι and M. to commit, entrust; to delay, put off. [ceedingly.]

ὑπερ-τῑμάω to honour ex-]

ὑπερ-τρέχω to outrun; to surpass; to pass over.

ὑπ-έρυθρος 2 somewhat red. [high.]

ὑπερ-υψηλος 2 exceedingly

ὑπερ-υψόω to exalt exceedingly. [pear above.]

ὑπερ-φαίνομαι P. to appear.

ὑπερ-φέρω to carry over; intr. to project; to excel; be superior.

ὑπερ-φίαλος 2 overbearing, arrogant, excessive, overpowerful. [ceedingly.]

ὑπερ-φιλέω to love exceedingly.

ὑπερ-φρονέω to be haughty or overproud; to disdain.

ὑπέρ-φρων 2 high-minded; arrogant.

ὑπερ-φυής 2 immense, excessive, enormous, extraordinary; strange.

ὑπερ-φύομαι M. to surpass. [ceedingly.]

ὑπερ-χαίρω to rejoice exceedingly.

ὑπερ-χλίω, -χλιδάω to be arrogant or proud.

ὑπ-έρχομαι M. to go or come under, to creep into; to come up, advance slowly; to deceive; to fawn, flatter.

ὑπερῴα, ἡ palate. [back]

ὑπ-ερωέω to go or shrink

ὑπερῷον, ὑπερῷον, τό upper story, upper room.

ὑπερωιόθεν adv. from the upper story. [question.]

ὑπ-ερωτάω to insert a

ὑπ-εύθυνος 2 liable to give account, responsible.

ὑπ-έχω to hold under, put under, hold out; to lend, grant, afford, allow; to take upon oneself, submit to, suffer.

ὑπ-ήκοος 2 obedient, subject.

ὑπ-ημύω to bend the head.

ὑπ-ήνεμος 2 sheltered from the wind.

ὑπήνη, ἡ beard.

ὑπηνήτης, ου bearded.

ὑπ-ηοῖος 3 about dawn, early.

ὑπ-ηρεσία, ἡ rower's service; crew, sailors; service.

ὑπ-ηρέσιον, τό cushion on a rower's bench.

ὑπ-ηρετέω to serve, do service; to aid, obey, comply with; to gratify, afford.

ὑπ-ηρέτημα, τό service, assistance.

ὑπ-ηρέτης, ου, ὁ rower, sailor; servant; assistant; porter; aide-de-camp, inferior officer. [ing.]

ὑπ-ηρετικός 3 fit for serv-

ὑπ-ίλλω to draw in the tail; to check, restrain.

ὑπ-ισχνέομαι M., ὑπ-ίσχομαι to promise; to engage, betroth; to assure, assert.

ὕπνος, ὁ sleep, sleepiness.

ὑπνόω, ὑπνώω intr. and P. to sleep.

ὑπό adv. and prp. with gen. under; from under; by; through, by reason of, because of, in consequence of; with. — with dat. under; by force of, under one's power, subject to. — with acc. towards and under; towards; about, near upon; about the time of; behind; in the power of.

ὑπό - βαθρον, τό prop; rocking frame of a cradle.

ὑπο-βαίνω to go under or down, stand under.

ὑπο-βάλλω to throw or put under; to rejoin, retort; to suggest, contrive. — M. substitute; to invent, forge.

ὑπο-βλέπω and M. to look askance, scornfully, suspiciously, or angrily; to glance at.

ὑπο-βλήδην adv. replying interruptingly.

ὑπό-βλητος 2, ὑπο-βολιμαῖος 3 substituted, spurious, counterfeit.

ὑπο-βρύχιος 3, ὑπό-βρυξ, υχος under water.

ὑπό-γαιος 2 subterraneous.

ὑπο - γίγνομαι to be born after. [secretary.]

ὑπο-γραμματεύς, ὁ under-

ὑπο-γραμματεύω to be an under-secretary. [model.]

ὑπο-γραμμός, ὁ pattern,

ὑπο-γραφή, ἡ subscription; outline, sketch, design.

ὑπο-γράφω to subscribe, write under; to sketch out, delineate.

ὑπό-γυος 2 close at hand.

ὑπο-δαίω to set on fire under. [mit.]

ὑπο-δάμναμαι P. to sub-

ὑπο-δεής 2 feeble, weak; inferior; insignificant.

ὑπό-δειγμα, τό sign; model, pattern, example.

ὑπο-δείδω, ὑπο-δειμαίνω to fear a little. to shrink from.

ὑπο-δείκνῡμι to show secretly; to delineate; to give to understand, to suggest, intimate; to show, prove.

ὑπο-δέμω to build under.

ὑπο-δεξίη, ἡ hospitality.

ὑπο-δέξιος 3 receiving, capacious, ample.

ὑπό-δεσις, ἡ a binding under; sandal, shoe.

ὑπο-δέχομαι M. to receive, welcome, entertain; to endure, bear; to become pregnant; to undertake, promise, admit, allow; to border upon.

ὑπο-δέω to bind under; to put on shoes.

ὑπό-δημα, τό sandal, shoe.

ὑπό-δικος 2 subject to trial. [servant.]

ὑπο - δμώς, ῶος, ὁ under-

ὑπο - δοχή, ἡ reception, entertainment; supposition, opinion. [ly.]

ὑπό-δρα adv. looking stern-

ὑπο-δράω to wait on.

ὑπο - δρηστήρ, ῆρος, ὁ waiter, servant.

ὑπο - δύνω, ὑπο - δύομαι M. to slip or slide under or into, to dive under; to put on under; to put on shoes; to steal into; to come on, emerge from; to undertake, undergo; to insinuate oneself. [priestess.]

ὑπο - ζάκορος, ἡ under-

ὑπο-ζεύγνῡμι to yoke under. — P. to take on oneself.

ὑπο-ζύγιος 2 put under

the yoke; τὸ ὑποζύγιον beast of burden.

ὑπο-ζώννῡμι to gird under, undergird. [little.]

ὑπο-θερμαίνω to heat a/

ὑπό-θερμος 2 somewhat hot; passionate.

ὑπό-θεσις, ἡ foundation; supposition; question, subject of discussion; argumentation, principle, summary; design, proposal.

ὑπο-θήκη, ἡ, ὑπο-θημοσύνη, ἡ hint, advice, warning. [make a noise.]

ὑπο-θορυβέω to begin to/

ὑπο-θωπεύω to flatter.

ὑπο-θωρήσσομαι M. to arm oneself secretly.

ὑπο-κάθημαι M., ὑπο-καθίζομαι M. to sit down at; to lie in ambush.

ὑπο-καίω to burn from below. [der.]

ὑπο-κάμπτω to bend un-/

ὑπο-καταβαίνω to go down by degrees.

ὑπο-κατακλίνομαι P. to submit. [neath.]

ὑπο-κάτω adv. below, be-/

ὑπό-κειμαι to lie under, below, or at the bottom; to be put under the eyes; to be laid down, taken for granted, or settled; to be subject to; to submit; to be proposed; to be at hand.

ὑπο-κηρύσσομαι M. to have a thing proclaimed.

ὑπο-κῑνέω to move gently; to incite a little; -intr. to move a little.

ὑπο-κλαίω to weep at.

ὑπο-κλέπτομαι P. to be defrauded. [under.]

ὑπο-κλίνομαι P. to lie/

ὑπο-κλονέομαι P. to press on in wild flight.

ὑπο-κλοπέομαι M. to be hidden. [secretly.]

ὑπο-κνίζομαι to be tickled/

ὑπο-κορίζομαι M. to extenuate, palliate; to disparage.

ὑπο-κρητηρίδιον, τό base of a mixing vessel.

ὑπο-κρίνομαι M. to answer; to interpret; to play a part, be a player; to feign, dissemble.

ὑπό-κρῐσις, ἡ answer; hypocrisy.

ὑπο-κρῐτής, οῦ, ὁ actor; hypocrite. [secret.]

ὑπο-κρύπτω to hide, keep/

ὑπό-κυκλος 2 running upon wheels. [pregnant.]

ὑπο-κύομαι to become/

ὑπο-κύπτω to stoop or bend under; to submit.

ὑπό-κωφος 2 rather deaf.

ὑπο-λαμβάνω to take from below; to take on one's back; to receive, accept; to take up; to answer, rejoin; to take up, fight with; to think, suppose, conceive, understand; to follow close; to draw away, entice.

ὑπο-λάμπω to shine from beneath; to shine into.

ὑπο-λέγω to say or name after; to suggest; to say beforehand; to mean.

ὑπό-λειμμα, τό remnant.

ὑπο-λείπω to leave remaining, leave behind. — P. to be inferior.

ὑπο-λευκαίνομαι P. to become white underneath.

ὑπο-λήνιον, τό tub of a wine-press, press-tub.

ὑπό-ληψις, ἡ answer, reply; objection; opinion.

ὑπ-ολίζων 2 somewhat smaller.

ὑπο-λιμπάνω = ὑπολείπω.

ὑπο-λογίζομαι M. to take into account.

ὑπό-λογος, ὁ a taking into account; adj. taken into account.

ὑπό-λοιπος left remaining or behind.   [captain.]

ὑπο-λόχαγος, ὁ under-]

ὑπο-λύω to loosen from below; to untie; to slacken gradually. — M. to untie one's shoes; to free from secretly.

ὑπο-μαλακίζομαι P. to become a little cowardly.

ὑπό-μαργος 2 a little mad.

ὑπο-μείων 2 somewhat inferior, subordinate.

ὑπο-μένω to stay behind; to abide, await; to survive; to endure; to wait for; to stand one's ground; to undertake; to resist.

ὑπο-μέγνυμι to come near or approach secretly.

ὑπο-μιμνήσκω to remind; to mention. — P. to remember, recollect.

ὑπο-μνάομαι M. to woo or court secretly.

ὑπό-μνημα, τό, ὑπό-μνησις, ἡ remembrance; re-

minding, mention, admonition; memorial, memoir.

ὑπ-όμνυμαι M. to take an oath to stay legal proceedings.

ὑπο-μονή, ἡ perseverance, patience; endurance.

ὑπο-νείφω to snow a little.

ὑπο-νήϊος 2 lying at the foot of mount Neion.

ὑπο-νοέω to suspect; to conjecture, guess.

ὑπό-νοια, ἡ suspicion; conjecture, guess, opinion.

ὑπο-νομηδόν adv. by underground channels.

ὑπό-νομος, ὁ underground passage, mine.

ὑπο-νοστέω to go down, decrease, fall.   [der.]

ὑπο-πάσσω to strew un-]

ὑπό-πεμπτος 2 sent secretly.   [cretly.]

ὑπο-πέμπω to send se-]

ὑπο-περκάζω to become dark-coloured by degrees.

ὑπο-πετάννυμι to spread out under.   [neath.]

ὑπό-πετρος 2 stony be-]

ὑπο-πιάζω to oppress.

ὑπο-πίμπλημι to fill by degrees.   [much.]

ὑπο-πίνω to drink rather]

ὑπο-πίπτω to fall down, prostrate oneself; to get under.   [Mount Placos.]

ὑπο-πλάκιος 3 under]

ὑπό-πλεος 2 rather full.

ὑπο-πλέω to sail along under.

ὑπο-πνέω to blow gently.

ὑπο-πόδιον, τό footstool.

ὑπο-ποιέω to cause secretly. — M. to win cunningly.

ὑπό-πτερος 2 winged, feathered.

ὑπ-οπτεύω to be suspicious, to suspect; to divine, conjecture.

ὑπ-όπτης, ου, ὁ suspicious.

ὑπο-πτήσσω to crouch or cower down; to hide oneself from fear; to be shy or abashed.

ὕπ-οπτος 2 suspected, critical; suspicious, fearing.

ὑπ-όρνῡμι to stir up, rouse gradually. — intr. and M. to rise.

ὑπο-ρρήγνῠμαι P. to break or open from beneath.

ὑπό-ρρηνος 2 suckling a lamb.   [undermine.]

ὑπ-ορύσσω to dig under,)

ὑπο-σημαίνω to order by a signal.

ὑπο-σκελίζω to trip one up.

ὑπο-σπανίζομαι to suffer want a little.

ὑπο-σπάω to draw away from under.

ὑπό-σπονδος 2 under a truce, by way of a treaty.

ὑπο-σσείω to move below.

ὑπο-στάθμη, ἡ sediment.

ὑπό-στασις, ἡ foundation; substance, matter, reality, real nature; confidence.

ὑπο-σταχύομαι M. to grow up, thrive.

ὑπό-στεγος 2 under a roof; entering a house.

ὑπο-στέλλω to draw or take down; to keep back.

— M. to shrink back from, conceal, dissemble.

ὑπο-στένω, -στενάζω, -στεναχίζω to sigh or moan; to ring.

ὑπο-στολή, ἡ despondency.

ὑπο-στόρνῡμι to spread out under.   [under-captain.]

ὑπο-στρατηγέω to be an)

ὑπο-στράτηγος, ὁ subordinate commander.

ὑπο-στρέφω to turn round about or back. — intr. and P. to wheel round, turn and flee; to return; to take care of; to evade, elude.

ὑπο-στροφή, ἡ a turning round; retreat; return; flight.   [στόρνῡμι.]

ὑπο-στρώννῡμι = ὑπο-)

ὑπό-σχεσις, ὑπο-σχεσίη, ἡ promise.

ὑπο-ταγή, ἡ subordination.

ὑπο-τανύω to spread out under.

ὑπο-ταράσσω to trouble a little, to perplex.

ὑπο-ταρβέω to fear.

ὑπο-ταρτάριος 2 living below in Tartarus.

ὑπο-τάττω to place or arrange under; to subject. — P. to obey.

ὑπο-τείνω to stretch under; to hold out, suggest hopes; to cause; to strain, sharpen, highten.

ὑπο-τειχίζω to build a cross-wall.

ὑπο-τείχισις, ἡ, ὑπο-τείχισμα, τό cross-wall.

ὑπο-τελέω to pay off; to pay tribute.

ὑπο-τελής 2 tributary.

ὑπο-τέμνω and *M.* to cut away below; to cut off, intercept; to thwart.

ὑπο-τίθημι to put or place under; to delay, keep in suspense; to substitute; to pawn, mortgage; to suppose, suggest, admonish, promise. — *M.* to lay down as a principle or rule; to propose to one-self; to intend, purpose; to suggest, advise.

ὑπο-τοπέω, -εύω and *M.* to suspect.

ὑπο-τρέμω to tremble in the knees; to shrink from.

ὑπο-τρέχω to run (in) under; to sail by or past; to ingratiate oneself.

ὑπο-τρέω, ὑπο-τρομέω to tremble; to shrink back.

ὑπό-τρομος 2 trembling with fear.

ὑπό-τροπος 2 returning.

ὑπο-τύπτω to strike or push down; to dip down.

ὑπο-τύπωσις, ἡ outline; model.

ὕπ-ουλος 2 festering inwardly; rotten underneath; illusory. [ven.]

ὑπ-ουράνιος 2 under heaven.

ὑπ-ουργέω to serve, be helpful; to perform, afford.

ὑπούργημα, τό, ὑπ-ουργίᾱ, ἡ service rendered, complaisance. [helpful.]

ὑπ-ουργός 2 serviceable.

ὑπο-φαίνω to show from under, to bring to light, show a little. — *intr.* and

P. to come in sight, be seen a little. [for light.]

ὑπό-φαυσις, ἡ an opening.

ὑπό-φείδομαι *M.* to forbear, be regardful.

ὑπο-φέρω to carry away, save, rescue; to carry downwards; to hold out, proffer; to pretend; to endure, suffer. — *P.* to sail down stream; to be seduced or misled. [cretly.]

ὑπο-φεύγω to escape secretly.

ὑπο-φήτης, ου, ὁ interpreter, prophet.

ὑπο-φθάνω and *M.* to be beforehand.

ὑπο-φθέγγομαι *M.* to speak gently. [envy.]

ὑπο-φθονέω to feel secret envy.

ὑπό-φθονος 2 with secret envy.

ὑπο-φορά, ἡ pretence, objection. [dually.]

ὑπο-χάζομαι to retire gradually.

ὑπο-χειρ, χειρος, ὑπο-χείριος 2 under the hand, at hand; under one's power, subject.

ὑπο-χέω to pour, strew, or spread under; to administer to. [under.]

ὑπ-οχλέομαι to be rolled.

ὕπ-οχος 2 subject, dependent, subdued.

ὑπο-χρίω to besmear under or a little.

ὑπο-χωρέω to withdraw, retire, recoil; to advance slowly.

ὑπό-ψαμμος 2 sandy.

ὑπ-οψίᾱ, ἡ suspicion, jealousy.

ὑπ-όφιος 2 suspected, despised.

ὑπτιάζω to bend back.

ὕπτιος 3 bent back; on one's back; turned up, inverted; level, flat.

ὑπ-ωμοσία, ἡ oath taken to stop proceedings at law.

ὑπ-ώπια, τά face.

ὑπ-ωπιάζω to vex, annoy.

ὑπ-ώρεια, ἡ foot or slope of a mountain.

ὑπ-ωρόφιος 2 and 3 under the roof. [pig.]

ὗς, ὑός, ὁ, ἡ swine, sow.

ὑσμίνη, ἡ battle, combat.

ὕσσωπος, ἡ hyssop.

ὕστατος 3 last, utmost, extreme.

ὑστέρα, ἡ womb.

ὑστεραῖος 3 following, later, next.

ὑστερέω to be behind, late, or later; to come too late; to miss, fail; to be in want of; to come short of, be inferior; to delay, be wanting. — P. to be in want.

ὑστέρημα, τό, ὑστέρησις, ἡ a coming short, deficiency, want.

ὑστερίζω = ὑστερέω.

ὕστερος 3 the latter; coming after, following, later; younger; too late; inferior, weaker; ὕστερον adv. afterwards, later, in future. [ing after.]

ὑστερο-φθόρος 2 destroy-]

ὑσ-τριξ, ιχος, ὁ, ἡ hedgehog, porcupine.

ὑφαίνω to weave; to contrive, devise.

ὑφ-αιρέω to take away from under; to draw away, seduce; to withhold. — M. to purloin, abstract: to make away with.

ὕφ-αλος 2 submarine.

ὑφάντης, ου, ὁ weaver.

ὑφαντικός 3 skilled in weaving.

ὑφαντός 3 woven.

ὑφ-άπτω to set on fire from underneath. [rob.]

ὑφ-αρπάζω to filch away,]

ὕφασμα, τό texture, web.

ὑφάω = ὑφαίνω.

ὑφ-ειμένως adv. dejectedly.

ὑφ-έλκω to draw away under. [cretly.]

ὑφ-έρπω to creep on se-]

ὑφ-ηγέομαι M. to lead the way, to guide; to advance slowly. [guiding.]

ὑφ-ήγησις, ἡ a leading,]

ὑφ-ηγητήρ, ῆρος, ὑφ-ηγητής, οῦ, ὁ guide.

ὑφ-ηνίοχος, ὁ charioteer.

ὑφ-ίημι to send down; to put under; to lower; to admit, submit. — intr. and M. to yield, abate, slacken; despond; to creep or steal in.

ὑφ-ίστημι to place under; to place secretly. — intr. and M. to stand under; to post oneself secretly; to stand one's ground; to resist; to take upon oneself, to engage in; to promise.

ὑφ-οράω and M. to look askance or with suspicion.

ὑ-φορβός, ὁ swineherd.

ὑφ-ορμίζομαι M. to come to anchor.

ὕφ-υδρος 2 under water.

ὑφ-αγόρᾱς, ου boasting.

ὑφ-ερεφής 2 with high roof.

ὑφηλός 3 high, lofty, steep; proud, stately. [minded.]

ὑφηλο-φρονέω to be high-

ὑφ-ηρεφής = ὑφερεφής.

ὑφ-ηχής 2 neighing with raised head.

ὕφι adv. high, on high; ὕφιστος 3 highest.

ὑφί-βατος 2 high-legged.

ὑφί-βρεμέτης, ου high-thundering.

ὑφί-ζυγος 2 ruling on high. [topped.]

ὑφί-κάρηνος 2 high-

ὑφί-κέρως, ων with high horns. [liage.]

ὑφί-κομος 2 with high fo-

ὑφί-κομπος 2 boastful.

ὑφι-πετήεις 3, -πέτης, ου flying on high.

ὑφι-πέτηλος 2 with high foliage.

ὑφί-πολις, ι eminent in one's city.

ὑφί-πους, ποδος walking on high.

ὑφί-πυλος 2 with high gates. [towers.]

ὑφί-πυργος 2 with lofty

ὕφιστος 3 see ὕφι.

ὑφόθεν adv. from on high; on high.

ὑφόθι adv. on high.

ὑφ-όροφος 2 = ὑφερεφής.

ὕφος, τό height, top; sublimity.

ὑφόσε adv. upwards.

ὑφοῦ = ὕφι.

ὑφόω to heighten, raise.

ὕφωμα, τό height, elevation.

ὕω to water, wet; to let rain; to rain. — P. to be rained on; to rain.

Φ

Φ, φ (φῖ) twenty-first letter of the alphabet; as a numeral φ' = 500. [νός.]

φαάντατος 3 sup. of φαει-

φαγέδαινα, ἡ eating ulcer.

φαγεῖν aor. of ἐσθίω.

φάγος, ὁ glutton.

φαέθων 3, φαεινός 3 shining, beaming.

φαείνω to shine; to illuminate. — P. to become visible.

φαεννός 3 = φαεινός.

φαεσί-μβροτος 2 shining on mortals.

φαιδιμόεις 3, φαίδιμος 2 shining, brilliant; illustrious; famous, glorious.

φαιδρός 3 beaming, gay.

φαιδρόω, φαιδρύνω to cheer up, gladden.

φαινόλης, ου, ὁ cloak.

φαίνω to bring to light, make visible, show, make clear or audible; to display, exhibit, explain; to announce, denounce, make known: to promise, grant; intr. to give light, shine. — P. to come to light, appear, to shine forth; to be conspicuous; to make one's appearance; to be denounced.

φάκελος, ὁ bundle.

φαλαγγηδόν *adv.* in rows.

φαλάγγιον, τό spider.

φάλαγξ, αγγος, ἡ round piece of wood, trunk; spider; line of battle, order of battle, phalanx, body of soldiers, compact mass.

φαλακρόομαι *P.* to become bald.

φαλακρός 3 bald.

φάλαρον, τό brazen boss; cheek-piece of horses.

φαληριάω to become white with foam.

φαλλός, ὁ wooden pole; membrum virile, penis.

φάλος, ὁ fore-piece, ridge or crown of a helmet.

φανερός 3 or 2 visible, manifest, conspicuous; public; known, famous.

φανερόω to make visible, manifest, or known. — *P.* to become known or famous.

φανέρωσις, ἡ manifestation. [torch.]

φᾱνός 3 = φαεινός; ὁ φ.

φαντάζομαι *P.* to appear, show oneself.

φαντασίᾱ, ἡ appearance; display, show; splendour; imagination.

φάντασμα, τό appearance; apparition, phantom, vision, spectre.

φάος, ους, τό light, daylight, sunlight; lamp of life; eye-sight; lamp, torch; life, deliverance, happiness; darling.

φάραγξ, αγγος, ἡ ravine, cleft, chasm.

φαρέτρᾱ, ἡ; φαρετρεών, ῶνος, ὁ quiver.

φαρμακείᾱ, ἡ the use of drugs or spells; poisoning, witchcraft; medicine.

φαρμακεύς, ὁ poisoner, sorcerer. [or poisons.]

φαρμακεύω to use drugs

φάρμακον, τό drug, medicine, remedy; poison, enchanted potion; dye, colour.

φαρμακο-ποσίᾱ, ἡ the drinking of medicine or poison.

φαρμακός, ὁ = φαρμακεύς.

φαρμάσσω = φαρμακεύω; to enchant, bewitch; to temper, harden.

φᾶρος, φάρος, τό web, cloth; sheet; sail; cloak.

φάρσος, τό part, portion, division. [throat; chasm.]

φάρυγξ, υγγος, ὕγος, ἡ

φάσγανον, τό knife, sword.

φάσις, ἡ information, assertion.

φάσκω = φημί.

φάσμα, τό = φάντασμα.

φάσσα, ἡ wood-pigeon.

φασσο-φόνος 2 pigeon-killing. [betroth.]

φατίζω to say, speak; to

φάτις, ἡ = φήμη.

φάτνη, ἡ manger. crib.

φαυλίζω to depreciate, slight.

φαῦλος 3 and 2 bad; slight, trifling; useless, mean, common, worthless; vulgar; insignificant, simple, plain; careless, evil, malevolent. [ness; badness.

φαυλότης, ητος, ἡ meanφάω to shine.

φέβομαι to flee; to shun.

φέγγος, τό light, splendour.

φείδομαι M. to keep clear or aloof, turn away from; to spare, use sparingly.

φειδώ, οῦς, όος, ἡ, φειδωλή, ἡ a sparing; thrift.

φειδωλός 3 sparing, thrifty.

φελόνης, ου, ὁ = φαινόλης.

φενᾱκίζω to cheat, deceive.

φενᾱκισμός, ὁ imposture.

φένω to slay, murder.

φέρβω to feed, nourish.

φερ-έγγυος 2 giving surety or bail; trusty, competent.

φερέ-οικος 2 carrying one's house with one.

φέριστος, φέρτατος 3 best, bravest, most excellent.

φερνή, ἡ dowry.

φέρτε = φέρετε.

φέρτρον, τό bier, litter.

φέρω to bear, carry, bear along; to suffer, endure; χαλεπῶς or βαρέως φέρειν to bear impatiently; take a thing amiss; to fetch, bring, present; to occasion, cause; to pay; to bring forth, produce; to carry away (booty), rob, gain, win; to lead to, to stretch, aim at, refer to, tend to; to have in one's mouth. — P. to be carried or borne on or along; to move quickly, to hasten, run;

fly. — M. to carry away for oneself; to bring with one; to win, gain.

φεῦ int. ah! alas! woe! oh!

φεύγω to flee, take flight, run away; to flee before one; to shun, shrink from, fear; to be banished; to be an exile; to be accused or prosecuted.

φευκτός 3 to be avoided.

φεῦξις, ἡ = φυγή.

φή, φῆ adv. just as.

φήγινος 3 oaken.

φηγός, ἡ a species of oak.

φήμη, ἡ speech, talk; report, rumour; legend; saying, word; voice; prophetic voice, omen.

φημί to say, speak, tell; to call by name; to answer; to think, believe, imagine, fancy; to assert, say yes; οὔ φημι to say no, deny, forbid. — M. = Act. to think oneself.

φημίζω to speak out; to divulge a report.

φῆμις, ἡ = φήμη.

φήνη, ἡ sea-eagle.

φήρ, φηρός, ὁ monster.

φθάνω to come or reach before or beforehand, be sooner or first.

φθαρτός 3 corruptible.

φθέγγομαι M. to raise one's voice, to cry aloud, to sound; to call, speak; to murmur.

φθέγμα, τό = φθογγή.

φθείρ, ρός, ὁ louse.

φθειρο-τραγέω to eat fir-cones.

φθείρω to destroy, ruin; to corrupt, spoil, waste; to kill; to seduce. — P. to perish, be lost or cast away.

φθινάς, άδος consuming, wasting.

φθιν-οπωρινός 3 late in autumn. [tumn.]

φθιν-όπωρον, τό late au-)

φθινύθω, φθίνω to decay, wane, pine away, perish; trans. to consume, waste, destroy.

φθισ-ήνωρ, ορος, φθισί-μβροτος 2 man-destroying.

φθίσις, ή decline; consumption.

φθιτός 3 decayed, dead.

φθίω = φθίνω.

φθογγή, ή, φθόγγος, ὁ voice; cry, sound; speech.

φθονερός 3 envious.

φθονέω to envy, be jealous, grudge, bear ill-will; to refuse.

φθόνησις, ή, φθόνος, ὁ envy, grudge, jealousy, ill-will; denial.

φθορά, ή, φθόρος, ὁ corruption, decay, destruction; death; transitoriness.

φιάλη, ή cup, bowl, vessel, urn.

φιδίτιον, τό common Spartan meal; hall for those meals.

φιλ-άγαθος 2 loving goodness. [love.]

φιλ-αδελφία, ή brotherly)

φιλ-άδελφος 2 brotherly, sisterly.

φιλ-αίτιος 2 fond of blaming, censorious.

φίλ-ανδρος 2 loving one's husband.

φιλ-ανθρωπία, ή love for mankind, benevolence, charity, humanity.

φιλ-άνθρωπος 2 benevolent, humane, kind.

φιλ-απεχθημοσύνη, ή quarrelsomeness, malignity.

φιλ-απεχθήμων 2 quarrelsome. [travelling.]

φιλ-απόδημος 2 fond of)

φιλ-αργυρία, ή covetousness. [money, covetous.]

φιλ-άργυρος 2 fond of)

φίλ-αρχος 2 fond of rule.

φίλ-αυλος 2 fond of the flute.

φίλ-αυτος 2 self-loving.

φίλ-έλλην, ηνος, ὁ fond of the Greeks.

φιλ-έταιρος 2 loving one's comrades.

φιλέω to love; to receive hospitably, to entertain; to court; to kiss; to be fond of; to be wont.

φίλη, ή friend, mistress.

φιλ-ήδονος 2 fond of pleasure. [ing.]

φιλ-ήκοος 3 fond of hear-)

φίλημα, τό kiss. [oar.]

φιλ-ήρετμος 2 loving the)

φιλία, ή love, affection; friendship. [tionate.]

φιλικός 3 friendly, affec-)

φίλιος 3 of a friend, friendly; kindly. [Philip.]

φιλιππίζω to side with)

φιλιππισμός, ὁ a siding with Philip.

φίλ-ιππος 2 fond of horses.

φιλίτιον, τό friendly meal.

φιλογυμναστέω to be fond of bodily exercise.

φιλο-γυμναστίᾱ, ἡ love for bodily exercise.

φιλο-δέσποτος 2 loving one's master.

φιλο-δικέω to be fond of lawsuits. [suits.

φιλό-δικος 2 fond of law-

φιλό-δωρος 2 fond of giving. [mals.

φιλό-ζῳος 2 fond of ani-

φιλό-θεος 2 loving God.

φιλό-θηρος 2 fond of hunting.

φιλ-οικτίρμων 2, φιλ-οίκτιστος 2 compassionate; fond of complaining.

φίλ-οικτος 2 piteous; fond of lamenting. [beautiful.

φιλο-καλέω to love the

φιλό-καλος 2 loving the beautiful. [of gain.

φιλο-κερδέω to be greedy

φιλο-κερδής 2 greedy of gain. [mocking.

φιλο-κέρτομος 2 fond of

φιλο-κίνδῡνος 2 fond of danger, bold. [gain.

φιλό-κτέανος 2 fond of

φιλό-λογος 2 fond of words or learning; scholar.

φιλο-λοίδορος 2 slanderous.

φιλο-μαθής 2 loving knowledge. [smiling.

φιλο-μμειδής 2 sweet-

φιλό-μουσος 2 fond of the Muses. [blaming.

φιλό-μωμος 2 fond of

φιλο-νεικέω, φιλο-νικέω to be fond of dispute; to be ambitious or obstinate; to quarrel·

φιλο-νῑκίᾱ, ἡ rivalry; ambition, jealousy; obstinacy.

φιλό-νῑκος 2 contentious, rivalling; fond of strife; obstinate.

φιλο-ξενίᾱ, ἡ hospitality.

φιλό-ξενος 2 hospitable.

φιλο-παίγμων 2 fond of sport, sportive, gay.

φιλο-πόλεμος 2 fond of war, warlike.

φιλό-πολις, ιδος loving one's city, patriotic.

φιλο-πονέω to love work, be diligent.

φιλό-πονος 2 diligent, industrious. [drinking.

φιλο-ποσίᾱ, ἡ love of

φιλο-πρᾱγμοσύνη, ἡ activity, fussiness, officiousness.

φιλο-πρᾱγμων 2 busy, officious, meddlesome.

φιλο-πρωτεύω to strive to be the first. [πόλεμος.

φιλο-πτόλεμος = φιλο-

φίλος 2 loved, beloved, dear, pleasing; loving, friendly, fond; ὁ φίλος friend, companion; husband; lover; kinsman. [jesting.

φιλο-σκώμμων 2 fond of

φιλο-σοφέω to love wisdom or knowledge, to be a philosopher, seek after knowledge; to inquire into, study.

φιλο-σοφίᾱ, ἡ love of wisdom or knowledge, scientific or systematic study, philosophy; investigation, research.

φιλό-σοφος 2 fond of knowledge, loving wisdom, scientific, literary, learned; ὁ φ. philosopher. [tenderly.]

φιλό-στοργος 2 loving/

φιλο-στρατιώτης, ου, ὁ soldier's friend.

φιλό-σώματος 2 loving one's body. [children.]

φιλό-τεκνος 2 fond of/

φιλο-τεχνέω to love arts, to be ingenious.

φιλότης, ητος, ἡ love, friendship; hospitality.

φιλοτήσιος 3 of love or friendship, friendly.

φιλο-τῑμέομαι P. to love honour or distinction; to take a pride in, make it one's boast; to endeavour earnestly.

φιλο-τῑμίᾱ, ἡ love of honour or distinction; ambition, emulation, point of honour; liberality, ostentation.

φιλό-τῑμος 2 loving honour or distinction; ostentatious; emulous.

φιλο-φρονέομαι M. and P. to be affectionate, show kindness, be benevolent or well disposed; to greet.

φιλο-φροσύνη, ἡ friendliness, love, benevolence.

φιλό-φρων 2 friendly, kindly, affectionate.

φιλο-χρήματος 2 fond of money, covetous.

φιλό-χρηστος 2 righteous, honest.

φιλο-χωρέω to be fond of a certain place. [ing.]

φιλο-ψευδής 2 fond of ly-/

φιλό-ψογος 2 fond of blaming. [one's life.]

φιλο-ψῡχέω to be fond of/

φιλο-ψῡχίᾱ, ἡ love of life.

φίλτρον, τό love-charm, spell; enticement.

φιλύρᾱ, ἡ lime-tree.

φῑμόω to muzzle, gag. — P. to be silent.

φῑτρός, ὁ trunk of a tree.

φῑτύω to engender, beget.

φλαυρίζω, φλαῦρος see φαυλίζω, φαῦλος. [badly.]

φλαυρουργός 2 working/

φλεγέθω = φλέγω.

φλέγμα, τό flame, fire, heat; phlegm.

φλεγμαίνω to be inflamed.

φλεγμονή, ἡ heat, inflammation.

φλέγω to set on fire; to burn, scorch; to inflame, torment. — intr. and P. to shine, flame, blaze, flash; be inflamed.

φλέψ, φλεβός, ἡ vein.

φλίβω to rub, press.

φλιή, ἡ door-post.

φλόγεος 3 flaming, blazing.

φλογίζω to burn up. — P. to blaze.

φλογιστός 3 burnt.

φλόγωσις, ἡ = φλεγμονή.

φλόϊνος 3 of rushes or reed.

φλοιός, ὁ bark, bast.

φλοῖσβος, ὁ roaring noise; battle-din. [blaze.]

φλόξ, φλογός, ἡ fire, flame/

φλόος, φλοῦς, ὁ rush, reed

φλυᾱρέω to talk nonsense, speak idly; to slander.

φλυᾱρίᾱ, ἡ idle talk; nonsense.

φλύαρος 2 talking idly, prattling. tule.

φλύκταινα, ἡ blister; pus-tule.

φοβερός 3 frightful, terrible; fearful, afraid.

φοβέω to terrify, put to flight. — *P.* to be frightened, be put to flight, to flee; to fear, be alarmed or afraid; to feel awe.

φόβη, ἡ hair, mane.

φόβημα, τό terror.

φοβητός 3, φόβητρον, τό frightful. [terror; awe.]

φόβος, ὁ flight; fear, fright, φοιβό-λαμπτος 2 seized or inspired by Phœbus.

φοῖβος 3 bright; pure.

φοινήεις 3 blood-red.

φοινίκεος 3 purple, crimson.

φοινικήιος 3 of the palm-tree. [garment.]

φοινικίς, ίδος, ἡ purple]

φοινικιστής, οῦ, ὁ wearer of purple.

φοινικόεις 3 = φοινίκεος.

φοινικο - πάρῃος 2 red-cheeked.

φοῖνιξ, ῑκος purple-red, crimson; ὁ φ. purple dye; ὁ, ἡ φ. date-palm, date; phœnix (a fabulous bird); lyre.

φοίνιος 3, φοινός 3 blood-red; bloody; blood-thirsty.

φοινίσσω to redden.

φοιτάς, άδος, ἡ strolling woman.

φοιτάω to go to and fro or up and down; to hasten; to roam wildly about; to go regularly, to frequent; to (go to) visit; to come in, be imported.

φοίτησις, ἡ a going to and fro.

φολκός 3 crook-legged.

φονάω to be blood-thirsty.

φονεύς, ὁ, ἡ murderer.

φονεύω to murder, slay.

φονή, ἡ = φόνος.

φονικός 3, φόνιος 3, φονός 3 murderous; bloody; relating to murder or blood.

φόνος, ὁ murder, slaughter, massacre; dagger; deadly wound; blood shed in murder; place of murder.

φοξός 3 with a pointed head.

φορά, ἡ a carrying, bearing; payment; fertility; load, burden; tax, tribute; fruit, crop; quick motion, rush, onset. [lent motion.]

φοράδην *adv.* with a vio-]

φορβάς, άδος nourishing.

φορβή, ἡ food, fodder, victuals.

φορεύς, ὁ bearer.

φορέω = φέρω. [ment.]

φόρημα, τό burden; orna-]

φορημηδόν *adv.* crosswise; in layers. [lute.]

φόρμιγξ, ιγγος, ἡ lyre,]

φορμίζω to play on the lyre. [corn-measure.]

φορμός, ὁ basket; mat;]

φόρον, τό the Forum.

φόρος, ὁ tribute; income, revenue.

φορός 2 favourable.

φορτ-ηγέω to carry loads.

φορτ-ηγικός 3 carrying loads.

φορτίζω to load.

φορτικός 3 carrying loads;

burdensome; importune; vulgar; abject.

φορτίον, τό load, burden; freight; baggage.

φορτίς, ίδος, ἡ ship of burden.

φόρτος, ὁ = φορτίον.

φορτο-φορέω to carry loads.

φορύνω, φορύσσω to stain, defile.

φόως, τό = φῶς.

φραγέλλιον, τό scourge.

φραγελλόω to scourge.

φράγμα, τό, φραγμός, ὁ a fencing in; fence, hedge, enclosure, wall, partition; stoppage.

φραδής 2, φράδμων 2 prudent, cunning.

φράζω to make clear; to show; to pronounce, declare, tell, utter; to beckon; to promise; to order, advise. — M. and P. to think, believe, consider; to perceive, remark, notice; to understand; to purpose, contrive.

φράσσω to fence in, fortify, block up, defend, protect. — M. to fence or fortify for oneself.　[a clan.

φράτηρ, ερος, ὁ member of

φρᾱτρίᾱ, ἡ tribe, clan.

φρέᾱρ, ατος, τό well, water-tank.　　　[duit; mine.

φρεᾱτίᾱ, ἡ reservoir, con-

φρεν-απατάω to deceive.

φρεν-απάτης, ου, ὁ deceiver.　　　[prudent.

φρεν-ήρης 2 sound of mind,

φρενο-βλαβής 2 crazy, mad.

φρενόθεν adv. away from one's mind.

φρενο-μόρως adv. in mind.

φρενόω to make wise, inform, teach.

φρήν, φρενός, ἡ midriff; breast; soul, mind, heart; sense, understanding, reason.

φρήτρη, ἡ = φρατρία.

φρίκη, ἡ a shuddering; ripple or ruffling of the sea; awe, fear.　[rible.

φρικώδης 2 awful, hor-

φριμάσσομαι M. to snort.

φρίξ, φρικός, ἡ = φρική.

φρίσσω to be ruffled; to bristle; to shudder, shiver, feel a chill.

φροιμιάζομαι = προοιμιάζομαι.

φροίμιον, τό = προοίμιον.

φρονέω to think, be sound in mind, be wise; to understand, consider, know; to be minded or disposed; to mean, intend, purpose.

φρόνημα, τό, φρόνησις, ἡ mind, will; thought, insight; purpose; high spirit, pride, arrogance.

φρόνιμος 2 in one's senses; prudent, sensible, wise.

φρόνις, ιος, ἡ practical wisdom.

φροντίζω to think, consider, reflect; to give heed to, care about, be thoughtful.

φροντίς, ίδος, ἡ thought, care, heed; reflection; anxiety; concern.

φροντιστής, οῦ, ὁ thinker.

φροντιστικῶς *adv.* carefully. [gone, departed.]

φροῦδος 3 gone away;

φρουρά, ἡ watch, guard; watchfulness; prison; garrison; levy, conscription.

φρουρ-αρχία, ἡ commandership in a fortress.

φρούρ-αρχος, ὁ commander of a garrison.

φρουρέω to watch, keep guard, to serve as a garrison; to watch, guard, keep; to observe, beware of.

φρούρημα, τό watch, guard.

φρουρικός 3 belonging to a watch or garrison.

φρούριον, τό watch-post, fort; garrison.

φρουρίς, ίδος, ἡ guard-ship.

φρουρός, ὁ watcher, guard.

φρύαγμα, τό a snorting, neighing. [neigh.]

φρυάσσω and *M.* to snort,

φρύγανισμός, ὁ a collecting of wood.

φρύγανον, τό dry wood, fire-wood.

φρύγω to roast; to parch.

φρυκτός 3 roasted; ὁ φ. firebrand; signal-fire.

φρυκτωρέω to give signals by fire.

φρυκτωρός, ὁ one who watches signal-fires.

φύγαδε *adv.* to flight.

φυγαδεύω to chase, banish.

φυγαδικός 3 for an exile.

φυγάς, άδος fugitive, banished, exile; deserter.

φυγγάνω = φεύγω.

φυγή, ἡ flight, escape, banishment; place of refuge.

φυγο-πτόλεμος 2 shunning war.

φύζα, ἡ flight; terror.

φυζανικός 3 flying, cowardly.

φυή, ἡ growth, stature.

φῦκιόεις 3 rich in seaweed. [paint.]

φῦκος, τό sea-weed; red

φυκτός 3 to be escaped.

φυλακή, ἡ a watching, keeping guard; nightwatch; watch, guard; watchfulness, caution; watchpost, life-guard, garrison; prison. [prison.]

φυλακίζω to throw into

φυλακός, ὁ, φυλακτήρ, ῆρος, ὁ = φύλαξ.

φυλακτήριον, τό watchpost, fort; preservation; amulet. [for preserving.]

φυλακτικός 3 cautious, fit

φύλαξ, ακος, ὁ, ἡ watcher, guard; sentinel; keeper.

φύλ-αρχος, ὁ chief of a tribe; commander of cavalry.

φυλάσσω to watch; to keep guard; to serve as a garrison; to be on one's guard, to take heed; *trans.* to watch, guard, keep, secure, preserve, protect; to observe. — *M.* to keep guard; to keep, bear in memory; to take heed; to shun, avoid.

φῦλή, ἡ tribe, clan; people; division of soldiers.

φυλίη, ἡ wild olive-tree (buckthorn?).

φυλλάς, άδος, ἡ heap of leaves; foliage, leafy bushes.

φύλλον, τό leaf; *pl.* foliage.

φϋλο-κρινέω to distinguish races.

φϋλον, τό race, family; tribe, people, nation; troop; kind, sex.

φϋλοπις, ιδος, ἡ din of battle; battle, strife.

φϋμα, τό tumour, ulcer.

φύξηλις, ιδος = φυζανικός.

φύξιμος 2 able to flee; τὸ φ-ον place of refuge.

φύξις, ιος, ἡ = φυγή.

φϋραμα, τό dough.

φϋράω to mix up, knead.

φϋρω to mix, mix up, mingle, knead; to confound; to wet.

φϋσα, ἡ pair of bellows.

φϋσάω to blow, puff, snort; to puff up, blow up, make swell. [pipe.]

φϋσητήρ, ῆρος, ὁ blow-]

φϋσιάω = φυσάω.

φϋσί-ζοος 2 life-giving.

φϋσικός 3 belonging to nature; produced by nature, natural, inborn.

φϋσιόω = φυσιάω.

φϋσις, ἡ birth, origin; nature, inborn quality, natural parts; temper, disposition; stature; sex; natural order; creative power; the universe; creature.

φϋσίωσις, ἡ vanity, pride.

φϋταλίη, ἡ orchard, vineyard.

φϋτάλμιος 2 producing; from one's birth.

φϋτεία, ἡ plantation; plant.

φϋτευμα, τό = φυτόν.

φϋτευσις, ἡ a planting.

φϋτεύω to plant; to beget; to produce.

φϋτόν, τό plant, tree; creature; child. [father.]

φϋτο-σπόρος, ὁ begetter,]

φϋτουργός 2 begetting.

φύω to produce, beget, bring forth, make to grow; to get, gain. — *intr.* and *P.* to grow, spring up, come into being, be born or produced; to be by nature; to fall to one by nature.

φώκη, ἡ seal, sea-dog.

φωλεός, ὁ hole, den.

φων-ασκέω to practise one's voice. [the voice.]

φων-ασκία, ἡ practise of]

φωνέω to speak loud, raise one's voice, sound, cry, call, speak, pronounce; to address; to invite, bid.

φωνή, ἡ voice, sound, tone, cry, speech, language, dialect, word. [speech.]

φωνήεις 3 gifted with]

φώνημα, τό = φωνή.

φώρ, φωρός, ὁ thief.

φωράω to detect a thief, trace, discover.

φωριαμός, ἡ chest, trunk.

φώς, φωτός, ὁ man; husband; hero.

φῶς, φωτός, τό = φάος.

φωστήρ, ῆρος, ὁ luminary, star; splendour.

φωσ-φόρος 2 bringing light; morning-star.

φωτεινός 3 bright, lighted.

φωτίζω to give light, bring to light. [ing.]

φωτισμός, ὁ an enlighten-]

X

X, χ (χῖ) twenty-second letter of the alphabet; as a numeral χ´ = 600.

χάζω to cause to retire from; to bereave. — *M.* to give way, retire, retreat (from), desist.

χαίνω to yawn, gape; to gasp for; to utter.

χαίρω to rejoice, be glad, delighted, or pleased; to like, be wont, delight in. χαῖρε, χαίρετε hail! welcome! farewell! χαίρειν ἐᾶν to bid farewell or welcome; to set at nought.

χαίτη, ἡ long hair; mane.

χάλαζα, ἡ hail.

χᾱλ-αργός 2 swift-footed.

χαλαρός 3 slackened, languid.

χαλάω to loosen, slacken, unstring, let fall, let loose, let go, give up; to leave off, cease; to become slack; to gape; to give way, yield; to come to rest.

χαλεπαίνω to be hard, bad, severe, harsh, grievous, angry, or embittered. — *P.* to be treated severely.

χαλεπός 3 hard, severe, grievous, difficult, troublesome, dangerous; rough, rugged, disagreeable; bitter, harsh, cruel, angry, morose. — *adv.* χαλεπῶς with difficulty, hardly, scarcely; severely, harshly, angrily; ill.

χαλεπότης, ητος, ἡ difficulty, trouble; hardship, severity, harshness.

χαλέπτω to oppress.

χαλῑν-αγωγέω to curb, restrain.

χαλῑνός, ὁ bridle, rein.

χαλῑνόω to bridle (a horse).

χάλιξ, ικος, ὁ, ἡ gravel; mortar, cement.

χαλι-φρονέω to be silly.

χαλι-φροσύνη, ἡ thoughtlessness. [silly.]

χαλί-φρων 2 thoughtless, silly.

χάλκ-ασπις, ιδος with brazen shield.

χαλκειά, ἡ art of a smith.

χαλκεῖον, τό forge, smithy; copper vessel.

χάλκειος 3, **χάλκεος** 3, **χαλκοῦς** 3 of copper or bronze, brazen.

χαλκεό-φωνος 2 with a voice of brass. [smith.]

χαλκεύς, ὁ smith; goldsmith.

χαλκευτικός 3 skilled in smithing. [smith.]

χαλκεύω to forge, be a smith.

χαλκεών, ῶνος, ὁ smithy.

χαλκηδών, όνος, ὁ calcedony. [headed with brass.]

χάλκ-ήρης 3 covered or headed with brass.

χαλκί-οικος 2 with a brazen temple.

χαλκίον, τό copper vessel.

χαλκίς, ιδος, ἡ nighthawk. [brass.]

χαλκο-βαρής 2 heavy with brass.

χαλκο-βατής 2 with brazen base.

χαλκο-βόης 2 with a voice of brass.

χαλκο-γλώχῑν, ῑνος with points of brass.

χαλκό-δετος 2 brass-bound.

χαλκο-θώρᾱξ, ᾱκος with a brazen breastplate.

χαλκο-κνημῑς, ῑδος with greaves of brass.

χαλκο-κορυστής, οῦ armed with brass. [gold.]

χαλκο-λίβανον, τό half-

χαλκο-πάρηος 2 with cheeks of brass.

χαλκό-πλευρος 2 with sides of brass. [of brass.]

χαλκό-πληκτος 2 forged

χαλκό-πους brazen-footed.

χαλκό-πυλος 2 with gates of brass.

χαλκός, ὁ copper; bronze; brass; brazen vessel; copper coin; brazen arms.

χαλκό-στομος 2 with brazen mouth. [smith.]

χαλκο-τύπος, ὁ copper-

χαλκο-χίτων, ωνος brazen-coated.

χάλκωμα, τό brazen vessel.

χάλυψ, υβος, ὁ steel.

χαμᾶδις, χαμᾶζε adv. to the ground.

χαμᾶθεν adv. from the ground. [or earth.]

χαμαί adv. on the ground

χαμαι-ευνάς, άδος, χαμαι-εύνης, ου sleeping on the ground. [footstool.]

χαμαί-ζηλος 2 low; ὁ

χαμαι-κοίτης, ου = χαμαι-εύνης. [χαμᾶθεν.]

χαμᾶθεν, χαμόθεν =

χάμψαι, οἱ crocodiles.

χανδάνω to hold, contain.

χανδόν adv. greedily.

χάος, ους, τό chaos.

χαρᾱ, ἡ joy, delight, pleasure; darling.

χάραγμα, τό bite; mark, stamp, character.

χαράδρᾱ, ἡ rent, cleft, ravine, gully; bed of a mountain-stream; torrent.

χαραδριός, ὁ plover.

χαραδρόω to tear up into clefts.

χαρακτήρ, ῆρος, ὁ stamp, mark; characteristic trait, character; token.

χαράκωμα, τό palisaded fort, wall.

χάραξ, ακος, ὁ, ἡ pointed stake, pole; pale; palisade, fortified camp.

χαράσσω to point, sharpen; to scratch; to notch; to exasperate, irritate.

χαρίεις 3 graceful, lovely, charming, pleasing, pretty; elegant, accomplished, refined, witty; welcome, dear.

χαριεντίζομαι M. to jest.

χαρίζομαι M. to show favour or kindness; to gratify, indulge; to offer willingly, give freely; to offer; to abandon; to pardon; to be pleasing, agreeable, or acceptable.

χάρις, ιτος, ἡ joy, pleasure: grace, loveliness; favour, kindness, goodwill, boon; gratitude, thanks; respect; the being beloved. — χάριν τινός in favour of, for the sake of.

χάρισμα, τό gift of grace, free gift.

χαριτόω to show favour.

χάρμα, τό, χαρμονή, ἡ = χαρά. [bat; battle.]

χάρμη, ἡ desire for com-]

χαρμόσυνος 3 joyful.

χαρ-οπός 3 glad-eyed; bright-eyed.

χάρτης, ου, ὁ leaf of paper.

χαρτός 3 delightful.

χάσκω to yawn, gape.

χάσμα, τό cleft, chasm.

χασμάομαι M. to gape wide, to stand gaping.

χατέω, χατίζω to want; to desire, long, wish.

χαυλι-όδων, οντος, ὁ with projecting teeth.

χειά, ἡ hole. [rim.]

χεῖλος, τό lip; edge, brim,]

χεῖμα, τό = χειμών.

χειμάδιον, τό = χειμασία.

χειμάζω, χειμαίνω trans. to expose to a storm or to the winter; to trouble, afflict; intr. to be stormy; to pass the winter. — P. to suffer from a storm.

χειμά - ρροος, -ρρους 2 swollen in winter; torrent, mountain-stream. [ters.]

χειμασία, ἡ winter-quar-]

χειμερίζω = χειμάζω.

χειμερινός 3, χειμέριος 2 and 3 wintry; stormy.

χειμών, ῶνος, ὁ winter; frost, cold; storm, tempest; distress, suffering.

χείρ, χειρός, ἡ hand, fist; arm; side; close fight; present time; nearness; deed, bravery, might, pow-

er, violence; handwriting; grappling-hook; body of men, band.

χειρ-αγωγέω to lead by the hand. [the hand.]

χειρ-αγωγός 2 leading by]

χειρ-απτάζω to handle.

χειρῐδωτός 2 sleeved.

χείριος 3 in the power of one.

χειρίς, ῐδος, ἡ glove, sleeve; money-bag.

χείριστος 3 see χέρης.

χειρό-γραφον, τό a hand-writing, bond.

χειρο-δάϊκτος 2 mangled by the hand.

χειρό-δεικτος 2 pointed out by the hand, manifest.

χειρο-ήθης 2 accustomed to the hand, manageable.

χειρό-μακτρον, τό towel, napkin.

χειρο-νομέω to gesticulate.

χειρόομαι M. to master, subdue. — P. to be subdued. [as a hand.]

χειρο-πληθής 2 as large]

χειρο-ποιέομαι M. to do with one's own hands.

χειρο-ποίητος 2 made by hand.

χειρότερος 3 = χείρων.

χειρο-τέχνης, ου artisan, mechanic; artist.

χειρο-τονέω to stretch one's hand; to give one's vote, to vote for, elect.

χειρο-τονία, ἡ a voting by show of hands, election.

χειρουργέω to do with the hands, execute.

χειρούργημα, τό, χειρουργίᾱ, ἡ manual labour; craft. [subduing.]

χείρωμα, τό a mastering,

χείρων see χέρης.

χειρῶναξ, ακτος, ὁ artisan, mechanic.

χειρωναξίᾱ, ἡ handicraft.

χελῑδών, όνος, ἡ swallow.

χελώνη, ἡ tortoise; pent-house.

χέραδος, τό gravel, shingle.

χερειότερος 3, χερείων 2 = χείρων (χέρης).

χέρης, ηος, εος mean, little; weak; bad. — comp. χείρων 2 less, weaker, worse, inferior. — sup. χείριστος 3 worst, lowest.

χερμάδιον, τό field-stone.

χερνῆτις, ιδος, ἡ work-woman. [basin.]

χέρνιβον, τό wash(ing)-

χερνίπτομαι M. to wash one's hands; to sprinkle with holy water.

χέρ-νιψ, ιβος, ἡ water for washing; holy water.

χερό-πληκτος 2 struck with the hand.

χερρό-νησος, χερσό-νη-σος, ἡ peninsula.

χερσαῖος 3 living on dry land. [insular.]

χερσονησο-ειδής 2 pen-

χέρσος 2 dry; firm; bar-ren, destitute; ἡ χ. main-land, continent.

χεῦμα, τό what is poured; vessel for pouring.

χέω to pour, pour out, shed; to cause to rain or snow; to throw up (earth); to scatter, shower; to let

fall. — P. to be poured out or thrown up, stream forth, to be spread around. — M. to pour for oneself.

χηλευτός 3 plaited.

χηλή, ἡ hoof, talon, claw; break-water.

χηλός, ἡ chest, box.

χήν, χηνός, ὁ, ἡ goose.

χην-αλώπηξ, εκος, ὁ fox-goose.

χήνεος 3 of a goose.

χήρᾱ, ἡ widow.

χηραμός, ὁ cleft, hole.

χηρεύω to be destitute, bereft, or widowed.

χῆρος 3 destitute, bereft; widowed.

χηρόω to make destitute or desolate; to unpeople; to bereave of a husband.

χηρωστής, οῦ, ὁ collateral relation.

χήτει adv. (dat. of χῆτος) from want or need of.

χθαμαλός 3 low, on the ground. [day.]

χθές (ἐχθές) adv. yester-

χθιζός 3 of yesterday.

χθόνιος 3 and 2 earthly; native, indigene; of the nether world. [the earth.]

χθονο-στιβής 2 treading

χθών, χθονός, ἡ soil, ground, earth; country.

χῑλί-αρχος, χῑλί-άρχης, ου, ὁ commander of a thousand men.

χῑλιάς, άδος, ἡ the num-ber one thousand.

χῑλι-ετής 2 a thousand years old.

χῑλιοι 3 a thousand.

χῑλιοστός 3 thousandth.

χῑλός, ὁ grass, green fodder; pasture.

χῑλόω to feed with grass.

χίμαιρα, ἡ she-goat.

χιονίζω to snow upon.

χιονό-κτυπος 2 beaten by snow.

χιτών, ῶνος, ὁ under-garment, frock, tunic; coat of mail, coat, jerkin.

χιτωνίσκος, ὁ short coat.

χιών, όνος, ἡ snow.

χλαῖνα, ἡ mantle, cloak; carpet. [ing of cloaks.]

χλαμυδουργίᾱ, ἡ the mak-}

χλαμύς, ύδος, ἡ upper garment, cloak; military cloak.

χλανίδιον, τό small cloak.

χλανιδο-ποιίᾱ, ἡ the making of fine upper garments.

χλανίς, ίδος, ἡ state-garment. [to mock.]

χλευάζω to joke, jest;}

χλευασμός, ὁ mockery, scoffing.

χλιαρός 3 lukewarm.

χλιδάω to pride oneself; to be luxurious.

χλιδή, ἡ delicacy, luxury; finery, beauty; wantonness.

χλόη, ἡ young verdure; tender shoot.

χλούνης, ου, ὁ wild boar.

χλωρηΐς, ΐδος pale green.

χλωρός 3 light green, yellow; pale; green, fresh, vigorous. [grey beard.]

χνοάζω to get a downy or}

χνόη, ἡ box of a wheel; axle.

χνόος, ὁ foam, crust.

χόανος, ὁ crucible.

χοή, ἡ a pouring; libation.

χοϊκός 3 of earth or clay.

χοῖνιξ, ικος, ἡ a corn-measure; daily bread; fetter, shackle.

χοιράς, άδος, ἡ rock, cliff.

χοίρειος 3, χοίρεος 3 of swine.

χοῖρος, ὁ pig, swine.

χολάδες, ων, αἱ bowels.

χολάω to be bilious or angry. [wrath.]

χολή, ἡ, χόλος, ὁ gall, bile;}

χολόω to make angry. — P. and M. to become angry.

χολωτός 3 angry.

χόνδρος, ὁ grain, corn, morsel.

χορδή, ἡ gut; chord, string.

χορευτής, οῦ, ὁ choral dancer.

χορεύω and M to form a chorus; to dance in a chorus; to dance; to celebrate with a choral dance.

χορ-ηγέω to lead a chorus; to pay the expenses for a chorus.

χορ-ηγίᾱ, ἡ office of a χορηγός; equipment; means, wealth.

χορ-ηγός, ὁ leader of a chorus; one who defrays the costs for bringing out a chorus. [chorus.]

χορο-ποιός 2 arranging a}

χορός, ὁ dancing-place; dance in a ring, choral dance; chorus, choir.

χορτάζω to feed, fatten.

χόρτασμα, τό food, fodder.

χόρτος, ὁ fence, enclosure, cattle-farm; pasture; fodder, food.

χοῦς, gen. χοός, ὁ rubbish, sand; a liquid measure.

χόω to throw up, heap up (earth); dam up, fill up.

χραίνω to besmear, soil, pollute.

χραισμέω to help, aid; to defend.   [to befal.]

χραύω to scratch, wound;

χράω¹ to desire, demand.

χράω² to lend, supply (M. to borrow); to give oracle, pronounce. — P. to be pronounced as an oracle. — M. to consult an oracle.

χράομαι M. to want, long for; to use; to be possessed of; to have dealings with, converse with; to treat, practise.

χρεία, ἡ use, advantage; intercourse; service, business, office; need, necessity; want, poverty; desire.

χρεῖος, τό = χρέος.

χρεμετίζω to neigh.

χρέος, τό = χρεία; debt; amends, damages; trespass; the due.   [want, need.]

χρεώ, οῦς, ἡ necessity;

χρέως, τό = χρέος.

χρεωφειλέτης, ου, ὁ debtor.

χρή it is necessary, it must, it is right or proper; it is fated; there is need.

χρῄζω to want, need; to desire, wish, long for; to prophesy.

χρηΐσκομαι = χράομαι.

χρῆμα, τό a thing, matter, business; piece, copy; fact; enterprise; amount, money. pl. goods, money, power.

χρηματίζω to do business; to transact state business; to negotiate, debate, consult, answer; to bear a name or title. — M. to negotiate; to make money, transact business.

χρηματισμός, ὁ transaction of business; divine answer; a doing business; money-making, gain.

χρηματιστής, οῦ, ὁ tradesman, man of business.

χρηματιστικός 3 fitted for money-making; portending gain.

χρήσιμος 3 and 2 useful, serviceable, profitable; honest; made use of.

χρῆσις, ἡ = χρεία.

χρησμο-λόγος 2 giving or interpreting oracles.

χρησμός, ὁ oracular response.   [phesying; want.]

χρησμοσύνη, ἡ art of pro-

χρησμ-ῳδέω to prophesy.

χρησμ-ῳδία, ἡ prophecy.

χρησμ-ῳδός 2 prophesying.

χρηστεύομαι M. to be kind.

χρηστηριάζομαι M. to consult an oracle.

χρηστήριος 3 prophetic; τὸ χρηστήριον oracle; victim, sacrifice.

χρηστο-λογία, ἡ flowery or dissembling speech.

χρηστός 3 useful, serviceable, beneficial; honest, righteous, good, brave; kind.

χρηστότης, ητος, ἡ honesty, goodness.

χρῖμα, τό unguent.

χρίμπτω to touch the surface, to scratch. — *P.* to come near.

χρῖσμα, τό = χρῖμα.

χριστός 3 anointed.

χρίω to besmear, anoint, colour; to sting, prick.

χρόα, χροιά, ἡ = χρώς.

χρόμαδος, ὁ a gnashing.

χρονίζω to spend time; to tarry.

χρόνιος 3 and 2 for a long time, lasting long; after a long time, late.

χρόνος, ὁ time, duration; period; term.

χρονο-τριβέω = χρονίζω.

χρῡσ-άμπυξ, υκος with a golden frontlet.

χρῡσ-άορος 2 with a golden sword. [ing.]

χρῡσ-αυγής 2 gold-gleam-)

χρύσεια, τά gold mine.

χρύσεος, χρυσοῦς 3 golden, gilt; gold-coloured; precious; blessed, lovely.

χρῡσ-ηλάκατος 2 with a golden arrow or spindle.

χρῡσ-ήλατος 2 beaten out of gold. [gold.]

χρῡσ-ήνιος with reins of)

χρῡσίον, τό = χρυσός.

χρῡσῖτις, ιδος auriferous.

χρῡσο-δακτύλιος 2 with gold rings. [gold.]

χρῡσό-δετος 2 bound with)

χρῡσο-ειδής 2 like gold.

χρῡσό-θρονος 2 on a throne of gold.

χρῡσό-κομος 2 golden-haired.

χρῡσό-λιθος, ὁ topaz.

χρῡσο-μίτρης, ου with a head-band of gold.

χρῡσό-παστος 2 embroidered with gold.

χρῡσο-πέδιλος 2 with sandals of gold. [prase.]

χρῡσό-πρασος, ὁ chryso-)

χρῡσό-πτερος 2 with wings of gold. [a golden staff.]

χρῡσό-ρραπις, ιδος with)

χρῡσό-ρρυτος 2 flowing with gold.

χρῡσός, ὁ gold; gold vessel; gold coin. [with gold.]

χρῡσό-στροφος 2 twisted)

χρῡσο-φορέω to wear gold.

χρῡσο-φόρος 2 wearing gold. [ing gold.]

χρῡσο-φύλαξ, ακος watch-)

χρῡσο-χάλῑνος 2 with a golden bridle.

χρῡσο-χόος, ὁ goldsmith.

χρῡσόω to gild. [stain.]

χρώζω to touch; besmear,)

χρῶμα, τό colour; complexion; embellishment; paint. [flesh; complexion.]

χρώς, χρωτός, ὁ skin; body;)

χύσις, ἡ a pouring; heap.

χυτλόομαι *M.* to bathe and anoint oneself.

χυτός 3 poured out; heaped up; melted.

χύτρα, ἡ, χυτρίς, ιδος, ἡ, χύτρος, ὁ pot, jug.

χωλεύω to be lame, to halt.

χωλός 3 lame, halting; maimed. [tomb.]

χῶμα, τό mound; dam;)

χώννῡμι = χόω.

χώομαι *M.* to be wroth or angry.

χώρᾱ, ἡ space, room, place; dwelling-place; locality; station, post-station; district, region, territory, country, land; field, farm, estate.

χωρέω to give way, withdraw, retire; to go forward, start, come, go; to succeed; to hold, contain, have room for.

χωρίζω to part; to sever, separate. — *P.* to be divided; to be at variance; to go away.

χωρίον, τό = χώρα.

χωρίς *adv.* and *prp.* with *gen.* separately, asunder, apart, alone; differently, otherwise; except; far from, without.

χωρισμός, ἡ separation.

χωρίτης, ου, ὁ countryman, peasant.

χωρῖτικός 3 rustic, boorish.

χῶρος¹, ὁ = χώρα.

χῶρος², ὁ north-east wind.

χῶσις, ἡ a heaping up, raising a mound.

Ψ

Ψ, ψ (ψῖ) twenty-third letter of the alphabet; as a numeral ψ′ = 700.

ψακάς, άδος, ἡ drizzling rain.

ψάλλω to pull, pluck; to play the lyre with the fingers; to sing, praise.

ψαλμός, ὁ a playing on the lyre; song, psalm.

ψαλτήριον, τό stringed instrument.

ψάλτρια, ἡ lute-player.

ψάμμινος 3 sandy.

ψάμμος, ἡ sand; heap of sand; down, strand.

ψαμμώδης 2 sandy.

ψάρ, ψαρός, ὁ starling.

ψαύω to touch; to affect.

ψάω to rub, crumble.

ψέγω to blame.

ψεδνός 3 thin, spare; bald.

ψεκάς, άδος, ἡ = ψακάς.

ψέλιον, τό bracelet; ring.

ψελιο-φόρος 2 wearing bracelets.

ψελλίζομαι *M.* to stammer.

ψευδ-άγγελος, ὁ false messenger.   [brother.]

ψευδ-άδελφος, ὁ false

ψευδ-απόστολος, ὁ false apostle.   [bush.]

ψευδ-ενέδρα, ἡ sham am-

ψευδής 2 lying, false; fictitious, sham.

ψευδο-διδάσκαλος, ὁ false teacher.   [herald.]

ψευδο-κῆρυξ, υκος, ὁ false

ψευδο-λόγος 2 lying.

ψευδό-μαντις, ὁ, ἡ lying prophet(ess).

ψευδο-μαρτυρέω to bear false witness.

ψευδο-μαρτυρίᾱ, ἡ false witness.   [ing witness.]

ψευδό-μαρτυς, υρος, ὁ ly-

ψευδο-πάρθενος, ἡ pretended maid.

ψευδο-προφήτης, ου, ὁ false prophet.

ψευδ-όρκιος 2 perjured.

ψεῦδος, τό lie, falsehood, untruth.

ψευδο-στομέω to tell lies.

φευδό-φημος 2 telling lies.

φευδό-χριστος, ὁ a false Christ.

φεύδω to represent as a lie; to give one the lie; to cheat, defraud. — *P.* to be cheated or deceived; to be false. — *M.* to lie, cheat, feign; to belie, falsify.

φευδ - ώνυμος 2 falsely named.

φεῦσμα, τό = φεῦδος.

φευστέω to lie.

φεύστης, ου, ὁ liar, cheat.

φήγμα, τό gold-dust.

φηλ-αφάω to grope one's way; to feel, touch.

φήν, φηνός, ὁ gall-insect.

φήρ = φάρ. [to vote.]

φηφιδο-φόρος 2 entitled]

φηφίζω to count, reckon; to put to the vote; to decide. — *M.* to give one's vote with a pebble; to vote for, resolve, decide; to adjudge.

φηφίς, ίδος, ἡ pebble.

φήφισμα, τό vote, decree; proposition. [votes.]

φηφο-ποιός 2 falsifying]

φῆφος, ἡ small stone, pebble; counting - stone; counter; accounts; voting-stone; vote; resolution, decree, election; sentence.

φήχω to rub down; to curry.

φιάς, άδος, ἡ drop.

φιθυρίζω to whisper, mutter. [ing, slander.]

φιθυρισμός, ὁ a whisper-]

φιθυριστής, οῦ, ὁ whisperer, slanderer.

φιθυρός 3 whispering.

φιλός 3 bare, naked; bald; stript of; treeless; uncovered, unarmed; without heavy armour; simple, plain; οἱ φιλοί light troops.

φιλόω to make bare or bald; to strip of, deprive (of).

φιμύθιον, τό, φίμυθος, ὁ white lead.

φιμυθιόω to paint with white lead.

φιχίον, τό crumb, morsel.

φόγος, ὁ blame, reproach.

φολόεις 3 smoky, sooty.

φοφέω to make a noise; to ring.

φόφος, ὁ noise, sound; idle talk.

φύθος, τό = φεῦδος.

φυχ-αγωγέω to lead souls to the nether world; to lead, win, or entertain souls.

φυχεινός 3 = φυχρός.

φυχή, ἡ breath, spirit; life; living being, person; soul of man, heart, spirit; desire, appetite; courage; departed soul, ghost.

φυχικός 3 living, mental; animal, natural.

φῦχος, τό cold, frost; winter.

φυχρός 3 cool, cold, chill; unfeeling, heartless; spiritless; vain, fruitless, unreal; frigid.

φυχρότης, ητος, ἡ coldness.

φύχω to breathe, blow; to cool, refresh.

φωμίζω to eat; to feed.

φωμίον, τό, φωμός, ὁ bit, morsel.

φώρα, ἡ itch, scab.

φώχω to rub (to powder).

Ω

Ω, ω (ὦ μέγα) twenty-fourth letter of the alphabet; as a numeral ω' = 800.

ὤ, ὦ o! ah!

ὦδε adv. thus, so, in this wise; so very; so much; hither; here.

ᾠδεῖον, τό house of songs.

ᾠδή, ἡ song, lay, poem.

ᾠδί = ὦδε.

ὠδίν or **ὠδίς, ῖνος, ἡ** pains of child-birth, labour-pains; birth.

ὠδίνω to be in labour or travail; to be in pains, to suffer; to toil, work painfully.

ᾠδός, ὁ = ἀοιδός.

ὠθέω, ὠθίζω to thrust, push, force away; to thrust back or into; to push on. — M. to hurry on; to push from oneself. — P. to struggle, be in dispute.

ὠθισμός, ὁ a thrusting, pushing, struggling; battle.

ὦκα adv. of ὠκύς.

ὠκεανός, ὁ ocean.

ὠκύ-αλος 2 sailing fast.

ὠκυ-βόλος 2 quick-hitting.

ὠκύ-μορος 2 dying early; bringing early death.

ὠκυ-πέτης, ου swift-flying.

ὠκύ-πορος 2 swift-passing.

ὠκύ-πους, ποδος swift-footed.

ὠκύ-πτερος 2 swift-winged.

ὠκύ-ρ(ρ)οος 2 swift-flowing.

ὠκύς 3 swift, quick.

ὠκυ-τόκος 2 causing quick birth, fertilizing.

ὠλένη, ἡ elbow, lower arm.

ὠλεσί-καρπος 2 losing its fruit.

ὦλλος = ὁ ἄλλος.

ὦλξ, ὤλκος, ἡ furrow.

ὠμ-ηστής, οῦ eating raw flesh; savage, brutal.

ὠμό-βοειος, -βόεος, -βόϊνος 3 of raw oxhide.

ὠμο-γέρων, οντος, ὁ fresh old man. [pieces of flesh.]

ὠμο-θετέω to put on raw

ὠμό-θυμος 2 brutal.

ὤμοι woe is me.

ὠμο-κρατής 2 strong-shouldered. [arm.]

ὦμος, ὁ shoulder, upper

ὠμός 3 raw, undressed, unripe; rude, cruel, brutal, savage.

ὠμότης, ητος, ἡ rawness; cruelty. [flesh.]

ὠμο-φάγος 2 eating raw

ὠμό-φρων 2 savage-minded.

ὦν = οὖν.

ὦνα = ὦ ἄνα(ξ).

ὠνέομαι M. to buy, purchase; to farm; to offer to buy.

ὠνή, ἡ = ὦνος.

ὠνητός 3 bought, hired; to be bought.

ὤνιος 2 and 3 to be bought, for sale; τὰ ὤνια market-wares.

ὦνος, ὁ a buying, purchase, barter; price.

ᾠόν, τό egg.

ὦρ, ἡ = ὄαρ.

ὤρᾱ, ἡ care, concern, regard.

ὥρᾱ, ἡ limited time or period; season; spring and summer; fruit(s), produce; climate, weather; year; time of day; hour; moment; prime of life, youth; right time.

ὡραῖος 3, ὥριος 3 suitable to the season, ripe; youthful, blooming, mature; ἡ ὡραῖα season for gathering fruit(s); τὰ ὡραῖα fruit(s) of the season.

ὠρύομαι M. to howl, low, roar, shout.

ὥς, ὥς adv. thus, so, in this way; καὶ ὥς nevertheless; οὐδ' ὥς not even so; in this case; for instance; therefore.

ὡς[1] adv. as, just as; with sup. as ... possible; with part. by reason of, for the sake of. — conj. = ὅτι; = ὥστε; = ὅπως; = ὅτε; = ἐπειδή.

ὡς[2] prp. with acc. = πρός.

ὡσαννά hosanna (save now!). [the same manner.]

ὡσ-αύτως adv. just so, in

ὡσ-εί adv. as if, as though; just as; about.

ὥσ-περ adv. even as, just as; as soon as; for instance.

ὥστε adv. as, like as, just as. — conj. therefore, so that, so as, on condition that.

ὠτ-ακουστέω to listen anxiously.

ὠτάριον, τό, ὠτίον, τό ear.

ὠτειλή, ἡ wound; sear.

ὠτίς, ίδος, ἡ bustard.

ὠτώεις 3 with ears or handles.

ὠφέλεια, ἡ help, assistance; profit, advantage.

ὠφελέω to help, aid, assist, benefit. — P. to be helped, derive profit.

ὠφέλημα, τό = ὠφέλεια.

ὠφελήσιμος 2 = ὠφέλιμος.

ὠφέλησις, ὠφελίᾱ, ἡ = ὠφέλεια.

ὠφέλιμος 2 useful, serviceable, profitable.

ὠχράω to turn pale.

ὠχρός 3 pale.

ὦχρος, ὁ paleness.

ὤψ, ὠπός, ἡ eye; face, countenance.

NOTES

NOTES